Baltimore's Own:
The World's First Dental School
1840–2006

John M Hyson, DDS MS

Baltimore's Own:
The World's First Dental School
1840–2006

A History of the Baltimore College of Dental Surgery

John M. Hyson, Jr., DDS, MS, MA

Regina L. Davis, MA
Editor

University of Maryland Dental School
Baltimore, Maryland

2006

Baltimore College of Dental Surgery
University of Maryland Dental School
650 W. Baltimore Street
Baltimore, Maryland 21201

Printed in the United States of America.

Designed by Brushwood Graphics Design Group.

Back cover image: Ward L. Massey, PhD

Library of Congress Control Number: 2006908701

ISBN: 978-0-9774882-1-6
0-9774882-1-7

Science! true daughter of Old Time thou art!
Who alterest all things with thy peering eyes.

Sonnet—To Science
Edgar Allan Poe

A Note of Thanks

The Baltimore College of Dental Surgery, University of Maryland Dental School, thanks its many friends, alumni, and donors who have supported the vision of the institution throughout its history. We are a product of collective thought, intellect, and achievements. Specifically we thank those individuals who have provided financial support to make this publication a reality. We are especially grateful to Eli Eisenberg/VPC, Inc., for being a sponsor of this book.

Contents

**Note: For photo credits, refer to the bibliography.*

Foreword

This book seeks to address a major void in dental history: the history of the world's first dental school, the Baltimore College of Dental Surgery. While several other dental schools have had their histories published, a complete and scholarly history of the Baltimore College has never been penned. The origin of the college in 1840, the role of its co-founders, Drs. Horace H. Hayden and Chapin A. Harris, the medical members of its faculty, the Medical and Chirurgical Faculty of Maryland, and the influence of competition from other Baltimore dental colleges, until the ultimate merger into the University of Maryland system, will be examined and documented in this work.

Dr. H. Berton McCauley
Class of 1936
Alumni Association Historian

Acknowledgments

I would first like to thank the dean of the Baltimore College of Dental Surgery, Dr. Christian S. Stohler, for his perception of the importance of this history. It is surprising that the world's first dental school has never had a comprehensive written history. Hopefully, this book will clear up many misconceptions, historical errors, and set the record straight. Many thanks go to my editor, Regina Lavette Davis, MA, for the many hours she spent in transforming the original manuscript into a scholarly production. Without her timely help, this book would have suffered through its final completion to our deadline; it was a pleasure working with her.

I would also like to thank Dr. H. Berton McCauley for his review of the manuscript and the many little things he has done for its emergence as a book. Bert has always been there when I needed him. Also, I cannot forget my old teacher, Dr. Gardner P. H. Foley, professor of dental history and dental literature, when I was a student in his class in 1946. Gardner is responsible for whatever research capabilities the author has, from his beginning paper for Foley's class on a biography of Dr. James E. Garretson to the present day. Gardner set the tone and format for my research. Thank you to former deans Drs. Errol L. Reese and Richard R. Ranney and Dr. Warren M. Morganstein (former acting dean), for their critical review of the initial draft and comments. I cannot forget the assistance given to me by the campus historical librarian, Richard J. Behles, MLS, who cheerfully honored all of my many requests for the original catalogues and volumes documenting the BCDS history. Also thanks to Dr. Harry W. F. Dressel, Jr., one of my old BCDS instructors, for his perusal of the initial draft and timely comments; Dr. John F. Hasler, professor, Department of Diagnostic Sciences and Pathology, for his review and comments on the early draft; Dr. Joseph Cappuccio, my former oral surgery colleague, for his insight and material on oral surgery and the alumni; Dr. Norbert R. Myslinski, associate professor, Department of Biomedical Sciences, for his additions to the text; Dr. Leslie P. Gartner, associate professor, Department of Biomedical Sciences, for his recommendations and perceptions; Dr. James F. Craig, professor, Department of Health Promotion and Policy, for sharing his research on the BCDS's original building, providing the Milner architectural report, and his "institutional memory."

Thank you to Dr. Norman Tinanoff, professor and chair, Department of Health Promotion and Policy, and Dr. Harry Goodman, associate professor and chair of the Clinical Operations Board, for the material on the university's role in providing children's programs; Dr. Michael M. Belenky, associate professor, Department of Endodontics, Prosthodontics, and Operative Dentistry, for providing the material on the foreign dental school commitments; Dr. Glenn E. Minah, professor, Department of Biomedical Sciences, for providing the material on the Dominican Republic program; Dr. Werner Seibel, associate professor,

Department of Biomedical Sciences, for the Quest for Care material; Dr. Henry N. Williams, adjunct professor, Department of Biomedical Sciences, for access to his important and very relative files on minority student and faculty records; the late Dr. Gerald W. Gaston, clinical professor, Department of Oral and Maxillofacial Surgery; Dr. Leonard A. Cohen, professor, oral health care delivery, and Dr. John J. Sauk, chair and professor, Department of Diagnostic Sciences and Pathology, for their review of the manuscript; Dr. George Buchness, former associate professor, Department of Endodontics, Prosthodontics, and Operative Dentistry, and my old high school classmate, for his comments on his BCDS faculty days. Thanks also to James N. Reynolds, MBA, former associate dean for Fiscal and Personnel Affairs, for his help on the logistics of this publication.

Thanks go to Dr. Ronald Dubner, professor and department chair and Fran Addison, program manager, Department of Biomedical Sciences, for their material on biomedical research; Elon Burley, formerly of the Dean's Office, and John A. Phillips, assistant director of Facilities Support Services, for their assistance with the old correspondence files in the basement storage area. They were both very accommodating in turning up needed school records. A special thanks is due to Dr. Norinaga Moriyama, of Tokyo, for his timely information on the first Japanese graduates.

Lastly, I want to thank my late father, John M. Hyson, DDS, BCDS Class of 1927, who was a member of the faculty in the histology department until I became a sophomore. He quit the faculty because he did not want me to have any preferential treatment. He was a very honorable man. He would have been very proud of this book, as he loved the school dearly. I dedicate this book to his memory.

John M. Hyson, Jr., DDS, MS, MA

BALTIMORE 1840

(Courtesy—Purnell Art Gallery)

Chapter 1

The Beginnings of a Profession

"For hundreds, yes for thousands of years, the care-taking of diseased teeth had been very largely in the hands of ignorant, uneducated, and unscrupulous persons. It was often the barber and watchmaker, the shepherd and blacksmith, if not the quack and charlatan, to whom the people applied in times of sadly needed dental aid."[1] **~William Simon, 1904**

The Origins of Dental Education

Until 1810, there were but a few dentists practicing in the United States,[2] and the knowledge they possessed of the dental art had been principally obtained from practitioners in Europe. No works on operative or prosthetic dentistry had been written in this country, and but a few in France and England. However, it was difficult to procure these works in this country. Until 1829, and the publication of Samuel Sheldon Fitch's, *A System of Dental Surgery*, there was no work of importance to the student of dentistry produced in the United States. In the meantime, the demand for dentistry increased and by 1825 there were perhaps 200 competent dentists in this country. As late as 1830, the means of obtaining information on dental subjects was extremely limited.[3]

In 1851, the *American Journal of Dental Science* expressed the role of the early dentists in this manner:

> The constant demand for their services by persons able to remunerate them, called forth all their ingenuity in devising the readiest and most complete substitutes for deficiencies of the natural teeth, and made them skillful in performing the operations then in use upon these organs when diseased. Carving artificial teeth from bone, neatly introducing human teeth, extracting and filling with more or less completeness, and constructing the cumbrous spring-work by which their rudely constructed sets were made to do their reluctant office—these occupied the attention of the dentist. He had no help from without. Himself designer and artificer, he was compelled to rely upon his own mechanical skill for whatever he needed in his manipulations. Even his instruments were of his own workmanship.[4]

Before the organization of the world's first dental school, the Baltimore College of Dental Surgery in 1840, there was no academically recognized source of a formal education in dentistry. There were but three methods of entering into the practice of dentistry. The first was called the "self-made" method; men who thought they had a natural ability and talent, who, after obtaining a few instruments and materials, would announce themselves by advertisement or sign as "prepared and ready to do all that dental art and skill could accomplish."[5] The second was called the "preceptor" method; the dental art being taught by experienced dentists to students for a fee. It was based on the training offered by the guild masters in the Middle Ages. Preceptorships in the early 19th century were scarce. Most dentists were itinerant practitioners; many in the large East Coast cities traveled a regular circuit into the hinterlands and throughout the South. Besides, they were jealous of their craft and reluctant to reveal their secrets to students.[6] The third method was by attending lectures by leading surgeon dentists and some physicians who offered courses of instruction. In October 1787, Dr. Foulke, of Philadelphia, advertised in the *Maryland Journal and Baltimore Advertiser* that his lectures in "Anatomy, Surgery, Dissection and Midwifery" would commence on the first Monday in November. "Five lectures will be given on the Formation, Diseases and Operations on the teeth, in order to enable country practitioners to become useful and expert dentists."[7]

Painting of itinerant dentist, who carried instruments, medications and perhaps a dental chair in his wagon. The dentist's family at times traveled with him.

Long before 1840, some dentists saw the need for a radical change in this method of passing on dental instruction. The preceptor imparted to the student apprentice all he knew, which in some cases was dubious and misleading. However, the majority of the profession went along with this system[8] as long as it was properly conducted with integrity. The fee for this training varied, as well as the length of the apprenticeship. Eleazar Parmly, when in England, offered "to receive students, and to render them fit for practice in London for one thousand, in other large cities for seven hundred and fifty, and in the provinces for five hundred dollars."[9] Such a fee was sufficient to discourage the great majority of seekers of dental education at the hands of teachers capable of instructing them correctly, and as a consequence they were forced to enter the profession without proper knowledge or training in the dental sciences or to learn from "inferior practitioners whose charges were not so great."[10] As an example of the latter case, there was a dentist who offered to fully instruct students in the dental art in just four weeks at a charge of $30.[11] However, $500 was a common preceptor's fee in the United States, which very few could afford.[12]

Some dentists did not restrict themselves to the technical arts of the profession but were "well informed in general medicine, and their pupils were required to attend medical lectures, and read medical books, and thus a class of educated dentists was gradually formed."[13] However, this class of dentists was necessarily small. Men engaged in a lucrative daytime practice and doing their lab work at night could not devote much time to the instruction of students. These dentists laid the foundation of the respectability of dentistry as a profession.[14]

By 1840 a complete revolution had taken place in dentistry. Prosthetic dentistry, which had been considered the most important branch, now gave way to operative dentistry in importance. It was now considered far more important to conserve the teeth than to "merely hide its ravages."[15]

An earlier experiment to teach dentistry by means of lectures in medical colleges (Horace H. Hayden at the University of Maryland) had failed because the proportion of those attending medical colleges to learn dentistry was exceedingly small. Medical students displayed little interest in the dental course. Dental students, conversely, gave little attention to medical lectures. It was obvious that though "good physicians might be sent forth from the college, that good dentists could not; while those who studied the dental specialty would not be skillful physicians."[16] By and large, the medical practitioners of the day looked "rather contemptuously upon those who performed any kind of dental operations."[17] Some criteria were needed to guarantee the public that they were in the hands of a competent practitioner. Those qualified to practice dentistry needed to be identified. A separate dental college was the ultimate answer to this dilemma.

Why Baltimore? A History

The question may be raised why the world's first dental college was founded in Baltimore, the nation's third largest city, built on swamps and marshes, which had been settled in 1729 and incorporated as a city on December 31, 1796.[18] As early as 1755, Baltimore became a medical center when Charles F. Wiesenthal, one of Europe's "most celebrated practitioners of medicine" and physician to Frederick the Great of Prussia, arrived in Baltimore. With no medical school in the United States, and few students who could afford a European education, Wiesenthal was immediately in demand as a preceptor to both established physicians and those who aspired to the profession. In about 1769, he built a little two-story laboratory behind his house on Gay Street, where each winter 15 or 20 students paid him $10 dollars each to use his laboratory and attend lectures. The school was eminently successful, but unfortunately in December 1788, when Wiesenthal and his students were dissecting the body of a murderer whose "corpse they had purchased from the public executioner," the building was stormed by an angry mob protesting human dissection. They destroyed the furnishings and "dragged the body through the streets." Perhaps charlatans had a hand in the raid, as the school was a threat to the "numerous quacks who were posing as physicians." Dr. Wiesenthal died a few months after that invasion, but the school survived. Inspired by his efforts, in 1799, some reputable Baltimore physicians banded together to form the Medical and Chirurgical Faculty of the State of Maryland, chartered by the General Assembly. This organization had the power to license medical practitioners and prosecute those who practiced without a license. Meanwhile, John Beale Davidge, an Annapolis native, who was trained in medicine at Edinburgh and Glasgow, Scotland, had arrived in Baltimore in 1797 "to practice and teach." By 1807, Davidge was the "recognized successor to the great Wiesenthal."[19]

In 1807 Dr. Davidge and two associates, James Cocke and James Shaw, at their own expense, built a laboratory behind Davidge's house at the southeast corner of Liberty and Saratoga Streets. The little school opened on November 2, 1807, but 19 days later it was raided and demolished by an angry mob. However, on the very day of the raid, a bill to incorporate Davidge's school was introduced in the General Assembly. The violence was perceived as "an intolerable obstruction to scientific progress," and on December 18, 1807, the Assembly approved the charter of the College of Medicine of Maryland, the sixth in the United

States. Colonel John Eager Howard, the former governor and Revolutionary War hero, offered land at Lombard and Greene Streets for building the new school.[20]

By 1800, Baltimore had more than 26,000 residents, over 6,000 houses, and ranked fourth in foreign trade among the major cities.[21] From October 1805 to 1806, the exports from Maryland, nearly all of which were from Baltimore, amounted to $14,580,905.[22] It was said that, "among all the cities of America, or of the Old World, in modern or ancient times, there is no record of any one which has sprung up so quickly to so high a degree of importance as Baltimore. . . ."[23] By 1810, its population had increased to 46,555, of which only about five percent were slaves. George Washington had predicted that Baltimore was and would be the "risingest town in America, excepting the Federal City." The city's geographical location and its magnificent harbor stimulated its "rapid growth and the prosperity" that accompanied it. Baltimore was one of the fastest-growing cities in America. Its position was essentially central, the "most northern of the southern cities, the most southern of the northern cities, and the most eastern of the western cities." Its location was favorable for the "development of foreign trade, both export and import, and for the distribution of commodities at home." On a waterway with 2,000 miles of well-timbered coastline, it was well suited to shipbuilding.[24] Fells Point was "one of the most crowded shipping wharves on earth, with 3,000 houses, most of brick, two or three stories high." As land values rose dramatically, the cost of living was "higher than London's and much higher than in Paris."[25]

In 1814, Baltimore was the site of the British attack on Fort McHenry and the creation of our national anthem by Francis Scott Key, a Baltimore lawyer, who was negotiating for the release of British prisoner Dr. William Beanes of Upper Marlboro. Reportedly, Major George Armstead, the fort's commander, raised the big 15-star flag on September 14 while the fort's musicians played "Yankee Doodle." This incident inspired Key to write his famous poem, the "Star Spangled Banner."[26] During the 25-hour British naval bombardment, the *Niles Weekly Register* reported that the "houses in the city were shaken to their foundations."[27]

Baltimore was called the "Monumental City" because the first monument to the founding father, George Washington, was erected in Baltimore in 1815.[28] Baltimore was honored by a visit from General Lafayette in 1824. During his three-day stay, he was awarded an honorary degree from the University of Maryland.[29] At the ball given in his honor, Lafayette offered a toast to the ladies of Baltimore for his gratitude for the help he had received as a young soldier in 1783 when he passed through Baltimore with his expeditionary force on their way to Virginia "limping and in rags, some of his soldiers were barefoot." The town's women had gone to work sewing trousers, shirts, jumpers, and hats from bolts of cloth donated by the local merchants from their warehouses. Lafayette promised to reimburse the city to the entire sum of 2,000 guineas, which he did when the war was over. He even had Congress pass "a special resolution commending the town for its civic virtue."[30]

Baltimore was, by land, "the hub of a giant wheel whose spokes are the hard-surface pikes, running away from her in every direction; to Havre de Grace and to Philadelphia, to York, to Reisterstown, to Annapolis, to Washington—and greatest of all, by far, that Frederick Pike, leading off straight to the West, and the wonderful National Road," which ran from Cumberland to Ohio. Stagecoach and Conestoga wagon traffic caused many inns and taverns to spring up in the western part of the city because of its convenience and access to the National Road. Along Franklin Street, the *Golden Horse*, the *White Swan*, the *Black Horse*, and the

Golden Lamb, proudly displayed their "gaudy signs." Paca Street had its *General Wayne*, the *Three Tuns*, and *May Pole*.[31]

Baltimore had the nation's first railroad, the Baltimore & Ohio, whose cornerstone was dedicated by Charles Carroll, of Carrollton, the sole surviving signer of the Declaration of Independence, on July 4, 1828. The dedication took place near the corner of Pratt Street and Amity Alley, with several thousand people in attendance. A parade followed and the town was "packed to overflowing."[32] The railroad ran 380 miles long from Baltimore's port through "sparsely settled, mountainous wilderness all the way to the Ohio River."[33] The rail line was "designed to compete with shipping on the Erie Canal, which advantages New York State."[34] Baltimore was the home of the famous "Baltimore Clipper,"[35] the swift, two-masted, sharply raked, privateers that had caused the British in 1812 to call for wiping out that "Nest of Pirates" on the Chesapeake.[36] In the mid 1800s, new and larger Baltimore clipper ships, retaining much of the speed of their predecessors, carried Baltimore's flour and tobacco to foreign ports, such as Buenos Aires, Marseilles, and China. They carried in return, coffee, sugar, copper, and hides from South America and the West Indies.[37] In fact, by the 1840s, Baltimore's most important foreign trade market was South America, exporting thereto flour, beef, pork, grain, textiles, barrel staves, and brown sheetings. A new grade of flour made from winter wheat was developed in 1840, which became the city's greatest export to Brazil.[38] "Baltimore Flour" was even advertised for sale in the *Boston Daily Advertiser* in September 1840.[39] A "superior canvas" was also exported, advertised as "Cotton Duck made at Baltimore."[40]

In 1835, an Englishman visiting the city remarked: "Baltimore is the handsomest place I have yet seen—here are the finest monuments—the prettiest girls and the cleanest City in the Union."[41] Former slave and abolitionist Frederick Douglas even worked in a Baltimore shipyard in 1836, apprenticed to William Gardner, shipbuilder.[42] By the 1840s, "Baltimore and Boston Packets" were sailing regularly every Saturday between the two ports. The *Boston Daily Advertiser* in September 1840 advertised that ships were leaving from "Bowley's Warf" in Baltimore.[43]

In 1803, beautiful Betsy Patterson, the "Belle of Baltimore," married Jerome Bonaparte, Napoleon's younger brother.[44] Baltimore was a literary center, as between 1815 and 1833 at least 72 periodicals were started in the city.[45] Among the most famous literary accomplishments was that of Edgar Allan Poe, who lived in the city from 1831 to 1835. His short story, "The Murders in the Rue Morgue," was published in the 1841 issue of *Graham's*.[46] In 1840, Richard Henry Dana, Jr., wrote his novel, *Two Years before the Mast*, which changed the public's perception of life on a clipper ship.[47] That year was also when Samuel Cunard, funded by the British Admiralty, inaugurated his steamship line connecting Europe and America.[48] In 1840, Great Britain issued the first postage stamp depicting a very young portrait of Queen Victoria,[49] and a Belgian instrument maker, Adolphe Sax, invented the saxophone.[50]

Baltimore was also the first city in America to be lighted by gas, initially demonstrated at Rembrandt Peale's Museum[51] in 1816. The *Baltimore American* called it a "very brilliant and pleasing light." The Gas Light Company of Baltimore was chartered in 1817, and on February 7, 1817, put the first gas lamp at Market and Lemon Streets (now Baltimore and Holliday Streets).[52] In the 1800s, Baltimore, because of its location midway between the North and the South and its proximity to Washington, was a popular place for holding political conventions. On May 4, 1840, the Whig Convention met to ratify the nomination of William Henry Harrison and John Tyler. A parade marched through Baltimore to Canton Race Track, where a crowd of 20,000 was addressed by Daniel Webster and Henry Clay. By contrast, the Democratic National Convention also met the next day at the Assembly Rooms in Baltimore and nominated Martin Van Buren, the current president, as its presidential candidate.[53] Van Buren was soundly defeated by Harrison in the "Log Cabin and Hard Cider" campaign, which featured the song, "Tippecanoe and Tyler Too."[54]

In 1842, Charles Dickens visited Baltimore and stayed at Barnum's City Hotel, founded in 1825 on the southwest corner of Fayette and Calvert Streets. Barnum's was the largest hotel in the country. It was said that its guests were "so comfortable that several were induced to extend their stay in the city for days and weeks instead of passing rapidly through it." Dickens praised its ambiance and called it, "the most comfortable of all hotels . . . in the United States." It had 200 rooms, twice the number of the largest European hotels. He also probably shared with Washington Irving at Barnum's an "enchanted julep which held out far into the night." Diamond-back terrapin and oysters were featured at the "hotel's table d'hote dinner, priced at $1.50."[55]

Baltimore was also the location for the manufacture of the first Colt revolvers. In 1834, Samuel Colt contracted with a gunsmith, A.T. Baxter, to work on two rifles and several pistols. Baxter assigned the job to John Pearson, to whom Colt paid more than $400 dollars during a seven-week period. Colt had gotten the idea for his revolving six-chambered cylinder from a ship's capstan. Meanwhile, he pursed his business of demonstrating the effects of "laughing gas" (nitrous oxide), advertising himself as the "Celebrated Dr. Coult of New York, London, and Calcutta."[56]

Early Baltimore Dentists

Indeed, Baltimore was a hub of dental activity, being the most northern of Southern cities (south of the Mason Dixon line) in the United States. During the years before the end of the 18th century and the early 19th, Baltimore had many prominent European- and American-trained dentists practicing in the city; namely, John Baker (London, 1773); John H. Gilbert (Germany, 1773); John M'Ginnis (Europe, 1773); Michael Poree (Paris, 1774); Benjamin Fendall (America, 1776); Mr. Sowdon (Europe, 1783); C. E. Whitlock (London, 1784); Dr. Hornby (Europe, 1786); M. Jeanin (France, 1787); James Gardette (France, 1788); Isaac Bassett (America, 1791); Mr. Chandler (America, 1791); James Molan (1791); Frederick Raymond (Europe, 1792); Richard Cort Skinner (England, 1794); Dr. Beziers [Bessieres] (Europe, 1796); Philip Larus (Europe, 1796); Thomas Bruff (America, 1797); Dr. Battemps (1797); Thomas Hamilton (London, 1799); I. J. Comyn (France and Spain, 1800?); Enoch Noyes (1800?); Leonard Mackall (1800?); B. T. Longbothom (London, 1802); Leonard Koecker (1807); Oliver Holmes (1819); E. Laroque (Europe, 1824); Mr. Shymanski (1824); Dr. Parsons (1826); and Edmond Byrne (1836).[57]

John Baker, an itinerant dentist who plied the Baltimore circuit, had practiced first in Europe, then in Boston, New York, Philadelphia, Baltimore, Annapolis, and Williamsburg. He reportedly tutored Paul Revere in the dental art, was one of George Washington's dentists, was the first dentist to advertise gold fillings, and in 1773 (*Maryland Gazette*, September 14, 1773) the first to practice in Maryland.[58] He advertised in the September 7, 1773, *Maryland*

Journal and Baltimore Advertiser that he had "just arrived in this Town, and intends returning to Annapolis, the beginning of October next; that those who are disposed to apply to him, may not be disappointed, he is now at Mrs. Orrick's, in Gay Street."[59]

John H. Gilbert, a German-trained dentist, in the September 25, 1773, edition of the *Maryland Journal and Baltimore Advertiser*, reported that he had just arrived from Philadelphia. His "Anti-Scorbutic Tincture . . . cures all disorders of the mouth, gums, and teeth, in a few times using removes that grievous, and intolerable nauseous disorder called a stinking breath, chiefly proceeding from ulcerous gums, rotten and decayed teeth, in a few applications it gives the teeth a beautiful whiteness, and entirely removes those sandy tartarous scales which give them disagreeable black and yellow color, which proceed from Scurvy." His temporary lodging was at Mrs. Frazier's home on Gay Street.[60]

John M'Ginnis, surgeon dentist, advertised in the December 19, 1774, *Maryland Journal and Baltimore Advertiser* that he had moved to his apartment at "Capt. White's Tobacconist, on Gay Street. Where he may be consulted in all disorders of the teeth, gums, sockets, ulcers, cancers, fungus, fistulas, suppurations and inflammation in the gums, not the gums only are affected by these disorders, but also the teeth, jaw, head, etc."[61] Michael Poree came to America in 1768 and located in New York. In 1774, he moved to Baltimore for a short time and then on to Philadelphia. He was the first dentist to publish a lay article on dentistry in the December 11, 1769, *New York Gazette and Weekly Mercury*. After 1775, he disappears between the years 1776 and 1780, undoubtedly due to the war.[62]

Traveling instument kit of the colonial dental practitioner

Benjamin Fendall, a medically trained dentist, originally from Port Tobacco, Charles County, Md., practiced as far north as Philadelphia, but he also saw patients in Baltimore. On September 11, 1776, the *Maryland Journal and Baltimore Advertiser* reported that Dr. Fendall, the "Operator upon the teeth is just arrived in this town," and was residing with Mrs. Orrick on Gay Street. The *Maryland Journal and Baltimore Advertiser* for November 30, 1779, states: "The justly celebrated, ingenious, and much-esteemed Doctor Benjamin Fendall left this town on Saturday last for Annapolis, on his way to his Seat in Charles County." In 1784, he was reported by the *Baltimore Advertiser* as having "taken up his residence, for a few weeks, at Miss Young's, in Calvert street," where he was offering his services to the public. Again in 1786, the *Baltimore Advertiser* reports: "Doctor Fendall, who has been, and is now indefatigable in his Studies in the Art and Mystery of a Surgeon Dentist, has brought it to great perfection, having been regularly bred to Physik and Surgery, will visit Baltimore." He was in Baltimore as late as 1809, according to his announcement in the *Baltimore Evening Post*, that he had become "a resident of Baltimore."[63] Apparently, Fendall traveled a circuit from his home in Charles County to Annapolis, Baltimore, and Philadelphia.

Mr. Sowden advertised in the July 26, 1783, *Maryland Journal and Baltimore Advertiser* that he would "give his advise gratis in all cases relative to the teeth and gums, either at his own apartments, Mr. Augustine's, in Calvert Street, or at people's respective homes; and if any operation or attendance is deemed necessary, if the party is not perfectly satisfied, with pleasure will return his fee."[64] C. E. Whitlock, by profession an actor from London, came to Boston about 1778. He announced that:

> C. E. Whitlock, Dentist, Respectfully acquaints the Public that his engagements at the Theater having expired, he is now at liberty to offer his services in the above profession, to which he has been regularly bred.[65] In 1784, he was in Baltimore and advertised that he performed "every operation in the above profession with the utmost care and attention."

He was located at Mrs. Alexander's on Calvert Street, and offered to treat patients at their own homes.[66] He was the first dentist to announce his fees, which he published in the August 13, 1795, *Federal Intelligencer and Baltimore Daily Gazette.* After about two years in Baltimore, he relocated to Philadelphia. The last known announcement by Whitlock appeared in the *Baltimore Republican or Anti-Democrat* on April 26, 1802.[67]

Dr. Hornby advertised in the August 1, 1786, *Maryland Journal and Baltimore Advertiser* that he performed "all operations on the teeth and gums," and that he could be consulted at "Mr. Grant's Tavern." "He will wait on any Lady—His stay will be short."[68] M. Jeanin, a French-trained dentist, advertised in the *Maryland Journal and Baltimore Advertiser* on March 6, 1787, that he:

> Takes this method of informing the Ladies and Gentlemen of Baltimore, and the Public in General, that he cleanseth the teeth, be they ever so black a colour, and gives them a most beautiful enamel; he supplies the place of decayed teeth with ivory ones, which will remain as firm as natural ones, without giving the smallest degree of sensible pain. His office was at "Mrs. Gold's in French-Town."[69]

James Gardette, a former French naval surgeon, who practiced dentistry in Philadelphia, informed the citizens of Baltimore that he would be in their town through an ad in the *Maryland Journal and Baltimore Advertiser* on September 5, 1788.[70] On September 16, he placed another ad in the *Baltimore Advertiser,* which stated that he had arrived and intended to remain a few weeks for the purpose of "practicing the several Branches of his Profession," which included, "Scaling or cleaning teeth—curing any Diseases incident to the Teeth, Gums, Sockets, etc.—regulating the Dentition of children—extracting and replacing natural and artificial teeth, etc., etc." His location was at "Mrs. Sanderson's, in Market Street, opposite South Street."[71] Gardette was in Baltimore again in January and April 1789, and January 1790.[72]

Isaac Bassett, presumed to be American born, on September 27, 1791, published an announcement in the *Maryland Journal and Baltimore Daily Advertiser,* that, "Having for sometime past, practiced in this Town . . . takes this method of returning his most grateful thanks to his Friends and the Public in general for the favours he has received. . . . His residence is at Mrs. Phillip's in Bank-Street opposite the Mansion of Mary Gough, Esquire." On April 5, 1783, in the same paper, he mentions the names of three of his patients, Peter Kempf, Susan Rutter, and John Morris.[73] On November 4, 1797, Dr. Bassett announced that he had purchased the rights to use Mr. Thomas Bruff's[74] patent instrument for perpendicular extraction of teeth. This purchase demonstrates Dr. Bassett's interest in keeping up with the progress in dentistry. Bassett's press notices and listing in the city directories indicate that he practiced in the city for at least 17 years, from 1791 to 1808.[75]

James Molan moved from Philadelphia to Baltimore in 1791 and informed the public that he intended to reside with his family and practice "in the line of his profession." He offered to produce testimonials of his ability in his September 23, 1791, ad in the *Maryland Journal and Baltimore Advertiser.* He cleaned the teeth, transplanted human teeth, which "in a few Days will be as fast as if formed by Nature," and extracted "carious Teeth and Stumps with Care and Ease." He offered to extract teeth for the poor gratis. His location was at Widow Woolsey's on Gay Street.[76] Mr. Frederick Raymond, reportedly the former surgeon dentist to the Duke of d'Orleans, in the French Court, offered his services to the citizens of Baltimore in 1792. He advertised in the July 18, 1792, *Baltimore Daily Repository* that he was both [*sic*] a dentist, oculist, and physician, who treated gratis people unable to pay. He was located at "Mr. Peter Mitchell's, Market Street, at the sign of Liberty and Security."[77]

Dr. Richard Cort Skinner, an English émigré practicing in New York, advertising himself as a "surgeon, dentist, and oculist," informed the Baltimore public that he was now on his return from a tour through the southern states, "for the benefit of the health of his family," and would be in Baltimore for two weeks in the spring of 1794. In his April 2, 1794, ad in the *Baltimore Daily Intelligence,* he offered to give, gratis, every patient a copy of his book, *A Treatise on the Human Teeth,* which he published in 1801. This was the first book on dentistry published in the United States. Apparently, Skinner had an earlier printing for distribution to his patients, which he handed out as early as 1794 in Baltimore and in 1796 in Richmond, Va. Skinner also had the distinction of being the first dentist in this country to receive an official appointment as the dentist to a medical dispensary, the Dispensary of the City of New York. He was temporarily located at Mr. Joshua Kirby's residence on Calvert Street.[78]

Dr. Beziers, a dentist trained in Europe, practiced with James Gardette in Philadelphia. In March 1796, he came to Baltimore and advertised that he "undertakes effectively to remove all complaints incidental to the Teeth and Gums, and pursues the most approved method for preserving them in a sound and useful state." He was located at Mrs. Alexander's, on St. Paul Lane.[79] Philip Larus reported in the October 4, 1796, *Federal Gazette and Baltimore Daily Advertiser* that he had recently arrived from Philadelphia, and that his stay in Baltimore would only be for a few weeks. He offered to treat "any imaginable disorders of the teeth" at "Mrs. Levely's, No. 140 Market Street."[80]

Thomas Bruff, a native of Chestertown, Md., practiced dentistry in Maryland, Pennsylvania, and Virginia. In 1797, he located to Baltimore. He patented the first dental instrument, a perpendicular extractor, recorded by the U.S. Patent Office on June 28, 1797. He sold the right of use to various dentists.[81] Thomas Hamilton, a surgeon dentist from London, Horace H. Hayden's mentor, moved to Baltimore from New York in 1799. On January 4, 1800, he announced his office location as 21 Market Street. In 1801, he moved back to New York, leaving Horace Hayden in charge of his practice.[82]

Even after the turn of the century, Baltimore continued to attract dental practitioners. I. J. Comyn, who claimed to have been "medically educated" in France and Spain, practiced in Baltimore in 1808.[83] B. T. Longbothom reportedly was a pupil of Mr. Whitewood of London, who practiced in London and Jamaica before coming to Baltimore. In 1802, he was the author of the second treatise on dentistry published in America. Although the 68-page book, published in Baltimore (No. 200, Market Street), was intended for the public, it was the best of the earlier treatises, and of practical value to the period dentists. Longbothom showed his familiarity with the important dental authors of the day, particularly John Hunter.[84] Leonard Koecker practiced dentistry in Baltimore from 1807 to 1812, and then in Philadelphia from 1812 to 1822. He moved to London in 1822 and practiced there until his death in 1850. Koecker was regarded as a "careful and diligent" student, a dentist of "unusual ability," and an author who contributed to the advancement of dentistry through his 1826 writings.[85]

In 1824, E. Laroque, trained in Europe and America, announced that he had moved his office to No. 12, Harrison Street, and "respectfully offers his services to the citizens of Baltimore and its vicinity, in that useful branch of surgery which he professes." Apparently, he had been practicing in Baltimore for at least four years. In 1825, he offered his "Anodine [*sic*] Drops" for relief of the toothache.[86] Mr. Shymanski, a dentist who had formerly practiced in the southern and southwestern states, also advertised in 1824 that he had taken up residence in the city on "N. Charles Street, a few doors below St. Paul's Church." In October 1825, he moved his office to "No. 11, corner of Liberty and Lexington Street."[87] In 1826, another dentist, Dr. Parsons, moved to Baltimore from New York. He advertised that "his practice embraces all operations on the teeth and gums, and the insertion of teeth, from one to a full set." His office was located at No. 20, North Gay Street.[88] Edmond Byrne, dental surgeon, advertised in 1836 that his office was on Lexington Street, first door from Charles St., [N]o. 28."[89] Enoch Noyes; Leonard Mackall, MD; and Oliver Holmes also practiced in Baltimore.[90] Thus, it can be seen that Baltimore City was indeed a "hot bed" of dental activity and professionals, an appropriate location for the first dental school. For this and many excellent reasons, Baltimore was the ideal choice for its location. Perhaps Dr. Gardner P. H. Foley, the college's longtime historian, sums it up best:

> Being situated between the North and the South was an advantage in its maintenance of a steady and usually adequate supply of students. From 1790 to 1840 the country had been on a surge of road building. There was also an impressive growth of river and stagecoach travel facilities. The coming of the railroads led to drastic changes in the character of travel accommodations to and from Baltimore. The development of Baltimore as a port city with a wide variance in connections with both domestic and foreign ports must have had a strong impact on the students' choice of a dental school.[91]

NOTES

1. William Simon, "History of the Baltimore College of Dental Surgery," in *Transactions of the Fourth International Dental Congress* [1904], vol. 3 (Philadelphia: S. S. White Dental Mfg. Co., 1905), p. 290.
2. At the time of the signing of the Declaration of Independence, there were 79 professional dentists in practice in the 13 colonies, 15 of them in Maryland. [Isaac Rehert, "Forget that Myth about Washington's Set of Wooded Teeth," *Alma Mater* 17 (May 1975): 6.]
3. Charles W. Ballard, "Dental Education," American Journal of Dental Science, n.s., 2 (October 1851): 59–60; Milton B. Asbell, *Dentistry: A Historical Perspective* (Bryn Mawr, PA: Dorrance & Co., Inc., 1988), p. 125.
4. "Historical Review of the Progress of Dental Surgery in the United States, with Reflections upon the Causes that have Accelerated it, and the means Necessary for its further Advancement," *American Journal of Dental Science*, n.s., 2 (October 1851): 97.
5. J[ohanathan] Taft, "Dental Education—Office Pupilage," *Dental Register* 44 (February 1890): 57.
6. Woodrow S. Monica, *Outline of Dental History* (Hackensack, N.J.: Fairleigh Dickinson University, School of Dentistry, 1967), p. 32.
7. J. Ben Robinson, "The Beginnings of Institutional Dental Education in America," in *Proceedings of the Fourteenth Annual Meeting of the American Association of Dental Schools* (American Association of Dental Schools, 1937), p. 25.
8. As late as 1901, of the 28,142 dentists then in practice in the United States, 16,831 were graduates of a reputable dental college and 11,311 had been preceptor or self-trained. [William J. Gies, "Dental Education: Including a Study of the Alleged Influence of Derogatory Medical Opinion on Its Institutional Initiation in 1840," *Journal of the American Dental Association* 27 (January 1940): 100.]

9. American Academy of Dental Science, *History of Dental and Oral Science in America* (Philadelphia: Samuel S. White, 1876), p. 179.
10. Ibid.
11. "Curiosities of Dentistry," *Dental News Letter* 4 (October 1850): 21.
12. "Historical Review of the Progress of Dental Surgery," *American Journal of Dental Science*, n.s., 2 (October 1851): 98.
13. Ibid.
14. Ibid.
15. Ballard, "Dental Education," 65.
16. Ibid., 67.
17. Simon, "History," p. 292.
18. J. Thomas Scharf, *History of Baltimore City and County from the Earliest Period to the Present Day: Including Biographical Sketches of Their Representative Men* (Philadelphia: Louis Everts, 1881), pp. 169–70.
19. H. Berton McCauley, "Professional Dentistry and the University of Maryland at Baltimore," *Bulletin of the History of Dentistry* 30 (October 1982): 73–74; George H. Callcott, *A History of the University of Maryland* (Baltimore: Maryland Historical Society, 1966), pp. 17–20.
20. McCauley, "Professional Dentistry and the University of Maryland," 74. At the first Regents meeting, Dr. Davidge was elected dean and chair of surgery, Cocke the chair of anatomy and physiology, Shaw the chair of chemistry, Nathaniel Potter the chair of theory and practice of medicine, and Samuel Baker the chair of materia medica. Originally, Dr. Davidge filled the chair of obstetrics and diseases of women, but in 1812 that chair was assumed by Richard Wilmot Hall. All but Davidge and Shaw, who did not have an MD degree, were trained by Benjamin Rush in Philadelphia. At first the college was homeless, the first session with seven students being housed in the homes of Davidge, Cocke, and Shaw. The second year, with 10 students, the school occupied an "abandoned shack" at the southwest corner of Fayette Street and McClelland's Alley. In 1809, Dr. Shaw died and was replaced by Elisha DeButts, MD, from Philadelphia. The third session, 1809–10 with 18 students, was divided between the Fayette Street shack and a hotel ballroom. In March 1810, at the first public commencement, five MD degrees were awarded. Finally, in 1812, the school took possession of its new building on the northeast corner of Lombard and Greene Streets. The building's construction was financed by a lottery and cost $45,000. It was designed after the Pantheon in Rome and built by Robert Cary Long, a Baltimore builder. On December 29, 1812, the General Assembly authorized the Medical College to annex to itself schools of divinity, law, and arts and sciences and thereby become a true university, "by the name and under the title of the University of Maryland." However, the state assumed no financial obligation to the school; therefore, it began as a proprietary institution. Each of the four faculties was represented in the board of regents by seven professors. [McCauley, "Professional Dentistry and the University of Maryland," 74–75.]
21. David P. Erlick, "The Peales and Gas Lights in Baltimore," *Maryland Historical Magazine* 80 (Spring 1985): 9.
22. Thomas W. Griffith, *Annals of Baltimore* (Baltimore: William Wooddy, 1824), p. 181.
23. Edward Hungerford, *The Story of the Baltimore & Ohio Railroad 1827–1927*, vol. 1 (New York: G.P. Putnam's Sons, 1928), p.11.
24 Thompson King, *Consolidated of Baltimore 1816–1950: A History of Consolidated Gas Electric Light and Power Company of Baltimore* (Baltimore: Consolidated Gas Electric Light and Power Co., 1950), p. 16.
25. Paul Johnson, *A History of the American People* (New York: Harper Perennial, 1999), p. 99.
26. Joseph A. Whitehorne, *The Battle for Baltimore 1814* (Baltimore: Nautical & Aviation Publishing Company of America, Inc., 1997), p. 191.
27. Scott Sheads, *Fort McHenry* (Baltimore: Nautical & Aviation Publishing Company of America, Inc., 1995), pp. 37, 105.
28. Francis F. Beirne, *Baltimore: A picture history 1858–1968* (Baltimore: Bodine & Associates, Inc., 1968), p. 7.
29. Sherry H. Olson, *Baltimore: The Building of an American City*, rev. ed. (Baltimore: Johns Hopkins Press, 1997), p. 88.
30. Claude Bourguignon-Frasseto, *Betsy Bonaparte: The Belle of Baltimore*, translated by Elborg Forster (Baltimore: Maryland Historical Society, 2003), p. 8.
31. Hungerford, *The Baltimore & Ohio Railroad*, pp. 8, 13.
32. Beime, Baltimore, p.13; Hungerford, *The Baltimore & Ohio Railroad*, p. 38.
33. Courtney B. Wilson, "The B & O Railroad Museum," *The Courier* 2 (Spring/Summer 2003): 11.
34. Bourguignon-Frasseto, *Betsy Bonapate*, p. 227.
35. In 1814, speed was the prime requirement for warships. The "hit-and-run privateer schooners" had taught the Navy that "speed in sailing meant survival when the odds were against them, or victory and the choice of position when the odds were favorable or even." The *Ann McKim* built in Baltimore in 1833, was hailed as the first of the new clipper ships and the "forerunner of the China and California Clippers." [Howard I. Chapelle, *The History of the American Sailing Navy: The Ships and their Development* (New York: Bonanza Books, 1949), pp. 292, 474.]
36. Beirne, *Baltimore*, p. 8.
37. Ibid., p. 26.
38. Gary Lawson Browne, *Baltimore in the Nation, 1789–1861* (Chapel Hill, N.C.: University of North Carolina Press, 1980), pp. 162–63.
39. "Baltimore Flour," *Boston Daily Advertiser* 45 (September 22, 1840).
40. "Cotton Duck," *Boston Daily Advertiser* 45 (September 10, 1840).
41. Kenneth Silverman, *Edgar A. Poe: Mournful and Never-Ending Remembrance* (New York: Harper Perennial, 1992), p. 79.
42. Olson, *Baltimore: The Building of an American City*, p. 98.
43 "Union and Dispatch Line of Baltimore and Boston Packets," *Boston Daily Advertiser*, 45 (September 10, 1840).
44. Bourguignon-Frasseto, *Betsy Bonaparte*, p. 40.
45. Beirne, *Baltimore*, p. 18.

46. Silverman, *Edgar A. Poe*, p. 171.
47. Melanie Parry, ed., *Chambers Biographical Dictionary*, reprint (Edinburgh, UK: Chambers Harrap Publishers Ltd, 1998), p. 486.
48. David W. Shaw, *The Sea Shall Embrace Them: The Tragic Story of the Steamship Artic* (New York: Free Press, 2002), p. 10.
49. Tom Koch, *The Wreck of the William Brown: A True Tale of Overcrowded Lifeboats and Murder at Sea.* (Camden, ME: International Marine/McGraw-Hill, 2004), p. 95.
50. Melanie Parry, ed., *Chambers Biographical Dictionary*, reprint (Edinburgh, UK: Chambers Harrap Publishers Ltd., 1998), p. 1639.
51. Rembrandt Peale built a museum and gallery of fine arts on Holliday Street in 1813. [Griffith, *Annals of Baltimore*, p. 208.]
52. Erlick, "The Peales and Gas Lights," 14; Beirne, *Baltimore*, p. 19.
53. Beirne, *Baltimore*, p. 23; Scharf, *History of Baltimore City*, p. 122.
54. John Bowman, *Pictorial History of the American Presidency* (New York: Gallery Books, 1986), p. 48.
55. Beirne, *Baltimore*, p. 28; Scharf, *History of Baltimore City*, pp. 515–516; Johnson, *A History of the American People*, p. 387.
56. Bern Keating, *The Flamboyant Mr. Colt and his Deadly Six-Shooter* (Garden City, N.Y.: Doubleday & Co., Inc., 1978), pp. 9–11, 13.
57. J. Ben Robinson, *The Foundations of Professional Dentistry* (Baltimore: Waverly Press, Inc., 1940), pp. 16, 17, 29, 31–34, 36, 42, 54, 68; Various newspaper ads, Gardner P. H. Foley Papers, National Museum of Dentistry Archives (*hereafter* cited as GPHFP, NMDA).
58. Robinson, *Foundations*, p. 16.
59. "Dr. Baker Surgeon Dentist," *Maryland Journal and Baltimore Advertiser* 1 (September 7, 1773), GPHFP, NMDA.
60. "John H. Gilbert, a German and regular bred physician," *Maryland Journal and Baltimore Advertiser* 1 (September 25, 1773), GPHFP, NMDA.
61. "Doctor McGinnis, Surgeon Dentist," *Maryland Journal and Baltimore Advertiser* 2 (December 19, 1774), GPHFP, NMDA.
62. Robinson, *Foundations*, p. 17.
63. J. Ben Robinson, "Dr. Benjamin Fendall (1753–1818): A Pioneer American Dentist," *Journal of the Baltimore College of Dental Surgery, Dental School, University of Maryland* 2 (March 1938): 1, 2–3; Leonard Rapoport," Dentistry in the Eighteenth Century" ["Doctor Fendall," *Maryland Journal and Baltimore Advertiser* 3 (September 11, 1776)], unpublished paper, GPHFP, NMDA; "Doctor Fendall," *Maryland Journal and Baltimore Advertiser* (July 20, 1784), GPHFP, NMDA; Aaron Schaeffer, "Dentistry in Maryland: 1800–1840" ["Dr. B. Fendall, Operator Upon Teeth (A regular bred Dentist)," *Baltimore Evening Post* (February 13, 1809)], unpublished paper, GPHFP, NMDA.
64. "Mr. Sowden, Surgeon Dentist," *Maryland Journal and Baltimore Advertiser* (July 26, 1783), GPHFP, NMDA).
65. Robinson, *Foundations*, p. 20.
66. Rapoport, "Dentistry in the Eighteenth Century," ["C. Whitlock," *Federal Intelligencer and Baltimore Daily Gazette* 2 (November 5, 1794)], GPHFP, NMDA.
67. Rapoport, "Dentistry in the Eighteenth Century," ["C.E. Whitlock, Dentist," *Federal Intelligencer and Baltimore Daily Gazette* 3 (August 13, 1795)], GPHFP, NMDA; Robinson, *Foundations*, p. 20.
68. "Dr. Hornby," *Maryland Journal and Baltimore Advertiser* 13 (August 1, 1786), GPHFP, NMDA.
69. "M. Jeanin, Dentist, From France," *Maryland Journal and Baltimore Advertiser* 14 (March 6, 1787), GPHFP, NMDA.
70. Rapoport, "Dentistry in the Eighteenth Century," ["Mr. Gardette, Dentist," *Maryland Journal and Baltimore Advertiser* 15 (September 5, 1788)], GPHFP, NMDA.
71. Rapoport, "Dentistry in the Eighteenth Century," ["Mr. Gardette, Dentist From Philadelphia," *Maryland Journal and Baltimore Advertiser*, 15 (September 16, 1788)], GPHFP, NMDA.
72. Rapoport, "Dentistry in the Eighteenth Century," various Gardette ads, GPHFP, NMDA.
73. J. Ben Robinson, "Early Dentists in Baltimore who Probably Practiced their Profession at Fell's Point," *MSDA Journal* 19 (December 1976): 166.
74. Thomas Bruff patented a "perpendicular extracting instrument" on June 28, 1797. It was the first patent (No. 245) issued by the U.S. Patent Office for a dental instrument in the country. [Robinson, "Early Dentists," p. 166.]
75. Robinson, "Early Dentists," p. 166.
76. "James Molan," *Maryland Journal and Baltimore Advertiser* 18 (September 23, 1791), GPHFP, NMDA.
77. "To the Gentlemen and Ladies of Baltimore-Town and County," *Baltimore Daily Repository* 1 (July 18, 1792), GPHFP, NMDA.
78. "Doctor Skinner, Surgeon, Dentist, and Oculist of New York," *Baltimore Daily Intelligencer* 1 (April 2, 1794), GPHFP, NMDA; Robinson, *Foundations*, pp. 27–28.
79. Rapoport, "Dentistry in the Eighteenth Century," ["Dr. Beziers, Dentist," *Federal Gazette and Baltimore Daily Advertiser* 4 (March 22, 1796], GPHFP, NMDA.
80. "Philip Larus, Dentist (Duly examined in Europe)," *Federal Gazette and Baltimore Daily Advertiser* 5 (October 4, 1796), GPHFP, NMDA.
81. Robinson, *Foundations*, p. 29.
82. Robinson, "Early Dentists," pp. 166–67.
83. Robinson, *Foundations*, pp. 42, 52.
84. Ibid., pp. 33–34, 37.
85. Ibid., pp. 34–35.
86. "E. Laroque," *American & Commercial Daily Advertiser* (September 15, 1824); "E. Laroque—Dentist, Anodine Drops for the Cure of the Tooth Ache," *American & Commercial Daily Advertiser* (March 11, 1825); GPHFP, NMNA.

87. "Mr. Shymanski, Dentist," *American & Commercial Daily Advertiser* (July 12, 1824); "Removal. Mr. Shymanski, Dentist," *American & Commercial Daily Advertiser* (October 3, 1825), GPHFP, NMDA.
88. "Dr. Parsons, Dentist, From N. York," *American & Commercial Daily Advertiser* (March 3, 1826), GPHFP, NMDA.
89. "Edmond Byrne, Dental Surgeon," *American & Commercial Daily Advertiser* (January 1, 1836), GPHFP, NMDA.
90. Robinson, *Foundations*, pp. 36, 42, 54, 74, 76.
91. Gardner P. H. Foley, "The World's First Dental College: Why? When? And Where?" *Journal of the Maryland State Dental Association* 33 (Spring 1990): 9.

Horace H. Hayden

Chapin A. Harris

Chapter 2

Organization of BCDS: 1840

"The amount of labor required of him [Horace H. Hayden] as a professor was very great, for one who had already numbered threescore years and ten. . . . He labored diligently and anxiously, too diligently and so anxiously in the discharge of his duty to his pupils. I need not tell you that he did not labor in vain. His lectures were rich in matter. He had read every thing that could throw light upon the healthy and diseased conditions of the dental structures, and, what was of more importance to his pupils, he had been a close observer and independent thinker for fifty years. The aggregate of the vast knowledge thus acquired from the labors of others, and more especially from his own, was comprehended in his lectures. He loved knowledge for its own sake, and studied nature from the force of that instinctive curiosity which is the animating principle of genius."[1] **~Thomas E. Bond, 1840**

The Cofounders: Hayden and Harris

It was not until the middle of the 19th century that the first institution giving instruction in the "science and art of dentistry" was founded and almost simultaneously the first dental journal and first national dental organization were established. The primary architects of these three major developments in the history of the profession were two Baltimore dentists, Horace H. Hayden, a transplanted Connecticut Yankee, and Chapin A. Harris, a New Yorker. Although neither dentist was college educated nor born of wealth, the "intellectual curiosity of each man, however, ranged from the natural sciences to the liberal arts." Both men were interested in art, as attested by their 1838 election as directors of the Maryland Academy of Fine Arts, an organization for "artists, amateur artists, and lovers of art generally, including ladies." To these two men, the profession owes everlasting gratitude. They stand out "prominently and conspicuously as intelligent, energetic, far-sighted, and unselfish men."[2]

Horace H. Hayden

Horace Henry Hayden was born on October 13, 1769, in Windsor, Conn. Hayden came from a military background. His ancestor, William Hayden, saved the life of his captain in the Pequot War of 1637. His grandfather, Daniel Hayden, was a lieutenant in the French and Indian War; and, his father, Thomas Hayden, an architect and builder, served as a sergeant and then first lieutenant in the Revolutionary War. During the war, Hayden and his mother

Horace H. Hayden

had to harvest the crops and attend to the family farm. As a boy, Hayden exhibited a "remarkable liking for natural history" while rambling in the woods. At the age of 10, he began studying the ancient languages and became quite proficient. When he was 14, he shipped out on a brig bound for the West Indies as a cabin boy and made two trips. After this episode, he returned to school until he was 16, when he learned the trade of a carpenter and later became an architect. He attacked his new career with ardor and read all the books he could procure on architecture, both ancient and modern. He left many drawings and notations as evidence of his "knowledge and skill in this art." At age 21, he again sailed for the West Indies and settled at Pointe a Pitre, Guadeloupe; but, after a brief stay came down with a fever and was forced to return to the United States. The next year, he returned to the West Indies, but again succumbed to the fever and had to return home. For several years, he practiced as an architect, and at age 24, left Connecticut for New York, remaining there during the spring and summer of 1792. Not meeting with much success in New York, he returned home and taught school near Hartford during the winter.[3]

Initially, Hayden had planned to pursue the vocation of his father as an architect; however, a professional visit to John Greenwood in New York changed his life's career. He greatly admired Greenwood's dental skills, which had made him George Washington's favorite dentist. While under treatment, Hayden borrowed from Greenwood the few books on dentistry to be found, most notably John Hunter's, *The Natural History of the Human Teeth* (1771). He had finally found his destiny.[4]

After studying with Greenwood in 1792, he also studied the medical sciences, such as anatomy, pathology, and physiology, and was "thoroughly conversant with the best French writers on dental science." He began his early practice in the northern states, particularly in the towns of New York. In 1800, he came to Baltimore as an assistant to Dr. Thomas Hamilton,[5] "one of America's leading dentists since 1769." Hamilton's August 15, 1800, ad in the *Maryland Gazette and Baltimore Daily Advertiser* states, "From various and frequent applications which he has received, many of which not being able to attend to, he has employed an assistant Mr. Hayden whose experience as a dentist in the northern states . . . assures him great success." On March 9, 1801, Drs. Hamilton and Hayden were practicing dentistry at 62 Market Street, near Gay Street. Dr. Hamilton left Baltimore for New York later in the year, leaving Hayden in charge of his practice. By March 1802, Hayden had moved his office to 149 Market Street, and as of June 1, 1804, he was located at Chatham Street (East Street).

In 1807, he was still at Chatham Street, but the 1812 city directory lists him at the corner of Charles and Chatham Streets. It is interesting to note that these early dentists made house calls, as evidenced by Hayden's announcement: "Any person wishing to be waited on at their residences will please to send a line or servant."[6]

Hayden's "natural earnestness and aptitude quickly attracted attention" and he soon built up a large clientele. Among his patients were many notable Baltimoreans, including the Ridgely family. Hayden began to study medicine, especially anatomy, and thus gained the "respect and goodwill" of the local medical profession. Dr. Hayden was issued a license by the Medical and Chirurgical Faculty[7] of Maryland in 1810, the first for the practice of dentistry in the United States. Hayden persuaded his two brothers[8] to take up dentistry and even began to teach a night class in dentistry, the forerunner of things to come.[9]

On August 16, 1813, just before the British attacked at North Point, Md., Hayden enlisted as a private in Captain Christian Andreon's Company of Infantry, 39th Regiment (Fowler's) Maryland Militia. The genes were there, as every Hayden ancestor had been a soldier. He served for only eight days until August 23 (paid $2.06 for services), when General Samuel Smith (according to biographer Thorpe), aware of Hayden's medical skills, ordered him to serve as an assistant surgeon at the regimental hospital.[10]

In 1816, Hayden was a charter member of the Delphian Club of Baltimore, one of the "earliest and most reputable literary groups," in the United States. It included eminent physicians, lawyers, ministers, and orators. Among its members were Francis Scott Key, author of the "Star Spangled Banner," and Rembrandt Peale, the artist and founder of the Peale Museum in Baltimore. Each of the charter members signed the constitution of the club after the pen name by which he was known in the club; Hayden's is recorded as "Jasper Hornblende."[11] In addition, he became the "companion of the most eminent physicians and medical professors of Baltimore."[12] As proof of his medical qualifications, in 1810 he had published an article, "Observations on Ulcerated Tonsils," in the New York Medical *Repository*. In addition, Hayden published other articles on medical subjects between 1809 and 1822.[13]

Hayden was an early advocate of the acid theory for dental caries, as evidenced by his 1813 *Medical Repository* article in which he states: "I feel no hesitation in saying that the decay in human teeth is occasioned almost universally by an acid, or otherwise morbid secretion from the mouth and gums."[14] This observation demonstrates Hayden's keen mind, for it was not until 1899 that Willoughby D. Miller (1853–1907), a transplanted American dentist in Germany, introduced his bacterio-chemical theory on dental caries.[15]

Reportedly, between 1819[16] and 1825, Hayden delivered a course of lectures on dental physiology and pathology to the medical students at the University of Maryland, which had been founded and chartered by the Maryland General Assembly in 1807. It was the sixth medical school founded in the United States and the first south of Pennsylvania. The attendance at these lectures was poor, for few medical students were interested in dentistry and the other professors thought it detracted from their medical studies. These lectures were interrupted in 1825 by an internal problem at the medical school. Discord and dissention among members of the faculty precipitated an ugly legal battle between the Regents of the University and a newly created, state-appointed Board of Trustees, which challenged the Board of Regents as the governing body of the university. This legal fight between the regents and trustees continued until 1837, when the "Board of Regents had its rights restored in a ruling by the Court of Appeals of the State of Maryland," at which time the "Regents regained control of the university and, it is said, Hayden resumed his lectures." This incident was the first time a dentist had lectured in a medical school[17] in the United States.[18]

Dr. Hayden was one of the founders of the Maryland Academy of Sciences and served as its president in 1825. He was also involved with the programs of the American Philosophical Society and the Academy of Natural Science in Philadelphia. Honorary MD degrees were conferred upon Dr. Hayden by the Jefferson College of Medicine of Philadelphia in 1837 and the University of Maryland in 1840. In 1842, Hayden was made an honorary member of the Virginia Society of Surgeon Dentists as a token of his esteem. His educational, literary, and professional skills resulted in his founding, along with Chapin A. Harris, of the Baltimore College of Dental Surgery chartered in 1839, the world's first institution exclusively dedicated to dental education. At age 70, he was the college's first president and professor of dental physiology and pathology. In 1840, Dr. Hayden was instrumental in the founding of the American Society of Dental Surgeons, the first national dental organization (which union he had advocated as early as 1817), and served as its first president until his death in 1844. He received the honorary DDS degree as an adjunct to society membership. In 1839, he helped organize the world's first dental journal,[19] the *American Journal of Dental Science*, which eventually became the official organ of the society.[20]

By 1833, Dr. Hayden was living "uptown" on Mulberry Street at "the corner of a pretentious block of homes and a private school which stood immediately south of Latrobe's Basilica of the Assumption." An 1820 source mentions that Hayden "looked down on humbler neighbors . . . [on] Charles Street."[21] In 1838, Dr. Hayden was elected a director of the Maryland Academy of Fine Arts.[22]

In 1842, Hayden was granted a patent for "preventing caries of the human teeth, and the exclusive privilege of using and rendering the empyreumatic oil (tar or balsam) and acid obtained by distillation of wood, which oil or acid, when properly modified, proportioned, and applied, is used for the purpose of counteracting decay in human teeth, and the diseases consequent thereto, and to the human mouth." He claimed his product had "an antiseptic property which counteracts caries, allays pain and irritability of the vessels of the teeth and mouth, lessens morbid sensibilities, and arouses and restores a healthy action."[23]

A man of many talents, Hayden was also the author of the first general work on geology published in the United States, *Geological Essays* (1820). Hayden had to master the French language to translate the best books on geology. He discovered a new mineral, named Haydenite in his honor. Later, his mineral collection became the basis of the collection of Roanoke College, Va. Dr. Hayden was a botanist and wrote on silkworm culture; he was also a great sportsman, excelling with rod and gun. He married Maria Antoinette Robinson, of Baltimore, in 1805 and had six children, two of whom died in infancy. Dr. Hayden died on January 26, 1844, at age 75 in Baltimore and was buried in Green Mount Cemetery in that city.[24] Many years later, Dr. J. Ben Robinson, the Baltimore College of Dental Surgery dean (1924–53), eulogized Hayden as:

> . . . One of the most profound characters among the great in the annals of dentistry. . . . Horace Hayden's life's work personified the ideals of scientific dentistry, recognizing at every point all of the elements which go to make up professional integrity based on maximum values to be found in scientific education, and the culmination of his resolute ideal was the founding of the Baltimore College of Dental Surgery.[25]

Chapin A. Harris

Chapin Aaron Harris was born in Pompey, Onondaga County, N.Y., on May 6, 1806, of English ancestors. His granduncle, Captain Joshua Harris, fought at Bunker Hill, and his grandfather, James Harris, was killed in battle during the war. His father, John Harris, born in 1773, married, and immigrated to America.[26]

Chapin A. Harris

The family moved to Madison, Ohio, when Harris was about 17. He began studying medicine with his elder brother, John Harris,[27] in about 1824. After completing his course of study, he was licensed by the Ohio Medical Board of Censors to practice medicine and surgery. However, he was intrigued by dentistry and began practicing dentistry in Greenfield, Ohio, in 1828. A year later, he moved to Bloomfield, Ohio, where he practiced dentistry, medicine, and surgery for two or three years. He then began touring the South and Southwest as an itinerant, where he built up an excellent reputation. Bored with life on the road, he next established himself in Fredericksburg, Va., where he practiced dentistry exclusively, but continued his medical studies.[28]

In the early 1830s, Harris and his brother James came to Baltimore to study under Dr. Hayden. In 1833, both Chapin and James were licensed by the Medical and Chirurgical Faculty to practice dentistry in Maryland. Harris was referred to as a "pupil of Dr. H. H. Hayden." Harris continued his southern itinerant circuit until the founding of the college. He devoted a large portion of his time to dental and medical literature, and attended the Washington Medical College[29] of Baltimore for an indeterminate time and date. Although it has been said that Harris received his MD degree from the college, the records of the period do not support that statement. He is listed as an undergraduate student at the college in 1838. The list of former graduates published that year does not include his name, either as a graduate or the recipient of an honorary MD degree. However, in 1839 in the preface of his book, *The Dental Art,* he signed his name with the title MD. He also used the MD title in an 1840 article published in the *Maryland Medical and Surgical Journal.* In 1833, the degree was also appended to his name on his license issued by the Medical and Chirurgical Faculty of Maryland. It can be concluded that when Harris was licensed to practice medicine in Ohio, he "assumed the MD degree and continued to use it." His honorary MA degree was awarded by the Shurtleff College of Alton, Ill. His DDS degree came from his membership in the American Society of Dental Surgeons. Reportedly, he received an honorary DDS degree in 1854 from the Philadelphia Dental College.[30]

Seeking a more permanent character for his work, in 1839 he published his first book, *The Dental Art: A Practical Treatise on Dental Surgery,* which was 385 pages. A second edition was published in 1845 under the title, *Principles and Practice of Dental Surgery*, containing 600 pages. Later editions were issued in 1847, 1850, 1852, 1855, 1858, 1863, 1866, 1871, 1885, 1889, and 1898. It was the most popular dental book ever published. His next book, *Dictionary of Dental Science, a Dictionary of Dental Science, Biography, Bibliography, and Medical Terminology*, was published in 1849; other editions followed in 1854, 1877, 1891, and 1898.[31]

Dr. Harris was an "untiring worker," described as a big man: 6 feet, 2 inches tall and weighing 208 pounds, who would work hard all day and then work on his book at night until one or two o'clock in the morning. Dr. Harris was largely responsible for the establishment of the world's first dental journal, the *American Journal of Dental Science*, published in Baltimore in 1839, under the direction of a committee consisting of Eleazar Parmly, Solymon Brown, and Elisha Baker, with Chapin A. Harris and Eleazar Parmly as co-editors.[32] In October 1839, the *Maryland Medical and Surgical Journal* published an article supporting its sister journal, the *American Journal of Dental Science*:

> The above is the title of a new periodical devoted particularly to the interests of our *Brethren* of the *File* and *Forceps*. It has reached its third number; one of which has not in the least disappointed the high expectations created by its predecessors. We look upon this undertaking as fraught with interest, and pregnant with good to the community at large, and more particularly to the members of the profession.
>
> We commend it to the favorable attention of the medical community, and ask for it an extended patronage. We do this more cheerfully because of the intimate connexion [*sic*] which exists in reality between this branch of our profession, and *those* to the interests of which *we* are more immediately devoted. We trust the time has come when dental surgeons will bestir themselves in meeting the obligations of the whole community which are upon them, and not confine themselves to the building up of personal reputation and individual fortune. They have the time and the *talent*, and should freely lend the one, and bestow the other, in the most unwearied efforts to drive every quack from *their* field.[33]

The journal also called to the attention of its readers the fact that there was an "immediate effort" either to establish schools of dental surgery or attach chairs of dental surgery to the medical schools already in existence. It called for the members of "these kindred professions" to "see eye to eye, and unite diligently" in the efforts to raise the standards of both professions.[34]

The *American Journal of Dental Science* published the works of John Hunter, Gariot J. Nasmyth, T. Berdmore, Leonard Koecker, Baume, Jobson, J. White, S. Brown, R. Blake, Blandin, and T. E. Bond. Harris translated for the *American Journal of Dental Science*, the French works of Delabarre, Lefoulon, Duval, Desirabode, and Jourdain. By the fourth issue, the circulation reached 174 subscribers. In 1840, the journal was taken over by the American Society of Dental Surgeons as its official organ, and the journal was issued quarterly instead of monthly. Its title was changed to the *American Journal and Library of Dental Science* and the price of a subscription was increased from $3.00 to $5.00. For the next 10 years, Dr. Harris remained continuously as its chief editor until 1850, when he took it over as a "personal enterprise," until his death.[35]

Dr. Harris was one of the founders of the American Society of Dental Surgeons, the first national dental society, and had made the motion "that a national society of dentists be formed." He was chairman of the constitution committee, the first corresponding secretary, and the president in 1844.[36] Harris was also the editor of the *Guardian of Health*, a publication that first appeared in 1841.[37]

Upon the death of Dr. Hayden in 1844, Harris was elected the president of the Baltimore College. From 1856 to 1857, Dr. Harris served as the second president of the American Dental Convention,[38] which was the successor to the American Society of Dental Surgeons after it folded in 1855. Dr. Harris' library was one of the finest in Baltimore. He corresponded with foreign authors and publishers and had standing orders for purchasing anything on dentistry at his own expense. Dr. Harris was an avid reader and chess player. His favorite authors were Sir Walter Scott, Lord Byron, Napier, Rollin, Motley, Macaulay, and Strickland. In 1838, he was elected a director of the Maryland Academy of Fine Arts. He loved children and animals, especially dogs and horses. He brought up and educated nine children in addition to nine of his own. Dr. Harris was married to Lucinda Heath of Loudoun County, Va. He died on September 29, 1860, and was buried at Mount Olivet Cemetery in Baltimore. Unfortunately, Harris, "liberal in life to an extreme," died in poverty. In October 1860, 50 prominent dentists started a fund for the relief of his family. Although more than one thousand dollars was collected, after expenses only $85 was sent to his widow. Dr. Eleazar Parmly said: "He has labored more arduously as a practitioner, more untiring as a writer, and more devotedly as a teacher of the principles and practice of dental surgery than any person who has in any way or in any country been connected with our professional art."[39]

Thomas E. Bond, Jr.

Thomas E. Bond

The third founder of the Baltimore College of Dental Surgery was Dr. Thomas Emerson Bond, Jr., a well-trained, reputable, medical practitioner, a "speaker of unusual force and a capable instructor," who was sympathetic to Hayden and Harris' cause.[40] Dr. Bond was born in Harford County, Md., in November 1813. He received his AM degree from the Baltimore City College in 1830 and MD from the University of Maryland in 1834. In 1832, as a medical pupil, he assisted his father, Dr. Thomas E. Bond, Sr., during the Baltimore cholera epidemic. In 1838, he assumed his father's practice. For 32 years, he held the chair of pathology and therapeutics at the Baltimore College of Dental Surgery, and was the dean from 1841 to 1842. He was also the professor of materia medica and hygiene at the Washington University, Baltimore (1842–51). Dr. Bond was a minister in the Methodist Episcopal Church, and was the editor of the *Baltimore Christian Advocate* and the *Episcopal Methodist* and in 1841was the coeditor of the *Guardian of Health*. He was the author of *Treatise on Dental Medicine* (1851), and "Life of John Knox." Dr. Bond died on August 19, 1872, in Harford County, Md.[41]

Henry W. Baxley

Henry W. Baxley

The fourth founder of the Baltimore College of Dental Surgery was Dr. Henry Willis Baxley, who had been a pupil of Hayden's. He was a "distinguished anatomist" and the "outstanding oral surgeon" of his day. In 1839, he removed a patient's lower jaw for osteosarcoma, reportedly the first such operation in America. His addition to the faculty as an "authority in the field of oral surgery" added greatly to the proposed course of instruction for the dental students.[42] Dr. Baxley was born in Baltimore in June 1803, and educated at St. Mary's College in Baltimore. He received his MD degree in 1824 from the University of Maryland. From 1826 to 1829, he was the attending physician at the Baltimore General Dispensary, and from 1831 to 1832 held the same post at the Maryland Penitentiary. In 1832, he reported on the cholera epidemic[43] in Baltimore. In 1834, he was appointed demonstrator of anatomy at his alma mater. He was disliked by the students because he collected a $5.00 fee from each student who attended the anatomy laboratory. The other professors at the school also detested him for his close association with the university's board of trustees. They even imagined that he was a spy at their lectures and meetings for the trustees with whom they had been at odds since 1826. When the trustees raised Baxley's lab fee to $10.00 per student, the other professors rebelled, as their own salaries had been reduced. Many students left to attend a private laboratory run by Dr. Samuel G. Baker, the son of a former faculty member. Finally, in 1837, the professor of anatomy, Eli Geddings, left the university for a better position and Dr. Baxley was named to the post by the trustees. Almost immediately, the faculty elected Dr. Baker to the medical faculty, and on September 21, 1837, the professors seized the buildings, which were state owned. The trustees met in an emergency session the next day and selected their lawyers. On September 23, the legal minds of both sides met and the professors abandoned their siege. Medical education in Maryland had reached its "lowest ebb." This incident was the famous suit of the "Regents vs. Trustees." Finally, in 1839, the Maryland Court of Appeals ruled in favor of the faculty (regents), and the trustees had to return the disputed property. The faculty received full title to the medical college buildings. This incident probably diverted Baxley's interests toward the new dental school then being in the process of formation. As one of the original faculty, Dr. Baxley served only one year (1840–1841) as professor of anatomy at the Baltimore College of Dental Surgery. From 1842 to 1847, he was professor of surgery at the Washington University, Baltimore, and from 1849 to 1850, physician to the Baltimore Almshouse. In 1850, he served as professor of anatomy at the Medical College of Ohio, in Cincinnati, and in 1852 held the chair of surgery at that institution. From 1860 to 1862, he served as a government inspector of hospitals, which required him to travel to California, South America, and the Pacific Islands. In California, he was offered a chair at the University of the Pacific but declined. As a southerner, he feared he would not be comfortable in a pro-Union state. In 1866, he went to Europe for his health, where he remained before moving back to Baltimore in 1875. Dr. Baxley died on March 13, 1876, at age 73. At his death, he bequeathed a large sum of money to Johns Hopkins Medical School for a chair of pathology, which was occupied by Dr. William H. Welch in 1904.[44]

Eleazar Parmly

Parmly and Brown: The Other Contributors

Among the dentists of the 1800–40 period who were most intimately associated with the promotion of a national dental society (American Society of Dental Surgeons), a dental journal (*American Journal of Dental Science*), and a dental college (Baltimore College of Dental Surgery), were Eleazar Parmly,[45] the president of the Society of Surgeon Dentists of the City and State of New York (founded in 1834), and Solyman Brown,[46] the corresponding secretary of that organization. The two men met in 1825 and remained friends as long as they lived. Along with Hayden and Harris, these two dentists may be regarded as the "leaders who designed and promoted the institutions which have since been regarded as establishing dentistry upon an acceptable professional basis." They attracted the attention of the world to American dentistry for the "superior excellence of its dental art, a distinction which had hitherto been reserved to dentistry in France and England."[47] However, as M. D. K. Bremner, dental historian, evaluated their roles:

> In short, both of these men were very helpful in furthering the three great projects. Both played and important part in ventures which are connected in our minds with Hayden and Harris, and it is unfortunate that their names have not been included among the founding fathers. Apparently everything is a matter of luck, even immortality. Hayden and Harris have gained renown as the founders of professional dentistry. Busts and plaques have been dedicated in their honor. The details of their lives have been preserved and recorded, while Eleazar Parmly (1797–1874) and Solym[a]n Brown (1790–1876), their co-workers and helpers, have been completely forgotten.[48]

Solyman Brown

This statement may be not entirely true, as J. Ben Robinson (1940) gives great credit to both Parmly and Brown for the Baltimore College's founding. Robinson states that Parmly's contributions among the dental pioneers were "next to that of Hayden's," and Brown's influence on early professional dentistry was "profound" and more than he has been credited with. However, Robinson does admit that their work "has not been appreciated by dental historians."[49]

The Baltimore College of Dental Surgery: 1839–40

Hayden had always looked upon dentistry as a branch of medicine, and when his lectures to the University of Maryland medical students proved unsuccessful, he was distraught. Dr. H. Willis Baxley wrote that when Hayden lectured to the medical students on dental pathology and physiology: "I was [in] one of his class [*sic*], and found the lectures very speculative and unsatisfactory. Certain it is that those engaged in tooth-pulling, filing, and filling, which then seemed the sole business of the craft, took no interest in Dr. Hayden's attempt to enlighten them. Nevertheless, he is entitled to credit for an effort, however unsuccessful, to give dentistry better claims to public confidence."[50] However, although Hayden's efforts to teach "scientific dentistry" were unsuccessful in the medical school, there is no doubt that this effort was the starting point for the founding of the dental college a few years later.[51]

Dr. Harris was in sympathy with Dr. Hayden that the profession needed a school and that an adjunct to the medical department of the University of Maryland would be the answer to the profession's future educational needs. Reportedly, their overtures to the medical school were rejected because the physicians feared the "chartering of a dental school would prove detrimental to the interests of the medical school." Their opposition simply stated, "That the subject of dentistry was of little consequence, and thus justified their unfavorable action."[52]

Robinson Defends the University of Maryland

Robinson (1940) in his book, *Foundations of Professional Dentistry*, disputes the fact that dentistry was forced to "accept autonomy as a consequence of the unfavorable action" of the University of Maryland Medical School. He claims that the statement, "the subject of dentistry was of little consequence" to justify their rejection, reportedly in a letter to Chapin Harris, was never in actuality written; furthermore, Harris never made such a request to the university. The medical literature of the 1840s and the dental college's founders' statements clearly indicate that "medicine entertained a kindly feeling toward the founding movements in dentistry and gave them every possible encouragement." It is unlikely that Harris would have approached the University of Maryland with his alleged request, because he was so closely connected with its competitor, the Washington Medical College in Baltimore, and had been a former student. Certainly, he would have first appealed to his friends there. Furthermore, the University of Maryland at that time was in "an exhausted condition due to internal strife, and would have been unable to offer any aid," even if Harris had been foolish enough to request it. According to Robinson, much of this error was introduced into dental history by the friends of Chapin Harris, who wanted to establish him as the founder of the Baltimore College of Dental Surgery. The contention that Harris received a letter of rejection from the University of Maryland after he had attempted to add a chair of dentistry to its medical school was fiction, not fact. Robinson attributes this error to Dr. James Taylor's 1861 obituary in *Dental Register of the West*, which stated "the medical department of the University of Maryland opposes the measure." Robinson further cites the 1884 article by Dr. Richard B. Winder, the Baltimore College Dean (1882–94), that appeared in Wilson's *Medical and Dental Register of the City of Baltimore.* Winder stated:

> A graduate in medicine who had adopted dentistry as his calling [Harris], perceiving, the relations of the two professions, applied to a medical college [University of Maryland] in this city, already venerable in the

rank of schools for the formal recognition of dentistry; and the founding by that institution of a chair, or chairs of dentistry. 'Dentistry indeed! A mere trade to ask for partnership with medicine.' The out come of this refusal was the founding, in 1839 [sic] of the 'Baltimore College of Dental Surgery' the first, and for some time the only, dental college in the world.[53]

Robinson's contention was that this reference was handed down by dental historians as gospel, despite its unsubstantiated source; it simply never happened. Other later historians, such as Eugene F. Cordell (1891), B. J. Cigrand (1893), and William Simon (1904) merely copied this mistake, which was never challenged.[54]

As further indication of Harris' lack of interest in the medical school idea, Robinson cites Harris' 1851 editorial in the *American Journal of Dental Science*, which indicated that he had been opposed to 'an alliance" with a medical school and had rejected "an overture" from a medical school:

When the first dental college was about going into operation, we were waited on by three members of the faculty of one of our oldest and most respectable medical schools, and tendered such a professorship as is suggested by Dr. Gardette, but we declined it upon the ground that no purely medical institution could afford the necessary facilities for thorough practical instruction in operative and mechanical dentistry, and that, consequently, if we accepted it, we would be employed in making the worst kind of quacks—men without skill, but with acknowledged pretensions to it.[55]

Furthermore, Robinson cites some of the contemporary published reports as evidence of medicine's support for the Baltimore College:

1. The conferring of an honorary MD degree on Horace H. Hayden in March 1840 by the Medical Faculty of the University of Maryland as an "expression of its high esteem for his scientific attainments."
2. The October 1839 issue of the *Maryland Medical and Surgical Journal*, the official organ of the Medical and Chirurgical Faculty of Maryland, recommended the new *American Journal of Dental Science* to its readers and commented: "We would particularly call their attention to an immediate effort either to establish schools of dental surgery in this country, or attach chairs devoted to this branch of a medical education, to the different colleges already in existence. Although many difficulties would necessarily be encountered in carrying into successful operation either of these suggestions, we nevertheless believe that one or the other of them could be fully carried out, to the great benefit of both professions, and the people generally."
3. Chapin A. Harris in his introductory lecture at the opening of the college stated: "For the friendly feeling that has been manifested toward it by most of the medical faculty of this city, as well as by gentlemen of that profession in other places, and for the flattering notices that have been taken of it by many of the medical and newspapers presses of the country, they not only feel profoundly grateful, but are stimulated by them to enter upon its duties, with a zeal which perhaps they might not otherwise have possessed."
4. Dr. Thomas E. Bond, Jr., in his valedictory address to the first graduating class in 1841 said: "To the medical profession, too, we are happy to acknowledge ourselves under great obligations. From the first they have been our warm and zealous friends. They have despised the fitful jealousy, so often and so falsely attributed to them, and everywhere and in every way, they have prompted the success of an infant enterprise."[56]

Robinson believed that the above statements proved that there was no justification for charging the university medical faculty with rejecting a dental department on the grounds that it was *unimportant and lacked the respect of the medical men.* Medicine recognized "an independent dental profession and respected it for its importance."[57]

Waite (1937), on the other hand, thought it "entirely logical" that the medical school of the University of Maryland would have been selected as the first choice for "this venture." He reasoned that both Drs. Henry Willis Baxley and Thomas Emerson Bond, Jr., were both graduates of that school and that Baxley had been a professor there. In addition, Bond's father had been one of the founders and an early professor there. Dr. Hayden had studied there and lectured on dentistry to the medical students. Unfortunately, Baxley had been dismissed from the faculty a few months before amid "much contention on his part." Waite reasoned that the school did not want Baxley back on the faculty, because of the "bitter personal feelings." Certainly, the school had nothing against Dr. Hayden, as it gave him an honorary MD degree within the year and there was no problem with Dr. Bond. Baxley was the main problem, but if the school said he was unacceptable publicly, perhaps it would only "renew the bitter controversy of the immediately preceding years."[58]

An Independent School

With this apparent dismissal, failure, or conscious decision, Drs. Hayden and Harris went to New York City and endeavored to establish a "chair of dentistry" in one of the New York medical schools. Earlier, in 1834 the Society of Surgeon Dentists of the City and State of New York had stated as one of its objectives to obtain "a charter to found an institution for qualifying students to practice dentistry." Certainly, Hayden and Harris knew of the society's interest in dental education; however, this effort, too, was a failure because the men who were selected for the faculty would not serve because "there was no money in it and they could not spare the time." The one exception was Dr. Solyman Brown, but no one else. Dr. Harris said he was willing to serve as dean if a college was established in Baltimore. Reportedly, Dr. Brown was the one who suggested, "Why not have an independent Dental College?" Therefore, $1,300 was subscribed by 13 prominent New York dentists—$100 each, for starting the college. It would be 10 years before the College paid the money back.[59] At the same time, apparently, although it supported the school in Baltimore, the society was giving some thought to organizing its own college, or merely encouraging the formation of schools in the various 26 states. The society felt that more than one dental college was needed as soon as this "mode of professional education" became a necessity and a reality.[60]

Meanwhile, Hayden and Harris returned to Baltimore to renew their efforts for an independent school. During the winter of 1839–40, they secured the signatures of Baltimore citizens to a petition to the Maryland Legislature for the "incorporation of a college of dental surgery" in Baltimore. Despite attempts by jealous medical rivals (according to Thorpe) to kill the proposal, the charter was granted in 1839, and with the aid of Drs. Bond and Baxley they organized the Baltimore College of Dental Surgery. Hayden became the president and professor of physiology and pathology, and Harris became the first dean and the professor of operative dentistry and dental prosthesis.[61]

The question repeatedly surfaces to which of the two men the greater honor is due, especially "in whose mind was born the thought of establishing a dental school." Simon states that neither of these men alone would have succeeded, for in many ways they complemented one another. The "exchange of thought and through combining their forces the creation of the college was made possible." Hayden was fond of teaching, as exemplified by his night classes and medical school lectures. He strongly believed in and labored for the "advancement of scientific pursuits in general," particularly dentistry. However, to some extent his "great intellectuality overshadowed his practical endowments, and here it was that Harris supplied the lacking force." Harris was not just a "man of science," but also a practical man of world affairs. He could organize and solve problems of a practical nature, which would have stymied Hayden. Even the chairs occupied by the two men at the school tell us something about them. Hayden was professor of dental pathology and physiology, branches that, at the time, were largely of a theoretical nature; whereas Harris was professor of operative dentistry and prosthetics and had to deal with reality. Although dental education was uppermost in Hayden's mind, he needed Harris "to show the way for carrying out his lofty ideas, to take the necessary steps in matters of detail, such as securing a charter, forming a faculty, creating a board of visitors, etc." The fact that Hayden was elected president of the college and remained so until his death does not minimize Harris' role in the success of the college, which was largely due to his "efficiency, tact, organizing power, and untiring labors." [62]

Hayden and Harris worked for many months at night in Hayden's office on their plans for a college. Finally in 1839, they were ready. Cordell sates:

> The founders of the school first endeavored to engraft it upon the University as a separate department of the same. Being unsuccessful on this, doubtless owing to the unsettled condition of the latter, which had shortly before this been rent in twain and was but just emerging from a nearly fatal lawsuit, they boldly launched out upon the untried sea, with an independent school. Their immediate and marked success shows their effort was opportune and that they supplied a real want.[63]

According to Dr. Ferdinand J. S. Gorgas, the Baltimore College of Dental Surgery dean (1865–82), when Chapin Harris co-founded the College in 1840, "it was done with the expectation of its one day becoming incorporated with the University of Maryland, the 3rd oldest Medical College in this country." Gorgas remembered Harris saying that "the day the Univ. of Md. would form a Dental department then he should consider that his efforts in behalf of Dental education had been successful."[64]

DeFord (1912) proposes the interesting scenario that if Chapin A. Harris had been successful in establishing a dental chair at the University of Maryland Medical School, then "every dentist would have been a medical man and the DDS degree unknown. In keeping with such terms as otologist, rhinologist, neurologist, etc., we would have been designated odontologists, and would have practiced under the MD degree. . . . "[65]

NOTES

1. Tho[ma]s E. Bond, Jr. "Obituary Notice of Prof. Horace H. Hayden, being a Valedictory Address to the Graduating Class of the Baltimore College of Dental Surgery," *American Journal of Dental Science* 4 (June 1844): 228.
2. William Simon, "History of the Baltimore College of Dental Surgery," in *Transactions of the Fourth International Dental Congress* [1904], vol 3. (Philadelphia: S. S. White Dental Mfg. Co., 1905), p. 292; John Milner Associates, "Architecture as History: The Formative Years of the Baltimore College of Dental Surgery as Recorded in the Housing History," Final Report, John Milner Associates, West Chester, Pa., 1980, p. 5; J. Thomas Scharf, *History of Baltimore City and County from the Earliest Period to the Present Day: Including Biographical Sketches of Their Representative Men* (Philadelphia: Louis Everts, 1881), p. 675.
3. Burton Lee Thorpe, "A Biographical Review of the Careers of Hayden and Harris," in *Transactions of the Fourth International Dental Congress* [1904], vol. 3 (Philadelphia: S. S. White Dental Mfg. Co., 1905), pp. 413–15.
4. Ibid., p. 415.

5. Thomas Hamilton, a surgeon dentist from London, first located in Boston in 1768. Later, he moved between Boston, New York, and Philadelphia. After September 1773, he disappeared from sight until 1782 when he reappeared in New York. It is assumed that he went "underground" during the Revolution as "a loyal *Britisher.*" In 1799, he practiced in Philadelphia, but the same year moved to Baltimore. On January 4, 1800, he announced his office location as 21 Market Street, Baltimore. He moved to East Street, and then to 62 Market Street near Gay Street. In 1801, he moved back to New York and may have been in New York as late as 1810. He was the first of the early dentists to advertise, "no cure no pay." He also announced his fees in his ads. [J. Ben Robinson, *The Foundations of Professional Dentistry* (Baltimore: Waverly Press, Inc., 1940), pp. 17–18; J. Ben Robinson, "Early Dentists who Probably Practiced their Profession at Fell's Point," *MSDA Journal* 19 (December 1976): 166–67.]
6. Robinson, "Early Dentists," 166–67; Robinson, *Foundations*, p. 18.
7. The Medical and Chirurgical Faculty of Maryland was founded in 1799 as the nation's seventh medical society. Its primary responsibility was the licensing of physicians in the state. Hayden's was the first dental license issued. [Deborah K. Woolverton, "The Medical and Chirurgical Faculty of the State of Maryland and the Evolution of Professional Dentistry in Maryland: An Exhibition Celebrating the Maryland State Dental Association's Centennial Meeting, Convention Center, Baltimore, Maryland, September 22–25, 1983," *Journal of the Maryland State Dental Association* 26 (December 1983): 120.
8. One of Hayden's brothers, Anson B. Hayden, began studying with Hayden in 1818 and attended lectures at the University of Maryland. He later practiced in Savannah, Ga., and then in Washington, D. C. He died at age 52 of pulmonary tuberculosis on June 29, 1842 in Savannah. He was the first member of the American Society of Dental Surgeons to die. [(Leonard Mackall), "Obituary (Anson B. Hayden)," *American Journal of Dental Science* 3 (September 1842): 80.]
9. Thorpe, "Biographical Review," pp. 415- 16; Milner, 'Architecture as History," p. 5.
10. Thorpe, "Biographical Review," p. 416; Index to Compiled Service Records of Volunteer Soldiers who Served during the War of 1812, microcopy 602, roll 95, Record Group 94 (Adjutant General's Office), National Archives and Records Administration (*hereafter* cited as RG__, NARA); Compiled Military Service Record, Horace H. Hayden, 39 Regiment (Fowler's) Maryland Militia (War of 1812), RG 94, NARA.
11. Robinson, *Foundations*, p. 45.
12. J. Ben Robinson, "Dr. Horace H. Hayden and His Influence on Dental Education," *Dental Cosmos* 74 (August 1932): 784.
13. Lawrence Parmly Brown, "The Horace H. Hayden—John Harris Controversy: Hayden's Priority as a Dental Educator," *Dental Cosmos* 75 (August 1933): 798, 799. In 1809–10, Hayden published "Anatomical and Pathological Observations on the Teething of Infants"; in 1813, "An Investigation on the Nature, Growth and Formation of the Human Teeth, with an Explanation of the Causes of Their Decay; Particularly of Its Uncommon Prevalence in the Middle and Northern States of America"; in 1815, "An Essay on Diseased Tonsils in a Letter to Dr. Felix Pascalis"; in 1818, "Theoretical Observations on the use and functions of the Salivary, Lachrymal and other Glands in the Human System," all in the *Medical Repository.* In 1822, he published, "Remarks and Observations on 'Conjoined Suppuration of the Gums and Alveoli'," in the *American Medical Recorder.* [Ibid.]
14. William Robertson, "A Practical Treatise on the Human Teeth, showing the causes of their Destruction, and the means of their Preservation," *American Journal and Library of Dental Science* 2 (September 1841): 151.
15. Milton B. Asbell, *Dentistry: A Historical Perspective* (Bryn Mawr, Pa.: Dorrance & Co., Inc., 1988), p. 170.
16. These lectures may have occurred as early as 1818. In an article submitted to the New York *Medical Repository* in 1818, Hayden lists his title as "Horace H. Hayden, Esq., Surgeon Dentist, Lecturer on Odontology, in the University of Baltimore." The abbreviated designation undoubtedly refers to the University of Maryland Medical School. [Brown, "Horace H. Hayden—John Harris Controversy," 798.]
17. Reportedly, lectures on dentistry had been given regularly as early as 1797 at the School of Medicine at Guy's Hospital, London, by Joseph Fox and other prominent English dentists. [Bernard Wolf Weinberger, "The Educational Evolution of the Dental Surgeon: Development and Progress toward the Formation of the First Dental College," *Dental Cosmos* 71 (May 1929): 517.]
18. Robinson, "Dr. Horace H. Hayden," 787; Callcott, George H. *A History of the University of Maryland* (Baltimore: Maryland Historical Society, 1966), pp. 22–23; Carl P. Lewis, Jr., "The Baltimore College of Dental Surgery and the Birth of Professional Dentistry, 1840," *Maryland Historical Magazine* 59 (September 1964): 273.
19. According to L. Parmly Brown, Hayden originally was opposed to the publication of a journal, "alleging that he had labored too hard and too long in the acquisition of professional knowledge to sow it broadcast through the land by means of a magazine." Nevertheless, he seems to have been reconciled early on to the publication of a journal, for he was appointed one of its "collaborators" at the second meeting of the American Society of Dental Surgeons. [Lawrence Parmly Brown, "New Light on Dental History," *Dental Cosmos* 62 (August 1920): 944–45, 946–47.]
20. Thorpe, "Biographical Review," pp. 416, 417; Milner, "Architecture as History," p. 5.
21. Milner, "Architecture as History," p. 5.
22. Scharf, *History of Baltimore City*, p. 675.
23. Thorpe, "Biographical Review," pp. 417–18.
24. Thorpe, "Biographical Review," p. 418.
25. Robinson, "Dr. Horace H. Hayden," 783, 787.
26. Thorpe, "Biographical Review," pp. 418–19.
27. Reportedly, during the winter of 1835–36, John Harris delivered a course of dental lectures to the medical students at the Transylvania University at Louisville, Ky. In 1836, he made an unsuccessful attempt to charter a dental college at Transylvania University. In 1850–52, the school did, in fact, establish the first dental school to be affiliated with a medical school; however, it graduated just two students before closing its doors. [Weinberger, "The Educational Evolution of the Dental Surgeon,"572, 573; Edward C. Mills, "John Harris, MD, DDS," *Bulletin of the Ohio State Dental Society* 1 (November 1927): 107.]

28. Thorpe, "Biographical Review," pp. 419–20.
29. The Washington Medical College was founded in 1827 by Dr. Horatio Gates Jameson. It was charted by the state of Maryland in 1833. The college closed in 1851 due mainly to competition from the University of Maryland; however, the college was reopened in 1867 by Dr. Edward Warren, an ante-bellum professor at the University of Maryland. [Callcott, *A History of the University of Maryland*, pp. 69, 82, 206.]
30. Robinson, *Foundations*, pp. 48, 49; C[hapin] A. Harris," Ulceration of the gums and exfoliation of the Alveolar processes of children—resulting from general debility or defective nutrition," *Maryland Medical and Surgical Journal* 1 (October 1840): 424.
31. Thorpe, "Biographical Review," p. 420
32. Ibid., p. 421.
33. "The American Journal of Dental Science," *Maryland Medical and Surgical Journal* 1 (October 1839): 110.
34. Ibid., 110–11.
35. Thorpe, "Biographical Review," p. 421.
36. Ibid., pp. 421–22.
37. Simon, "History of the Baltimore College," 296.
38. The American Dental Convention was the second national dental society founded in August 1855 in Philadelphia. The society continued until 1876, when it was replaced by the more progressive American Dental Association, which was founded in 1859. [J.A. Taylor, *History of Dentistry: A Practical Treatise for the Use of Dental Students and Practitioners* (Philadelphia: Lea & Febiger, 1922), pp. 178–80.]
39. Thorpe, "Biographical Review," pp. 422–23., 424; Scharf, *History of Baltimore City*, p. 675.
40. J. Ben Robinson, "The Beginnings of Institutional Dental Education in America," in *Proceedings of the Fourteenth Annual Meeting of the American Association of Dental Schools* (American Association of Dental Schools, 1937), p. 36.
41. Simon, "History of the Baltimore College," 308; Howard A. Kelly, and Walter L. Burrage, *American Medical Biographies* (Baltimore: Norman Remington Co., 1920), p. 122; Eugene F. Cordell, *The Medical Annals of Maryland 1799–1899* (Baltimore Williams & Wilkins Co., 1903), p. 326; John R. Quinan, *Medical Annals of Baltimore from 1608 to 1880, Including Events, Men and Literature* (Baltimore: Isaac Friedenwald, 1884), pp. 65–66.
42. Robinson, "Dental Education in America," p. 36.
43. Baxley's report in an article titled, "Report on the Epidemic Cholera Lately Prevalent in the Maryland Penitentiary," was published in the *American Journal of Medical Science*, and in the newspapers. [Albert C. Eskin, "Dr. Henry Willis Baxley," *Journal of the Baltimore College of Dental Surgery, Dental School, University of Maryland* 5 (March 1941): 5.]
44. Callcott, *A History of the University of Maryland*, pp. 70–75; Kelly and Burrage, *American Medical Biographies*, p. 75; Simon, "History of the Baltimore College," 308; Eskin, "Dr. Willis Baxley," 5–6.
45. Eleazar Parmly was born in Braintree, Vt., on March 13, 1797. At age seventeen, he taught school for a year. In 1815, he began the study of dentistry with his older brother, Levi Spear Parmly in Montreal, Canada. After touring the West, he went to London and remained in Europe from 1819–21. After returning to America, he established an office in New York City and became its leading dentist. In 1833, Solymon Brown began studying dentistry with Parmly. Parmly led the fight against the Crawcours'and their Royal Mineral Succedaneum in 1834. His bitterness was so great that it motivated the founding of the Society of Surgeon Dentists of the City and State of New York founded in 1834, of which he was president. He inspired the members of the American Society of Dental Surgeons to wage the "amalgam war." He was one of the editors and on the publishing committee of the *American Journal of Dental Science*. He served as provost of the Baltimore College of Dental Surgery from 1848–52. In 1866, he served as the first president of the New York College of Dentistry and remained on the faculty until 1869. In 1866, he was the first president of the first dental educational organization, the Association of Colleges of Dentistry. He received his DDS degree as a member of the American Society of Dental Surgeons, and an honorary DDS from the Baltimore College of Dental Surgery at its first commencement in 1841. He probably had an honorary MD degree from Shurtleff College in 1842. He practiced until 1866 and accumulated a fortune estimated at 3 million dollars. Dr. Parmly died on December 13, 1874 and was buried in Ransom Cemetery, Shrewsbury Township, Monmouth County, New Jersey. [Robinson, *Foundations*, pp. 46–48; "An International Dental Family (Eleazar Parmly, MD, DDS)," *Dental Radiography and Photography* 32, no. 3 (1959): i, 59–60.]
46. Solyman Brown was born in Litchfield, Conn., on November 17, 1790. He had the best academic education of all the pioneer dentists, having received both a baccalaureate (1810–12) and a Master of Arts degree from Yale College. He was ordained a minister in the Congregational Church in 1813, and for seven years combined the duties of minister and teacher. In 1820, because of a throat disorder, he abandoned the pulpit and taught school in some of the better eastern academies until 1833. In 1825, Brown, then a teacher at the Wall Street Academy, met Eleazar Parmly. In 1833, Brown began studying dentistry with Parmly and soon became one of New York's leading dentists. In 1834, Brown wrote *Dentalogia*, a dental poem in blank verse, and in 1838, another poem, Dental Hygeia. He took an active part (if not the principal part) in the founding of the *American Journal of Dental Science*, and contributed "A Treatise on Mechanical Dentistry," which ran serially in the 1841 *Journal*. The meeting at which the *Journal* was born was held at his home, No. 17, Park Place, New York. He was one of three members of the first publishing committee, and was the practical editor for the first volume, although his name does not appear officially. He was also one of the founders of the Society of Dental Surgeons of the City and State of New York (organized in 1834), and was the corresponding secretary in 1836. Brown was a charter member of the American Society of Dental Surgeons (organized in 1840), and was on the committee that drafted its constitution. Again, the founding meeting was held at his residence. He was the society's recording secretary and its president in 1839. He received an honorary DDS degree from the Baltimore College of Dental Surgery in 1841. In 1844, he sold his New York practice to Dr. Charles C. Allen and retired to a Fourieristic community, which failed causing him severe financial losses. He could not return to New York City to practice because of an agreement with Dr. Allen; therefore, he began a practice in Ithaca and Owego, N.Y., and then returned to New York as manager of a dental sup-

ply house. Upon obtaining a release from Dr. Allen to resume practice, he formed a partnership with Drs. Norman W. Kingsley and Samuel Lockwood. In 1854, he organized the New York Teeth Manufacturing Company, which ceased business in 1857. Dr. Brown then returned to the ministry, becoming the pastor of Swedenborgian Church in Danby, N.Y. In 1874, he went to live with his daughter in Dodge Center, Minn. He died on February 13, 1876, at age 86, after a brief illness. Solymon Brown's influence was felt in the founding of the first journal, first college, and first national society much more than he has ever been credited with. [Robinson, *Foundations*, pp. 50–51; "Poet Laureate of Dentistry (Solymon Brown, AM, DD, MD, DDS)," *Dental Radiography and Photography* 27, no. 4 (1954): i, 72.]

47. Robinson, *Foundations*, p. 44.
48. M. D. K. Bremner, *The Story of Dentistry*. 3rd ed., rev. (Brooklyn: Dental Items of Interest Publishing Co., 1954), p. 138.
49. Robinson, *Foundations*, pp. 48, 51.
50. Simon, "History of the Baltimore College," p. 295.
51. Ibid.
52. Thorpe, "Biographical Review," p. 422.
53. Robinson, *Foundations*, pp. 61–62; W[illia]m H. Wilson, ed., comp., *Medical and Dental Register of the City of Baltimore with Medical Directory of Maryland* (n.p., 1884), p. 137.
54. Robinson, *Foundations*, pp. 62–63.
55. Ibid., p. 64; [Chapin A. Harris], "Dr. Gardette on the Propriety of Abolishing Dental Colleges, and substituting for them a Lectureship on Dentistry in each of the Medical Schools," *American Journal of Dental Science*, n.s., 1 (April 1851): 399.
56. Robinson, "Dental Education in America," pp. 33–34.
57. Ibid., 34.
58. Frederick C. Waite, "The Background of Modern American Dentistry," *Journal of Dental Education* 1 (February 1937): 102.
59. Brown, "New Light on Dental History," pp. 941, 947, 948.
60. Solyman Brown, "Information Concerning the American Society of Dental Surgeons," *American Journal of Dental Science* 1 (January–February 1841): 193–94.
61. Thorpe, "Biographical Review," p. 422.
62. Simon, "History of the Baltimore College," pp. 296–297.
63. Cordell, *The Medical Annals of Maryland*, p. 105.
64. Letter, F. J. S. Gorgas, Dean, Dental Department, University of Maryland, to George E. Traverse, May 23, 1882, in "Records of Papers—Letters, etc., in connection with Conduct of Dr. F. J. S. Gorgas in regard to Mail matters –Treachery and Falsehood affecting the interests of the Baltimore College of Dental Surgery—after the resignation of his position as Dean on April 27th 1882," Historical Collections, Health Sciences and Human Services Library, University of Maryland, Baltimore.
65. William H. DeFord, *Lectures on General Anaesthetics in Dentistry*, 2nd ed. (Pittsburgh: Lee S. Smith & Sons, 1912), p. 16.

ACADEMIA,

Chirurgiæ Dentium.

Baltimoriensis

OMNIBUS AD QUOS HÆ LITERÆ PERVENERINT

SALUTEM

Studuit apud nos vir probus ac ingenuus Robert Arthur qui in scientiis a nobis doctis sic feliciter incubuit, ut postquam curriculi proprii spatio in aula nostra peracto, coram Nobis Curatoribus ad examen revocatus, se, in his studiis satis versatum exhibuisset, nos Eum Chirurgiæ Dentium Doctorem creavimus atque omnes honores et jura et privilegia grado Chirurgiæ Dentium Doctoris concessa ei concessimus.

In quorum fidem literis hisce sigillo Academiæ communi munitis nomina nostra subscripsimus.

Datum Urbe Baltimoriensi Die Martis Idus VII Anno Domini MDCCCXLI

Horace H. Hayden M.D. D.D.S. Prof. Physiol. et Pathol. Dentium

H. Willis Baxley, M.D. Anat. & Physiol. Prof.

Chapin A. Harris M.D. D.D.S. Prof. Prax. Chirurg. Dentium.

Tho. E. Bond J. M.D. Prof. Pathol. et Therap. Special.

Robert Arthur's diploma: 1841

Chapter 3

The Founding of BCDS in 1840

"The true significance of the beginning of institutional dental education has been obscured by dental historians in their attempts to identify the parts played by the individual founders and to label finally those who deserve credit for priority in the educational movement. The emphasis has been placed on who was instrumental in laying the foundation rather than on why a foundation was necessary and what actually entered into it. While it is important to know who participated in the movement it is more important to understand the purposes and motives of the participants. The idea of institutional dental education was not the thought of one man but the conclusion reached by many; its beginning and its growth were not the work of one individual but the achievements of the cooperative efforts of a group of men."[1] **~J. Ben Robinson, 1940**

The Baltimore College of Dental Surgery: 1840

The purpose in founding the Baltimore College of Dental Surgery was "to provide adequate facilities for instructing the dental student in both the science of dentistry and its art of practice." In addition, it was thought that the influence exerted by such an institution would "effectively discourage the empirics" and serve to drive them from the field as a source of dental education. It was also hoped that these reforms would elevate dentistry into a "more useful and more highly esteemed profession." A combination of the preceptorial training, which dealt mainly with the art of practice, and the institutional, which was designed for the biological sciences, combined these two essential elements into the best scenario. Chapin Harris clearly stated the college's mission in his introductory lecture for the college's first session in 1840:

> In regard to the plan of instruction which it is proposed to pursue, it is only necessary to observe, that, while it will be such as will enable the pupil to become thoroughly grounded in theory, the surgical and mechanical portions of the art will be exhibited in all their minutiae, and opportunity given each, of repeating them sufficiently often to become familiarized with, and skilled in the various manipulations pertaining thereto, so that on leaving school he may not only be a good theorist but a good practitioner.[2]

The greatest weakness of pioneer dentistry was the "lack of interest in the biological factors involved in dental practice." The relatively few medically trained dentists, who were educated in the health sciences, appreciated the "health significance" of dental procedures, whereas the majority of dentists, who lacked a formal medical education, were woefully lacking in this respect. The college sought to address this need to incorporate scientific education with the practical application of the dental art. At the time of the college's founding there were two schools of thought among dentists in the relationship between medical and dental education. The first wanted to add dental lectures to the medical curriculum and bring dentistry under medical control as a specialty of medicine. The other wanted an independent dental college, whose curriculum would teach both the biological and the technical. Hayden's previous experience in lecturing to students of the University of Maryland Medical School "did not indicate medicine's lack of respect for dentistry so much as it proved that medical education regarded dentistry as naturally autonomous." Another factor favoring independent dental education was the lack of proper physical facilities in medical schools for teaching the clinical phase of dentistry, a vital part of the dental curriculum.[3]

Dr. Charles Ballard discussed the two theories for dental education and the advantages of an independent curriculum:

> An experiment had been made of teaching dentistry by means of lectures in medical colleges; but it became obvious to those who attempted it, that it was ineffectual, so far as the main object was concerned, and it was attended with one disadvantage which would of itself more than counterbalance the good to be derived. The proportion of those attending medical colleges for the benefit of dental lectures was exceedingly small; and those who attended for the purpose of perfecting themselves in the various branches of medicine, took but slight interest in the dental course. Dental students, in like manner, gave their attention to their own branch at the expense of the medical lectures. It hence became obvious, that though good physicians might be sent forth from the college, that good dentists could not; while those who studied the dental specialty would not be skillful physicians. . . . The method of instruction pursued in the Baltimore College of Dental Surgery, has now been in successful operation something over ten years; it was not adopted without due consideration on the part of its faculty. A sufficient proof of its superiority over the plan proposed of adding a course of dental lectures to the regular lectures of the medical colleges, is given in the fact of Dr. H. H. Hayden's acceptance of one of the chairs of the dental college—*after having tried the former plan and found it wanting.*[4]

The rational conclusion is that Hayden and Harris were both convinced that an "independent college" would better serve the "peculiar requirements involved in training candidates for dental practice" and that for this purpose it would be better to establish "such an institution rather than to seek a chair in a medical school."[5]

The Act of 1840

On January 23, 1840, William F. Giles, a member of the Maryland House of Delegates representing Baltimore, presented a bill in the Maryland Legislature entitled, "An Act incorporating the Baltimore College of Dental Surgery." It was endorsed by Drs. James H. Miller[6] and William W. Handy,[7] both Baltimore physicians; Dr. Thomas Hughes Edmunds, a Baltimore dentist; and others. The bill was read and then referred to the Committee on Corporations. Section 2 of the act stated:

> And be it enacted, that the following persons be and are hereby appointed and constituted the Professors of said College, to wit: Horace H. Hayden, MD, to be Professor of Pathology and Physiology; Chapin A. Harris, MD, to be Professor of Practical Dentistry; Thomas E. Bond, Jr., MD, to be Professor of Special Pathology and Therapeutics; and Horace H. Hayden to be Professor of Anatomy and Physiology.[8]

The bill passed its preliminary readings and came up for final passage on January 30, 1840. Dr. John James Graves,[9] a Baltimore member of the House of Delegates, proposed several amendments to the bill; namely, to insert "Dental" before Hayden's first two subjects; to insert "Dental" after "special" appearing before Bond's two subject; to insert "Special Dental" before Hayden's last two subjects. Harris' designation was unchanged. H. Willis Baxley's name was added when the bill reached the Senate. Graves' amendment gave the college curriculum a "purely dental complexion and distinguished the proposed dental college as wholly apart from medicine."[10]

The bill was returned by the Senate Clerk to the House on February 1, 1840, with the endorsement, "will pass with the proposed amendment," namely, "in the 6th line of the 2nd section, strike out the name of Horace H. Hayden and insert the name of H. Willis Baxley," to be professor of special dental anatomy and physiology. The House approved the amended bill and it was passed on for final reading and ordered to be printed. On March 6, 1840, the bill, "That a College of Dentistry be, and the same is hereby established in the city of Baltimore, to be known and designated by the name and style of the Baltimore College of Dental Surgery," was signed by John Nick Watkins, Clerk of the House; by Joseph H. Nicholson, Clerk of the Senate; and by William Grayson, Governor of Maryland.[11]

McCauley states very eloquently the resulting effects of the bill:

> The great objective of a publicly chartered institution for the education of practitioners of dentistry was realized. A foundation for instruction in both the science and the art of dentistry was created, an unprecedented standard of dental education established. Dentistry was at last legally recognized as a profession in itself, separate from medicine. Elevation of the profession and an end to the era of 'barbers and blacksmiths' in dental practice were rendered predictable. The public would reap the benefit.[12]

The act declared the professors and their successors were to be a "corporation and body politic" under the name of the Baltimore College of Dental Surgery. Furthermore, the act stated:

> That the said Professors and their successors shall be capable, in law, of purchasing, receiving by gift, or otherwise, and holding, improving and disposing of property, real, personal or mixed; and they may take and receive any sum or sums of money, or any kind of goods and chattels that may be sold or given to them by any person or persons, bodies politic or corporate, and employ the same for the benefit of said College. . . . *provided however*, that their corporate stock or property acquired, shall never at any time exceed the sum of twenty-five thousand dollars.[13]

The act gave the professors the power to elect a president and other officers of the college; the power to fill vacancies as they occur; and to choose and appoint lecturers in the various branches of dental science.[14] It also stipulated that the professors and their successors should hold at least "one term in every year, for the period of four months, for the purpose of delivering lectures and instructions in the different branches of Dental Science, for which they are hereby empowered to charge such fees as they may deem proper for attending such lectures and receiving such instructions."[15] It also created a Board of Visitors, consisting of: R. S. Stewart, MD; Joshua T. Cohen, MD; Thomas E. Bond, Jr., MD; Thomas C. Risteau, MD; Rev. John G. Morris; Rev. Beverly Waugh; John H. Briscoe, MD; Samuel Chew, MD; Rev. George C. M. Roberts, MD; John James Graves, MD; Rev. Dr. J. P. K. Henshaw; Rev. James G. Hammer; John Fonerden, MD; Leonard Mackall, MD; and Enoch Noyes. Their duty was to meet at least once a year and see that the requirements of the charter were fulfilled.[16]

Furthermore, the law stipulated that the professors had the power to confer the degree of "Doctor of Dental Surgery" on any student, who attended all the lectures for two terms, and on others, who were found worthy "after an examination by the Professors." Those who had attended "any respectable Dental or Medical School for an equal period of time" were given credit "the same as equivalent to his having attended one of the terms herein mentioned." The professors also had the power to confer an honorary DDS degree on any dentist who "rendered service to the science, or distinguished himself in his profession."[17] The act was to remain in effect for 30 years from the date of its passage.[18]

Almost immediately, the faculty and the board of visitors began to organize. On February 3, 1840, three days after the passage of the act incorporating the Baltimore College of Dental Surgery and before the governor could affix his signature, Hayden called a meeting of the faculty at his home for the purpose of electing a president and a dean. On motion, Dr. Hayden was appointed chairman and Dr. Harris secretary; another motion was made to proceed with the election of officers. The faculty nominated and elected Horace H. Hayden the president and Chapin A. Harris the dean of the college. With no other business to discuss, the faculty adjourned. Oddly enough, the minutes of the meeting fail to even mention Drs. Bond or Baxley, who certainly must have been present. Simon (1904) suggests that this omission shows that the "chief work" was done by Hayden and Harris and that the other two members of the faculty were chiefly teachers.[19] The board of visitors elected Thomas E. Bond, Sr., MD, its president and John Fonerden, MD, its secretary. By April 1840, the board issued an announcement outlining the college's objectives, listing the standards for admission, the student fees, the qualifications of the faculty, and calling attention to the "woeful lack of educational standards that prevailed in the dental profession." Meanwhile, on May 20, 1840, Dean Harris advertised in the *American and Commercial Advertiser* the names of the faculty, a description of the course of instruction, a fee schedule, and other pertinent information on the college.[20] The announced fees were: for attending each professor's lecture for each session, $30; diploma fee, $30; and a matriculation fee, $5.[21]

Demonstrating the medical profession's support for the new college, an April 1840 editorial in the *Maryland Medical Journal* can be cited:

> We hail with no ordinary pleasure this effort to carry out the observations made in the preceding number of this journal on this important subject. We feel confident that under the direction of the talented gentlemen in the several chairs, it will prove a lasting benefit to that branch of the profession whose immediate interests it contemplates. We have understood that the prospect for a large class is much more flattering than its warmest friends have anticipated. We wish it the greatest possible success, and hope sincerely that nothing may arise to dim the prospect of its rising influence.[22]

On May 15, 1840, the faculty called a second meeting at Dean Harris' home to discuss a national advertising campaign to promote the new school and attract students. Thirteen journals and newspapers were selected from as far afield as Philadelphia, Charleston, and Louisville. The advertisements appeared more frequently as the date of the college's opening approached.[23] In July 1840, Chapin Harris (as editor) published an announcement in the *American Journal of Dental Science* that classes would begin on the first Monday in November.[24]

The 1840 announcement of the college's board of visitors stated that Professor Horace Hayden had collected a "valuable cabinet of pathological specimens" with which he could "illustrate fully the course of instruction which has been assigned to him." Professor Baxley was in possession of a "valuable anatomical cabinet" to give a "demonstrative course of instruction" in anatomy. Professor Bond, a "practitioner of medicine" would be able to give "all information" on the subject of general pathology and therapeutics as allied to dentistry. Professor Harris, "a gentleman well known both as a Dental Practitioner and author," would be in charge of the "Operations of Dentistry."[25]

The Board of Visitors gave this reason for the incorporation of a College of Dental Science:

> It is well known to all, that the wants of society resulting from diseases and distortions of the teeth, and the morbid conditions of collateral structures, are multiplied and great; but it is only those who have made it a subject of particular inquiry who are aware of the fact, that the number of those professing to control these diseases, and correct these distortions, who are competently educated Dentists, is small in proportion, to the many engaged in the practice of this profession. It has been ascertained that there are about 1200 professing Dentists in the United States; of these but a few have enjoyed the advantages of collegiate instruction in this Science. Some, it is true, have overcome the difficulties encountered in the commencement of their studies, and by the persevering application of rare abilities in the pursuit of knowledge, have contributed to enlarge the boundaries of usefulness, and established for themselves just claims to distinction. But the greater number of those engaged in the active duties of the profession—most of whom would gladly have availed themselves of suitable means of instruction, could such have been commanded—have enjoyed but limited opportunities for acquiring information, neither do they possess the original power of investigation, acuteness of observation, and discriminating judgment, which fall to the lot of but a few, and which are indispensable to supply the deficiencies of education.
>
> It is also a fact that many totally incompetent individuals from the humbler occupations of life, influenced either by mercenary or aspiring feelings, have, without any kind of preparation, assumed the title of Dentists, and engaged in the practice of Dental Surgery, and thus the science has been unjustly disparaged, and the profession has sustained unmerited reproach. Charlatanism has been too often successful in imposing upon the credulity of society, who, in the absence of all testimonials of competency have unfortunately been unable to demand what the opportunity should be afforded to them to require, viz: a professional credential in the absence of all knowledge of persons, a necessary prima facie evidence of qualifications. And thus imposture has been emboldened to occupy a position, arrogate pretensions, and engage in a practice, to the detriment of community, and the injury of the deserving cultivators of this department of science.[26]

On August 19, 1840, the American Society of Dental Surgeons met in New York City and offered its approval and support of the Baltimore College of Dental Surgery by stating that it would "co-operate with the other friends of that institution in promoting its designs."[27]

The First Commencement: 1841

Church where introductory lectures were held.

On September 22, 1840, the faculty announced that lectures would commence on November 1, 1840; however, the college officially opened its doors on November 3, 1840. To maximize public awareness, the event was held in the centrally located, Baptist Church on Calvert Street, between Lexington and Saratoga Streets. The church was the "first of the prominent Baltimore buildings with which the college was to become associated." It was also within walking distance of the homes[28] of the faculty. The introductory lectures were given at 7:30 p.m. Dr. Hayden was to be the first lecturer, but reportedly, Harris gave the opening lecture, which is the only one preserved. The Board of Visitors, the medical faculty, the clergy, and the public were invited to attend. Five students were registered for the first class: Robert Arthur and Richard Covington Mackall, Baltimore; Joseph B. Savier,[29] Norfolk, Virginia; Joseph Washington Clowes[30] and Thomas Payne,[31] New York City.[32] Lectures were delivered and clinical instruction given, primarily in the homes and offices of the faculty, from November 3, 1840, until the latter part of February 1841. Actually, there is no record of a college building as such in 1840; rather, the "faculty was the college and the college 'existed' at whatever place the faculty deemed appropriate." On February 17, 23, and 24, 1841, the first two students to apply for a degree, Robert Arthur and Richard Mackall, were examined in faculty homes. They were eligible for their degrees after having attended only one session, "each having defended a thesis and sustained a satisfactory examination, the faculty resolved to admit them to the degree of Doctor of Dental Surgery."[33]

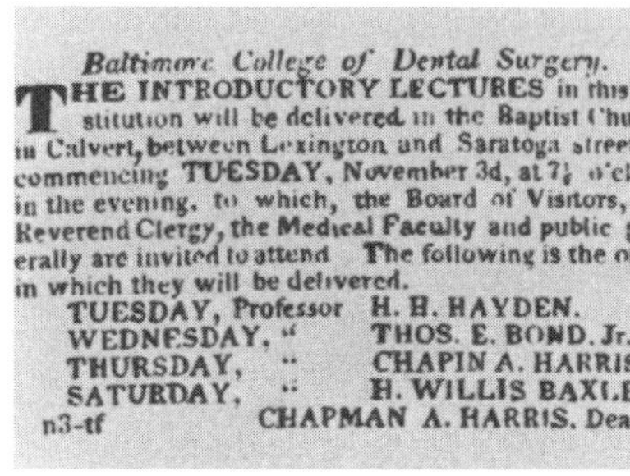
Baltimore College of Dental Surgery.

THE INTRODUCTORY LECTURES in this Institution will be delivered in the Baptist Church in Calvert, between Lexington and Saratoga streets—commencing TUESDAY, November 3d, at 7½ o'clock in the evening, to which, the Board of Visitors, the Reverend Clergy, the Medical Faculty and public generally are invited to attend. The following is the order in which they will be delivered.

TUESDAY, Professor H. H. HAYDEN.
WEDNESDAY, " THOS. E. BOND, Jr.
THURSDAY, " CHAPIN A. HARRIS.
SATURDAY, " H. WILLIS BAXLEY.

n3-tf CHAPMAN A. HARRIS, Dean.

Announcement of introductory lectures, Baltimore College of Dental Surgery. November, 1840.

Robert Arthur and Richard Covington Mackall were the first graduates on March 9, 1841, at the first commencement held in the Assembly Rooms, both receiving their DDS degrees from Dr. Hayden. Since his name had "alphabetical priority," Arthur received the first earned dental diploma in history.[34] The degree awarded was the DDS, instead of CDD, for *Chirurgiae Dentium Doctor,* the Latin degree conferred by the Baltimore College. The DDS degree had been previously awarded for the first time in history by the American Society of Dental Surgeons at its first convention in August 1840, some seven months before the College conferred it on March 9, 1841. According to Dr. Robert Arthur, Harris did not originally contemplate conferring the DDS degree, but was persuaded to do so by a friend, the Rev. John N. McJilton of New York.[35]

Robert Arthur, MD, DDS

Robert Arthur, MD, DDS, was born at Calverton, Baltimore County, Md., on July 22, 1819. His father and two brothers immigrated to America about 1800 because of the Great Irish Rebellion in 1798. Originally, young Arthur was apprenticed to a printer, but met Chapin A. Harris and studied dentistry with him before matriculating at the Baltimore College of Dental Surgery. After graduation in 1841, he began practice in Baltimore, but in 1846 moved to Philadelphia. In 1847, he moved to Washington, D.C., where he practiced for the next seven years. He was instrumental in the founding of the Philadelphia College of Dental Surgery in 1852, and served on the faculty as the professor of principles and practice of dental surgery. In 1855, he became the dean, but resigned in 1857 over a dispute on honorary degrees and helped organize the Pennsylvania College of Dental Surgery. He became a member of the American Society of Dental Surgeons at its second annual meeting in Philadelphia in 1841, and helped organize the Pennsylvania Association of Dental Surgeons in 1845, and served as its first corresponding secretary. He was active in organizing the Dental Association of Maryland in 1866 and was its first president. He translated from the French, Blandin's *Anatomy of the Dental System,* which was published in 1845 by the *American Library of Dental Science.* He also published *Treatment of Dental Caries Complicated with Disorders of the Pulp* in 1853.

Dr. Arthur is credited with the discovery of the cohesive property of gold foil. He also developed a system known as "Arthurizing," whereby the teeth were separated for prophylactic purposes, by filing the proximal surfaces. He was awarded an honorary MD degree by the Maryland College of Medicine of Baltimore. After he left Philadelphia, he moved back to Baltimore and died on June 22, 1880. Dr. Arthur was buried in Green Mount Cemetery in Baltimore.[36]

Richard C. Mackall, DDS, MD

Richard Covington Mackall, DDS, MD, was born in Wilna, Cecil County, Md., on January 14, 1822. As a boy, he studied at Elkton, Bel Air, and New London Academies. At age 18, he was sent to Baltimore to study dentistry under his uncle, Leonard Mackall, MD. He entered the first class of the Baltimore College of Dental Surgery and was the second graduate to receive the DDS degree in 1841. After graduation he moved to St. Louis, Mo., where he practiced dentistry for about three years as the state's first graduate dentist. Mackall then returned to Baltimore in 1845, entered the University of Maryland Medical School, and received his MD degree in 1847. He practiced medicine in Sudley, Va., and after the death of his wife moved to Savannah, Ga. In 1857, he purchased a farm at Langley, Fairfax County, Va. During the Civil War, as a Southern sympathizer, his property was confiscated and he was made a prisoner. He was paroled on June 11, 1861. From 1873 to 1876, he was the editor and owner of a local newspaper, the *Cecil Democrat.* For many years, he was the president of the Cecil County Board of School Commissioners and, in 1888 was elected to the Maryland House of Delegates. Dr. Mackall died on February 16, 1902, in Elkton, Md.[37]

Robert Arthur and Richard Covington Mackall

Dr. Bond's Valedictory Address: 1841

The valedictory address at the first commencement was given by Professor Bond:

> You have been taught that dental surgery is not a mere art separate from, and independent of, general medicine; but that it is an important branch of the science of cure. Your knowledge has been based on extensive and accurate anatomical investigation. You have seen and traced out the exquisitely beautiful machinery by which the organism is everywhere knit together. You have learned the secrets of nervous communication, and studied the simple, yet admirable, arrangement by which nutrition is drawn by each part from the common receptacle of strength. You have also carefully examined the phenomena of health and disease, as they are manifested in the dental arch, its connections and relations. Your attention has been directed to the effect of irritation on the general health, and you have seen how readily organs apparently unconnected and independent, may be involved in mutual disease. You have been taught to regard the human body as a complete whole, united in all its parts, and pervade everywhere by strong and active sympathies; and your principles of practice have been carefully formed on a sound knowledge of general medicine.[38]

On May 18, 1841, at a faculty meeting at Dr. Hayden's, Professor Bond was elected as the new dean.[39] In October 1841, about three weeks before the beginning of the second session, H. Willis Baxley, MD, professor of special anatomy and physiology, resigned from the faculty. Dr. Washington R. Handy, adjunct professor of anatomy and physiology at the Washington University of Baltimore, was elected to fill the vacancy.[40]

The Amalgam War: 1841

Simultaneously, with the awarding of the first earned DDS degrees in 1841, the so-called "Amalgam War" was in full swing. The war broke up friendships and divided the dental profession into two distinct groups: the dentists who endorsed amalgam by using it as a restorative material rather than gold (which was the accepted standard) and the anti-amalgam dentists. This divisive issue began in 1833, when two of the Crawcour brothers[41] arrived in the United States from Europe with a cheap coin-silver amalgam they called "Royal Mineral Succedaneum." The Crawcours set up lavish and elegant dental "Parlors" in New York City and competed with the ethical dentists who were using gold foil fillings. With the "grace and mannerisms of the French," they catered to the wealthy and influential residents of the city. The patients reclined on sumptuous chairs, and their dentistry was painless because the dentists merely sloped and thumbed a soft plastic mix of their impure material into cavities without removing the decay. They were out-and-out money-grabbing charlatans who exploited the public, charging exorbitant fees. As the Crawcours' business boomed, the conscientious practitioners—who were still working with gold and tin—lost patients. Later, as the fillings placed by the brothers began to fall out, discolor the teeth, and cause tooth fracture because of the cheap amalgam's expansion, the public realized that it had been cheated. With that, the Crawcour brothers beat a hasty retreat back to Europe in 1834, leaving "a long trail of victimized patients and exasperated dentists."[42] However, the damage had been done—amalgam now had a bad reputation, despite the fact that if used properly it was an excellent restorative material.

In 1841, the American Society of Surgeon Dentists, which had been founded the year before as the first national dental society in the United States (they gave the first honorary doctor of dental surgery DDS degree), appointed a committee to study the amalgam problem. The committee, consisting of Drs. Eleazar Parmly, Elisha Baker, Solyman Brown, Chapin A. Harris, and Jahiel Parmly, reported that all filling materials in which mercury was an ingredient were "vile and nasty" substances and capable of "producing the worst of effects."[43] Four years later, without even testing silver amalgam, their derogatory report resulted in the society's blanket statement that the use of amalgam constituted malpractice.[44] On the other hand, Dr. Christopher S. Brewster of Paris, France, thought that to condemn the use of amalgam in all cases merely because its use was abused by some "unprincipled quacks" was unwise. He felt that "much good has been and may be done by a judicious use of this composition."[45]

In 1842, Dr. Chapin A. Harris warned that there were few cases in which the "filling of teeth with an *amalgam of mercury and silver*, is justifiable." He believed that amalgam exerted "a vitiating influence upon the fluids of the mouth and given rise to an unhealthy action in the gums."[46] Harris' opposition to amalgam is evidenced by an 1881 recollection of Dr. Joseph Washington Clowes (1821-1900), Class of 1846 (honorary):

> Forty-one years ago, Amalgam, as a filling for teeth, was brought to my notice. It was spoken of by Doctor [Chapin A.] Harris, of Baltimore, in most uncomplimentary language. By him the initial class of the first Dental College in the world was taught that it was poisonous; they were admonished to adjure and refrain from it in their various fields of labor, denouncing its users and condemning its use. In my office, during the first year of professional practice, poison, salivation, galvanic action, charlatan, quack, humbug, imposter, were words of frequent utterance, and the mere sight of an amalgam plug in a patient's mouth would excite my indignation, and arouse within me the spirit of antagonism and warning.[47]

In 1844, the society's members were warned that they must sign a pledge never to use amalgam or they would risk being expelled from membership. Many members resigned, and by 1847 only five of New York's 200 dentists remained in the society, which Dr. Charles C. Allen said had "Gold" for its motto. So much bitterness was created that eventually the society rescinded the pledge, but the damage had been done and the organization folded in 1856, all because of the amalgam controversy.[48]

NOTES

1. J. Ben Robinson, *The Foundations of Professional Dentistry* (Baltimore: Waverly Press, 1940), p. 60.
2. Ibid.
3. Ibid., pp. 60–61.
4. Charles W. Ballard, "Dental Education," *American Journal of Dental Science*, n.s., 2 (October 1851): 67.
5. J. Ben Robinson, "The Beginnings of Institutional Dental Education in America," in *Proceedings of the Fourteenth Annual Meeting of the American Association of Dental Schools* (American Association of Dental Schools, 1937), pp. 34–35.
6. James H. Miller was professor of anatomy and physiology at the Washington Medical College, Baltimore. Md. [Robinson, Foundations, p. 64.]
7. William W. Handy was professor of obstetrics and diseases of women at the Washington Medical College, Baltimore, Md. [Robinson, *Foundations*, p. 64.]
8. Robinson, *Foundations*, p. 64.
9. John James Graves was an 1827 medical graduate of the University of the City of New York. He was co-editor of the *New York Medical Journal* from 1829–31 and practiced in New York City for three years. He then moved to Baltimore, where he became prominent in medicine, served as a member of the Maryland Legislature for 1839–42, and was a member of the original Board of Visitors of the Baltimore College of Dental Surgery. [Robinson, *Foundations*, p. 64.]
10. Robinson, *Foundations*, pp. 64–65.
11. Robinson, *Foundations*, p. 65; State of Maryland, *Laws Made and Passed by the General Assembly of the State of Maryland* (Annapolis, Md.: William M'Neir, 1840), section 1, chap. 155.
12. H. Berton McCauley, "Dental Education Institutionalized: The 'What' of the Baltimore College of Dental Surgery," *Journal of the Maryland State Dental Association* 33 (Spring 1990): 12.
13. State of Maryland, *Laws Made*, section 3, 4, chap. 155.
14. State of Maryland, *Laws Made*, section 5, chap. 155.
15. State of Maryland, *Laws Made*, section 7, chap. 155.
16. State of Maryland, *Laws Made*, section 8, chap. 155.
17. State of Maryland, *Laws Made*, section 9, 10, chap. 155.
18. State of Maryland, *Laws Made*, section 13, chap. 155.
19. "Record of the Proceedings of the Faculty of the Baltimore College of Dental Surgery," Baltimore College of Dental Surgery Papers, National Museum of Dentistry Archives (hereafter cited as BCDSP, NMDA); William Simon, "History of the Baltimore College of Dental Surgery," in *Transactions of the Fourth International Dental* Congress [1904], vol. 3 (Philadelphia: S. S. White Dental Mfg. Co., 1905), p. 300.
20. Robinson, *Foundations*, p. 65; McCauley, "Dental Education," p. 12.
21. Simon, "History of the Baltimore College," p. 302.
22. Ibid.
23. "Record of the Proceedings of the Faculty of the Baltimore College of Dental Surgery," BCDSP, NMDA; Carl P. Lewis, Jr., "The Baltimore College of Dental Surgery and the Birth of Professional Dentistry, 1840," *Maryland Historical Magazine* 59 (September 1964): 278–79. The list of publications included the: American and Commercial Advertiser (Baltimore), *Baltimore Pilot, Baltimore American, Baltimore Patriot, Maryland Medical and Surgical Journal, American Journal of Dental Science, American Journal of Medical Science, Charleston Currier, Louisville Journal, National Gazette* (Philadelphia), *National Intelligencer* (Washington, DC), Globe (Washington, DC), and *United States Gazette* (Philadelphia). [Ibid., p. 279.]

24. "Baltimore College of Dental Surgery," advertisement in *American Journal of Dental Science* 1 (July 1840): 7.
25. Baltimore College of Dental Surgery, *Annual Announcement of the Board of Visitors of the Baltimore College of Dental Surgery* (Baltimore: Wood and Crane, Printers, 1840), pp. 5–6.
26. Baltimore College of Dental Surgery, *Annual Announcement of the Board of Visitors* [1840], pp. 3–4.
27. [Solyman Brown, comp.]. "National Dentists' Society," *American Journal of Dental Science* 1, no. 7 (1840): 168.
28. Dr. Hayden lived at the corner of Mulberry and Charles Streets, Dr. Harris lived on Hanover Street, and Dr. Bond lived on Lombard Street. [John Milner Associates, "Architecture as History: The Formative Years of the Baltimore College of Dental Surgery as Recorded in the Housing History," Final Report, John Milner Associates, West Chester, Pa., 1980, p. 56.]
29. Joseph B. Savier continued his studies at the college, but did not graduate until 1842. He was the first to graduate after two years. [Robinson, *Foundations*, p. 69.]
30. Joseph W. Clowes had studied under Dr. J. Smith Dodge of New York City the previous year and did not return for his second year. He had entered practice in New London, Connecticut. In 1846, he received the honorary DDS degree from the BCDS. He became the "millionaire dentist" of New York City. An amalgam devotee, he was the originator of the amalgam bridge, which he called a 'causeway." [Robinson, *Foundations*, p. 69; L. Parmly Brown, "New Light on Dental History," *Dental Cosmos* 62 (August 1920): 948.]
31. Thomas Payne attended only one year and did not graduate. [Robinson, *Foundations*, pp. 60–70.]
32. Robinson, *Foundations*, pp. 69–70; McCauley, "Dental Education," 12.
33. Simon, "History of the Baltimore College," p. 303; Milner, "Architecture as History," pp. 6, 8.
34. Robinson, *Foundations*, pp. 69–70.
35. Brown, "New light on Dental History," 949–50.
36. Charles R. E. Koch, ed., *History of Dental Surgery*, vol. 3 (Fort Wayne, IN: National Art Publishing Co., 1910), pp. 200, 202, 204, 205–6; Simon, "History of the Baltimore College," pp. 312–14.
37. Koch, *History of Dental Surgery*, pp. 208–9; "Obituary. Dr. Richard C. Mackall," *Dental Cosmos* 44 (May 1902): 523–24; Gardner P. H. Foley, ed., *Proceedings of the 125th Anniversary Celebration of the Baltimore College of Dental Surgery* (Baltimore: Horn-Shafer Co., 1966), p. 192; Compiled Service Records of Confederate Soldiers Who Served in Organizations from the State of Maryland, roll 16, 22, Microcopy 321, Record Group 109 (War Department Collections of Confederate Records), National Archives and Records Administration.
38. Simon, "History of the Baltimore College," p. 303.
39. "Record of the Proceedings of the Faculty of the Baltimore College of Dental Surgery," BCDSP, NMDA.
40. [Chapin A. Harris], "Baltimore College of Dental Surgery," *American Journal and Library of Dental Science* 2 (December 1841): 207.
41. The Crawcours were a family of five Polish dentists, who acquired a "superficial knowledge" of dentistry in France before unleashing themselves on the English public in the 1780s. They advertised extensively proclaiming their skill and claimed to be surgeon-dentists to the "Royal Family and patronized by the Courts of Austria, France, Russia, Prussia, and Belgium." [J. Menzies Campbell, *Dentistry Then and Now* (Glasgow: Bell & Bain, Ltd., 1981), pp. 265, 266.]
42. D.M. Cattell, "Amalgam: Its History and Metallurgic Phenomena," *Dental Cosmos* 64 (August 1922): 855–56.
43. American Society of Dental Surgeons, "Minutes, 1840–56," NMDA, pp. 27–28, 79.
44. Ibid., pp. 73–74; Milton B. Asbell, *Dentistry: A Historical Perspective* (Bryn Mawr, PA: Dorrance & Co., Inc., 1988), p. 146.
45. E. Baker, "Letter from Dr. Baker," *American Journal of Dental Science* 6 (June 1846): 307.
46. [C(hapin) A. Harris], "Answers to Questions of a Correspondent," *American Journal and Library Dental Science* 2 (March 1842): 264.
47. Gardner P. H. Foley, "BCDS Notes," *Alma Mater* 11 (Spring 1970): 5.
48. A. Porter Sweet, "Amalgam and the 'New Departure'," *Dental Radiography and Photography* 32, no. 4 (1959): 66; C[harles] C. Allen, "A Society of Dental Surgeons in New York," *New York Dental Recorder* 2 (October 1, 1847): 2.

LEXINGTON ST. NEAR CALVERT
1851-1853

Chapter 4

The Handy Years: 1842–53

"In entering upon the duties of the chair, to which I have been called, in the 'Baltimore College of Dental Surgery,' allow me to observe, that howsoever much of interest or curiosity the establishment of this institution—the first of the kind that had ever existed, either in this or any other country—may have awakened, it constitutes an era in the history of a most useful and valuable department of medicine; and if it be properly conducted, cannot be otherwise than productive of great good."[1] **~Chapin A. Harris, 1841**

The Second Commencement: 1842

On February 18, 1842, the college held its second commencement at the Assembly Rooms,[2] a Baltimore architectural landmark. Degrees were conferred on J. B. Savier, W. R. Scott, and William W. H. Thackston. In addition, under Article 10 of the Act of Incorporation, which allowed the college to confer the honorary DDS degree "on any dentist who may have rendered service to the science or distinguished himself in his profession," the college conferred honorary degrees on 18 prominent American and European dentists (14 American and 4 European): Solyman Brown, Starr Brewster (Paris), Sir Samuel Cartwright (London), J. Smith Dodge, J. Foster Flagg, Isaac J. Greenwood, William Pitt Greenwood, James S. Gunnell, Daniel Harrington, Anson B. Hayden, Chester Hayden, Edward Hudson, Leonard Koecker, Edward Maynard, Eleazar Parmly, Jahial Parmly, Levi Spear Parmly (Matanzas, Cuba), and Rudolph Parmly.[3]

The valedictory address was given by Washington R. Handy, MD, professor of anatomy and physiology, who stated what many other dental professionals perceived, but did not say:

> The science of dentistry is regarded by some as a new thing, a new science; consequently unknown, untried, and of course liable to all the objections and drawbacks which necessarily attach to uncertainties of every kind, whether real or supposed.
>
> This supposition, strange as may seem, has been stated, not-withstanding it is well known the practice of dentistry is as old as the science of medicine itself.
>
> It is true, it has but recently received at the hands of the legislature a legitimate name, form, and habitation, and may still be regarded by some as yet in the school of doubt and experiment.[4]

Over the years, the Baltimore College of Dental Surgery took some criticism for the number of honorary degrees it conferred. During the first 10 years of its existence (1842–52), the college conferred 136 honorary degrees, 13 on foreign dentists. However, it must be remembered that before the college was founded there were many "highly competent" dentists scatted throughout the United States and Europe. McCauley (1990) perhaps sums it up the best:

> The seemingly over-generous distribution of the honors of the College should be judged in the light of the unique position of the College as an outstanding symbol of excellence in dentistry in a country estimated to have 1,200 dentists of whom perhaps 200 were qualified. Those who were honored deserved to be honored. The lofty standards of the College were in no way compromised.[5]

Of course all the candidates had to present a thesis and "specimens of their mechanical work."[6] After 1855, honorary degrees became scarcer, and from 1858 to 1913, only 14 were given. The reasons for this sharp decline are several: including the conferring of earned degrees on the type of practitioner formerly awarded the honorary degree; the opposition of dental schools and the leading dentists to the procedure; the activities of the diploma mills; and the opposition of the National Association of Dental Faculties.[7]

Washington R. Handy: The New Dean

For the 1842–43 session, the Baltimore College of Dental Surgery had a new dean, replacing Thomas E. Bond, Jr., MD, who had served only one year as dean, from 1841 to 1842. His replacement, Washington R. Handy, MD, served as dean from 1842 to 1853. Dr. Handy was born in Somerset County, Md., in 1811. Handy's father was William W. Handy, MD, professor of obstetrics and diseases of women and children at the Washington Medical College of Baltimore, who was one of the original signers in 1839 of the petition to incorporate the Baltimore College of Dental Surgery. Handy's preliminary education was completed at the Classical Academy in Newark, Del. He then entered the U.S. Military Academy, West Point, N.Y., in 1831, but was forced to resign because of ill health. Upon his recovery, he matriculated at the Washington Medical College, Baltimore, and graduated with an MD degree in 1834. Shortly afterwards, he was appointed a demonstrator in anatomy at his alma mater. In 1841, he was elected professor of anatomy at the Baltimore College of Dental Surgery, became dean in 1842, and served as dean until 1853; however, he continued his anatomy lectures until a few years before his death in 1857.[8]

In 1854, Dr. Handy published a treatise on anatomy, *A Textbook of Anatomy, and Guide in Dissection, for the Use of Students of Medicine and Dental Surgery*, which was dedicated to Chapin A. Harris and was used by many dental colleges in the country. Handy states in his preface that the book "directs *special attention to the Mouth*, showing step by step the important anatomical and physiological relations which it has with each and all the organs and functions of the general system."[9]

Hayden-Harris Debate over Maxillary Sinuses: 1842–43

We would naturally presume that Horace Hayden and Chapin Harris were close friends, bound together by the common goal of founding the world's first dental school. Apparently, this was not so, as evidenced by an incident over a lecture. From 1842 to 1843, Drs. Hayden and Harris had an argument over papers they presented to the American Society of Dental Surgeons on the same subject. As the story goes, both men lectured on the maxillary sinus at the July 20, 1842, meeting of the society in Boston. Apparently, unaware of the other's intentions (although Harris said he told a student), Hayden gave his paper at 12 p.m. and Harris at 4 p.m. When Harris published his paper, "Dissertation on the Diseases of the Maxillary Sinus," in the *American Journal of Dental Science* in September 1842, Hayden responded with a very lengthy rebuttal in the December issue of the journal. Hayden criticized the journal for "propagating or circulating misguided views and unsound theories," referring to the publication of the works of John Hunter (1728–93) and Leonard Koecker (1728–1850) without updating them. He also was critical of the contents of Harris' paper, referring to Harris as "my friend, the doctor."[10]

Harris immediately responded to what he presumed to be an attack on his expertise on the subject in the June 1843 issue of the journal. He opened his remarks by stating that "as a matter of special courtesy and in compliance with a request made by Dr. H. H. Hayden to one of the editors of this Journal, and by him communicated to us, we consented to publish without inspection, a paper from the former, purporting to be a review of [his] dissertation on the Diseases of the Maxillary Sinus." Harris said that if Hayden had confined his remarks to his dissertation alone, he would not have deemed a response necessary, but to attack the editorship was unforgivable. He defended the role of the editors to allow "full liberty to the expression of opinion and freedom of discussion." He also thought that the "extraordinary coincidence" of both reading the same papers was not extraordinary as Hayden had been apprized, several weeks previously by a student, that Harris was preparing such a paper to read at the meeting.[11]

Still not willing to drop the issue, Hayden published a rebuttal to Harris' "disingenuous ebullitions" as a private printing to send out to the subscribers of the *American Journal of Dental Science.* Hayden had been refused permission to publish his paper in the journal (of which Harris was an editor); therefore, he took this method of passing on his comments. Hayden stated that the student Harris referred to was in fact Hayden's nephew, who told him that Harris was merely writing a lecture on "the antrum." They did not discuss the Boston meeting at any time. It was a "sheer fabrication" on Harris' part in stating that he knew Harris' lecture subject for the Boston meeting.[12] Apparently, the ill feelings persisted until Hayden's death the next year, as Harris did not publish Hayden's obituary in the journal.

Changes in the 1840s

In 1843, the college offered a spring course of lectures with reduced fees. It was to start in March 1843 and run for two months. The cost of tickets for the course was $65, and the price of tickets for the winter course was reduced from $30 to $25. It was also determined by the faculty that four years of dental practice was equivalent to a winter course. Good board could be obtained with private families in Baltimore for three dollars a week.[13]

Before 1843, the college did not even have its own building, as it held its lectures and demonstrations in the professors' homes, which served as classrooms, or in prominent buildings such as the Calvert Street Church or the Assembly Rooms, a Baltimore architectural landmark.[14] Even as late as 1844, students were examined in Professor Bond's home. One must bear in mind that the major source of income for the new school was the "degrees-by-fee" granted to qualified practitioners.[15] Professor Baxley in an 1874 letter stated: "The didactic lectures were delivered in a small room, publicly situated, but the teaching of practical anatomy demanded privacy and other prudential considerations also suggested the use for that purpose of a secluded stable loft."[16] Finally, in the college's "Proceedings" for January 27, May 6, and November 11, 1843, "there is a strong suggestion that plans were underway, if not fulfilled in that year, for a lecture room and museum." The obituary of Francis Arnold, a well-known dental instrument manufacturer located at 15 Sharpe Street in Baltimore, mentions the college being located at Sharpe Street at this time. The address referred to was 13 South Sharpe Street. This very ordinary location contrasted strongly with the image the college projected with its lectures in more prominent locations.[17] However, the rooms were close to the homes and offices of the faculty, the University of Maryland Medical College, and Arnold's dental instrument company. For the semi-public functions demanding a more prestigious location, such as lectures and commencements to which the public attended, there was always nearby "new and architecturally significant buildings."[18] In 1843, the college's commencement was held in Masonic Hall,[19] one of Baltimore's grandest structures.[20]

Death of Hayden: 1844

January 26, 1844, saw the death of Dr. Hayden and a faculty vacancy. Until a replacement could be found, the duties of his chair were divided between Dr. Harris (lectures on pathology) and Dr. Bond (physiology of the teeth and mouth).[21]

In June 1844, the college announced that its regular course of lectures would begin in November and continue for four months. Its mission was the "elevation of the standard of the dental profession; of making scientific dentists, by educating young men thoroughly in all the different branches of dental knowledge, and thus sending them forth into the community fully qualified to do credit to themselves, to their profession, and by their practical skill and success, to their patients." For those who feared that the "head is educated too much, and the hand too little," the college replied that it had a separate chair for teaching "Surgical and Mechanical" dentistry exclusively. A full-time professor devoted his entire time to teaching the students "every variety of operation upon the natural or living teeth." A special room was set up as a "surgical and mechanical" workshop, which contained "all the instruments and appliances" necessary to teach a large class. The other departments were dental physiology and pathology, special pathology and therapeutics, and anatomy and physiology. The dissecting room, "not inferior to that of any medical school," was always supplied with fresh subjects; a general lecture room and museum rounded out the facilities. The library, "one of the finest dental libraries in the world," of course was available off campus to the students.[22]

The 1844 catalog also referred to the fact that, "scientific dentistry" was a branch of medicine and the "College embraces a Medical and Dental Department—each of which is committed to two Professors—the first being Practitioner of Medicine, the latter of Dentistry." The fees continued to be basically the same as the 1840 opening ones: "Ticket of each Professor, for each session, $25; Demonstrator's Ticket, $10; Dissecting Ticket, optional, $10; Diploma Fee, $30; Matriculation, $5."[23]

The Museum: 1844

The earliest mention of a museum at the Baltimore College of Dental Surgery appears in the *American Journal of Dental Science* in 1844. Chapin Harris, the editor, in his article on the BCDS stated:

Dental Museum

> The College, we may add further, has a general lecture room and a museum, which, with one of the finest dental libraries in the world—though not in the College, but to which the students can have free access—furnished some idea of the facilities and advantages which it gives to those who come to its halls for instruction in dental science.[24]

Earlier in 1842, Harris had reported in the journal that the college had a denture worn by George Washington:

> We have half of a beautifully carved upper set, that was worn for several years in connection with a lower set, by General Washington, which were presented to us by Dr. Isaac I. Greenwood, son of the late Mr. John Greenwood, extensively known as an eminent practitioner of dental surgery of the city of New York. Mr. J. Greenwood's initials, which were engraved upon these teeth at the time of their fabrication, together with part of the date, filled with tartar or salivary calculus while they were worn, are now perfectly distinct. . . . They were secured in the mouth by means of spiral springs. The other half of the upper, and the whole of the lower set, are in the possession of Dr. Isaac I. Greenwood.[25]

The Discovery of Surgical Anesthesia: 1844

In December 1844, Horace Wells (1815–48), a Hartford, Conn., dentist, discovered that nitrous oxide[26] could be used to produce freedom from pain during surgical procedures. On October 16, 1846, William T. G. Morton (1818–68), a former apprentice of Wells, administered ether[27] as an anesthetic to a patient who had a tumor of the neck. It was removed painlessly by the aforementioned Dr. Warren, who this time remarked to those present, "Gentlemen, this is no humbug." Oliver Wendell Holmes (1809–94) coined the term, "anesthesia" for this state of total absence of sensibility. Morton was hailed as the discoverer of surgical anesthesia. In the ensuing controversy for the title of discoverer of anesthesia, Wells committed suicide and Morton died penniless. In 1870, the American Medical Association gave credit to Dr. Wells.[28] Inhalation anesthesia has been called dentistry's greatest gift to mankind.

The Fifth Year: 1845

Despite the apparent success of the new school, there still remained some skeptics concerning its future. The *Boston Medical & Surgical Journal* defended an "institution organized on the principles of the Baltimore College," stating "it is a school for making safe dentists, and the people will have confidence in those who have been taught there." [29]

In March 1845, the college announced that it had 45 pupils since it opened its doors. Some were regular graduates of medical schools; others had been in practice and attained prominence in the profession; and about 20 had received the DDS degree and were practicing throughout the country. Here again, the college defended itself from those who said equal training could be attained by spending time with a preceptor. The college believed that a student learned more from "one course of instruction in the college, than can be possibly gained in four or five years' study in the private office of any dentist." Again, although two courses of lectures were required for graduation, a course in any "respectable medical school" was accepted as equivalent to one year of lectures at the college.[30] The college's 1845 annual announcement (the sixth), in describing the school's building (13 South Sharpe Street), states that the building had four rooms, a lecture room, a museum, a mechanical workshop, and a dissecting room, which was "ample and well ventilated, and abundantly supplied with subjects."[31] Actually, dissection was not compulsory for the students. Those who wished to "study the practical aspects of anatomy" could do so by purchasing a dissecting ticket for 10 dollars; otherwise, the students merely attended the didactic lectures. However, the students were urged to take advantage of the opportunity to dissect and "see and handle for himself, all the different parts of the body, especially those composing the dental apparatus, and such as are most intimately related with it."[32]

The museum was described as "containing many valuable anatomical and dental specimens, to which others from abroad will soon be added." In June 1845, Dr. Harris noted that some of the anatomical specimens coming from Paris would be arriving before the start of the next course of lectures. In December, he announced that the museum had received "between twelve and fifteen thousand morbid dental specimens" from his brother, Dr. John Harris, of Ohio.[33]

Also in the sixth announcement of 1845 the following interesting advertisement appeared under "Private Tuition":

> Dr. Harris having provided himself with every facility for teaching the various branches pertaining to Theoretical and Practical Dentistry, will give private instruction to such as may wish to avail themselves of its advantages, during the lectures, or preparatory to entering the College. His Dental Library is the most extensive in this country, if not in the world; it embraces every work of value that has ever been published on that subject. He has also a large and highly valuable cabinet of healthy and morbid dental preparations, to which his pupils have free access; in addition to which, constant opportunities are afforded them, of witnessing and performing every operation connected with *Surgical and Mechanical Dentistry.* Terms of tuition made known on application.[34]

Apparently, Harris was taking advantage of the situation now that Hayden was no longer around. What would Hayden have thought about this profit-making scheme? Would he have approved of it? Was it ethical? After all, the students were paying their tuition to be taught everything the professors knew, not information held back for "private students."

At the February 17, 1846, commencement exercises at the Masonic Hall, Chapin Harris gave the commencement address and his brother, John Harris, presented the diplomas.[35] The same year, the college announced that Dr. Amos Westcott,[36] of Syracuse, N.Y., had been elected to the Chair of Operative and Mechanical Dentistry, and that Cyrus O. Cone[37] had been appointed a demonstrator of mechanical dentistry. The college continued to attract the best dental practitioners in the country for its faculty. Meanwhile, the college had moved to a new building, "located in the very center of the city, but a few rods from the Battle Monument."[38]

The University Building: 1847

Actually, on July 29, 1847, the college entered into a 10-year lease to rent specific rooms in the "University Building" at 11 East Lexington Street near Monument Square. The building was a three-story structure erected in 1845 on the north side of Lexington Street, "two buildings east of Calvert." This was the same building occupied by Newton University, a "scientific institution" founded in 1845. Not only did the two schools "share the same building,[39] and very likely the same rooms, they also shared some administration: as late as 1855, and possibly earlier, the council of Newton University included Chapin Harris." As set down in the agreement with Simpson Larned on July 28, 1847:

> The college was to occupy all five rooms on the third floor, as well as two rooms on the fourth or attic floor. A large salon or second-floor lecture room was also to be made available (manned and lighted) for twelve nights a year. There was to be free use each Wednesday of a third-floor lecture room, with lights and fuel furnished. Use of as much of the cellar as was necessary for the storage of fuel was also agreed to in the lease. For these accommodations, the college agreed to pay $520 a year in four equal payments. Larned was to pay all taxes, repairs, charges, and assessments. Alterations were to be allowed only when written consent was granted and work was undertaken to improve facilities.[40]

The selection of this uptown site for the college, which was almost in the mathematical center of the city, was in keeping with the founder's efforts of maintaining a "high level of visibility" during the formative years of the college and the establishment of dentistry as a profession. While hinting at ownership, the college, in fact, "did not own real estate for almost forty years after its founding."[41]

In 1847, Eleazar Parmly described the college on Lexington Street:

> Large, commodious and well-lighted rooms, with furnaces, work-benches, etc. etc., are provided; a skillful Mechanical Demonstrator is daily with the students for the purposes of Mechanical Dentistry; he operates before the class, and, in every possible way, lays before them the best mode of practice; while, to crown all, a Dental Infirmary, attached to the building, enables the student to perform the several operations under the eyes of the demonstrator and Professors. The museum contains a large number of models, diseased specimens, etc., to which the students have access. In short, the College offers every desirable facility to the pupil, and the fault must be his own should he fail to acquire a proper knowledge of his profession.
>
> The College buildings are large, well ventilated, comfortable, and centrally situated. The professors feel that they have now done all that could be expected from them in order to elevate the dental art to its proper place as a branch of medical and surgical science. They have, by their own exertions, established a school which holds forth every advantage to the pupil which could be hoped for from such a foundation, and at a price far below what is commonly paid to a dentist of repute for private instruction. Whether the institution shall fulfill the intentions of its founders, and realize the hopes of its friends, must now in a great measure depend on the exertions of scientific dentists, and of the medical profession at large, in its behalf.[42]

The 1847 museum was described as containing a "large number of morbid specimens, and anatomical preparations of a valuable and costly kind, imported expressly for the use of the Institution."[43] Dr. Harris mentions that among the recent contributions to the museum was a full set of artificial dentures made by James Gardette (1756–1831), of Philadelphia, in about 1811; a mandibular denture made by Edward Hudson (1772–1833), of Philadelphia, in about 1822; a set of teeth made by Robert Wooffendale (1742–1828) before 1787; and a 1795 maxillary porcelain denture made by M. Nicholas Dubois de Chemant (1753–1824), of London (the first to make usable mineral teeth in 1789). He also said that all donated artifacts would be "carefully arranged, with the names of the donors attached to them."[44]

Following the trend set by the American Medical Association, the college announced in 1847 that it had established a "Committee of Physicians and Dentists" to participate in the examination of all degree candidates. The committee for the following year consisted of dentists and physicians: Joshua I. Cohen, MD; J. R. W. Dunbar, MD; Emile B. Gardette, MD; William W. Handy, MD; Simon P. Hullihen, DDS; Edward Maynard, MD; Elisha Townsend, DDS.[45] This plan is remarkably similar to the plan adopted by Dr. Richard Bayly Winder for his Maryland Dental College in 1873, only his was called a Board of Regents.

The Baltimore College of Dental Surgery was a "first-class private institution." It set the pattern for future dental schools by combining the medical sciences with the technical training, as seen from its curriculum of equally balanced theory and practice; its faculty was equally balanced between medical and dental practitioners. The course of study, two years of approximately four months each, was patterned after that of the best medical schools of the day, and "splendidly served the educational needs" of the profession. The requirements for the DDS degree were "as high, if not higher," than those for the MD degree. The successful completion of one year of an approved medical school was acceptable in lieu of one of the two annual sessions required for graduation. Similarly acceptable was evidence of preceptorial experience or training. To graduate, students had to pass comprehensive examinations in "theory and practice," and defend a thesis satisfactorily.[46]

The 1847 commencement was held in the Hall of the College Building on the evenings of February 15 and 16. On the first evening, the prosthetic work of the candidates was exhibited to the audience with comments by Drs. Westcott and Harris. After Dr. Bond's address, Dr. Parmly, the chairman of the awards committee, offered remarks to the students. On the second evening, the exercises opened with music, Dr. Harris conferred the degrees, and Dr. Parmly presented a cased set of dental instruments, manufactured by Mr. Arnold, of Baltimore, to John Wayland, the graduating student with the "highest proficiency." There were 10 graduates, including one from Ireland.[47]

On October 2, 1847, Isaac Greenwood, the son of John Greenwood, George Washington's favorite dentist, wrote to Chapin A, Harris to inform him that he was sending that day, via the schooner *Michigan*, a portrait of his late father for the college. The painting was done by Mr. Lovett, a student of Alston (of Boston), and was said to be an excellent likeness.[48] The portrait now hangs in the Dr. Samuel D. Harris National Museum of Dentistry.

The 1848–49 catalog noted that the school had "survived the dangers of its infancy," and was now "beyond doubt permanently established." The professional success of its graduates had "settled the question, both of the utility of its design and the efficiency of its action." The ninth annual session saw the resignation of Dr. Amos Westcott and the temporary assumption of his chair of operative and mechanical dentistry by Dr. Chapin A. Harris.[49]

In 1849, the college announced some changes in the museum, namely: "During the present summer, extensive additions will be made to the Museum, consisting of French preparations, illustrative of the branches taught in the Institution."[50]

The 1849 commencement was held at 7:30 p.m. on the evening of March 1, 1849, at the college's lecture room at the Lexington Street address. After a prayer, Professor Washington R. Handy, dean, read the right to confer degrees, given the college by the authority of the State of Maryland, in Latin. Dr. Eleazar Parmly, provost, conferred the degrees on the 13 candidates, namely: Philip H. Austen, MD; Charles W. Ballard, MD; A. A. Blandy, MD; M. Jerome Cherry, J. U. S. Feemster, M. A. Hopkinson, J. H. A. Fehr, MD; Thomas Littey, MD; Albion Martin, William S. Miller, R. R. Sams, J. F. Warren, and George W. Watkins. The valedictory address was delivered by Dr. Emile B. Gardette, the son of James Gardette, the Revolutionary War French dental surgeon. Philip H. Austen, representing the student body, then spoke of the advantages the graduates of the college enjoyed and their obligations to the professors, the college, and the community. To the professors, he said, "We feel, for their unvarying kindness, unwearied attention, and generous forgetfulness of self interest, a debt of gratitude, which the class wish[es] never to forget. With such kind feelings, we bid you, gentlemen, an affectionate farewell and pass forth into the world bearing before us that 'banner with a strange device: - Excelsior.' "[51]

For the tenth session beginning in 1849, Cyrus O. Cone assumed the vacant chair of operative and mechanical dentistry, and Philip H. Austen, MD, DDS,[52] who had just graduated the year before, became a lecturer on dental chemistry and a demonstrator of mechanical dentistry. The curriculum consisted of: Principles and Practice of Dental Surgery, Special Pathology and Therapeutics, Anatomy and Physiology, Operative and Mechanical Dentistry, and Dental Chemistry. The clinics were held in the morning and the lectures were given in the afternoon. The college proudly announced that the dental infirmary was steadily increasing its role in the care of the indigent of the city; not by the professors, but by the students under the "immediate eye and direction" of the professors. The clinic was open daily. The "Committee of Physicians and Dentists" added Drs. J. H. Foster and S. Blandin to its dental ranks and deleted Dr. Gardette.[53]

Alumni Society of the BCDS: 1849

On Thursday, March 1, 1849, at 9 a.m., the Society of the Alumni of the Baltimore College of Dental Surgery held its first meeting with Dr. Harvey Colburn, Class of 1848, as the chair. The minutes of the preliminary meetings were read and adopted. After some debate, the resolutions laid on the table by the preliminary organizers were passed. The society then proceeded with the adoption of its constitution and bylaws.[54] The mission of the society was the "mutual improvements of the graduates and students of the Baltimore College of Dental Surgery, and the advancement of the art and science of dentistry."[55]

On a motion of Dr. Charles W. Ballard, Class of 1849, the constitution was signed by the following men, who became, de facto, the founders of the society: Charles W. Ballard, Philip H. Austen, Harvey Colburn, J. U. L. Feemster, M. Jerome Cherry, Robert R. Sams, Frederick N. Seabury, R. W. Armstrong, Levi S. Burridge, Thomas D. Thompson, Cyrenius O. Cone,

Cyrus O. Cone

Albion Martin, George W. Watkins, M. A. Hopkinson, J. F. Warren, J. H. A. Fehr, and Charles A. Barnes. The following officers were elected: Harvey Colburn, president; Philip H. Austen, vice-president; Cyrus Cone, treasurer; R. W. Armstrong, corresponding secretary; and M. Jerome Cherry, recording secretary. Two committees were established: a standing committee, consisting of Drs. Cone, Hopkinson, and Feemster; and a committee on dental practice, consisting of Drs. Warren, Fehr, and Ballard. A resolution was proposed by Drs. Cone, Colburn, and Austen to grant honorary membership to the following dentists: Thomas E. Bond, J. I. Cohen, J. R. W. Dunbar, Drs. J. H. Foster, Emile B. Gardette, W. R. Handy, Chapin A. Harris, Daniel Harwood, Samuel P. Hullihen, Edward Maynard, Robert Nasmyth, Jr. (London), Eleazar Parmly, Jahiel Parmly, and Elisha Townsend. The resolution was passed and after an address by Dr. J. H. Foster, the meeting was adjourned until 3 p.m.[56]

After Dr. Colburn called the meeting to order for the p.m. session, special committees were elected. Drs. Austen, Feemster, and Hopkinson were elected for the committee on mechanical dentistry; Drs. Cone, Colburn, and Fehr formed the committee for the selection of subjects for scientific investigation and Drs. Armstrong, Cherry, and Austen the committee for arrangements for the next annual meeting. Letters were received from Drs. Wilkes Allen, W. H. Morgan, and J. D. Wemple requesting membership and they were unanimously elected. After Drs. Austen, Feemster, and Fehr were selected to deliver papers at the next meeting, the meeting adjourned.[57]

On a rainy evening on March 24, 1850, the Society of the Alumni of the Baltimore College of Dental Surgery held their second annual meeting in the college's hall. The address was given by Dr. Elisha Townsend.[58] Among the resolutions passed in the following three days of the meeting were that the annual meeting be held during the week preceding the annual commencement of the college; and any graduate of the Baltimore College could be enrolled in the society with the payment of the "initiatory fee of $3" to the treasurer. F. P. Abbott, Charles G. Davis, and Randolph Walton were elected unanimously to active membership, and honorary membership conferred on Dr. Cleveland, William H. Dwinelle, Thomas W. Evans (Paris), Levi S. Parmly, and James Robinson (London), and Amos Westcott. Dr. Austen read a paper from Dr. James Robinson, who was unable to be present, on the "State of the Dental Profession in England." Dr. Cyrus O. Cone, the treasurer, reported that the treasury had a balance of $6.55. The election of officers for the ensuing year concluded the meeting. The following were elected: J. H. A. Fehr, president; Charles W. Ballard, vice president; Cyrus O.

Cone, treasurer; Philip H. Austen, corresponding secretary; and H. Colburn, recording secretary.[59]

NOTES

1. Chapin A. Harris, "Introductory Lecture," *American Journal of Dental Science* 1 (January 1841): 198.
2. The Assembly Rooms, a two-story building, designed by Colonel Nicholas Rogers at a cost of $30,000, opened at the northwest corner of Fayette and Holliday Streets on January 17, 1798. It contained several large and elegant salons, devoted to the "entertainments of fashionable life," making it the "finest building of the character in the United States." In October 1824, the reception for Lafayette was held here. Later, a third story was added, which contained a very large hall used for lectures, concerts, and graduations. The lower floor was occupied by the Baltimore Library Company. Later in 1835, as the building fell into obsolesce, it was sold at auction to B. I. Cohen for $10,000; however, the building continued to be occupied by the Baltimore City College. It was destroyed by fire in 1873. [J. Thomas Scharf, *History of Baltimore City and County from the Earliest Period to the Present Day: Including Biographical Sketches of Their Representative Men* (Philadelphia: Louis Everts, 1881), pp. 679–80.]
3. J. Ben Robinson, *The Foundations of Professional Dentistry* (Baltimore: Waverly Press, Inc., 1940), p. 70; "Baltimore College of Dental Surgery," *American Journal and Library of Dental Science* 2 (March 1842): 261.
4. W[ashington] R. Handy, *Valedictory Address, Delivered Before the Baltimore College of Dental Surgery at its Second Annual Commencement, February 18, 1842* (Baltimore: Woods and Crane, 1842), p. 10.
5. Robinson, *Foundations*, p. 70; H. Berton McCauley, "Dental Education Institutionalized: The 'What' of the Baltimore College of Dental Surgery," *Journal of the Maryland State Dental Association* 33 (Spring 1990): 12.
6. William Simon, "History of the Baltimore College of Dental Surgery," in *Transactions of the Fourth International Dental Congress* [1904], vol. 3 (Philadelphia: S.S. White Dental Mfg. Co., 1905) p. 306.
7. Gardner P.H. Foley, "The Granting of Honorary D.D.S. Degrees by the Baltimore College of Dental Surgery," *Bulletin of the History of Dentistry* 33 (April 1985): 13–14, 16. The College awarded its last honorary degree in 1913 to Edward S. Gaylord (1840–1926) of New Haven, Connecticut. Gaylord demonstrated his gratitude by bequeathing a sum of $10,000 to the College to aid poor and worthy students. [Ibid., 17.]
8. Riley S. Williamson, "Washington R. Handy, M.D.," unpublished paper, Gardner P. H. Foley Papers, NMDA; John R. Quinan, *Medical Annals of Baltimore From 1608 to 1880, Including Events, Men and Literature* (Baltimore: Isaac Friedenwald, 1884), p. 110; H. Berton McCauley, "Dental Education Institutionalized : The 'What' of the Baltimore College of Dental Surgery," *Journal of the Maryland State Dental Association 33* (Spring 1990): 11.
9. Washington R. Handy, *A Textbook of Anatomy, and Guide in Dissection, for the Use of Students of Medicine and Dental Surgery* (Philadelphia: Lindsay & Blackiston, 1854, p. v.
10. H[orace] H. Hayden, "The following comments were elicited by the perusal of an Essay, read in part, by Dr. C. A. Harris, of Baltimore, before the American Society of Dental Surgeons, at their annual meeting, held in Boston, July 20th 1842," *American Journal of Dental Science* 3 (December 1842): 203–9; Chapin A. Harris, "Dissertation on the Diseases of the Maxillary Sinus," *American Journal of Dental Science* 3 (September 1842): 20.
11. [Chapin A.] H[arris]. "Dr. Hayden's 'Comments'," *American Journal of Dental Science* 3 (June 1843): 286–89.
12. H[orace] H. Hayden, "A Reply to Dr. C.A, Harris, on 'Hayden's Comments'," private printing, Baltimore College of Dental Surgery Papers, National Museum of Dentistry Archives (*hereafter* cited as BCDSP, NMDA).
13. "Baltimore College of Dental Surgery—Spring Lectures," *American Journal of Dental Science* 3 (December 1842): 151–52.
14. James F. Craig, "The First Dental College: A Faculty Without a Building," *Baltimore College of Dental Surgery Forum* 7 (Spring 1987): 2.
15. John Milner Associates, "Architecture as History: The Formative Years of the Baltimore College of Dental Surgery as Recorded in the Housing History," Final Report, John Milner Associates, West Chester, Pa., 1980, pp. 6, 8.
16. H. Willis, Baxley, "The First Dental College," *Items of Interest* 11 (January 1888): 2.
17. Craig, "The First Dental College," 2.
18. Milner, "Architecture as History," p. 3.
19. The Masonic Hall, a three-story brick building, was designed by Maximillian Godefroy in 1813 and the cornerstone was laid in 1814, but the building was not completed until 1822. That year, the government rented space on the first floor for the Circuit and District Courts of the United States. It was considered "quite a handsome addition to the city." It had office space and larger rooms for rental. [Claire W. Eckels, "Baltimore's Earliest Architects 1785–1820," PhD diss., Johns Hopkins University, 1950, pp. 135, 137, 139.]
20. Milner, "Architecture as History," p. 24.
21. Baltimore College of Dental Surgery, *Fifth Annual Announcement of the Baltimore College of Dental Surgery* (Baltimore: Woods & Crane, Printers, 1844), p. 5.
22. [Chapin A. Harris], "Baltimore College of Dental Surgery," *American Journal of Dental Science* 4 (June 1844): 298–99.
23. Baltimore College of Dental Surgery, *Fifth Annual Announcement*, pp. 4, 7.
24. [Harris], "Baltimore College of Dental Surgery," 299.
25. [Chapin A. Harris], "Artificial Teeth Worn by Washington," *American Journal of Dental Science* 3 (September 1842): 76–77.
26. The contemporary era in pain control began in 1772, when Joseph Priestley (1733–1804) discovered nitrous oxide and later Sir Humphry Davy (1778–1829) noted its analgesic properties; nitrous oxide " . . . appears capable of destroying physical pain. . . ." How-

ever, although by 1803 a few physicians had experimented with its use for treating various pulmonary diseases, nitrous oxide remained dormant in the medical pharmacopoeia. When the intoxicating effects of nitrous oxide were discovered by the public, students and showmen began using it for frolics and sideshows. Samuel Colt (1814–62) of revolver fame originally raised the money for his gun manufacturing business by touring the country and giving nitrous oxide exhibitions as entertainment. On December 10, 1844, Wells attended a nitrous oxide exhibition conducted by Professor Gardner Q. Colton, a traveling lecturer and demonstrator of "laughing gas." Wells was impressed by the fact that a friend who inhaled the gas felt no pain when he injured his leg. The next day, Wells took a bag of the gas to his office and had his apprentice, Dr. John M. Riggs, extract a tooth for him; he felt no pain. Colton instructed Wells how to make the gas and he immediately began using it on his patients. However, when he demonstrated his technique to Dr. John Collins Warren (1778–1856) and his medical students at the Massachusetts General Hospital in Boston, the patient (a medical student) cried out and Wells was humiliated, a "humbug" affair. Despondent, he returned home and later sailed for France to pursue the merits of his claim as the discoverer of anesthesia. [Milton B. Asbell, *Dentistry: A Historical Perspective* (Bryn Mawr, Pa.: Dorrance & Co., Inc., 1988), 156–158.]

27. Although the anesthetic properties of diethyl ether had been noticed by Michael Faraday (1791–1867) in 1818, its use remained dormant. In 1842, Crawford W. Long (1815–78), a Georgia physician, impressed by the "ether frolics," used ether as an inhalant for surgical procedures; however, he did not report it until 1849. [Daniel De Moulin, "A Historical-Phenomenological Study of Bodily Pain in Western Man," *Bulletin of the History of Medicine* 48 (Winter 1974): 544; Asbell, Dentistry, pp. 156–57.]
28. Asbell, Dentistry, p. 119; J. A. Taylor, *History of Dentistry: A Practical Treatise for the Use of Dental Students and Practitioners* (Philadelphia: Lea & Febiger, 1922.), p. 113.
29. "College of Dental Surgery," (Boston Med. & Surg. Journal), quoted in *American Journal of Dental Science* 5 (December 1844): 158.
30. "Baltimore College of Dental Surgery," *American Journal of Dental Science* 5 (March 1845): 249.
31. Baltimore College of Dental Surgery, *Sixth Annual Announcement of the Baltimore College of Dental Surgery* (Baltimore: John W. Woods, Printer, 1845), pp, 4–5.
32. William E. Hahn, "Department of Anatomy," *Alma Mater* 2 (February 1960): 38; Baltimore College of Dental Surgery, *Sixth Annual Announcement*, p. 5.
33. Baltimore College of Dental Surgery, *Sixth Annual Announcement*, p. 5; [Chapin A. Harris], "Baltimore College of Dental Surgery," *American Journal of Dental Science* 5 (March 1845): 250; Idem, "Museum of the Baltimore College of Dental Surgery," *American Journal of Dental Science* 6 (December 1845): 181–82.
34. Baltimore College of Dental Surgery, *Sixth Annual Announcement*, p. 8.
35. Edward C. Mills, "John Harris, MD, DDS," *Bulletin of the Ohio State Dental Society* 1 (November 1927): 110.
36. Amos Westcott, BS, CE, MD, DDS, was born on April 28, 1815, in Newport, N.Y. At age 19, he entered Rensselaer Polytechnic Institute and graduated with a BS degree. In 1835, he graduated as a civil engineer from his alma mater. After teaching chemistry for three years, he began to study medicine and in 1838 entered the Medical College at Geneva, N.Y., but later transferred to the Albany Medical College where he received his MD degree in 1840. He started a practice in Syracuse, N. Y., but soon decided he preferred dentistry as a career. After serving as Professor of Operative and Prosthetic Dentistry at the Baltimore College from 1846–49, he founded the New York College of Dental Surgery at Syracuse where he served as Dean and Professor of Theory and Practice of Dental Surgery and Dental Technology. Unfortunately, the school closed after a disastrous fire in 1855. He was a member of the American Society of Dental Surgeons (from which he received the honorary DDS degree), the American Dental Convention, and the American Dental Association. He was the first president of the New York State Dental Association, organized in 1859. He was the author of numerous dental articles and became an associate editor of the *American Journal of Dental Science.* Dr. Westcott experimented with dental materials, including plaster of Paris for impressions, and was one of the discoverers of the principle of the cohesion of gold at room temperature. He also patented a number of non-dental inventions, including a butter churn, a door spring, and a door bolt. After a physical breakdown, he left his Syracuse practice and toured the capitols of Europe. After returning home, in a moment of insanity, he committed suicide on July 6, 1873. ["Farm boy to dentist, via engineering and medicine (Amos Westcott, BS, CE, MD, DDS)," *Dental Radiography and Photography* 29, no. 3 (1956): i, 50.]
37. Cyrus Orlando Cone, DDS, MD, was born on September 27, 1820, in East Haddem, Conn. After an unsuccessful attempt to run a bookstore, he became a student of Dr. Solyman Brown, a leading New York City dentist in 1841. After his preceptorship, he began to practice dentistry in Chatham, Falmouth, and Edgartown, Mass. Not satisfied with his training, he entered the Baltimore College of Dental Surgery in 1844, and graduated with a DDS degree in April 1845. After his graduation, he took over Dr. John Harris' practice in Georgetown, Ky. His prosthetic skills were not unnoticed, and in 1846, he was invited back to his alma mater to become their first demonstrator in mechanical dentistry. In 1849, he succeeded Dr. Amos Westcott as Professor of Operative and Mechanical Dentistry, which position he held for another three years. In 1857, he enrolled at the Washington Medical University in Baltimore and received his MD degree in 1858. He was a member of the American Society of Dental Surgeons and served as secretary in 1852–53. After suffering from tuberculosis, he moved to Hartford, Conn., where he died on August 1, 1858. ["Cyrus Orlando Cone, DDS, MD," *Dental Radiography and Photography* 36, no. 2 (1963): i, 44.]
38. [Chapin A. Harris], "Baltimore College of Dental Surgery," *American Journal of Dental Science* 7 (September 1846): 112.
39. During the Civil War in 1862, the Newton University building became a U.S. Army General Hospital with 1,200 beds. It was demolished in 1867 for Baltimore City Hall on Holliday Street. [Scott S. Sheads, and Daniel C. Toomey, *Baltimore During the Civil War* (Linthicum, Md.: Toomey Press, 1997), p. 177.]
40. Milner, "Architecture as History," p. 27.
41. Craig, "The First Dental College," 9.
42. Robinson, *Foundations*, pp 70–71.

43. Baltimore College of Dental Surgery, *Eighth Annual Announcement of the Baltimore College of Dental Surgery* (Baltimore: John W. Woods, Printer, 1847), p. 4;
44. [Chapin A. Harris, "Contributions to the Museum of the Baltimore College of Dental Surgery," *American Journal of Dental Science* 8 (October 1847): 110–11; Asbell, Dentistry, pp. 72, 90, 136.
45. Baltimore College of Dental Surgery, *Eighth Annual Announcement,* p. 4.
46. McCauley, "Dental Education," 12.
47. "Baltimore College of Dental Surgery," *American Journal of Dental Science* 7 (March 1847): 282–84.
48. Isaac Greenwood, letter to Chapin A. Harris, October 2, 1847, BCDSP, NMDA.
49. Baltimore College of Dental Surgery, *Ninth Annual Announcement of the Baltimore College of Dental Surgery* (Baltimore: John W. Woods, Printer, 1848), pp. 2, 3.
50. Baltimore College of Dental Surgery, *Tenth Annual Announcement of the Baltimore College of Dental Surgery* (Baltimore: John W. Woods, 1849), p. 5.
51. "Report of the Commencement of the Baltimore College," *Dental News Letter* 2 (April 1849): 59–60.
52. Philip H. Austen, AM, MD, DDS, was a 1849 graduate of the Baltimore College of Dental Surgery, who joined the faculty of his alma mater the same year as a lecturer in chemistry and a demonstrator of mechanical dentistry. He became the professor of dental mechanism, 1852; dean of the college, 1853–65; and professor of the principles of dental science and chemistry, 1860–73. He had received his MD degree in 1845 from the University of Maryland and practiced medicine for 10 years, specializing in diseases of the mouth. [Gardner P. H. Foley, ed., *Proceedings of the 125th Anniversary Celebration of the Baltimore College of Dental Surgery* (Baltimore: Horn-Shafer Co., 1966), p. 129.]
53. Baltimore College of Dental Surgery, *Tenth Annual Announcement,* pp. 3, 6, 7, 8.
54. R. W. Armstrong, "Proceedings of the First Annual Meeting of the Society of the Alumni of the Baltimore College of Dental Surgery; furnished for the American Journal and Library of Dental Science," *American Journal of Dental Science* 9 (January 1849): 261.
55. "Constitution and By-Laws of the Society of the Alumni of the Baltimore College of Dental Surgery," *American Journal of Dental Science* 9 (January 1849): 248.
56. Armstrong," Proceeding of the First Annual Meeting," 261.
57. Ibid., 262.
58. Elisha Townsend, MD, DDS, was born in Philadelphia on July 16, 1804. He started out as a watchmaker, his father's trade, but switched to acting as a career. In 1832, he began studying dentistry and shortly after opened an office in the Philadelphia area. He became, as a result of his earlier training, an expert in gold work. He helped introduce to dentistry the more delicate instruments of his former trade. He served as the first vice-president of the American Society of Dental Surgeons. Townsend was one of the organizers of the American Dental Convention, which succeeded the old society after it folded. He was the recording secretary 1856–57. In 1852, he was chosen as Dean and Professor of Operative Dentistry at the Philadelphia College of Dental Surgery. After its failure, he helped organize the Pennsylvania College of Dental Surgery, and was made the dean. After serving only one year, he was forced resign because of ill health. He died on October 13, 1858. ["Watchmaker—Actor—Dentist (Elisha Townsend, MD, DDS)," *Dental Radiography and Photography* 30, no. 3 (1957): I, 60.]
59. "Proceedings of the Society of the Alumni of the Baltimore College of Dental Surgery," *Dental News Letter* 3 (April 1850): 66–68.

Philip H. Austen

Chapter 5

The Austen Years: 1850s

"Dentistry, as a true science and art, is built upon the foundation of a generous early education, is enlightened by a complete medical course of instruction, is specially trained by a full term of practical pupilage, and recognizes no sliding-scale in the quality of the service it renders. Such dentistry will exercise influence in its own, and command respect among kindred professions; for it becomes thus a curative work, second in importance and extent of its usefulness to no specialty of the great Art of Healing."[1] ~**Philip H. Austen, 1879**

The 1850 Catalog

The eleventh catalog of the college in 1850 commented on the small class size and the preceptor's lack of interest in the school:

> Many preceptors are indifferent to the success of the collegiate scheme, and many more are entirely hostile to it. If students can be persuaded that they can obtain sufficient information by remaining a few months in the office of a dentist, they will rarely incur the expense and labor of college education; and unfortunately there are many, and among them those least capable of teaching, who are always ready to undertake the training of the pupil upon the terms most likely to be acceptable to himself. The Faculty have knowledge that, in some instances, young men who have been sent to the school by their parents or guardians, have been induced to go into the office of practitioners of low standing, who have promised to give them all necessary instruction in a few months, and for a paltry sum. The consequence has been as might have been expected. No instruction was given; and the money intended for college expenses has been wasted in dissipation.[2]

Although the college faculty saw the great importance of "office instruction as an adjunct to college teaching," they felt that to elevate dentistry to the "dignity of a specialty of Medicine and Surgery," it was necessary to combine the two means of dental education.[3]

The "Committee of Physicians and Dentists" for the final examination of the candidates for graduation underwent a drastic change, as a new group of physicians and dentists not connected with the college replaced the former ones. The new committee consisted of dentists John A. Cleaveland, DDS; N. Clute, MD; N. A. Fisher, MD; and Daniel Harwood, MD, and physicians William W. Davis, MD; George C. M. Roberts, MD; and Richard Stewart, MD.[4]

A Meaningful Diploma: 1850

In the late 1840s to 1850, the college received some queries from England about the "purchase of a diploma." The college responded that when the applicants had gone through the "curriculum of study prescribed by its charter, and submitted to the usual examination, they will be entitled to a diploma." The college also noted that some individuals were using the title that had no diploma from the college and it offered to furnish all the names of those who had been granted a degree in Great Britain.[5]

Not all American dentists were exactly enamored with the new dental college, as evidenced by the reaction of one southern dentist who exclaimed: "Wherever the graduates of the Baltimore College have gone out into the South, they have taken away the business of old practitioners. *Their diplomas* are a passport everywhere and the people believe that a graduate from that college knows more than any one else."[6] In the same venue, some dentists or charlatans called themselves BCDS graduates to mislead the public into thinking that they had superior skills. One such person, H. K. Neigh, in 1850 was reported to be masquerading as a BCDS graduate and "swindling the people in various ways" in Tennessee, Alabama, and Mississippi.[7] So much for the fame the school had created for 10 years.

From March 25 to 27, 1850, the American Society of Dental Surgeons held its annual meeting at the college's lecture hall. Besides the Baltimore members, the meeting was attended by dentists from New Orleans, Charleston, Wheeling, Washington, New York City and state, and Philadelphia. Dr. Chapin A. Harris read a lengthy biography of Dr. Alexander Nasmyth.[8] Dr. Elisha Townsend reported on the amalgam controversy, which ultimately led to the demise of the society.[9] The next day, March 28, the college held its annual commencement. The examining committee, appointed on the recommendation of the American Medical Association, consisted of Simon P. Hullihen, MD; Edward Maynard, MD; J. H. Foster, Elisha Townsend, DDS; S. Blandin, MD; and Eleazar Parmly, the Provost of the College, as the dental component and Joshua I. Cohen, MD; John R. W. Dunbar, MD; and William W. Handy, MD, as the medical portion. Dr. Hullihen[10] gave the valedictory address. Many of the members of the Society of Dental Surgeons stayed over for the graduation to lend their support to the college. For the 1849–50 session, there were nine graduates to receive their DDS degrees, including one from Belgium.[11]

The Gardette Plan: 1850

Some dentists, even with the Baltimore College's 10-year success, were still skeptical of the wisdom of continuing an independent dental college separate from the medical. In 1850, Dr. Emile B. Gardette advocated establishing in the medical schools "an adjunct professorship to the chair of surgery, in which the specialty of dental surgery may be taught to the medical student seeking knowledge in your institutions." He proposed: "The establishment of separate schools for each specialty in medical science (and why should there not be for the oculist, or the aurist, as well as the dentist?) would appear to be the dismembering of a great family, thereby lessening its influence for good, as well as that power which is justly derived from an *esprit de corps* subsisting in every branch of an elevated and honorable profession."[12]

Chapin A. Harris, the editor of the *American Journal of Dental Science*, wasted no time in offering a rebuttal to Gardette's remarks. He pointed out that before the establishment of the Baltimore College of Dental Surgery, he was approached by "three members of the faculty of one of our oldest and most respectable medical schools" (University of Maryland), and tendered such a professorship as Gardette suggested. He declined on the grounds that "no purely medical institution could afford the necessary facilities for thorough practical instruction in operative and mechanical dentistry." Such a school would turn out the "worst kind of quacks—men without skill, but with acknowledged pretensions." He felt a little knowledge is a dangerous thing, especially a little knowledge in "wielding such formidable engines as dental instruments."[13] Fortunately, the Gardette plan was never implemented.

On March 27, 1851, the college held its twelfth annual commencement in the Assembly Room at Hanover and Lombard Streets. Professor Cone announced that 1,700 cases were treated in its infirmary during the last session. It was noted that the number of patients was increasing, which was a boon to the students and those "not able to pay for operative dentistry." Dr. Eleazar Parmly gave the valedictory address. There were 17 graduates, including one from England (Thomas D. Miller).[14]

Vulcanite Revolutionizes Denture Fabrication: 1851

As early as 1848, Thomas W. Evans[15] (1823–97), an American dentist practicing in Paris, France, had begun experimenting on denture materials. Finally, he produced a hard, black, elastic material, which was easy to make and impervious to mouth fluids. Because professional ethics kept him from promoting this product, he turned to Charles Goodyear (1800–60), who had discovered the vulcanization process of rubber. Goodyear added vermilion (mercuric sulphide) to the process and thus obtained Vulcanite, a maroon-colored India rubber compound, suitable for denture base construction. Now dentistry had a denture base that was inexpensive, durable, and relatively easy to manufacture. No longer would dentists have to carve ivory or bone to fit the impression or hammer out swedged denture bases out of gold or silver. In 1851, Nelson Goodyear secured a patent for using Vulcanite for making artificial dentures. Vulcanite remained the primary denture base material until the advent of the acrylics in the 1940s.[16]

On March 18, 1852, the college held its graduation at its hall. After a prayer by the Rev. B. H. Nadadal, Dr. Washington R. Handy, Dean of the Faculty (1842–53), read the names of the graduates. The diplomas were handed out by the Provost, Dr. Eleazar Parmly, to the 12 graduates, including one from Germany (Aldabert J. Volck). Music was provided by the "Independent Blues' Band." Dr. Robert Arthur, the college's first graduate, gave the valedictory address. After the ceremony, a "repast" was served at Dr. Bond's residence.[17]

The New Assembly Rooms: 1852

In June 1852, the college announced that it contemplated "important improvements" for the 1852–53 session. The college having survived "all the dangers of infancy" was determined to establish itself as a permanent fixture. It hoped to open the next session of lectures in a "much larger, and more suitable building than the present." In addition, a "costly apparatus for demonstrating all the details of dental and general chemistry, and microscopical anatomy of the teeth" was to be provided the students.[18] The college called the new location "one of the most central and accessible locations in the city." It contained large lecture rooms, a mechanical laboratory (about 80 feet long and well lighted from the roof), a large well-lighted operating room, dissecting rooms, and rooms for apparatus. There were also some faculty changes for the 1852–53 session: Dr. Cyrus O. Cone resigned, and Alfred A. Blandy, MD, took over the chair of operative dentistry; Reginald N. Wright, AM, MD, was appointed lecturer on dental chemistry, and Dr. Philip H. Austen was promoted to professor of mechanical dentistry.[19]

When the college, despite a pinched budget, opted for larger quarters in 1852, it chose a new building known as the "New Assembly Rooms" on the northeast corner of Lombard and Hanover Streets. John Eager Howard built the structure in February 1851 in an older part of town to "fill the void left when the old Assembly Rooms became a public school." The building had been the former home of the Washington Medical College,[20] which closed in 1851. In July 1852, Drs. Harris and Handy entered into a verbal agreement with H. L. Wood, agent for Howard, to rent space in the so-called "College Building." The rent was to be geared to enrollment, with $700 for the basic term charge. Escalation was dependent on enrollments exceeding 30 students, with $20 added for each student over the 30 limit. It was assumed the capacity enrollment would be no more than 40. The college shared the New Assembly Rooms with businesses, rather than educational enterprises; it was to be a long-time address for the college.[21] The *American Journal of Dental Science* commented that the college's faculty could congratulate themselves on the move as they now offered greater facilities for instruction, at a much greater cost to themselves, but without any additional expense to the student.[22]

The college proudly reported in its 1853–54 announcement:

> The Faculty take pleasure in announcing that the superior size and arrangement of the New College has enabled them greatly to enlarge their plan and means of instruction. Its location is central; its rooms are large and well ventilated, furnished with gas, abundantly supplied with water, and provided with every convenience necessary to the comfort of the student. The Museum has received important additions: also a large and very valuable chemical and Philosophical Apparatus has recently been purchased.
>
> The Operating and Mechanical Rooms have been refitted in the completest manner, to meet the wants and rapidly increasing practice of the Infirmary. The Dissecting Room is now undergoing entire reconstruction, and will be extended to twice its present size.[23]

The college claimed the infirmary was "unrivaled." It was in operation all year to accommodate the enlarged student body. The infirmary was considered having the same relation to the dental student as the hospital had to the medical student. The only difference was the medical students "must be content to observe," whereas, the dental students were "required to act." The infirmary was described:

> The Operating Room is lighted by six large windows, and contains ten operating chairs. The students will attend in classes; of which one will occupy the room during an entire morning, each member of the class having his separate chair and patient. The same decorum and courtesy will be expected in the Infirmary as in a private office.[24]

In the laboratory, each student was assigned a place by the dean, and the "permanent fixtures" were supplied by the college. The smaller tools and materials were furnished by the student. The "Janitor' was provided with a "full supply of all such articles" so that the student was spared the delay and inconvenience of obtaining them.[25] The dissecting room was "amply supplied with material, which is usually abundant[26] in our city." The lectures were illustrated by a large collection of wet and dry preparations, by models and drawings, and by demonstrations on the cadaver.[27] In 1853, the college agreed to pay J. E. Howard and additional

$100 for "certain alterations in the operating and dissecting rooms," and made plans to double the size of the latter. Symbolically, the "address was personalized when the faculty added the name of the college in block letters to the front façade." This marked the college's first use of signage in its history.[28]

Philip H. Austen, the New Dean: 1853

The new dean replacing Dr. Handy was Philip H. Austen, AM, MD, DDS. Dr. Austen was born on June 26, 1822, in Baltimore, Md. In 1841, at age 19, he graduated from Yale University; in 1845 he received his MD degree from the University of Maryland School of Medicine; and in 1849 he received his DDS degree from the Baltimore College of Dental Surgery. In 1852, he was made a professor at his dental alma mater. During a 21-year period, he successively held chairs of dental mechanism, chemistry, anatomy and physiology, dental science, and for 12 years was dean of the faculty. In 1871, he served as the editor of the tenth edition of Harris' *Principles and Practice of Dentistry.* He possessed a scholarly knowledge of Latin, Greek, French, and Hebrew. Foley (1966) called him, "The brightest and most thoroughly cultivated mind which has ever honored dentistry." Dr. Austen, at the date of his resignation as dean in October 1865, was the senior professor and president of the faculty. After leaving the School in 1865 because of poor eyesight, Dr. Austen was the supervisor and civil engineer of the Preston County Coal Mines in West Virginia. However, he retained his position on the faculty as professor of dental science and mechanism until 1874, when he became professor of dental science and chemistry. Dr. Austen died in Baltimore in October 1878 at age 56.[29]

The Museum: 1853

In 1853, Dr. J. L. Levison of Brighton, England, donated "three old instruments for the extraction of teeth," taken from the ruins of Pompeii. The antique instruments consisted of "a punch with two prongs, a pair of forceps, and an instrument intended for the extraction of teeth perpendicularly." In addition, Dr. Samuel P. Hullihen of Wheeling, Va., sent the museum a rare specimen of "osseous union of a permanent central and lateral incisor of the upper jaw."[30]

The thirteenth annual commencement was held on March 25, 1853, at the new college building with 22 graduates, including one from Bermuda (R. H. Tucker). During the session concluded, the infirmary performed 2,059 operations.[31]

The fourteenth annual commencement was held in the New Assembly Rooms in the College Building on the evening of March 1, 1854, with 18 graduates. Dr. William W. H. Thackston, an 1842 graduate, gave the valedictory address.[32]

The 1854–55 session began under the new dean, Dr. Philip H. Austen, on November 1 with lectures and continued to March 1, 1855. The anatomy laboratory, infirmary, and mechanical rooms were scheduled to open on the first Monday in October. Some lectures were scheduled for October; therefore, it was important that the students be there during the preliminary month. The infirmary was also to be open in the summer for those students who remained in the city between the first and second course of lectures. Certificates of four years' dental practice or one full course at any reputable dental or medical college would be accepted as equivalent to the first course. The course fee was $110, dissecting fee (optional) $10, diploma fee $30, and matriculation fee $5. The required textbooks were: Harris' *Principles and Practice of Dental Surgery*, 5th edition; Bond's *Dental Medicine*, 2d edition; Handy's *Anatomy*; Carpenter's Physiology; Mutter's *Liston's Surgery*; Jourdain's *Surgical Diseases of the Mouth*; Mitchell or Dunglison's *Therapeutics and Materia Medica*; Fownes's, Graham's or Turner's *Chemistry*; and Wood's or Watson's *Practice of Medicine*. The students were also informed they could rent rooms for from $2.50 to $4 per week.[33] The fifteenth annual commencement was held in the College's Assembly Rooms on March 1, 1855, with 27 graduates.[34]

Gold Foil: 1855

The 1855–56 session was noteworthy as for the first time the catalog mentions the use of gold foil as a restorative material. "The various methods of using Gold Foil the student learns by practice; also, the manipulation[35] peculiar to Crystalline Gold."[36] Also the same year, Dr. Edward Maynard of Washington, D.C., gave the college museum his extensive collection of 200 maxillae. These specimens where prepared to demonstrate the maxillary sinuses, showing their great variety in size and shape, and the effects of disease. The catalog mentioned that there was probably not "in the world a similar collection." The collection was exceedingly valuable to the dental students and practitioners alike to study the "great variety of shape, size and relation to the dental arch."[37]

The sixteenth annual commencement of the Baltimore College of Dental Surgery was held on March 4, 1856 in the Assembly Rooms of the college. Dr. Solyman Brown gave the valedictory address, and again the "Blues' Band" performed. There were 17 graduates hailing from New York to Mississippi.[38] The graduates included Thomas O. Walton,[39] who became the U.S. Naval Academy's first dentist.[40] The same year, Dr. Edward Maynard, dentist to Presidents Fillmore and Pierce, was appointed to the Chair of Theory and Practice of Dental Surgery.[41] This change came about because of the resignation of Dr. Blandy. Also, a new chair of microscopical and comparative anatomy of the teeth was created because of the "increasing interest and importance of microscopical studies," with Christopher Johnston, MD, in charge. George W. Neidich, DDS, was also added as a demonstrator of dental surgery. Prosthetic dentistry included working with block teeth, continuous gum,[42] and gutta percha. In the session 1855–56, the students performed: 2,430 extractions, 965 restorations, and made 28 full denture sets, 14 lower dentures, 15 pivot teeth, and 19 partial dentures.[43]

Thomas O. Walton

Doubts about the Future: 1857

In 1857, there were still some "doubters" in the dental profession about the future of dental colleges. Dr. John D. White, one of the editors of the *Dental News Letter*, expressed the opinion that the dental colleges would not "end in the kind of success hoped for by the teacher, as well as by the student." He felt that dentistry was an art that depended more upon the "*natural abilities* of the learner" than the method of instruction. He felt that the course time was too short for the pupil to acquire a "proper development of his practical judgment." Too much was crowded into a relatively short space of time. He also felt that many students would chose medicine over dentistry because of the high cost of a dental education.[44] In fact as late as 1890, Dr. Jonathan Taft, the dental dean at the University of Michigan, brought up this question: "Will not a well-directed and properly-arranged pupilage under a private preceptor, in addition to the college course, give better results than the indiscriminate admission to our colleges of those wholly innocent of any knowledge of dental art or science?"[45] Many other dentists were no doubt of a similar opinion.

The college's seventeenth annual commencement was held at the Baltimore Assembly Rooms on February 27, 1857. Dr. Philip H. Austen announced the 20 graduates; Dr. Chapin A. Harris conferred the degrees, and Dr. Thomas E. Bond gave the valedictory address. Music was again by the Blues' Band.[46] The eighteenth annual commencement was held on February 25, 1858. The valedictory address was by Professor A. Snowden Piggot[47] (Anatomy and Physiology). There were 19 graduates, including three from Cuba.[48] The nineteenth commencement was held on March 1, 1859. There were 20 graduates, including one from Scotland and one from Puerto Rico. Professor Chapin A. Harris gave the valedictory address.[49] Interestingly, that year, Dr. Ferdinand J. S. Gorgas, who later would spend 45 years as a dean of the college and its rival, the University of Maryland Dental Department, joined the faculty.[50]

As an indication that the museum was actively collecting objects other than dental pathological specimens during the period, in 1857, Dr. Austen announced that the museum had received the following donations: a square furnace, containing "one baking and two smaller annealing muffles" from the New York Teeth Manufacturing Company; a "highly finished" operating chair from Dr. Merrit Asay of Philadelphia; a dental ratchet lathe" designed by Dr. W. H. Helme of Providence Rhode Island; a "self adjusting rivet-hole punch" from Dr. Samuel Mallet of New Haven, Conn.; and one of Dr. D. W. Perkins of Rome, N.Y. patented dental chairs.[51] In the fall of 1858, Dr. Addison Blandy of London sent the Museum two sets of dentures, one made of ivory with human teeth and the other of ivory with English porcelain teeth. Both sets were described as "clumsy and awkwardly constructed, showing but little mechanical skill and but a very imperfect knowledge of the art as perfected by dentists of the present day." He also included several hundred teeth demonstrating pathology.[52]

The college entered its twentieth year in 1860 with the announcement:

> It is unnecessary to offer any arguments in support of Dental Collegiate Education. No longer an experiment, it has become, with the majority of the profession, an acknowledged necessity, and must ultimately be considered and indispensable prerequisite to the practice of Dental Surgery. The Faculty have endeavored to present a Course of Instruction, concise, comprehensive and practical; each year adding to their apparatus, and enlarging their curriculum of study, to meet the wants of an Art eminently progressive.[53]

There were now 14 chairs in the infirmary and it was open every afternoon from 12 a.m. to 4 p.m. No student was excused from graduation, unless by a special vote of the faculty. The twenty-first catalog listed the graduates by year; the highest total was 39 in 1860. The grand total of graduates from 1840 to 1860 was 216.[54]

The twentieth commencement was held on the evening of February 28, 1860.[55]

Death of Chapin A. Harris: 1860

Unfortunately, September 29, 1860, saw the death of Dr. Harris. He had served the college as its professor of the principles and practice of dental surgery for 20 years.[56] The *American Journal of Dental Science* called his loss, "too recent, too overpowering, and of too direct personal concern to us for expression in words." Dr. Austen, dean of the Baltimore College of Dental Surgery, and the faculty eulogized Harris in a resolution at a special faculty meeting on October 17, 1860: "That as the projector of Collegiate Dental Education and the laborious and successful founder of this College, Dr. Harris deserved the highest regards of the profession and the gratitude of the public. It may be said of him that he united Dental Surgery to Science, and raised the practice of it to the worth and respectability of a profession."[57]

NOTES

1. Bert G. Anderson, "Philip H. Austen: A Voice in the Wilderness," *Journal of Dental Education* 3 (October 1938): 19.
2. Baltimore College of Dental Surgery. *Eleventh Annual Announcement of the Baltimore College of Dental Surgery* (Baltimore: John D. Toy, 1850), pp. 5–6.
3. Ibid., p. 6.
4. Ibid.
5. [Chapin A. Harris], "The Diploma of the Baltimore College of Dental Surgery," *American Journal of Dental Science* 10 (January 1850): 139.
6. J. H. Foster, "Address, delivered before the Society of the Alumni of the Baltimore College of Dental Surgery, at their First Annual Meeting," *American Journal of Dental Science* 9 (April 1849): 297–98.
7. [Chapin A. Harris, ed.], "An Imposter," *American Journal of Dental Science* 10 (January 1850): 140–41.
8. Alexander Nasmyth (1789–1848), the discoverer of "Nasmyth's Membrane" (primary enamel cuticle) in 1839, was a member of the Royal College of Surgeons of London. [Walter Hoffmann-Axthelm, *History of Dentistry* (Chicago: Quintessence Publishing Co., Inc., 1981), p. 394.]
9. "April 1850 [American Society of Dental Surgeons]," *Dental News Letter* 3 (April 1850): 69; A[mos] Westcott, comp., "Tenth Annual Meeting of the American Society of Dental Surgeons, held in the City of Baltimore, the 25, 26, 27 days of March, 1850," *American Journal of Dental Science* 10 (April 1850): 208–10.
10. Simon P. Hullihen (1810–57) was born in Milton, Pa. He received his MD degree at age 22 from the Washington Medical College, and began to specialize in oral surgery in Wheeling, Va. In 1843, the Baltimore College of Dental Surgery conferred upon him an honorary DDS degree. In the last 10 years of his life, he performed the following number of operations: 200 cataract, 50 cleft palate, 100 harelip, 200 antrum cases, 150 cancer, 100 strabismus, remade 20 mandibles, 25 noses, and 50 lips, and about 200 general surgical operations. He also invented several instruments, compound root forceps, uvula scissors, spear-shape scalpel, needle holder, curved tooth forceps, and dumbbell-shaped cautery. In 1850, he established the Wheeling Hospital. He was one of the founders of the journal, *Dental Register*, and was on the publishing committee. He died on March 27, 1857. He has been called the "Father of Oral Surgery." [Simon P. Hullihen, MD, DDS," *Dental Radiography and Photography* 22, no. 4, (1949): i, 80.]
11. "Annual Commencement of the Baltimore College of Dental Surgery. Session, 1849–50," *American Journal of Dental Science* 10 (April 1850): 211–12, 215–16.
12. E[mile] B. Gardette, "On the Importance of Establishing a Lectureship on Dental Surgery in Medical Colleges," (*American Journal of Medical Sciences*), quoted in *American Journal of Dental Science*, n.s., 1 (April 1851): 395, 396.
13. [Chapin A. Harris], "Dr. Gardette on the Propriety of Abolishing Dental Colleges, and substituting for them a Lectureship on Dentistry in each of the Medical Schools," *American Journal of Dental Science*, n.s., 1 (April 1851): 399.
14. "Annual Commencement of the Baltimore College of Dental Surgery," *American Journal of Dental Science*, n.s., 1 (April 1851): 403–4; "Baltimore College of Dental Surgery," *Dental Times and Advertiser* 1 (August 1851): 35.

15. Thomas William Evans, MD, DDS, PhD, was born on December 23, 1823, in Philadelphia, Pa. At age 14, he was apprenticed to a gold and silversmith in Philadelphia who also manufactured dental instruments. In 1841, he became an apprentice in the office of Dr. John DeHaven White. He also attended lectures at the Jefferson Medical College in 1844–45. In 1850, he was awarded an honorary DDS degree by the Baltimore College of Dental Surgery; an honorary DDS by the Philadelphia College of Dental Surgery, 1853; an honorary MD by the Washington University in Baltimore, 1853; and an honorary PhD by Lafayette College, 1870. In 1847, Evans became associated with Dr. C. Starr Brewster, an American dentist practicing in Paris, France. Three years later, he established his own office in Paris, and became friendly with Louis Napoleon, nephew of Napoleon (Bonaparte), later to become Napoleon III of the Second Empire in 1852. Dr. Evans appointment to the Imperial Court brought him prestige, wealth, and social contact with Royal Courts of Europe. Evans visited the battlefields of the Crimean War in 1854 and recommended a reorganization of the field hospitals of the French Army. His Paris real estate investments paid off handsomely and he soon amassed a fortune of at least $4,000,000. His philanthropic contributions included the Lafayette Home for Girls during the American Civil War, the emperor sent him to the United States to confer with President Lincoln on the probable outcome of the conflict. His report of an expected Northern victory kept France from recognizing the Confederacy. In 1870, he assisted the Empress Eugenie in escaping the Paris mobs to England. His humanitarian work during the Franco-Prussian War resulted in the French government awarding him the Commander of Legion of Honor in 1871. Dr. Evans died at his Paris home on November 14, 1897. He left the majority of his fortune to the Thomas W. Evans Museum and Dental Institute, University of Pennsylvania, founded in 1878. [Malcolm Wallace Carr, "Thomas W. Evans: His Life and Influence on the Development of Dentistry as a Learned Profession," *Journal of the American College of Dentists* 46 (April 1979): 88, 90–96; "Thomas William Evans, MD, DDS, PhD," *Dental Radiography and Photography* 21, no. 3 (1948): i.]
16. Milton B. Asbell, *Dentistry: A Historical Perspective* (Bryn Mawr, Pa.: Dorrance & Co., Inc., 1988), pp. 138–39.
17. "Annual Commencement of the Baltimore College of Dental Surgery," *Dental News Letter* 5 (April 1852): 332–33; "Annual Commencement of the Baltimore College of Dental Surgery," *American Journal of Dental Science*, n.s., 2 (April 1852): 500–01.
18. "Baltimore College of Dental Surgery," *Dental Times and Advertiser* 1 (June 1852): 200.
19. Baltimore College of Dental Surgery, *Thirteenth Annual Announcement of the Baltimore College of Dental Surgery* (Baltimore: John W. Woods, Printer, 1852), pp. 2, 3.
20. George H. Callcott, *A History of the University of Maryland* (Baltimore: Maryland Historical Society, 1966), p. 82.
21. John Milner Associates, "Architecture as History: The Formative Years of the Baltimore College of Dental Surgery as Recorded in the Housing History," Final Report, John Milner Associates, West Chester, Pa., 1980, pp. 39, 42.
22. "Baltimore College of Dental Surgery," *American Journal of Dental Science*, n.s., 2 (July 1852): 672.
23. Baltimore College of Dental Surgery, *Fourteenth Annual Announcement and Catalogue of the Baltimore College of Dental Surgery* (Baltimore: John W. Woods, Printer, 1853), p. 3.
24. Ibid., pp. 3, 7.
25. Ibid., pp. 7–8.
26. Actually, in 1833, the University of Maryland Medical School, Baltimore, was the first medical college in the country to make dissection compulsory in the curriculum. [Eugene F. Cordell, *University of Maryland 1807–1907: Its History, Influence, Equipment and Characteristics with Biographical Sketches and Portraits of Its Founders, Benefactors, Regents, Faculty and Alumni*, vol. 1 (New York: Lewis Publishing Co., 1907), p. 68.]
27. Baltimore College of Dental Surgery, *Fourteenth Annual Announcement*, p. 6.
28. Milner, "Architecture as History," p. 43.
29. Anderson, "Philip H. Austen," 12–13; Gardner P. H. Foley, ed., *Proceedings of the 125th Anniversary Celebration of the Baltimore College of Dental Surgery* (Baltimore: Horn-Shafer Co., 1966), p. 129.
30. [Chapin A. Harris], "Ancient Dental Instruments," *American Journal of Dental Science*, n.s., 3 (January 1853): 333–34; Idem, "Osseous Union of Teeth," *American Journal of Dental Science*, n.s., 3 (January 1853): 333.
31. "Annual Commencement of the Baltimore College of Dental Surgery," *American Journal of Dental Science*, n.s., 3 (April 1853): 505–6.
32. "Annual Commencement of the Baltimore College of Dental Surgery," *American Journal of Dental Science*, n.s., 4 (July 1854): 675; Baltimore College of Dental Surgery, *Fifteenth Annual Announcement and Catalogue of the Baltimore College of Dental Surgery* (Baltimore: John W. Woods, Printer, 1854), pp. 12, 13.
33. Advertisement, "Baltimore College of Dental Surgery, Fifteenth Session, 1854–5," *Dental News Letter* 8 (January 1855): n.p.n.
34. "Baltimore College of Dental Surgery," *American Journal of Dental Science*, n.s., 5 (April 1855): 340–41.
35. Crystalline or sponge gold foil was introduced by C. T. Jackson in 1846 and patented by Alfred Watt in 1853. Its advantage was that it permitted the contouring of the restoration. Robert Arthur, the Baltimore College's first graduate, promoted a new technique in 1855 by which the gold foil was annealed over an alcohol lamp. This method provided the gold with cohesive properties by removing any surface impurities. Condensation was by serrated hand instruments. Cohesive gold foil became the most popular restorative material for decades. [Asbell, *Dentistry*, pp. 148–49.]
36. Baltimore College of Dental Surgery, *Sixteenth Annual Announcement and Catalogue of the Baltimore College of Dental Surgery* (Baltimore: John W. Woods, Printer, 1855), p. 3.
37. Ibid., p. 1.
38. "The Annual Commencement of the Baltimore College of Dental Surgery," *Dental News Letter* 9 (April 1856): 196.
39. Thomas Oliver Walton was born on September 24, 1834 in St. Mary's County, Md. In 1856, he graduated from the Baltimore College of Dental Surgery, and the same year entered practice in Annapolis, Md. In 1873, he was appointed an acting assistant surgeon to serve as the official dental surgeon at the U.S. Naval Academy. He served until 1899, when he was replaced by Dr. Richard Grady. Dr. Walton died at age 67 on December 21, 1900, of heart failure. ["Dr. T.O. Walton," *Dental Cosmos* 43 (April 1901): 442; Department of

the Navy, Bureau of Medicine and Surgery, *The Dental Corps of the United States Navy: A Chronology 1912–1962* (Washington: Bureau of Medicine and Surgery, 1962), pp. 4, 7.]

40. Foley, *Proceedings of the 125th Anniversary Celebration.*, p. 233.
41. "Baltimore College of Dental Surgery," *Dental News Letter* 9 (July 1856): 275.
42. Continuous gum dentures originated in France with M. Delabarre in 1820. The method consisted of "baking porcelain on a platinum base, giving a continuous porcelain surface without break between palate, teeth and gums, hence the name 'continuous gum'." [J. A. Taylor, *History of Dentistry: A Practical Treatise for the Use of Dental Students and Practitioners* (Philadelphia: Lea & Febiger, 1922), p. 144.]
43. Baltimore College of Dental Surgery, *Seventeenth Annual Announcement and Catalogue of the Baltimore College of Dental Surgery* (Baltimore: John W. Woods, Printer, 1856), pp. ii, 2, 3.
44. J[ohn] D. W[hite], "Dental Colleges," *Dental News Letter* 10 (April 1857): 220–21.
45. J[ohanathan] Taft, "Dental Education—Office Pupilage," *Dental Register* 44 (February 1890): 60.
46. "Baltimore College of Dental Surgery," *Dental News Letter* 10 (April 1857): 223.
47. A. Snowden Piggot, MD, assumed the chair of anatomy and physiology upon the death of Professor Washington R. Handy. Piggot was formerly a professor at the Washington Medical University. [Baltimore College of Dental Surgery, *Nineteenth Annual Announcement of the Baltimore College of Dental Surgery* (Baltimore: John W. Woods, Printer, 1858), pp. 3–4.]
48. "Baltimore College of Dental Surgery," *Dental News Letter* 11 (April 1858): 190–91.
49. "The Baltimore College of Dental Surgery," *Dental News Letter* 12 (April 1859): 204.
50. Baltimore College of Dental Surgery, *Nineteenth Annual Announcement*, p. 2.
51. Letter, Philip H. Austen to Chapin A. Harris, January 5, 1857, Baltimore College of Dental Surgery Papers, National Museum of Dentistry Archives.
52. [Chapin A. Harris], "Baltimore College of Dental Surgery," *American Journal of Dental Science*, n.s., 8 (October 1858): 584–85.
53. Baltimore College of Dental Surgery, *Twenty-First Annual Circular and Catalogue of the Baltimore College of Dental Surgery* (Baltimore: James Lucas & Son, 1860), p. 3.
54. Ibid., p. 14.
55. "Baltimore College of Dental Surgery," *Dental Cosmos*, n.s., 1 (April 1860): 480.
56. James Taylor, "Obituary [Dr. Chapin A. Harris]," *Cincinnati Dental Lamp* 2, no. 1 (1860): 17.
57. "Editorial Department," *American Journal of Dental Science*, n.s., 10 (October 1860): 588.

HANOVER & LOMBARD STREETS
1853-1872

Chapter 6

The Civil War Years: 1861–65

"You have been taught that Dental Surgery is not a mere art separate from, and independent of, general medicine; but that it is an important branch of the science of cure. Inquiring into the diseases of the antrum alone was sufficient to convince you that the teeth and their dependencies are often primarily interested in the production and aggravation of some of the most fearful and fatal of human disorders."[1] **~Thomas E. Bond, 1841**

Baltimore City: 1860–61

In 1860, Baltimore was the third largest city in the United States and the largest industrial city in the South. Supplied by three major railroads, its clipper ships carried its commerce all over the world. A strong flood of German and Irish immigrants helped to industrialize the city and add to its stature as a city on the rise. In the 1860s, Maryland sympathies were divided between the North and the South, with a decided preponderance on the southern side. In fact, only 2,294 votes in the entire state had been cast for Abraham Lincoln in the presidential election. Slavery was not a major issue in Maryland, as there were 83,942 free African Americans in Maryland, 87,189 slaves, and 515,918 whites in 1860. Baltimore City's population of 200,000 contained 50,000 free blacks, the largest total in the country. Therefore, there were almost as many free blacks in the state as slaves. Emancipation, in spite of the laws denouncing it, had slowly progressed. Thus, Maryland was rather moderate, especially Baltimore City, on the issue of abolition and was for "compromise and peace at any price consistent with honor."[2]

The period immediately after Lincoln's election in November 1860 was a time of "intense agitation" throughout the country. Some in the North favored compromise to war, even if it meant the dissolution of the Union. South Carolina seceded on December 17, 1860, followed by Georgia and the five Gulf states. On February 9, 1861, Jefferson Davis was elected president of the Confederacy. Other states were watching Virginia's course of action to see which way she went. The border states were on debatable ground, including Maryland.[3]

Baltimore College of Dental Surgery: 1860–61

Before the Civil War, the Baltimore College of Dental Surgery played a major role in dental education, as it was the South's only dental school and supplied the majority of the dentists in the service of the Confederate States Army. In 1860, there were roughly 5,000 dentists in the country, of which about 1,000 were located in the southern states.[4] In the year before the war, students of the South comprised the majority of the graduating classes of the two eastern dental schools then in existence, the Baltimore College of Dental Surgery[5] and the Pennsylvania College of Dental Surgery.[6] During the war, Baltimore, because it was south of the Mason Dixon Line, was occupied by federal troops, thus effectively cutting off the supply of dentists to the South for the next four years. A new dental school was started in New Orleans in 1861, but it did not graduate any students until after the war in 1867.[7]

The Problems of the South: 1861

Among other problems, the southern dentists were almost completely dependent on the North for their contacts with organized dentistry. The war isolated them from their northern colleagues and resources. The South had only one dental society, the Georgia State Dental Society, founded in 1859 with 11members. Another society, the Virginia Society of Surgeon Dentists, founded in 1842 (the first state dental society organized in the United States), was moribund; it had held its last meeting in 1846.[8] The South had only one dental journal, *The Southern Dental Examiner*, published by the firm of Brown and Hape of Atlanta, coincidently its only dental supply house. The journal's corresponding editor was Dr. George S. Fouke of Westminster, Md., who was behind the Union lines. The journal's first issue appeared in May 1860, with the editorial comment that the dentists of the South needed a medium through which they could "express and interchange their views to their mutual benefit."[9] By January 1862, the journal experienced difficulties in obtaining suitable paper for its press and after the March issue failed to reappear.[10] Coincidently, the *American Journal of Dental Science*, based in Baltimore, also ceased publication in 1861 and did not reappear until 1867. One factor in the journal's demise was, of course, the death of Dr. Harris in 1860.[11]

To further compound the civilian dental shortage, in 1862 the South initiated military conscription for dentists. Some dentists tried to test the law because physicians of "seven years practice" were exempted from conscription. The dentists claimed that they were practicing a medical specialty, as "*special practitioners.*"[12] One dentist, Dr. John W. Hunter of Salem, N.C., and an 1856 graduate of the Pennsylvania College of Dental Surgery, decided to carry the legality of the matter to the Supreme Court of North Carolina, on the advice of a friend, Dr. Benjamin F. Arrington,[13] a prominent Raleigh, N. C., dentist and an 1853 graduate of the Baltimore College of Dental Surgery. Arrington advised Hunter to refuse conscription and wrote the brief that claimed that dentistry was "an exact specialty of medicine." Arrington even loaned Hunter the money (nearly $100) to carry the case to the higher court. The judge, Chief Justice Richard M. Pearson, ruled in favor of Hunter's exemption, saying, "I am satisfied not only that regular, educated dentists are physicians, but that the human family are much indebted to them." This decision that dentists were exempt from military and jury duty was, "the first decision of the kind ever rendered in the United States giving dentistry the legitimate right to professional distinction." With this verdict now in, the Confederate Congress changed the wording in the clause exempting physicians to read, "the term physicians not to include dentists." The Confederate Surgeon General, Samuel Preston Moore, immediately made provision to assign the newly conscripted dentists to hospital duty.[14]

Brown and Hape, as the only manufacturer of dental instruments and materials in the entire Confederacy, had problems supplying its customers because the federal blockade effectively cut off dental supplies from reaching the South from Europe. Surgical instruments and medicine had been declared "contraband of war" by the United States government. Consequently, a shortage of dental supplies developed quite early in the war. As platinum was necessary for the manufacture of porcelain teeth, Dr. Brown had to resort to melting down scraps of that metal.[15] Rapid inflation also compounded the South's problems. The cost of a gold filling was $120, an extraction $20, and for an upper gold or vulcanite base denture, from $1,800 to $4,000. High prices were not confined to dentistry alone, for instance, it was not uncommon to pay $1,800 for a coat, $300 for shoes, $1,000 for cavalry boots, and from $300 to $500 for an ordinary hat.[16] Mary Boykin Chesnut of South Carolina mentions in her *Diary* that a toothbrush cost $10 and a dental visit to look at the teeth cost $350 in Confederate money.[17] Old toothbrushes were rethreaded with hog bristles from slaughtered animals. Twigs were also popular for cleaning the teeth, toothpicks were carved from bone or wood, and ground charcoal was used as a dentifrice.[18] Such were the problems in the South.

Wartime BCDS: 1861–65

Initially, the Baltimore College of Dental Surgery was not especially affected by the war, although one of its professors, A. Snowden Piggot, AM, MD,[19] professor of anatomy and physiology, went off to war as a surgeon on the Confederate side.[20] After the war, the college was challenged by the statement that a portion of the faculty "were down assisting the rebels." The college acknowledged that no less than "four of the present Faculty" were so engaged, and that "*all* the members of the Faculty of the Baltimore College are *natives* of the South."[21]

The college graduated 29 students in 1861 (contrasted to 39 in 1860), of whom 14 were from the southern states other than Maryland. The commencement was held on February 26 at the New Assembly Rooms in the presence of "a large and fashionable audience." The *Dental Cosmos* commented:

> We are glad to see, and consider it a subject for congratulation, notwithstanding the unsettled and unquiet condition of our country, that dental and medical schools have never been in a more prosperous condition than at present, and are giving the best evidences of continued usefulness. Upon an examination of the number of students in attendance and of those graduating in some of the most prominent institutions from our own city [Philadelphia] for the past session, we were surprised to see that they outnumbered those of any previous year.[22]

However, the next year, 1862, there was a drastic fall in matriculants, as the college graduated only ten students, nine of whom were from Maryland and one from Pennsylvania. The college missed the southern students, who in the past made up a large portion of the student body. In 1863, the college graduated nine students, in 1864, twelve students, and in 1865, nine students. The twenty-fifth commencement was held on March 3, 1865, with Professor Austen delivering the valedictory address.[23] No doubt the college felt the loss of tuition from lack of students very keenly, and had to suffer through hard times.[24]

As mentioned, Baltimore was primarily sympathetic to the South. In fact, 78 Baltimore College of Dental Surgery graduates, former students, or future graduates served the Confederate[25] forces during the war, as contrasted to 17 who saw service with the Union.[26,27] Of course, the dentists who served during the Civil War for both sides served as enlisted men, hospital stewards, line officers, or regimental surgeons (those with medical degrees), as there were no dental surgeons in either army. Some men took their instrument cases with them and rendered what service they could to their fellow soldiers, but any service they performed was strictly unofficial. The federal government did not authorize dental surgeons for the U.S. Army until 1901, with the formation of a 30-man corps of contract dental surgeons. However, in the South it was somewhat different, as the Confederacy drafted dentists and appointed them as enlisted hospital stewards. Perhaps Confederate President Jefferson Davis, who earlier was in favor of military dentists for the U.S. Army when he was the Secretary of War (1853–57), was himself more sympathetic to their need.[28]

James Baxter Bean, MD, DDS

For the South, by far the most important dentist was James Baxter Bean, MD, DDS, an 1860 graduate of the college, who established the first wartime maxillofacial trauma ward at the Medical College Hospital in Atlanta in 1864. Bean, who had practiced medicine in Micanopy, Fla., before receiving his dental degree in 1863, developed an interdental splint made of vulcanized India rubber, which he used quite successfully in treating jaw fracture wounds at the Atlanta hospitals. Before that time, the most common treatment of a fractured jaw was reduction and fixation by means of a gutta-percha splint. Splints made of pasteboard softened with vinegar and water and held in place with a head bandage were also used by some surgeons.[29]

In June 1864, Dr. Edward N. Covey, a Confederate surgeon, a former United States Army assistant surgeon (1856–1861), while on an inspection tour of the Department of Tennessee, observed Dr. Bean's work in the Atlanta hospitals. He was so impressed with Bean's method of treating jaw fractures that a special ward was established in the Atlanta Medical College Hospital exclusively for jaw fractures; and, he directed that all future such cases in the Atlanta area were to be sent there for treatment by Dr. Bean. Results were so good that during the evacuation of Atlanta in the summer of 1864, the patients in this ward were transferred to the Blind Asylum Hospital in Macon, Ga., where Dr. Bean continued treatment. More than 40 cases were successfully treated in a six-month period. These two hospitals have to be regarded as probably the first medical facilities in history to have had a special ward devoted exclusively for the treatment of maxillofacial war injuries.[30]

Meanwhile, reports of Dr. Bean's successful treatment were sent to Confederate Surgeon General Samuel P. Moore, who ordered Dr. Bean to Richmond to show his splint to the Confederate Army Medical Board. At a meeting of the board held at the office of Dr. W. Leigh Burton (presumably at 8th and Franklin Streets), Dr. Bean presented his drawings and models and explained his splint. The board members argued that "the principles of it were not entirely new," but unanimously recommended its adoption for general usage. Army dentists were to be "instructed in its construction," and a ward set up at the Robertson Hospital,[31] at the corner of 3rd and Main Streets, Richmond, for the "exclusive treatment" of jaw injuries. From August 1, 1861, to April 2, 1865, 1,334 patients, including the jaw cases, were treated at the hospital. Surgeon General Moore officially confirmed Dr. Bean's duties in a February

6, 1865, directive (circular no. 24). All fractured jaw cases were to be treated by the Bean method.[32]

In April 1865, the popularity of Dr. Bean's interdental splint among southern surgeons caused one Confederate dentist, upon hearing of Secretary of State William H. Seward's unfortunate carriage accident in which he sustained a fractured jaw, to write to Brigadier General Joseph K. Barnes, the surgeon general of the Union Army, calling his attention to the Bean splint. The Surgeon General replied that the "same splint" was being made by Dr. Thomas B. Gunning[33] of New York.[34]

After the war, Dr. Bean returned to Baltimore and established a highly remunerative civilian practice. He published several articles, strangely enough none on his interdental splint; developed a method of casting aluminum denture bases; invented an apparatus for the manufacture and administration of nitrous oxide gas; and was one of the founders of the Maryland Association of Dentists (Maryland State Dental Association) in 1866 and was its president in 1868. He died in September 1870, the victim of an avalanche while descending Mount Blanc in Switzerland. Dr. Bean has to be regarded as one of the pioneer dental surgeons on the treatment of wartime maxillofacial wounds.[35]

Other BCDS Graduates in the War

Other 1860 graduates who served in the Confederate States Army were: Amzi Wallace Alexander of North Carolina; Thomas Edward Bessellieu of South Carolina; John Bland; Hugh Phillips Bone of Alabama; Memory Bonner of South Carolina; Conrad S. Boyd of North Carolina; William N. Cunningham of Louisiana; John Hamilton Dickson of South Carolina; John W. Doniphan of South Carolina; Thaddeus Haynie of Virginia; Thomas M. Henley of Virginia; John S. Moore of North Carolina; George W. Patterson of Georgia; and Bryant S. Traywick of North Carolina.[36] The Class of 1860 was certainly well represented in the Confederate service.

Some of the Baltimore College graduates who had medical degrees even served as regimental surgeons. Memory Bonner, Class of 1860, who apparently had received an MD degree before coming to Baltimore in May 1852, began service as a contract surgeon. On July 18, 1862, he was appointed an assistant surgeon, serving initially at Macon, Ga., with the 8th Georgia Battalion. Later in 1863–64, he served with Terrill's Light Artillery.[37] Alexander Mills Campbell, Class of 1857, had an MD before receiving his DDS degree. He served as an assistant surgeon assigned to Nelson's Light Artillery of the 7th Mississippi Regiment.[38] George Patterson (Class of 1860), a Scottish immigrant from Georgia, in 1864 was appointed an acting assistant surgeon in the Confederate Army and served with the troops in the Northern Sub-District of Texas.[39] One 1857 graduate, Israel Francis Disoway, a private in Company "E," 12th Virginia Regiment, on May 12, 1864, was killed in the battle of Spottsylvania Court House, Virginia.[40] John Hamilton Dickson (Class of 1860), while serving with Company "E," 2nd South Carolina Cavalry, died in a Charleston Hospital on August 3, 1864.[41]

During the war, an 1852 Baltimore College of Dental Surgery graduate, Adalbert Volck, a Bavarian immigrant who had studied chemistry at the University of Munich, was appointed as a special agent by his personal friend, Jefferson Davis. He aided those individuals desiring to cross the Union lines and assisted in running the blockade with medical supplies. His home was a sanctuary for Confederate soldiers and secret agents. He was a brilliant artist and a cartoonist for the Southern cause. His drawings were called "Civil War Sketches," and lampooned the Northern leaders and generals. On several occasions he was imprisoned at Fort McHenry for his leanings.[42]

By contrast, only William Brown Dennis of Rhode Island, and William H. Waters of Vermont of the Class of '60 served in the Union forces.[43] However, there was an earlier graduate who served as a regimental surgeon. Charles Knower, an 1859 graduate, who apparently received his MD degree at some point, served as an assistant surgeon with the 1st Regiment, Missouri Engineers (Bissell's Regiment) for three years (1861–64). In 1866, he was one of the founders of the Missouri Dental College at St. Louis.[44] Another dentist, Homer Judd with an 1847 MD from Berkshire Medical College in Pittsfield, Mass., who had studied dentistry under Dr. Cyrus Cone in Baltimore, served as an assistant surgeon with the 34th and 40th Missouri Infantry in 1854–65. He participated in the battles of Nashville, Franklin, and Spanish Fort. He was the dean of the Missouri Dental College for seven years, editor of the *Missouri Dental Journal* for five years, and president of the American Dental Association from 1868 to 1869.[45]

Edward Maynard, AM, MD, DDS

Edward Maynard

Perhaps the Baltimore College of Dental Surgery's graduate who made the greatest contribution to the Union war effort was its 1841 honorary graduate and professor (1856–60) of theory and practice of dentistry, Dr. Edward Maynard. Maynard[46] had served as dentist to presidents Fillmore and Pierce and was one of the 19th century's premier ordnance inventors.[47] In March 1845, Dr. Maynard patented a tape priming system for firearms to replace the standard percussion cap. The U.S. government purchased the rights from Dr. Maynard for $4,000 for 4,000 muskets. In May 1851, he patented a breech-loading rifle to become famous as the "Maynard rifle." In October 1860, he patented a method of converting muzzle-loading firearms into breech-loaders.[48] Dr. Maynard's personal friend, Abraham Lincoln, reportedly commented, "Dr. Maynard, you have increased the entire army without adding a single man to the ranks."[49] The carbine version of the "Maynard rifle" was used extensively by Union troops (20,202 purchased by the federal government), and was highly prized by Confederate cavalrymen because of its "accuracy and range."[50]

A multitalented individual, Maynard possessed both an inventive and an artistic nature. He was an accomplished engraver and wood-carver, architect, surveyor, and artist (member of the Sketch Club of Washington). He was the first to discover the existence of dental fibrils (before they were identified microscopically), described the variations of form and shape of the maxillary sinus, invented the barbed broach for pulp extirpation (made from a watch spring), invented the Maynard drill for cavity preparation, was an early advocate of enamel fillings for anterior teeth (as practiced by Dr. Volck), perfected a method of non-cohesive gold foil filling, was an early advocate of the use of arsenic as a pulp devitalizer and use of gold foil as a root canal filling material in posterior teeth, and in addition, made his own instruments in a blacksmith forge.[51]

Thomas W. Evans: His Role in the War

Another dentist who played a major role as a civilian during the war was Dr. Thomas William Evans, an 1850 honorary graduate of the Baltimore College of Dental Surgery and famed for his development of the denture base, Vulcanite. Dr. Evans, who was practicing in Paris, France, was a friend and confident of Napoleon III of France. During the Civil War, Dr. Evans was sent as a personal emissary of Napoleon III to Washington, D.C., on a "confidential diplomatic mission" to ascertain the probable outcome of the war. The British were urging Napoleon III to join England in recognizing the Confederacy. Dr. Evans conferred with President Lincoln, General Grant, and other government officials and personally toured the battlefields. He saw the evidence of a Northern victory and on his return to France so informed Napoleon III that the North was winning the war. The Emperor thanked him for his services and said that he was glad he had not acted precipitately in the war's early days, as the friendship of America was "most important to France." Dr. Evans had performed a most important service to his country in keeping France out of the war.[52]

Newell Sill Jenkins: Progenitor of Cosmetic Dentistry

Another noteworthy graduate, although he did not serve in the Civil War, was Newell Sill Jenkins, Class of 1863. After graduation, Dr. Jenkins moved to Germany to practice with Dr. Frank P. Abbot, an 1851 graduate who practiced in Berlin. Dr. Abbot was one of the most distinguished American dentists in Europe. The German dentists were intrigued by Jenkins' demonstration of the rubber dam, which had only recently been invented by Sanford C. Barnum[53] of New York. After spending several weeks with Abbot, Jenkins established his dental practice in Dresden. Jenkins soon acquired a large practice and his reputation brought him many patients from among the German nobility and royal families of Germany, Austria, Russia, and Italy during the 45 years he practiced in Dresden. In 1886, King Albert of Saxony awarded Dr. Jenkins the Knight of the Albrecht's Order, first class. The king later became a patient. One of Jenkins' patients and closest friends was composer Richard Wagner. Although he was living in Europe, Jenkins kept up with the progress of dentistry in America. He noticed the increase in the display of gold in American mouths. Jenkins sought to find a porcelain material that would be esthetically pleasing and, after visiting practically all the ceramic works of Austria and Germany, came up with the formula for "Jenkins' Porcelain Enamel." He founded a company called the Klewe Company to manufacture and distribute his porcelain enamel. Jenkins' "personal friend," Samuel L. Clemens (Mark Twain), offered to buy the American rights to his enamel and manufacture it in America. Dr. Jenkins also invented "Kolynos Toothpaste" (from the Greek Kolyo nosus, meaning "disease preventer"), and presented his formula to the dental profession at the 1908 meeting of the American Dental Society of Europe in London. The American Dental Association endorsed Kolynos,[54] the only toothpaste at the time so honored. In 1916, after the outbreak of World War I in Europe, Jenkins was forced to leave Europe and return to America. He died in Havre, France, on September 25, 1919. Jenkins' remains were brought back to the United States and he was interred in the family plot in Bangor, Me. Dr. Jenkins was truly the progenitor of cosmetic dentistry.[55]

The Baltimore College of Dental Surgery had survived the great Civil War, although it had felt the financial loss from lack of students, but it had survived. It was now ready for a new dean and the prosperity changes make.

NOTES

1. Thomas E. Bond, "Valedictory Address," *American Journal of Dental Science* 1 (August/September 1841): 243.
2. Scott S. Sheads, and Daniel C. Toomey, *Baltimore During the Civil War* (Linthicum, Md.: Toomey Press, 1997), p. vii; George W. Brown, *Baltimore and the Nineteenth of April, 1861: A Study of the War* (Baltimore: Johns Hopkins University, 1887; reprint, Maclay & Associates, 1982), pp. 30–31.
3. Brown, *Baltimore and the Nineteenth of April, 1861*, pp. 31–32.
4. American Academy of Dental Science, *History of Dental and Oral Science in America* (Philadelphia: Samuel S. White, 1876), p. 271.
5. In 1860, out of a graduating class of 39, 28 students were from the southern states, 9 from the northern states, and 2 foreign. [Baltimore College of Dental Surgery, *63rd Annual Catalogue of the Baltimore College of Dental Surgery* (n.p., 1902), p. 22.]
6. L. Laszlo Schwartz, "War Problems of Dentistry: The South in the Civil War," *Journal of the American Dental Association* 32 (January 1, 1945): 37.
7. J[ohn] D. W[hite], "Dental Colleges," *Dental Cosmos*, n.s., 2 (May 1861): 560; "New Orleans Dental College," *Dental Cosmos*, n.s., 9 (October 1867): 151.
8. Schwartz, "War Problems of Dentistry," 37; Charles R. E. Koch, ed., *History of Dental Surgery*, vol. 2 (Fort Wayne, Ind.: National Art Publishing Co., 1910), p. 866.
9. [J. P. H. Brown], "Objects and Aims," *Southern Dental Examiner* 1 (May 1860): 1.
10. [J. P. H. Brown], "To Our Readers," *Southern Dental Examiner* 2 (January 1862): 107.
11. [Jonathan] T[aft], "American Journal of Dental Science," *Dental Register of the West* 15 (November 1861): 666.
12. W. Leigh Burton, "Dental Surgery as Applied in the Armies of the late Confederate States," *American Journal of Dental Science*, 3rd ser., 1 (August 1867): 182–83.
13. Benjamin Franklin Arrington, MD, DDS, was an 1853 graduate of the Baltimore College of Dental Surgery who received his MD degree at Transylvania Medical College before entering dental school. He practiced medicine and dentistry until 1858, when he limited his practice to dentistry. Dr. Arrington was president of the old North Carolina Dental Society in 1858 and 1866, and the new NCDS in 1875. He was the first president of the Southern Dental Association in 1869. For several years, he was a Regent of the Maryland Dental College under Dr. Winder. He invented alloys bearing his name and instruments for manipulating them. Dr. Arrington originated the "Arrington Toothbrush." [Gardner P. H. Foley, ed., *Proceedings of the 125th Anniversary Celebration of the Baltimore College of Dental Surgery* (Baltimore: Horn-Shafer Co., 1966), p. 128.]
14. "Obituary. Dr. J. W. Hunter," *Dental Cosmos* 45 (January 1903): 70; Burton, "Dental Surgery as Applied in the Armies of the late Confederate States," 183; J. Martin Fleming, *The History of the North Carolina Dental Society: With Biographies of Its Founders* (Raleigh, N.C.: North Carolina Dental Society, 1939), pp. 61–63; [Mrs.] J. M. Walker, "An Interesting Supreme Court Decision," *Dental Brief* 4 (October 1899): 573.
15. W. Leigh Burton, "Dental Notes on the late Civil War," *American Journal of Dental Science*, 3rd ser., 1 (January 1868): 441, 443.
16. Burton, "Dental Surgery as Applied in the Armies of the late Confederate States," 182.
17. Mary B. Chesnut, *A Diary from Dixie*, edited by Ben A. Williams (Boston: Houghton Mifflin Co., 1949), p. 462, 468.
18. Mary E. Massey, *Ersatz in the Confederacy: Shortages and Substitutes in the Southern Homefront* (Columbia, S.C.: University of South Carolina Press, 1952), p. 154.
19. Aaron Snowden Piggot, AM, MD, was born in Philadelphia in 1822. He graduated from Yale College in 1841 and from the University of Maryland in 1844. In 1851, he was the professor of anatomy and physiology at the Washington Medical University. From 1858–60, he held the same position at the Baltimore College of Dental Surgery. During the Civil War (1862–65), he served as a surgeon in the Confederate States Army. In July 1862, he was assigned to the laboratory of the medical purveying department in Richmond, which manufactured various medicines, and was superintendent of all the pharmacies and chemists. In November 1863, he was in charge of the new medical laboratory at Lincolnton, N.C. In July 1865, Piggot was paroled at Lincolnton. After the war, he returned to the Baltimore College faculty as professor of chemistry and metallurgy (1865–69). He served as co-editor of the *American Journal of Dental Science* in 1856, and 1867–69. Dr. Piggot died on February 13, 1869. [John R. Quinan, *Medical Annals of Baltimore from 1608 to 1880, Including Events, Men and Literature* (Baltimore: Isaac Friedenwald, 1884), pp. 145–46; Daniel D. Hartzler, *Medical Doctors of Maryland in the C.S.A.*, 1st ed. (Funkstown, Md.: Tri-State Printing, Inc., 1979), p. 67.]

20. Quinan, *Medical Annals of Baltimore*, p. 146.
21. "The Defamatory Article in the Dental Times," *American Journal of Dental Science*, 3rd ser., 2 (August 1868): 210.
22. "Dental Commencement," *Dental Cosmos*, n.s., 2 (April 1861): 498.
23. "Baltimore College of Dental Surgery," *Dental Cosmos*, n.s., 6 (May 1865): 560.
24. Baltimore College of Dental Surgery, *63rd Annual Catalogue*, pp. 22–23.
25. *See* Appendix A for BCDS graduates, former students, and future graduates.
26. *See* Appendix B for BCDS graduates, former students, and future graduates.
27. John M. Hyson, Jr., comp., War Department Collection of Confederate Records (Record Group 109) and U.S. Army Adjutant General's Office (Record Group 94), National Archives and Records Administration (*hereafter* cited as NARA).
28. [Chapin A. Harris], "Importance of Army and Navy Dentists," *American Journal of Dental Science*, n.s., 9 (July 1859): 444.
29. John M. Hyson, Jr., and Gardner P. H. Foley, "James Baxter Bean: The first military maxillofacial hospital," *MSDA Journal* 40 (Spring 1997): 77.
30. Ibid., 78.
31. This hospital had originally been opened on July 30, 1861, 10 days after the first battle of Manassas, by Miss Sally L. Tompkins of Richmond, who equipped and operated it entirely at her own expense. [Wyndham B. Blanton, *Medicine in Virginia in the Nineteenth Century* (Richmond: Garrett & Massie, Inc., 1933), p. 303.]
32. Hyson and Foley, "James Baxter Bean," 79–80.
33. Actually, Drs. Bean and Gunning both invented the same Vulcanite interdental splint simultaneously and independently of each other, one in the South and one in the North; however, because of the war neither was aware of the other's work on jaw fractures. The interdental splint is still used in edentulous fracture cases by oral surgeons today and is referred to as the "Gunning splint" rather than the "Bean splint." The reason for the nomenclature is because Dr. Gunning published several articles (1868–94) on his splint, whereas Dr. Bean only published articles in the dental literature on plaster manipulation and aluminum as a denture base. Both men were graduates of the same dental college (BCDS), Bean in 1860 and Gunning in 1880 (honorary). See John M. Hyson, Jr., and Gardner P. H. Foley, "Thomas Brian Gunning and his splint for jaw fractures," *MSDA Journal* 40 ((Winter 1997): 35–38
34. Hyson and Foley, "James Baxter Bean," p. 80.
35. Ibid.
36. *See* Appendix A for Civil War service and later careers.
37. Compiled Service Records of Confederate General and Staff Officers, and Non-Regimental Enlisted Men, roll 27, Microcopy 331, Record Group 109 (War Department Collection of Confederate Records), NARA (*hereafter* cited as M__, RG__).
38. Hartzler, *Medical Doctors of Maryland*, pp. 24–25.
39. Compiled Service Records of Confederate General and Staff Officers and Non-Regimental Enlisted Men, roll, 194, M 331, RG 109, NARA.
40. Compiled Service Records of Confederate Soldiers Who Served in Organizations from the State of Virginia, roll 519, M 324, RG 109, NARA.
41. Foley, *Proceedings of the 125th Anniversary Celebration*, p. 243.
42. Gardner P.H. Foley, "Adalbert Volck dentist and artist," (*Journal American College Dentists*), quoted in *Dental Radiography and Photography* 35, no. 4 (1962): 74, 87–89.
43. *See* Appendix B for Civil War service and later careers.
44. Personal Papers, Medical Officers and Physicians, ("Medical Officer's File"), prior to 1912, C. Knower, Entry 561, RG 94 (Adjutant General's Office), NARA; Compiled Service Records of Volunteer Union Soldiers Who Served in Organizations from the State of Missouri, Charles Knower, 1st Missouri Engineers, roll 353, M 405, RG 94, NARA; Foley, *Proceedings of The 125th Anniversary Celebration* , p. 185.
45. "Obituary. Dr. Homer Judd," *Dental Cosmos* 32 (July 1890): 574; Personal Papers, Medical Officer's and Physicians ("Medical Officer's File"), prior to 1912, H. Judd, E 561, RG 94, NARA.
46. Edward Maynard was born on April 26, 1813, in Madison, N.Y. His father, Moses Maynard, was a farmer, the sheriff of Madison County, a member of the New York State Legislature, and also served as a major in the New York militia during the War of 1812. In 1831, after completing his education at the Hamilton Academy, Maynard was appointed to West Point by DeWitt Clinton, a friend of his father's. Health problems forced his resignation in October the same year. After studying civil engineering, law, architecture, and anatomy, he decided on dentistry as his profession in 1835. After a short preceptorship with a Utica, N.Y., dentist, he began his own practice. He made all his own instruments, except forceps, in a blacksmith shop in Sherburne, N.Y.; he was a "born mechanic." In 1836, Dr. Maynard relocated in Washington, D.C., where he maintained a practice until 1890. Dr. Maynard received several honorary degrees: AM from Columbia College, Washington, D.C.; MD from Western Medical College in 1840; and DDS from the Baltimore College of Dental Surgery in 1841. From 1843 to 1850, Dr. Maynard was an associate editor along with Chapin A. Harris and Solymon Brown of the *American Journal of Dental Science*. In 1845, Dr. Maynard was requested to visit St. Petersburg, Russia, to perform a root canal procedure. He so impressed the emperor's physician, a Dr. Arndt, that he was employed as the court dentist for the imperial household. Emperor Nicholas offered him the title of "Actual Dentist to His Imperial Majesty" with rank of major if he would agree to stay in Russia for 10 years to practice and teach his methods; however, he refused the offer and returned to America. Dr. Maynard's Washington practice was highly selective and included several presidents, many cabinet members, congressmen and senators, army and navy officers, and foreign dignitaries. From 1856–60, he held the chair of theory and practice of dentistry at the Baltimore College of Dental Surgery, his alma mater. Later from 1887–89, he held the same faculty position at the Dental Department, National University in Washington. In 1890, Dr. Maynard retired from practice. He died of Bright's disease on May 4, 1891, at age 78 and was buried in the Congressional Cemetery in Washington, D.C. One can only speculate what if he had remained at West Point. Would he have contributed even greater

ordnance inventions to U.S. Army arsenals? [Charles R. E. Koch, ed., *History of Dental Surgery*, vol. 3. (Fort Wayne, Ind.: National Art Publishing Co., 1910), pp. 217, 219, 220–21, 223.]

47. C. Willard Camalier, Sr., *100 Years of Dental Progress in the Nation's Capital* (Washington, DC: C. Willard Camalier, 1966), p. 137.
48. "Obituary. Dr. Edward Maynard," *International Dental Journal* 12 (June 1891): 414–15; Arcadi Gluckman, *United States Muskets, Rifles and Carbines* (Harrisburg, Pa.: Stackpole Co., 1959), p. 224.
49. B. J. Cigrand, "Abraham Lincoln and Dentists," *American Dental Journal* 10 (February 15, 1913): 345.
50. Gluckman, *United States Muskets*, p. 389; Bell J. Wiley, *The Life of Johnny Reb* (Baton Rouge, La.: Louisiana State University Press, 1988), p. 292.
51. Camalier, *Dental Progress in the Nation's Capital*, 219–20.
52. Malcolm Wallace Carr, "Thomas W. Evans: His Life and Influence on the Development of Dentistry as a Learned Profession," *Journal of the American College of Dentists* 46 (April 1979): 91, 92–93. For more details of Evans' French career see Gerald Carson, *The Dentist and the Empress: The Adventures of Dr. Tom Evans in Gas-Lit Paris* (Boston: Houghton Mifflin Co., 1983).
53. Sanford Christie Barnum, DDS, was born on August 24, 1838, in Oakland Valley, N.Y. In 1858, at age 20, he began an apprenticeship with his uncle, Dr. Joseph W. Clowes, who had attended the first class at the Baltimore College of Dental Surgery in 1841, but did not return for the his second year (he was given an honorary DDS degree in 1846). After four years, Barnum opened his own office in Monticello, N. Y. While at Monticello, he conceived the idea of the rubber dam and first used it in the mouth of a patient. In 1864, he went back into practice with his uncle in New York City. Dr. Clowes convinced him to present his discovery to the profession as a gift, keeping in mind that at the time gold foil restorations, which required an absolutely dry field of operation, were the restorative material of choice. Although Barnum could have made a fortune from his invention, he gave it freely to the profession. In 1868, Barnum graduated from the New York College of Dentistry. In 1870, the American Dental Association presented Dr. Barnum with a gold medal. He received other awards from the California State Dental Association, and the American Dental Society of Europe. Dr. Barnum was afflicted with chronic meningitis during his last 10 years of practice and died at age 47 in Monticello on December 24, 1885. ["Originator of the Rubber Dam (Sanford Christie Barnum, DDS)," *Dental Radiography and Photography* 43, no. 4 (1970): ii, 82.]
54. In July 1928, Kolynos merged with the American Home Products Corporation, which is still in business as a consumer health care holding company called Wyeth. Kolynos today is a subdivision of Colgate Palmolive and is manufactured in Brazil. [John M. Hyson, Jr., and Scott D. Swank, "Dr. Newell Sill Jenkins Progenitor of Cosmetic Dentistry," *CDA Journal* 31 (August 2003): 629.]
55. Hyson and Swank, "Dr. Newell Sill Jenkins," 626–29.

Ferdinand James Samuel Gorgas

Chapter 7

The Gorgas Years: 1865–82

"The profession in which the practical dentist is engaged, is one so generally in demand—so endeared to community by the relief which it brings to human suffering—and requiring so much skill and talent to elevate it to its possible perfectibility, that nothing but the character of its professors has restricted its influence and usefulness in ages past, or shall in times to come, mar its reputation, or circumscribe its emolument."[1] ~**Solyman Brown, 1839**

Post War Recovery: 1866

By 1866, things were fairly back to normal for the Baltimore College of Dental Surgery. Ferdinand James Samuel Gorgas, AM, DDS, MD, was now the dean and professor of dental surgery, along with five new faculty members, namely: Russell Murdoch, AM, MD, professor of anatomy; Henry Reginald Noel, AM, MD, professor of physiology; Henry Hobart Keech, DDS, demonstrator of operative dentistry; T. Sollers Waters, DDS, demonstrator of prosthetic dentistry; and Claude Baxley, MD, demonstrator of anatomy; and of course, Dr. Piggot was back from the war.[2] The college's 1866–67 catalog noted the increased number of matriculants since the close of the war, and the prospects of a "much larger number at the next session." The faculty decided to expand the course of lectures on anatomy and physiology by creating a new chair of physiology, apart from that of anatomy, by adding Dr. Noel to the faculty. The curriculum was arranged to include 21 lectures every week throughout the session, besides the clinical practice.[3] For the 1865–66 session, there were 35 matriculates; however, in 1866 there were only 10 graduates.[4] The graduation was held at the New Assembly Rooms on March 2, 1866, with Dr. Thomas E. Bond giving the valedictory address.[5]

Ferdinand J. S. Gorgas: The Dean

Ferdinand James Samuel Gorgas, the dean of the Baltimore College of Dental Surgery (1865–82), has to be regarded as the dominant personage of the college during the period he served the institution. Dr. Gorgas was born on July 27, 1834, in Winchester, Va. He received his early education in the public schools of Carlisle, Pa. In 1854, he received his AB degree from Dickinson College, and later his AM degree (1857). In 1855, he graduated from the

Baltimore College of Dental Surgery with a DDS degree, and practiced briefly in Madison, Ind., and Harrisburg, Pa. In 1857, he was appointed to the faculty of the Baltimore College of Dental Surgery as a demonstrator of prosthetic dentistry. In 1863, he received an MD degree from the University of Maryland, and promptly enrolled as a volunteer surgeon[6] in the U.S. Army. In 1865, he was appointed as Professor of Dental Surgery and dean of his alma mater, serving until 1882, when he was appointed the first dean of the Dental Department, University of Maryland. He served as dean until 1911 (in all, 45 years as a dean). He served as editor of the *American Journal of Dental Science* from 1867 to 1900, wrote several textbooks,[7] and edited Chapin A. Harris' textbooks. Dr. Gorgas died on April 8, 1914.[8]

Ferdinand James Samuel Gorgas

Dr. Gorgas was described as medium height, strong of bone, well muscled, and a "strikingly erect posture." His facial expression exhibited "a kindly spirit," and his "dark and somewhat protruding dreamy eyes betokened artistic appreciation inherent in his mental makeup." His upper lip was "adorned by a flowing mustache dark in color," and his voice was "well modulated and of exceptional carrying power." His enunciation in the lecture hall was superb and "marked him as a scholar and a man of unusual insight." He was always well groomed and wore the conventional dark clothes, "well tailored and kept in excellent condition." In contrast with his somber clothes, he favored bright neckties, preferring "Scottish plaids." He constantly wore a finger ring, a watch fob, and a "gold band set with rich jewels" around his necktie. Masonic emblems decorated all three ornaments. Dr. Gorgas was an "inveterate tobacco chewer." A high brass cuspidor was in his office within "easy spittal range" of his desk chair. In theory and practice he was an individualist, but was always ready to accept other ideas if they met the test of "sound reasoning and could be upheld by logical precepts." He was not a good mixer, but was always ready and willing to help others seeking his counsel. During his later years, he did not participate in the affairs of organized dentistry, although he had been active in his early years. He formulated the bylaws and the code of ethics adopted by the Maryland State Dental Association at its initial meeting. As a writer and teacher, he had no desire to acquire leadership in national dental organizations. Dr. Gorgas kept student accounts in a leather-bound pocket ledger that he carried inside his coat pocket. Dates and payments were "neatly entered in diminutive but legible script."[9]

According to Dr. Heatwole, Dr. Gorgas was involved in the treatment of Secretary of State William H. Seward's jaw fracture in 1865. Seward, who had fractured his jaw in a previous carriage accident, was attacked while still bedridden on the night of Lincoln's assassination (April 14, 1865) by Louis Powell, a co-conspirator of Booth's, and his jaw was re-fractured. Dr. Gorgas was called in to render emergency treatment in reducing and fixing the fracture. It is unknown whether Gorgas was called upon because of his reputation or because he was a volunteer surgeon in the U.S. Army. Dr. Gorgas retained the plaster cast of Seward's jaw for exhibition in the school museum.[10] It is unclear at what point Dr. Gorgas was involved in the Seward case, as it is well known that Dr. Thomas Bryan Gunning, an 1880 honorary graduate of the Baltimore College of Dental Surgery, treated Seward's jaw fracture with his interdental splint.[11]

In 1866, Dr. Gorgas had a slight problem with the officials at the Eastern Potter's Field, where the college was obtaining cadavers for dissection. The manager complained that hereafter when the bodies were removed, the coffin and grave clothes be put back and the dirt properly placed over them." Dr. Gorgas replied that not one body had been brought to the college that year.[12]

Association of the Colleges of Dentistry: 1866-68

From 1840 on, when the Baltimore College of Dental Surgery was founded, the curriculum of each dental school was organized as the founders saw fit independent of one another. The medical curriculum was taken as a guide with strong emphasis on the medical sciences. Clinical training was left mainly to the offices of preceptors. Uniformity in the subject matter was not a concern "as long as it confirmed somewhat to the traditional medical pattern."[13]

On October 17, 1866, Dr. Gorgas, representing the Baltimore College of Dental Surgery, attended the meeting of a new group of dental educators called the Association of the Colleges of Dentistry at the campus of the Philadelphia Dental College in Philadelphia. The purpose of this new academic organization of dental colleges, the first of its kind, was to give uniformity to the length of the dental curriculum and the subjects taught; "harmony and uniformity" were the key issues to be discussed. The other four colleges were represented by Drs. Jonathan Taft of the Ohio Dental College; T. L. Buckingham, George T. Barker, E. Wildman, W. S. Forbes, and J. Truman of the Pennsylvania Dental College; John H. McQuillen, J. Foster Flagg, Thomas Wardle, C. A. Kingsbury, James E. Garretson, and A. Leeds of the Philadelphia Dental College; Eleazar Parmly, Norman W. Kingsley, and William H. Dwinelle of the New York Dental College. Actually, the groundwork for this meeting had been established at the meeting of the American Dental Association in Boston the previous August.[14]

On March 20, 1867, Drs. Gorgas and P. H. Austen attended the group's next meeting in Philadelphia, at which time the five schools agreed to the following regulations to govern the Association:

I. That the rule of our Dental Colleges allowing one session in a medical college to be considered equivalent to one course in a Dental College be abolished.

II. That two full years of pupilage with a reputable Dental practitioner, inclusive of two complete courses of lectures in a Dental College, be required to entitle the candidate to an examination for graduation for the degree of DDS.

III. That a graduate of a respectable medical college, who has been under the pupilage of a reputable

Dentist for one year, and shall have attended one full course of lectures in a Dental College, shall be entitled to examination for the degree of DDS.

IV. That eight years of Dental practice, including regular pupilage, will be regarded as equivalent to one course of lectures.

V. That the regular term of instruction in the Dental Colleges, be five months, the sessions in each to commence on the third Monday of October, annually.

VI. That students entering the Colleges later than the 10th of November, will not be credited for a full course, nor be eligible to graduation at the same term.

VII. That a candidate for graduation will be required to furnish a certificate of having pursued the required pupilage, or period of practice.

VIII. Regarding the education of the profession as the primary and only object in the establishment of Dental Colleges, therefore, *Resolved*, That whilst this Association does not forbid, it cannot approve the conferring of degrees upon persons who have not complied with the regulations agreed upon by this body, with the exception of gentlemen who have distinguished themselves as contributors to Dental science.[15]

Regulation number eight was very warmly discussed and voted on. When it passed, the Pennsylvania Dental College withdrew from the association, alleging that it was a rebuke of their past practice of conferring honorary degrees and a restriction on their "intended future course in this respect."[16]

At the April 2, 1868, meeting held at the New York Dental College, only four colleges were represented: the Baltimore College of Dental Surgery, New York College of Dentistry, Ohio College of Dental Surgery, and Missouri Dental College (added at the last meeting). The two Pennsylvania colleges were not represented. The Philadelphia Dental College dean, Dr. J. H. McQuillen, sent a note stating that the school withdrew its connection with the association without giving any explanation. He was probably influenced by the action taken by the Pennsylvania Dental College at the previous meeting. Dr. Gorgas reported that the Baltimore College of Dental Surgery had "adhered strictly to the regulations, both in the letter and the spirit; and had no cause for regret." He remarked that the adoption of these rules had prevented 12 to 15 students from attending the college, who would have otherwise matriculated. He also thought that a five-month session was not too long. The group planned to meet at the next meeting of the American Dental Association at Niagara Falls.[17]

Unfortunately, the association was short-lived and no future meetings apparently took place. The colleges simply could not agree over the "indiscriminate granting of degrees." Dental education was "too young, too unstable, and too highly commercial in its objectives to make permanent the continuance if an association devoted primarily to educational ideals."[18]

Meanwhile in 1867, Harvard University opened its dental school with requirements based on "two college years of four months each and three years' apprenticeship in the office of a dental practitioner."[19] Dr. Nathan Cooley Keep, president of the Massachusetts Dental Society, was the primary organizer. Dr. Keep, who was awarded an honorary DDS degree by the Baltimore College of Dental Surgery in 1843, was to become Harvard's first dental dean. He expressed his feelings on dental education in his 1865 address to the society:

> My own predilections would favor a thorough and united dental and medical education. I should hope in such a case that the degree of MD would be the lawful and merited appendage to the names of those young men who enter our specialty. If this, however, is not yet attainable, it may not be entirely out of place to

> inquire whether Harvard University might not appoint professors of dentistry, and confer upon candidates the degree of Doctor of Dental Surgery. We are admonished also, that the time has come for a chair of dentistry in our hospitals.[20]

Harvard was the first dental school to be associated with a university and its medical school. The dental school functioned as a part of the university from the start.[21] This trend would continue and eventually lead to the demise of the proprietary dental colleges.

The Washington Dentures: 1867

The most famous artifact in the Baltimore College of Dental Surgery Museum was George Washington's 1795 dentures. According to one source, the set of dentures made by John Greenwood (probably made in 1795 and repaired in 1798) for George Washington, called "one of the best known prosthetic appliances [ever] made," was given to the Baltimore College Museum in 1867. The set was originally given to Dr. Clowes of Philadelphia, whose grandson presented them to the college. Another source says the set was given to the college by Dr. John Allen before 1876. Allen had obtained the set from "a grandson [not Isaac (Jr.)] of Dr. Greenwood" and donated them to the college in "whose museum it now belongs." The plates were carved from a walrus tusk; the palatal portion of the upper plate was 18-karat gold.[22]

The other Washington ivory half-denture given to Chapin A. Harris was apparently lost to the museum during the Civil War, when it was taken out of the museum by Dr. Alfred Addison Blandy, Harris' son-in-law, and taken with him to England. In 1890, Dr. Richard B. Winder, the BCDS dean, related from hearsay: "In 1861, as I learn at the Commencement of the late civil war, the school was very nearly suspended and fearing that a raid might be made on the College by the Soldiers, these two sets were taken out of the College and placed for better and safer keeping in the hands of two of the Professors—Dr. Blandey [sic] had the safe keeping of one set and took it off to Europe with him and has never returned it."[23] If this story is true, then both Washington denture sets were in the museum before the Civil War.

Post-War Commencements

The twenty-seventh annual commencement of the Baltimore College of Dental Surgery was held on February 28, 1867, at the Concordia Opera House,[24] Baltimore. Again, the "Blues Band" proved the music, which "tended greatly to enliven the scene." The graduating class of 31 almost doubled that of the previous session. A change in the faculty was announced, with the resignation of Dr. H. H. Keech as demonstrator of operative dentistry. His position was assumed by Dr. Hugh McGinnis Grant of Abingdon, Va.[25]

For the next session of 1867–68, Dr. Gorgas, as noted above, decided to lengthen the course of instruction from four to five months, with no increase of fees. For the first time, the catalog mentions teaching "the use of anaesthetic agents for dental operations." In addition, the "Harris Lectures," in honor of the late Chapin A. Harris, were inaugurated for certain evenings throughout the session.[26] The twenty-eighth commencement was held at the Concordia Opera House on March 12, 1868. A month earlier, Charles Dickens had given a course of readings in the saloon of the same building. There were 26 graduates that year, including one from Cuba.[27] The twenty-ninth graduation was held on March 3, 1869, at the same location with the same number of graduates, including Jacob Z. Hoffer,[28] the only known alumnus to serve in the Mexican War of 1846–47. Dr. Thomas E. Bond delivered the valedictory address, which was scheduled to be given by the late Dr. Piggot.[29] For the thirtieth session of 1869–70, the college announced that Russell Murdoch, AM, MD, was replacing the deceased Dr. Piggot as professor of chemistry; E. Lloyd Howard, AM, MD, was assuming the new chair of histology, comparative, descriptive, and pathological anatomy; and Thomas Lattimer, MD, was added as a demonstrator of anatomy, replacing Dr. Claude Baxley. Also, the catalog stated that the number of operating chairs in the infirmary had been increased.[30] The commencement was held on March 2, 1870, at the Concordia, with 24 graduates, including candidates from Russia, England, and Germany.[31] The thirty-first session began on October 17, 1870, with some faculty changes. Dr. M. J. DeRosset replaced Dr. Murdoch as professor of chemistry; Dr. Henry Clark replaced Dr. Grant as demonstrator of operative dentistry; and three new assistant dental demonstrators were added: Drs. Alonzo G. Bouton, Louis Augspath, and Henry G. Ulrich. The students were reminded that as graduates, they could receive their MD degrees after attending one session at the Washington University of Medicine, Baltimore.[32] The thirty-first commencement was held on March 2, 1871, with 27 graduates. An honorary DDS degree was conferred on Dr. Norman W. Kingsley[33] of New York.[34] In 1871, James H. Harris[35] joined the faculty as a demonstrator of operative dentistry and in 1872 was named to head the new chair of clinical dentistry. He was to deliver special lectures during the week and supervise the operative and prosthetic clinics, which were under the charge of two "experienced" demonstrators.[36] The thirty-second commencement was held on February 29, 1872, with 18 graduates.[37]

In 1872, after nearly 20 years in the New Assembly Rooms, the college moved to 2 North Greene Street, across from the Westminster Church. It was described as containing "a very large operating room lighted by twelve windows, affording ample light for all operations."[38] In 1873, Dr. Basil Manly Wilkerson,[39] a former Confederate cavalryman and an 1868 graduate, joined the faculty as a demonstrator of prosthetic dentistry.[40] A multitalented individual, Wilkerson later achieved fame as the inventor of the first hydraulic dental chair, patented in 1877. The same year, he also invented an air-turbine drill.[41]

Emilie Foeking

The First Woman Graduate: 1873

The thirty-third commencement was historic because on Thursday evening, February 27, 1873, the college conferred its first DDS degree on a woman, Emilie Foeking of Prussia. Her thesis was appropriately titled, "Is Woman Adapted to the Dental Profession?"[42] At first, she had been refused admission to the Pennsylvania College of Dental Surgery, but was taken to Baltimore to meet Dr. Gorgas, the Baltimore dean, by Dr. James Truman,[43] who was the primary advocate for women in the dental profession.[44] She was the first of her sex to receive a diploma in medicine or dentistry in Baltimore, after attending two full sessions and passing a "very creditable final examination." Her paper was published in the *American Journal of Dental Science* in April 1873. In contrast to the Pennsylvania College, the Baltimore College of Dental Surgery was recognized as having "no objection whatever to receiving female students." In 1873, one prominent daily paper reported:

> Why the male students of the Pennsylvania College should object to those of the opposite sex, we cannot understand, as it has been entirely different in the Baltimore College during the past two sessions, where respect and consideration, instead of enmity, have characterized the behavior of the male portion of the class toward the female members.
>
> We are not so uncharitable as to ascribe this opposition on the part of Northern students to a want of that courtesy and respect so justly woman's due, and which have been manifested by Southern dental students in the Baltimore College (where a great majority of the class are from the South), thereby maintaining their claim to be gentlemen, but rather to the fear on the part of the Northern men that perhaps their domain of practice is about to be invaded by the opposite sex.[45]

The *Missouri Dental Journal* commented on Dr. Foeking's article that women were "by nature much better fitted" for "cooking, tailoring, etc." and would be unable to achieve the "highest honors as professionals."[46] After graduation, Dr. Foeking returned to Berlin, Germany, to practice dentistry.[47]

The following year, another woman—also from Germany—Louise Jacobi, was among the 19 graduates on February 26, 1874. She was the second-ranked student in her class. Her thesis was "Neuralgia of the Trigeminus."[48] Originally, she had attended the Philadelphia College in 1872–73[49] for a year, but transferred to Baltimore after she encountered problems in Philadelphia.[50] The *American Journal of Dental Science* commented on the "two ladies from the North German Empire" in 1873:

> The experiment of receiving female students, inaugurated last session, has proven so successful, and the effect upon the male students is so beneficial that the faculty are perfectly satisfied with their action in this respect.
>
> The greatest respect and consideration has, at all times, been shown by the male members of the class to these lady students, their behavior being such as to reflect honor upon themselves, and to merit the title of gentlemen.[51]

Dr. Gorgas has to be complimented on his foresight and tolerance in accepting women in his school. After graduation in 1874, Dr. Jacobi joined Dr. Henriette Hirschfeld[52] in a partnership in Berlin, Germany.[53]

The Austen Controversy: 1875

In January 1875, Dean Gorgas wrote to former dean (1853–65) and current professor of dental science and chemistry, Dr. Philip H. Austen, expressing his concern that Austen apparently felt that he was no longer held in the "highest regard" by the BCDS faculty. Austen had apparently told Gorgas that he would be unable to fill the chair of dental science and chemistry for the present session because of moving his family residence to another state. Also, he had canceled his subscription to the *American Journal of Dental Science* and said he would take "no further interest in dentistry and had dissolved all connection with the same." He was now turning his attention to a "wholly different occupation." However, he offered to deliver extra lectures at such times as might suit his convenience. The faculty refused this offer because of the "irregularity of such an arrangement." They proposed that he accept the position of Emeritus Professor of Dental Science and Chemistry" and deliver 10 lectures per session, one lecture per week, and receive $10 per lecture. On January 25, 1875, Dr. Austen replied that the faculty had placed themselves in an "embarrassing position" and tendered his resignation from the faculty. Finally, after some consideration the faculty agreed to apologize to Austen in view of his long and valued service to the college, and offered him the opportunity to choose the time for delivery of his optional lectures.[54]

The New Building: 1875

In 1875, the college moved again to a new larger, four-story building completed in February 1875 situated on the south-east corner of Eutaw and Lexington Streets. The building[55] was described as having a Mansard roof with large windows "extending from the ceilings to very near the floors. Its central location, with large, well-ventilated rooms, made it an excellent choice for patient convenience and infirmary practice. With the emphasis on clinical practice, the college opted for space and lighting requirements rather than the old "age of enlightenment" policy of architectural style. The building was supplied with gas and water, and provided with "every convenience necessary to the comfort of the student." The new building enabled the faculty to greatly enlarge their plan for student instruction.[56]

The thirty-fifth commencement was again held at the Concordia Opera House on February 25, 1875, with 17 graduates, including John E. M. Chevers from the West Indies.[57]

The Alumni Meeting: 1876

Meanwhile, on March 6, 1876, a meeting of the graduates of the Baltimore College of Dental Surgery was held in the college building with the purpose of forming an alumni association, which apparently had been dormant since it was first organized in 1849. About one hundred graduates assembled with quite a number from out of state. The meeting was organized by Dr. Samuel J. Cockerille of Washington, D.C. as the chair and Dr. Gorgas as secretary. Officers were elected as follows: Samuel J. Cockerille, Class of 1853, president; Theodore A. La Far, Class of 1860, first vice-president; Samuel D. French, Class of 1854, second vice-president; Thomas H. Davy, Class of 1874, recording secretary; William B. Wise, Class of 1874, corresponding secretary; William H. Hoopes, Class of 1856, treasurer; Ferdinand J. S. Gorgas, Class of 1855; James H. Harris, Class of 1860; and William H. Hoopes, Class of 1856, executive committee. Dr. Cockerille remarked on the necessity for organization and the "claims of their Alma Mater upon those she sends forth to practice the dental art." A constitution and bylaws were adopted. It was decided to hold the annual meetings timed with the college commencements.[58] Was this meeting called by Dr. Gorgas to offset the inroads that Winder's Maryland Dental College had made upon dental education in the city of Baltimore? Was Winder even invited to the meeting as an alumnus of the college? Probably not, as Gorgas and Harris were involved in the organization.

Centennial Exposition: 1876

George Washington's dentures were exhibited by the college at the Philadelphia Centennial Exposition in 1876. After viewing Washington's "false teeth" at the 1876 Centennial, Dr. Henry Lovejoy Ambler remarked: "The wonder is, they say, that any man ever held them in his mouth five minutes. The teeth are bits of bone, scarcely trying to look like teeth, attached to gold plate, with strips riveted across to strengthen the teeth in place, while coiled wire at the end of the jaw make a spring, and assists in opening and closing the machine."[59]

The thirty-sixth commencement was held on March 10, 1876, at the Academy of Music,[60] Baltimore, with 19 graduates, including another German woman, Elise von Heyden, whose thesis was "Secondary Dentin."[61] The thirty-seventh commencement was held at the same location on March 9, 1877, with another German woman, Pauline Boeck, receiving her DDS degree.[62]

The Museum: 1877

The college's 1877 catalog described the museum's collections in detail:

> The Museum of the College is the growth of years, and is a large and rare collection of anatomical specimens, its assortment of skulls and jaws alone numbering many hundreds. Plates and drawings and photographic prints of anatomical and physiological subjects, which are fully used in illustration of lectures, are in great numbers, exceeding variety, and constantly added to. The collection of dental morbid specimens is alone worth a visit to examine. A large number of beautiful pathological specimens have been recently added to the collection.[63]

The thirty-eighth session began on October 15, 1877, and ran until March 1878. The first two weeks were devoted to clinics and introductory lectures on dental subjects. The regular course of lectures began on November 1 and continued without intermission (except for Christmas break) until the following March. The college proudly announced that almost 800 students had received diplomas from its hands. Its graduates were scattered all over the world. They were located in almost every city in Europe; in England, France, Germany, Switzerland, Spain, Italy, and Russia; in Asia, South America, West Indies, and Canada; and every state from New England to Florida, and from New York to California. Many of its graduates were world-renowned for their discoveries and publications. Every court dentist in Europe (with but one or two exceptions) was a graduate of the college. The college also announced the initiation of a two-week spring course for the current session; it was considered in the "highest degree beneficial" to those who attended it. The catalog also cited the college's support from the medical profession; another example of the cooperation and recognition it received from physicians.[64] The graduation was held on March 5, 1878, at the Academy of Music with two more German females, Elvira Castner and Adolfhine Peterson, among the 17 graduates receiving degrees.[65] By contrast, the Pennsylvania College of Dental Surgery had 78 graduates.[66]

The Merged Schools: 1879

On February 17, 1879, the BCDS faculty met to discuss the merger of BCDS with the Maryland Dental College, and the creation of a chair for Dr. Richard B. Winder, its dean. A committee of three consisting of Drs. Gorgas, Latimer, and Harris was appointed to discuss the merger with a similar committee from the Maryland Dental College. Dr. Gorgas had previously toured the Maryland College facilities with Dr. Winder. It was decided that the Maryland College's property be appraised by the firm of Snowden and Cowman, which it did and came up with the figure of $655.77 for its effects. BCDS agreed to pay one-half of the Maryland College's building rent for six months.[67]

The thirty-ninth commencement was held on March 6, 1879, at the Academy of Music, with 41graduates, including the graduating class of the Maryland Dental College, which had merged into the Baltimore College of Dental Surgery.[68] The morning of the commencement, at the annual meeting of the Baltimore College of Dental Surgery alumni, the alumni of the Maryland Dental College were made members of the Alumni Association[69] of the Baltimore College of Dental Surgery.[70] Meanwhile, the Maryland College dean, Dr. Richard B. Winder, had joined the faculty as professor of dental surgery. The Baltimore College's 1879–80 catalog noted: "Since the union of the Maryland Dental College with the Baltimore College of Dental Surgery, in March, 1879, this latter is the only Dental College in Baltimore."[71] The consolidation of the two Baltimore dental colleges was made after scrutiny by attorneys, who pronounced it legal. Every member of both faculties signed the merger agreement. One of the conditions of the merger was the appointment of a board of visitors by the faculty, which had "limited advisory powers."[72] The fortieth annual commencement was held at the Academy of Music on March 4, 1880, with 40 graduates receiving a DDS degree from Dr. Gorgas. Dr. Thomas Brian Gunning[73] of New York was awarded an honorary degree.[74]

On March 3, 1881, a committee of the board of visitors, consisting of Drs. M. Whilldin Foster, J. B. Ten Eyck, and R. Finley Hunt, attended the final examinations of the 1880–81 graduating class and reported on the qualifications of the candidates for receiving a degree.[75] The forty-first commencement was again held at the Academy of Music on March 2, 1881, with Professor Gorgas conferring degrees on 53 candidates.[76]

Relocation of College: 1881

In June 1881, the college again relocated, a few blocks north of the previous location, on the southeast corner of Franklin and Eutaw Streets. The college catalog called the building "one of the finest structures in Baltimore City." The school occupied the entire three-story building, except for the stores on the ground floor. The infirmary occupied half of the second story and the other half contained the "extensive" museum ("a large and beautiful Hall"), an extraction room, hat and coat room, water closets, etc. The third floor contained a large lecture hall, capable of seating 300 students, three laboratories (one of which was devoted to "plaster-work, furnace work, vulcanizing, etc."), a dissecting room, and other rooms for various purposes. The rooms had 20-foot ceilings with numerous corresponding size windows. The building was steam heated, had "beautiful chandeliers and gas fixtures," and fronted two wide streets. The catalog called its new home the "finest and best equipped College building in the world devoted exclusively to dental instruction."[77] This move had been precipitated by what Dr. Gorgas called the "crowded and unhealthy" lecture room in the old building, which required the students to spend an average of three to four hours in an unhealthy environment. These conditions caused "illness of quite a number of the students."[78]

Dr. William H. DeFord, Class of 1882, who later became the first dean of the College of Dentistry, Drake University, in 1931, reflected on his college clinical days:

> The Dental foot engine was attracting the attention of the profession, and many dental offices had not installed one. I recall that the Baltimore College of Dental Surgery allowed members of the senior class to use the engine, but it was considered entirely too dangerous a venture for a junior. We relied on the excavator, chisel and hand-bur for cavity preparation.
>
> The burs were the same length as chisels and excavators, and those who were not strong enough to twist

them with the fingers used an instrument for this purpose, which consisted of a ring of metal[79] placed on the second finger. A tongue of metal extended to the palm of the hand, terminating in a miniature metal cup, which resembled a bowl in shape. One end of the handle of the bur rested in this little bowl and was twirled with the fingers. The palm of the hand was entirely too tender to support the end of the bur, as considerable pressure was necessary to effect cutting. Cavity preparation had not been systematized, and all that was attempted was just a shape that would prevent fillings from falling out. I[t] was indeed a slow procedure for the dentist and a tiresome nerve-racking experience for the patient.[80]

The college also announced that during its existence it had now graduated 1,085 students and had 1,817 students attend its halls. Furthermore, it was treating more than 2,000 charity patients in its infirmary every year. The inmates of the Baltimore Orphan Asylum, St. Mary's Orphan Asylum, St. Vincent's Orphan Asylum, the Boys' Home, the Aged Men's Home, the Aged Women's Home, St. James' Home for Boys, St. Joseph's House of Industry, St. Paul's School for Boys, the Christ Church Orphan Asylum, and others were treated without cost to the patient and the institution from which they came.[81]

The 1882 commencement took place at Ford's Opera House on Thursday afternoon, March 9, 1882. Dr. Gorgas conferred degrees on 47 graduates. It would be the last time he would exercise this duty for the Baltimore College of Dental Surgery.[82]

NOTES

1. Solyman Brown, "Remarks on Professional Morality," *American Journal of Dental Science* 1 (August 1839): 1.
2. Baltimore College of Dental Surgery, *Twenty-Seventh Annual Circular & Catalogue of the Baltimore College of Dental Surgery* (Baltimore: John W. Woods, Printer, 1866), p. 2.
3. Ibid., p. 4.
4. Ibid., pp. 14, 15.
5. "Baltimore College of Dental Surgery," *Dental Cosmos*, n.s., 7 (April 1866): 483.
6. The author was unable to find Gorgas' name among the official roster of the 1861–65 volunteer surgeons of the U.S. Army. [Ron R. Van Sickle, ed., comp., *General Index to Official Army Register of the Volunteer Force of the United States, 1861–1865* (Gaithersburg, Md.: Ron R. Van Sickle, 1987), p. 307.]
7. Dr. Gorgas wrote the first textbook on dental medicine, *Dental Medicine, A Manual of Dental Materia Medica and Therapeutics*, in 1883. In 1885, he published, *Questions and Answers for Dental Students*, which he revised and published periodically. He also edited and revised Harris' *Principles and Practice of Dental Surgery*, the 11th (1885) through the 13th (1896) editions, and Harris' *A Dictionary of Dental Science, Biography, Bibliography and Terminology*, 5th (1891) and 6th (1898) editions. In 1885, he published, *Lectures on Dental Surgery, Special Pathology, Materia Medica and Therapeutics for the Use of Dental Students.* [Gardner P.H. Foley, ed., *Proceedings of the 125th Anniversary Celebration of the Baltimore College of Dental Surgery* (Baltimore: Horn-Shafer Co., 1966), p. 168.]
8. Ibid.; T[imothy] O. Heatwole, "An Abbreviated Biography of Ferdinand J. S. Gorgas, MA, DDS, MD," Special Collections, Health Sciences and Human Services Library, University of Maryland at Baltimore (*hereafter* cited as HSL); "Obituary. Dr. Ferdinand J. S. Gorgas," *Dental Cosmos* 56 (June 1914): 771–72.
9. Heatwole, "Abbreviated Biography of Ferdinand J. S. Gorgas," HSL.
10. Ibid. A 1904 newspaper article on the museum mentions "three casts of the jaw of William H. Seward, Lincoln's Secretary of State." ["Historic Teeth," *Baltimore Sun*, July 10, 1904.] Apparently, the Seward casts were lost sometime in the 1960s during the time the museum was under duress. [The author.]
11. John M. Hyson, Jr., and Gardner P. H. Foley, "Thomas Brian Gunning and his splint for jaw fractures," *MSDA Journal* 40 (Winter 1997): 35–37.
12. Letter, C.D. White, Health Office, Eastern Potter's Field, to F. J. S. Gorgas, Dean, Baltimore College of Dental Surgery, November 28, 1866, Baltimore College of Dental Surgery Papers, National Museum of Dentistry Archives (*hereafter* cited as BCDSP, NMDA).
13. John T. O'Rourke, and Leroy M.S. Miner, *Dental Education in the United States* (Philadelphia: W.B. Saunders Co., 1941), p. 109.
14. [J(onathan) Taft], "Association of the Colleges of Dentistry [Proceedings]," *Dental Register* 21 (January 1867): 29, 30.
15. [Jonathan Taft], "The Association of the Colleges of Dentistry," *Dental Register* 21 (April 1867): 179, 181.
16. Ibid., 181–82.
17. J[onathan] Taft, "Proceedings of the Association of the Colleges of Dentistry," *Dental Register* 22 (May 1868): 197, 201, 202.
18. Harlan H. Horner, *Dental Education Today* (Chicago: University of Chicago Press, 1947), p. 33.
19. O'Rourke and Miner, *Dental Education*, p. 109.
20. Richard L. Hapgood, *History of the Harvard Dental School* (Boston: Harvard University Dental School, 1930), p. 226.

21. O'Rourke and Miner, *Dental Education in the United States*, p. 37.
22. W. J. Pryor, ""The Closed Bite Relation of the Jaws of George Washington, with Comments on his Tooth Troubles and General Health," *Journal of the American Dental Association* 20 (April 1933): 569; Lawrence Parmly Brown, "The Antiquities of Dental Prosthesis, Part III, Section II, Eighteenth Century," *Dental Cosmos* 76 (November 1934): 1162; [Alfred W. Chandler], "George Washington's Dentures," *Journal of the American Dental Association* 76 (May 1968): 961.
23. Letter, Richard B. Winder to Isaac J. Greenwood, October 15, 1890, BCDSP, NMDA. Nothing more became of the "lost denture" until 1934, when Dr. J. Ben Robinson, the BCDS dean, wrote to Chapin Harris' daughter, Mrs. Mary (Charles Edward) Barrett-Lennard living in London. Robinson stated that he heard that "a part set of Washington's teeth," which once belonged to the Baltimore College was now in the London Hospital Medical College Museum, University of London. Mrs. Barrett-Lennard replied that it was her understanding that the denture had been given to her father, not to the college. In any case, she stated that her sister sold the denture along with a Washington letter for the "contemptible sum of five pounds." [Letter, J. Ben Robinson to M. Barrett-Lennard, March 13, 1934; Letter, M. Barrett-Lennard to J. Ben Robinson, March 22, 1934, BCDSP, NMDA.]
24. The Concordia Opera House, located on the southwest corner of Eutaw and German (Hanover) Streets, was erected by the Concordia German Association in 1864. [J. Thomas Scharf, *History of Baltimore City and County from the Earliest Period to the Present Day: Including Biographical Sketches of Their Representative Men* (Philadelphia: Louis Everts, 1881), p. 695.]
25. "Baltimore College of Dental Surgery," *American Journal of Dental Science*, 3rd ser., 1 (May 1867): 40–41.
26. Baltimore College of Dental Surgery, *Twenty-Eighth Annual Circular of the Baltimore College of Dental Surgery* (Baltimore: John W. Woods, Printer, 1867), pp. 4, 5, 6–7.
27. "Baltimore College of Dental Surgery," *Dental Cosmos*, n.s., 10 (April 1868): 207–8; Scharf, *History of Baltimore City*, p. 695
28. Jacob Zollinger Hoffer was born at Carlisle, Pa., on April 7, 1826. He enlisted as a private in Company "E," 2nd Pennsylvania Infantry, on December 24, 1846. He served under Gen. Scott and participated in the battles of Vera Cruz, Cerro Gordo, Chapultepec, and Mexico City Gates. He was discharged on a medical certificate in April 1948. In 1855, he began to study dentistry under Dr. G. W. Neidich of Carlisle, and in 1858 opened his own dental practice in Columbia, Pa. In 1869, he graduated from the Baltimore College of Dental Surgery at age 43, and was a charter member of the Pennsylvania State Dental Society. Dr. Hoffer died on March 22, 1901 in Columbia. [Foley, *Proceedings of the 125th Anniversary Celebration*, pp. 176–77; "Obituary. Jacob Zollinger Hoffer, DDS," *Dental Cosmos* 43 (July 1901): 835.]
29. "Baltimore College of Dental Surgery," *Dental Cosmos*, n.s., 11 (April 1869): 194–95.
30. Baltimore College of Dental Surgery, *Thirtieth Annual Circular of the Baltimore College of Dental Surgery* (Baltimore: Office *American Journal of Dental Science*, 1869), pp. 1, 7.
31. "Baltimore College of Dental Surgery," *Dental Cosmos*, n.s., 12 (April 1870): 204.
32. Baltimore College of Dental Surgery, *Thirty-First Annual Circular of the Baltimore College of Dental Surgery* (Baltimore: Office of the *American Journal of Dental Science*, 1870), pp. 2, 4, 7, 9.
33. Norman William Kingsley was born on October 26, 1829, in Stockholm, N.Y. He apprenticed with his uncle, a physician/dentist, in Elizabeth, N. J. After a partnership with Dr. B.C. Leffler in Owego, N. J., in 1850, he went to New York in 1852 to practice with Solyman Brown. At the New York World's Fair in 1853, he won a gold medal for his porcelain teeth mounted in gold. In 1859, he became interested in cleft palate work and evolved a technique for making artificial appliances still used today. He was one of the founders of the New York College of Dentistry and the first dean from 1866 to 69. Kingsley published the first book on orthodontics and was the president of the New York State Board of Censors for 16 years. He was also a talented artist and sculptor. Dr. Kingsley died on February 20, 1913. ["Not the occupation that honors this man—he honors his occupation (Norman William Kingsley, MD, DDS)," *Dental Radiography and Photography*, 26, no. 3 (1953): i, 64.]
34. "Baltimore College of Dental Surgery," *Dental Cosmos*, n.s., 13 (April 1871): 196.
35. James Howell Harris, DDS, MD, was born in Albemarle County, Va., on October 23, 1834. He began studying dentistry in the office of Dr. William Chapman of Stanton, Va. After several years as an apprentice, he opened his own office in Harrisonburg, Va. In 1861, he graduated from the Baltimore College of Dental Surgery. Returning to Harrisonburg, on May 28, 1861, he joined the Confederate Army, enlisting as a private in Company "I," 4th Regiment, Virginia Cavalry, at Ashland for one year. On November 3, 1864, he was assigned to duty as a dentist at the Harrisonburg General Hospital to "perform all dental operations requires." Harris was discharged on November 28, 1864, and resumed his practice in Harrisonburg. In 1871, he returned to Baltimore as an instructor in operative dentistry at his alma mater. In 1872, he became the professor of "clinical dentistry" (1872–82). In 1872, he also received his MD degree from the College of Physicians and Surgeons in Baltimore. In 1882, he resigned from the Baltimore College of Dental Surgery's faculty to join Dr. Ferdinand J. S. Gorgas in organizing the dental department of the University of Maryland. He held the chair of operative and clinical dentistry from 1882–1910. He was known as a remarkably efficient operator and devised a test for detecting impurities in the mercury used in amalgam, which had been a major factor in the failure of the material at the time. Dr. Harris died on December 12, 1910, in Baltimore. [Foley, *Proceedings of the 125th Anniversary Celebration*, pp. 173–74; Eugene F. Cordell, *University of Maryland 1807–1907: Its History, Influence, Equipment and Characteristics with Biographical Sketches and Portraits of its Founders, Benefactors, Regents, Faculty and Alumni*, vol. 1 (New York: Lewis Publishing Co., 1907), pp. 398, 401; "Civil War File," Gardner P.H. Foley Papers, NMDA (*hereafter* cited as GPHFP); Compiled Service Records of Confederate Soldiers Who Served in Organization from the State of Virginia, roll 42, Microcopy 324, Record Group 109 (War Department Collection of Confederate Records), National Archives and Records Administration (*hereafter* cited as M__, RG__, NARA); Daniel D. Hartzler, *Medical Doctors of Maryland in the C.S.A.*, 1st ed. (Funkstown, Md.: Tri-State Printing, Inc., 1979), p. 43.
36. Baltimore College of Dental Surgery, *Thirty-Third Annual Circular of the Baltimore College of Dental Surgery* (Baltimore: Snowden & Cowman, 1872), pp. i, 1.
37. "Baltimore College of Dental Surgery," *Dental Cosmos* 14 (April 1872): 198.

38. Marc D. Star, "Stones and Bricks: An Architectural Record of Maryland's Dental Colleges," senior thesis, Baltimore College of Dental Surgery, Dental School, University of Maryland, 1993, p. 11; Baltimore College of Dental Surgery, *Thirty-Third Annual Circular*, p. 1.
39. Basil Manly Wilkerson, DDS, MD, was born in Foster's Settlement, Tuscaloosa County, Ala., on March 28, 1842. During the Civil War, he served as a third sergeant in Company "K," 8th Regiment, Alabama Cavalry, from 1863–65. His unit commanded by Capt. Charles E. Owen, surrendered on May 4, 1865, at Citronelle, Ala., to Maj. Gen. Edward R. Canby's troops. He was paroled on May 14, 1895. After the war, he attended the Baltimore College of Dental Surgery and graduated in 1868. In 1873, he graduated from the College of Physicians and Surgeons in Baltimore with an MD degree. He served on the faculties of the Baltimore College of Dental Surgery from 1872 to 1879, and the Dental Department, University of Maryland, from 1883 to 1888. He was the proprietor and co-editor of the *Independent Practitioner* from 1879–82. Dr. Wilkerson died at Harrisonburg, Va., on June 13, 1910, of a coronary. ["Obituary. Dr. Basil Manly Wilkerson," *Dental Cosmos* 52 (October 1910): 1176; Foley, *Proceedings of the 125th Anniversary Celebration*, p. 237–38; Compiled Service Records of Confederate Soldiers Who Served in Organizations from the State of Alabama, roll 27, M 311, RG 109, NARA.]
40. Baltimore College of Dental Surgery, *Thirty-Fourth Annual Circular of the Baltimore College of Dental Surgery* (Baltimore: Snowden & Cowman, 1873), p. i.
41. John M. Hyson, Jr., and Audrey B. Davis, "Basil Manly Wilkerson: Dental Inventor Extraordinaire," *Journal of the History of Dentistry* 47 (July 1999): 61, 63.
42. "Baltimore College of Dental Surgery," *Dental Cosmos* 15 (May 1873): 247.
43. On August 6, 1869, Dr. Truman proposed a resolution at the American Dental Association meeting at Saratoga, N.Y., that as the "National Delegated Body," the organization should ensure the rights of any duly qualified women as full members of organized dentistry. The resolution was "laid on the table" and not acted on, a major setback for the admission of women to the profession. [John M. Hyson, Jr., "Women Dentists: The Origins," *CDA Journal* 30 (June 2002): 447.]
44. Elizabeth C. Stanton, Susan B. Anthony, and Matilda J. Gage, eds., History of Woman Suffrage, vol. 3 (New York: Charles Mann, 1886), quoted in "Women in Dentistry," *Odontographic Journal* 7 (April 1886): 41–42.
45. Federation of American Women Dentists, "Women in Dentistry—1855–1880," *Journal of the American Dental Association* 15 (September 1928): 1752, 1753.
46. "Journalistic," *Missouri Dental Journal* 5 (June 1873): 230–31.
47. Foley, *Proceedings of the 125th Anniversary Celebration*, p. 164.
48. "Baltimore College of Dental Surgery," *Dental Cosmos* 16 (April 1874): 190; "Women Dentists in Germany," (*Cincinnati Gazette*), quoted in *Johnston's Dental Miscellany* 1 (June 1874): 239.
49. In 1872–73, the Pennsylvania College of Dental Surgery accepted three women, Annie D. Ramborger, Veleske Wilcke, and Louise Jacobi, as students. After their first year, there was a determined effort to remove them by some of their male classmates. A petition was sent to the faculty to effect their removal, and it was decided not to allow them to continue. The decision was appealed to the board of trustees, and a special committee established to decide the issue. The committee reported that as the women had paid their matriculation fees, attended classes, and looked forward to graduation; therefore, it was the college's legal duty to give them as second course of lectures. The board accepted the decision and the women were invited to resume their studies. Misses Ramborger and Wilcke accepted, but Louise Jacobi refused the offer and transferred to Baltimore. [Stanton, Anthony, and Gage, "Women in Dentistry," 42–43.]
50. Federation of American Women Dentists, "Women in Dentistry," 1750, 1752; Stanton, Anthony, and Gage, "Women in Dentistry," 42–43.
51. Federation of American Women Dentists, "Women in Dentistry," 1752.
52. Henriette Hirschfeld was the first woman to complete the full two-session dental course and receive a DDS degree from the Pennsylvania College of Dental Surgery. Lucy Beaman Hobbs Taylor was the first woman to receive a DDS degree, but she had received credit for her previous practice time and therefore did not attend the full course of lectures. When Hirschfeld reported to the college, she was met "with a storm of hisses" from the male students, and the anatomy professor refused to teach her. She had to take anatomy in the Woman's Medical College; however, she gradually won the respect of the male students and graduated with honors. [Federation of American Women Dentists, "Women in Dentistry," 1740–41; Stanton, Anthony, and Gage, "Women in Dentistry," 41.]
53. Federation of American Women Dentists, "Women in Dentistry," 1742.
54. Baltimore College of Dental Surgery, "Faculty Minutes Jan, 15, 1875, to and incl. April 26, 1916," January 19, 25, 1875, Special Collections, HSL.
55. This building is still standing on the south-east corner of Eutaw and Lexington Streets, with many of its original architectural details intact. It is the oldest surviving dental college building in Baltimore. [Star, "Stones and Bricks," p. 11.]
56. Baltimore College of Dental Surgery, *Thirty-Seventh Annual Catalogue of the Baltimore College of Dental Surgery* (Baltimore: n.p., [1876]), p. 2; John Milner Associates," Architecture as History: The Formative Years of the Baltimore College of Dental Surgery as Recorded in the Housing History," Final Report, John Milner Associates, West Chester, Pa., 1980, p. 46.
57. "Baltimore College of Dental Surgery," *Dental Cosmos* 17 (April 1875): 206.
58. T[homas] H. Davy, "Alumni Meeting," *Dental Cosmos* 18 (May 1876): 262.
59. "The Dental Exhibit at the Centennial," *Dental Advertiser* 7 (October 1876): 167; Henry L. Ambler, comp., ed., *Facts, Fads and Fancies about Teeth* (Cleveland: Helman-Taylor Co., 1900), pp. 178–79.
60. The Academy of Music, located on the west side of the 500 block of North Howard Street, was built in 1874. The building featured a façade of "red brick with sandstone trim, sets of triple-arched windows, and a steep French roof of polychromatic slate with dormer windows, finials, and a fancy iron-work cresting rail." The building was designed to provide "a grand concert hall, opera house, and theater for the city." [Mary Ellen Hayward and Frank R. Shivers, Jr., eds., *The Architecture of Baltimore: An Illustrated History* (Baltimore: The Johns Hopkins University Press, 2004), p. 201].

61. "Baltimore College of Dental Surgery," *Dental Cosmos* 18 (April 1876): 202.
62. "Baltimore College of Dental Surgery," *Dental Cosmos* 19 (April 1877): 207.
63. Baltimore College of Dental Surgery, *Thirty-Eighth Annual Catalogue of the Baltimore College of Dental Surgery* (Baltimore: n.p., [1877]), p. 3.
64. Ibid., pp. 1–4.
65. "Baltimore College of Dental Surgery," *Dental Cosmos* 20 (April 1878): 232–33; Baltimore College of Dental Surgery, *Thirty-Ninth Annual Catalogue of the Baltimore College of Dental Surgery* (Baltimore: n.p., [1878]), p. 19.
66. "Pennsylvania College of Dental Surgery," *Dental Cosmos* 20 (April 1878): 233.
67. Baltimore College of Dental Surgery, "Faculty Minutes Jan, 15, 1875 to and incl. April 26, 1916," Special Collections, HSL.
68. "Baltimore College of Dental Surgery," *Dental Cosmos* 21 (April 1879): 219–20.
69. In 1883, Dr. James B. Hodgkin, Class of 1869, was elected president of the merged organization for 1883–84; however, there are no records of any meetings during his term of office. [Joseph H. Seipp, Jr., "A Brief History of the First Dental Alumni Association in the World (Organizations Associated with the Baltimore College of Dental Surgery)," *Alma Mater* 8 (November 1966): 5.]
70. Ibid.
71. Baltimore College of Dental Surgery, *Fortieth Annual Catalogue of the Baltimore College of Dental Surgery* (Baltimore: N.p., 1879), p. 1, 12.
72. Baltimore College of Dental Surgery, *Forty-Second Annual Catalogue of the Baltimore College of Dental Surgery* (Baltimore: n.p., [1881]), pp. 13–14.
73. For details of Gunning's career see John M. Hyson, Jr., and Gardner P. H. Foley, "Thomas Brian Gunning and his splint for jaw fractures," *MSDA Journal* 40 (Winter 1997): 35–38.
74. "Baltimore College of Dental Surgery," *Dental Cosmos* 22 (April 1880): 202.
75. Baltimore College of Dental Surgery, *Forty-Second Annual Catalogue*, p. 13.
76. "Baltimore College of Dental Surgery," *Dental Cosmos* 23 (April 1881): 212.
77. Baltimore College of Dental Surgery, *Forty-Second Annual Catalogue*, p. 5.
78. Letter, Ferdinand J. S. Gorgas to Richard B. Winder, June 9, 1880, BCDSP, NMDA.
79. The finger ring for holding the long-shanked drills while twirling them was invented in 1846 by Amos Westcott, the former chair of operative and mechanical dentistry (1846) at the College. [J. A. Taylor, *History of Dentistry: A Practical Treatise for the Use of Dental Students and Practitioners* (Philadelphia: Lea & Febiger, 1922), p. 135.]
80. Gardner P. H. Foley, "BCDS Notes," *Alma Mater* 12 (Spring 1971): 6.
81. Baltimore College of Dental Surgery, *Forty-Second Annual Catalogue*, p. 4–6.
82. "Baltimore College of Dental Surgery," *Dental Cosmos* 24 (April 1882): 213.

Dental Infirmary
Baltimore Medical College
715 North Eutaw Street
1895-1913

Chapter 8

The Maryland Dental College: 1873–79

"Dentistry has always impressed me as one of the most important, and necessary specialties of Medical Science, but to attain any high degree of proficiency in it requires so much careful investigation, observation, and severe application, that it may indeed be reckoned among the Herculean tasks."[1] **~Richard Bayly Winder, 1869**

The Maryland Dental College: 1873

For many years after the founding of the Baltimore College of Dental Surgery in 1840 dental education centered on the world's first dental college. In 1845, the Ohio College of Dental Surgery was organized in Cincinnati, Ohio. In the other states, only five other dental schools were organized before the Civil War. After 1865, however, there was a "renascence of enthusiasm for dental training, and a continually increasing number of schools were chartered and put in operation in many of the larger cities throughout the United States." Whereas, only seven dental schools had been chartered before 1865, 22 were organized between 1866 and 1884. The time was ripe for another dental college in Baltimore in the 1870s.[2]

Richard B. Winder, DDS, MD

In 1873, Richard Bayly Winder, a Confederate veteran and a 1869 graduate of the Baltimore College of Dental Surgery, organized a new dental school, later described as the "most bitter enemy" with which the Baltimore College of Dental Surgery ever had to contend. Richard B. Winder[3] was a Princeton and University of Virginia-educated Virginian, who during the Civil War had volunteered his services to the South and served as the quartermaster of the infamous Confederate Andersonville Prison in Georgia. After the war, he entered the Baltimore College of Dental Surgery and graduated in 1869, at age 41. He then became an associate of Dr. Ferdinand J. S. Gorgas, the dean of the Baltimore College of Dental Surgery and a fellow Virginian. Shortly afterwards, he established his own dental office at the corner of Madison and Park Avenues in Baltimore, and because of his excellent reputation, soon attracted a fashionable clientele. Earlier, he had been appointed the chairman of the dental service at the Baltimore Special Dispensary by its medical board. Seeking to improve his scientific knowledge, Winder entered the College of Physicians and Surgeons[4] of Baltimore, and received his MD degree in 1873.[5]

The Maryland Dental College was located at 42 North Calvert Street, near Saratoga, in Baltimore. Winder appointed himself dean of the faculty and professor of physiology and hygiene. Winder's founding of a rival dental school was interpreted by many to be a result of his being rebuffed at efforts to secure a faculty appointment at his alma mater, from which he had graduated only four years earlier, a "self-aggrandizement." Winder was described as having "a very aggressive, forceful, and domineering personality," whose ambition was eventually to be the dean of the Baltimore College of Dental Surgery; establishment of the Maryland Dental College was considered the first step in his ambitious plan. Perhaps, he may have been inspired to open his new college by Dr. Warren's opening his own medical school (College of Physicians and Surgeons) in Baltimore the previous year. His faculty was basically Baltimore oriented: Drs. Byron F. Coy, professor of dental surgery; M. Whilldin Foster, professor of dental mechanism and metallurgy; Samuel M. Field, professor of chemistry and dental material medica; Edward P. Keech, professor of clinical dentistry; Henry H. Keech, professor of pathology and therapeutics; Samuel H. Williams, emeritus professor of the institutes of dentistry; L. McLane Tiffany, professor of comparative microscopic and general anatomy; Albert P. Gore, demonstrator of mechanical dentistry; and B. W. Barton, demonstrator of anatomy. Visiting instructors included Drs. Thomas B. Gunning (inventor of the Vulcanite interdental splint for jaw fractures)[6]; E. Parmly Brown; J. N. Farrar; George H. Evans; John H. Meyer and Kasson C. Gibson of New York; William W. H. Thackston of Virginia; R. F. Hunt of Washington, D.C.; J. R. Walker of New Orleans; and Marshall H. Webb of Lancaster, Pa.[7]

The college was described as having 20 or more rooms, including a patient reception room, "free" dental infirmary (open from 1 to 4 p.m. daily), operating and dissecting rooms, and a laboratory. Nitrous oxide was manufactured in the operating room and the laboratory contained a furnace for making "continuous gum." The school's opening session began on October 1, 1873, with clinical lectures. The regular course of daily didactic and clinical lectures was given between November 1, 1873, and March 1874. The infirmary was open during the entire year.[8]

The opening of the new school was not met with much enthusiasm by the faculty of the Baltimore College of Dental Surgery. Prospective students were cautioned by the Baltimore College of Dental Surgery to beware of "*irregular* colleges" in its 1873–74 catalog:

> As a number of *irregular* colleges of all kinds, whose fall is generally as sudden as their rise, are being instituted throughout the country under dispensations obtained in the same manner as those for common building associations, and by persons whose sole aim is self-aggrandizement (many of them having been unsuccessful in obtaining positions in reputable institutions, and some even the degree of the profession which they practice), students are cautioned against all inducements held out to spend time and money in attending any but regularly chartered and well established colleges, whose diplomas are known and recognized throughout the world.[9]

The Baltimore College of Dental Surgery was obviously concerned about the competition, as this paragraph did not appear in any of its previous or subsequent announcements. As to the implication that some of Winder's professors lacked a dental degree, actually it was true that Byron F. Coy and H. Whilldin Foster, although the DDS degree appears after their names in the catalog, did not officially own dental degrees. It was only given later in 1879 as an honorary degree at the time of the merger of the Maryland Dental College with the Baltimore College of Dental Surgery.[10]

In its 1874 catalog, the college's Board of Regents gave the reasons for founding the college:

> Conservative and intelligent practitioners of dentistry have deemed it proper to establish a second College of Dentistry in the city of Baltimore, and the Faculty of the College have seen fit to appoint a Board of Regents from the dental and other professions, to whom is entrusted the power to confer degrees, and without whose consent no diplomas can be granted. Whilst the Board of Regents thus created have had no agency in establishing the Maryland Dental College, yet they have cheerfully consented to assume the duties of their position from a willingness to second the efforts of the gentlemen of the Faculty in building up a school for promoting dental education and elevating the standard of professional attainment.[11]

Winder's Board of Regents: 1873–79

Winder's college differed from the other dental schools of the period, which had been set up according to the model, the Baltimore College of Dental Surgery. In his school an independent board of examiners, composed of 50 or so well-known dental practitioners from all parts of the country, were authorized to conduct the student examinations. Each year, the president of the board appointed a committee of three members to give the oral examinations to the graduating class. Full authority was vested with the board to examine the students on any subject they chose and to decide who would be awarded a degree. Winder's philosophy was that "the dental college should be able to educate a man in everything pertaining to dentistry." As with the older Baltimore College of Dental Surgery, the college required two years' attendance to obtain the DDS degree. The requirements for admission to the college and the curriculum were basically the same as for the Baltimore College of Dental Surgery. Winder's ability to attract the best men the dental profession had to offer to impart their knowledge to his students began a new era in dental education. His reforms were eventually copied by other dental schools and represented a radical change for dental instruction. On March 4, 1874, 10 students graduated in the first Maryland Dental College class (seven from Maryland, two from Virginia, and one from England) at the Masonic Temple, Baltimore. Graduates were allowed to enter the senior year at either the College of Physicians and Surgeons or the Washington Medical College, both located in Baltimore, and upon the completion of the prescribed courses, receive their MD degree. Winder, himself, was a member of the faculty of the College of Physicians and Surgeons.[12]

The second session of the college began on October 1, 1874, and continued until March 1875. The 1874 catalog announced the educational plan to be followed:

> The course of instruction pursued is that which, in the opinion of the Faculty, is best calculated to teach both the art and science of Dental Surgery. It is eminently practical. Lectures, both Didactic and Clinical, will be delivered daily throughout the session, while the Infirmary, under the charge of the Clinical Professor and Demonstrators, is open during the entire year. The Faculty, with one exception, being actively engaged in the practice of Dentistry, will assist the Clinical Professor in his lectures and operations, thus enabling the student to become more familiar with the different styles of operating.
>
> Under the direction of the Demonstrators, patients will be assigned to the students, who will be required to operate at the chair, and they will in this way be taught the various operations incident to Dental Surgery.

> This intimate union of theoretical and practical instruction will be insisted on during the entire course, and, indeed, is considered as the one essential to becoming a competent dental practitioner [13]

The dissecting rooms were open daily until 10 p.m., at which time they were closed for the night. The infirmary and laboratory were open during the entire year. The college provided all the dental supplies used in the clinic, but the student had to provide his own instruments, with the exception of extraction forceps, vulcanizers, and lathes.[14]

The fees charged by the college were lecture fee $120, matriculation fee $5, and diploma fee $30. The college announced that "good board" could be secured in the city for $6 per week. The textbooks used were: Tome's *Dental Surgery*; Harris' *Principles and Practice of Dental Surgery*; Quain, Gray, or Wilson's *Anatomy; Fowne's Chemistry*; Dunglison's *Medical Dictionary*; Taft's *Operative Dentistry*; Richardson's *Mechanical Dentistry*; Carpenter, Dalton or Bennett's *Physiology*; Biddle's *Materia Medica*; and Wedl's *Pathology*.[15]

The authority of the Board of Regents was complete. After a degree candidate had passed the faculty examinations, he was permitted to go before the Board of Regents. They had full authority to give examinations on any subject they chose and by any method to all students nearing graduation. They alone decided who received the dental degree and who failed the course. Also, before February 14, the students had to deposit in the dean's office his graduation fee of $30, a thesis of "his own composition" on a dental subject, and specimens of his operative and prosthetic work. Interestingly enough, for the few years before the opening of the Maryland Dental College, the Baltimore College of Dental Surgery failed to list their graduates in the school's annual catalog as had been its former custom. However, in the 1874–75 catalog the full list of graduates was restored. Prospective students could see that the old school had hundreds of graduates, whereas the new school had only 10.[16]

Again in 1875, the college's catalog stressed the importance of its innovation of having the Board of Regents be responsible for granting degrees:

> The interest awakened by the establishment two years ago of a second College of Dentistry in the city of Baltimore on principles and with features hitherto unknown in dental education, has not flagged either on the part of its friends or its opponents. This College, with its new principles and features, has, since its institution, been on trial, and the results thus far have been most satisfactory.[17]

The second annual commencement was held at the Masonic Temple,[18] Baltimore, on March 3, 1875, with four graduates.[19] In 1875, the college held an alumni meeting and elected the following officers: Dr. Frederick A. Levy of New York, president; Dr. T. W. Coyle of Maryland, vice-president; Dr. J. Emory Scott of Maryland, treasurer; Dr. Charles E. Duck of Maryland, corresponding secretary; and Dr. Frederick F. Drew of Maryland, recording secretary.[20]

The third annual session of the college began on October 1, 1875, and ended in March 1876. A new requirement appeared in the college's third annual catalog, namely: "Students before matriculating will be required to pass a satisfactory examination in the usual branches which constitute a good English education, and they will also be required to furnish evidence of their good moral character and personal standing."[21] For the session 1875–76, the college graduated only 10 students on March 2, 1876. Again, the ceremonies were held in the Masonic Temple, Baltimore.[22] The alumni association held its annual meeting the next day, March 3, 1876.[23]

The college's fourth annual session for 1876–77 began with some faculty changes. Edward P. Keech replaced Henry H. Keech as professor of pathology and therapeutics, and B. W. Barton replaced L. McLane Tiffany as professor of anatomy. In 1876, to stimulate sagging attendance, the college announced that it would accept tuition-free one student from each state selected and recommended by the state dental societies, who could meet the admission requirements.[24] However, this plan to basically give states a "scholarship" did little to increase enrollment. Competition from the Baltimore College of Dental Surgery made things very difficult for the college.[25] The college's fourth commencement was held on March 1, 1877, at the Academy of Music, Baltimore, with 17 graduates.[26] The same night, the alumni held their annual "Alumni Hop" at the Academy of Music Concert Hall.[27]

For the fifth session, beginning on October 1, 1877, the college made some faculty changes. A. P. Gore was replaced by T. Morris Murray, as a demonstrator, and several clinical lecturers were added, namely: William H. Atkinson, MD, New York; E. Parmly Brown, Flushing, Long Island; G. J. Barclay, Pittsburgh; John Allen, MD, New York; W. M. Reynolds, MD, New York; H. B. Noble, DDS, Washington, D.C.; and T. S. Waters, DDS, Baltimore.[28] The graduation was held on March 7, 1878, at the Academy of Music, Baltimore, with 10 DDS degrees awarded.[29] On March 8, the annual meeting of the alumni association was held in the college's lecture room.[30]

Again in 1878, there were faculty changes. Dr. R. B. Donaldson replaced Byron F. Coy as professor of dental surgery; Dr. R. Finley Hunt replaced Samuel M. Field as professor of physics and chemistry; and Dr. C. E. Duck was dropped from the faculty. The sixth annual session began on October 1, 1878, and continued until March 1879.[31]

The Board of Regents announced the "cheering success" of the Maryland Dental College. The test of five years had "resulted favorably to the new features introduced into its regime—new in dental colleges, though not in some other institutions of learning." The new features were:

> 1st. A preliminary examination by the Faculty of all applicants for matriculation as to preparation by previous education and fitness in moral character. 2nd. That the degree of D.D.S. will be conferred on any candidate for graduation, of good moral character, who can prove himself qualified by his knowledge and skill to practice dentistry, without reference to the time and place of the acquirement of his qualifications. 3rd. A Board of Regents who prescribe the regime of the College, examine candidates for graduation, and confer degrees on those who are qualified.[32]

The University of Virginia (Winder's college) and Johns Hopkins University used this same system to confer degrees whenever merited. Any matriculant who was 21 years of age and in good standing in his class had the privilege at the close of the session of coming forward as a candidate for graduation. After the faculty selected those they found "qualified" and believed would make good dentists, they sent the Board of Regents a list of those they believed could "meet the rigid examination to which they know they will be subjected." The Board of Regents passed "none who do not satisfy them of their proficiency."[33]

The Merger with the BCDS: 1879

The sixth annual and last commencement was held on March 5, 1879, at the Academy of Music. Among the 18 graduates was the dean's son, Richard B. Winder, Jr.[34] However, despite the college's initial success, small enrollments and competition from the Baltimore College of

Dental Surgery eventually forced the Maryland Dental College to quietly merge into its older brother, the Baltimore College of Dental Surgery in 1879. In its six years of existence, the Maryland Dental College had graduated about 70 students. Although the Maryland Dental College faded into history, the ramifications of its very existence would be felt not only by the Baltimore College of Dental Surgery, but also by the very nature of the dental education process. It had left its mark on dental education and changed it forever.[35]

As a postscript to this event, the Maryland Dental College faculty issued a letter to the "Dental Profession," in which they (presumably Dr. Winder) offered an explanation for the merger:

> Six years ago the Maryland Dental College was organized in the city of Baltimore, to meet what was believed to be a serious and pressing want in the line of Dental Education. During its existence of six years it has supplied that want, and steadily fulfilled the object for which it was established. It points with pride to its Alumni, now occupying high positions in the Profession in this and other countries, and to the improvement in the standard of Dental Education wherever its influence has extended.
>
> But there has been for more than a year past a general feeling, which has increased and deepened with passing time and current events, that if the two Dental Colleges located in Baltimore could combine and unite their efforts in the common cause in which both are engaged, their labors would be attended with far greater good to the Profession and larger benefits to all.
>
> This feeling has given rise to negotiations and these negotiations have resulted in the combination and mergement of the two Institutions, and the uniting of their Faculties. This combination of the older Institution, 'The Baltimore College of Dental Surgery,' and the younger Institution carries with it into the combination the peculiar features of its regime, modified and improved by six years of experience.[36]

After the spring graduation of the Maryland Dental College, the faculty merger also occurred. A new chair or title was created for the Maryland College dean, Dr. Winder, at the Baltimore College of Dental Surgery, apparently in accordance with a premerger agreement. He became the professor of dental surgery and operative dentistry (1879–94), a chair previously held by Dr. Ferdinand J. S. Gorgas, the Baltimore College dean. This exchange may have had a dramatic effect on what was to follow a few years later in 1882. However, finally, Winder was a faculty member at his alma mater.[37]

Two other instructors at the Maryland Dental College were added to the Baltimore College of Dental Surgery faculty, Drs. Whilldin Foster and William B. Finney. However, they were not well received by the Baltimore College alumni, many of whom had been opposed to the absorption of the Maryland Dental College. Letters of "protest and criticism" from the alumni poured into the school. Placing the Maryland College faculty or graduates in key teaching positions in the original school created bitter resentment for many years. Even the students were involved; the 1879 class of the Baltimore College of Dental Surgery assumed a dim view of the appearance of the 1879 Maryland Dental College class to receive their diplomas on the same stage.[38] However, the *Missouri Dental Journal* hailed the merger as for the "greater good to the profession and larger benefits to all," as it questioned whether there was a "necessity for more than one college in the same section of the country." It predicted an "increased measure of success to the combined college."[39]

As an additional provision of the merger, the Baltimore College of Dental Surgery agreed to purchase the property of the Maryland Medical College, which was appraised at $655.77 by the firm of Snowden & Cowman, and to pay one half of the rent due on its building for the next six months.[40]

Winder-Harris Controversy over Gold Foil: 1880–82

Some of the "old guard" at the Baltimore College of Dental Surgery resented the way that Winder had seemingly forced his way onto the faculty. Shortly after his arrival, dissention erupted between Winder and Dr. James Howell Harris,[41] the professor of operative and clinical dentistry, who opposed the merger. Dr. Harris was a fellow Virginian and a Confederate veteran, who had graduated from the Baltimore College in 1861. As the story goes, a student told Dr. Winder about an uncomplimentary remark Dr. Harris had made in reference to Winder's dentistry. It seemed that the two men had a different philosophy on the two most popular types of gold foil restorations, cohesive foil and soft foil. Dr. Winder advocated the use of cohesive gold and Dr. Harris was a proponent of soft gold. The ongoing debate in dental circles during this period over the merits of soft gold vs. cohesive (hard) gold caused one dentist to remark at a national dental meeting, "a young man who came here to learn how to fill a tooth would go home without knowing how any better than when he came." Some dentists recommended starting the restoration with soft gold, which was more adaptable to the cavity walls and then completing the restoration with the harder cohesive gold, which was more durable and lasting. Some used the combination of a tin foil lining filled in with hard gold. Others thought the instrumentation was the key factor, advocating smooth over serrated-tipped plugging instruments. Such was the state of affairs in the mid-1800s. Soon a bitter argument between the two men ensued, with charges and counter charges being leveled. Eventually, the faculty, board of visitors, and even the student body became involved in the controversy and took sides. Some felt that Winder was promoting the affair toward his own ambitions (to become dean). Others accused Harris of systematically poisoning the minds of newly arrived students and the alumni (oddly enough, particularly in Virginia) against Dr. Winder. Harris had insinuated that Winder was "ignorant, incompetent, incapable of teaching, and of bad character." Apparently, there was no love lost between these two former Confederate soldiers—Harris, the cavalryman, and Winder, the quartermaster. Possibly, the "prejudice" against anyone (even a fellow Virginian) associated with Andersonville had again surfaced and was the real cause of their difficulties. Then too, there was the fact that Winder may have used his relationship with his cousin, General Winder, to secure his noncombatant position, whereas Harris saw actual combat. This situation alone could have irritated Harris, who had served as an enlisted man, despite his dental degree. Of course, Winder had been commissioned a captain (1861) and a quartermaster (1862) before his service in the prison system,

James H. Harris

and it was likely this experience caused his cousin to choose him for the Andersonville assignment.[42]

In February 1880, it was rumored that a petition, charging Winder with "incompetency," "drunkenness," "ungentlemanly conduct," etc., had been circulated and signed by numerous students. They recommended Winder's removal from the Baltimore College of Dental Surgery's faculty. On February 23, several prominent Baltimore dentists (including Drs. T. S. Waters, J. B. McPherson, Samuel H. Williams, Samuel M. Field, E. P. Keech, and others) sent a petition to Dr. Ferdinand J. S. Gorgas, the dean of the college, expressing their support for Winder and recommending that he be retained on the faculty. The dentists stated that they considered Winder a "competent teacher" and an "excellent lecturer," possessing "capabilities for imparting knowledge," and having "general intelligence, liberality of education" and "gentlemanly bearing."[43] Two days later, on February 25, several well-known Washington, D.C., dentists (including Drs. R. Finley Hunt, R. B. Donaldson, J. Curtis Smythe, J. B. TenEyck, H. B. Noble, Hall Lewis, and others) sent a similar petition to Dr. Gorgas backing Winder as a faculty member. They also expressed their disdain for students being able to "sit in judgment upon the qualifications of their preceptors," and decide who would be faculty members of the institution they were attending. The dentists believed that this student movement could jeopardize the recent consolidation of the two colleges (Baltimore College of Dental Surgery and Maryland Dental College) and cause "irreparable injury." Winder was praised as "a gentleman of the purest and nicest sense of honor;" having undisputed standing in the profession; and, having the power to surround himself with the profession's best "scientific and practical" talent.[44]

On February 26, 1880, Dr. Edward Maynard of Washington, D.C., the former Baltimore College professor and alumnus, presidential dentist, and ordnance inventor, expressed his concerns over the current situation to Dean Gorgas:

> It would be an unspeakable pity a public calamity even—to have The Baltimore College of Dental Surgery go down—But it has started on the down ward way since the late change in the constitution of its Faculty and it is very evident, and growing more so daily, that you will need to act promptly and decidedly to undo the mischief already done and reassure the friends and advocates of the college and save it from disgraceful ruin.[45]

On February 29, 1880, the student body, junior and graduating classes (1879–80), stated that Dr. Harris had never criticized Dr. Winder and that he should be exonerated of any "real or imaginary wrongs." The students, Class of 1880–81, also denied that Harris had ever attempted to "poison" their minds against any faculty member. It stands to reason that the majority of the students sided with Dr. Harris, as he had been their professor long before Winder arrived on the scene.[46]

By the spring of 1880, the matter had still not been resolved, it just simmered. Finally, at the faculty meeting on March 8, 1880, attended by Drs. Gorgas, E. Lloyd Howard, Thomas L. Latimer, and James B. Hodgkin, a resolution was passed (without Winder or Harris' presence) to the effect that Dr. Harris had acted "improperly and inconsiderately during the past Session in speaking disparagingly and disrespectfully of his Colleague Dr. Winder," and unless Harris changed his tone in addressing Winder, the "best interests of the College" would be served by his resignation from the faculty.[47]

On October 28, the college's board of visitors held a special meeting to discuss the "difficulties now existing in [the] Faculty." A committee, consisting of Drs. J. B. TenEyck, E. P. Keech, H. B. Noble, and R. Finley Hunt, was appointed to investigate the situation. The charges against Dr. Harris were also investigated by the faculty and he was found guilty based on the evidence they uncovered; Harris denied the charges. Harris was censored for improper conduct because of his "speaking disparagingly and disrespectfully of his colleague [Winder]." He was advised that unless he would agree in the future to treat Winder with the proper respect he deserved as a faculty member, it was thought best for him to resign.[48] After receiving the faculty report, the board of visitors was not satisfied. Their committee felt that Harris was guilty of the "stigma of a violation of professional ethics, of undermining the reputation and official influence of a colleague in the Faculty, and of falsehood." Documentary evidence left no doubt of his guilt despite his denial. In response to the board of visitors report, Dr. Harris' supporters accused Winder of "sending an emissary over the country, undermining the reputation of Dr. Harris." They said that Harris had never attempted to "poison" students' minds.[49]

The one person who could have settled the matter, Dean Gorgas, despite his earlier endorsement of Winder and repudiation of Harris, seemed to remain indecisive in the dispute. Although not supporting Harris, he did not side against him. Some conjectured that he was bitter about having to give up the chair of dental surgery to Winder at the amalgamation of the two schools. Others perceived that two factions divided the school; one led by Drs. Gorgas and Harris and the other by Drs. Winder and Foster. However, these arguments were (and are) mere speculation. After all, at one time Winder had been an associate of Dr. Gorgas. Did the two men really have a falling out? In any event, Dr. Gorgas certainly did not take Dr. Maynard's advice to "act promptly and decidedly."[50]

The situation finally peaked on March 1, 1882, when Dr. Harris refused to allow Dr. R. Finley Hunt of Washington, a member of the board of visitors, to sit in (as was customary) on his final examination of the graduating class, locking him out of the room. Students partial to Harris ordered Dr. Hunt to leave the campus. Hunt was so infuriated, as he was performing the board's "specific duty" that he preferred charges against Harris. At the April 27, 1882, faculty meeting, Gorgas was the only dissenting vote censoring Harris; however, coupled with the Winder charges, Harris was eventually forced to resign in April 1882.[51]

With the Harris resignation, the stage was set for the emergence of a third dental college in Baltimore; however, the roles of the major players would now be reversed.

NOTES

1. Richard B. Winder, "Dental Education," *American Journal of Dental Science,* 3d ser., 2 (April 1869): 575.
2. Harry B. McCarthy, "A History of Dental Education in Maryland," master's thesis, Graduate School, University of Maryland, 1948, p. 31; William J. Gies, *Dental Education in the United States and Canada* (New York: Carnegie Foundation for the Advancement of Teaching, 1926), pp. 42, 46.
3. Richard Bayly Winder was born on July 17, 1828, at "Covington," the family estate in Eastville, Northhampton County, Va. In 1845, Winder was enrolled at Princeton (then known as the College of New Jersey), where he spent one year, and then transferred to the University of Virginia in 1846. At the outbreak of the Civil War, Winder volunteered his services to the Confederacy and was appointed as a captain in the 39th Regiment, Virginia Infantry. After his regiment was disbanded, he was assigned to the quartermaster department. In the fall of 1863, with Richmond threatened by the Union forces and food in short supply, the Confederate government decided that it would be best to move the Richmond prisoners of war camps further south. The site ultimately selected was Andersonville, Ga., described as "one of those miserable little hamlets" near Macon. In addition to its good forests, its very remoteness offered security from

Union raids. The man selected by Brigadier General John Henry Winder, the Confederate provost marshal and commander of prisons, as assistant quartermaster for the new prison was his second cousin, Captain Richard Bayly Winder. In December 1863, Winder was ordered to report to Andersonville for the construction of a prison for an expected 10,000 men. The local pine trees were to supply the logs for the stockade enclosure. Meanwhile, prisoners were being sent to Andersonville at the rate of 400 a day. At that time the prison consisted of sixteen and a half acres enclosed by a 15-foot stockade with no buildings. A five-foot stream, which was soon polluted, divided the prison yard roughly in half. With these problems, the well-known horrors of Andersonville began. Winder's name would forever be linked with the "miserable" place, even though he tried to obtain food, tents, and construction materials for the prisoners. The Confederate inspector general described the prison as "a place of horrors." In March 1865, Winder was promoted to major and reassigned as the chief quartermaster to Headquarters, Military Prisons East of the Mississippi at Salisbury, N. C. In April 1865, while on his way to Augusta, Ga., he was taken prisoner by the Union troops. Winder was paroled at Augusta in May 1865 and returned home to what was left of his Accomac County estate. Winder, now widowed, having to care for two small children, and finding prejudice against the former Andersonville officers even in the South, contemplated the possibility of leaving the country. However, in July 1865, he took the oath of allegiance to the federal government and was given a certificate of loyalty. In August 1865, he was arrested by two U.S. Army officers, and incarcerated in the Accomac County jail. Earlier, the Andersonville commandant, Heinrich Wirz, had been arrested and charged with responsibility for the atrocities at Andersonville. After a trial on August 23, Wirz was convicted and condemned to death by hanging. On August 31, Winder was transferred to the Old Capitol Prison in Washington, D.C. His cell was directly opposite Wirz's cell. In October 1865, the judge advocate general recommended that Winder be tried for complicity only, since there was no evidence of alleged cruelty to prisoners. Meanwhile, Wirz was executed (by hanging). Affidavits of former Union prisoners affirmed that Winder was never inhumane in dealing with them; therefore, he was eventually released on April 11, 1866, because of a lack of evidence. Winder again returned home to his Virginia plantation and made plans with a friend to go into business in Baltimore. However, the war, in addition to changing his financial situation, had also changed his priorities and interests, so since he was an excellent wood carver and metal worker, he decided to become a dentist. Therefore, he entered the Baltimore College of Dental Surgery and graduated with a DDS degree, at age 41, in 1869. [John M. Hyson, Jr., and Gardner P. H. Foley, "Richard Bayly Winder: Andersonville Quartermaster and Dental College Dean, *MSDA Journal* 40 (Fall 1997): 163–67.]

4. The College of Physicians and Surgeons was founded in 1872 by Dr. Edward Warren, an antebellum professor of material medica and therapeutics at the University of Maryland, School of Medicine. Dr. Warren had resigned his chair in 1861 to join the Confederate Army. He served as the surgeon general of North Carolina and the medical inspector of the Army of Northern Virginia. Upon his return in 1865, he demanded the restoration of his professorship, but was refused reinstatement. Bitter toward the university, in 1867, he sought revenge by reopening a rival medical school, the Washington Medical College, which had been dormant since 1851. In 1872, he resigned from the Washington College and started the aforementioned College of Physicians and Surgeons in the same city. [George H. Callcott, *A History of the University of Maryland* (Baltimore: Maryland Historical Society, 1966), pp. 206–7.]
5. Hyson and Foley, "Richard Bayly Winder," 167–68; Petition, Various dentists to the Board of Visitors, Baltimore College of Dental Surgery, n.d. [1880], Baltimore College of Dental Surgery Papers, National Museum of Dentistry Archives (*hereafter* cited as BCDSP, NMDA).
6. See John M. Hyson, Jr., and Gardner P. H. Foley, "Thomas Brian Gunning and his splint for jaw fractures," *MSDA Journal* 40 (Winter 1997): 35–38.
7. Koch, Charles R. E., ed. History of Dental Surgery, vol. 3 (Fort Wayne, Ind.: National Art Publishing Co., 1910), p. 462; McCarthy, "Dental Education in Maryland," pp. 31–33.
8. McCarthy, "Dental Education in Maryland," p. 32; "New Dental College," *Dental Advertiser* 4 (July 1873): 119.
9. McCarthy, "Dental Education in Maryland," p. 32; Baltimore College of Dental Surgery, *Thirty-Fourth Annual Circular of the Baltimore College of Dental Surgery* (Baltimore: Snowden & Cowman, 1873), p. 4.
10. McCarthy, "Dental Education in Maryland," pp. 33–34; Baltimore College of Dental Surgery, *Forty-Second Annual Catalogue of the Baltimore College of Dental Surgery* (Baltimore: n.p., [1881]), p. xiii.
11. Maryland Dental College, *Annual Circular and Catalogue of the Maryland Dental College* (Baltimore: Snowden & Cowman, 1874), p. 7.
12. McCarthy, "Dental Education in Maryland," pp. 34, 35; "American Dental Convention—Twenty-Second Annual Session," *Dental Cosmos* 18 (November 1876): 606; Maryland Dental College, *Annual Circular and Catalogue* [1874], p. 8; "Maryland Dental College," *Dental Cosmos* 16 (April 1874): 193–94.
13. Maryland Dental College, *Annual Circular and Catalogue* [1874], p. 4.
14. Ibid., p. 5.
15. Ibid., p. 6.
16. McCarthy, "Dental Education in Maryland," p. 35; Maryland Dental College, *Annual Circular and Catalogue* [1874], p. 6.
17. Maryland Dental College, *Annual Circular and Catalogue of the Maryland Dental College* (Baltimore: Snowden & Cowman, 1875), p. 6.
18. The Masonic Temple, on the northeast corner of Lexington and St. Paul Streets, was designed by Maximilian Godefroy in 1812, but not completed until 1819 because of the war. The building featured four Greek Doric columns. [Mary Ellen Hayward and Frank R. Shivers, Jr., eds., *The Architecture of Baltimore: An Illustrated History* (Baltimore: The Johns Hopkins University Press, 2004), p. 75.]
19. "Maryland Dental College," *Dental Cosmos* 17 (April 1875): 210.
20. "Dental Alumni Association of Maryland Dental College," *Dental Cosmos* 17 (May 1875): 267.
21. Maryland Dental College, *Annual Circular and Catalogue* [1875], pp. 3, 5.
22. Maryland Dental College, *Annual Circular and Catalogue of the Maryland Dental College* (Baltimore: Snowden & Cowman, 1876), p.8; "Maryland Dental College," *Dental Cosmos* 18 (April 1876): 205.
23. "Dental Alumni Association of the Maryland Dental College," *Dental Cosmos* 18 (April 1876): 202.
24. Maryland Dental College, *Annual Circular and Catalogue* [1876], pp. 2, 5.

25. McCarthy, Dental Education in Maryland," p. 36.
26. "Maryland Dental College," *Dental Cosmos* 19 (April 1877): 211.
27. Commencement invitation, Maryland Dental College, 1877, BCDSP, NMDA.
28. Maryland Dental College, *Annual Circular and Catalogue of the Maryland Dental College* (Baltimore: Snowden & Cowman, 1877), p. 2.
29. "Maryland Dental College," *Dental Cosmos* 20 (April 1878): 236.
30. "Meeting of the Alumni of the Maryland Dental College," *Dental Cosmos* 20 (February 1878): 120.
31. Maryland Dental College, *Annual Circular and Catalogue of the Maryland Dental College* (Baltimore: Snowden & Cowman, 1878), pp. 2, 3.
32. Ibid., p. 7.
33. Ibid., pp. 5, 7.
34. Commencement Program, Maryland Dental College, 1879, BCDSP, NMDA.
35. McCarthy, "Dental Education in Maryland," pp. 36, 38; Koch, *History of Dental Surgery*, p. 462.
36. [Maryland Dental College Faculty], "To the Dental Profession," [1879], BCDSP, NMDA.
37. McCarthy, "Dental Education in Maryland," pp. 36, 37.
38. Ibid., pp. 37, 38.
39. "A Good Time in Baltimore," *Missouri Dental Journal* 11 (March 1879): 177.
40. "Faculty Minutes of BCDS," February 21, 25, 1879, Gardner P. H. Foley Papers, NMDA.
41. James Howell Harris, MD, DDS, was born near Charlottesville, Va., on October 22, 1834. He graduated from the Baltimore College of Dental Surgery in 1861 (the first of four brothers to do so), and began practicing dentistry in Harrisonburg, Va. During the Civil War, he served as a private in Company "I," 4th Regiment, Virginia Cavalry. On November 3, 1864, he was assigned to duty as a "dentist" at the Harrisonville General Hospital in Virginia to "perform all dental operations required." Among his patients were General Robert E. Lee, Mrs. Jefferson Davis, and Mrs. Stonewall Jackson. After the war, he resumed his practice, but in October 1871 returned to Baltimore to serve on the Baltimore College faculty, as a demonstrator of operative dentistry. At the end of the 1871–72 session, he was elected to full professorship of operative and clinical dentistry. In 1872, he received his MD from the College of Physicians and Surgeons of Baltimore. He remained in this position until 1882, when he resigned to become professor of operative and clinical dentistry at the newly created Dental Department, University of Maryland. He held the chair of operative dentistry until his death in 1910. He died at age 76 on December 12, 1910, in Baltimore and was buried in Harrisonburg, Va. [Eugene F. Cordell, *University of Maryland 1807–1907: Its History, Influence, Equipment and Characteristics with Biographical Sketches and Portraits of Its Founders, Benefactors, Regents, Faculty and Alumni*, vol. 1 (New York: Lewis Publishing Co., 1907), pp. 398, 402; Compiled Service Records of Confederate Soldiers Who Served in Organizations from the State of Virginia, Micro copy 324, roll 42, Record Group 109 (War Department Collection of Confederate Records), National Archives and Records Administration; Ann Louise Peace, "James Howell Harris—DDS, MD, 1834–1910)," *Alma Mater* 14 (April 1973): 3–4.]
42. McCarthy, "Dental Education in Maryland," pp. 40–41; J. B. Letter, Ten Eyck, Secretary, Board of Visitors, Baltimore College of Dental Surgery, to Ferdinand J. S. Gorgas [?], undated, BCDSP, NMDA; A. A. Blount, "The Merits of Soft and Cohesive Gold, as Filling Materials," (*Ohio State Journal of Dental Science*), quoted in *Dental Advertiser* 13 (January 1882): 1, 2, 3.
43. Petition, Baltimore dentists to Ferdinand J. S. Gorgas, February 23, 1880, BCDSP, NMDA.
44. Petition, Washington dentists to Ferdinand J. S. Gorgas, February 25, 1880, BCDSP, NMDA.
45. Letter, Edward Maynard to Ferdinand J. S. Gorgas, February 26, 1880, BCDSP, NMDA.
46. Letter, Students (Class of 1879–80), Baltimore College of Dental Surgery, to Ferdinand J. S. Gorgas and faculty, February 29, 1880; Testimonial, Students (Class of 1880–81), Baltimore College of Dental Surgery, to Dr. Gorgas and faculty, n.d.; all BCDSP, NMDA.
47. Baltimore College of Dental Surgery, "Faculty Minutes Jan. 15, 1875, to and incl. April 26, 1916," March 8, 1880, Special Collections, Health Sciences and Human Services Library, University of Maryland (*hereafter* cited as HSL).
48. Letter, J. B. Ten Eyck, Secretary, Board of Visitors, Baltimore College of Dental Surgery, to Ferdinand J. S. Gorgas, n.d., BCDSP, NMDA.
49. Ibid.; Petition, Various dentists to the Board of Visitors and Faculty, Baltimore College of Dental Surgery, n.d. [1880], BCDSP, NMDA.
50. McCarthy, "Dental Education in Maryland," pp. 41–42; J. Ben Robinson, *The Foundations of Professional Dentistry* (Baltimore: Waverly Press, Inc., 1940), p. 62; Letter, Edward Maynard to Ferdinand J. S. Gorgas, February 26, 1880, BCDSP, NMDA.
51. McCarthy, "Dental Education in Maryland," p. 41; Baltimore College of Dental Surgery, "Faculty Minutes," April 27, 1882, Special Collections, HSL.

Dental and Pharmaceutical Building: 1904

Chapter 9

University of Maryland Dental Department: 1882–1911

"The present and prospective condition of the dental profession is a subject, to those who feel a true interest in its welfare, of deep concern. No question can be considered of greater importance, in this connection, than that of the education of those who seek admission into its ranks. This subject has recently been a prominent topic of discussion in a number of associations, both local and general."[1] **~Robert Arthur, 1875**

The New Dental Department: 1882

Meanwhile, after leaving the Baltimore College of Dental Surgery, Dr. James H. Harris became involved with the University of Maryland officials about adding a dental department to the university. Apparently, some of the groundwork for the creation of the new department had been laid as early as 1871. At that time, Dr. Ferdinand J. S. Gorgas, while dean of the Baltimore College of Dental Surgery, perhaps in anticipation of Winder's intent to establish a rival school (Maryland Dental College), had approached the University of Maryland authorities concerning the incorporation of the Baltimore College of Dental Surgery into the University of Maryland system. Initially, Gorgas was unsuccessful in convincing the university's Faculty of Physic to approve the merger; however, he continued the negotiations. The Faculty of Physic, in principle, was sympathetic to the merger, but was concerned that it would precipitate a serious rift in the dental profession. If an outright merger between the two institutions was impossible, Gorgas proposed "establishment of a completely new dental curriculum, organized as a department of the University of Maryland School of Medicine." As such, it was reasoned, the "image of dentistry would be enhanced as a worthy branch of medicine and the new school could be expected to profit from the dignity of association with a prestigious medical institution." The Faculty of Physic was attracted by Gorgas' proposal, which was not only "consistent with a growing concept of medical specialties," but offered medical faculty members "an opportunity to improve their incomes by appointment to the dental faculty." Other dental colleges had enhanced their status by this type of association with a university; namely, Harvard (1867), Michigan (1875), Tennessee (1877), Pennsylvania (1878), and Vanderbilt (1879).[2]

Then too, Gorgas, who had originally held to dentistry as belonging to the "medicine-and mechanics position," after seeing the competing dental schools emphasize "dentistry-as-mechanics," now changed to the "equally dangerous camp of "dentistry-as-medicine." He had built his faculty so that every professor had an MD degree in conjunction with his dental degree. Gorgas worked for closer ties with the university's medical school.[3]

Finally, in March 1882, the University of Maryland acquired a charter from the Maryland State Legislature for a dental department to be added to the School of Medicine. The Act read: " 'An Act for founding an University in the city or precincts of Baltimore, by the name of the University of Maryland,' and authorizing the Regents of said University to grant degrees, diplomas and certificates to students of Dental Surgery, Pharmacy and other cognate branches of Medical Science in said University." The first meeting of the faculty of the new University of Maryland Dental Department was held at the office of Professor J. Edwin Michael, MD, at 246 Madison Avenue, Baltimore, at 9 p.m., Friday evening, April 28, 1882. Those present were: Professors Francis T. Miles, AM, MD; L. McLane Tiffany, AM, MD; J. Edwin Michael, AM, MD; James H. Harris, MD, DDS; and Ferdinand J. S. Gorgas, AM, MD, DDS. Professor Tiffany, Dean of the Faculty of Physic of the University of Maryland School of Medicine, announced that the following faculty had been elected for the new school: Ferdinand J. S. Gorgas, AM, MD, DDS, Professor of Dental Science, Dental Surgery and Prosthetic Dentistry; James H. Harris, MD, DDS, Professor of Operative and Clinical Dentistry; William E. A. Aikin, MD, LLD, Professor of Chemistry; Samuel C. Chew, AM, MD, Professor of Materia Medica and Therapeutics; Francis T. Miles, AM, MD, Professor of Physiology; L. McLane Tiffany, AM, MD, Professor of Oral Surgery; and J. Edwin Michael, AM, MD, Professor of Anatomy. Dr. Gorgas was unanimously elected the dean of the dental department. In addition, Dr. John C. Uhler was selected as Demonstrator of Prosthetic Dentistry, and Dr. Frank L. Harris as Demonstrator of Operative Dentistry.[4]

To accept this new position, Dr. Gorgas had to resign as dean of the Baltimore College of Dental Surgery. He had been on the faculty for 25 years, the last 15 as the dean. The fact that he was to be joined on the new faculty by Dr. James H. Harris undoubtedly influenced his decision. He forwarded his resignation to Professor Thomas S. Latimer, chair of Physiology at the Baltimore College of Dental Surgery, on April 27, 1882. With Gorgas' exodus, Winder was named the new dean (1882–94) of the Baltimore College of Dental Surgery. Many, reportedly, considered this the fulfillment of his lifelong ambition.[5]

Thus, the first faculty of the new dental department consisted of seven professors, five of whom were medical men and members of the Faculty of Physic. In addition to Drs. Uhler and Harris, there were other demonstrators in anatomy, and operative and prosthetic dentistry. The total number of instructors was 19, and many prominent local and national dentists volunteered their time as clinical instructors to give the students the benefit of their varied experience in dentistry. Such Baltimore College of Dental Surgery stalwarts as Edward Maynard, William W. H. Thackston, Adelbert J. Volck, and Basil M. Wilkerson were quickly signed up as clinical instructors. In addition, to the two courses taught by Gorgas and Harris, the dental students studied chemistry, anatomy, physiology, materia medica, and surgery usually in the same classes with the medical students.[6]

In 1882, the new school issued the following statement of purpose and a challenge to the Baltimore College of Dental Surgery to compete with a dental school associated with a medical institution:

> The rapid advance of the art and science of dental surgery and the recognition of it by the leading medical associations as a specialty of medicine, as well as the desire of every reputable dental practitioner to have it accepted as such, renders it necessary to increase the facilities by which dental students can acquire not only a thorough knowledge of the profession of their choice, but also a knowledge of the collateral sciences. While the object of this Department is to graduate students in dentistry, yet it should be an incentive to all who aim to become properly qualified to practice dentistry, to educate themselves as doctors of medicine in conjunction with their dental training. By placing dental surgery, as connected with oral surgery, in a position where it is accepted as a department of medicine, its status will be exalted, and a larger number of intellectual men be found in its ranks, and a new impetus to thought and investigation be thereby be created.[7]

The Opening Session: 1882

The first summer session began on April 28, 1882, in the "new ward" of the University Hospital, and the first winter session began on October 1, 1882, with 60 students. The dental lectures were delivered in Practice Hall (capable of holding 200 students), which was conveniently located at the northeast corner of the University Building (now called Davidge Hall). The medical lectures were held in "Chemical and Anatomical Halls" of the University Building. The general and oral surgery clinics were in University Hospital at the southwest corner of Lombard and Greene Streets.[8]

A special new two-story building, the "Dental Infirmary and Laboratory Building," was erected in time for the 1882–83 session on the university grounds at Greene Street, abutting on Cider Alley. It had 49 large windows for ample natural light. The infirmary occupied the second floor and was equipped with 25 cast-iron "new and improved" dental operating chairs, most of them Morrison chairs, and bracket tables. Each chair faced its own window, and had a battery for dental electrical appliances. The first floor contained the dental laboratory, which had "all conveniences for the preparation of metals, the manufacture of teeth, and the construction of artificial dentures of every kind," and closets for the students' books, instruments, and clothing. The dental building was connected to the University Building by a covered walkway. The university went into debt to the extent of $6,000 for the building's construction.[9]

The 1882 catalog reminded prospective students that the University Hospital, the largest in the city, was adjacent to the dental infirmary, and it held daily surgical and medical clinics which the dental students could attend. Actually, during the past year 25,000 patients had been treated in this facility. The hospital was staffed by the Sisters of Mercy, who were known as "tender and skilful nurses." No separate dental school could ever offer such an abundance of clinical material for the students' education.[10] How could the Baltimore College of Dental Surgery possibly hope to compete with these advantages?

To receive the DDS degree from the university, a student had to be 21 years of age and have attended two courses of lectures, the last session at the University of Maryland. As equivalent to the first course of lectures, a course in "any other reputable dental or medical college, five years' of dental practice, including regular pupilage, or a satisfactory examination on entrance" was an acceptable alternative. The candidate was also required to show examples of his work in the infirmary or fabricated in the laboratory (for preservation in the museum). The faculty then voted on each candidate. It was also possible to obtain both the DDS and MD degrees in three years. Admission to any course of lectures required a ticket issued by Dean Gorgas. A free summer session for the regular students for clinical instruction was also provided, extending from May to October. The fees were fixed at $115 for each session, and a $30 diploma fee. Nearby room and board was available for "as little as $3.50 a week, and the required textbooks for $25 or $30.[11] The dental diploma was copied after the medical school diploma with the necessary changes as to title, etc.[12]

In 1882, although the cost of a dental education was about the same as the cost of a medical degree, the Faculty of Physic of the University of Maryland made it "as easy as possible to qualify for either degree—or both." Therefore, the university was in a "strong competitive position with its rivals in either profession." The first dental department announcement stated: "The dental student taking advantage of this opportunity to obtain the Medical degree, can save, irrespective of time, the sum of *three hundred dollars.*" This competition forced the Baltimore College of Dental Surgery to follow suit by entering into an agreement with the College of Physicians and Surgeons of Baltimore to use their clinical facilities.[13] That the organization of the University's dental department exerted a "good influence" on dental education in Maryland during the 1880s cannot be denied. Before the new college's formation, the Baltimore College had had the field of dental education in Maryland all to itself, other than during the short, five-year period of the Maryland Dental College. Now the Baltimore College was confronted with a "new, strong, progressive dental school, possessing a good faculty and an association with an outstanding medical school." The older college must "look after her laurels."[14]

The Catalog Controversy

Actually, from the very beginning of the new school a bitter feud developed between the Baltimore College of Dental Surgery and its rival. Dean Gorgas was accused of stealing students from his old school. The Baltimore College of Dental Surgery catalogs had included Dr. Gorgas' home address (279 Eutaw Street) in addition to the school's address. Many prospective students therefore continued to write directly to him when inquiring about admission to the Baltimore College of Dental Surgery.[15]

Dr. Winder, as the dean of the Baltimore College of Dental Surgery, concerned about what he perceived on Gorgas' part as an attempt to intercept prospective students, on May 5, 1882, wrote a letter of complaint to the postmaster of Baltimore City, Col. Harrison Adreon. He requested that all letters addressed to the Baltimore College of Dental Surgery or Baltimore Dental College be sent directly to him.[16] On May 8, 1882, Dr. Gorgas responded to this allegation by stating that he only claimed mail directed to "President of Dental College," "Dean of Dental College," Dean of Dental Department of Univ. of Md.," "College of Dentistry," "Dental College"; he did not claim any mail directed to "Baltimore College of Surgery," or to "Dean of Baltimore College of Dental Surgery."[17] The postmaster then replied to Winder on May 31, 1882, that as they both claimed essentially the same mail, it would be necessary to appoint a "receiver" for the mail; otherwise, it would be sent to the Dead Letter Office.[18] Dr. Winder agreed on having a "receiver," but emphasized that any correspondence with the word "college" appearing on it, even if Gorgas' name was on it, should go to the "receiver" not to Gorgas. Gorgas should receive only the mail addressed to the Dental Department of the University of Maryland.[19] Gorgas accepted the "receiver" idea and listed three names acceptable to him. When the postmaster informed Dr. Winder, he rejected Gorgas' candidates and named three alternates, stating that he had proof that Gorgas had "already received letters of this sort, retained them and replied to them in the interests of his school."[20] Finally, an exasperated Adreon replied to Winder that he would deliver to him all Dental College mail in which the term "Baltimore" appeared, but could not take the responsibility of having Dr. Gorgas' letters delivered to anyone but him. If this arrangement was not satisfactory, then he would refer the entire matter to the Post Office law officer for a decision.[21] Meanwhile, Gorgas was apparently getting upset about the whole affair and suggested that the Postmaster General render a decision "concerning all letters addressed to me in my name, irrespective of any title which may be written on said letters in connection with my name, as I certainly claim all such letters as my private property."[22]

Finally, on June 7, 1882, Col. Adreon referred the matter to the Postmaster General in Washington, D.C., for a decision.[23] The Postmaster General bounced the problem back to Adreon, who notified both parties that he would deliver only mail with their respective names on it, and the rest would go to the dead letter office to be returned to the sender.[24] Meanwhile, the situation reached the legal stage when Dr. Winder's lawyer, Richard J. Gittings, contacted Dr. Gorgas, who in turn had his lawyer, James A. L. McClure, contact Gittings.[25] Eventually, the matter quieted down, but the ill feelings persisted for years.

As the rivalry continued, the two schools watched each other closely; whatever one school did the other followed. A new course added to the curriculum or a new piece of equipment acquired was sure to bring an immediate response. Faculty changes between the two schools were common and many charges of pirating were hurled, and there was constant bickering over student transfers from one school to the other.[26]

The college offered a "beneficiary student" a scholarship on the recommendation of the state dental society from each state as did the Baltimore College of Dental Surgery. Again, they copied each others moves. The textbooks required were: Harris' *Principles and Practice*, Tomes' *Dental Anatomy and Surgery*, Taft's *Operative Dentistry*, Richardson's *Mechanical Dentistry*, Attfield's or Fowne's *Chemistry*, Bartholow's *Materia Medica*, Foster's *Physiology*, Bryant's or Erichsen's *Surgery*, and Sharpey and Quain's or Gray's *Anatomy*. The college also offered prizes to graduates for scholarship, namely: the "University Prize," a gold medal for the highest examination score; the "S. S. White Prize," a dental engine for the best filling; the "Snowden and Cowman Prize," a set of Harris' forceps for the best prosthetic case; and the "S. S. White Prize," a set of Varney's plugging instruments for the second best denture case.[27]

The First Commencement: 1883

Sixty students, representing 15 states and two foreign countries, attended the opening session. Sixteen of these were transfers from the Baltimore College of Dental Surgery. There were 34 graduates at the first commencement held on March 15, 1883, at the Academy of Music, in Baltimore. After this session, D. Genese, DDS, a local dentist of "brilliant inventive genius," was added to the faculty to instruct on "continuous gum and plastic" work. For the second session, attendance had risen to 86, with 36 graduates. The graduation was held on March 14, 1884, at the Academy of Music. Many of the graduates (16) had availed themselves of the opportunity of getting the degree after one session with five years of practical experience.[28]

The first meeting of the Alumni Association of the university's dental department was held in 1884, but there is no record of the officers elected. In 1885, a second meeting was held, but Dr. R. Arthur Hungerford (Class of 1883), was unable to attend because of illness. Therefore, Dr. R. Delamer Dodson, the vice-president (Class of 1883), presided and was elected the president for the following year.[29]

The Museum: 1883

It is not surprising that Dr. Gorgas included a museum for the new school via his old college, the Baltimore College of Dental Surgery. The new museum was described in the catalog as, "The large and interesting Museum of the University contains many specimens of peculiar interest to dental students."[30] The 1883 catalog reported that the "Dental Museum will compare favorably, on account of the large donations of valuable dental and pathological and other specimens received during the past year from all parts of this country and Europe, with that of any other institution."[31] The "any other institution" no doubt, referred to its competition—the old, established Baltimore College of Dental Surgery.

Maryland State Dental Association: 1883

Meanwhile, on October 18, 1883, Dr. Gorgas acted as a temporary chairman of a meeting held at the "University of Maryland, Dental Department Building" to organize a state dental society. The dentists who attended this meeting may be regarded as the founders of the Maryland State Dental Association, and they were: Drs. Gorgas, Thomas H. Davy, Charles F. Dinger, John C. Uhler, David Genese, M. Gist Sykes, Alex C. McCurdy, Charles C. Harris, William A. Mills, James H. Harris, Basil M. Wilkerson, B. Merrill Hopkinson, Howard W. Hoopes, Harry C. Medcraft, Robert A. Hungerford, George A. Volck, Charles S. Grindall, and Godfrey J. Gremplar. A constitution, bylaws, and code of ethics were adopted, and the following officers elected: Thomas J. Smithers, Easton, president; Thomas H. Davy, Baltimore, first vice-president; David Genese, Baltimore, second vice-president; William A. Mills, Baltimore, corresponding secretary; and B. Merrill Hopkinson, Baltimore, recording secretary.[32] On November 3, 1883, a certificate of incorporation was issued by the Superior Court of Baltimore City for the "Maryland Dental Association of Baltimore City."[33]

Many prominent Maryland dentists were not involved with this organization because of the ongoing schism between the Gorgas and the Winder camps. The Maryland State Dental Association was regarded as a Gorgas plot to embarrass Winder. Moreover, in 1887, Winder founded a competing dental society, the "Maryland State Odontological Society." At a meeting held in Johns Hopkins Hall on October 27, 1887, Dr. Edward Nelson of Frederick was elected president of the new society.[34]

Maryland State Board of Dental Examiners: 1884

Another result of the October 18, 1883, organizational meeting of the new association was the appointment of a committee to draft a bill to "regulate the practice of dentistry in the State of Maryland," which was unanimously adopted for presentation to the state legislature at the 1884 session. However, two months later, another society was formed called the "Dental Legislative Society," which proposed a different bill in opposition to the state association's. The two bills differed in that the state association bill made no provision for paying the members of the examining board, whereas, the legislative society's bill paid the sum of five dollars each per member.[35]

Finally, on March 31, 1884, Governor Robert M. McLane signed into law, "An Act to ensure the better education of practitioners of Dental Surgery, and to regulate the practice of Dentistry in the State of Maryland." The Maryland State Board of Dental Examiners was this established with "five reputable practicing dentists, residents of Maryland, none pecuniary connected with any dental school, appointed by the governor for terms of four years, initially for two, and three for four years." The board chose its officers, a president and a secretary, determined the time and place of meetings, a majority constituted a quorum, the proceedings were open to the public, and an annual report to the governor was required.[36]

For the first time a "certificate of registration or a diploma from a college or university authorized to grant diplomas in dental surgery was required to practice dentistry on Maryland." Dentists in practice were allowed six months to register with the board, and those entering practice had to submit to an examination by the board of their "knowledge and skill in dentistry." The one dollar registration fee provided the dentist with a certificate of registration duly issued by the board and was "prima facie evidence of the right of the holder to practice in Maryland." Willful violation of the new dental law was a misdemeanor, punishable by a fine of $50 to $300, or "confinement up to six months in jail." Now, dental practice in Maryland was "at last ostensibly confined to persons qualified to perform as dentists."[37]

National Association of Dental Faculties: 1885

On July 28, 1885, Dr. Gorgas wrote a letter to the National Association of Dental Faculties explaining why his institution could not join the association. While agreeing that his school would "cheerfully comply" with all the graduation requirements, as adopted at the meetings held in August 1884, so far as to require "two full courses of five months each in separate years," his institution deemed it "inexpedient" to join the association. The reason given by Dr. Gorgas was that the faculty of the University of Maryland believed the present curriculum at the university to be "superior to any graded course of study, such as is obligatory upon all dental schools joining your Association, for the reason that the graded course restricts junior students to dental mechanism alone for the one session of the two comprising the full course to the exclusion of operative dentistry." Therefore, it afforded dental students the advantage of only one session of operative dentistry, when two sessions were insufficient. His school considered it best to have two sessions of both operative and mechanical dentistry. Gorgas thought the adoption of this plan to be "*regressive* instead of progressive" in dental education.[38] Again, was it Winder's involvement with the organization that was the real reason for not joining the association?

Meanwhile, with the increase in student population it was necessary to add two wings to the Infirmary and Laboratory Building, adding 200 feet to the building and adding a "museum, impression, reception and extraction rooms." For the third session, Dr. R. Dorsey Coale replaced Professor Aikin as the chair of chemistry. Also, the clause offering a " 'satisfactory examination' in lieu of the first of the two sessions" was dropped from the third annual circular. The third commencement was held on March 17, 1885, at the Academy of Music with again 36 graduates receiving the DDS degree. During the session of 1885–86, the credit for five years of dental practice was abolished, and the only exception was credit for the MD degree, which was accepted in lieu of the first years' lectures. Also mentioned for the first time was the preliminary requirement that the student had to have "a good English education." "The diploma of a reputable literary institution, or other evidence of literary qualification, will be received instead of an examination."[39]

The fourth annual commencement was held on March 17, 1886, at the Academy of Music. Colonel William Allan of the McDonogh Institute gave the annual address. The number of matriculates for this session was 91, the largest class yet, but the number of graduates, 27, was down because of "a strict compliance with the *two-session rule* as a requisite for graduation." [40]

For the fifth session of 1886–87, Professor I. E. Atkinson replaced Professor Chew in the chair of materia medica and therapeutics, and Dr. Genese left the faculty. Dissection was now "obligatory in all dental schools." The students now numbered 124 and 51 graduated on March 16, 1887. The catalog mentioned the fact that the school's students had come from "every section of the country, and from Canada, South America, Great Britain, Germany, Switzerland, Turkey, etc., and a number of its students have been previously in attendance upon the lectures, are graduates of the Universities of Europe, or of medical and dental colleges in the United States." It also stated that "no dental student who has attended its lectures, etc., has ever gone elsewhere to graduate," an obvious dig at the Baltimore College of Dental Surgery.[41]

Dentistry as a Medical Profession

Dentistry as a Medical Specialty: 1887

In 1887, dental graduates were recognized by the American Medical Association as practitioners of medicine and admitted to membership in that organization.[42] At the thirty-eighth annual meeting held in Chicago in June 1887, the following resolution was passed:

> That the regular graduates of such dental and oral schools and colleges as require of their students a standard of preliminary or general education, and a term of professional study equal to the best class of the medical colleges of this country, and embrace in their curriculum all the fundamental branches of medicine, differing chiefly by substituting practical and clinical instruction in dental and oral medicine and surgery, in place of practical and clinical instruction in general medicine and surgery, be recognized as members of the regular profession of medicine, and be eligible to membership in this Association on the same conditions and subject to the same regulations as other members.[43]

This resolution no doubt was an attempt to make "dentistry," as it was then conceived, "a part of the medical profession, the same as otology, ophthalmology, and the other specialties." Obviously, only a small percentage of dental practitioners could qualify for membership, the majority having trained under a preceptor. In 1887, there were 34 dental schools in the United States, of which 11 offered a three-year course—the same as the better medical schools; the reminder offered a two-year course. The proprietary nature of most of the dental schools, and their commercial character, tended to "cloud the issue and lessen the consideration" of this opportunity to join medicine. Furthermore, "dentistry had already been established and had its own professional organizations and had largely become a distinct and separate group."[44] Still some dentists, as early as 1875 had advocated "the abolishment of the degree of DDS." Dr. James E. Garretson of Philadelphia thought that dentists could "never be esteemed as doctors, in the desirable fullness of the term, until we replace the DDS with the MD."[45]

The sixth commencement was held on March 14, 1888, with again 51 graduates. Dr. Gorgas gave the annual address.[46]

In 1889, the National Association of Dental College Faculties required candidates for matriculation to have "a diploma from a reputable literary institution, a teacher's certificate, or other evidence of literary qualification, and in the absence of any of these, a preliminary examination embracing a good English education." The University of Maryland complied with this requirement as a member of the association, and announced, "At the end of the Junior year students will be examined for admission to the Senior Class." During the school year of 1888–89, the students completed 4,132 extractions, 7,010 restorations (gold, amalgam, and plastic), treated 2,507 teeth, made 560 sets of teeth, and repaired 137 dentures.[47] The seventh commencement was held on March 13, 1889, at the Lyceum Theater, Baltimore. The number of matriculates was 120, with 39 graduates receiving the DDS degree. In addition, seven students completed the postgraduate course during the 1888–89 session. This course had been open to the school's graduates annually, since the school was organized, on the payment of the matriculation fee only.[48] The eighth commencement was held on March 19, 1890, at the Lyceum with 44 graduates.[49]

During the ninth session, an addition was made to the dental building (the third since 1882), which increased its size to 44 x 100 feet, and the number of infirmary windows increased to 43. The school also announced that the students had to procure their own dental engines[50] in addition to their "Students' Set" of dental instruments. The university sup-

Faculty of the era

plied the extraction forceps, lathes, vulcanizers, ovens, and other large laboratory equipment. The commencement was held on March 18, 1891, at the Academy of Music, with 64 graduates.[51] For the tenth session, Randolph Winslow, AM, MD, took over the chair of anatomy from Dr. Michael. Meanwhile, a radical course change was implemented for this session, the addition of a third year. The National Association of Dental Faculties had requested this additional year at its meeting two years previous, and it was endorsed by the American Dental Association. The admissions requirements were also stiffened. Those who did not have a diploma or teacher's certificate had to complete an examination in arithmetic, geography, grammar, and history and write an essay. The medical school graduates were admitted to the second year without examination, and were required to take only the dental courses. The fee per session was $105 with a $5 matriculation fee, a dissection fee of $10, and a diploma fee of $30; the total for the three years was therefore $355. There was a somewhat decline in the student body this year (from 163 to 127), due perhaps to the additional year and the increase in expense. There were 73 graduates on March 17, 1892, again back at the Lyceum Theater, Baltimore.[52]

The following year—1893—was not a good year for the college, as the number of matriculates fell to 108, and it only graduated 16 students on March 16, 1893, at the Academy of Music. By comparison, the Baltimore College of Dental Surgery had only 20 graduates. The year 1893 strangely enough was not good for either school.[53] The following year, 1894, the number of matriculates increased to 145 and the graduates numbered 34.[54] The next year, the number of matriculates again increased to 180, the most in school history to that date, and the number of graduates was 45.[55]

In 1896, the session was lengthened to six months, and the rule for admission was changed to admit students who had attended one course in a medical school to the second year, subject to examination. Also, Dr. Charles W. Mitchell[56] assumed the chair of materia medica with Dr. Atkinson retaining therapeutics only. The annual commencement was held on April 1, 1896, at the Academy of Music, with 42 graduates. The next year, the commencement was held at the Lyceum Theater on March 31, 1897, with 62 receiving their diplomas. The graduation's location changed the following year in 1898 to the Music Hall, with 64 graduates.[57] The advent of the Spanish-American War in February 1898, apparently went unnoticed in the college's catalog as no mention of it is made; however, three graduates and four future graduates of the Dental Department of the University of Maryland and one graduate and two future graduates of the Baltimore College of Dental Surgery served with the colors during the war.[58]

First Asian Graduate: 1899

In 1899, things were back to normal and the commencement was held at the Lyceum Theater on March 30, with 65 graduates, including Tameji Takashima from Japan, the school's first Asian graduate.[59] Dr. Takashima, born in 1866, was 20 years old when he moved to Seattle, Wash., where he went to high school. He was encouraged to study dentistry by Dr. O. Brunce. After receiving his DDS degree in 1899, Dr. Takashima continued his studies at the University's School of Medicine and is listed as a third-year student for the 1899–1900 session; however, there is no record of his ever receiving an MD degree. He practiced in New Jersey and Boston in 1901. He later returned to Japan and practiced in Tokyo in 1903. His Japanese dental license was number 487. He became quite famous and served on the faculty of the Naval Medical School as an associate professor. Later, he served on the faculties of the Tokyo Jikei Medical School and the Nippon Dental College. He retired in 1926 as professor emeritus and died in 1960 at age 94.[60]

Story of School Colors: 1901

The origin of the University of Maryland school colors is an interesting anecdotal and bizarre story. It seems that before the 1890s the university had no emblem to designate it among other universities and colleges in the field of athletics. In October 1890, William Oakley Haines (Class of 1891), was investing a Vulcanite denture, and while he was working on the denture, an old Italian, who was selling lunches to the students, appeared on the scene. The Italian asked Haines, "What are your colors?" Upon the spur of the moment, Haines was about to reply, "We haven't any," but instead impressed with the beauty of the two shades of rubber in his plate, replied, "Maroon and black." The following day, the Italian set up his stand in front of the main entrance of the Medical Department with about 20 yards of narrow "maroon and black" ribbon wrapped around his arm and crying, "Here's your College colors, only five cents." In a short time, these became the university's official colors and the students had badges, buttons, and pins made. Later, a meeting among the schools of medicine, dentistry, and law was held in Anatomical Hall in which the unofficial maroon and black was officially adopted by the university. Reportedly, the denture responsible for this incident was placed in the school's museum.[61]

More faculty changes occurred in 1900–01, as Professor Mitchell rejoined the faculty, taking Atkinson's place in therapeutics; Drs. John C. Uhler and Isaac H. Davis were promoted to associate professors of prosthetic and operative dentistry, respectively; Dr. Clarence J. Grieves was appointed an associate professor in crown and bridge work. In addition, in 1901, the admission of medical and pharmacy students to the second year was abolished. The National Association of Dental Faculties now required two years of high school or its equivalent for admission. In 1902, Professor Tiffany resigned from the oral surgery chair and was replaced by Professor Winslow, and Dr. J. Holmes Smith was made professor of anatomy. Again, in 1902, the entrance requirement was upped to three years of high school for entrance.[62] The 1900 (56 graduates), 1901 (71 graduates), 1902 (58 graduates), and 1903 (64 graduates) commencements were held at the Lyceum Theater, Baltimore.[63]

In 1903, with the death of Professor Miles, Dr. John C. Hemmeter was elected to the chair of physiology. Dr Timothy O. Heatwole was promoted to associate professor of orthodontics. For the 1903–04 session, the requirements for a degree was increased to attendance at four annual sessions, in accordance with the National Association of Dental Faculties ruling for all dental schools in the United States. However, the requirement was rescinded after one year and before the 1904–05 session. The opposition to this unpopular change came from many dental colleges, including Harvard. So temporarily at least, the four-year curriculum was in limbo.[64]

The New Building: 1904

In 1903–04, between sessions, the school constructed a new building on the same site as the 1882 building (demolished in 1904), at Greene Street. The new building was in brick, three-and-a-half stories high, and shaped like an "L," extending along Greene Street and Cider Alley. It was 100 x 90 feet and was steam heated, had both electricity and gas, and cost $45,000. The infirmary was 100 x 30 feet, with windows on all four sides. On the first floor were the dental museum, extraction room, impression room, dean's office, student's reading room, clinic room, and a large lecture hall. Each student had his own locker. The basement contained the dental laboratories and occupied the entire floor. Also the building contained the school of pharmacy, and the laboratories for bacteriology, pathology, and physiological chemistry.[65] The new University Hospital Building was just across the street.[66]

The dental curriculum consisted of the following courses: anatomy (with dissections), physiology, dental material medica and therapeutics, chemistry, operative and prosthetic dentistry (didactic and practical), crown and bridgework, clinical operative and prosthetic dentistry, principles of dental science, metallurgy, dental medicine, dental and general histology and pathology, porcelain work, bacteriology, orthodontics, oral surgery, dental jurisprudence and history.[67]

The opening of the new building coincided with the Baltimore Great Fire of February 7, 1904, which devastated the city. The fire started in a six-story brick building between Hopkins Place and Liberty on the south side of German (now Redwood) Street. Fortunately for the university, the fire did not cross Liberty Street, but moved easterly toward Charles Street rather than toward Greene Street. The loss from the fire was estimated to be more than 70 million dollars.[68]

Gorgas' Museum: 1904

Dr. Gorgas was justly proud of his new museum, and in September 1904 published an article on it in the *University Orist.* He said that many of the museum's objects had never been on exhibit before. Among the more interesting objects were: "The head of an Egyptian mummy, covered with long, flowing, jet-black hair, exhibiting the teeth of both jaws"; the 1855 Maynard collection of 200 Russian maxillae from the Crimean War battlefields; a collection of skulls from "fetal to adult, and old age," and skulls showing the "development and eruption of teeth"; skulls of many animals; a mineral exhibit used to illustrate the lectures on mineralogy; hundreds of sets of teeth made with "continuous gum, gold, silver, vulcanite, celluloid, metallo-plastic," etc.; crown and bridgework and porcelain work; sets of teeth carved from ivory; a pathological collection of dental anomalies; Dr. Horace H. Hayden's 1810 license to practice dentistry in Maryland; oil portraits of Chapin A. Harris, Thomas E. Bond, William H. Atkinson, Jonathan Taft, Isaac I. Wetherbee, William C. Barrett, I. Foster Flagg, and Theodore Menges.[69] It is interesting to note that two months earlier in July 1904, the

Baltimore Sun had published an extensive article on the Baltimore College of Dental Surgery Museum.[70] Apparently, Gorgas wanted people to know that his school had a museum, too.

In 1905, L. Whiting Farinholt, DDS, was appointed as demonstrator in porcelain inlay work. In 1906, Professor Mitchell retired and the department was taken over by Professor Culbreth. Dr. Grieves also resigned. Again, the entrance requirements were raised to require "an examination corresponding to that required in a high school of the section of country from which candidates come." A knowledge of Greek or Latin was not required. The tuition was raised from $100 to $150 per session.[71] Meanwhile, the university graduated 64 dental students in 1904, 76 in 1905, 42 in 1906, and 51 in 1907.[72] The Class of 1907 included Robert Hilliard Mills,[73] the future chief of the U.S. Army Dental Corps, and Sadayoshi Teraka,[74] the school's second Japanese graduate.[75]

Robert H. Mills

In 1907, the University celebrated its centennial and the dental department offered its laurels in the advancement of dental science in this manner:

> The rapid advance of the art and science of dental surgery, and the recognition of it by the leading Medical Associations as a specialty of Medicine, as well as the desire of every reputable dental practitioner to have it accepted as such, renders it necessary to increase the facilities by which dental students can acquire not only a thorough knowledge of the profession of their choice, but also a knowledge of the collateral sciences. By placing dental surgery, as connected with oral surgery, in a position where it is accepted as a department of medicine, its status is exalted, a larger number of intellectual men enter its ranks and a new impetus to thought and investigation is thereby created.[76]

The 1909–10 catalog continued to stress dentistry's connection with medicine when it stated:

> The rapid advance of the art and science of dental surgery, and the recognition of it by the leading Medical Associations as a specialty of Medicine, as well as the desire of every reputable dental practitioner to have it accepted as such, renders it necessary to increase the facilities by which dental students not only a thorough knowledge of the profession of their choice, but also a knowledge of the collateral sciences. By placing dental surgery, as connected with oral surgery, in a position where it is accepted as a department of medicine, its status is exalted, a larger number of intellectual men enter its ranks and a new impetus of thought and investigation is thereby created.[77]

The catalog also said that the rules of the National Association of Dental Faculties and the National Association of Dental Examiners[78] were "strictly complied with" by the college. It also noted that at a recent examination of the Maryland State Dental Board of Registration, 22 of its graduates had taken the test and all passed the examination successfully. The tuition fee was the same as the Baltimore College of Dental Surgery, $150 a session.[79] On June 1, 1908, the college graduated 47 students.[80]

The First Woman Graduate: 1909

Interestingly, in its 28-year history, the Dental Department of the University of Maryland had failed to graduate even one female dentist until 1909, despite Dr. Gorgas' earlier record with the Baltimore College of Dental Surgery. Georgiana Palmer Monks, from Pennsylvania, was among the 61 graduates on May 31, 1909, at the Academy of Music.[81] Lena C. S. Sparck of Maryland was the college's second woman graduate in 1910.[82]

Death of Dean Gorgas: 1914

Dr. Gorgas became incapacitated in September 1910 and had to relinquish his deanship in 1911. He had been a dental faculty member for 50 years (1860–1910) and a dean for 45 years (1865–1911); probably the longest teaching record and the longest service as dean. Dean Gorgas died on April 14, 1914, after a stroke. His body was cremated and interred in Green Mount Cemetery, in Baltimore. Shortly after his death, a student organization, the Gorgas Odontological Society, was formed to perpetuate his memory.[83]

Dr. Ferdinand Gorgas

NOTES

1. Robert Arthur, "Dental Education," *Dental Cosmos* 17 (May 1875): 229–30.
2. Harry B. McCarthy, "A History of Dental Education in Maryland," master's thesis, Graduate School, University of Maryland, 1948, p. 42; H. Berton McCauley, "The Century-Old Dental Department of the University of Maryland at Baltimore," *Journal of the Maryland State Dental Association* 25 (December 1982): 97–98; George H. Callcott, *A History of the University of Maryland* (Baltimore: Maryland Historical Society, 1966), p. 218.
3. Callcott, *History of the University of Maryland*, pp. 217–18.
4. Eugene F. Cordell, University of Maryland 1807–1907: Its History, Influence, Equipment and Characteristics with Biographical Sketches and Portraits of Its Founders, Benefactors, Regents, Faculty and Alumni, vol. 1 (New York: Lewis Publishing Co., 1907), pp. 109–10, 385–86.
5. Cordell, University of Maryland, pp. 384, 385; McCarthy, "Dental Education in Maryland," p. 42.
6. Cordell, University of Maryland, p. 386; Callcott, *History of the University of Maryland*, p. 218; Dental Department of the University of Maryland, *Announcement of the Dental Department of the University of Maryland for the Session 1882–3* (Baltimore: William K. Boyle & Son, 1882), p. 2.
7. Dental Department, University of Maryland, *Announcement of the Dental Department [1882–3]*, p. 3.
8. Cordell, *University of Maryland*, pp. 386, 367; McCauley, "The Century-Old Dental Department," 99.
9. Cordell, *University of Maryland*, pp. 111, 387, 388; McCauley, "Century-Old Dental Department," 99.
10. Dental Department, University of Maryland, *Announcement of the Dental Department [1882–3]*, pp. 4, 5.
11. Cordell, *University of Maryland*, pp. 387–88; McCauley, "Century-Old Dental Department," 99.
12. University of Maryland, Dental Department, "U. of M. Faculty Minutes April 28, 1882, to March 15, 1911," Special Collections, Health Sciences and Human Services Library, University of Maryland (*hereafter* cited as HSL).
13. McCauley," Century-Old Dental Department," 99.
14. McCarthy, "History of Dental Education in Maryland," pp. 44–45.
15. Ibid., pp. 43–44, 45.
16. Letter, Richard B. Winder, Dean Baltimore College of Dental Surgery (*hereafter* cited as BCDS), to Col. Harrison Adreon, Postmaster City of Baltimore, May 5, 1882, "Records of Papers—Letters, etc. in connection with Conduct of Dr. F. J. S. Gorgas in regard to Mail matters—Treachery and Falsehood affecting the interests of the Baltimore College of Dental Surgery—after the resignation of his position as Dean on April 27th 1882" (*hereafter* cited as RPLG), Special Collections, HSL
17. Letter, Ferdinand J. S. Gorgas, Dean, Dental Department, University of Maryland, to Col. Harrison Adreon, Postmaster of Baltimore City, May 8, 1882, RPLG, HSL.
18. Letter, Col. H. Adreon, Postmaster, to R. B. Winder, Dean, BCDS, May 31, 1882, RPLG, HSL.
19. Letter, R. B. Winder, Dean, BCDS, to Col. H. Adreon, Postmaster, June 2, 1882, RPLG, HSL.

20. Letters, H. Adreon to F. J. S. Gorgas, Dean , Dental Department, University of Maryland, June 3, 1882; R.. B. Winder, Dean, BCDS, to H. Adreon, June 1882, RPLG, HSL.
21. Letter, H. Adreon, Postmaster, to R. B. Winder, Dean, BCDS, June 3, 1882, RPLG, HSL.
22. Letter, F. J. S. Gorgas, Dean, Dental Department, University of Maryland, to H. Adreon, Postmaster, June 5, 1882, RPLG, HSL.
23. Letter, H. Adreon, Postmaster, to Postmaster General, June 7, 1883, RPLG, HSL.
24. Letter, H. Adreon, Postmaster, to R. B. Winder, Dean, BCDS, n.d., RPLG, HSL.
25. Letters, R.J. Gittings to F. J. S. Gorgas, Dean, Dental Department, University of Maryland, May 27, 1882; J. A. L. McClure, to R. J. Gittings, May 31, 1882, RPLG, HSL.
26. McCarthy, "Dental Education in Maryland," p. 45.
27. Dental Department of the University of Maryland, *Announcement of the Dental Department [1882–3]*, pp. 13, 14.
28. Cordell, *University of Maryland*, 388–89; Dental Department, University of Maryland, *Annual Circular of the Dental Department [1883–4]*, pp. 18–19; "Dental Department of the University of Maryland," *Dental Cosmos* 25 (April 1883): 213; "University of Maryland—Department of Dental Surgery," *Dental Cosmos* 26 (April 1884): 245–46.
29. Joseph H. Seipp, Jr., "A Brief History of the First Dental Alumni Association in the World (Organizations Associated with the Baltimore College of Dental Surgery," *Alma Mater* 8 (November 1966): 5. After 1885, apparently no further meetings of this association were held until 1906, when on May 7–9, the association held a meeting in its new building at Lombard and Greene Streets. Exhibition space was rented at $5 for a 4 by 4 foot space and $1 for each additional foot with tables at 75 cents each. Attendance of 300 dentists and 100 students was anticipated according to Dr. Leroy W. Farinholt, the chairman, who hoped for a large display of exhibits. [L(eroy) W. Farinholt, "Alumni Association, Dental Department, University of Maryland," *Items of Interest* 28 (May 1906): 392.]
30. Ibid., p. 4.
31. Dental Department of the University of Maryland, *Annual Circular of the Dental Department of the University of Maryland for the Session 1883–4* (Baltimore: Isaac Friedenwald, 1883), p. 5.
32. J. Ben Robinson "Some Highlights in the History of the Maryland State Dental Association," *Journal of the Maryland State Dental Association* 1 (April 1958): 5.
33. Certificate of Incorporation, Maryland Dental Association of Baltimore City, Superior Court of Baltimore City, November 3, 1883, Baltimore College of Dental Surgery Papers, National Museum of Dentistry Archives.
34. Robinson, "History of Maryland State Dental Association," 5–6. Finally, in 1889 the two dental societies, the Maryland State Dental Association and the Maryland State Odontological Society agreed to amalgamate under the name of the former. [Ibid., 6.]
35. H. Berton McCauley, "The Maryland State Dental Association: In the Beginning," *Journal of the Maryland State Dental Association* 26 (August 1983): 77.
36. Ibid.. 78.
37. Ibid.
38. Gorgas, F[erdinand] J. S., "University of Maryland," *Dental Advertiser* 16 (October 1885): 120.
39. Cordell, *University of Maryland*, pp. 388, 389; "University of Maryland—Dental Department," *Dental Cosmos* 27 (April 1885): 252.
40. "University of Maryland—Dental Department," *Dental Cosmos* 28 (April 1886): 250.
41. Cordell, *University of Maryland*, pp. 389, 390; "University of Maryland—Dental Department," *Dental Cosmos* 29 (April 1887): 273–74; Dental Department of the University of Maryland, *Annual Circular and Catalogue of the Dental Department of the University of Maryland for the Session 1886–7* (Baltimore: Guggenheimer, Weil & Co., 1886), p. 3.
42. John T. O'Rourke, and Leroy M. S. Miner, *Dental Education in the United States* (Philadelphia: W.B. Saunders Co., 1941), p. 195.
43. W[illia]m B. Atkinson, comp., "Society Proceedings. American Medical Association," *Journal of the American Medical Association* 8 (June 25, 1887): 722.
44. O'Rourke and Miner, *Dental Education in the United States*, pp. 195–96.
45. "New York Odontological Society [Proceedings]," *Dental Cosmos* 17 (July 1875): 367.
46. "University of Maryland—Dental Department," *Dental Cosmos* 30 (April 1888): 291.
47. Cordell, *University of Maryland*, p. 390.
48. "University of Maryland—Dental Department," *Dental Cosmos* 31 (April 1889): 312–13; Dental Department, University of Maryland, *Eighth Annual Circular and Catalogue of the Dental Department of the University of Maryland for the Session 1889–90* (Baltimore: Munder Bros., 1889), p. 19.
49. "University of Maryland—Dental Department," *Dental Cosmos* 32 (April 1890): 321.
50. In 1892, a dental engine cost between $37 for a Johnston and $43 for a S. S. White side-wheel. [S.S. White, I*llustrated Catalogue Dental Engines and Equipments* (Philadelphia: S.S. White Dental Mfg. Co., 1892), pp, 6, 7. Actually, the foot-powered dental engine was invented in 1871 by James B. Morrison. The earlier hand drills could reach 100 rpm, whereas Morrison's drill could attain 2,000 rpm. Eventually, the foot-drill would be replaced by the electric dental engine in the early 1900s. [Malvin E. Ring, "Behind the Dentist's Drill," *Invention & Technology* 11 (Fall 1995): 28–20.]
51. Cordell, *University of Maryland*, p. 391; "University of Maryland—Dental Department," *Dental Cosmos* 33 (April 1891): 312; Dental Department, University of Maryland, *Ninth Annual Circular and Catalogue of the Dental Department of the University of Maryland for the Session of 1890–91* (Baltimore: Munder Bros., 1890), p. 10.
52. Cordell, *University of Maryland*, p. 391; "University of Maryland—Dental Department," *Dental Cosmos* 34 (May 1892): 397–98.
53. "University of Maryland—Department of Dental Surgery," *Dental Cosmos* 35 (April 1893): 319; "Baltimore College of Dental Surgery," *Dental Cosmos* 35 (April 1893): 319.
54. "University of Maryland—Department of Dental Surgery," *Dental Cosmos* 36 (June 1894): 477.
55. "University of Maryland—Dental Department," *Dental Cosmos* 37 (May 1895): 455.

56. In 1898, Dr. Mitchell was replaced by David M. R. Culbreth, MD, PhG, as professor of materia medica. [Cordell, *University of Maryland*, p. 392.]
57. Cordell, *University of Maryland*, pp. 391–92; "University of Maryland–Department of Dental Surgery," *Dental Cosmos* 38 (April 1896): 434; "University of Maryland–Department of Dental Surgery," *Dental Cosmos* 39 (June 1897): 501; "University of Maryland–Department of Dental Surgery," *Dental Cosmos* 40 (May 1898): 396–97.
58. *See* Appendix C for directory of Spanish-American War dental veterans.
59. University of Maryland–Department of Dental Surgery," *Dental Cosmos* 41 (May 1899): 497–98.
60. University of Maryland, School of Medicine, *Ninety-Fourth Annual Announcement of the School of Medicine, Session 1900–1901* (Baltimore: Kohn & Pollock, 1900), p. 25; Letters, Norinaga Moriyama to John M. Hyson, Jr., August 16, December 12, 2004.
61. University of Maryland, *Bones Molars and Briefs* (Baltimore: Senior Department of Medicine, Dentistry, and Law, 1901), p. 70.
62. Cordell, *University of Maryland*, p. 392.
63. "University of Maryland, Dental Department," *Dental Cosmos* 42 (June 1900): 594; 43 (June 1901): 679–80; 44 (June 1902): 628; 45 (June 1903): 514.
64. Cordell, *University of Maryland*, p. 393.
65. Cordell, *University of Maryland*, p. 393.
66. Dental Department, University of Maryland, *Twenty-Second Annual Announcement and Catalogue of the Dental Department of the University of Maryland. Session 1903–1904* (Baltimore: n.p., 1903), p. 5.
67. Ibid., 9.
68. Harold A. Williams, *Baltimore Afire* (Baltimore: Schneidereith & Sons, 1954), pp. 1, 4.
69. Ferdinand J. S. Gorgas, "The Museum of the Dental Department of the University of Maryland," *University Orist* 1 (September 1904): 3–4.
70. "Historic Teeth: Those of George Washington in Baltimore Dental College Museum," *Baltimore Sun*, July 10, 1904.
71. Cordell, *University of Maryland*, p. 394
72. "University of Maryland, Department of Dental Surgery," *Dental Cosmos* 46 (June 1904): 525; 47 (June 1905): 743; 48 (June 1906): 706–7; 49 (August 1907): 890
73. Robert Hilliard Mills was born in Whigham, Ga., on July 29, 1883. In 1904, he attended the Southern Dental College, Dental Department of the College of Physicians and Surgeons in Atlanta for two years, but transferred to the Dental Department, University of Maryland, for his senior year and graduated in 1907. He won the James H. Harris Gold Medal Prize for non-cohesive gold foil filling for 1906–07. In May 1909, he signed a three-year contract with the U.S. Army as a contract dental surgeon. After duty in the Philippines in 1910, on June 15, 1911, he was commissioned a first lieutenant. In May 1917, he was promoted to captain and to lieutenant colonel in October 1917. In 1918, he served as the dental surgeon for the 82nd Division, American Expeditionary Forces, in France. After the war, he served as the ROTC officer at Northwestern University Dental School, and from 1932–36 was director of the Army Dental School, Washington, D.C. He played an important role in developing the mobile dental operating unit. Dr. Mills was promoted to colonel in 1935, and in 1942 to Brigadier General and Chief of the Army Dental Corps (1942–46). In 1943, General Mills was promoted to major general, the first dental officer to be so recognized. In 1945, he was awarded the Distinguished Service Medal for outstanding service in the surgeon general's office. In 1946, he was awarded an honorary doctor of science degree by the University of Maryland. General Mills retired in 1946 and died in April 1965 in Washington, D.C. ["Brigadier General Robert H. Mills," *Army Dental Bulletin* 13 (April 1942): 142; J. Ben Robinson, "General Robert H. Mills Honored," *Alma Mater* 2 (October 1960): 31–32; Gardner P. H. Foley, ed., *Proceedings of the 125th Anniversary Celebration of the Baltimore College of Dental Surgery* (Baltimore: Horn-Shafer Cp., 1966), p. 195.]
74. Sadayoshi Teraka later studied at the Angle School of Orthodontia and was a faculty member of the Tokyo Dental College in 1912–13. He wrote a textbook, *Compendium of Orthodontics*, and became a faculty member of the Nippon Dental College. He practiced in Tokyo and after World War II started a dental magazine, *Dental Pen Club*. Dr. Teraka wrote many articles on the various fields of dental practice.[Letter, Norinaga Moriyama to John M. Hyson, Jr., July 6, 2004.]
75. "University of Maryland, Department of Dental Surgery," *Dental Cosmos* 49 (August 1907): 890.
76. Dental Department, University of Maryland, *Twenty-Sixth Annual Announcement and Catalogue of the Dental Department of the University of Maryland. Session 1907–1908* (Baltimore: n.p., 1907), p. 6.
77. Dental Department of the University of Maryland, *Twenty-Eighth Annual Announcement and Catalogue of the Dental Department of the University of Maryland. Session 1909–1910* (Baltimore: n.p. [1909]), p. 7.
78. The National Association of Dental Examiners was organized in February 1883 by the representatives of six state boards of dental examiners. The six states were Illinois, Indiana, Kentucky, New York, Ohio, and Vermont. The lack of "uniformity in dental-practice acts, the need of a registry of licensed dentists in each state," the appointment by the state governors of candidates submitted by the various state dental societies, and "reciprocal relations in licensure among the states" were all topics of concern to all states. The association's main purpose was to protect the public from incompetent practitioners. In August 1883 at their meeting in Niagara Falls, N.Y., the resolution was passed to not accept any diploma from a college which did not require "two full regular courses of lectures," or the equivalent "one full course and five years' practice." [Harlan Hoyt Horner, *Dental Education Today* (Chicago: University of Chicago Press, 1947), pp. 33–34.]
79. Ibid., pp. 13, 15.
80. "University of Maryland, Dental Department," *Dental Cosmos* 50 (July 1908): 775.
81. "University of Maryland, Dental Department," *Dental Cosmos* 51 (July 1909): 909.

82. Dental Department of the University of Maryland, *Twenty-Ninth Annual Announcement and Catalogue of the Dental Department of the University of Maryland. Session 1910–1911* (Baltimore: n.p., [1910]), p. 20.
83. T[imothy] O. Heatwole, "An Abbreviated Biography of Ferdinand J. S. Gorgas, MA, DDS, MD," Special Collections, HSL; Foley, *Proceedings of the 125th Anniversary*, p. 168.

Richard Bayly Winder

Chapter 10

The BCDS Winder Years: 1882–94

"You all know, as well as I do, that the most difficult parts of dentistry to learn are the practical parts. You can by application rapidly cram theory, but to properly educate the hand and eye requires practice; and you cannot outside the large cities find a sufficiency of clinical material to enable the student to do this."[1] **~Richard Bayly Winder, 1885**

Winder: The "Southern Planter"

The years 1882 to 1894 may well be called the "Winder Years," because Richard Bayly Winder was the dominant personality and force of the Baltimore College of Dental Surgery. After Winder became the dean of the Baltimore College of Dental Surgery in 1882, he continued to strive for excellence at his institution. Winder was a driven man, possessing "untiring energy" and being a "very good judge of human nature." He had a "kindly nature" and a "natural dignity, but was by no means stiff." He was "extremely popular" and respected by his students. Charles L. Klingelhofer, Class of 1894, a former student, recalled that he had the wonderful gift of being in close contact with "his boys" as he called them. He had the senior class visit his house, one at a time, and talked to them "as a father would to his son." Klingelhofer said: "He had a large mirror above his desk so hung that he could see who came into his study. I fancy he knew before you sat down for the first time what kind of a chap you were. I noticed this mirror only after my third visit. After talking with him one received the impression he understood you entirely, and with a few words he made you feel at ease and know you could easily confide in him." Any student in trouble could always go to him and be sure to find a sympathetic listener and receive good advice. On his way from his house to college, he was always accompanied by 10 or 15 students. What higher tribute to a professor could there be than to have his students of their own free will continually seeking his company? His popularity was such that when he entered the lecture room, he would be received "with clapping and stamping, an ovation no other member of the faculty received." It was said that he had "a command of language that held his listeners spell-bound." His words were "pronounced very distinctly through his southern drawl." Obviously, Winder's earlier education in the classical languages at Princeton and Virginia placed him a cut above the average dental lecturer of his day.[2]

Winder was described as looking like a "southern planter," with "a slow but yet decided way of walking and rather deep set piercing eyes that seemed to take you all in at one glance." His clothes were "well-fitting" and he wore a "wide-brimmed black felt hat." He had only one disturbing habit and that was he chewed tobacco in class and while lecturing was known to stop now and then to squirt a long stream of tobacco juice into a spittoon on his left side. He told the students it was a habit he could not shake, having acquired it during his years in the military. Winder's closing remarks to one graduating class were: "We should hold our standard high, be strictly ethical, live decently, and never be tempted to take advantage of any possible situation with female patients."[3]

Professor Winder was an early contributor to the dental literature of the day. He published his first article in April 1869 (the year he graduated), appropriately titled "Dental Education." Among the papers he presented at various dental society meetings were: "Causes of the Deterioration of the Teeth" (American Dental Convention, 1875); "Deterioration of Teeth Ethnologically Considered" (Dental Society of the State of Maryland and the District of Columbia, 1875); "Secretions of the Mouth" (American Dental Convention, 1876); "A National Dental Association" (American Dental Convention, 1879); "Microscopy" (Southern Dental Association, 1881); "Dental Education" (Southern Dental Association, 1884); "Alveolar Abscess" (North Carolina State Dental Association, 1888); and "The Etiology of Pus-Formation" (Sixth, Seventh, and Eighth District Dental Societies of the State of New York, 1893). Dr. Winder's other publications were: "A Series of Questions Pertaining to Course of Lectures on . . . Dental Surgery," 1881; "Anchylosed Maxillaries: A Remarkable Case," 1885; "The Teeth as an Index of Civilization," 1893; and "Treating Burnishers," 1893.[4]

Dr. Winder was an enthusiastic researcher, especially in dental anthropology. In October1875, for his lecture, "Deterioration of Teeth Ethnologically Considered," before the Dental Society of the State of Maryland and District of Columbia at Willard's Hall, Winder borrowed a series of prehistoric and ancient skulls from the Army Medical Museum. Even though the crania were to be lent only for a few hours, the Surgeon General's office took the precaution of sending one of the museum's staff along "to protect them from careless handling." On another occasion, he examined 1,000 skulls of various Indian tribes and reported that only 27 decayed teeth were found. He attributed the low caries rate to the diet. As early as 1881, he delivered a paper on the history and use of the microscope in dentistry. However, he cautioned dentists to be careful of eye strain.[5]

Winder Defines Dentistry: 1881

In 1881, even before becoming the BCDS dean, Dr. Winder became involved in the ongoing national debate with those in the dental profession who thought that dentistry should be a specialty of medicine and not a separate profession. Winder's opinion was that the two professions should not be combined. As early as 1875, Winder had made the point that although medicine was the foundation of dentistry, as "one science can and does overlap another," dentistry was still a separate profession. Medicine was based on anatomy, chemistry, and physiology, whereas dentistry, in addition to this foundation, also involved "mechanics and artistic taste." Winder agreed that dentistry was a specialty of medicine "in the broader sense of the term," but dentistry was "essentially distinct." After all, those universities having both medicine and dentistry in their curricula conferred different degrees for the two professions. Winder also referred to the historical fact that early attempts to include dentistry in the medical curricula of colleges in Baltimore and Philadelphia were turned down, resulting in the founding of the world's first dental college, the Baltimore College of Dental Surgery, and later its sister schools. Winder urged that the two professions be kept separate, but cooperate with each other.[6]

Winder also noticed that medical textbooks did not contain anything on dentistry; there were no dental lectures in the medical curriculum; and medical schools did not even pretend to teach dentistry. The public did not consider "an MD a dentist, nor a dentist an MD." Medicine and dentistry were "distinct, though kindred professions." Winder pointed out that although dentistry had learned from medicine, dentistry had given medicine much in return. He mentioned anesthesia, the interdental splint, and the dental engine for surgical procedures. Winder stated that "dentistry stands on three pillars—mechanism, artistic taste, and theory."[7] However, Winder saw no objection to the graduate dentist seeking a medical degree after he had satisfied the first requirement that "a man shall master the essentials of success in the avenue he has chosen." After all, Winder, himself, had followed this route and obtained his MD degree. Additional education simply made "a wider and broader man."[8]

One of Winder's first acts in 1882 after becoming dean was to add Dr. Henry J. B. McKellops[9] of St. Louis, the former president (1879) of the American Dental Association, to the Board of Visitors. Dr. McKellops had served during the Mexican War in 1846 and had written the first resolution to add dentists to the medical department of the U.S. Army in 1858.[10] One of Winder's attributes, as was seen from his Maryland College days, was his ability to attract the best professional men in the country to serve his school.

The forty-third commencement was held at Ford's Opera House, Baltimore, on March 8, 1883, with Dr. Winder conferring DDS degrees on 36 candidates, including one from Spain (Juan Piosay Gonzalez).[11] The next year, Winder conferred degrees on 42 graduates at the Academy of Music, Baltimore, on March 6, 1884.[12] One of the graduates, Henry A. Parr,[13] a former Confederate secret service agent, would become one of President Ulysses S. Grant's dentists.[14]

Winder's "Quantum Sufficit": 1884

Winder's concept of a dental college's mission was somewhat different than the majority of his colleagues in dental education. He believed that a dental college should concentrate on teaching dentistry to the student and not try to give him a general education. All that was necessary was that he receives a "quantum sufficit" of general information for him to have sufficient knowledge to "understand the special teaching." Winder pointed out (rather prophetically) in commenting on the standard four-year collegiate course, considered the norm for an educated man: "Now, however, the arts and sciences have so multiplied, and the spheres of knowledge have so increased, that no sane man would think of undertaking to master them in four years. As the world advances in knowledge this difficulty increases, and, inasmuch as a boy cannot learn all, the practical question of the day is, what studies shall he pursue, and what shall he neglect?" After obtaining the "essentials of success in his special calling," it was the dentist's prerogative, and even his duty, to "cultivate and enlarge his mind in every way." This viewpoint was in direct contrast with those who were in favor of lengthening the dental curriculum. As early as 1869, Winder had stated that dental education was "without question equal, if not superior to" that of the other professional schools. After all, Winder said:

> While it takes but two courses of instruction at these schools to teach *everything* pertaining to the whole science of Medicine, our Dental Schools devote the same length of time to one single specialty of this general science. Which ought to be, and which is the best prepared? He who has applied himself two years in acquiring all the various branches of general Medicine, or he who has devoted the same time and attention to one single specialty?[15]

Winder's idea of a "model school" was a college located in a large city ("nowhere else can be found sufficiency of clinical material"); teaching "all the subject-matter pertinent to dentistry"; having a "select" faculty from the dental profession rather than from the medical profession (an obvious reference to the University of Maryland faculty); having "chairs of anatomy, physiology, chemistry, pathology, therapeutics, dental surgery, operative dentistry, and mechanical dentistry"; teaching only as much didactics as a dentist needed to practice on a sound scientific basis; and teaching "everything" known in the clinical branches, placing emphasis on diagnosis and "minor surgical operations." He felt that students should be allowed to enter whatever class in which they qualified; it was the student's knowledge not the time spent in school which should qualify him for a degree. This viewpoint was a variance from a resolution passed by the National Board of Dental Examiners (which Winder helped establish) that required attendance at a two-year curriculum for a dental degree. The only exceptions were for allowing as one year of equivalent, five years of practice or a course in another accredited dental or medical college.[16]

On the subject of oral surgery training in dental schools, Winder felt that "capital operations" on the head and face belonged in the realm of the general surgeon, not the dentist. The dentist was educated in the dental infirmary, whereas the surgeon was educated in the hospital. Dental schools had no hospitals attached to them; therefore, the dentist who desired to become a surgeon should attend a medical school to receive his training.[17]

The Hopkinson Controversy: 1884

In 1884, the continuing battle with the Dental Department, University of Maryland, erupted again when Dr. B. Merrill R. Hopkinson, an 1880 alumnus of the Baltimore College, published an article accusing the Baltimore College of Dental Surgery of graduating students without them attending the prescribed course of lectures. His article appeared in the June 1884 issue of the *Independent Practitioner.* He charged the current faculty of "certain irregularities" in direct opposition to the "law as it appears it her charter, and according to the terms of graduation published in the forty-fourth annual catalogue."[18] He specifically cited the Baltimore College of Dental Surgery's issuing of diplomas on March 6, 1884, to C. S. W. Baldwin, F. C. Barlow, and C. A. Meeker of New Jersey; J. F. Dowsley and F. A. Twitchell of Massachusetts; and T. H. Schaeffer of Maryland. Hopkinson claimed that these six men had originally applied to Dr. Gorgas at the University of Maryland, but upon being told that they would have to attend a full course of lectures and demonstrations demurred and instead applied to the Baltimore College of Dental Surgery from which institution they subsequently graduated in 1884.[19]

The Baltimore College of Dental Surgery was quick to respond to these allegations in the July issue of the same journal. Dean Winder and his faculty called Hopkinson's charge a "vicious attack on the Baltimore College of Dental Surgery" made by "enemies" of the college, emanating from a "rival institution." The faculty claimed that the faculty of the college did "nothing inconsistent with the custom and practice of the college, running back at least to 1869." The college did not concede that the granting of diplomas, "practiced by their predecessors and continued by them, is an irregularity, but contend that it is founded on sound principles and common sense." The men in question had fulfilled the College's requirement of five years in practice in lieu of one course. All six of the men mentioned in Hopkinson's article had been examined by each of the department professors and approved by the Board of Visitors before graduation.[20]

The Baltimore faculty stated that Dr. Hopkinson was a faculty member (assistant demonstrator of operative dentistry) of the Dental Department, University of Maryland, and the information he quoted could have only come from Dr. Gorgas, the dean. Furthermore, the college had a "round robin" paper signed by Dr. Hopkinson and a number of other members of the graduating class of 1879–80, "condemning as a teacher the present dean of the Baltimore College of Dental Surgery, Professor R. B. Winder—shades of the 1880 Winder-Harris gold foil controversy revisited.[21]

Furthermore, the Baltimore College said that all these men had originally applied to Dr. Gorgas and been told that they could receive their degrees at the university by remaining on campus "several days, matriculating, and during their stay dissecting the upper extremity, then return home, and next session pass the month of November at the University, a few days of January, and the greater part of the month of February," to receive their diplomas in March.[22] A furious Dr. Gorgas responded to these charges in the August issue of the *Practitioner* to what he called an "unprovoked attack upon the Dental Department of the University of Maryland." He claimed that Dr. Hopkinson was not a faculty member of his school when he wrote the article, but as a BCDS alumnus was "well acquainted with the manner in which his *alma mater* has been conducted of late years." Dr. Hopkinson was merely responding to what he considered to be "an abuse of power and an injury to the alumni of the old school." He alone was responsible for the article containing the "charges of irregularity" at the old school. Winder's rebuttal was merely an attempt to cover up the fact that the BCDS was willing to issue diplomas "without attendance upon the lectures, demonstration, etc.," a process that Gorgas' school would not do. Furthermore, all these applicants in question had expressed "preference for the diploma of the University over that of the Baltimore College."[23] Such was the state of affairs between the two deans of the rival Baltimore dental schools.

The New York Dental Society: 1884

In May 1884, the Dental Society of the State of New York's Board of Censors failed to place the Baltimore College of Dental Surgery on its list of approved dental schools; however, the Dental Department, University of Maryland made the list. The Baltimore College was summoned to appear to defend the accusations that it had conferred degrees upon men who were "graduated irregularly."[24] In May 1885, Dr. Winder appeared before the society representing his school, the Baltimore College of Dental Surgery, to show why his school should not be "stricken from the list of reputable schools recognized" by the society. Winder stated that the "good name" of his institution had been brought into question. He pleaded guilty of conferring degrees on candidates without them attending college lectures. He pointed out that the custom of conferring degrees on worthy candidates, who had been in practice for 10 or more years, had been the practice of the school since its inception and was incorporated in its charter. This custom had been in existence for 30 years before the New York Society was even incorporated. Winder, himself, had always been in favor of "conferring degrees upon merit and merit alone," and did not believe in any other system. He cited his alma mater, the University of Virginia, and Johns Hopkins University of Baltimore as practicing this principle. On March 15, 1884, his college desiring to conform to the requirements of the National Association of Dental Examiners passed a resolution abolishing the system of granting degrees without attendance upon lectures; however, under the school's original charter they would be obliged to allow a qualified candidate to present himself for examination. After a brief discussion, the society expressed its vote of confidence that the Baltimore College would abide by its decision to abandon the condemned practice of issuing diplomas to absentee candidates.[25]

National Association of Dental Faculties: 1884

Despite his differences with other dental educators, Dr. Winder was the primary founder, along with Dr. James Truman (the future editor of the *International Dental Journal*), and Dr. C. Newlin Peirce, of the National Association of Dental Faculties. Winder thought that the various dental schools throughout the country should be united more closely through a national organization to adopt a uniform standard for graduation. Before that time, there were no general academic standards affecting admission to dental schools, and "practically all candidates were accepted without special regard for their intellectual qualifications." At the organization meeting in New York on August 4, 1884, the following 11 schools were represented: Baltimore College of Dental Surgery—Drs. Richard B. Winder and M. Whilldin Foster; Boston Dental College—Drs. J. A. Follett and A. N. Blodgett; Chicago College of Dental Surgery—Drs. A. W. Harlin and F. H. Gardiner; Harvard University, Dental Department—Dr. Thomas Fillebrown; Dental Department, State University of Iowa—Dr. A. O. Hunt; New York College of Dentistry—Drs. Frank Abbott and J. Bond Littig; Dental College of the University of Michigan—Dr. Jonathan Taft; Ohio College of Dental Surgery—Dr. H. A. Smith; Pennsylvania College of Dental Surgery—Drs. C. Newlin Peirce and Henry Leffmann; Philadelphia Dental College—Dr. James E. Garrettson and S. H. Guilford; and University of Pennsylvania, Dental Department—Drs. James Truman and E. T. Darby. Letters were also received from the deans of the Kansas City Dental College and the University of California pledging their support. A constitution was adopted, which included the membership clause: "Any reputable dental college may be represented in this body upon submitting to the executive committee satisfactory credentials, signing the constitution, conforming to the rules and regulations of this body and paying such assessments as may be made." The requirement was passed that applicants for admission to the first year of the study of dentistry had to "possess a good English education," as determined by a preliminary examination. A candidate possessing a diploma from a reputable school, "or other evidences of literary qualification," was admissible without examination.[26]

The constitution was then signed by the college representatives, including Winder and Foster representing the Baltimore College of Dental Surgery; however, Dr. Fillebrown, representing Harvard did not sign. He said that although he was in "hearty sympathy with the movement," he had to have the matter brought before Harvard's governing board before Harvard could become a member of the organization. Officers were elected and C. N. Peirce was chosen president; Winder, vice-president; H. A. Smith, secretary; A.W. Harlin, treasurer; and Frank Abbott, James Truman, and J. Taft, members of the executive committee. Winder, Truman and Taft were selected for a curriculum committee.[27] In 1885, Winder became the organization's president. Brophy (1904) called the association "among the foremost educational organizations of our country." Winder had once again influenced a major change in dental education.[28]

Interestingly enough in 1885, the University of Maryland Dental Department refused to join the National Association. Through its dean, Dr. Gorgas, the school agreed to comply with the requirement of two full five-month courses in separate years, but felt its present curriculum to be "superior" to the plan proposed for members in the association. The objection was based primarily on the member schools' standard of one session of operative dentistry rather than the two required at Maryland. Dr. Gorgas referred to this system as "retrogressive" rather than "progressive" in dental education. Was this curriculum conflict the real reason, or was it the fact that Dr. Winder was the founder and current president of the organization?[29]

Finally, in August 1889, at the meeting of the National Association of Dental Faculties held Saratoga Springs, N.Y., the university's dental department became a member of the association. The members, after a long discussion, adopted a rule requiring attendance "upon three full regular courses in separate years before examination for graduation," and the length of the regular courses was made "not less than five months each." The new rules were to go into effect at the beginning of the 1891–92 session. The tuition fee was recommended to be fixed at a minimum of $100 a year. Dr. Winder's motion to grant honorary degrees to a "prominent practitioner without attendance upon lectures" was rejected by the committee. Winder was named to the *Ad interim* committee and Gorgas to the executive committee.[30]

In accordance with the resolutions adopted by the National Association of Dental Faculties on August 4, 1884, the dental course was divided into a junior and a senior term, with "graded" courses for each. The preliminary qualification for entering the junior class was an examination in English. The courses assigned to the junior term were: anatomy, with dissections; physiology; histology; chemistry; and prosthetic dentistry. The senior courses were: pathology; surgery; materia medica and therapeutics; and operative dentistry. However, the college still gave credit for a course at a reputable dental school or a medical degree as equivalent to one course.[31]

In 1885, the college announced that it had graduated 1,238 students in its 47-year history, and had 2,166 students attend its classes. It also reiterated that since the close of the 1881–82 session, the college had formed an alliance with the College of Physicians and Surgeons by which its students could avail themselves of the clinical facilities of the latter. This move was in direct response to the formation of the Dental Department, University of Maryland[32]

The 1885–87 commencements were held at the Academy of Music, Baltimore, with 28, 44, and 47 graduates respectively.[33] The Class of 1886 is noteworthy for graduating Emory

Emory A. Bryant

A. Bryant,[34] the U.S. Navy Dental Corps' first commissioned dental officer.[35] The 1888–89 exercises were held at the Lyceum Theater, Baltimore, with Professor Winder conferring 53 and 44 degrees, respectively.[36]

By 1886, lingering attacks were still being made on Winder by some Baltimore College of Dental Surgery alumni, which were aimed at the "very existence of their *Alma Mater* by some of her ungrateful children." The Board of Visitors said it had positive proof that false statements had been made against the college, the faculty, and the Board. The 1886–87 college catalog stated: "But the grand old College, having, since its consolidation with a sister institution, confined its acts strictly within the limits of its legitimate authority, has withstood these attacks, and, as its Faculty will henceforth pursue the same straightforward, manly and honorable course that they have heretofore done, we believe that it has before it a future commensurate with its past."[37] Interestingly enough, the catalogs continued to contain this statement until 1892, thus demonstrating that the old wound had not healed, with Winder as the scapegoat.[38]

Winder: "The Times Demand a National Organization"

Winder was not only active in dental education, but added to his national reputation by his participation in the affairs of organized dentistry at all levels, national, state, and local. Winder was a strong advocate for the union of the Southern Dental Association and the American Dental Association, which in 1897 became the National Dental Association (forerunner of the present American Dental Association). As early as 1879, at the American Dental Convention meeting held at Saratoga, N.Y., Winder had stated that the "times demand a national organization, which shall embrace in its membership all who are worthy, and know no North, South, East, or West, but whose purpose shall be the greatest good to the greatest number." He was also influential in the unification of the Maryland and the District of Columbia dental societies (Maryland State—District of Columbia Dental Association) and was its president in 1876. As previously mentioned, Winder was the president of the National Association of Dental Faculties in 1885.[39]

Winder was also an early advocate for the appointment of dental surgeons to the United States military. In 1881, he stated, "I have had hopes for some years past that the day would come when there would be Dental Surgeons in the United States Army and Navy, on an equal footing with medical men proper." Unfortunately, it would take another 36 years for his wish to come true (the U.S. contracted for dental surgeons in 1901 and commissioned them in 1911).[40]

Dr. Winder, besides being an educator, a leader, and an excellent dentist, was also a skilled surgeon. In December 1884, he operated on a former Union soldier who had been wounded on July 3, 1864, at the battle of Gettysburg. One James D. McIntire of Baltimore had been struck by shell fragments (in the arms, chest, and face), and treated by a Confederate surgeon while lying wounded on the battlefield. When Winder examined him, 20 years later, his jaws were anchylosed so that he could not open his mouth. His teeth had elongated causing him further problems. He was much emaciated, having been living on whiskey and milk. He was gradually starving to death. On December 18, Winder assisted by Dr. J. H. Coyle, operated with students in attendance. Under chloroform anesthesia, Winder extracted the elongated teeth and was able to break apart (using large shears) the bony attachment of the "condyles rigidly anchylosed in the glenoid cavities." Winder reported the patient survived the operation successfully, was no longer in danger of starving, and was in "much better health."[41]

As a demonstration of Dr. Winder's skills in operative (in which reportedly he "excelled") and prosthetic dentistry, at the 1888 North Carolina State Dental Association meeting held in Raleigh, N.C., he exhibited "some beautiful specimens of crown and bridge work." It was described: "The bridge was confined by a screw and tap, so neatly arranged that to all appearances it was immovable. It, however, could be easily displaced for a more perfect cleaning or to repair a fractured tooth." Dr. Winder was also the inventor of a combined clamp and separator in 1890; it was described as consisting of two jaws that could be forced together by means of a screw.[42]

The "Mother of Them All"

In 1885, Winder had to defend the reputation of his college. It seemed that the school had been taken off the "list of reputable schools" recognized by the State of New York Board of Censors. This action was widely publicized and resulted in the loss of some students. One procedure in question was the school's conferring degrees on dental practitioners who had been in practice for ten years without requiring attendance of normally prescribed lecture courses. In May 1885, at the society's meeting in Albany, N.Y., Winder pleaded his school's case; after all, the Baltimore College of Dental Surgery was the "mother of them all." To confer degrees on "honorable candidates" without attendance was incorporated in the college's charter. However, a year earlier, the school's faculty had voted to apply a "higher standard" on the examinations in order to confirm more closely to the National Board of Examiners' requirements. Although Winder still felt the diploma should be given for "merit and merit alone," his view was not shared by the majority of dental educators and he was obliged to defer to the majority opinion. As to another matter wherein a diploma could be worthless outside of the state where it is granted, Winder said the result could be disastrous to the dental profession; better to let accreditation rest with the National Association of Dental Examiners.[43]

Again, in July 1888, at a meeting of the New Jersey State Dental Society, Winder voiced his opposition to various states interfering in dental education by dictating the length of the dental college term. At the time, it varied from a five-month to a nine-month term per year for two or three years. Most medical schools had a five-month term. Dental colleges connected with a medical college would obviously have a problem if they deviated from the medical curriculum. Some states such as Illinois and Massachusetts, had already adopted the three-year requirement, although in some cases a year spent with a preceptor counted as one-year completed. Winder felt that state meddling with dental education would merely "handicap the colleges," and not necessarily improve the standards of dental education.[44]

In 1887–88, Dr. Winder was also defensive of American dental education against those who catered to the idea that American dental schools should confirm to European (especially German) standards and adopt their methods. In his opinion, American dentistry was not "inferior" to the European in any way. Winder cautioned that the real reason for the German requirements was to "keep the American dentists out" of Europe. He stated, "we don't want to teach as they teach, or to turn out such dentists as they turn out."[45]

The Alumni Association: 1888

In 1888, the Alumni Association of the Baltimore College of Dental Surgery adopted new bylaws. The mission of the association was to "increase the acquaintance among graduates" and to "promote the interests of the College and its members." The officers of the association were a president, vice-president, secretary, and treasurer, who with three other elected members would constitute the Executive Committee of the association. The officers would serve until replaced by newly elected successors. A committee of five would constitute the "Committee on the College." Any graduate of the college was eligible for membership upon a written application to the Executive Committee, but had to be voted on by the members. A new member had to sign the bylaws and code of ethics of the association before he was approved. Any membership could be terminated by a majority vote at the regular meeting upon violation of the code of ethics. The annual dues were one dollar, and two meeting were to be held annually. An essay was to be read at every annual meeting. The Executive Committee was to provide the meeting site, and the College Committee was to "devise, consider, report upon, and execute plans for promoting the interest of the College." Nine members were to constitute a quorum for business transaction.[46]

Chapin A. Harris Memorial: 1889

In 1889, the Alumni Association of the Baltimore College of Dental Surgery resolved to celebrate the semi-centennial of its founding by the erection of a memorial to Chapin A. Harris. A memorial association was organized to appoint a board of trustees and sub-committees for each state in the United States and in Europe to collect funds for the memorial. Mrs. C. E. Barrett Lennard, Chapin Harris' daughter, promised her assistance and financial support. The College faculty subscribed $6,000 to start the campaign.[47] On March 20, 1890, the college alumni held a meeting with Dr. Norman W. Kingsley presiding. Papers were read by Dr. Edward Nelson of Frederick, Md., and Dr. C. A. Amand of Baltimore, Md. The officers elected for the next year were: A. R. Eaton, Class of 1889, president; Thomas H. Davy, Class of 1874, vice-president; Richard B. Winder, Class of 1869, secretary; and Thomas S. Waters, Class of 1865, treasurer.[48]

The Census Bureau Controversy: 1890–92

Dr. Winder is generally given credit for convincing the government to add dentistry to the list of professions recognized by the census bureau. In 1890, the U.S. Census Bureau sought to ascertain the cost of a bridge, crown, or denture as a manufactured product of the dentist. The Baltimore dentists refused as a group to answer any questions and hired a lawyer to represent them in the courts. They won their case because there was no federal penalty at the time for refusal. In 1892, legislation (H. R. 7696) was proposed in Congress to make it mandatory to answer the census queries at a penalty fine of $1,000–10,000 or a year of imprisonment. As can be expected, Dr. Winder was the leader of the southern dental profession against this federal intrusion.[49] At the annual meeting of the Maryland State Dental Association in Baltimore on May 9–10, 1892, the organization passed a resolution protesting the Census Bureau's classification of dentists as "manufacturers." By that time, nearly all the states recognized them by law as "professional men," requiring licenses to practice. In 1880, Dr. Thomas B. Gunning of New York was credited with being successful in convincing the superintendent of the census, General Francis A. Walker, that dentistry was a profession. Now Winder, as a member of the Maryland State Dental Association's committee to protest this misclassification, was in the thick of the battle. On May 11, 1892, he addressed the New York State Dental Society on this important issue which would "set the profession of dentistry back half a century, and reduce it from a profession and practice to the level of mechanics, a trade, and a manufacturer." He wanted the New York dentists to join their southern confreres in lobbying their congressmen to vote against the Wilmot bill.[50]

The Three-Year Curriculum: 1891

The fiftieth commencement exercises were held on March 20, 1890, at Ford's Opera House, Baltimore, with Dr. Winder conferring degrees on 64 candidates. The 1891 exercises were held at Harris' Academy of Music, Baltimore, with a record 76 graduates.[51] For the 1891–92 session, the college adopted the new requirements of the National Association of Dental Faculties, which increased the curriculum from two to three years of five months each. The courses were divided into freshmen, junior, and senior terms. Students were examined at the end of each session for advancement.[52]

The three-year curriculum reflected the growing trend in dental education to emphasize the technical or "practical" phase of dentistry rather than the "scientific."[53] Not all dental educators believed that this was the correct path to follow. Dr. A. H. Thompson, in his paper before the American Dental Association in 1890, stated:

> If it were true that practical education were the main thing, the only thing worth considering, as the practical man would have us believe, it were better to return to the old system of office apprenticeship. No time was wasted on theory or science in that system and the student had no end of practical experience. As a practical education it supplied numerous advantages over the college system. The student was untrammeled by books and lectures and went in for a practical education—and that as quickly as possible. Its brevity was its main recommendation.[54]

Thompson felt that despite the student's commercial instincts, it was necessary that "pure science" should not be neglected in the curriculum. "Without pure science we cannot have advanced practice." Scientific knowledge is the superstructure upon which practice is built upon.[55]

Another dentist, who felt that dental education was embarking on the wrong direction, was John Sayre Marshall, MD, the future "Father" of the U.S. Army Dental Corps. In a symposium on dental education before the Section on Stomatology, at the meeting of the American Medical Association in June 1900, he remarked:

> The difficulty, however, lies in the fact that so much time is being spent in the manipulative training of the student that his scientific education is being neglected, and instead of making scientific practitioners out of our students, we are training them largely as mechanics and artisans. Do not misunderstand me on this latter point, for I would not have his technical training made any less thorough or complete than it is today, for manipulative skill of the very highest order is required in the first-class dental surgeon. But he needs much more than this if he is to intelligently meet the grave responsibilities of his calling. The health of his patient, and often life and death, wait on his decision in the treatment of many forms of dental and oral diseases. . . . What the profession needs today is not less technique, but a more thorough training in those sciences which make the intelligent physician and surgeon.[56]

The 1892 graduation was held at the Lyceum Theater, Baltimore, with Winder conferring still a new record 102 degrees. It was obvious that the college was prospering under Winder's leadership.[57]

Founding of the Psi Omega Dental Fraternity: 1892

The Psi Omega Dental Fraternity was organized by four students at the College who met in April 1892 for that purpose. On June 8, 1892, 40 members signed the original charter and were inducted into the fraternity's Alpha chapter. A few months later, the Baltimore students were approached by a representative of Alpha chapter of the Delta Sigma Delta of the University of Michigan with the suggestion that the new fraternity merge with the older fraternity (founded in 1882); however, the proposition was respectfully declined.[58]

On February 21, 1893, Delta Chapter, the first subordinate chapter of the Xi Psi Phi Fraternity, was organized at the college. The fraternity had been founded at Ann Arbor, Mich., in 1889. The Alpha Omega Fraternity was first organized at the college on December 7, 1909.[59]

The Medical Council of England: 1892

In June 1892, Winder, as dean, made application to have the Baltimore College of Dental Surgery recognized by the Medical Council of England and placed on the same status as the dental departments of Harvard and Michigan universities. These two schools were the only two American dental colleges whose diplomas had been somewhat reluctantly accepted by the medical council under the Dentist's Act of 1878. The British felt their system was superior to the American, their curriculum being of four years compared to the two or three years in the states. In addition, the professional examination in England was conducted by a "body of examiners" who were not engaged in teaching dental students; whereas, in America the degrees were conferred by the schools' faculty. Winder rated his school as the "peer and equal of any Dental school in the world." The text of Dr. Winder's letter dated June 2, 1892:

> The faculty of the Baltimore College of Dental Surgery most respectfully makes application to have this school recognized by the Medical Council of England, and placed on the same footing with the Dental Departments of Harvard and Michigan Universities in the United States of America.
>
> In making this application we would state that this College is the oldest Dental Institution in the world, and that the Dental Profession dates its origin from the founding of this School, the charter of which was granted by the Maryland legislature in 1839.
>
> Without making invidious comparisons, we claim to be the peer and equal of any Dental School in the World—that we have always maintained a foremost position in advancing the interests and welfare of the profession as an educational institution—that our curriculum and instructions are fully equal to the

demands of the times—that we probably number among our alumni more distinguished scientific men than any other school—and that our standing at home is unquestioned. In consideration of these facts we think it is hardly fair to discriminate against us; whether judged by our work already done, or by the work we are now doing, we think we are fully entitled to your consideration and recognition. Our diplomas in this country, are recognized wherever the degrees of Harvard and Michigan are. We mail you our catalogue, which contains a list of all our Graduates, and will be pleased to give any further information, should it be desired.[60]

On May 29, 1893, in a debate precipitated by Winder' letter, the council decided not to recognize any American dental degrees, including Harvard and Michigan. The British believed all the American dental school's curricula inferior to their own. No doubt Winder was in complete disagreement with this decision, and one can envision him muttering under his breath, "those dammed English."[61]

The year 1893, also marked a first during the Winder era as Claire G. Hamilton of Vermont became the first woman to graduate among a class of 20 at Ford's Grand Opera House on March 20, 1893.[62]

The Death of Dean Winder: 1894

After the death of his wife, Elizabeth, Winder married her sister, Sarah Custis. Two children were born to this marriage, Richard Bayly Winder II (who became a dentist and an instructor at the Baltimore College of Dental Surgery) and Mary Custis Winder. After the death of his second wife in April 1869, Winder married Kate Dorsey of Frederick County, Md. Winder, while still dean of the Baltimore College of Dental Surgery, in the spring of 1894 became ill, suffering from what was called "la grippe." He was unable to attend the college's March 20 commencement exercises held at the Lyceum Theater. On July 18, 1894, at age 66, Dr. Winder died as a result of "fatty degeneration of the heart," complicated by Bright's disease. The funeral took place from his residence at 716 Park Avenue in Baltimore on July 21, and he was buried at Loudon Park Cemetery in Baltimore. He was survived by his widow.[63] With all his faults and shortcomings, Winder had certainly left his imprint upon dental education as we know it today; he had elevated it to a higher plateau than it was before he entered the profession. What more can be said of any man?

NOTES

1. "Dental Society of the State of New York. Seventeenth Annual Meeting Odontographic Journal[Proceedings]," *Odontographic Journal* 6 (July 1885):117
2. "Obituary. [Prof. R. B. Winder]," *American Journal of Dental Science* 28 (August 1894): 186–87; Charles L. Klingelhofer, "Reminiscences of the Baltimore College of Dental Surgery in the Years 1891–1894," n.d., Gardner P. H. Foley Papers, National Museum of Dentistry Archives (*hereafter* cited as GPHFP, NMDA); "In Memoriam. Dr. R. B. Winder Dead," *Southern Dental Journal and Luminary* 13 (September 1, 1894): 392.
3. Klingelhofer, "Reminiscences of the Baltimore College of Dental Surgery," GPHFP, NMDA.
4. Richard B. Winder, "Dental Education," *American Journal of Dental Science*, 3d ser., 2 (April 1869): 575–81; "Causes of the Deterioration of the Teeth," in *Transactions of the American Dental Convention* (New York: Sears and Cole, [1875 ?], pp. 311–23; "American Dental Convention : Twenty-First Annual Session [Proceedings]," *Dental Cosmos* 17 (November 1875): 594–96; "Annual Meeting of the Dental Society of the State of Maryland and District of Columbia," *Dental Cosmos* 17 (December 1875): 652; "American Dental Convention, Twenty-Second Annual Session [Proceedings]," *Dental Cosmos* 19 (January 1877): 26–27; "A National Dental Association," *Dental Cosmos* 21 (September 1879): 500–06; "Southern Dental Association. Annual Meeting (Conjointly with the North Carolina State Dental Association) [Proceedings]," *American Journal of Dental Science*, 3d ser, 15 (October 1881): 269–75; "Southern Dental Association—Sixteenth Annual Session [Proceedings]," *Dental Cosmos* 26 (July 1884): 423–27; "Dental Education," *Southern Dental Journal* 3 (June 1884): 188–97; F.N.H., "North Carolina State Dental Association, Raleigh, N.C.," *Archives of Dentistry*, n.s., 5 (August

1888): 391; "Twenty-Fifth Annual Union Convention of the Sixth, Seventh, and Eighth District Dental Societies of the State of New York," *Dental Cosmos* 35 (December 1893): 1315, 1317–19; "Anchylosed Maxillaries: A Remarkable Case," *Odontographic Journal* 6 (July 1885): 130; "The Teeth as an Index of Civilization," *American Journal of Dental Science* 27 (December 1893): 337–39; "Treating Burnishers," (*Southern Dental Journal*), quoted in *Catching's Compendium of Practical Dentistry for 1893* (Atlanta , Ga.: Franklin Printing & Publishing Co., 1894), p. 279; J[ames] B. Hodgkin and R[ichard] B. Winder, *A Series of Questions Pertaining to the Course of Lectures on Dental Mechanism and Metallurgy by Prof. J.B. Hodgkin and on Dental Surgery by Prof. R.B. Winder* (Baltimore: Snowden & Cowman, 1881), pp. 1–26.

5. Letter, Capt. George A. Otis to Surgeon General J. K. Barnes, October 26, 1875, Box 46, Entry 12 , Record Group 112 (Surgeon General's Office), no. 1875: 4371, National Archives and Records Administration; Winder, "The Teeth as an Index of Civilization," 338; "Southern Dental Association—Annual Meeting," 269, 274.
6. "National Dental Association of the United States of America—Second Annual Session [Proceedings]," *Dental Cosmos* 23 (September 1881): 481–82; American Dental Convention, *Transactions of the American Dental Convention* (New York: Sears and Cole, 1875), pp. 278, 287.
7. "Southern Dental Association –Sixteenth Annual Session," 425.
8. "Southern Dental Association—Fifteenth Annual Session [Proceedings]," *Dental Cosmos* 25 (September 1883): 482–83.
9. Henry Jerome Byron McKellops was born on August 31, 1823 at Salina, N.Y., but in 1840 moved to St. Louis, Mo. After taking a course in bookkeeping, he studied medicine at the St. Louis Medical College in 1846–47. Shortly afterward, he was encouraged to study dentistry by his brother-in-law, Dr. George Silvers, a dentist. He served in the Mexican War as a captain in the St. Louis Legion, making the noted expedition "under Colonel Alton R. Easton from New Orleans to the Brazos and up the Rio Grande to Matamoras." On July 21, 1858, at the meeting of the Western Dental Society, he proposed the first resolution to memorialize Congress for the appointment of dentists to the U.S. Army. In 1856, he was one of the founders of the St. Louis Dental Society, and served as its president in 1879. In 1860, he helped organize the Western Dental Association and later was its president; he was the first president of the Missouri State Dental Association in 1865; president of the American Dental Association in 1879 and the Southern Dental Association in 1885; and chairman of the section on clinics of the National Dental Association (successor to the American and Southern Dental Associations). In 1855, the Ohio College of Dental Surgery conferred on him an honorary DDS degree. Dr. McKellops practiced in St. Louis except for a brief sojourn in London and Paris from 1863–65 when he fled the country as a Confederate sympathizer. Dr. McKellops used gold for his restorations, for which he became internationally famous. He introduced the continuous-gum process to St. Louis dentists. His library was unquestionably the largest in the world, and his necktie collection numbered more than 2,000. Dr. McKellops died at age 78 from Bright's disease on April 23, 1901. [F. L. H. "Obituary. Dr. Henry J. B. McKellops," *Dental Cosmos* 43 (June 1901): 702–4.]
10. Baltimore College of Dental Surgery, "Faculty Minutes Jan. 15, 1875, to and incl. April 26, 1916," October 2, 1882, Special Collections, Health Sciences and Human Services Library, University of Maryland; F.L.H. "Obituary. Dr. Henry J.B. McKellops," 703, 704.
11. "Baltimore College of Dental Surgery," *Dental Cosmos* 25 (April 1883): 208.
12. "Baltimore College of Dental Surgery," *Dental Cosmos* 26 (April 1884): 240–41.
13. Henry A. Parr is certainly one of the most interesting characters to have ever graduated from the Baltimore College of Dental Surgery. His exact birthplace in about 1843 is not known, ranging from Nova Scotia to Nashville to New York. The confusion over Parr's birth date and place is not surprising in view of his later activities. With the outbreak of the Civil War, Parr left his Tennessee home to serve with Confederate General John Hunt Morgan's 2nd Kentucky Cavalry. He was among the 12 volunteers that Morgan selected for a night raid on Nashville to burn a federal steamboat, the *Minnetonka*. With this raid Parr evidently began a rather clandestine and shadowy career as a Confederate secret service agent. Later, he was taken prisoner, but managed to escape and worked his way up to New Brunswick, Canada. By 1863, Parr had returned to the States and was working under cover for the secret service as a drugstore clerk. In 1863, Parr was paired with the man the northern press referred to as the "notorious Lieutenant Braine." They and their confederates hijacked the steamer *Chesapeake* on its run from New York to Portland, Me., and took it to Halifax, Nova Scotia. The U.S. Navy cornered the *Chesapeake* and took possession of her in British waters. This triggered an international incident and almost started a war between Britain and the United States. Meanwhile, Parr and the Confederate "pirates" were released by the Canadian authorities, despite the demands of the U.S. government for extradition. In 1864, Parr was paid from a special gold fund that could only be approved by President Jefferson Davis. Later, in 1864, Parr was involved in two more ship hijackings. After the war, Parr decided to remain in Canada and began practicing pharmacy (perhaps as a result of his drugstore apprenticeship in Nashville). Parr was later recognized as the "pioneer " pharmacist in Yarmouth County, Nova Scotia. In 1878, when Parr tried to return to the United States, he was arrested by federal agents and charged with murder of the *Chesapeake's* second engineer. In the trial in Boston, he was exonerated on the basis of no proof that he was the killer. Upon returning to Canada, Parr began practicing dentistry and became known as "Dr. Parr." He was the first dentist in western Nova Scotia to perform crown and bridgework. In 1880, a fire destroyed his pharmacy, and apparently convinced him to return to the United States. He then began attending the Baltimore College and at age 38, received his DDS degree in 1884. He was awarded a gold medal for his proficiency. From 1885–1922, Parr served on the faculty of his alma mater as a "clinical Instructor" and was on the board of visitors appointed by the faculty. Dr. Parr was very active as a clinician at dental meetings as was known as a specialist in crown and bridge. He was also an inventor of a tooth separator and clamp, mouth prop, antiseptic telephone mouthpiece attachment, key guard, and fan mechanism for rocking chairs. Overall, Parr practiced in New York City for 50 years and included among his patients former President Ulysses S. Grant and Harry K. Thaw, the accused murderer of Sanford White, the famous architect. Dr. Parr died on August 6, 1932, at his New York City home. He was a Confederate to the very end; among his personal artifacts given posthumously to the BCDS museum was a lock of Jefferson Davis' hair. Unfortunately, when Parr's safe was robbed in 1926, the burglars took President Grant and President Arthur's dentures; otherwise, the BCDS museum would have had three presidential dentures. [John M. Hyson, Jr., and Ben Z. Swanson, Jr., "Portrait of a Confederate Secret Agent: Henry A. Parr, DDS," *Journal of the History of Dentistry* 44 (July 1996): 53–59.]

14. Ibid., 59.
15. "Southern Dental Association—Sixteenth Annual Session," 423–24, 430–31; Winder, "Dental Education," 578.
16. "Southern Dental Association—Sixteenth Annual Session," 425–26.
17. Ibid., 426.
18. B. Merrill Hopkinson, "Dental Education," *Independent Practitioner* 5 (June 1884): 293.
19. Ibid., 294–95.
20. James B. Hodgkin, et al, "Dental Education," *Independent Practitioner* 5 (July 1884): 358–59, 360–63.
21. Ibid., 361–62.
22. Ibid., 363.
23. Ferdinand J. S. Gorgas, "Dental Education," *Independent Practitioner* 5 (August 1884): 415–16.
24. "Dental Society of the State of New York. Sixteenth Annual Meeting [Proceedings]," *Odontographic Journal* 5 (July 1884): 82–83, 89–90.
25. "Dental Society of the State of New York. Seventeenth Annual Meeting," 112–15, 119.
26. Charles R. E. Koch, ed., *History of Dental Surgery*, vol. 3 (Fort Wayne: National Art Publishing Co., 1910), p. 463; "National Association of Dental Faculties [Proceedings]," *Dental Cosmos* 26 (August 1884): 560, 561; American Association of Dental Schools, *A Course of Study in Dentistry* (Chicago: Curriculum Survey Committee, 1935), pp. 359–60.
27. "National Association of Dental Faculties," 561, 562, 563.
28. Gardner P.H. Foley, ed. *Proceedings of the 125th Anniversary Celebration of the Baltimore College of Dental Surgery* (Baltimore: Horn-Shafer Co., 1966), p. 240; [Truman W. Brophy], "Section IX: Education, Literature, and History [Chairman's Address]," in *Transactions of the Fourth International Dental Congress* [1904], vol. 3 (Philadelphia: S.S. White Dental Mfg. Co., 1905), p. 216
29. F[erdinand] J.S. Gorgas, "University of Maryland," *Dental Advertiser* 16 (October 1885): 120.
30. "National Association of Dental Faculties [Proceedings]," *Dental Cosmos* 31 (September 1889): 727, 728, 729,
31. Baltimore College of Dental Surgery, *Forty-Six Annual Catalogue of the Baltimore College of Dental Surgery* (Baltimore: n.p., [1885]), p. 11.
32. Ibid., pp. 3, 4, 6.
33. "Baltimore College of Dental Surgery," *Dental Cosmos* 27 (April 1885): 247; 28 (April 1886): 247; 29 (April 1887): 270.
34. Emory Addison Bryant was born in Kalamazoo, Mich., on August 10, 1863. After graduating from the Baltimore College of Dental Surgery in 1886, he began practicing in Washington, D.C. He also obtained law degrees from the National University of Washington (1906) and George Washington University (1907). He specialized in patent law. In 1912, he was the first dentist commissioned in the new U.S. Navy Dental Corps. Dr. Bryant was the personal dentist to President Theodore Roosevelt. He specialized in crown and bridge work and invented the Bryant bridge repair instruments and the Bryant mandibular splint. He retired from the Navy as a commander in March 1929 and died on November 25, 1935, at the Naval Hospital. He was buried at Arlington National Cemetery with full military honors. [Foley, *Proceedings of the 125th Anniversary Celebration*, pp. 140–41; "Final Tribute is Paid Commander Bryant, *Washington Star*, November 27, 1935.]
35. Foley, *Proceedings of the 125th Anniversary Celebration*, p. 140.
36. Baltimore College of Dental Surgery," *Dental Cosmos* 30 (April 1888): 284; 31 (April 1889): 306.
37. Baltimore College of Dental Surgery, *Forty-Seventh Annual Catalogue of the Baltimore College of Dental Surgery* (Baltimore: n.p., [1886]), p. 15.
38. Baltimore College of Dental Surgery, *Fifty-third Annual Catalogue of the Baltimore College of Dental Surgery* (Baltimore: Snowden & Cowman, 1892), p. 14.
39. Foley, *Proceedings of the 125th Anniversary Celebration*, p. 239; "Obituary. Dr. R. B. Winder," *Dental Cosmos* 36 (September 1894): 758; Koch, *History of Dental Surgery*, p. 463; Winder, "A National Dental Association," 501; Gardner P. H. Foley, ed., *Hall of Fame of Great Maryland Dentists*, Maryland State Dental Association, 1976), p. 12; William Simon, "History of the Baltimore College of Dental Surgery," in *Transactions of the Fourth International Dental Congress* [1904], vol. 3 (Philadelphia: S.S. White Dental Mfg. Co., 1905) p. 311.
40. "Southern Dental Meeting—Annual Meeting (Conjointly with the North Carolina State Dental Association)," 257.
41. Winder, "Anchylosed Maxillaries,"130.
42. "Obituary. Prof. R.B. Winder," 186; F. N. H., "North Carolina State Dental Association," 392; [H. M.] Kempton, "Ohio State Dental Society [Proceedings]," *Archives of Dentistry*, n.s., 7 (January 1890): 31.
43. "Dental Society of the State of New York. Seventeenth Annual Meeting,," 99, 109, 112–17.
44. Jersey State Dental Society, *Transactions of the New Jersey State Dental Society* (Philadelphia: J. B. Lippincott Co., 1888), pp. 87–91.
45. "American Dental Association. Twenty-Seventh Annual Meeting [Proceedings]," I*ndependent Practitioner* 8 (September 1887): 483; R[ichard] B. Winder, "German Dental Education," Items of Interest 10 (January 1888): 35.
46. Baltimore College of Dental Surgery, *By-Laws of the Alumni Association of the Baltimore College of Dental Surgery* (Baltimore: Griffin, Curley & Co., 1888), pp. 3–7.
47. B. Holly Smith, "The Chapin A. Harris Memorial Association," *Dental Review* 3 (August 15, 1889): 531–32. By 1911, the Chapin A. Harris memorial was still in limbo and was now taken over by the Maryland State Dental Association, which appointed a committee to oversee the project. The committee consisted of M. G. Sykes, B. Holly Smith, W. W. Dumbracco, T. O. Heatwole, J. W. Smith, H. A. Wilson, and William G. Foster as chairman. The association was seeking funds from dental societies, colleges, and members of the profession to erect a suitable monument. In 1913, the *Dental Cosmos* reported that $1,000 had been raised to date. It was estimated that it would take $8,000 to erect a suitable memorial in bronze on a granite base. Finally, on June 1, 1922, the monument was unveiled in Baltimore. It was sculpted by Edward Berge and was ten feet, eight inches tall, with a seven foot, two-inch granite base and shaft, sur-

mounted by a heroic-sized bust of bronze. The wreath and name was in bronze and the inscription cut into the granite shaft. [J. Ben Robinson, "Let's Keep the Records Straight," *Alma Mater* 1 (May 1959): 30; "The Chapin A. Harris Memorial Fund," *Dental Digest* 18 (January 1912): 20; (Edward C. Kirk), " The Chapin A Harris Memorial," *Dental Cosmos* 55 (March 1913): 330, 333; "The Chapin A. Harris Memorial," *Dental Digest* 28 (May 1922): 299.]

48. W. W. Dunbracco, "Baltimore College of Dental Surgery Alumni," *Dental Cosmos* 32 (May 1890): 398–99.
49. "The Dental Profession Alarmed: A Bill Imposing Fine or Imprisonment for Refusal to Answer Census Queries," *New York Sun*, May 12, 1892, Bayly Philip Winder Papers, London, UK (*hereafter* cited as BPWP).
50. Maryland State Dental Society Committee, "To the Senators and Representatives of Maryland, and other states, in Congress Assembled, May 9–10, 1892," pp. 1, 3, BPWP; "The Dental Profession Alarmed," BPWP.
51. "Baltimore College of Dental Surgery," *Dental Cosmos* 32 (April 1890): 319; 33 (May 1891): 406.
52. Baltimore College of Dental Surgery, *Fifty-Second Annual Catalogue of the Baltimore College of Dental Surgery* (Baltimore: Snowden & Cowman, 1891), pp. 10–11.
53. John T. O'Rourke, and Leroy M.S. Miner, *Dental Education in the United States* (Philadelphia: W.B. Saunders Co., 1941), p. 110.
54. A.H. Thompson, "Scientific Instruction in Our Colleges," in *Transactions of the American Dental Association* (Chicago: H.D. Justi—The Dental Review Co., 1890): 66.
55. Ibid., 63, 65, 66.
56. John S. Marshall, "Technical vs. Theoretic Training," *Dental Brief* 5 (September 1900): 508–9.
57. "Baltimore College of Dental Surgery," *Dental Cosmos* 34 (May 1892): 396–97.
58. Charles C. Kelsey, "Dental Fraternities at Michigan," *School of Dentistry Alumni Bulletin* (1977–78): 59, 64.
59. J. A. Taylor, *History of Dentistry: A Practical Treatise for the Use of Dental Students and Practitioners* (Philadelphia: Lea & Febiger, 1922), pp. 224–25.
60. "General Medical Council," *British Journal of Dental Science* 36 (June 15, 1893): 562, 565, 566–67.
61. Ibid., 569, 574.
62. "Baltimore College of Dental Surgery," *Dental Cosmos* 35 (April 1893): 319.
63. Koch, *History of Dental Surgery*, pp. 463–64; J. J. Cadden, "Richard Bayly Winder," unpublished student paper, 1945, GPHFP; "Obituary. Prof. Richard Bayly Winder," *Dental Review* 8 (August 15, 1894): 607; J. T[ruman], "Obituary. Richard Bayly Winder, M.D., D.D.S.," *International Dental Journal* 15 (September 1894): 604, 605; "The Baltimore College of Dental Surgery [Fifty-fourth Annual Commencement Exercises]," *American Journal of Dental Science* 27 (April 1894): 570.

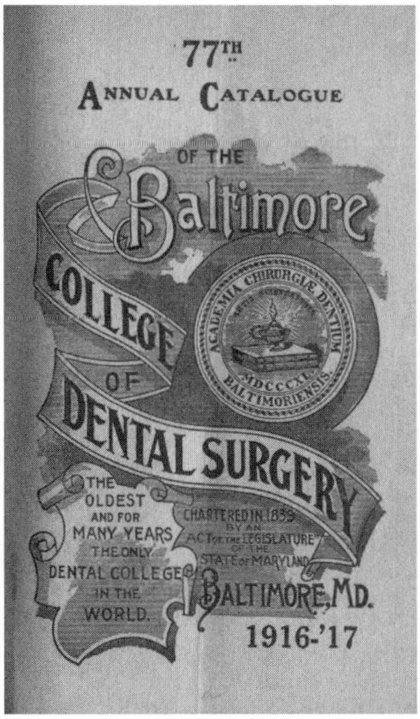
77TH
ANNUAL CATALOGUE
OF THE
Baltimore
COLLEGE
OF
DENTAL SURGERY
ACADEMIA CHIRURGIÆ DENTIUM
MDCCCXL
BALTIMORIENSIS.
THE OLDEST AND FOR MANY YEARS THE ONLY DENTAL COLLEGE IN THE WORLD.
CHARTERED IN 1839 BY AN ACT OF THE LEGISLATURE OF THE STATE OF MARYLAND
BALTIMORE, MD.
1916-'17

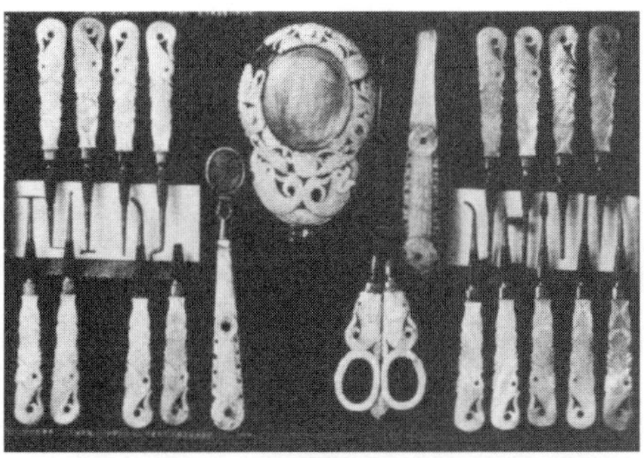

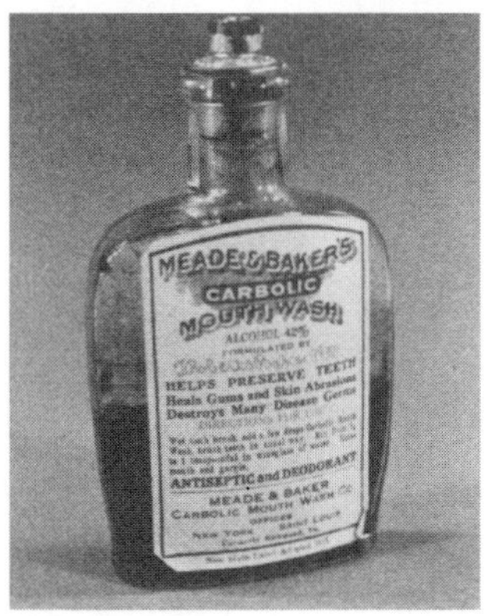
MEADE & BAKER'S
CARBOLIC
MOUTH WASH
ALCOHOL 42%
HELPS PRESERVE TEETH
Heals Gums and Skin Abrasions
Destroys Many Disease Germs
ANTISEPTIC and DEODORANT
MEADE & BAKER
CARBOLIC MOUTH WASH CO.

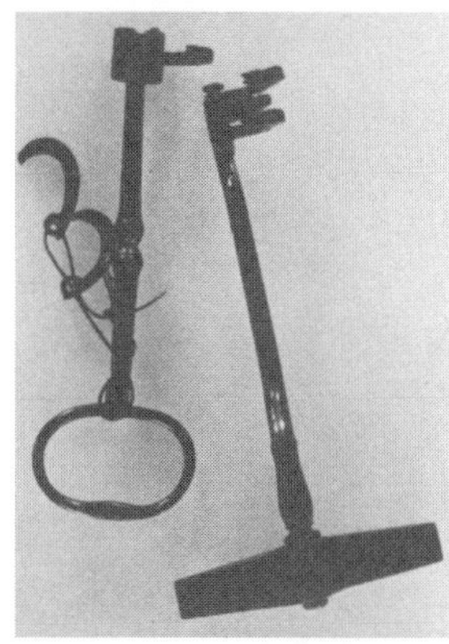

N.Y.
PA.
N.J.
W.VA
R.T.
W.Va.
B.C.D.S. '08
Man's Usefulness Does Not End In Death
Crawford - N.J.
Spear - Me
Hennen - W.Va
Stick - Penna
Shuttleworth - N.Y.
McQueen - W.Va
Fennessy - R.I.

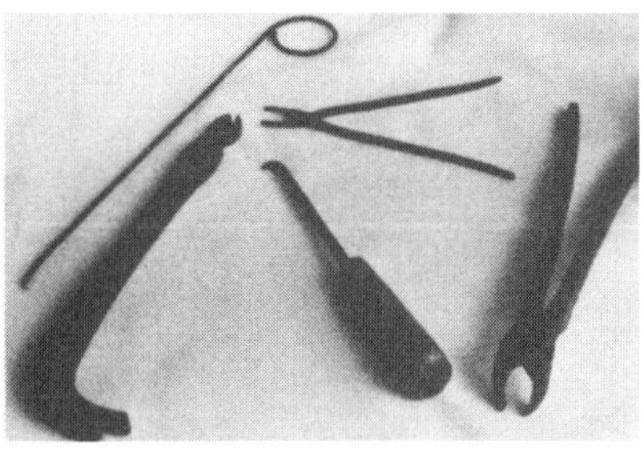

SOCIETAS AMERICANA CHIRURGORUM QUI DENTIUM VITIA CURANT.

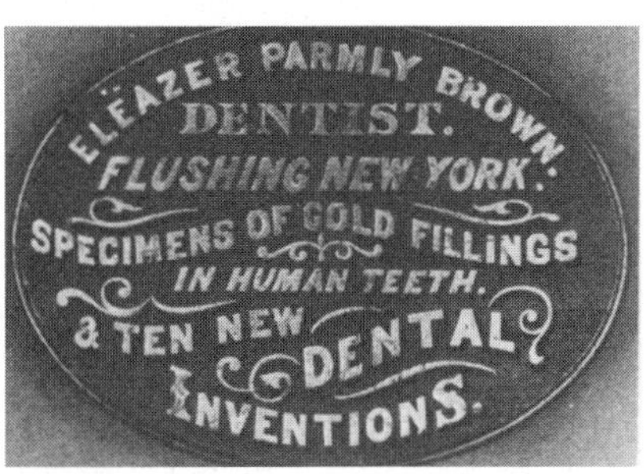
ELEAZER PARMLY BROWN.
DENTIST.
FLUSHING NEW YORK.
SPECIMENS OF GOLD FILLINGS
IN HUMAN TEETH.
& TEN NEW DENTAL
INVENTIONS.

TESTIMONIAL DINNER
Dr. Katherine Toomey
NEW JERSEY ALUMNI ASSOCIATION
BALTIMORE COLLEGE OF DENTAL SURGERY
DENTAL SCHOOL
UNIVERSITY OF MARYLAND
ROBERT TREAT HOTEL
NEWARK, NEW JERSEY

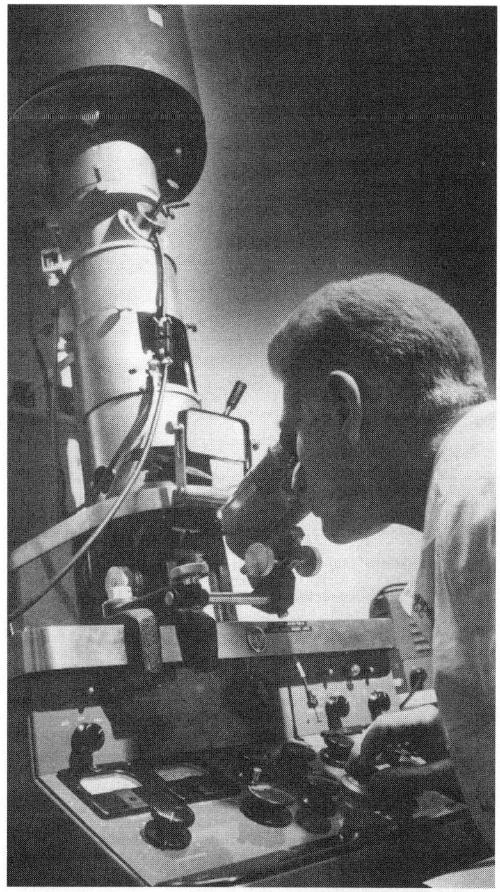

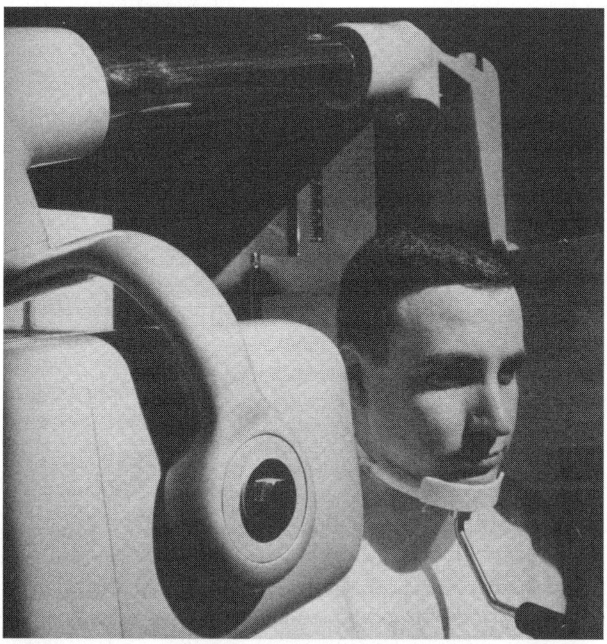

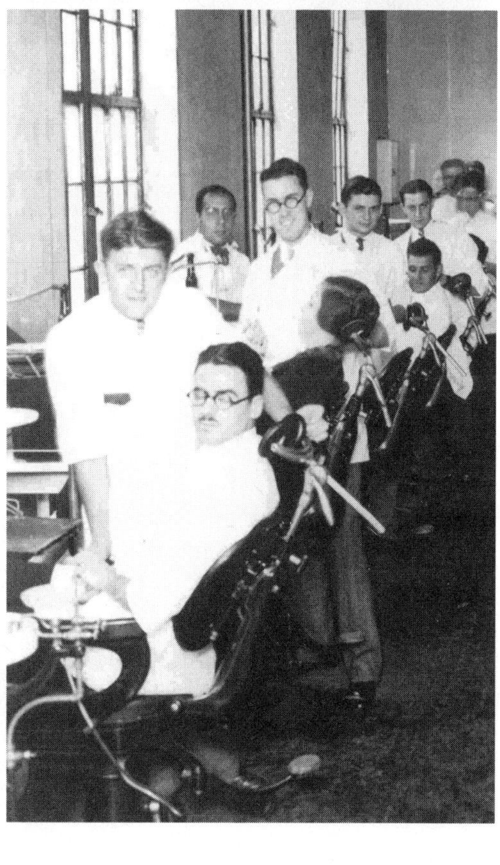

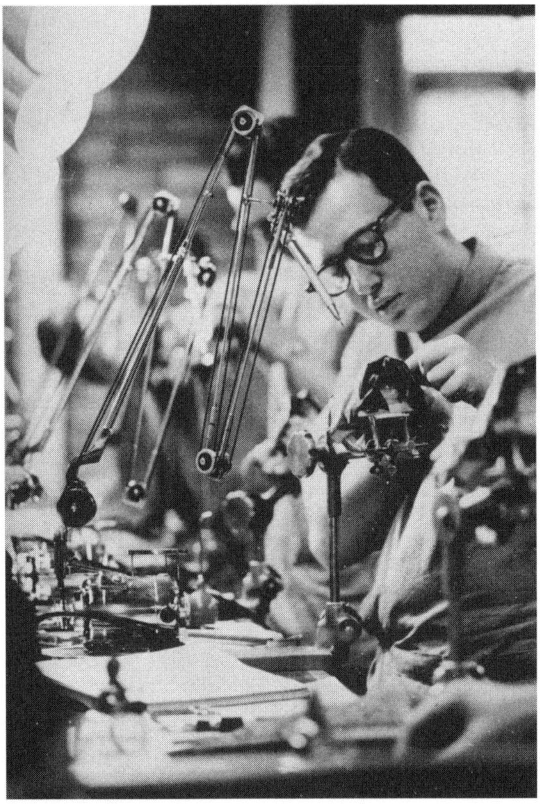

SESQUICENTENNIAL
THE MIRROR
BALTIMORE COLLEGE OF DENTAL SURGERY
DENTAL SCHOOL
UNIVERSITY OF MARYLAND
1840-1990

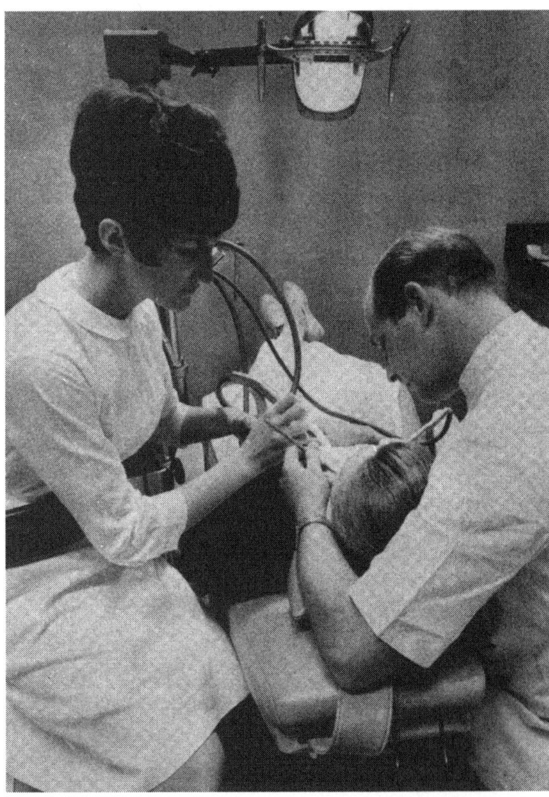

HARRIS
1806–1860

Mdental
BALTIMORE COLLEGE OF DENTAL SURGERY, UNIVERSITY OF MARYLAND
The Research and Alumni Magazine of the World's First Dental School
Summer 2006
Technology for the Future Today
The Dental School ushers in a new era of patient care and education

Faculty and students on the steps of the Baltimore Medical College.

Chapter 11

The Dental Department of the Baltimore Medical College: 1895–1913

"Oral hygiene is at bottom of all success in our operations. Our success, frequently, is altogether dependent on the hygienic condition; according to the cleanliness maintained will be the success of the operation performed. . . . How frequently has the operation of cleaning the teeth been carelessly performed! Most practitioners look upon it as an operation that any tiro can perform and one of no importance at all. I regret to say that the impression is obtained in many instances from the college clinics. The demonstrators look upon it as an operation for freshmen only."[1] **~William A. Montell, 1902**

Problems in Dental Education

The latter part of the 19th century saw the chartering and establishment of a great number of dental schools throughout the United States. Personal profit was the chief motivator in the majority of cases; in fact, in many incidences the schools were chartered by lay groups hoping to sell their interest to some individual dentist or professional organization. Many of the charters were never used and expired, whereas others were used by dental schools for the temporary organization of a school that failed to last. During this period, 61 dental colleges were started, but 14 had failed before 1900. Among the survivors, there were numerous mergers. Once a charter had been granted there was little control by the state governments over the school or its activities, which of course was particularly advantageous to the proprietary schools. Charters were fairly easy to obtain and the state failed to ask the underlying motives for the charter application. One reason for the explosion of dental colleges was the enactment of state laws requiring licensing by state boards for competency. Boards were very exacting in their demands upon candidates with no dental degree and rejected them for "insufficient knowledge or skill." Soon candidates learned that the easiest way to pass the examination was to enter a dental school and obtain a degree. This created a demand for more dental colleges and resulted in the formation of many schools, which were simply diploma mills. Therefore, it is not difficult to explain why a charter was granted in 1895 for another dental school in Baltimore, known as the Dental Department of the Baltimore Medical College.[2]

Baltimore Medical College: 1881

The Baltimore Medical College was founded in 1881, "condemning Darwinism" and stating that it was a "Christian College." In 1882, the college decided that it would be "indelicate" to admit women; thus, opening the door for the Women's Medical College of Maryland.[3]

Organization of the Dental Department: 1895

In May 1895, Dr. John William Smith, an 1888 alumnus of the Baltimore College of Dental Surgery, approached David Streett, MD, dean of the Baltimore Medical College; Wilmer Brinton, MD, the college's professor of obstetrics; T. A. Ashby, the college's professor of diseases of women and children; and R. H. P. Ellis, MD, the college's professor of materia medica, about organizing a dental department for the Baltimore Medical College. A week later, a committee was appointed by the college's faculty to talk to Dr. Smith about the feasibility of organizing a dental department. The committee thought the prospects good and appointed Smith to invite other dentists to help him form a dental faculty. Dr. John Edgar Orrison, an 1886 alumnus of the Baltimore College of Dental Surgery, agreed to join Smith in forming a committee to find a third man. Several prominent dentists were interviewed, but all declined on the grounds that there were already two dental colleges in the city and it would be impossible to make the proposed school a success. Dr. Smith met with Dr. Ferdinand J. S. Gorgas, the University of Maryland Dental Department dean, to see if he or his faculty had any objections to the establishment of a dental department in conjunction with the Baltimore Medical College. He sought the approval of at least one of the two dental schools in Baltimore before proceeding with the plans for the chartering of a third school. Dr. Gorgas not only approved, but said he would help Smith secure the necessary charter. With this backing, the committee decided to either undertake the organizing and financing of the new institution themselves or abandon the idea completely. They determined to proceed with the venture.[4]

On June 3, 1895, the Dental Department of the Baltimore Medical College was incorporated under the "general incorporation act of Maryland" by Drs. S. K. Merrick, Wilmer Brinton, T. A. Ashby, J. Edgar Orrison, and J. William Smith. The following officers were selected: Dr. T. A. Ashby, president; Dr. J. William Smith, dean; and Dr. J. Edgar Orrison, secretary and treasurer. For a location, they rented the Friends' School House at 715 North Eutaw Street, Baltimore. About August 1, 1895, the dental infirmary was opened and equipped with Wilkerson chairs, dental engines, vulcanizers, lathes, and the other necessary equipment to perform all operations in operative and prosthetic dentistry, but with still no students. By the end of September, the students arrived and by October 10 there were 34 matriculates in the school. Many of the junior and senior students were transfers from other schools. The faculty brought in patients from various charitable institutions, and soon there was a large clinical practice underway. Students from Louisiana, West Virginia, Virginia, Maine, Ohio, Connecticut, New York, Vermont, Rhode Island, North Carolina, Pennsylvania, Massachusetts, Nebraska, Canada, as well as Maryland, were matriculates. The lectures were held in the Baltimore Medical College rooms and the clinics in the Friends' School.[5]

William A. Montell

The faculty consisted of: J. William Smith, DDS, dean and professor of prosthetics, metallurgy, and crown and bridge; J. Edgar Orrison, DDS, professor of operative dentistry and dental science; William A. Montell, DDS (BCDS 1884), professor of dental pathology, dental therapeutics, and dental technique; A. C. Pole, MD, professor of anatomy; J. D. Blake, MD, professor of operative and clinical surgery; Robert W. Johnson, AB, MD, professor of principles and practice of surgery and oral surgery; Samuel T. Earle, MD, professor of physiology; J. Frank Crouch, MD, professor of materia medica and therapeutics; and W. B. D. Penniman, PhD, professor of chemistry. The lecturers were: S. C. Pennington, nitrous oxide anesthesia; Tilghman B. Marden, AB, MD, histology; A. Lee Browne, AB, chemistry; Delano Ames, MD, pathology. The clinical instructors were: C. E. Duck, DDS; A. P. Gore, DDS; J. Emory Scott, DDS; A. Price, DDS; F. F. Drew, DDS.; S. B. Ward, DDS; William A. Mills, DDS; George R. Carter, DDS; B. Meyer, DDS; H. E. Lupus, DDS; H. S. Abendschein, DDS; and G. A. Hamill, DDS. The demonstrators were: H. Phillips, DDS, demonstrator in operative dentistry; Carl E. Smith, DDS, demonstrator in prosthetics; Walter A. Low, DDS, assistant in operative dentistry; B. Bar, DDS, assistant in prosthetics; D. H. R. Patton, MD, DDS, assistant in prosthetics; A. B. Fonshill, DDS, assistant in prosthetics; Charles H. Theberath, DDS, assistant in crown and bridge; Kennon W. Egerton, DDS, assistant in prosthetics; Charles W. Kammer, DDS, PhG, assistant in operative dentistry; J. George Schmetzer, DDS, assistant in operative dentistry; S. De Leon Avery, assistant in operative dentistry; R. B. Warfield, MD, anatomy; Walton Bolgiano, AB, MD, anatomy; James B. Bennett, MD, assistant in anatomy; A. Lee Browne, AB, chemistry; and Delano Ames, MD, pathology.[6]

In its opening catalog, the Dental Department of the Baltimore Medical College openly stated its attributes and educational advantages to the prospective dental student:

> The Dental Department of the Baltimore Medical College possesses a college and laboratory plant not surpassed by any dental school. Its facilities for the education of the dental student are fully equal to the requirements of the best courses of instruction in modern dentistry. The dental student will have the advantage of the same instruction in medicine as is given by the Faculty of the Baltimore Medical College to the medical student. In those branches which especially prepare him for dental practice he will enjoy the best instruction under competent teachers.
>
> The course of instruction has been arranged for the thorough education of the Dental Student in the theory and practice of dentistry. It is the determination of the Faculty of the Dental Department to make this one of the most progressive dental schools in this country.[7]

The New Howard Street Building: 1896

In the fall of 1896, the dental department moved into its new five-story, Byzantine-style building at 802–806 North Howard Street, near Madison Street, constructed at a cost of $200,000. Now the College could hold all its lectures and clinics in the new building. The first floor was primarily for the students and contained a reading room, smoking room, a lavatory, and the dental laboratory. The laboratory was divided into three rooms, a 16 x 20 foot impression room, a 20 x 24 foot vulcanizing room, and a 40 x 20 foot lathe and locker room. The second floor contained the dean's office, faculty room, and the infirmary toward the center and rear of the building. The infirmary was 2,140 square feet, lighted by 25 large windows, steam-heated, had wash stands with hot and cold water, and was equipped with the new and improved Wilkerson chairs with movable bracket trays. It also contained a 20 x 20 foot reception room, an extraction room, a drug room, and 10 private consultation rooms for the use of physicians and the various department specialists. The third floor contained a 40 x 80 foot lecture hall with a stage, ante-room, vestibule, and private rear stairway. The hall could seat 600 students. The fourth floor contained the tiered amphitheatre with a skylight. The amphitheatre could seat 500 students. This floor also had waiting and anesthesia rooms and a histology/pathology/physiology laboratory. The bacteriology laboratory was situated in the mezzanine story. The anatomical laboratory contained tables for 100 students to dissect at the same time, was thoroughly lighted with windows and skylights, was ventilated and had hot and cold running water, an elevator for moving the anatomical material, and a tile floor for flushing and good sanitation. The chemical laboratory was 42 x 84 foot, well lighted and ventilated with hot and cold water, equipped with tables for chemical apparatus, and contained 444 student lockers. It was supplied with gas and had a storeroom for chemicals. The entire building was steam-heated, had hot and cold water on every floor, and had provision for lighting at night by means of gas or electricity. The buildings' doors opened directly into the hospital in the rear and an elevator ran from the lower floor to the top floor. The college museum contained an extensive collection of pathology specimens and models and casts, which were used for teaching purposes.[8]

The catalog also stressed that the dental students would get ample opportunity to see patients at the school's outpatient medical dispensary, which treated more than 25,000 patients annually, and also treated the ward patients in the adjacent Maryland General Hospital. The regular winter course of instruction was to begin on October 1, 1896, and run until March 31, 1897. The spring and summer course was to begin on April 1, 1897, and run until the opening of the next regular session. The course of instruction for freshman students included lectures on prosthetic and operative dentistry, anatomy, physiology, materia medica, chemistry, dental technique, and clinical and laboratory work. For the second year, pathology, histology, and therapeutics were added, and for the third year, bacteriology, metallurgy, and surgery were included, in addition to the clinical work. All students after practice on extracted teeth were permitted to operate at the chair. Special instruction was given in porcelain crown and bridgework, continuous gum, and aluminum work by the faculty. Prominent and well-known dentists from different sections of the country were brought in to give special lectures on the various branches of dentistry. Oral examinations were held at the end of the first and second years for advancement.[9]

The requirements for admission to the College were those of the National Association of Dental Faculties and the National Association of Dental Examiners, which attests to the school's interest in the improvement of dental education. A preliminary examination in English was required before admission, unless the candidate had a collegiate degree, a high school diploma, or a teacher's certificate. Medical and pharmacy graduates were eligible to graduate after two years of clinical work and attendance of two regular winter sessions. To graduate, a candidate had to be 21 years of age, of good moral character, and have attended all the required courses of lectures in a reputable dental college, and the last of which was the Baltimore Medical College. In addition, he had to demonstrate to the professors' satisfaction his knowledge of practical dentistry, deposit in the college's museum examples of his operative and prosthetic work, and pass an oral examination by the faculty. It was also possible to obtain both the DDS and MD degrees in five years. The fee for a full course of lectures was $90, and the matriculation fee was $5. Beneficiary students were accepted upon the recommendation of a State Dental Society, a payment of $50, and the usual matriculation fee.[10]

All during its existence, the school and faculty seem to have been intent on keeping "abreast of the trends in dental education." The college's record is notable, particularly among proprietary schools that "too often had reputations of being more interested in the financial returns of a school than in adherence to and advancement of high standards of instruction." [11]

The First Commencement: 1896

In 1896, the college graduated three students, two from Virginia and one from Ohio.[12] In 1897, there were six graduates, including Emil E. Janssen from Germany.[13] On July 30, 1897, at the joint meeting of the National Association of Dental Faculties and the National Association of Dental Examiners, held at Old Point, Va., the Dental Department of the Baltimore Medical College was elected to membership in both groups.[14]

The third annual commencement was held at Ford's Opera House, Baltimore, on April 6, 1898. Degrees were conferred on 18 graduates by the college president, S. K. Merrick, MD.[15] The fourth commencement was held on April 6, 1899, at the Academy of Music, Baltimore, with 14 graduates.[16] The fifth commencement was held at the Lyceum Theater on May 4, 1900, with 28 graduates.[17] In 1901, William A. Montell, DDS, took over as dean from J. William Smith, DDS, but Smith retained the professorship of prosthetics and crown and bridge.[18] The sixth commencement was held at Lehmann's Hall, Baltimore, on May 6, 1901, with 21 graduates.[19] The 1901–02 catalog proudly announced that the college was installing electric lathes and ovens for porcelain work in its "most modernly equipped dental laboratories."[20] The seventh commencement was held again at Lehmann's Hall on May 1, 1902, with 26 graduates.[21] The next year, John Edgar Orrison became the new dean and the college held its commencement at the Lyceum Theater on May 1, 1903, with 23 graduates receiving DDS degrees. Included in this class was the third Japanese graduate from a Baltimore school, Shintaro Tanaka from Hiroshimo.[22] Dr. Montell was appointed a delegate for the 1903 meeting of the National Association of Dental Faculties, thus demonstrating the college's commitment to the advancement of dental education.[23] For the 1903–1904 year, the college increased its requirement to attendance from three to four full courses of "not less than seven months each, in separate academic years" as a requirement for graduation for all students matriculating after the 1902–03 session.[24] In 1904, Dr. Smith, after an absence of three years because of health reasons, returned as dean of the college and remained in that position for the next nine years.[25] The ninth commencement exercises were held on April 29, 1904, at the Lyceum Theater, Baltimore, with 24 graduates.[26] The next year, the college graduated 30 students on May 11, 1905.[27]

For the 1905–06 session, the college reverted to a three-year curriculum with three courses of 30-week duration in separate academic years.[28] The college graduated 17 individuals that year at Albaugh's Theater.[29] The following year, there were 20 graduates on May 21, 1907, at the Academy of Music.[30] For the 1907–08 session, the course was lengthened to 32 weeks, and the tuition was increased from $100 to $150 a session.[31] In 1908, there were 17 graduates, 30 in 1909, 20 in 1910, and 21 in 1911.[32] Meanwhile, the college had rather optimistically erected another building in January 1909. The new, four-story, 64 x 94 foot Laboratory Building was located on North Howard Street, nearly opposite the College Building. The basement floor contained a large lecture hall; on the first floor were two lecture rooms, a surgical laboratory, and a YMCA room for students; and on the second a lecture room, library, a pathology museum, and an office for the Law Department.[33]

The 1912–13 catalog expressed the school's thanks "to its many friends and patrons for past favors, and promised to merit their good will in the future;" but this was not to be, as the college had its final graduation ceremony at Albaugh's Lyceum Theater, Baltimore, on June 1, 1912. Twenty-three graduates received their DDS degrees from Professor S. K. Merrick.[34]

The Merger with the University of Maryland: 1913

Apparently, a merger of the Baltimore Medical College with the University of Maryland School of Medicine was contemplated as early as 1910. In 1913, the American Medical Association issued an ultimatum that unless the two schools merged they would lose their accreditation within the year. The deans hurriedly shaped an agreement and in 1913, the merger of the two medical schools was consummated, leaving the dental department of the college out in the cold to what would have been "an independent, but isolated, status." This situation would have put the dental department in the same situation as other proprietary dental schools as far as financial difficulties were concerned. Moreover, the dental faculty was fully aware of the increasing importance of having a "medical school connection." Consequently, in 1913, the faculty "wisely decided to pool the interests of good dental education by merging with the Dental School, University of Maryland." Contrasted to the rocky merger of the Maryland Dental College with the Baltimore College of Dental Surgery in 1878, the merger was effected with the "utmost harmony and good-will" on the part of all concerned parties. The Baltimore Medical College's dental and laboratory equipment was transferred to the University for its use, and the building became part of Maryland General Hospital. Some of the Baltimore Medical College's dental faculty were placed on the University of Maryland faculty.[35] For instance, John William Smith became professor of prosthetics (1913–19) at the university and John Edgar Orrison was appointed professor of crown and bridge (1920–25).[36] It is presumed that the college museum's collections were added to the University of Maryland's dental museum after the merger.

In reviewing the list of the 367 graduates of the Dental Department, Baltimore Medical College, during its 18-year existence, one immediately notices the preponderance of out-of-state graduates as contrasted to those from Maryland. Probably, the excellent reputations of the two older schools discouraged Maryland residents from applying to a new relatively unknown college. Of course, the students from other states could not help but spread the fame of Baltimore, Md., as a "dental education center." The Dental Department of the Baltimore Medical College certainly had an honorable record, starting with its "amiable relationship" with the other schools, continuing with its "high standards of dental education" during its relatively brief existence, and finally, ending with its peaceful merger with the University of Maryland. It had upheld the tradition of combining excellence with education and demonstrated to the older Baltimore College of Dental Surgery that the days of an independent dental college were numbered.[37]

NOTES

1. "Union Meeting of the Maryland State Dental Association and the District of Columbia Dental Society," *Dental Cosmos* 44 (November 1902): 1180.
2. Harry B. McCarthy, "A History of Dental Education in Maryland," master's thesis, Graduate School, University of Maryland, 1948, pp. 47–48; Charles R.E. Koch, ed., *History of Dental Surgery*, vol. 1 (Fort Wayne, Ind.: National Art Publishing Co., 1910), pp. 402–3.
3. George H. Callcott, *A History of the University of Maryland* (Baltimore: Maryland Historical Society, 1966), pp. 207–8.
4. Koch, *History of Dental Surgery*, p. 594; McCarthy, "A History of Dental Education in Maryland," p. 48; "[History of the Dental Department, Baltimore Medical College]," typed 5 pp. manuscript, undated, Baltimore College of Dental Surgery Papers, National Museum of Dentistry Archives (*hereafter* cited as BCDSP, NMDA).
5. Koch, *History of Dental Surgery*, pp. 594, 596.
6. Dental Department of the Baltimore Medical College, *Annual Announcement. Dental Department of the Baltimore Medical College. Session 1896–97* (Baltimore: n.p., [1896]), p. 1.
7. Ibid., p. 3.
8. Koch, *History of Dental Surgery*, p. 596; Dental Department of the Baltimore Medical College, *Annual Announcement [1896–97]*, pp. 3–5.
9. Dental Department of the Baltimore Medical College, *Annual Announcement [1896–97]*, pp. 5, 6, 7.
10. Ibid., p. 12, 13.
11. McCarthy, "A History of Dental Education in Maryland," p. 51.
12. Dental Department of the Baltimore Medical College, *Annual Announcement [1896–97]*, p. 14.
13. Dental Department of the Baltimore Medical College, *Annual Announcement Dental Department of the Baltimore Medical College. Session 1897–98* (Baltimore: n.p., [1897]), p. 17.
14. ["Meeting of National Association of Dental Faculties"], n.d., BCDSP, NMDA.
15. "Baltimore Medical College—Dental Department," *Dental Cosmos* 40 (July 1898): 587.
16. "Baltimore Medical College, Dental Department," *Dental Cosmos* 41 (May 1899): 498.
17. "Baltimore Medical College, Dental Department," *Dental Cosmos* 42 (June 1900): 596.
18. Dental Department of the Baltimore Medical College, *Dental Department of the Baltimore Medical College. Session 1900–1901* (Baltimore: n.p., [1900]), p. 2.
19. "Baltimore Medical College, Dental Department," *Dental Cosmos* 43 (June 1901): 681.
20. Dental Department of the Baltimore Medical College, *Dental Department of the Baltimore Medical College. Session 1901–1902* (Baltimore: n.p., [1901]), p. 6.
21. "Baltimore Medical College, Dental Department," *Dental Cosmos* 44 (June 1902): 632.
22. "Baltimore Medical College, Dental Department," *Dental Cosmos* 45 (July 1903): 603. Dr. Tanaka later served as president (principal) of the Osaka Higher Women's Dental College in 1926. A booklet of its matriculation and list of school faculty for dental education and clinical instruction was issued in May 1925. Dr. Tanaka convinced the Ministry of Education to approve the college as a dental school; however, the school was discontinued shortly thereafter. His dental license issued by the Japanese government was number 824. He was listed as a member (not graduate) of the Tokyo Dental College Alumni Association until 1931. Dr. Tanaka died around the 1930s in Hiroshima, Japan. [Letters, Norinaga Moriyama to John M. Hyson, Jr., December 6, 12, 2004.]
23. Dental Department of the Baltimore Medical College, *Dental Department of the Baltimore Medical College. Session 1902–1903* (Baltimore: n.p., [1902]), p. i.
24. Dental Department of the Baltimore Medical College, *Dental Department of the Baltimore Medical College. Session 1903–1904* (Baltimore: n.p., [1903]), p. 16.

25. Gardner P.H. Foley, ed., *Proceedings of the 125th Anniversary Celebration of the Baltimore College of Dental Surgery* (Baltimore: Horn-Shafer Co., 1966), p. 221.
26. "Baltimore Medical College, Dental Department," *Dental Cosmos* 46 (June 1904): 524.
27. "Baltimore Medical College, Dental Department," *Dental Cosmos* 47 (July 1905): 906–7.
28. Dental Department of the Baltimore Medical College, *Dental Department of the Baltimore Medical College. Session 1905–1906* (Baltimore: n.p., [1905]), pp. 18–19.
29. "Baltimore Medical College, Dental Department," *Dental Cosmos* 48 (July 1906): 802.
30. "Baltimore Medical College, Dental Department," *Dental Cosmos* 49 (July 1907): 779.
31. Dental Department of the Baltimore Medical College, *Annual Catalogue and Announcement. Dental Department of the Baltimore Medical College. Thirteenth Annual Session 1907–1908* (Baltimore: n.p., [1907]), pp. 20, 21.
32. "Baltimore Medical College, Dental Department," *Dental Cosmos* 50 (July 1908): 769; 51 (July 1909): 908; 52 (July 1910): 817; 53 (August 1911): 973.
33. Dental Department of the Baltimore Medical College, *Annual Catalogue and Announcement. Dental Department of the Baltimore Medical College. Seventeenth Annual Session 1911–1912* (Baltimore: n,p., [1911]), p. 8.
34. Dental Department of the Baltimore Medical College, *Annual Catalogue and Announcement. Dental Department of the Baltimore Medical College. Eighteenth Annual Session 1912–1913* (Baltimore: n.p., [1912]), p. 7; "Baltimore Medical College, Dental Department," *Dental Cosmos* 54 (August 1912): 959.
35. Callcott, *A History of the University of Maryland*, p. 266; McCarthy, "Dental Education in Maryland," pp. 51–52.
36. Foley, *Proceedings of the 125th Anniversary Celebration*, pp. 196, 200.
37. McCarthy, "Dental Education in Maryland," pp. 52–53.

M. Whilldin Foster

Chapter 12

The BCDS Foster Years: 1894–1923

"There is something beautiful in the contemplation of the introduction and growth of the Dental science in the United States. From Europe the first glimmering lights of the profession, as has been shown, were introduced almost by chance, like wandering rays from a distant source. But those rays fell upon a country full of the boundless materials of science—a luxuriant field for its development—an enterprising, inventive people—and no wonder that the result has been the astonishing perfection to which it has now attained."[1] **~Chapin A. Harris, 1845**

The M. Whilldin Foster Years: 1894–1914

M. Whilldin Foster, MD, DDS, the acting dean after Winder's death, replaced Dr. Winder as dean of the Baltimore College of Dental Surgery on August 14, 1894. He also held the chair of therapeutics and pathology. Dr. Foster was born on May 17, 1837, in Philadelphia. He graduated from the Philadelphia Dental College. In 1861, he became associated with Dr. Robert Arthur, the first BCDS graduate. After five years, he established an office in Baltimore at 9 West Franklin Street. In 1873, he became connected with Winder's newly organized Maryland Dental College. In 1879, with the merger of that college with the Baltimore College of Dental Surgery, he was elected the professor of pathology and therapeutics in the latter school. Upon the death of Dr. Winder, he assumed the deanship of the Baltimore College of Dental Surgery. Dr. Foster died at his home in Baltimore on June 30, 1914, at age 78.[2]

The fifty-sixth annual session began on October 1, 1895, and continued until March 20, 1896. Besides Dr. Foster, the faculty consisted of William B. Finney, DDS, professor of dental mechanism and metallurgy; B. Holly Smith, MD, DDS, professor of dental surgery and operative dentistry; Thomas S. Lattimer, MD, professor of physiology and comparative anatomy; William Simon, PhD, MD, professor of chemistry; Charles F. Bevan, MD, clinical professor of oral surgery; J. W. Chambers, MD, professor of anatomy; and George H. Rohe, MD, professor of materia medica. The lecturers were: R. Bayly Winder, PharG, DDS, materia medica; William F. Smith, AB, MD, regional anatomy; J. N. Farrar, MD, DDS, irregularities; John H. Meyer, DDS, continuous gum; Dr. George Evans, crown and bridgework;

and Dr. K. C. Gibson, artificial palates and fractured maxillaries. The clinical instructors were T. S. Waters, DDS, chief clinical instructor; Corydon Palmer, DDS; E. Parmly Brown, DDS; A. L. Northrop, DDS; E. L. Hunter, DDS; W. W. Walker, DDS; David Genese, DDS; F. C. Barlow; C. M. Gingrich, DDS; J. Hall Moore, MD; R. B. Donaldson, DDS; H. A. Parr; J. Emory Scott, DDS; C. L. Alexander, DDS; and C. A. Meeker, DDS. The demonstrators were William G. Foster, DDS, operative dentistry; and George E. Handy, MD, DDS, mechanical dentistry. The assistant demonstrators were: J. W. Smith, DDS; W.W. Dunbracco, DDS; J. C. Sutherland, DDS; J. E. Orrison, DDS; G. Marshall Smith, DDS; W. S. Twilley, DDS; J. K. Burgess, DDS; W. F. Smith, AB, MD, anatomy; Louis F. Ankrim, MD, anatomy; and R. G. Davis, MD, anatomy.[3]

The 1895 catalog announced that with the session beginning October 1, 1895, "women will be admitted as students subject to the same requirements as men."[4] The infirmary was open from 9 a.m. to 5 p.m. daily and many operations were performed free of charge and others at the cost of materials only. All the anesthetics used in dentistry were available for extractions and surgical operations on the head and face.[5] The catalog also mentioned that a joint College YMCA had been started by the college and the College of Physicians and Surgeons. Religious services were held at the Central YMCA on Sunday afternoons, at which time addresses were made by some of the leading ministers of the city and by students. The objectives were to prevent young men from "being enticed into evil ways by the allurements of a large city," and to raise the general moral standing of the profession.[6]

The fifty-fifth annual commencement was held on March 21, 1895, at Ford's Grand Opera House, Baltimore, with Professor M. Whilldin Foster conferring degrees on 45 candidates. The 1896 commencement was held at the Lyceum Theater, Baltimore, with 44 graduates.[7]

The Alumni Association: 1896–97

The Alumni Association of the College held a banquet on March 19, 1896, at Café "Calvert" in Baltimore. Music was provided by the college's Mandolin and Guitar Club. The alumni officers for 1895–96 were: Charles A. Meeker of Newark, N.J., president; Edward Nelson of Baltimore, vice-president; W. W. Dunbracco of Baltimore, secretary; and T. S. Waters of Baltimore, treasurer.[8] The following March, the alumni held a second banquet at the "Severn" in Baltimore. The officers for 1896–97 were: George E. Adams of South Orange, N.J., president; C. W. F. Holbrook of Newark, N. J., vice-president; W.W. Dunbracco, secretary; and George Milholland of Baltimore, treasurer.[9]

The 1897 exercises were held at the Academy of Music, Baltimore, on March 19, 1897, with 63 graduates.[10] Among the improvements for the 1896–97 session were electric motors for all the lathes in the laboratory and attachments in the infirmary for electric mallets for gold foil plugging. In 1898, the college added electric lights and fountain cuspidors for all the dental chairs in the infirmary. It also inaugurated a class in modeling and carving teeth in "plastic materials" for the freshmen students. This course was to teach them the "form, contour and anatomy" of the teeth.[11] The 1898 exercises were again held at Ford's Opera House, with 74 graduates.[12] The college catalog emphasized to the students that the money paid for books and instruments (about $50 per session) was a "permanent investment lasting for life." It was impossible to practice dentistry without them. This expense was one that all dentists had to absorb, so the sooner the better to acquire them. Those who tried to get through without purchasing them were practicing poor economy by not getting accustomed to handling all the instruments during their collegiate courses. The college, of course, furnished all the extraction forceps, lathes, and vulcanizers.[13]

First American Woman Graduate: 1899

The fifty-ninth commencement was held at the Lyceum Theater, Baltimore, on March 31, 1899, with Dean Foster handing out 62 diplomas. This graduation was especially significant, as Eva E. Semon of Maryland became the first American woman to graduate from the Baltimore schools. She was the first woman since 1878, when it was decided to refuse matriculation to any more women students. Dr. Semon practiced in Baltimore.[14] On April 30, 1900, there were 74 graduates at the Lyceum Theatre, and for the first time a year of high school was a requirement for entrance into the college. Before that date, rudimentary English was the only entrance requirement.[15] In 1901, the graduates numbered 79, including two women. Edith R. Brush became Florida's first licensed woman dentist. She practiced in Daytona Beach and was the first female member of the Florida State Dental Society. In 1904–05, she served as the society's corresponding secretary.[16] Clara C. Walker of Pennsylvania won the gold medal for non-cohesive gold foil the year 1901.[17] On April 29, 1902, the college graduated 67 candidates at Chase's Theatre, including Bessie Burns Bennett of Maryland; in 1903 there were 57 graduates at the Academy of Music, including Mary Parker Bosley of Maryland; and in 1904, 68 at the Maryland Theatre.[18]

Dr. Morgan Writes Army Dental Bill: 1901

The U.S. Army Dental Corps formed in 1901 as an experimental group of 30 contract dental surgeons. Its humanitarian, practical, and financial success in treating the Army's dental needs eventually led to the establishment of a permanent commissioned corps in 1911 and had a far greater impact on the dental profession than it has ever been given credit. The fact that dentistry was officially recognized by the United States Government as a distinct branch of the health services, requiring its own corps (although operating within the medical corps), gave credibility to dentistry that it hitherto had not been able to attain. The public was now aware that Uncle Sam considered dentists worthy of commissioned officer status in his Army. The prestige thus gained was invaluable to the profession, and influenced dentistry's development as we now know modern dental science. The role of one of the Baltimore College of Dental Surgery's own in the organization of the Dental Corps (the world's first) is significant. Dr. Robert Withers Morgan of Lynchburg, Va., an 1881 alumnus and Confederate[19] veteran, formulated the bill (H.R. 972) for Army dentists which Representative Peter J. Otey presented to Congress on December 5, 1899, which eventually passed in 1901 organizing the U.S. Army Dental Corps. In recognition of his important role, he was chosen by the Surgeon General as one of the three examining and supervising dental surgeons to select the other 27 members of the 30-man dental corps. Dr. Morgan signed a contract in February 1901, and on February 12 received his orders to report to the Surgeon General. After the examinations were concluded on July 31, 1901, he was assigned as dental surgeon to Columbus Barracks, Havana, Cuba, for duty with the Pacification Forces. The 57-year-old dentist's army career was rather brief. On October 30, 1901, Dr. Morgan developed marked anemia with leucocytosis as a result of the tropical climate, and was given a two-month sick leave in November

1901. He returned to Lynchburg and his contract was annulled on February 3, 1902, and he never fully regained good health before his death on July 14, 1904.[20]

The Museum: 1904

In 1904, the *Baltimore Sun* published an extensive article on the College Museum at Eutaw and Franklin Streets in Baltimore. They called the Washington dentures the "prize exhibit," but went on to describe the museum contents in great detail:

> Mounted on a silver rod and closely protected in a glass case contained in another glass case, the teeth of the first President are kept in the large room on the second floor of the college—a room wherein the advance of dentistry from the beginning to the present time is shown perhaps more comprehensively than in any other college museum, . . . Curiously, just across the room from the case in which is kept the relic of Washington is a death mask of King George III, . . . A single tooth—a jaw tooth at that of Amadeus, King of Spain, is pinned to a card in a case across the wall and almost directly under the death mask of King George III. Amadeus' chief claim to fame, according to the legend on the card, is that he was the husband of Isabella, who started Columbus on the way to America by pawning family jewels. Three casts of the jaw of William H. Seward, Lincoln's Secretary of State, rest side by side with a cast of the mouth of the wife of Tom Thumb. Perhaps the most interesting part of the collection to those whose experience with dentists has been one of pain and tribulation is a group of 'keys,' the forerunners of the modern forceps. On huge specimen resembles a corkscrew, with the large wooden handle made especially with a view to getting a good 'purchase' or leverage on the resisting and aching tooth. . . . The row of skulls is part of the extensive anatomical exhibit. . . .[21]

Also exhibited was the diploma of Robert Arthur, the first graduate of the BCDS in 1941, which was presented to the college by Dr. William H. Trueman of Philadelphia; portraits of famous dentists; and the collection of death masks of famous people collected by Dr. Richard B. Winder, the former BCDS dean. Included in the collection were Benjamin Franklin, Sir Isaac Newton, Chapin A. Harris, King George III, and Wordsworth, the poet.[22]

For the 1905–6 session, the college proudly announced:

> The oldest of Dental Colleges, this institution enters on the sixty-sixth year of its career with its prospects for usefulness brighter than ever before. It has added to its Faculty and Clinical Corps strong and active men and is better equipped than at any period of its existence. It makes no special claim to the consideration of the dental profession and public aside from its actual worth as an instructor of young men in a specialty, and claims only the modest place of aiding in developing with others (what it did for so many years alone and opposed) a single science and art. The results of its work in these sixty-five years are world-wide in their influence upon dentistry.[23]

The college also announced that it had purchased the site adjoining the college on Franklin Street. A building of "modern design" was to be added to the present one. This addition containing the same amount of square feet as the present building, would double the capacity, and allow for the "latest improved equipment of the dental and chemical laboratories, and the students' reading room."[24]

Local Anesthesia: 1905

Although much attention has been paid to the history of general anesthesia, relatively little has been written about local anesthesia. Nevin calls the discoverers of local anesthesia the "unsung heroes." Many individuals contributed to its development including, Charles Gabriel Pravaz (1791–1853) of France, who invented the hypodermic syringe in 1851; and

Alexander Wood (1817–84) of Scotland, who invented the hollow hypodermic needle in 1853. In 1869, Claude Bernard (1813–78), a French physiologist, injected morphine prior to the administration of chloroform or ether for general anesthesia. In 1884, the breakthrough came when Carl Koller (1857–1944), a Viennese ophthalmologist, discovered the anesthetic properties of cocaine. William S. Halsted (1852–1922), a Bellevue Hospital surgeon, blocked the inferior alveolar nerve with a four percent cocaine solution in November 1884—the first mandibular nerve block. However, cocaine was found to be an addictive and dangerous drug.[25]

The synthesis of Novocain (procaine) by Alfred Einhorn (1856–1917) of Germany in 1905 finally provided a local anesthetic without the dangerous side effects of cocaine. It was first introduced into the United States in 1907 and became the most popular anesthetic for dental procedures. Finally, pain was under man's control with a choice of anesthesia, local or general. Paradoxically, two dentists, Wells and Morton, introduced inhalation (general) anesthesia used primarily by physicians, whereas two physicians, Koller and Halsted, introduced block (local) anesthesia used primarily by dentists.[26]

Although the 1905 catalog noted that the dental infirmary was open daily from 1 to 5 p.m. daily, and "All anaesthetics in use are administered in the Extraction of teeth and in Surgical Operations of the head and face," no specific mention of the use of local anesthesia was made. Presumably, the anesthetics referred to were general, not local.[27]

The 1905 commencement exercises were held at Chase's Theater, Baltimore, with 77 graduates receiving their DDS degrees, including Sarah Sophy Ackerman of Maryland. Dr. Foster conferred 45 degrees in 1906 at Albaugh's Theater, including three from Cuba (E. de Caturla, M. Martinez, and O. Monagas).[28] The same year, the Alumni Association held its annual reunion at the College Building on May 10 and 11, 1906. Clinics and papers by "men of exceptional ability" were planned in addition to an alumni dinner.[29]

The Alumni Association: 1906

After a 10-year absence, the Alumni Association held another meeting and reunion on May 10–11, 1906. The program opened on May 10 with clinics and demonstrations by prominent dentists, including Dr. L. Parmly Brown of New York, who lectured on porcelain bridges. The officers for 1905–06 were: Harvey J. Burkhart of New York, president; William G. Foster, vice-president; W. W. Dunbracco, secretary; and George V. Milholland, treasurer. Commercial exhibitors included: Klewe & Company of New Haven, Conn., demonstrating Dr. Jenkins' porcelains; S. S. White Dental Mfg. Company of Philadelphia; Electro Dental Mfg. Company of Philadelphia; Harvard Company of Canton, Ohio; J. W. Ivory of Philadelphia; and Ritter Dental Mfg. Company of Rochester, N.Y.[30]

In 1907, the commencement exercises were held again at Albaugh's Theater, with 41 graduates. The 1907 catalog emphasized that the "intimate union of theoretical and practical instruction will be insisted on during the entire course, and, indeed, is considered as the one thing essential to becoming a competent dental practitioner." It also noted the new entrance requirement of a high school diploma or its equivalent.[31] Professor Foster conferred 47 diplomas in 1908; 52 in 1909, including two women, Mary A. Bane and Cecil L. Goetz; and 38 in 1910.[32]

The Founding of Alpha Omega Dental Fraternity: 1908

In 1908, a group of Jewish students at the college created an organization known as the Alpha Omega Fraternity, which became a national fraternity in December 1909 when it joined with "Ramach," a dental fraternity founded at the Pennsylvania College of Dental Surgery in Philadelphia in 1907. The Baltimore group became known as the *Zeta* Chapter and the Philadelphia group, the *Ramach* Chapter—the first two chapters of the fraternity. The purpose of the organization was to protect the Jewish students' interests and to "study collectively and to foster a genuine fraternal spirit by assisting one another in their scholastic endeavors." Although Alpha Omega emphasized its role as "the voice of the Jew in dentistry," the fraternity was not restricted to Jewish membership, as undergraduates of all faiths were welcome to belong. The fraternity took a strong stand against "discrimination of any person or group of persons."[33]

The First X-ray Machine: 1910

The 1910–11 session is historically important because the college purchased its first x-ray machine. It was installed on the second floor adjoining the infirmary. The school announced that a "competent instructor and lecturer" would be in attendance for emergency cases. The instructor was Louis D. Coriell, DDS, listed in the catalog as a lecturer in dental radiography and electro-therapeutics.[34] No doubt the college was being a little cautious concerning the use of x-ray, as oral roentgenlogy had been developed in the United States as early as 1896 by Dr. C. Edmund Kells, Jr. Unfortunately, some patients had been burned by the rays, and even Dr. Kells was a victim of uncontrolled exposure to the rays.[35] According to Dr. Howard R. Raper, professor of operative technic and roentgenlogy at Indiana Dental College, by 1913, less than one-third of the dental colleges were teaching dental radiography.[36] Therefore, the Baltimore College of Dental Surgery was in the vanguard in respect to using this wonderful diagnostic tool.

The college also announced that the junior class would take the dissecting course at the College of Physicians and Surgeons building, which had been rebuilt during 1899. This building was not only well-lighted and ventilated, but was equipped with all the "latest modern improvements."[37] The 1911–12 catalog reminded prospective students that clinical material was abundant in a city of 650,000 inhabitants, thereby enabling the student to "carefully prepare himself for future practice, and installing a degree of confidence which experience only can impart." Also, the college had "special lectures by eminent scientists" during the regular course and clinics by "celebrated operators."[38] Meanwhile, the session fees had been increased to $150 in accordance to a ruling from the National Association of Dental Faculties. Room and board could be secured for $3.50 to $5 per week at quality private boarding houses, cheaper than any other city. The college held its commencement at Albaugh's Theater, Baltimore, on May 17, 1911. Dean Foster conferred degrees on 47 graduates. In 1912, the College graduated 64 candidates, including Alexander Gordon Lyle,[39] its only Congressional Medal of Honor winner and first chief of the U.S. Navy Dental Corps.[40]

Alexander Gordon Lyle

The William G. Foster Years 1914–23

On June 8, 1914, Dean M. Whilldin Foster resigned as dean and his son William G. Foster, an 1881 alumnus of the Baltimore College of Dental Surgery, replaced Dr. Foster as acting dean. Dr Foster was born in Phillipsburg, N. J., on September 23, 1860. In 1876, he entered the Agricultural College of Maryland and received his DDS degree from the Baltimore College of Dental Surgery in 1881. Dr. Foster served as an assistant demonstrator of mechanical dentistry at his alma mater, 1883–88; demonstrator of mechanical dentistry, 1889; and demonstrator of operative dentistry, 1895. In 1885, he served as a first lieutenant in the 5th Regiment, Maryland National Guard, and later as captain of Company "E." In 1888, he was the inspector of rifle practice. He resigned from the Guard in 1890. Dr. Foster was the president of the Maryland State Dental Association in 1903–4, and was a charter member of the Alpha Chapter of the Psi Omega Fraternity. He served as dean of the Baltimore College of Dental Surgery until the 1923 merger with the Dental Department, University of Maryland. Dr. Foster died on March 7, 1939, at his home in St. Michaels, Md.[41]

The year 1914 also marked the college's move to new quarters at 851 N. Howard Street. In 1913, when the Baltimore Medical College merged with the University of Maryland, dental students of the Medical College transferred to the Dental Department, University of Maryland. In 1914, the Baltimore College of Dental Surgery became heir to the former Baltimore Medical College quarters, when the Baltimore Medical College, in transferring its programs to the University of Maryland, deeded its building to the Baltimore College of Dental Surgery. For the first time in its 75-five year history the college owned its own building.[42]

Once again, the college occupied a building that had been formerly associated with another scientific institution. The four-story, brick, Georgian Revival style building had a frontage of 65 feet and a depth of 168 feet. It was the "most commodious structure" ever occupied by the college. It had excellent lighting, with paired, plate glass windows. The first floor contained the students reading room, 25 x 40 feet, the dean's office, and the museum. The basement had a billiard room for the students. A 62 x 41 foot lecture hall with a seating capacity of 400 persons was on the second floor. The third story contained the infirmary and extraction and impression rooms, lighted on three sides by windows. The prosthetic laboratory was on the fourth floor. The building was steam heated and lighted by gas and electricity. On the side of the rear building was a campus large enough for a handball and basketball court.[43]

The curriculum for freshmen students was: anatomy, physiology, chemistry, dental materia medica, didactic and practical prosthetic dentistry, operative dentistry, pathology, and therapeutics. For junior students, special attention was given to bacteriology and orthodontics. In the senior year, the major portion of time was devoted to operative and prosthetic dentistry. It is interesting to note that the 1914 catalog mentioned that there would be no hazing in the school during the coming session. This action was determined by the student body at a mass meeting.[44] Dean Foster conferred 55 diplomas in 1914 at Albaugh's Theater, Baltimore; 79 in 1915; 53 in 1916; and 75 in 1918.[45] One of the 1916 graduates was Livius Lankford,[46] who established the U.S. Army's first overseas dental clinic in France in 1917.[47]

The Beginning of the Four-Year Course: 1917–18

Seemingly, the seventy-eighth annual session beginning in 1917 was not affected by the United States declaration of war on Germany on April 6, 1917. Many of its graduates[48] served the colors during the war. However, for the 1917–18 session there was a major change in the dental college curriculum. The National Association of Dental Faculties ruled that "*commencing with the session 1917–18 will be FOUR YEARS in all schools of dentistry.*" Now the course was divided into freshman, sophomore, junior, and senior terms. Attendance at four full courses, of not less than seven months each, in separate academic years, was now required of all students before examination for graduation.[46]

The 1918–19 catalog stated that the seventy-ninth session would start on October 1, 1918, and continue until June 1919. It proudly announced that 3,147 graduates had gone forth from the college into practice, and they were "scattered all over the civilized world." The college pointed with pride to the standing of its graduates. In addition, 8,507 students had matriculated at the institution. The college reiterated that its diploma was not purchasable.[50]

The Alumni Association: 1919–22

In February 1919, a banquet was held by the Rhode Island branch of the Alumni Association in Providence, R.I. Special guests were Drs. William G. Foster, the BCDS dean; George E. Hardy, professor of physiology; and James Kendall Burgess, professor of prosthetic dentistry.[51] In 1920, it was announced in *Dental Facts* that there would be a meeting of the alumni association and to contact Dr. Frank P. Duffy, president of the New England Alumni Association, Baltimore College of Dental Surgery, for details.[52] On November 30, 1921, Drs. B. Lucian Brun, James H. Ferguson, Jr., and Norval H. McDonald held a meeting to reorganize the alumni as the National Alumni Association of the Baltimore College of Dental Surgery. Dr. Ferguson was elected the first president of the new organization.[53]

On May 30–31–June 1, 1922, during commencement week, the National Alumni Association held a meeting in Baltimore. Dr. Ferguson called the meeting to order at 8:30 p.m., Tuesday, May 30. After Dr. B. Holly Smith read the first paper, "Oral Diagnosis," the meeting adjourned until Wednesday morning. The session opened with a paper by Dr. James K. Burgess on "A General Survey of the Field of Oral Restoration and a Consideration of What to do in the Case of the Incomplete Denture." This paper was followed by Dr. Emory C. Thompson's paper on "Three-quarter Crowns and Porcelain-Tipped Bridge Work."[54] The next paper was by Dr. Paul R. Stillman, a New York periodontist, who read a paper, "Preventive Dentistry." The society then adjourned until the evening session, which was a banquet. On Thursday morning, Dr. B. Lucian Brun presented, "Dental Responsibility of Correct Diagnosis;" followed by Dr. Harvey J. Burkhart's "Dental Clinics in Public Institutions and in Public Schools;" and Dr. A. C. Fones, "The Dental Hygienist in Public Schools." Officers were elected as follows: Dr. Frank P. Duffy, president; Dr. Carroll H. Frink, first vice-president; Dr. Charles P. Rice, second vice-president; Dr. E. B. McQuillan, third vice-president; Dr. N. H. McDonald, secretary; and Dr. George V. Milholland, treasurer. On June 1, the Chapin A. Harris Memorial was unveiled and presented to the City of Baltimore by Dr. Harvey J. Burkhart. When the association adjourned, it was announced that the next meeting would be in five years.[55]

In 1919, the college conferred 67 diplomas; 26 in 1920; 54 in 1921; and 44 in 1922.[56] For the eighty-second course beginning on October 3, 1921, the college announced that a course in oral hygiene was being added to the curriculum for the last half of the senior year. It included:

> Lectures on general hygiene and sanitation, with especial emphasis on the care of children's teeth and on the prevention of oral diseases. Dietetics are discussed in the relation of their influence on the development and structure of the teeth. A study is made of the work being accomplished by oral hygienists in the public schools, and the necessity of such preventive treatment emphasized.[57]

This statement was the first official reference to pediatric dentistry issued by the college in its 82-year history.

The courses assigned to the freshmen students included, anatomy, physiology, chemistry, histology, applied physics and biology, and didactic and practical prosthetic and operative dentistry. The sophomore class took anatomy, chemistry, physiology and hygiene, dental histology, bacteriology, metallurgy, prosthetic and operative dentistry. The junior class had pathology and therapeutics, materia medica, orthodontics, radiology, oral prophylaxis, crown and bridgework, physical diagnosis, anesthesia, and operative and prosthetic dentistry. The senior class courses included pathology, therapeutics, materia medica, oral surgery, orthodontics, oral hygiene, dental history, dental ethics and jurisprudence, anesthesia, physical diagnosis, prosthetic and operative dentistry. This course of study was subject to modification by the National Association of Dental Examiners, National Association of Dental Faculties, and the Educational Council of America.[58]

Merger of the Baltimore College of Dental Surgery and Dental Department, University of Maryland: 1923

The eighty-third annual session, its last as a proprietary, independent dental school, began on October 2, 1922, and ran until June 1923. To this point, 3,411 students had graduated from its halls and had become leaders in the dental profession. Its reputation was worldwide. In addition, 9,243 students had matriculated at the college.[59] In 1923, the Baltimore College of Dental Surgery merged with the Dental Department, University of Maryland.

NOTES

1. Chapin A. Harris, *The Principles and Practice of Dental Surgery,* 2nd ed. (Philadelphia: Lindsay & Blakiston, 1845), p. 26.
2. J. A. Taylor, *History of Dentistry: A Practical Treatise for the Use of Dental Students and Practitioners* (Philadelphia: Lea & Febiger, 1922), pp. 104–5; Baltimore College of Dental Surgery, "Faculty Minutes Jan. 15, 1875, to and incl. April 26, 1916," Special Collections, Health Sciences and Human Services Library, University of Maryland (*hereafter* cited as HSL).
3. Baltimore College of Dental Surgery, *Fifty-sixth Annual Catalogue of the Baltimore College of Dental Surgery* (Snowden & Cowman Mfg. Co., 1895), p. 1.
4. Ibid., p. 10. Unfortunately, the catalogs used initials only in identifying the graduates making it impossible to identify the women from the men. [The author]
5. Ibid., p. i.
6. Ibid., p. 5.
7. "Baltimore College of dental Surgery," *Dental Cosmos* 37 (June 1895): 534; 38 (April 1896): 429.
8. Alumni Association of the Baltimore College of Dental Surgery, *Alumni Banquet,* March 19, 1896, Baltimore College of Dental Surgery Papers, National Museum of Dentistry Archives (*hereafter* cited as BCDSP, NMDA).
9. Alumni Association of the Baltimore College of Dental Surgery, *Second Annual Alumni Banquet Baltimore College of Dental Surgery at the "Severn" Baltimore Thursday Evening March 18, 1897,* BCDSP, NMDA.
10. "Baltimore College of Dental Surgery," *Dental Register* 51 (July 1897): 350.
11. Baltimore College of Dental Surgery, *Sixtieth Annual Catalogue of the Baltimore College of Dental Surgery* (Baltimore: n.p., [1898]), pp. 5, 9. The dental tooth carvings in ivorine and wax were still part of the freshman curriculum as late as the 1950s. [the author.]
12. Baltimore College of Dental Surgery," *Dental Cosmos* 40 (May 1898): 391.
13. Baltimore College of Dental Surgery, *Fifty-Eighth Annual Catalogue of the Baltimore College of Dental Surgery* (Baltimore: Snowden & Cowman Mfg. Co., 1897), p, 8.

14. Baltimore College of Dental Surgery," *Dental Cosmos* 41 (May 1899): 499; Gardner p. H. Foley, ed., *Proceedings of the 125th Anniversary Celebration of the Baltimore College of Dental Surgery* (Baltimore: Horn-Shafer Co., 1966), p. 217.
15. "Baltimore College of Dental Surgery," *Dental Cosmos* 42 (June 1900): 599; Baltimore College of Dental Surgery, *Sixty-First Annual Catalogue of the Baltimore College of Dental Surgery* (Baltimore: n.p., [1900]), p. 10. In 1902, the entrance requirement was changed again to require "an education which entitles them to enter the third year in a High School, or its equivalent." [Baltimore College of Dental Surgery, *63rd Annual Catalogue of the Baltimore College of Dental Surgery* (Baltimore: n.p., [1902]), p. 11.]
16. Baltimore College of Dental Surgery," *Dental Cosmos* 43 (June 1901): 676; Foley, *Proceedings of the 125th Anniversary Celebration*, p. 140.
17. Baltimore College of Dental Surgery, *Sixty-Second Annual Catalogue of the Baltimore College of Dental Surgery* (Baltimore: n.p., [1901]), pp. 14, 17.
18. "Baltimore College of Dental Surgery," *Dental Cosmos* 44 (June 1902): 633; 45 (June 1903): 520; 46 (June 1904): 528.
19. Robert Withers Morgan was born on June 14, 1844, in Shady Grove, Campbell County, Va. During the Civil War, he served in the Confederate Army as a private (enlisted August 12, 1862) in Company "C," 11th Regiment, Virginia Infantry of Pickett's Division, for three years. He was wounded at Second Bull Run and did not return to duty until March 19, 1863. Morgan was wounded again at Gettysburg on July 3, 1863, but back on the regimental roster in January 1864. He was captured at Milford Station on May 21, 1864, and paroled at Point Lookout, Md., for exchange on February 13, 1865. After the war, he served an apprenticeship under Dr. Robert Lemon in Gladys, and opened his own office in Lynchburg in 1879. He then entered the Baltimore College of Dental Surgery, graduated in February 1881, and returned to Lynchburg, where he practiced for the next 20 years. [Compiled Service Records of Confederate Soldiers Who Served in Organizations from the State of Virginia, roll 507, Microcopy 324, Record Group 109 (War Department Collection of Confederate Records), National Archives and Records Administration (*hereafter* cited as RG__, NARA).]
20. John M. Hyson, Jr., *The United States Military Academy Dental Service: A History 1825–1920* (West Point, N.Y.: United States Military Academy, 1989), pp. xvii, 151–52; General Correspondence, 1894–1917, no. 77614, RG 112 (Surgeon General's Office), NARA; Document File,1890–1917, no. 362000, 391987, 406257, Entry 25, RG 94 (Adjutant General's Office), NARA; Pension File, certificate no. 584073, RG 15 (Bureau of Pensions and Veterans Administration), NARA; Robert P. Stickley, and Jack D. Amowitz, *The Lynchburg Dental Society presents One Hundred and Forty-Three Years of Dentistry 1820–1963* (Lynchburg, Va.: J. P. Bell Co., Inc., 1964), pp. 44–47; "War Time Doctor (Dr. Robert Withers Morgan)," *News and Daily Advance*, Lynchburg, Va., October 12, 1936, p. 11.
21. "Historic Teeth: Those of George Washington in Baltimore Dental College Museum," *Baltimore Sun*, July 10, 1904.
22. Ibid.
23. Baltimore College of Dental Surgery, *66th Annual Catalogue of the Baltimore College of Dental Surgery* (Baltimore: n.p., [1905]), p. 4.
24. Ibid., p. 5.
25. Mendell Nevin, "The History and Development of Local Anesthesia," *Dental Items of Interest* 65 (July 1943): 674–76.
26. Milton B. Asbell, *Dentistry: A Historical Perspective* (Bryn Mawr, Pa.: Dorrance & Co., Inc., 1988), p. 178; Nevin, "History Local Anesthesia," 675, 677;
27. Baltimore College of Dental Surgery, *Sixty-Sixth Annual Catalogue*, p. 1.
28. "Baltimore College of Dental Surgery," *Dental Cosmos* 47 (June 1905): 744; 48 (June 1906): 706.
29. W. W. Dunbracco, "Alumni Association of Baltimore College of Dental Surgery," *Items of Interest* 28 (March 1906): 239.
30. Alumni Association of the Baltimore College of Dental Surgery, *Program of the Alumni Meeting and Class Reunion Baltimore College of Dental Surgery May 190th and 11th 1906*, BCDSP, NMDA.
31. "Baltimore College of Dental Surgery," *Dental Cosmos* 49 (June 1907): 659; Baltimore College of Dental Surgery, *68th Annual Catalogue of the Baltimore College of Dental Surgery* (Baltimore: n.p., [1907]), pp. 9, 11.
32. "Baltimore College of Dental Surgery," *Dental Cosmos* 50 (July 1908): 765; 51 (June 1909): 774; 52 (June 1910): 708–9.
33. "Alpha Omega," *Maryland Probe* 3 (October 19, 1973): 4; Charles C. Kelsey, "Dental Fraternities at Michigan," *School of Dentistry Alumni Bulletin* (1977–78): 66; Walter I. Levine, *Fifty Year History of Alpha Omega Fraternity 1907–1957* (Philadelphia: Bingham Co., 1957), p. 8.
34. Baltimore College of Dental Surgery, *71st Annual Catalogue of the Baltimore College of Dental Surgery* (Baltimore: n.p., [1910]), p. 5.
35. Asbell, *Dentistry: A Historical Perspective*, p. 141.
36. Howard R. Raper, "The Teaching of Dental Radiology," *Dental Brief* 18 (September 1913): 602.
37. Baltimore College of Dental Surgery, *71st Annual Catalogue*, p. 6.
38. Baltimore College of Dental Surgery, *72nd Annual Catalogue of the Baltimore College of Dental Surgery* (Baltimore: n.p., [1911]), p. 6.
39. Alexander G. Lyle was born in Gloucester, Mass., on November 12, 1889, and graduated from the Baltimore College of Dental Surgery in 1912. He practiced in his hometown for three years, and in 1915 was commissioned a lieutenant (j.g.) in the U.S. Navy Dental Corps. He was assigned to the 5th Regiment, U.S. Marines and went to France with that outfit. He participated in the Aisne Defensive, the Aisne-Marne Offensive, the St. Mihiel Offensive, and the Meuse-Argonne Offensive operations. For extraordinary heroism and devotion to duty on April 23, 1918, during the action in the Verdum sector, Dr. Lyle was awarded the Congressional Medal of Honor. His citation read: "Under heavy shellfire, on 23 April 1918, on the French Front (Verdun), Lieutenant Commander Lyle rushed to the assistance of Corporal Thomas Regan, who was seriously wounded, and administered such effective surgical aid while bombardment was still continuing as to save the life of Corporal Regan." He also received two Army Silver Stars, the Italian *Merito de Guerra* medal, and the Victory medal with five stars. After the war, he served in China with the 4th Marines. From 1932–36, he headed the dental department at the Naval Hospital at Newport, R.I. In 1939, he was promoted to captain, and in 1943 to rear admiral and chief of the U.S. Navy Dental Corps. He was the first dentist to hold flag rank in the U.S. Navy. Adm. Lyle retired in 1947 and in 1948 was advanced on the retired list to vice admiral. In 1946, he was awarded a doctor of science degree by his alma mater. Adm. Lyle died on July 15, 1955, in

Portsmouth, R.I. ["Obituary [Dr. Alexander Gordon Lyle]," *Journal of the Baltimore College of Dental Surgery, Dental School, University of Maryland* 15 (January 1956): 13; Foley, *Proceedings of the 125th Anniversary Celebration*, pp. 188–89.]

40. "Baltimore College of Dental Surgery," *Dental Cosmos* 53 (June 1911): 744; 54 (July 1912): 840.
41. Baltimore College of Dental Surgery, "Faculty Minutes," June 8, 1914, Special Collections, HSL; Foley, *Proceedings of the 125th Anniversary Celebration*, p. 164; Baltimore College of Dental Surgery Alumni Card File, BCDSP, NMDA; Geo[rge] A. Meekins, *Fifth Regiment, Infantry, Md. Nat. Guard, U.S. Volunteer: A History of the Regiment from its First Organization to the Present Time, Illustrated* (Baltimore: A. Hoen & Co., 1899), p. 12.
42. John Millner Associates, "Architecture as History: The Formative Years of the Baltimore College of Dental Surgery as Recorded in the Housing History," final report, John Millner Associates, West Chester, Pa., 1980, p. 49.
43. Ibid.; Baltimore College of Dental Surgery, *75th Annual Catalogue of the Baltimore College of Dental Surgery* (Baltimore: n.p., [1914]), pp. 4–5.
44. Ibid., p. 10.
45. "Baltimore College of Dental Surgery," *Dental Cosmos* 56 (July 1914): 895; 57 (August 1915): 956; 58 (July 1916): 843; 59 (September 1917): 946; 60 (July 1918): 643.
46. Livius Lankford, DDS, was born on February 20, 1893, in Norfolk, Va. After attending Richmond College and the University of Virginia, he matriculated at the Baltimore College of Dental Surgery and graduated in 1916. He was examined at Walter Reed General Hospital on May 3, 1917, found qualified and commissioned on May 7, 1917, as a first lieutenant in the U.S. Army Dental Reserve Corps. He served overseas in France with Base Hospital No. 18, Johns Hopkins Hospital Unit. Reportedly, he was the first American dentist to practice in France. It seems that he was among the group of medical officers assigned to a French hospital (Base Hospital No. 1) at St. Nazaire on July 5, 1917, to treat the troops who had landed and those to follow. This clinic was the first American dental office to open in France, and Dr. Lankford worked there for the next six weeks. After the war, he practiced in Baltimore, but moved to New Mexico in 1948. Dr. Lankford died on December 1, 1962, in Santa Fe, N. M. [Personal Data Cards of Candidates Seeking Appointment to the Dental Reserve Corps, 1917–1918, Entry 134, RG 112 (Surgeon General's Office), NARA; "History in brief of Base Hospital No. 18," in *Base Hospital Eighteen Thanksgiving Dinner* (program), November 28, 1918; "Death Claims Dr. Lankford," *New Mexico Dental Journal* (February 1963): 12.]
47. Base Hospital 18 Association, *History of Base Hospital No. 18 American Expeditionary Forces (Johns Hopkins Unit)* (Thomsen-Ellis Co., 1919), p. 40.
48. *See* Appendix D for list of graduates from all the Baltimore dental schools who served in World War I.
49. Baltimore College of Dental Surgery, *78th Annual Catalogue of the Baltimore College of Dental Surgery* (Baltimore: n.p., [1917]), pp. 10–11.
50. Baltimore College of Dental Surgery, *79th Annual Catalogue of the Baltimore College of Dental Surgery* (Baltimore: n.p., [1918]), pp. 2, 4.
51. "Annual Banquet Baltimore College of Dental Surgery Alumni Association, February 26th," *American Dentist* 8 (February 15, 1919): 10.
52. "[Meeting Alumni, of Baltimore College of Dental Surgery]," *Dental Facts for Dentists* 8 (August 1920): 26.
53. Joseph H. Seipp, Jr., "A Brief History of the First Dental Alumni Association in the World (Organizations Associated with the Baltimore College of Dental Surgery)," *Alma Mater* 8 (November 1966): 7.
54. "National Alumni Association of the Baltimore College of Dental Surgery," *Dental Cosmos* 64 (December 1922): 1336, 1338, 1341, 1342.
55. "National Alumni Association of the Baltimore College of Dental Surgery," *Dental Cosmos* 65 (January 1923): 86, 89, 92, 95; National Alumni Association of the Baltimore College of Dental Surgery, *Reunion May 30th, 31st and June 1st, One –Nine—Two—Two*, BCDSP, NMDA.
56. "Baltimore College of Dental Surgery," *Dental Cosmos* 61 (August 1919): 804; 62 (August 1920): 1030; 63 (July 1921): 756; 64 (August 1922): 909.
57. Baltimore College of Dental Surgery, *Eighty-First Annual Catalogue of the Baltimore College of Dental Surgery* (Baltimore: n.p., [1921]), pp. 3, 6.
58. Ibid., p. 8.
59. Baltimore College of Dental Surgery, *Eighty-Second Annual Catalogue of the Baltimore College of Dental Surgery* (Baltimore: n.p., [1922]), p. 3.

Timothy O. Heatwole

Chapter 13

The University of Maryland Heatwole Years: 1911-23

"A thorough knowledge of the science of dentistry is more difficult to be acquired, than is generally supposed. Many regard it a mere mechanical occupation, and believe that any one possessed of a slight degree of tact and manual dexterity and practice it. But this is a mistaken view of the subject. Dentistry, as it exists at the present day, is a science, partaking of medicine, surgery, and the manual arts; and he who practices it, should have some knowledge of all these branches, and moreover, be possessed of a mind that naturally inclines him to their study."[1] **~Chapin A. Harris, 1839**

Timothy O. Heatwole Becomes Dean: 1911

In 1911, after the semi-retirement of Dr. Gorgas due to illness, Timothy Oliver Heatwole, MD, DDS, became the new dean of the Dental Department, University of Maryland. Dr. Heatwole was born in Rockingham County, Va., in 1865. After attending the Shenandoah Normal College, in Harrisonburg, Va., he worked as a bookkeeper in Harrisonburg, Va. He then entered the Dental Department, University of Maryland, in 1892 and received his DDS degree in 1895. He received his MD degree from the Medical School in 1897. While still in medical school, he served on the faculty of his alma mater as an assistant demonstrator of operative dentistry from 1895 to 1903, as associate professor of orthodontics (1903–1906), as professor of materia medica and therapeutics (1906–23), assistant dean (1910), and as dean from 1911 to 1923. He served as the treasurer of the National Association of Dental Faculties for five years and was secretary-treasurer of the Alumni Association of the Dental Department, University of Maryland, in 1904. In 1905, always interested in politics, he was elected from the Second Legislative District of Baltimore City to the House of Delegates in the Maryland Legislature. From 1907 to 1920, he was a member of the first Branch City Council of Baltimore City. Dr. Heatwole was the president of the Maryland State Dental Association from 1909 to 1910. In 1923, St. John's College awarded him an honorary degree of Doctor of Science. After the amalgamation of the Baltimore College of Dental Surgery and the Dental Department of the University of Maryland, he served as the interim dean from 1923 to 1924. Dr. Heatwole retired in 1937 and died on April 28, 1949, in Baltimore.[2]

When Dr. Heatwole took over the deanship of the school from Dr. Gorgas in 1911, he was surprised to find unpaid notes totaling "several thousand dollars, which had been signed by men who had graduated eight and ten years prior to the date of their discovery." Letters sent to the graduates with the delinquent accounts produced the reply that they had a "verbal understanding that the notes were not to be presented for payment." This policy was put into effect by Dr. Gorgas after the ban on scholarships and was a subterfuge to get around the prohibited policy. Unfortunately for the school, the statute of limitations made the notes legally uncollectible. Dr. Heatwole noted that this incident probably explained the "failure of the school to provide expansion facilities during that period."[3]

Dr. Heatwole, upon taking office as dean, discovered that the school had only one microscope, which was housed in the dean's office, where interested students might borrow it. Needless to say this was a rare occurrence. In 1911, Dr. Heatwole purchased a "sufficient number of microscopes" to correct the situation.[4]

During this period, fixed salaries for instructors were non-existent and the pay of professors was "pro-rated on the distribution of money in hand, over and above operating expenses and based on fixed percentages for the variously rated instructors." Therefore, the faculty compensation fluctuated as a "consequence of fat and lean years." A corps of unpaid instructors cluttered the catalogued instructors, who were serving for the prestige it gave them. They frequently failed to show up for duty on the assigned clinic dates. The financial returns for the clinic work during Heatwole's first year as acting dean netted $444 for the entire year, whereas the dental supply bills ran into the thousands. For this reason, Dr. Heatwole recommended a "cost charge for material" for those patients able to pay. This proposal was strenuously opposed by the department of operative dentistry, which based its opposition on the fact that institution had been organized as a "charitable one" from its inception and had been operated as such. They also felt that charging would reduce the clinic patient load to the detriment of the students. Despite the objections, Dr. Heatwole put nominal charges into effect to apply only to those patients who could afford to pay them. Heatwole's plan produced the desired effect on the clinic income[5] and did not deter patients from seeking treatment.[6]

Heatwole's first commencement exercises were held at The Lyric, Baltimore, on June 1, 1911, with 43 candidates receiving their DDS degrees.[7] The thirtieth regular course of instruction began on October 2, 1911, and continued for seven months. In keeping pace with its competition, the college added oral hygiene and dental history to the curriculum. Dental history reportedly gave the student a "knowledge of the co-relation of Dental Science to that of Medicine and also serves as a stimulus to professional loyalty and pride." The college also reported that during the 1910–11 session there were 4,140 teeth extracted; 7,892 fillings inserted; 3,754 crowns made; 6,256 dentures and bridges made; 2,320 denture repairs; and 45 surgical operations on the mouth and jaws.[8]

The thirty-second commencement was held on June 1, 1914, with 75 graduates, including one woman, Eva Carroll Carter of Virginia.[9] The Class of 1915 included two women, Lois Eunice McKeown of North Carolina and Elsie D. Roof-Scimeca of Germany.[10] The Class of 1916 graduated 47 candidates.[11]

World War I: 1917

In response to the declaration of war on Germany and her allies on April 6, 1917, on April 15, the Dental Committee, Medical Board, Council of National Defense, which was appointed to mobilize the entire nation's dental personnel for the war emergency, recommended that dental faculty members should be deferred from the draft, as should dental students until they graduated.[12] However, dental students continued to be drafted until October 1917, when H.R. 4897 passed, which allowed dental students (second, third, or fourth year only) to enlist in the Enlisted Reserve Corps of the Medical Department and continue their college course the same as medical students.[13]

On August 24, 1918, the U. S. Congress created the Students' Army Training Corps to provide control and training to deferred students while they remained on campus.[14] In September 1918, all dental schools designated as "well recognized" by the Surgeon General were allowed to apply for the establishment of a Students' Army Training Corps (SATC) unit for their school. Students between 18 and 21 years old were eligible to enroll until the school's prescribed quota was full. The students' tuition would be paid by the government and they would be furnished uniforms, quarters, rifles, cots, and blankets and were paid $30 a month. The students would receive at least six hours of military drill a week and would be examined in military and professional subjects every three months.[15] Similarly, the U.S. Navy also offered students an enrollment in the Naval Reserve Force and a chance to continue their education without call to active duty before graduation. In January 1918, 21 students participated in this plan.[16] Barracks soon appeared a few blocks from the campus and by the fall of 1918 "almost every student wore a uniform and marched to class."[17]

World War I BCDS Graduation

In June 1917, the University of Maryland organized Base Hospital No. 42. It was mobilized on April 1, 1918, at Camp Meade, Md., where it was trained and equipped. On June 20, 1918, the organization entrained for Camp Mills, N.Y. On June 28, it left Hoboken, N. J., on the U.S.S. *Metagama* for Liverpool, England. After arriving in Liverpool on July 10, it was entrained for Southampton, and then transported to Cherbourg, France. On July 15, 1918, it moved up to the advance section at Bazoilles-sur-Meuse, where it became part of a large hospital center designated as a special hospital for maxillofacial cases. Originally, it was a 1,000 bed hospital, but soon was increased to 2,000 beds.[18]

Two members of the Dental Reserve Corps were on the hospital staff, First Lieutenants George Edward P. Truitt and Charles Edward Waters, who joined the unit on April 2, 1918.[19] Truitt was a 1907 graduate and Waters was a 1910 graduate of the Dental Department, University of Maryland.[20] From the period July 19, 1918, to January 8, 1919, the hospital treated 2,593 surgical and 4,550 medical cases. The hospital was relieved on January 8, 1919, and on April 8, 1919, sailed from St. Nazaire on the U.S.S. *Santa Paula*, arriving in New York April 20, 1919. The hospital was demobilized on May 2, 1919, at Camp Meade, Md.[21]

The Four-Year Course: 1917

Oddly enough, despite the war, for the thirty-sixth annual session beginning on October 1, 1917, there was a major change in the curriculum. The National Association of Dental Faculties, of which the college was a member, now ruled that a candidate for graduation needed to attend four sessions of 32-week instruction, exclusive of holidays, in separate years. The freshman year comprised 1,136 hours; the sophomore 1,186 hours; the junior 1,124 hours; and the senior year 1,092 hours. The last year had to be taken in the student's graduating (degree-granting) institution. Also, the candidate had to be 21 years old and of good moral character.[22]

In addition, a new course, medical English, was added to the curriculum. The course included a study of Latin and Greek word roots, prefixes and suffixes, the "science of word building and derivation." The course was taught by Geoffrey C. Buehrer, AM.[23] Interestingly, there was still no mention in the school's catalogs of a course in radiology. One student described the current clinical facilities:

> We had a cable foot engine to do all our work and prepare cavities. In many instances the cuspidor was a brass one that clipped on the left-hand of the chair; there was no running water. The students would chain their foot engine to the foot rest of a dental chair during the night so that it wouldn't be stolen or taken out by some thief. Our operating light was more or less a gooseneck arrangement to supplement the so-called ceiling light. The x-ray which had been invented several years before our class entered dental school, had not come in general use, . . . We weren't aware at the time of the dangers of the x-ray. The open wire, which connected the arm of the x-ray machine with the so-called head or tube and carried the electricity was fully exposed. If you stood too close to the exposed wire as you were snapping the picture, you could feel the electricity raising the hair on your head. For the molar region in taking an x-ray picture your exposure time could be from three to four seconds.[24]

During the June 1917 commencement exercises, degrees were conferred on 46 candidates, including one from Brazil, Russia, Cuba, and two from Puerto Rico. In 1918, the college graduated 82 candidates, including four women, Ella B. Cox, Norma R. Mitchell, Carmen A. Mora, and Brownie L. Lewis, by far the largest class of women in the history of the

Baltimore schools. In 1919, there was a very large class of 89 graduates. In 1920, there were only 12 receiving the DDS degree; however in 1921 the total was 32. By contrast, the Baltimore College of Dental Surgery graduated 54.[25] It would seem the older college was holding its own against the newcomer.

Prelude to Dental Merger: 1917

Whereas its building had been adequate in 1900, in 1917, with the course lengthened from three to four years, with "additional subjects added to the curriculum, and with the Dental Educational Council's insistence that dental students have adequate laboratory facilities, the Baltimore College of Dental Surgery, like other proprietary dental schools, was unable to meet the demands imposed on it." It had lost its use of the College of Physicians and Surgeons' anatomy laboratory for its students when that institution merged with the University of Maryland in 1916. Deprived of this arrangement that it had used since 1882, it had to provide a substitute facility. Then too, new concepts of the "medico-dental relationship" were being formulated and dentistry realized that it needed to change its teaching methods to compete with medicine. Dental schools that were not associated with medical schools were at a disadvantage, and could see their coming demise.[26]

Dr. Heatwole also noted that although proprietary schools were a business, they were not always run as such. In 1912, Dr. Heatwole had expressed his opinion on a remedy for the current situation:

> I shall speak now of conditions in Baltimore, Maryland. There are three dental schools in this city, with an aggregate enrollment of over four hundred pupils. The original dental school of the world, the Baltimore College of Dental Surgery, established in 1839, the Dental Department of the University of Maryland, established in 1882, and the Dental Department of the Baltimore Medical College, established within recent years. None of these schools receive State aid, but are wholly dependent upon the tuition of students for maintenance. All are members in good standing in the National Association of Dental Faculties.
>
> The advance of dental science has recently been so rapid as to demand a broadened curriculum, calling for an additional teaching force, thus making it more and more difficult to meet the situation fully. In addition to this, entrance requirements have gradually been raised and this has served to cut down the number of students somewhat. The logical outcome appears to me to be amalgamation of the three schools, making one high grade institution. There are enough men of capacity and energy connected with the several faculties to do this.
>
> I have in mind a reorganization of the local forces through amalgamation, looking to the establishment of a dental school that shall rank with the best in the world and serve to keep the eyes of the nation fixed on Baltimore as the fountainhead of dentistry.[27]

Although the amalgamation he advocated did not occur, the merger of the Dental Department of the Baltimore Medical College with the University of Maryland Dental School in 1913 was the first of the changes that did take place. The Baltimore Medical College simply surrendered to the pressures, closed its doors, and transferred the students to whom it was obligated to the University of Maryland.[28]

In the summer of 1916, Dr. Heatwole was invited to a meeting in Dr. William B. Finney's office with Dr. William G. Foster, the dean of the Baltimore College of Dental Surgery. The purpose of the meeting was to discuss the "possibility of consolidating the two schools." Finney and Foster desired that the preliminary negotiations be kept confidential until a reasonably acceptable plan had been formalized and submitted to both faculties. After much debate it was decided that the best solution to the problem seemed to be the outright purchase of the Baltimore College of Dental Surgery by the University of Maryland. An inventory of the Baltimore College of Dental Surgery's property, including the equipment, library, and museum was prepared, and after some discussion agreed on a sum of $6,000. The faculties were then approached for ratification of the agreement. The University of Maryland faculty accepted the proposal, but the Baltimore College of Dental Surgery bulked on signing the deal. The Baltimore faculty felt that the amount offered was not adequate for all the chattels offered to the University. The entry of the United States into World War I in 1917 forestalled further negotiations and the matter was temporarily abandoned.[29]

Meanwhile, the University of Maryland had been given a "B" classification by the National Association of Dental Faculties. Dean Heatwole, at the faculty meeting on September 6, 1918, summarized the requirements necessary to place Maryland with the Class "A" schools and said that every effort was being made to achieve this goal.[30]

Again, in September 1918, negotiations were resumed for the University of Maryland to absorb the Baltimore College of Dental Surgery. Dean Heatwole sent the following letter to Dr. William G. Foster, Dean, Baltimore College of Dental Surgery:

> I am taking occasion to give notice that, at a Faculty meeting of the Dental Department of the University of Maryland, held on September 6th, 1918, the proposition made by representatives of the Baltimore College of Dental Surgery was accepted and ratified.
>
> The tentative agreement contemplated the transfer of charter of the Baltimore College of Dental Surgery, good will, classes and equipment, as per attached itemized statement, to the Dental Department of the University of Maryland for the sum of $8210.00.
>
> The tentative agreement further stipulated that the University of Maryland Dental Department was to take a lease on the College building of the present Baltimore College of Dental Surgery for three years, with the privilege of five years, at a yearly rental of $3,000.00, the lease to contain a clause to the effect that same to be binding for one year only in case the Federal Government should interfere with the operation of dental schools.[31]

However, the two schools continued to dicker over the terms of the merger and the Baltimore College of Dental Surgery "rescinded action to dispose of their interests to the University of Maryland."[32] During the war, the Dental Educational Council, of necessity, eased its pressure on many of the proprietary dental colleges; however, in 1920 the strict policies were once again enforced. Once again, the consolidation of the two schools became a matter for discussion.[33]

Merger with Maryland State College: 1920

In 1920,[34] the University of Maryland, including the Dental Department, merged with the Maryland State College at College Park, Md., to become truly, the University of Maryland. Hitherto, the Dental Department, University of Maryland, was a proprietary school since its organization in 1882, as was the privately owned Baltimore College of Dental Surgery. Actually, a merger with Johns Hopkins University in Baltimore had been under negotiations shortly before the merger with the Maryland State College at College Park. However, adjustments relative to the entrance requirements for medical students caused a delay in the negotiations, and the University of Maryland approached the Maryland State College. Proprietary schools, run for profit, always had a tendency to withhold as much as possible from the students' fees and the clinic receipts. They avoided spending money on new equipment, and in fact, only spent enough to meet the minimum requirements set by the dental education organizations. As the requirements set by the National Association of Dental Faculties became more and more rigid, both the Baltimore College of Dental Surgery and the Dental Department, University of Maryland, found it difficult to keep up enrollments.[35]

In 1920, the Dental Department, University of Maryland, raised its tuition from $150 to $175 a session. The passing grade for the college was 75 percent, and a grade ranging between 60 and 75 percent was regarded as conditional. A grade lower than 60 percent was classified as a failure.[36]

The Gies Inspection: 1921

On December 14–15, 1921, the Dental Department, University of Maryland, underwent an inspection by Dr. William J. Gies representing the Carnegie Foundation Institute. The inspection was authorized by the Dental Educational Council of America. All faculty members were made available for the inspection and instructed to "do their part in giving the best possible impression."[37]

In 1922, the college again raised its tuition from $175 to $200 a session. The diploma fee was now $30, the dissecting fee $15, and the laboratory fee $5.[38] The college graduated 29 in 1922 and 45 in 1923, including one woman, Charlotte B. Brickner.[39] One 1923 graduate, Harry B. McCarthy of Highgate, Vt., later recalled his experiences when he first reported to class as a freshman in 1919:

> I reported to Baltimore to Dr. T. O. Heatwole, the Dean of the University of Maryland Dental School, around September 28, 1919. My first year at the University of Maryland passed rather uneventfully. There were 52 boys in the class, most of them from Maryland and the southern states. Many of them were ex-servicemen from World War I. Knowing that I would have to be careful with my finances and conserve all available funds, I secured a job working part-time with the American Railway Express Company in the evenings, loading and unloading freight. I worked three nights a week at this job from six until midnight, for which they paid us $.46 an hour. However, that wasn't too bad, as the first year it only cost me $1.50 a week for a room and $4.50 a week for board.[40]

Merger of the Baltimore College of Dental Surgery and the Dental Department of the University of Maryland: 1923

The chairman of the Board of Regents of the new state controlled University of Maryland, Samuel M. Shoemaker, was a close personal friend of Dr. George Edward Hardy, an 1888 alumnus of the Baltimore College of Dental Surgery and a faculty member (professor of physiology) of his alma mater. After many discussions, these two men decided that negotiations for the merger of the two colleges should be renewed. After contacting Dr. Heatwole, Hardy formed a committee from the Baltimore College of Dental Surgery to meet with a similar committee from the University of Maryland. After several committee meetings the University of Maryland raised its offer to $10,000. The Baltimore faculty asked for $30,000; however, after prolonged discussion the two rival schools finally agreed on the figure $12,000 for the purchase. The agreement was ratified to take effect on June 15, 1923.[41] The 1923 graduates numbered 45, including one woman, Charlotte B. Brickner.[42]

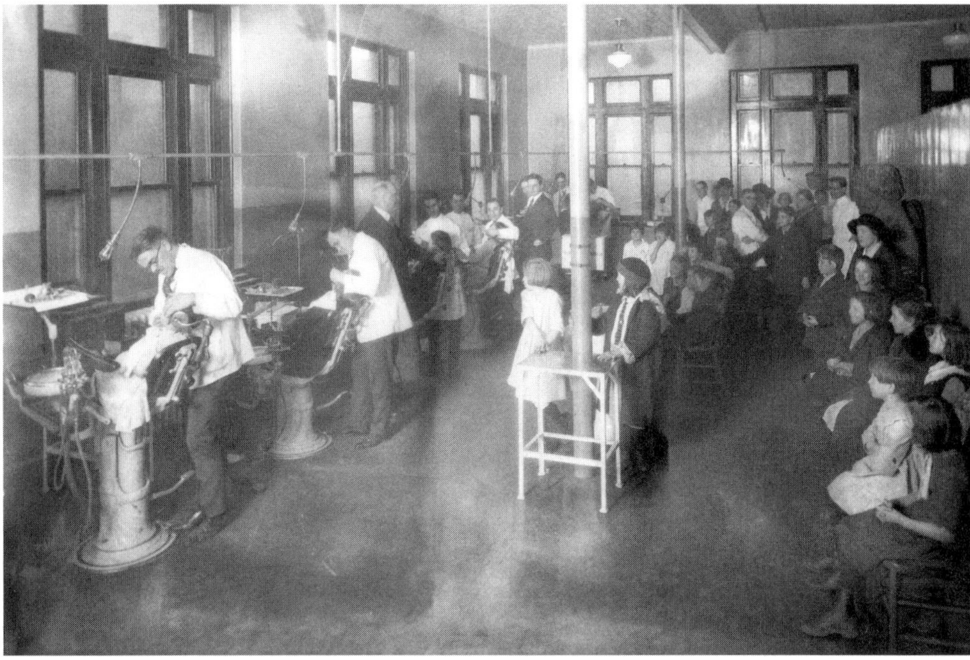

Patients being treated in the clinic.

Because the University of Maryland building on Greene Street at Cider Alley could not accommodate the large number of Baltimore College of Dental Surgery students, a lease was taken out on the old Baltimore College of Dental Surgery building at 851 N. Howard Street to enable students to complete their education "without swelling the already crowded facilities" at the University of Maryland's Dental Department. To coordinate and administer the policies for the two schools, Dr. Heatwole placed his secretary, Miss Katherine Toomey,[43] in charge of the dean's office at the Baltimore College of Dental Surgery, and Dr. Grayson W. Gaver, a 1922 alumnus of the University of Maryland and a faculty member of his alma mater, in charge of the clinics. There was of necessity some overlapping of lecture and laboratory courses during this period of adjustment, and some lectures were held jointly in either building. All new students were enrolled at the University of Maryland.[44]

It was obvious that some form of dental educational reorganization had to take place in Maryland, as the situation in 1915–23 was deplorable in the two schools. Had it not been for the sentiment attached to the Baltimore College of Dental Surgery as the "founder and forerunner of all formal dental education in the world," it would have been given a "Class C" rating. However, the men who owned and operated the Baltimore College of Dental Surgery all those years must be given credit for their unselfishness and honesty in relinquishing control of their school so that it could be "reestablished on an honorable and acceptable basis." They made the ultimate sacrifice in giving up their school to an "institution that had been born out of dissention within the ranks of their school's own Faculty in 1882, and that had remained its rival and chief competitor ever since."[45]

The merger of the two schools had far-reaching effects on dental education in Maryland. Undoubtedly, the most important was that it closed the ranks within the profession now that it had only one dental school to support. The three alumni organizations could now unite and combine their efforts to improve dental education in the state. Then too, the competitive efforts to recruit students could now be channeled into raising the educational standards, which had slipped in recent years. All in all, the school now had the full support of the dental profession in Maryland, affiliation with an "outstanding medical school," and "membership in the family of a great state university."[46]

The name selected for the new dental school was "The Baltimore College of Dental Surgery, Dental School, University of Maryland." This title was officially adopted by an act of the Maryland Legislature on April 9, 1924. The Act declared: "It is believed to be in the interest of higher education in the State of Maryland that a consolidation and a merger of the Baltimore College of Dental Surgery and the University of Maryland shall be effected. . . ." And further, ". . . that the name of the Baltimore College of Dental Surgery shall be known as a definite department of the University of Maryland in all ways and manner as may be possible after the consolidation."[47] It was thought best by the men consummating the merger that the name of the first dental college in the world deserved to be preserved in the name of the new dental school.[48]

NOTES

1. Chapin A. Harris, "Observations on the qualifications necessary to a Practitioner of Dental Surgery—and on the manner in which they should be obtained," *American Journal of Dental Science* 1, no. 3 (1839): 49.
2. Eugene F. Cordell, *University of Maryland 1897–1907: Its History, Influence, Equipment and Characteristics with Biographical Sketches and Portraits of its Founders, Benefactors, Regents, Faculty and Alumni*, vol. 2 (New York: Lewis Publishing Co., 1907), p. 446; Gardner P. H. Foley, ed., *Proceedings of the 125th Anniversary Celebration of the Baltimore College of Dental Surgery* (Baltimore: Horn-Shafer Co., 1966), p. 175; "Dinner in Honor of Dr. Timothy O. Heatwole," *The Bulletin the National Alumni Association of the Baltimore College of Dental Surgery* 2 (April 1927): 7; Baltimore College of Dental Surgery Alumni Card File, Baltimore College of Dental Surgery Papers, National Museum of Dentistry Archives (*hereafter* cited as NMDA).
3. Timothy O. Heatwole, "Timothy O. Heatwole Memoirs," June 13, 1940, Gardner P. H. Foley Papers, National Museum of Dentistry Archives (*hereafter* cited as GPHFP), pp. 9–10.
4. Ibid., pp. 12, 13.
5. During Heatwole's last year as dean (1923–24), the budgeted expected income from clinical revenue was $40,000. [Ibid., p. 14.]
6. Ibid., pp. 13–14.
7. "University of Maryland, Dental Department," *Dental Cosmos* 53 (August 1911): 970.
8. Dental Department of the University of Maryland, *Thirtieth Annual Announcement and Catalogue of the Dental Department of the University of Maryland, Session 1911–12* (Baltimore: n.p., [1911]), pp. 7, 11, 19.
9. "University of Maryland, Dental Department," *Dental Cosmos* 56 (August 1914): 1012.
10. Dental Department of the University of Maryland, *Thirty-Fourth Annual Announcement and Catalogue of the Dental Department of the University of Maryland, Session 1915–1916* (Baltimore: n.p., [1915]), p. 16.
11. "University of Maryland, Dental Department," *Dental Cosmos* 58 (July 1916): 847.
12. [Edward C. Kirk], "Committee on Dentistry, General Medical Board of Council of National Defense," *Journal of the National Dental Association* 4 (June 1917): 643.
13. [L. p. Bethel], "Congress Gives Dentistry the Same Recognition as Medicine," *Dental Summary* 37 (November 1917): 855.
14. U.S. War Department, *General Orders and Bulletins* [General Orders no. 79, par. 2, August 24, 1918] (Washington, D.C.: U.S. Government Printing Office, 1919), p. 1.
15. [Rodrigues Ottolengui], "The Present Status of Dental Service in the United States Army, and the Effect of War Conditions upon Education," *Dental Items of Interest* 40 (October 1918): 825–26. After the Armistice on November 11, 1918, the S.A.T.C. was demobilized and abruptly began discharging its men on December 1, 1918. Some dental colleges that had already made up their 1919 budgets were upset at the government, which had promised to pay fair compensation for the additional services the colleges were to provide. [(Otto U. King), "Demobilization of the Student Army Training Corps Between December 1 and 21, 1918," *Journal of the National Dental Association* 5 (December 1918): 1288.]

16. Baltimore College of Dental Surgery, Dental School, University of Maryland, letters, W. C. Braisted, Bureau of Medicine and Surgery, Navy Department, to the Medical and Dental Student enrolled in the Naval Reserve Force, February 14, 1918; T. O. Heatwole, Dean, Dental Department, University of Maryland, to F. L. Pleadwell, Medical Inspector, U.S.N., January 10, 1918, Office of the Dean, Files.
17. George H. Callcott, *A History of the University of Maryland* (Baltimore: Maryland Historical Society, 1966), p. 275.
18. Frank W. Weed, ed., *The Medical Department of the United States Army in the World War: Administration American Expeditionary Forces*, vol. 2 (Washington, D.C.: U.S. Government Printing Office, 1927), p. 668.
19. Post Return, Base Hospital No. 42 for the month of April 1918, Entry 2130, Record Group 120 (American Expeditionary Forces), National Archives and Records Administration.
20. Dental Department of the University of Maryland, *Thirty-Fourth Annual Announcement and Catalogue*, p. 26.
21. Weed, The *Medical Department of the United States Army in the World War,* p. 668.
22. Dental Department of the University of Maryland, *Thirty-Sixth Annual Announcement and Catalogue of the Dental Department of the University of Maryland.* Session 1917–1918 (Baltimore: n.p., [1917]), pp. 5, 6, 8.
23. Ibid., p. 12–13.
24. Harry B. McCarthy, "Former Director of Clinics Remembers Peers," *Journal of the Maryland State Dental Association* 26 (August 1983): 65.
25. "University of Maryland, Dental Department, *Dental Cosmos* 59 (October 1917): 1053; 60 (September 1918): 848; 61 (August 1919): 797; 62 (September 1920): 1153; 63 (July 1921): 756.
26. Harry B. McCarthy, "A History of Dental Education in Maryland," master's thesis, Graduate School, University of Maryland, 1948, pp. 101–2.
27. Ibid., pp. 103–4.
28. Ibid., p. 104.
29. Ibid., pp. 104–5.
30. University of Maryland, Dental Department, "Minutes of Faculty Meetings, May 11, 1911, to June 22, 1922, incl.," September 6, 1918, Special Collections, University of Maryland, Health Sciences and Human Services Library (*hereafter* cited as HSL).
31. Ibid.
32. Ibid.
33. McCarthy, "History of Dental Education," p. 105.
34. On April 9, 1920, the General Assembly of Maryland chartered the modern University of Maryland by "combining under a single administrative authority the old University of Maryland located at Baltimore, which consisted of the School of Medicine (1807), the School of Law (1813), the Pharmacy Department (1841), and the Dental Department (1882), with the Maryland Agricultural College (1856) located at College Park." [J. Ben Robinson, "The Baltimore College of Dental Surgery and the Baltimore College of Dental Surgery, Dental School, University of Maryland," *Journal of the Maryland State Dental Association* 18 (August 1975): 98.]
35. McCarthy, "History of Dental Education," pp. 99–101.
36. Dental Department of the University of Maryland, *Thirty-Ninth Annual Announcement and Catalogue, School of Dentistry, University of Maryland, Session of 1920–1921* (Baltimore: n.p., [1920]), pp. 6, 7.
37. University of Maryland, Dental Department, "Minutes of Faculty Meetings," November 30, 1921, Special Collections, HSL The author was unable to locate any reference to the results of this inspection in the school's archives [the author].
38. University of Maryland, *Catalogue 1922–1923* (College Park, Md.: n.p., [1922]), p. 128.
39. "University of Maryland, School of Dentistry," *Dental Cosmos* 64 (July 1922): 802.
40. Harry B. McCarthy, *Harry B. McCarthy, DDS, M.A.: an autobiography* (n.p., [1985]), p. 11.
41. Heatwole, "Timothy O. Heatwole Memoirs," GPHFP, NMDA; McCarthy, "History of Dental Education," pp. 105–6.
42. "University of Maryland, School of Dentistry," *Dental Cosmos* 65 (August 1923): 896.
43. Katherine Toomey served the dental school as an administrative assistant from 1917 to 1961, a period of 44 years. In 1942 and 1957, she was honored by the students, faculty, and alumni. In 1958, she was awarded an honorary doctor of laws degree by Mount St. Mary's College, Emmitsburg, Md. On April 1, 1961, she retired after serving three deans, Drs. Heatwole, Robinson, and Aisenberg. Several thousand dental students knew Miss Toomey as a "gracious, energetic, intelligent, and helpful friend." She also served as secretary of the Dean's Council, secretary-treasurer of the Faculty Assembly, and as a member of several faculty committees. ["Farewell to Miss Toomey," *Journal of the Baltimore College of Dental Surgery, Dental School, University of Maryland* 20 (May 1961): 3; "Miss Toomey Honored by Mount Saint Mary's College," *Journal of the Baltimore College of Dental Surgery, Dental School, University of Maryland* 17 (May 1958): 53.]
44. McCarthy, "History of Dental Education," pp. 106–7.
45. Ibid., pp. 107–8.
46. Ibid., pp. 108–9.
47. Robinson, "The Baltimore College of Dental Surgery," 99.
48. McCarthy, "History of Dental Education," p. 107.

J. Ben Robinson

Chapter 14

The Heatwole-Robinson Era: 1923–40

"I have no hesitation in asserting, and defy successful contradiction, that the theoretical knowledge necessary to qualify a practicing dentist for the duties he is called upon to perform is comparatively easily acquired. While on the other hand the skill necessary to operate serviceably in cases, which will present themselves almost every day in practice, can be acquired only by years of hard, careful, thoughtful, laborious effort."[1] **~Robert Arthur, 1860**

Timothy O. Heatwole: 1923–24

The reign of Timothy O. Heatwole as dean of the new Baltimore College of Dental Surgery, Dental School, University of Maryland, lasted only one year, from 1923 to 24. After retiring as dean in 1924, he served as secretary of the Baltimore Division of the University until 1937.[2] In the meantime, the search for a new dean continued. The deanship was turned down by several dental deans.

The question can be raised why Dr. Heatwole resigned after only one year at the helm; after all, he had been dean of the university's dental department since 1911. Antagonism between the two alumni organizations and the two faculties apparently was at the center of an ongoing controversy. The origins of this scenario began at an October 8, 1923, monthly meeting of the Maryland State Dental Association. Apparently, the Heatwole administration was coming under some criticism from the state's dentists for the failure of Maryland graduates to pass the Maryland State Board of Dental Examiners. On October 11, 1923, Heatwole sent a form letter defending the issue as to "whether or not the School had retrogressed or made advancement within recent years." Heatwole also provided the failure percentages for Maryland graduates for the past five years from 1918 to 1923. In 1918 there were 17.6 percent; in 1919, 26.4 percent; in 1920, 27.3 percent; in 1921, 14.3 percent; in 1922, 8.3 percent; and in 1923, not yet reported. Heatwole said that he hoped that "some credit may be given to those who have labored diligently to carry on the work of the School during the latter sessions, which show a gradual gain in ratings."[3]

Heatwole's chief protagonist on this issue of the school's national rating was apparently J. Ben Robinson. On October 19, 1923, Dr. Robinson wrote to Dr. Heatwole that he was not in sympathy with "destructive criticism which does not have as its final aim better conditions and better opportunities for the young man seeking dental training;" however, he wanted to know the reasons for the improved showing on dental boards. Was it "changes in teaching personnel, better facilities or improvements in general?" After all, the main objective was to advance to a class A rating. To Robinson, the future looked "pretty dark."[4] Dr. Heatwole replied to Robinson on October 24 that his letter had a "tone of finality in it which is characteristic of the writer as he is known to us." Heatwole called Robinson a "destructionist," and said that Robinson and his confreres were "credited with honesty of purpose and a real and genuine interest in the up building of the school of which you are alumni, but by the intensity of your desires have been led into doubtful paths of endeavor which may easily prove hurtful rather than helpful, a something we must believe is not intended."[5] Dr. Robinson's reply two days later was curt and decisive. He stated that he resented Heatwole's "remonstrances and apparent effort to deprecate my knowledge of school conditions, judgments of matters with which I am familiar, and reflections on my treatment of matters of importance." Robinson said that he was not a "destructionist," but if "curing ills is a destructive measure," then he pleaded guilty and accepted the consequences. He had no intention of interfering with the school's affairs or "meddling in matters not my concern."[6] Such was the state of affairs between the two men. Did Robinson and his colleagues intentionally undercut Heatwole and cause him to lose the deanship?

J. Ben Robinson: 1924

In 1924, a new dean was appointed by the University, Dr. J. Ben Robinson of Clarksburg, W. Va., the son of a Confederate veteran. Robinson took the job under certain conditions: (1) an assurance that "continuing annual State appropriations would be made to the Dental School budget in amounts that would be required to maintain a quality dental education program; and (2) a promise that the construction of a suitable dental school building be given *first priority* in a building program then in the planning stage for the Baltimore campus."[7] According to Dr. McCauley, Heatwole and the administration wanted to put the money into a new hospital, but Robinson threatened to resign unless he got the new dental building.[8]

J. Ben Robinson was born on April 16, 1883, at Craigmoor in Harrison County, W. Va., and had five brothers and seven sisters, all but one of whom became teachers. After teaching in the rural elementary schools of Harrison County from 1902 to 1905, he entered Marshall College and received his teaching certificate in 1908. From 1908 to 1911, he served as a high school mathematics teacher and athletic coach at New Martinsville, W. Va., and during the summer months of 1909 and 1910 attended West Virginia University. During this period, he met a dentist who so impressed him that he decided on a career in dentistry. Robinson entered the Dental Department, University of Maryland, in 1912[9] and graduated in 1914 *magna cum laude.* In his senior year, Robinson won the gold medal for the highest grade at the final examinations. After graduation, he served on the faculty of his alma mater as a demonstrator of operative dentistry from 1915 to 1917; professor of clinical dentistry, 1917 to 1919; professor of operative dentistry, 1919 to 1922. He served as professor of dental anatomy and operative technic, Baltimore College of Dental Surgery, Dental School, University of Maryland, 1924–1931; and professor of dental history and dental ethics, 1931–1953. He was a member of the Maryland Board of Dental Examiners from 1922 to 24. Dr. Robinson was president of the Maryland State Dental Association in 1921–22; the American Association of Dental Schools, 1932–33; American College of Dentists, 1934–35; American Dental Association, 1942–43; and American Academy of the History of Dentistry, 1951–52 (first). He was a member of the American Dental Association's Council on Dental Education, 1938–51; Dental Advisor to the Surgeon General's Library, 1944; consulting editor, "History of World War II: The Medical Department"; and consultant to the U. S. Public Health Service for a study of dental education in the United States. Dr. Robinson received honorary Doctor of Science degrees from Temple University, 1943; Marshall College, 1952; and the University of Maryland, 1975. During World War II, he served as chairman of the advisory committee on dental education to the War Manpower Commission, and as a member of the advisory committee on dentistry to the National Selective Service. Quoting Professor Foley's (1966) remarks about Dr. Robinson:

> Dr. Robinson's enthusiastic support of measures for the achievement and maintenance of high standards in dental education; his ardent interest in dental history; his ability to speak and write effectively on the important questions related to dentistry; his forceful and highly capable leadership on all levels of dental organization; his noteworthy fulfillment of the professional man's obligations to his community—these qualifications have made Dean Robinson a man whom his fellow alumni and other professional associates proudly hail as an outstanding figure in American dentistry.[10]

Dr. Robinson's career at Maryland lasted almost 30 years (1924–53). The list of his other achievements[11] is most impressive. After his retirement in 1953 (because the mandatory retirement age for the State of Maryland employees was 70 at that time), he was appointed the first dean of a new dental school, the School of Dentistry, West Virginia University. He served there until 1958, when the first class graduated and he was made Dean Emeritus.[12]

On February 6, 1924, Dr. Robinson received the following letter from Dr. Albert F. Woods, President of the University, College Park, Md.:

> Confirming our verbal understanding and by authority of the Board of Regents you are hereby appointed Dean of the School of Dentistry of the University of Maryland, effective February 1st, 1924.
>
> The present Acting Dean, Dr. T. O. Heatwole, will render you all possible assistance in taking over the work and making such reorganizations in it as may be necessary to secure a Class A rating, and as far as funds at our disposal will permit. Dr. Heatwole will explain this to you. You may expect my hearty cooperation and that of the Board of Regents in your endeavor to bring this School up to the highest possible grade. The general committee representing the faculty and the Educational Committee of the Dental Association will also be glad to cooperate to this end.
>
> I realize that you are not able to give full time to this work, but it is the opinion of the committee that the work can be satisfactorily handled at present on a part time basis. The salary available at present is $5,000 per annum. While I know that this will be a sacrifice for you financially, I know that you are intensely interested in the School and that for the present at least you will be willing to accept the appointment on this basis.[13]

Six days later, on February 12, 1924, Dr. Robinson received the following mandate from Dr. Woods:

> I have your letter of the 8th and am pleased to know that you are willing to accept the position as Dean of the School of Dentistry.

> You have full power to go ahead with the reorganization of the dental School and it will be your duty to make such recommendations to the president and the Board of Regents as, in your judgment, are necessary for placing the School upon a firm foundation, for we want the work to confirm to the highest standards of Dental education. We want to come as near reaching these standards as may be possible under the physical and financial limitations which we must work. I understand that your letter of acceptance recognizes these necessary limitations.[14]

At the time, Dr. Robinson was only part-time at the University as he had a private practice at 219 W. Monument Street in Baltimore. In 1928, Dr. Robinson moved his office to the new Medical Arts Building, which had just been completed. He had a suite of offices with four operating rooms on the eighth floor, which he shared with Dr. Harry B. McCarthy, a 1923 graduate of the University of Maryland and part-time faculty member. In 1940, Dr. H. C. "Curley" Byrd, the president of the University of Maryland, persuaded Dr. Robinson to give up his practice and come down to the university full-time.[15]

Grieves Library Foundation: 1925–26

One of the first problems Dr. Robinson encountered as soon as he became dean was to address the plight of the college's library. In 1895, it was apparently shut down and then fell into disuse. Robinson commented on the existing condition of the library collections: "These books were old, unkempt, soiled, covered with dust, some of them having been resurrected from a lot of books piled in a coal bin." In his effort to reorganize the library, Robinson used the time and peculiar ability of a janitor, who "possessed unusual intelligence and incomparable interest in and knowledge of the traditions of the Baltimore College of Dental Surgery, which he had served for 30 years. . . . this janitor arranged the first complete list of books which served as the foundation for the present library, recording both the number of different texts and duplicates which were on hand."[16]

Clarence J. Grieves

In 1925, the Maryland State Dental Association established the Clarence J. Grieves[17] Library Foundation as a memorial to one of its most distinguished members. In 1926, the Grieves Library was merged into the Baltimore College of Dental Surgery Library and was called the Clarence J. Grieves Library. Dr. Robinson added to this collection the books he had salvaged from the old Baltimore College of Dental Surgery and the Dental Department of the University of Maryland. The latter had been housed with the medical collections and consisted mainly of books collected by Dr. Gorgas and Dr. Merrill Hopkins. The library from these three sources amounted to only 697 books and bound periodicals. Endowments from the University of Maryland, the Maryland State Dental Association, and the Carnegie Foundation made it possible to build up the library's collections very rapidly. Robinson was able to add new books and complete the old journal files, and in 1926 added a professionally trained librarian to manage the collections. By 1937, the college had 5,481 volumes in its library and possessed one of the most complete collections[18] of dental journals in the country.[19]

The eighty-fifth annual session began on September 28, 1925. The faculty under Dean Robinson consisted of the following professors: E. Frank Kelly, PharD, chemistry (emeritus); Robert P. Bay, MD, oral surgery; Robert L. Mitchell, PharG, MD, bacteriology and pathology; Alex H. Patterson, DDS, prosthetic dentistry; Burt B. Ide, DDS, operative dentistry; J. Edgar Orrison, DDS, crown and bridge and ceramics; Horace M. Davis, DDS, exodontia, anesthesia, and radiology; Earl W. Swinehart, DDS, orthodontia; Howard J. Maldeis, MD, embryology and histology; Neil E. Gordon, PhD, chemistry; Edward Hoffmeister, AB, DDS, materia medica and therapeutics; Jose A. Davila, DDS, clinical operative dentistry; Oren H. Gaver, DDS, physiology; J. Leroy Wright, MD, anatomy; and G. C. Eichlin, MS, physics. The 1925 graduation included one woman, Providencia Viera of Puerto Rico.[20]

Meanwhile, the National Alumni Association of the College held its reunion dinner at the Penn Athletic Club in Philadelphia on August 24, 1926, with Drs. Harvey J. Burkhart, J. Ben Robinson, Timothy O. Heatwole, and B. Lucien Brun as speakers. The officers were: Frank P. Duffy, president; James H. Samuel, vice-president; B. Lucien Brun, second vice-president; Oren H. Gaver, secretary; George V. Milholland, treasurer.[21]

American Association of Dental Schools: 1925–26

For the 1925-26 session, the college announced that it was a member in good standing of the American Association of Dental Schools and conformed to its rules and regulations. This new group was formed in 1923 by the amalgamation of the Canadian Dental Faculties Association, the American Institute of Dental Teachers, the National Association of Dental Faculties, and the Dental Faculties Association of American Universities into the American Association of Dental Schools. This association was organized:

> To facilitate intercourse and conference among teachers of the dental sciences and arts in North America; to promote advancement of teaching and research in American schools of dentistry; to encourage thorough study and discussion of the needs and problems of dental education; to improve public understanding and appreciation of the quality and value of dentistry; and to maintain dental education in full accord with the highest requirements of professional education in the public service.[22]

The amalgamation of these groups brought into the American Association of Dental Schools all the Class "A" and Class "B" dental schools in the United States and Canada.

> It unified the administrative and teaching forces in dental education in North America; eliminated all causes of reasonable disagreement among the schools except such as are inherent in the real problems of dental education; provided exceptional opportunity for unprejudiced consideration of procedures of administration and methods of teaching; and improved the accord, in the Dental Educational Council of America, between the representatives of the associated schools and of the national organizations of examiners and practitioners[23]

The Gies Report: 1926

In 1920, Dr. William J. Gies, a chemistry professor at Columbia University, began a study of dental education in the United States and Canada under the auspices of the Carnegie Foundation for the Advancement of Teaching. The 1910 Flexner study of medical schools for the Carnegie Foundation did not deal in any way with dental education; for, at that time, "medical and dental education appeared to be far apart, and dentistry, as it was then practiced, appeared to have only slight relations to medicine." The study carried on for five years was "timely and appropriate" and met the needs of the time. Gies in his report (Bulletin No. 19, a volume of 692 pages) seriously questioned the "adequacy of the limited technical approach in dentistry and contended that dentistry should become the equivalent of an oral specialty of medicine."[24]

Gies also thought that the development of dentistry into the category of the equivalent of an oral specialty of medicine would require a "new and more comprehensive definition of dentistry," a corresponding extension of the scope of its services, and a "commensurate improvement" of its educational system. He wanted the correlations between systemic disease and the teeth to be emphasized, and consultation between the patient's physician and dentist to be included in the diagnosis.[25]

In his report, Dr. Gies recommended that the dental course should be based on "two years' preprofessional study" and three years of graduate dental study. This plan became known as the "two-three-graduate" plan and was adopted by five dental schools, including the Baltimore College of Dental Surgery, Dental School, University of Maryland. Although some disagreed with Gies on his three-year curriculum, the majority favored his call for a "new concept of dentistry" and the improvement in dental education. Significant progress was made in the practice of dentistry as a result of the Gies report.[26]

Educational Council of America Five-Year Plan: 1926

The college also announced in 1925 that, beginning with the regular session of 1926-27, it would require for graduation five years of study in addition to the four years of high school work. For the first time, the college included among its listed courses, "radiodontia" and "periodontia."[27] Accordingly, the five-year course began with the session beginning on September 27, 1926. This change in the curriculum was brought about by a ruling of the Dental Educational Council of America, which stated that "preliminary dental training consisting of one year of college work of not less than 30 semester hours shall be required, which shall include courses in Chemistry, English, and Biology." The Baltimore College of Dental Surgery decided to increase its course to five years and include in the first year, academic courses that met the requirements of the Dental Educational Council. All academic work was of university grade and under the direct supervision and control of the Arts and Science Department of the University of Maryland. The first year courses were: English, inorganic chemistry, zoology, mathematics, public speaking (1st semester), technical drawing (2nd semester), and dental anatomy.[28]

Meanwhile, dental courses were being given in three separate buildings; however, a new building was planned to be ready for occupancy for the regular session of 1929–30. The college graduated 91 candidates in 1927, including one woman, Marcolina Fernandez Martinez of Puerto Rico and John Miller Hyson[29] of Hampstead, Md.[30] In 1928, the college graduated

90 candidates at the fifth Regiment Armory, including 14 in September 1928, which included one woman, Francisca Guerra-Alvarez of Puerto Rico.[31]

The Alumni Association: 1928

The Alumni Association held their annual reunion on June 1, 1928. The program began with a presentation by Dr. A. Y. Russell (University of Maryland, Class of 1913) on "Radiographic Interpretation," followed by a technique exhibit by the graduating class. The officers were: Frank O. Duffy, president; William F. Walz, first vice-president; James K. Burgess, second vice-president; Oren H. Gaver, secretary; and George V. Milholland, treasurer.[32]

Organization of Omicron Kappa Upsilon: 1929

The Phi chapter of the Omicron Kappa Upsilon, a national honorary fraternity of dentists founded at Northwestern University Dental School in 1914, was organized at the College in 1929 as the twenty-first chapter. The inducted members were selected from alumni, honorary, and faculty. The alumni members were chosen from each graduating class, the upper 12 percent of the entire class, and who "in addition to scholarship, have demonstrated exemplary traits of character and potential qualities of future professional growth and attainments." Generally, only one honorary member was selected each year, and faculty members were selected on merit.[33]

The New Building at Lombard & Greene: 1929

In 1929, construction on the new building at the northwest corner of Lombard and Greene Streets coincided with Governor Albert C. Ritchie's massive building program for the campus of the University of Maryland both at College Park and Baltimore. He was influenced by his desire to improve the university's ranking and at the same time provide construction jobs to fight the depression. Approximately $258,000 was appropriated for a new building to house the schools of dentistry and pharmacy.[34] The Dental School was to occupy 55 percent of the building and the Pharmacy School the remaining 45 percent.[35]

The brick and limestone structure of Georgian-inspired design was completed for the opening of the 1930 session. It was designed by the firm of Smith and May. The building faced the University Hospital. The building provided 45,000 square feet of floor space, was fireproof, and well-lighted and ventilated. Large lecture rooms and classrooms, a library and reading room, science laboratories, technique laboratories, clinic rooms, locker rooms, etc., were included. The large main clinic wing, designed with a "steel-framed shed roof structure incorporated into the brick walls of the formal side façade," accommodated 136 chairs. Casement windows, "composed of 18/18 lights, and skylights provided north light for the spacious clinic." Clinical space was provided for other specialties, prosthetics, surgery, pathology, orthodontics, periodontics, pedodontics, and radiography. All the dental equipment was new.[36]

From October 4 to 6, the Alumni Association held a three-day meeting to dedicate a marker plaque for the site of the original college building and to dedicate the new building.[37] The new expanded campus and dental building paid off by raising both the enrollment and ranking of the university. In 1930, the college obtained an "A" rating.[38]

Dedication of the new building

BCDS in the 1930s

In 1930, the American Association of Dental Schools appointed a committee to study the dental curriculum. The object was to bring the curriculum up-to-date in terms of the "new knowledge and its implications in the field of dentistry." The project was financed by the Carnegie Corporation.[39]

In 1931, the college catalog stated that to graduate, students needed a general average of 80 percent during the full course of study. In addition, they had to have attended a full five-year course of study, the last year of which had to be at Maryland, and, of course, they had to be 21 years old. The tuition fee was now $250 for state residents and $300 for non-residents. Forty-four students graduated in 1931, the Depression notwithstanding.[40] The 1932 catalog contained an expanded version of the listing of dental history as taught by Dean Robinson. His love of history was well known and one can imagine that he saw to it that history got its proper recognition in the curriculum. The catalog simply stated (probably Robinson's own words):

> The present status of professional knowledge and practice in dentistry is quite complex. From its crude beginning in ancient times down through the ages it has been improved and perfected through various educative processes. An appreciation of its purposes will be greatly influenced by the practitioner's knowledge of its philosophy as revealed through an understanding of its development to its present state of usefulness. A working knowledge of the history of dentistry is a necessary part of the education of the modern

dentist. Lectures in Dental History will discuss the beginning of the art of dental practice among ancient civilization, its advancement in relation to the development of the so called medical sciences in early classical civilizations, its struggle though the middle ages and the final attainment of recognized educational concepts in modern times.[41]

In 1932, the college added a new course to the curriculum, "preventive dentistry." Children's dentistry was considered "one of the most important departments of student instruction." The children's clinic, just down from the dean's office, was separate from the main operative clinic and was equipped with 24 chairs. The catalog stated:

"Diagnosis of children's oral ailments, modifications required in cavity preparation, partial pulpotomys and thorough prophylaxis are during the year demonstrated on young patients. This also affords the opportunity of practicing the management of young patients and gives a psychological approach to problems met with in children's practice."[42]

Sixty-three candidates received their degree in 1932; 89 in 1933, including Amy Hok Wan Kwan of China; and 77 in 1934, including Gertrude Chun Yen Huang of China.[43]

The Ice Hockey Team: 1931–34

Strange as it may sound, from 1931 to 34, the Baltimore College of Dental Surgery, Dental School, University of Maryland, represented the university in the Iceland Hockey League, a semi-pro hockey league—hockey, the sport most associated with dental trauma. The games were played at the Sports Centre at North Avenue and Charles Street in Baltimore. At first Maryland's rivals considered the idea of a hockey team of dental students as somewhat of a joke, but they were quick to learn that the dental school team was composed of seasoned players from New England and Canada who had been pushing hockey pucks virtually all their lives. Some had even played semi-pro hockey.[44]

The Sports Centre rink, approximately 125 by 85 feet, was considered too small for a regular six-man hockey squad, so the teams were cut to five men. The secretary of the Baltimore Amateur Ice Hockey Association commented: "Dr. H. B. McCarthy appeared on the scene with a bunch of fast-skating boys, who could, apparently, play hockey all night and then ask for more."[45] Maryland won its opening game in the 1931–32 season against Johns Hopkins, ten to five.[46]

Captain Fred Cuddy of Providence, R. I., Class of 1935, who had played at Cranston High School and Hebron Academy, became the league's most valuable player. He set the league record for the most assists in a season and was second in goals scored. Taffy Kobrinsky, a classmate, who had played for St. Bonaventure in Winnipeg and the University of Manitoba, was the league's top scorer. Other performers for the Gold and Black included Dick Stevens of Rutland, Vt. (Class of 1935); Ray Gillespie of New Haven, Conn. (Class of 1934); Louis d'Argy of Waterville, Maine (Class of 1936); Joe Scanlon of Pawtucket, R. I. (Class of 1935); Ralph Hodges from Providence, R. I. (Class of 1936); Bill Walsh of St. Johnsbury, Vt. (Class of 1936); and Gus MacKenzie from Prince Edward Island (Class of 1932).[47]

The team was coached by Dr. Harry B. McCarthy,[48] Class of 1923 and assistant professor of dental anatomy and ultimately dean of the Baylor College of Dentistry; by Dr. Joseph D. Fusco, Class of 1926 and instructor in exodontias; and by Dr. Walter L. Oggeson, assistant professor of crown and bridge. In its first season, Maryland won contests against Mount

Ice hockey team

Washington, Walbrook, Forest Park, Green Spring Valley, Johns Hopkins, and the All Stars. At season's end, Maryland and Walbrook were tied for the lead and a five-game playoff was decided upon. Maryland lost—three games to two. Nevertheless, in April, the team was honored at a testimonial dinner at the Southern Hotel. Dr. J. Ben Robinson, the dental dean, presented each player with an inscribed medal and lauded them for their "skillful playing" and "good conduct" while participating in the "several conflicts" of the past season. Dr. H. C. "Curley" Byrd, the University of Maryland football coach, was one of the guest speakers.[49]

In its second season (1932–33), after a slow start, the Dental School team gained momentum and finally won the Baltimore Amateur Hockey Championship. Green Spring Valley was defeated in two straight games for the title. Cuddy was the league's high scorer and again the most valuable player. As a postscript, the Maryland team defeated the Jamaica Hockey Club, Junior Amateur Champions of New York, by a score of three to two at Iceland.[50] During the 1933–34 season, Maryland's last, the dental students finished second to the Baltimore Athletic Club. However, Pud Quirk, a Maryland draftee from Rhode Island scholastic circles, was voted the league's most valuable player. In its three-year existence, this noteworthy ice hockey team contributed significantly to the spirit and pride of the Dental School and the University of Maryland. But, the era was over; an inability to maintain player strength, as key players of the team graduated or transferred elsewhere, resulted in disbandment. Nevermore would the Baltimore College of Dental Surgery field a team in contact sports. Presumably, the hockey players had few problems finding crown and bridgework patients.[51]

Robinson Acquires Harris Artifacts: 1933

In 1933, Dr. Robinson arranged for the donation of some of Chapin A. Harris' personal artifacts from Mrs. Mary Barrett-Lennard, Harris' daughter, in England. The items included the French black-marble clock from his library, a cup and saucer, two china vases, a silver tray from a nephew inscribed to "Uncle Chapin," a small, round, gilt mirror, a group of family photographs, a mahogany music rest, a piece of a rosewood cabinet, a small bust of George Washington, a rosewood cabinet from his office, and the secretary upon which he wrote many of his works.[52] This grouping complemented the museum's already fine collection of historic artifacts.

For the New York Dental Centennial in 1934, the museum loaned Horace Hayden's 1810 Maryland dental license, Robert Arthur's 1841 diploma, a model of the original college building (made by Thomas Worthington), and a set of dentures made by Robert Woofendale in about 1767 in England.[53]

The Four-Year Plan: 1935

In 1934, the Curriculum Survey Committee of the American Association of Dental Schools recommended that beginning in 1937, two years of liberal arts and sciences education be a requirement for admission to dental school and the dental curriculum be extended to four years.[54] In accord with these new guidelines, in 1935 the college announced that it was dropping the five-year plan in favor of a four-year curriculum. Graduation from an accredited high school or preparatory school, and completion of prescribed courses in predental collegiate training would now be required before admission to the college for the 1936–37 session. Dental education was advancing from a one-year predental collegiate requirement to a two-year predental collegiate requirement. Sixty semester hours of academic work "earned in an accredited college or university" was now required. The credits had to include eight hours of inorganic chemistry, eight hours of zoology, six hours of English and physics, either secondary or collegiate, equivalent to one secondary school unit or six hours of college mathematics.[55]

Drs. J. Ben Robinson, the dean; Alexander H. Paterson, professor of crown & bridge and prosthetics; and Leo A. Walzak, professor of periodontics, served as reviewers for the Curriculum Survey Committee. Interestingly, the report stated that only approximately one-half of the dental schools surveyed in the United States and Canada offered a course in dental history. Whereas some schools gave an "adequate presentation" of the subject, others were "obviously very limited." Although dental history was not essential in the same sense as other courses, it was beneficial, in that it gave the dental student a "historical perspective of his profession."[56]

The University of Maryland offered a two-year predental course in which the students would take the following subjects in the freshman year: composition and rhetoric, algebra, trigonometry, inorganic chemistry, general zoology, vertebrate zoology, reading and speaking, and technical drawing; in the sophomore year: organic chemistry, general physics, modern language (French or German), economics, and psychology or sociology. This course was offered at the Baltimore campus of the university.[57]

Among the 1936 graduates was Carlotta Augusta Hawley of the District of Columbia, the daughter of the famous orthodontist.[58] In 1938, the college raised its tuition from $250 to $275 for residents and from $350 to 375 for non-residents. There were 66 graduates that year.[59]

ADA Council on Dental Education: 1939

In 1939, the American Dental Association Council on Dental Education adopted the following guidelines on the dental curriculum:

> The content of the curriculum should be selected on the consideration of how its mastery will assist the student in the attainment of well determined aims and purposes.
>
> Organization of the curriculum should be flexible, based on appreciation of dentistry as a growing and expanding science. The curriculum should afford opportunities for adjustments to advances in knowledge and for constant investigation and research relative to its value in the educational program.
>
> The amount of time assigned to the several subjects of the dental course should be determined by their respective contributions to the aims of dental education, to the effectiveness of instruction, and to the time required by students for independent study.
>
> The dental curriculum should be conceived of as a unit and in terms of the interdependence of its related parts. Correlation of the various courses is essential to an effective educational program, as well as to satisfactory student achievement.[60]

The council also felt that the curriculum of a dental institution should be "in keeping with its stated objectives and the educational qualifications of students admitted." An institution's curriculum would be evaluated in terms of its contribution to the main mission, to teach dental students. The new knowledge in prevention and treatment had to be balanced against the aims of dental education and the public needs. A curriculum of no less than 3,800 hours and no more than 4,400 hours was recommended.[61] In 1939–40, the total lecture and laboratory hours for the four years at Maryland was 4,368 hours.[62]

Women Graduates: 1939

In 1939, the college graduated two women, Naomi Ada Dunn of Connecticut and Verda Elizabeth James of Delaware.[63] Dr. James was to become its most "outstanding woman graduate." Verda Elizabeth James received a Carnegie Fellowship for graduate work at the University of Louisville, College of Dentistry, for 1939–41. From 1941 to 1942, she served as a public health dentist for the state of Maryland. In 1942–43, she was an instructor in histology and pedodontics at her alma mater. In 1944–45, she practiced in Hagerstown, Md. In 1948, she joined the faculty of the University of Illinois, College of Dentistry, becoming an instructor of histology from 1949 to 1952. From 1952 to 1957, she served as an assistant professor; associate professor (1957–61); associate head of department (1961–62); director of paradental education (1962–83); professor of histology (1963–65); and professor and acting head of the histology department (1965). Dr. James published many papers in the dental literature. In 1960, she was the president of Chicago section of the International Academy of Dental Research.[64]

Operative Dentistry: 1940

Dean Robinson made some changes with respect to the administration of the teaching of operative dentistry in the school in 1940. From 1917 to 1930, the authority for the administering the work of the clinics was managed by a professor of clinical operative dentistry.

Upon the resignation of Dr. Jose A. Davila, professor of clinical operative dentistry, in 1931 the position was not filled until the beginning of the regular 1940–41 session, at which time Dr. Harry B. McCarthy was elected professor of clinical operative dentistry by the faculty and confirmed by the university president. McCarthy was responsible for administering all the affairs of the infirmary floor, including faculty and "proper conduct of the clinic both as to teaching and to general discipline." Dr. Burt B. Ide, professor of operative dentistry, remained in charge of lectures to both junior and senior classes, and Dean Robinson was professor of dental anatomy and operative techniques. The policies of administering the operative department would be decided by a committee of three composed of Drs. Ide, McCarthy and Robinson.[65]

Status of School: 1940

In 1940, the Baltimore College of Dental Surgery, Dental School, University of Maryland ranked third among the nation's dental schools in enrollment. Its enrollment total of 311 total students was exceeded only by the University of Southern California, with 339 and Atlanta-Southern Dental College, with 319 total students. The breakdown at Maryland was 86 freshmen, 85 sophomores, 64 juniors, and 76 seniors. Indeed, the world's first dental school was doing very well in recruiting students.[66]

NOTES

1. R[obert] Arthur, "Practical Dentistry," American Journal of Dental Science, n.s., 10 (April 1860): 178.
2. Gardner P. H. Foley, ed., *Proceedings of the 125th Anniversary Celebration of the Baltimore College of Dental Surgery* (Baltimore: Horn-Shafer Co., 1966), p. 175. Dr. Heatwole died on April 28, 1949. ["In Memory of Dr. Timothy O. Heatwole (1865–1949)," *Alma Mater* 2 (February 1960): 43.]
3. Letter, Timothy O. Heatwole, Acting Dean., School of Dentistry, University of Maryland, October 11, 1923, Baltimore College of Dental Surgery Papers, National Museum of Dentistry Archives (*hereafter* cited as BCDSP, NMDA).
4. Letter, J. Ben Robinson, to Timothy O. Heatwole, Acting Dean, University of Maryland, October 19, 1923, BCDSP, NMDA.
5. Letter, Timothy O. Heatwole, Acting Dean, University of Maryland, to J. Ben Robinson, Baltimore, Md., October 23, 1923, BCDSP, NMDA.
6. Letter, J. Ben Robinson to Timothy O. Heatwole, Acting Dean, University of Maryland, October 26, 1923, BCDSP, NMDA.
7. J. Ben Robinson, "The Baltimore College of Dental Surgery and the Baltimore College of Dental Surgery, Dental School, University of Maryland," *Journal of the Maryland State Dental Association* 18 (August 1975):100.
8. Memo, H. Berton McCauley to John M. Hyson, Jr., n.d.
9. Despite some of the Robinson biographies stating that he entered dental school in 1911, the official college catalogue of 1912 lists him as a freshman. The college was on the three-year plan at that time. [Dental Department, University of Maryland, *Thirty-First Annual Announcement and Catalogue of the Dental Department of the University of Maryland, Session 1912–1913* (n.p., [1912]), p.21.]
10. "Dr. J. Ben Robinson dies; dental school dean was 94," *The Sun* (Baltimore), June 17, 1977; Foley, *Proceedings of the 125th Anniversary Celebration*, p. 211; Letter [J. Ben Robinson curriculum vitae], Errol L. Reese, BCDS Dean to Albin O. Kuhn, Chancellor, University of Maryland at Baltimore, November 13, 1975, BCDSP, NMDA; Dental Department of the University of Maryland, *Thirty-Third Annual Announcement and Catalogue of the Dental Department of the University of Maryland, Session 1914–1915* (Baltimore: n.p., [1914]), p. 14; Program, *J. Ben Robinson Recognition*, April 9, 1976, West Virginia University, Morgantown, W. Va.
11. Dr. Robinson was selected by the dentists of Maryland as the state's "Outstanding Contributor to Dentistry 1900–1950"; named "Dentist of the Century" by the Maryland State Dental Association (1859–1959); Supreme Grand Master of Psi Omega Fraternity, 1931–48; Alpha Omega Fraternity Medal,1941; Alfred C. Fones Medal (Connecticut State Dental Association),1942; John R. Callahan Medal (Ohio State Dental Association), 1944; Congressional Medal, Selective Service System, 1945; William John Gies Award (American College of Dentists), 1957; Hayden-Harris Award (American Academy of the History of Dentistry), 1967; Award for Excellence (American College of Dentists), 1970; Distinguished Service Award (American Dental Association), 1972; author of 70 published articles, and one book, *Foundations of Professional Dentistry*, 1940; contributed chapter on "Historical Development of the Autonomous Dental Profession" to *Dentistry an Agency of Health Service*, 1946, and the chapter on "Visual Aids in Teaching" to *Teaching in Colleges and Universities*, 1945. [Foley, *Proceedings of the 125th Anniversary Celebration*, p. 211; Letter, Reese to Kuhn, 1975, BCDSP, NMDA.]
12. Foley, *Proceedings of the 125th Anniversary Celebration*, p. 211.
13. Letter, Albert F. Woods, President, University of Maryland, to J. Ben Robinson, Baltimore, MD, February 6, 1924, BCDSP, NMDA).

14. Letter, Albert F. Woods, President, University of Maryland, to J. Ben Robinson, Baltimore, Md., February 12, 1924, BCDSP, NMDA.
15. Harry B. McCarthy, *Harry B. McCarthy, D.D.S., M.A.: an autobiography* (n.p., [1985]), pp. 18–19.
16. George M. Anderson, ed., *Proceedings Dental Centenary Celebration 1840–1940* (Baltimore: Waverly Press, Inc., 1940), p. 248.
17 Clarence Jones Grieves was born on October 23, 1868, in Wilmington, Del. After his graduation from the Baltimore Polytechnic Institute, he was employed by the B & O Railroad. Fortunately, he was persuaded by Dr. Richard Grady (BCDS 1879) to study dentistry, and in 1888 graduated from the Dental Department, University of Maryland. He was president of the Maryland State Dental Association in 1902, and president of the alumni association of his alma mater in 1905. He served on the faculty of the university from 1888–1906, and on the faculty of the Baltimore College of Dental Surgery from 1906–17 as professor of comparative anatomy and histology. In 1907, he was chairman of the clinic committee at the Jamestown Dental Convention, and chairman at the National Dental Association in 1911. In 1913, he established a dental clinic at Johns Hopkins Hospital and was chief of staff until 1925. In 1917, with the outbreak of World War I, he entered the U.S. Naval Reserve as a lieutenant in the Dental Corps, stationed at Great Lakes Naval Training Center. He was an instructor at the Army and Navy Dental School, and a lecturer in the Dental Department, Naval Medical School, Washington, D. C. In 1921, he received an honorary MA degree from the University of Michigan. He was a charter member of the American College of Dentists in 1920. He received the Newell Sill Jenkins Medal from the Connecticut State Dental Association; the Callahan Medal from the Ohio State Dental Association; and the Jarvie Medal from the Dental Society of the State of New York. In 1926, he was honorary president of the section on bacteriology, pathology, and diagnosis at the Seventh International Dental Congress at Philadelphia. He made important contributions to the research of the various metals used in dentistry, and in 1908 presented a paper, "Base Metals Versus Noble Metal Appliances in Orthodontia," before the American Society of Orthodontists. He presented another paper, "The Behavior of Certain Metals in the Mouth," at the at the 1909 National Dental Association meeting. At the Sixth International Dental Congress in London in 1914, he presented, "The Structural and Other Changes Arising in Connection with Metals Used in the Mouth." He was also interested in research on focal infection, and in 1913 presented a paper, "Periapical Infection," before the National Dental Association. He was honored at a banquet on May 4, 1926, given by the Maryland State Dental Association commemorating the donation of his library to the University of Maryland as the Grieves Foundation Library. Dr. Grieves died on November 4, 1927. [Foley, *Proceedings of the 125th Anniversary Celebration*, pp. 170–71; Idem, *Hall of Fame of Great Maryland* Dentists, Maryland State Dental Association, 1976, pp. 17–18; Geo[rge]E. Handy, "Doctor Clarence Jones Grieves," *The Bulletin the National Alumni Association of the Baltimore College of Dental Surgery* 2 (December 1927): 13.]
18. According to Gardner P. H. Foley, during the Myron Aisenberg administration (1953–63) as dean, the Grieves Library collection was transferred from the dental school to the University's Health Sciences Library. [Letter, H. Berton McCauley to John M. Hyson, Jr., October 10, 1998, author's files.]
19. Anderson, *Proceedings Dental Centenary Celebration*, pp. 248–49.
20. Baltimore College of Dental Surgery, Dental School, University of Maryland, *Eighty-Fifth Annual Announcement and Catalogue University of Maryland School of Dentistry and the Baltimore College of Dental Surgery* (n.p., [1925]), pp. 3, 5, 19.
21. Alumni Association of the Baltimore College of Dental Surgery, *Reunion Dinner National Alumni Association of the Baltimore College of Dental Surgery Penn Athletic Club Philadelphia, Pennsylvania Tuesday Evening, August Twenty-Fourth Nineteen Hundred Twenty-Six*, BCDSP, NMDA.
22. Baltimore College of Dental Surgery, Dental School, University of Maryland, *Eighty-Fifth Annual Announcement and Catalogue*, p. 8; William J. Gies, *Dental Education in the United States and Canada* (New York: Carnegie Foundation for Advancement of Teaching, 1926), p. 52.
23. Gies, *Dental Education*, p. 53.
24. John T. O'Rourke, and Leroy M. S. Miner, *Dental Education in the United States* (Philadelphia: W. B. Saunders Co., 1941), p. 59.
25. Gies, *Dental Education*, pp.14, 15.
26. O'Rourke and Miner, *Dental Education in the United States*, p. 60.
27. Baltimore College of Dental Surgery, Dental School, University of Maryland, *Eighty-Fifth Annual Announcement*, pp. 8, 14, 17.
28. Baltimore College of Dental Surgery, Dental School, University of Maryland, *Eighty-Six Annual Announcement and Catalogue University of Maryland School of Dentistry and the Baltimore College of Dental Surgery* (n.p., [1926]), pp. 1, 6, 10.
29. Dr. John M. Hyson served as an instructor at his alma mater in dental technics (1931), clinical pathology (1932–36), and in embryology and histology (1937–46) [the author].
30. Baltimore College of Dental Surgery, Dental School, University of Maryland, *Eighty-Seventh Annual Announcement and Catalogue University of Maryland School of Dentistry and the Baltimore College of Dental Surgery* (n.p., [1927]), pp. 6, 18.
31. Baltimore College of Dental Surgery, Dental School, University of Maryland, *Eighty-Ninth Annual Announcement and Catalogue University of Maryland School of Dentistry and the Baltimore College of Dental Surgery* (n.p., [1929]), p. 20.
32. "Officers: The National Alumni Association," *Bulletin National Alumni Association of the Baltimore College of Dental Surgery* 3 (May 1928): i, ii.
33. Louis DePaola, "Dental Honorary Society," *Maryland Probe* 4 (March 1975): 4.
34. George H. Callcott, *A History of the University of Maryland* (Baltimore: Maryland Historical Society, 1966), pp. 300–1.
35. "Do You Know," *The Vanguard* 2 (February 17, 1928): 2.
36. John Milner Associates, "Architecture as History: The Formative Years of the Baltimore College of Dental Surgery as Recorded in the Housing History," Final Report, John Milner Associates, West Chester, Pa. 1980, p. 51; Baltimore College of Dental Surgery, Dental School, University of Maryland, *Eighty-Ninth Annual Announcement and Catalogue*, pp. 6–7.
37. Joseph H. Seipp, Jr., "A Brief History of the First Dental Alumni Association in the World (Organizations Associated with the Baltimore College of Dental Surgery)," *Alma Mater* 8 (November 1966): 7.
38. Callcott, *A History of the University of Maryland*, pp. 301–2

39. O'Rourke and Miner, *Dental Education*, p.115.
40. Baltimore College of Dental Surgery, Dental School, University of Maryland, *Ninety-First Annual Announcement and Catalogue University of Maryland School of Dentistry and the Baltimore College of Dental Surgery, Session of 1931–1932* (n.p., [1931]), pp. 10, 24.
41. Baltimore College of Dental Surgery, Dental School, University of Maryland, *Ninety-Second Annual Announcement and Catalogue University of Maryland School of Dentistry and the Baltimore College of Dental Surgery, Session of 1932–1933* (n.p., [1932]), p. 26.
42. Ibid., p. 20.
43. Ibid., p. 27; "Baltimore College of Dental Surgery," Dental Cosmos 75 (July 1933): 724; Baltimore College of Dental Surgery, Dental School, University of Maryland, *Ninety-Fourth Annual Announcement and Catalogue University of Maryland School of Dentistry and the Baltimore College of Dental Surgery, Session of 1934–1935* (n.p., [1934]), p. 27.
44. John J. Houlihan, "Ice Hockey," in *The 1932 Mirror* (Baltimore: n.p., 1932), p. 100.
45. Fred C. Lee, "The Amateur Ice Hockey Association of Baltimore," *Sports Centre News*, 1933: 6.
46. Houlihan, "Ice Hockey," p. 100.
47. Ibid.
48. Harry Bryan McCarthy from Highgate, Vt., played hockey for three years for a local club team, known as the "Taquahunga Club," which won the Vermont State Championship two years running. He was the manager of the team the last year of its existence. [McCarthy, *Harry B. McCarthy*, pp. 7, 8–9.]
49. Houlihan, "Ice Hockey,"100–101.
50. Thrall, Ralph B., ed., "Hockey Team," in *The 1933 Mirror* (Baltimore, n.p., 1933), p. 115.
51. Baltimore College of Dental Surgery, Dental School, University of Maryland, *The 1934 Mirror* (Baltimore: n.p., 1934), p. 114–15.
52. Letters, J. Ben Robinson to M. Barrett-Lennard, May 25, September 12, 1933; Letters, M. Barrett-Lennard to J. Ben Robinson, March 7, 22, 27, May 10, August 30, 1933; Letters, Army & Navy Co-operative Limited, to J. Ben Robinson, December 20, 1933, January 13, 1934; Invoice, Army & Navy Co-operative Society Limited, to J. Ben Robinson, January 22, 1934, BCDSP, NMDA.
53. New York Dental Centennial, *Catalogue Exhibition of Historical and Scientific Dentistry* (n.p., 1934), p. 4.
54. O'Rourke and Miner, *Dental Education*, pp. 115–16.
55. Baltimore College of Dental Surgery, Dental School, University of Maryland, *Ninety-Fifth Annual Announcement and Catalogue University of Maryland School of Dentistry and the Baltimore College of Dental Surgery, Session of 1935–1936* (n.p., [1935]), pp. 9, 10.
56. American Association of Dental Schools, *A Course of Study in Dentistry* (Chicago: Curriculum Survey Committee, 1935), pp. ix, x, 316.
57. Baltimore College of Dental Surgery, Dental School, University of Maryland, *Ninety-Fifth Annual Announcement and Catalogue*, pp. 10–11.
58. Baltimore College of Dental Surgery, Dental School, University of Maryland, *Ninety-Sixth Annual Announcement and Catalogue Baltimore College of Dental Surgery, Dental School, University of Maryland, Session 1936–1937* (n.p., [1936]), p. 27.
59. Baltimore College of Dental Surgery, Dental School, University of Maryland, *Ninety-Ninth Annual Announcement and Catalogue Baltimore College of Dental Surgery, Dental School, University of Maryland, Session 1938–1939* (n.p., [1938]), pp. 11, 26.
60. O'Rourke and Miner, *Dental Education*, pp. 124–25.
61. Ibid., pp. 125–26.
62. Baltimore College of Dental Surgery, Dental School, University of Maryland, *Centennial Number. Annual Announcement and Catalogue Baltimore College of Dental Surgery, Dental School, University of Maryland, Session 1939–1940* (n.p., [1939]), pp. 17–18.
63. Ibid., p. 30.
64. Foley, *Proceedings of the 125th Anniversary Celebration*, p. 181–82.
65. Letter, J. Ben Robinson, BCDS Dean, to H. B. McCarthy, October 22, 1940, BCDSP, NMDA.
66. "Dental School Enrollment, 1940–41," *Journal of Dental Education* 5 (October 1940): 6.

FORD'S THEATRE

Monday and Tuesday Evenings

March 18th and 19th

The Dental Centenary Committee

Presents

"WILDERNESS"

A Cavalcade of the Profession of Dentistry

By

CHARLES MARQUIS WARREN

Produced and Directed

By

EDWIN TUNIS

Chapter 15

The BCDS Centennial: 1940

"There can be little purpose, however, in our coming together at this time to enjoy the treat which they have prepared for us unless, in doing so, we pledge ourselves with increased devotion, to the unfinished tasks which confront us at every turn. Not to the past but to the future, must we set our faces as we gather to pay tribute to those of our number who have labored so earnestly in the days gone by. They laid the foundation upon which we build. 'Let every man heed how he buildeth thereon.'"[1] ~**Arthur H. Merritt**, President ADA, 1940

The Centenary Celebration: 1940

On March 21, 1938, the Maryland State Dental Association adopted a resolution urging the American Dental Association to hold its annual meeting in Baltimore, the home of the world's first dental college. It stated that the American Dental Association had a "moral responsibility to join in the Centennial Celebration," an event that could not be "observed suitably in any place other than Baltimore."[2]

A headquarters for the Dental Centenary Committee was established in September 1939 in Room 19-A, Medical Arts Building, Baltimore, Md., by Dr. B. Lucien Brun,[3] the chairman of the Centenary Committee. Miss Edna R. Walls was hired as the secretary and instructed to keep the office opened from 8:30 to 5:30 daily and 8:30 to 1 on Saturdays. She was paid $12.50 a week for her services until the work exceeded 20 hours a week, and then it was to be adjusted accordingly.[4]

The Centenary Celebration was scheduled to start on March 18 and run until March 20, 1940, in Baltimore, Md. The Centenary Celebration Committee, in announcing these dates, stated:

> The profession of dentistry is looking forward to its one hundredth anniversary. Dentists of every country regard this Centennial as a time when they should meet with common purpose to commemorate the founding of their profession: pay just tribute to Horace H. Hayden and Chapin A. Harris, co-founders of the first dental college; review a hundred years of progress in Dental Education, Dental Journalism, Dental Organization and, in full pride of those achievements, chart the course for broader professional service in the future.[5]

The celebration was sponsored by the Maryland State Dental Association and the American Dental Association. Dr. Brun was very emphatic in the fact that the affair was being run by the Maryland Committee in responding to a letter from the International College of Dentists in which he stated: "The American Dental Association, while substantially backing the Centenary Celebration, both financially and morally, has never for a minute taken over any part of its preparation. The entire program, from beginning to end, . . . has been planned, developed and arranged by the Maryland Committee."[6] The motif selected by the Maryland Dental Centenary Committee was "a three-legged pedestal—symbolic of dental Education, Literature, and Organization, the triad upon which rests our professional progress—supporting the ever-burning flame of crowning brilliance, exemplifying achievements of the past, the fullness of the present and suggesting the future with its opportunities for continued and improved service to mankind."[7]

Background to Centennial Planning

In 1928, Dr. Alex H. Paterson,[8] the retiring president of the Maryland State Dental Association, suggested in his report recognizing 1940 as the dental centenary year with a proper celebration. A centennial committee was formed to commemorate the founding of the first dental school in the world, the Baltimore College of Dental Surgery. In 1929, the centennial committee recommended that the Maryland State Dental Association create a distinct and separate special fund to be known as the "Centennial Fund." An annual assessment of two dollars was to be collected from each member of the state organization to support the fund. Various plans were discussed, including holding the American Dental Association annual meeting in Baltimore in conjunction with the Dental Centenary. However, it was thought that the Centenary Celebration would be upstaged by the sheer magnitude of the American Dental Association meeting; therefore, this idea was discarded. An independent meeting was decided upon that could be "approved and sponsored by, and have the moral and financial support" of the American Dental Association. A steering committee was appointed to develop a skeleton program, which was "revised and elaborated upon." This plan was then presented at the next national meeting to the American Dental Association Centennial Committee, which had been appointed in 1936. As they had received no other concrete program, the ADA Centennial Committee recommended to the ADA Trustees that the Maryland plan be accepted. With this formal agreement in hand, the Maryland committee was free to proceed with its development.[9]

The Dental Centenary Committee

The Dental Centenary Committee was composed of the following members: B. Lucien Brun, general chairman; Meyer Eggnatz, secretary; George B. Jersin, treasurer; committee chairmen: George M. Anderson, scientific program; Alex H. Patersopn, historical exhibits; J. Ben Robinson, dental history; F. Noel Smith, historical drama; James H. Ferguson, local arrangements; Earl W. Swinehart, publicity; Harry B. McCarthy, commercial exhibits; Harry E. Kelsey, international relations; J. Stephenson Hopkins, morning sessions; C. Adam Bock, president, Maryland State Dental Association; Daniel E. Shehan, president, Baltimore City Dental Society.[10]

The Dental Centenary Celebration Committee of the ADA was composed of the following members: Harvey J. Burkhart, Leroy M. S. Miner, Harry B. Pinnney, Charles A. Sweet, L. Pierce Anthony, Walter M. Morgan, and William H. G. Logan. Honorary chairmen were Arthur H. Merritt, president, American Dental Association; Harry Bear, president, American Association of Dental Schools; and Harold J. Noyes, president, American Association of Dental Editors.[11]

In addition to the 48 state dental societies and the District of Columbia being represented, there were representatives from Hawaii, Puerto Rico, Panama Canal Zone, and the Philippines. Thirty-nine dental schools in the United States and representatives from Argentina, Australia, Belgium, Bolivia, Bulgaria, Canada, Chile, Cuba, Denmark, Dominican Republic, Finland, France, Germany, Great Britain, Greece, Holland, Italy, Ireland, Japan, Java, Latvia, Lithuania, Luxemburg, Mexico, Norway, Palestine, Peru, Portugal, Scotland, Spain, Sweden, Switzerland, and Uruguay were included.[12]

The Scientific Sessions

The Centenary Celebration morning sessions were held at Ford's Theater in Baltimore. The opening program began on Monday, March 18, 1940, at 10:30 a.m., with an invocation by Msgr. Joseph M. Nelligan, chancellor of the Archdiocese of Baltimore, and remarks by Herbert R. O'Conor, governor of Maryland; Howard W. Jackson, mayor of Baltimore; and Dr. H. Curly Byrd, president of the University of Maryland. The opening address, "A Century of Science and Education," was given by Dr. William M. Lewis, president of Lafayette College.

The second morning session on March 19, 1940, was highlighted by an address by the Surgeon General of the United States, Dr. Thomas Parran, who spoke on "Dentistry as a Health

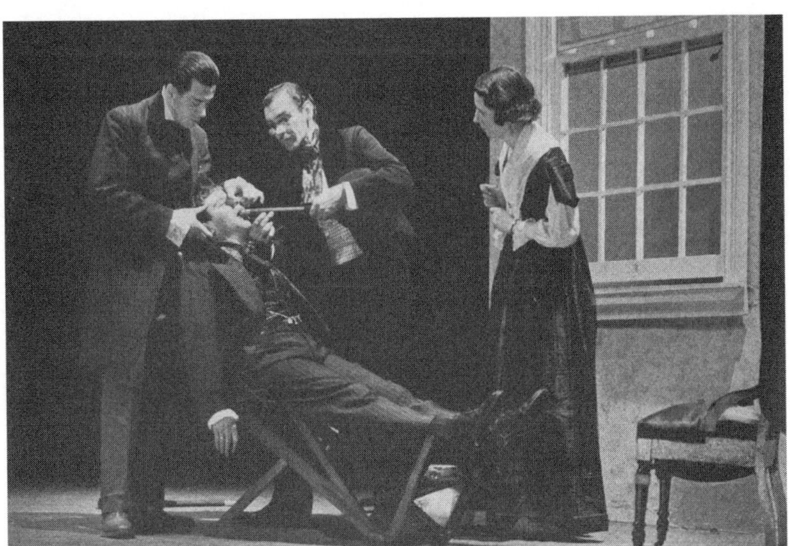

Scene XVII from the "Wilderness." *The Discovery of Nitrous Oxide Anesthesia.*

Service." The third session on March 20, 1940, featured addresses by Dr. J. Ben Robinson, dental dean of the University of Maryland, on "The Significance of the Centenary Celebration" and Dr. Raymond A. Kent, president of the University of Louisville, on "The Relation of Dental Education to the University Program." At the end of the session, Dr. Byrd conferred honorary degrees on Drs. Kent, Merritt, Harvey J. Burkhart, and William J. Gies.[14]

The scientific sessions were held in the afternoon at the Fifth Regiment Armory from 2 to 5 p.m., beginning on March 18, 1940. They were divided into 19 sections, six on Monday, seven on Tuesday, and six on Wednesday afternoon. There were three papers read per session, arranged so that sections closely allied with each other were spaced. Two sessions were held in the armory's lower floor in rooms having a capacity of 400 each, and four sections met on the mezzanine floor in rooms with a seating capacity of from 200 to 450. One section met in the Lord Baltimore Hotel. There was no discussion after the papers were read. The contributors were presented with an engraved certificate to commemorate their participation in the Centenary.[15]

Among the papers presented, the following examples may be cited: Leroy M. Ennis, DDS, "X-rays are Still Fraught with Danger;" Issac Schour, BS, MS, PhD, DDS, and Maury Massler, DDS, BS, "Effect of the Endocrines on the Teeth, Jaws and Facial Skeleton;" James D. McCoy, BS, MS, DDS, "Objectives in Orthodontic Treatment;" Harold J. Noyes, PhB, BS, DDS, MD, "The Etiology of Malocclusion Considered from a Clinical Viewpoint;" George C. Paffenbarger, DDS, and H. J. Caul, BS, "Dental Cements;" William J. Gies, BS, MS, PhD, ScD, LLD, "The Need for Improved Library Facilities in the Interest of Dental Research;" Harry Archer, BS, DDS, "The History of Anesthesia;" Rudolf Krownfeld, BS, MD, DDS, "Correlation Between Clinical Pathological Diagnosis in Chronic Apical Periodontitis;" V. H. Kazanjian, DMD, MD, "The Interrelation of Dentistry and Surgery in the Treatment of Deformities of the Face and Jaws;" and Kurt H. Thoma, DMD, "Fundamentals of Paradontal Pathology."[16]

Historical Exhibits

The historical exhibits, under Dr. Alex H. Paterson's chairmanship, were held at the Fifth Regiment Armory from 9 a.m. to 5 p.m. daily. As the planning for the Centenary Celebration progressed through the years before 1940, it became obvious that historical exhibits became increasingly important to the celebration. No true story of the advances in dentistry could be presented without historical artifacts. Invitations were sent out to all the dental schools and allied organizations in the United States and Canada. Twenty-four schools and 11 allied organizations responded to the call. Each school was assigned a different subject to avoid duplication of themes.[17]

In the center of a historical court was a statue of St. Apollonia, the patron saint of dentistry, and a replica of the first building occupied by the first dental school, the Baltimore College of Dental Surgery. On the right, against the wall was a portrait of Horace H. Hayden by Rembrandt Peale and two showcases of Hayden's personal artifacts. On the opposite side was a portrait of Chapin A. Harris by Eastman Johnson and two showcases of Harris' personal possessions. Also on the right were two pieces of furniture that once belonged to Hayden and a showcase containing the first dental society's documents, over which hung the portraits of the first two graduates, Robert Arthur and Richard Mackall, and their diplomas. On the opposite side were two pieces of furniture that once belonged to Harris and a showcase with the first dental journal, the 1939 *American Journal of Dental Science*, and 29 other volumes. Above the case were portraits of the founders of the Baltimore College of Dental Surgery. At the four corners of the historical court were period operating rooms (25-year intervals) demonstrating the stages in the development of dental equipment during the first hundred years. Portraits of the dental pioneers lined the walls on each side of the central aisle.[18]

Scene XI from the "Wilderness." *The First Class.*

The Apollonia sculpture was made for the centenary by Lucille Fagret Brun and Johanne Kendall. Apollonia appears as a "sympathetic, thoughtful and attractive young lady."[19] The replica of the first dental building was constructed as a model crafted by Thomas Worthington, a local Baltimore magician.[20]

The central section of the main floor of the armory hosted the other historical exhibits. Special 35 x 7 x 8 foot booths, well-lighted and marked with the exhibitor's name were separated by wide aisles. The commercial exhibits completely encircled the historical exhibits.[21] The Baltimore College of Dental Surgery had two exhibits; the subject of the first was "Evolution of the Dental Curriculum," which illustrated the advances that have been made in the four phases of dental education in dentistry's first century: the predental phase, consisting of charts demonstrating the changes in the length of the college curriculum and the entrance requirements; the preclinical phase, showing the history of the biological sciences as they developed up to1940; the clinical phase, demonstrating the historical development and background of the various clinical courses; and the postgraduate phase showing the development in advanced dental training.[22] The second exhibit was "Growth of Dental Colleges," which gave a chronological history of the 39 existing dental colleges. Founding dates, mergers, and amalgamations were listed and photographs of the various schools were depicted.[23] Various other dental colleges, government dental services, the American Dental Association, the Maryland State Dental Association, and private exhibitors had similar exhibits.[24]

As an additional exhibit, Dr. George M. Anderson mounted an exhibit, "The Art of Adalbert Johann Volck, 1828-1912." Dr. Volck,[25] a protégé of Chapin A. Harris and an 1852 graduate of the Baltimore College of Dental Surgery, taught chemistry at his alma mater.

During the Civil War, he supported the South and was appointed a special agent by Jefferson Davis, a personal friend. He aided agents, artisans, mechanics, and recruits desiring to cross the Union lines, and several times ran the blockade with medical supplies. Volck's home was a sanctuary for Confederate soldiers and secret agents. On several occasions, he was imprisoned at Fort McHenry. Volck became incensed at the political cartoons of Thomas Nast. Therefore, he took up the pen and under the pseudonym of V. Blada originated cartoons and caricatures called "Civil War Sketches," which lampooned the Northern leaders and generals, including President Lincoln. The cartoons were done as copper etchings. Volck sketched Stonewall Jackson on the night before he was killed. After the war, he turned his artistic talent to working in bronze and silver.[26]

During the Centenary Celebration, the Enoch Pratt Free Library of the City of Baltimore mounted two exhibits on dental history in its windows facing Cathedral Street. The Baltimore College of Dental Surgery Museum furnished the artifacts. The following fall, the museum again furnished material for a window exhibit on Horace Wells, the discoverer of inhalation anesthesia. Later, the Baltimore Wells exhibit was loaned to the city of Hartford, Conn., for exhibition in a department store during the period of the Wells Centenary Celebration.[27]

Historical Drama

Early in 1938, the Centenary Committee appointed a "ways and means committee" to develop a historical pageant or drama. The committee consulted a Mr. Edwin Tunis,[28] a local artist, who gave them an estimate of $1,000 to $10,000 to prepare the script, cost of costumes and stage settings, and hire a competent local coach. A drama committee was then formed, consisting of Drs. F. Noel Smith, George E. Hardy, Jr., Ethelbert Lovett, Kyrle W. Preis, and Mr. Gardner P. H. Foley, to proceed with the planning to prepare and produce a drama, whose theme would include dental education, organization, and journalism. Mr.

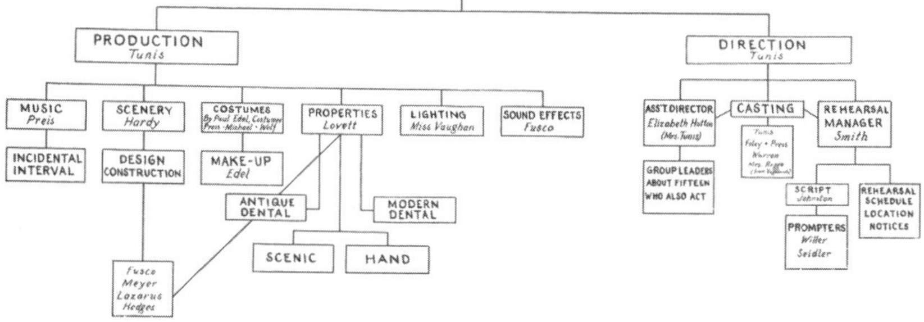

Tunis agreed to produce and direct the drama for $1,000 on the basis of a $5,000 production, or for a proportionally larger sum for a larger scale production. He would be entirely responsible for direction and production. Charles Marquis Warren, who had worked for MGM Studios in Hollywood, was selected to prepare the script for the drama. Production costs were estimated to be $4,950. In January 1939, the general Centennial Committee approved the plan and allotted the sum of $5,000 for the drama. Before the summer of 1939, Warren had completed the script and it was ready for the printer. It had 26 scenes and a cast of more than a hundred.[29] On March 18 and 19, the historical drama, "Wilderness: A Cavalcade of the Profession of Dentistry," was presented at Ford's Theater.[30]

Public Relations

The Dental Centennial Celebration afforded dentistry an extraordinary opportunity to promote "a comprehensive campaign of lay dental education." As dentistry was practiced in all countries, it was desirable that dentistry's message be spread throughout the world; however, because of conditions in Europe at that time, the impact of the celebration was only felt in countries of the Western Hemisphere. In the United States, the American Dental Association saw to it that dental information was distributed to all parts of the country through local dental groups. Dental dinners were sponsored by 316 of the 429 component societies that comprised the association. Speakers addressed school groups and other public organizations.

The American Dental Association's public relations bureau, the Greater New York Bureau of Dental Information, the various state societies' public relations bureaus, and the Pacific Coast Dental Congress all aided the successful campaign. The nation's newspapers, the national photographic services and magazines, radio broadcasts, lectures before schools, civic bodies, and health groups all contributed to the cause. In Baltimore, the amount of newspaper coverage exceeded that of any similar event in the city's history. The ADA's figures showed 3,147 unduplicated clippings, which translated into more than 12,000 new stories. The publicity for the centennial was the best ever for a dental event; the story reached every state in the country. The message urged the public "not to neglect its teeth," and showed that the dentist was the "only one qualified to cope with mouth ailments." During the centennial in Baltimore, the visiting leaders of the profession addressed 15 high schools and one college, including Eastern High, McDonogh School, Catholic High, Seton High, Roland Park Country, Patterson Park High, Calvert Hall High, Frederick Douglas High, Dunbar High, Towson High, City College High, Forest Park High, Southern High, Western High, Polytechnic Institute, State Teachers College for Women, four civic groups, and made six radio broadcasts.[31]

Conclusion

At the conclusion of the Centenary Celebration, Dr. Arthur H. Merritt, president of the American Dental Association, on March 21, 1940, addressed the following letter to Dr. B. Lucien Brun, chairman of the Centenary Committee:

> This is the first letter I have written since my return, and now that the smoke of battle has cleared away and one is able to see more clearly the magnificent success which you and your Committee made of the Centennial, I want to be among the first to express in this way my heartfelt congratulations on the deserved success of your almost superhuman activities in the last year.

> Please accept for yourself and convey to the members of your Committee my best wishes. You have placed the entire profession under obligation to each of you for the splendid job which you did in connection with our centenary.
>
> I want also to thank you personally for the many kindnesses shown me, while in your City, by you and your Fellows on the Committee.[32]

The official 1941 audit for the Centennial Celebration for the period January 25, 1939, to April 30, 1941, showed receipts of $57,615.80 and expenditures of $57, 539.40, for a net profit of $76.40. The most expensive item was the publication of the book, *Proceedings Dental Centenary Celebration 1840–1940,* which cost $11, 065, of which as of April 18, 1941, there were on hand 334 unsold copies.[33] Finally in 1944, after all bills and obligations had been paid and accounted for, there was the sum of $409.93 left over. The committee recommended this money be spent to mount a suitable memorial in the halls of the dental school commemorating the 1940 centennial.[34]

Pilgrimage to the grave of Chapin A. Harris, February 1, 1940

NOTES

1. Maryland State Dental Association, and American Dental Association, *1840–1940 Dental Centenary Celebration* (Baltimore: 20th Century Printing Co., 1940), p. 2.
2. "Resolution Adopted by the Maryland State Dental Association in Special Meeting," March 21, 1938, Baltimore College of Dental Surgery Papers, National Museum of Dentistry Archives (*hereafter* cited as BCDSP, NMDA).
3. B. Lucien Brun was born in Baltimore on April 11, 1884, and graduated from the Baltimore College of Dental Surgery in 1905. In 1906, he began a long-term service as a faculty member of his alma mater. After five years of general practice in Baltimore, he took post-graduate courses at St. Mary's Hospital and Trinity Hospital in Milwaukee, Wis., and at the German Hospital, New York City. He

Pilgrimage to the grave of Horace Hayden, February 1, 1940

returned to Baltimore and in 1911 began an oral surgery practice, and taught local anesthesia to the dental students. From 1912 to 1946, he served as head of the division of oral surgery at Johns Hopkins Hospital, Baltimore, and from 1946 to 1950 was chief of the dental department. From 1917 to 1923, he was professor of oral surgery at his alma mater. During World War I, he served as a captain in the Dental Reserve Corps, U.S. Army, with Base Hospital No. 18 (Johns Hopkins Unit) in France. Dr. Brun was president of the Maryland State Dental Association (1919–21), and president of the Alumni Association (1930–33). He was a member of the Maryland Board of Dental Examiners from 1931 to 1937 and was vice-president of the American Dental Association in 1940. During World War II, he was a consultant for the Selective Service. He retired in 1950 and died on February 19, 1954. [Gardner P. H. Foley, ed., *Proceedings of the 125th Anniversary Celebration of the Baltimore College of Dental Surgery* (Baltimore: Horn-Shafer, 1966), p. 140; "Obituary (Dr. B. Lucien Brun)," *Journal of the Baltimore College of Dental Surgery, Dental School, University of Maryland* 13 (May 1954): 44–45. For details of Dr. Brun's military career in World War I, *see*: John M. Hyson, Jr., "Dental Service Base Hospital No. 18: Johns Hopkins Hospital 1917–19," *Journal of the History of Dentistry* 51 (November 2003): 115–17.]

4. Letter, B. Lucien Brun, Chairman Centenary Committee, to Edna R. Walls, July 7, 1939, BCDSP, NMDA.
5. Dental Centenary Celebration Committee, "Advance Information Regarding the National Dental Centenary Celebration," n.p., n.d., BCDSP, NMDA.
6. Letter, Dr. B. Lucien Brun, General Chairman, Dental Centenary Committee, to Elmer S. Best, Registrar, International College of Dentists, January 15, 1940, BCDSP, NMDA.
7. Maryland State Dental Association, and American Dental Association, *1840–1940 Dental Centenary Celebration*, p. 1.
8. Alexander Horn Paterson was born on May 11, 1878, at Wilkes-Barre, Pa. He was educated in the public schools and at Starkey Academy, Lakemont, N.Y. In 1911, he graduated *summa cum laude* from the Dental Department, University of Maryland. He served on the faculty of his alma mater as a demonstrator of prosthetic dentistry from 1911 to 1916 and as professor of dental technics from 1916 to 1920, professor of prosthetic dentistry (1920–27), and professor of crown and bridge and prosthetics (1927–41). In 1927, he was president of the Maryland State Dental Association. He was the first dentist in Baltimore and one of the first dentists in the country to specialize in prosthetics. Dr. Paterson's contributions to the "science of denture construction rank among the notable accomplishments of modern dentistry." He died on February 4, 1941, in Baltimore. [Foley, *Proceedings*, p. 203; J. Ben Robinson, "Alexander Horn Paterson, DDS, FACD," n.d., BCDSP, NMDA.]
9. George M. Anderson, ed., *Proceedings Dental Centenary Celebration 1840–1940* (Baltimore: Waverly Press, Inc., 1940), p. 3.
10. Anderson, *Proceedings Dental Centenary Celebration*, p. 5.
11. Ibid., p. 5.
12. Ibid., pp. 13–28.
13. Ibid., pp. 33, 42.
14. Ibid., pp. 48, 62, 77.
15. Ibid., p. 83.
16. Ibid., pp. 91, 145, 193, 205, 232, 252, 333, 409, 489, 616.

17. Ibid., p. 681.
18. Ibid., pp. 682, 688, 690, 694, 698.
19. Ibid., p. 684.
20. Ibid., p. 686.
21. Ibid., pp. 696, 698.
22. Ibid., p. 700.
23. Ibid., p. 702.
24. Ibid., pp. 706–74.
25. Adalbert Volck was born on April 14, 1828, in Augsburg, Bavaria. He attended the Polytechnic Institute in Nuremberg and studied chemistry at the University of Munich. During his formative years, he developed a strong interest in art and attended summer art colonies. As one of the marchers on Berlin in March 1848, he became subject for immediate conscription; therefore, in 1848, he immigrated to the United States. After brief stays in St. Louis and California, he went to Boston in 1850 where he became associated with Dr. Nathan C. Keep and studied dentistry in the latter's office while attending Harvard University. In 1851, at Dr. Chapin A. Harris' urging, he moved to Baltimore and completed the course requirements for his DDS degree, graduating in 1852. He then began practicing in Baltimore and soon developed a lucrative practice. His training in chemistry and his experimental work with porcelain in filling teeth made his reputation. In 1870, Volck painted the last life portrait of Robert E. Lee. In 1872, he founded the Maryland Academy of Fine Arts, and organized the "Wednesday Club" and the "Charcoal Club," for which he made a beautiful copper tankard. He was a founding member of the Association of Dental Surgeons of Baltimore, and its president in 1890, and charter member of the Maryland State Dental Association in 1883. Dr. Volck retired in 1902 and devoted the rest of his life to his art work. Cardinal Gibbons said of him, "He was the most universally learned man I ever knew." Dr. Volck died in 1912. [Foley, *Proceedings of the 125th Anniversary Celebration*, pp. 230–31.]
26. Maryland State Dental Association, and American Dental Association, *1840–1940 Dental Centenary Celebration*, p. 97; Gardner P. H. Foley, "Adalbert Volck dentist and artist," (*Journal of the American College of Dentists*), quoted in *Dental Radiography and Photography* 35, no. 4 (1962): 74, 87–89; Idem, *Proceedings of the 125th Anniversary Celebration*, pp. 230–32. For a more thorough description of Dr. Volck's work, *see* George M. Anderson, *The Work of Adalbert Johann Volck 1828–1912: who chose for his name the anagram V. Blada 1861–1865* (Baltimore: George M. Anderson, 1970).
27. Gardner P. H. Foley, "Dental Exhibits at the Pratt Library," *Journal of the Baltimore College of Dental Surgery, Dental School, University of Maryland* 9 (September 1945): 3.
28. Edwin Tunis had acted with the Vagabond Theater for 22 years, and at various times had directed their productions and designed their scenery. He had served as artist for the Maryland Tercentenary Celebration; was the principal character and associate producer of the Charles Carroll of Carrollton Pageant; and had directed the posing of the tableaux for the Washington Bicentennial. [Anderson, *Proceedings Dental Centenary Celebration*, p. 779.]
29. Ibid., pp. 779–80.
30. Ibid., p. 777, 793.
31. Ibid., pp. 796–96, 797–842.
32. Letter, Arthur H. Merritt, President ADA, to B. Lucien Brun, Chairman Centenary Committee, March 21, 1940, BCDSP, NMDA.
33. Report of Audit, Centennial Celebration Committee, April 30, 1941, BCDSP, NMDA.
34. Letter, B. Lucien Brun, Chairman, Dental Centenary Committee, to Board of Governors, Maryland State Dental Association, May 1, 1944, BCDSP, NMDA.

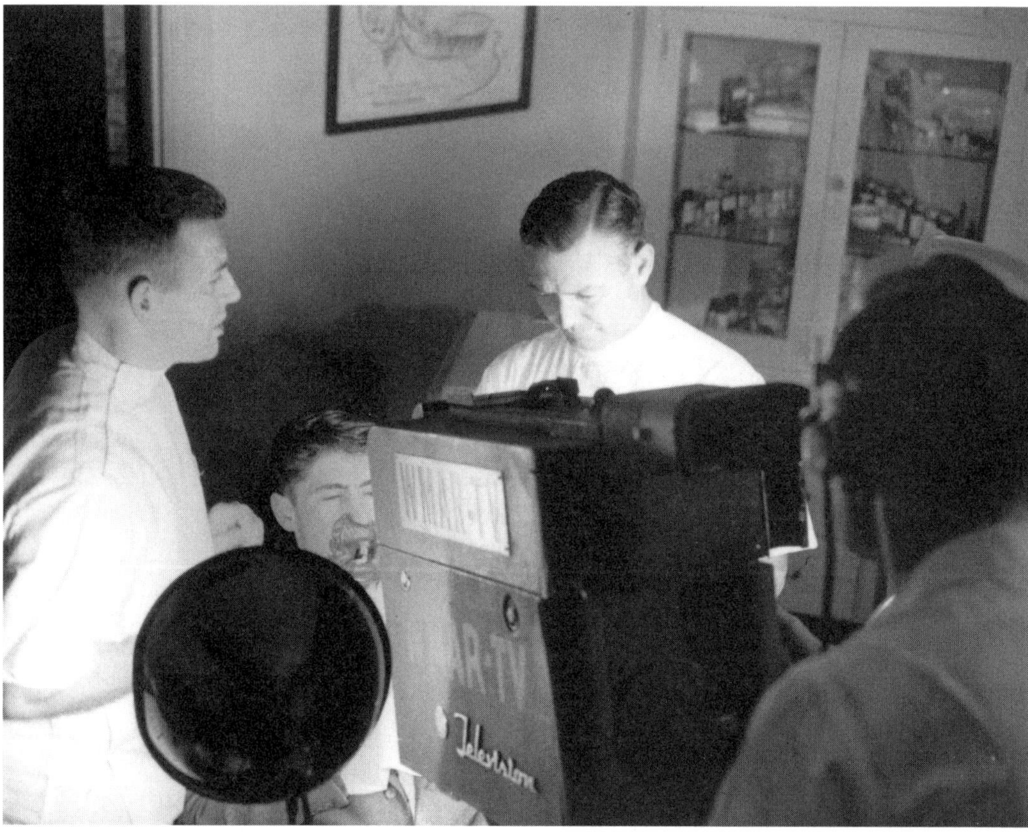

First broadcast dental operation, 1950

Chapter 16

End of the Robinson Era: 1941–53

"Has not the Old Baltimore College demonstrated the proposition, that a special school for a special division of science is more attractive, more efficient, and more successful, at least in our department and domain, than any system or device of the past or any method or arrangement of this present marvelous age of transition and progress? Has not the Baltimore College and the agencies and influences it originated and put into operation, absolutely created our profession? Has not the principle and system upon which this first of all dental schools was founded, been recognized and adopted in every section of our common country, and almost all over the civilized world, and always and everywhere, with a more or less gratifying and compensating success? The great commercial cities of the North, the East, the West, and the South, have their special schools for teaching dental science—some of the Universities have added faculties of instruction, and established departments for teaching dental surgery—all essentially modeled after the first grand and original design, conceived by the Fathers of American Dentistry."[1] **~William W. H. Thackston, 1877**

The War Years: 1941–45

The years of World War II from 1941 to 1945 brought many new changes in the curriculum of the Baltimore College of Dental Surgery. Uncle Sam wanted dentists for the services in much quicker order than before the war—acceleration was the popular theme of the day for all colleges and universities.

The 1941–42 catalog contained the college's wartime mission statement:

> Because of the over-all shortage of dentists and the great need to provide professional services to members of the armed forces of the country, the workers in the war industries, and the civilian population, it is necessary for the dental schools of the country to attempt through changes in their calendars to educate a larger number of dentists under an accelerated program of dental education. In the circumstances, the Council on Dental Education of the American Dental Association has recommended that those schools which are capable of adjusting their facilities to the emergency situation set up a continuous teaching program in order to graduate their students to professional practice at the earliest possible time. The Dental School, University of Maryland, is equipped to adopt the recommendation of the Council and has inaugurated an accelerated program of instruction.[2]

In January 1942, the American Dental Association, Council on Dental Education, recommended that the dental curriculum during the duration of the war be continuous (no summer vacation) and reduced to three years instead of the current four years.[3] During the accelerated period, a new class would start every eight months, beginning with the class of June 1942. Graduation would be approximately 36 months after the admission date. The first session semester started on June 15, 1942, and ran until October 24, 1942. The second semester began on October 26, 1942, and ran until February 27, 1943.[4] During the war years, only one woman—Rosalind Irene Toubman (from Connecticut)—graduated from the college (1942).[5]

The Army Specialized Training Program: 1942

In December 1942, the Armed Forces announced a plan, known as the Army Specialized Training Program (ASTP), to give military status to dental and medical students, defer them from Selective Service, and pay for their education at government expense. The reasons that the government took this action were manifold:

1. Selective Service could not be relied upon to defer dental and medical students for long-term commitments to professional education.
2. The Armed Forces needed to have "sufficient prospective professional replacements actually under military control" to assure their use without delay or difficulty as soon as their training was completed.
3. The government feared the students would not stay in school as civilians, but would enlist even if their deferment was guaranteed. The government did not want a shortage of professionals to develop.
4. It was felt the freedom of financial obligations would entice the students to stay in school.[6]

Dental students in good standing were eligible for a commission as a second lieutenant in the Army or as an ensign in the Navy while in school and upon graduation, be eligible for commission as a first lieutenant in the U.S. Army Dental Corps or as a lieutenant (j.g.) in the U.S. Navy Dental Corps.[7]

The Army Specialized Training Program at Maryland was designated the 3316th Service Unit, and the Navy V-12 program designated the University of Maryland Dental Unit. The Army unit was under the command of Lieutenant Colonel William A. Howland, and the Navy unit under Lieutenant R. D. Matthews.[8] For the academic year 1943–44, the first semester began on March 22, 1943, and ran until July 17, 1943, and the second semester started on July 19 and ran until November 24, 1943.[9] On January 25, 1944, the college graduated six students and on August 10, 1944, it graduated 80 candidates.[10]

The ASTP was terminated on July 18, 1944; all 39 dental schools had participated. In its 26-month duration, it had enrolled 7,734 dental students and graduated 2,458 and commissioned 1,914 in the Army Dental Corps and 269 in the Navy Dental Corps.[11]

The faculty of the college lost many members to the service on military leave. Those who joined the service included: Dr. Brice M. Dorsey, professor of oral surgery; Dr. Marion W. McCrea, associate professor of embryology and histology; Dr. A. Allen Sussman, assistant professor of anatomy; Dr. Carl E. Bailey, instructor in clinical operative dentistry; Dr. Douglas

A. Browning, instructor in clinical crown and bridge; Dr. Samuel H. Bryant, instructor in diagnosis; Dr. John W. Cronin, instructor in oral surgery; Dr. B. Wallace Inman, instructor in oral surgery; Dr. Hammond L. Johnston, instructor in clinical orthodontics; Dr. Max Miller, instructor in bacteriology and pathology; Dr. Eugene L. Pessagno, instructor in dental technics; Dr. Gordon S. Pugh, instructor in dental technics; Dr. Herbert E. Reifschneider, instructor in general anesthesia; Dr. Frank J. Roh, instructor in clinical operative dentistry; Dr. D. Robert Swinehart, instructor in orthodontics; Dr. William H. Triplett, instructor in physical diagnosis; and Dr. W. Kennedy Waller, instructor in physical diagnosis and principles of medicine.[12] In addition, many of the other graduates of the Baltimore schools, both those who were career military and those who enlisted or were drafted, served the colors during World War II.[13]

Base Hospital No. 42: 1942–45

In 1940, the War Department, through the Surgeon General's Office in its preparations for the upcoming war, invited the University to form a provisional group that could be mobilized as an army wartime hospital unit. The members of the unit would be commissioned in the Reserve Corps and be ready for mobilization. The invitation was accepted on May 22, 1940, at a meeting in Chemical Hall at Davidge Hall, and a committee formed that included Drs. Robinson and Brice M. Dorsey, professor of oral surgery at the Dental School. In October, the Surgeon General authorized the organization of the Maryland unit to be known as General Hospital No. 42—the same numerical designation as the base hospital that had represented the University in World War I. By January 1941, the medical, surgical, and dental personnel had been commissioned and a cadre of enlisted men placed in the enlisted reserve. A change in the table of organization resulted in two 250-bed hospitals being formed, the 42nd and 142nd General Hospitals. In April 1941, the two units left Baltimore, the 42nd to Fort Custer, Mich., and the 142nd to Fort Riley, Kans. After two weeks of training, the 42nd left Ft. Custer and entrained for San Francisco, and on May 12 boarded a ship for Australia. Col. Brice M. Dorsey was the ranking dental officer, assisted by Maj. Carl E. Bailey and Capt. Byron W. Inman. No dental treatment was provided in San Francisco on board ship. The first month was spent at Camp Pell, Melbourne, and in July the hospital was assigned to Camp Redbank, near Queensland. Two weeks later, it was transferred to Stuartholme, overlooking Brisbane. A convent school was converted into a hospital at Stuartholme, where the unit remained for 16 months. In November 1943, the 42nd moved to a new and better equipped hospital at Holland Park, Brisbane. In May 1945, the hospital left for Manila, and for the next month, the dental section was stationed in a staging area there. While they were setting up a hospital near Manila, the 42nd was assigned to the hospital ship *Marigold.* The ship spent two days at Okinawa and then headed for Yokohama, arriving there a few days before the signing of the Japanese surrender. The 42nd was the first medical unit to land in Japan. It established a screening camp for prisoners of war. Col. Dorsey was the first dental officer to land in Japan. After two weeks of processing prisoners, the unit moved to Tokyo, where, for six weeks, it was established in St. Luke's Hospital. While in Tokyo, the remaining original members of the unit were separated from the service and left for home on October 23, 1945.[14]

On May 6, 1942, the 142nd General Hospital left Fort Riley for San Francisco, and left the United States on May 26, for Auckland, New Zealand, arriving on June 13. Lieut. Col. Samuel H. Bryant was the ranking dental officer assisted by Maj. Douglas A. Browning and Capt. John W. Cronin. Initially for two weeks, it was quartered at Camp Papakura, near Auckland. It then sailed for the Fiji Islands, arriving in Suva on June 28, from which it was transported in trucks to Lautoka, on the western side of the island. In July the unit operated out of tents. In November the dental clinic received its first permanent building. A year later, the unit moved to a new hospital on the eastern side of the island near Suva, where it remained until September 1944. In October 1944, the unit was moved to Calcutta, India, from which the original members were returned home.[15]

The Honor Roll

The first graduate of the school to die in World War II was Lieut. Com. Hugh Rossman Alexander,[16] Dental Corps, U.S. Navy, who died in line of duty on the U.S.S. *Oklahoma* during the Japanese attack on Pearl Harbor on December 7, 1941. Dr. Alexander was a 1919 alumnus of the Dental Department, University of Maryland. The second alumnus to die was Wadsworth Caesar Trojakowski,[17] a 1923 graduate of the Baltimore College of Dental Surgery, who was killed in action during the battle of the Coral Sea on May 8, 1942, while caring for casualties on the U.S.S. *Lexington.* The third alumnus killed was Gilbert F. Gorsuch,[18] Dental Corps, U.S. Navy, Class of 1939, who was killed in action on November 12, 1942, when his ship, the U.S.S. *Erie*, was in an engagement with Japanese naval forces. Lieutenant Herbert Friedberg,[19] Dental Corps, U.S. Army, Class of 1937, was killed in a Japanese attack on Attu Island on May 29, 1943, the first Army alumnus to die in the war. Several other alumni died during the war including: John Thomas Wieland, Navy Dental Corps, Class of 1942, who was killed in a motor accident on December 2, 1942, while serving with the Seabees in the Southwest Pacific; William Becker Feindt, Army Dental Corps, Class of 1939, who died on June 6, 1944, while serving in India.[20]

Lieut. Com. Hugh Rossman Alexander

Wadsworth Caesar Trojakowski

Gilbert F. Gorsuch

Lieut. Herbert Friedberg

John Thomas Wieland

William Becker Feindt

Dean Robinson probably best summed up the sentiments of the College when he expressed the "deep appreciation of the sacrifices made by the nearly 600 graduates of the BCDS who have entered the services and who are stationed throughout the United States and in all theaters of operations on the many battle fronts."[21]

Robinson Buys Piperno Library: 1941

Coincidently, in 1941, Dr. Robinson acquired the library of Professor Arrigo Piperno of Rome, Italy. The collection included 26 dental books, many of which were rare Italian works dating from as early as 1665, advertisements, and engravings. Among the books was a copy of Antonio Campani's *Odontologia, ossia trattato sopra i dent,* published in 1786. This book was the first dental work published in the Italian language; only five copies were known to exist. More than 50 rare engravings, etchings, and water colors were in the collection. One of the engravings of St. Apollonia probably dated back to 1600. A number of early advertisements, prescriptions, and remedies were also included. Currently, the Piperno Collection is housed in the University of Maryland Health Sciences Library with the Grieves Library.[22]

Accreditation: 1943

From June 10 to 12, 1943, the college was visited by three members of the American Dental Association's Council on Dental Education. The Council reported on the following headings: admission, plant and equipment, faculty, organization and administration, library, financial management and support, clinical teaching, basic science teaching, research, and hospital relationships. The survey of the college revealed the following results:

1. Admission—the total enrollment was 301, of which 18 percent were Maryland residents. More than 55 percent of this total were residents of the states of Connecticut, Massachusetts, New Jersey, and New York.
2. Plant and Equipment—the clinical building was a "modern structure," well-adopted and maintained, but short on chairs to handle the clinical needs of the two upper classes and for development of graduate and postgraduate courses and research projects.

3. Faculty—41 of 42 faculty holding dental degrees earned their degree at Baltimore. Inbreeding, especially in clinical staffs, is generally characteristic in dental schools, but it is "markedly so at Baltimore."
4. Organization and Administration—the College's aims and objectives met the "broad purpose of dental education" and were in "complete harmony with the philosophy and the policy advocated by the Council."
5. Library—"clearly falls within the first tenth of the dental school libraries in the United States and merits special distinction because of the broad range of its collections which are rich in the history and development of dental education and practice."
6. Financial Management and Support—the College ranked third from the bottom of the list of state university-supported dental schools. The Council recommended that the School seek a larger portion of its income outside of its tuition, fees, and clinics.
7. Clinical Teaching—the College was graded "As" in anesthesia and history of dentistry; "Bs" in all other clinical departments except diagnosis, periodontics, pedodontics, and endodontics, which were classified as "Cs." In addition, the clinical departments were headed by "teachers not serving directly in clinics."
8. Basic Science Teaching—physiology and biochemistry received an "A" rating and anatomy, embryology, bacteriology, pharmacology, pathology, and medicine a "B" rating. All the basic science courses, except physiology, were taught at and by the Dental College, in contrast to other state university dental schools using medical school laboratories and faculty.
9. Research—the Council found "good teaching in several departments at Maryland but it did not find significant, constructive research going on to any considerable extent." Productive scholarship seemed to be "limited to a few members of the faculty."
10. Hospital Relationships—the nearby University Hospital and the South Baltimore General Hospital were not used to the full degree as "teaching agencies."

The Council ranked the college seventh among state university dental schools that it surveyed in 1943.[23]

All of the problems reported by the Council would have to wait for Dean Salley to address and rectify almost 20 years later.

Back to the Four-Year Curriculum

With the ending of hostilities in 1945, the college went back to its prewar four-year curriculum; however, the sophomores, juniors, and seniors were allowed to continue for the year 1945. The 1945–46 entering freshman class was a four-year program on a trimester basis, October 1945 to June 1946.[24]

The class entering in 1946 was largely composed of World War II veterans, plus a few youngsters. The average age of the graduating class in 1950 was about 27 years of age. The class started out with about 125 students, but was soon down to around 100. Dr. Marion W. McCrea's histology, Dr. William E. Hahn's anatomy, and Dr. Edmund G. Vanden Bosche's biochemistry course accounted for the majority of the losses. This veteran class was very serious about school, as many had families to support.

In 1949, there was an increase in tuition for the first time in several years to $330 for Maryland residents and $550 for non-residents.[25] In 1949, an Army Reserve Officers Training Corps (ROTC) program was initiated at the college under the command of Lieut. Col. Frederick H. Richardson. Maj. John L. Campbell, DC, USA, a veteran of the Southwest Pacific Theatre of Operations, succeeded Col. Richardson. The program consisted of 32 hours of instruction for each of the four years it was offered. The lectures were scheduled for one hour each week, consisting of lectures and training films dealing with military activities of the Dental Corps. The students were obligated to attend one 6-week summer camp at government expense. By 1951, the ROTC unit had an enrollment of 127 students, 14 seniors, 31 juniors, 44 sophomores, and 38 freshmen. In addition to this group, 24 seniors had completed the training for commissioning after graduation. Also, 17 students held commissions as second lieutenants in the Army and Air Force Senior Dental Programs. The total of 183 students associated with the military programs translated into 45 percent of the student body.[26]

Alumni Endowment Fund: 1946

In March 1946, a non-profit corporation was formed by the members of the National Alumni Association. This charitable corporation was set up to promote the advancement of science and education in dentistry, and to provide financial aid to worthy students. The funds of the corporation were to be managed by a 10-man board of trustees, all who were members of the Alumni Association. These funds were to be invested separate and distinct from the Alumni Association and University of Maryland general funds, and its investment was to be controlled by the Board of Trustees. Income from the invested monies was to be distributed according to the wishes of the donor, or if the gift was unrestricted, the income could be used in any manner deemed suitable by the board.[27]

First Televised Dental Operation: 1950

The first telecast of an actual dental operation ever viewed by a dental society was transmitted from a BCDS operating room in November 1950. Three operations, each about one-half hour long, were televised by WMAR-TV to more than 450 members of the Baltimore City Dental Society and dentists from other parts of Maryland, who watched on eight television receivers at Osler Hall of the Medical and Chirurgical Faculty Building, Baltimore. In addition, 150 dental students watched on receivers at the Dental School. In the first operation shown, Dr. Brice M. Dorsey, professor of oral surgery, extracted six teeth and sutured the ridge. Dr. Grayson W. Gaver, professor of prosthetics, then inserted an immediate denture. Dr. Ernest B. Nuttall, professor of fixed partial prosthetics, prepared a three-quarter crown in the second operation as the "tooth dust" flew off his grinding disc. Lastly, Dr. Kenneth V. Randolph, professor of operative dentistry, demonstrated the new S. S. White "Airdent," air-abrasive drill. Throughout the telecast, viewers' questions were relayed by phone to the operating room and answered by the faculty members.[28]

For the 1951–52 session, the college offered a combined arts and sciences-dental curriculum leading to the degrees of Bachelor of Sciences and Doctor of Dental Surgery. The pre-professional part of this curriculum was to be taken at the College of Arts and Sciences at College Park, Md., and the professional part in the Dental School, Baltimore. The BS degree was to be awarded at the completion of the second year of dental school. The college also offered graduate courses in anatomy, bacteriology, biochemistry, histology and embryology, physiology, and oral surgery, and postgraduate courses in airbrasive technic, head and neck anatomy, oral pathology, oral surgery, periodontics, and prosthodontics.[29]

In May 1951, the school was informed of the death of Major James Baido, Class of 1946, in Korea. His truck convoy was ambushed by the Chinese at Hagaru-ri on November 27, 1950. He was the first and only BCDS casualty of the Korean War.[30]

The early 1950s also saw the introduction of the self-curing acrylic resin restorations into the clinical armamentarium. L.D. Caulk introduced "Kadon" in about 1949 to the profession to replace the silicate cement restoration as the treatment of choice in the anterior teeth where esthetics was of paramount importance. The material came in various tooth shades and was very popular for its cosmetic value and strength, especially in restorations involving the incisal edge of anterior teeth. However, the material had mechanical and biological problems with marginal leakage, due to expansion and contraction, and its deleterious effect on the dental pulp; therefore, it did not completely replace the silicates as the material of choice where esthetics was concerned—that would have to wait for the composite restoration of the 1960s. Nevertheless, the use of Kadon was taught in the operative clinic.[31]

Around 1950, Dr. Robinson began negotiating with 90-year-old Dr. Vincenzo Guerini[32] of Naples, Italy, for the purchase of Guerini's collection of replica ancient prosthetic devices from Greece, Phoenicia, Eturia, and Rome. The collection included a walnut wood cabinet with the front part carved by the sculptor, Fosca. Finally, in February 1952, an agreement was reached to purchase the collection for $2,500 and have it shipped to the college's museum.[33] Several examples of Guerini's Etruscan bridgework can be seen on exhibition at the National Museum of Dentistry at the University of Maryland, Baltimore.

Baltimore Fluoridates: 1952

In 1916, the first article on mottled enamel was published by Drs. G. V. Black and Frederick S. McKay of Colorado Springs. The "Colorado Stain" opened the door to the realization that an excess of fluorine in the drinking water prevented dental caries.[34] In the late 1940s, the BCDS junior and senior students were treating children's teeth with topical sodium fluoride as a prophylactic measure to reduce caries.[35] On November 2, 1950, the House of Delegates of the American Dental Association recommended the fluoridation of community water supplies. Mayor Thomas D'Alesandro of Baltimore immediately contacted the Baltimore City Health Department and the Bureau of Water Supply to provide "information on the feasibility of adding fluoride to the city's water. Children between birth and the age of eight when the teeth are formed would be the primary beneficiaries of the reduction in tooth decay. Evidence of the effectiveness of this treatment had already been demonstrated in other cities, such as Grand Rapids, Mich., and Newburgh, N.Y. In 1952, Baltimore was a city of 970,000 people, the seventh largest in the nation, and its water supply served another 210,000 in surrounding counties. At the time, Dr. H. Berton McCauley, a BCDS alumnus of the Class of 1936 and a former faculty member,[36] was the director of the Baltimore City Health Department Bureau of Dental Care. Finally, after some delays caused by opponents of fluoridation, at 3 p.m., Wednesday, November 26, 1952, Baltimore's water supply contained the recommended one part fluoride to one million parts of water. It had been a hard battle, but Mayor D'Alesandro and Dr. McCauley had persevered and won.[37]

The Retirement of Dean Robinson: 1953

In 1953, Dr. J. Ben Robinson retired from the deanship of the college, which he had served for 29 years; he was made dean emeritus. It was the end of an era in dental education at the Baltimore College of Dental Surgery and the University of Maryland. A legend in his own time, Dr. Robinson, retired by the state of Maryland because of reaching the age of 70, then became the first dean of the School of Dentistry, West Virginia University. Dr. Myron S. Aisenberg was appointed the new dean to succeed Dr. Robinson.[38]

NOTES

1. Gardner P. H. Foley, ed., *Proceedings of the 125th Anniversary Celebration of the Baltimore College of Dental Surgery* (Baltimore: Horn-Shafer Co., 1966), pp. 247–48.
2. Baltimore College of Dental Surgery, Dental School, University of Maryland, *Annual Announcement and Catalogue Baltimore College of Dental Surgery, Dental School, University of Maryland, Session 1941–1942* (n.p., [1941]), p. ii.
3. George F. Jeffcott, *A History of the United States Army Dental Service in World War II* (Washington, DC: U.S. Government Printing Office, 1955), p. 138.
4. Baltimore College of Dental Surgery, Dental School, University of Maryland, *Annual Announcement and Catalogue* [1941–1942], i, ii.
5. Baltimore College of Dental Surgery, Dental School, University of Maryland, *Announcement of Accelerated Course of Instruction Offered by the Baltimore College of Dental Surgery, Dental School, University of Maryland* (n.p., [1942]), p. 35.
6. Jeffcott, *History of the United States Army Dental Service*, pp. 136–37.
7. Baltimore College of Dental Surgery, Dental School, University of Maryland, *Announcement of Accelerated Course*, p. i.
8. Morton H. Hollander, ed., *The Mirror of November, 1943* (n.p., 1943), p. 75.
9. Baltimore College of Dental Surgery, Dental School, University of Maryland, *Annual Catalogue Baltimore College of Dental Surgery, Dental School, University of Maryland, Session 1943–1944* (Baltimore: n.p., [1943]), p. 1.
10. Baltimore College of Dental Surgery, Dental School, University of Maryland, *Annual Catalogue Baltimore College of Dental Surgery, Dental School, University of Maryland, Session 1944–1945* (Baltimore: n.p., [1944]), pp. 46–47.
11. Jeffcott, *History of the United States Army Dental Service*, p. 140.
12. Baltimore College of Dental Surgery, Dental School, University of Maryland, *Annual Catalogue* [1944–1945], pp. 4–7.
13. Gardner, P. H. Foley, "The Dental Sections of the University Hospital Units," *Journal of the Baltimore College of Dental Surgery, Dental School, University of Maryland* 9 (November 1946): 66–67; Theodore A. Schwartz, Walter E. Karfgin, and Clarence G. Luther, et al, eds. *The 42nd General Hospital in World War II* (Brisbane, Australia: Truth and Sportsman Ltd., [1945?]), 2 pp.[no page nos.]
14. Foley, "University Hospital Units," 67.
15. During World War I, Hugh Rossman Alexander interrupted his dental career at the University of Maryland to join the U.S. Navy. In 1918, he served on convoy duty with the U.S.S. *Martha Washington*. After the War, he returned to graduate in 1919. In 1920, he was commissioned as a lieutenant (j.g.) and assigned to duty at the Naval Training Station, Hampton Roads, Va. Later, he served on the U.S.S. *Henderson*, a naval transport. In 1930, he was promoted to lieutenant commander. During the Japanese attack, it was said that he helped men to safety by pushing them out of the port-hole of the compartment in which they were trapped while the ship was on fire. [J. Ben Robinson, "Dedication Address by Dean Robinson," *Journal of the Baltimore College of Dental Surgery, Dental School, University of Maryland* 8 (December 1943): 4.]
16. Wadsworth C. Trojakowski was born in 1898 in Schenectady, N. Y. During World War I, at age 17, he enlisted in the U.S. Navy. He left the service as a chief pharmacist's mate to enter the Baltimore College of Dental Surgery and graduated in 1923. In July 1924, he was appointed a lieutenant (j.g.) in the U. S. Navy Dental Corps. In 1929, he was promoted to lieutenant and served with the Marine Expeditionary Brigade in Managua, Nicaragua. After a tour of duty at the U.S. Naval Hospital, Great Lakes, he was assigned to sea duty with the U.S.S. *Beaver*. His next duty was with the Asiatic Station in Hankow, China. In 1937, he was the dental surgeon at the U.S. Naval Hospital, Brooklyn, where he was promoted to lieutenant commander. In 1939, he was on sea duty with the battleship, U.S.S. *Mississippi*. In 1941, he was stationed at the Puget Sound Navy Yard, Bremerton, Wash. His next duty was with the aircraft carrier, U.S.S. *Lexington*. In January 1942, he was promoted to commander. He died while caring for casualties in the forward dressing station on board the *Lexington*. ["Wadsworth C. Trojackowski," *Journal of the Baltimore College of Dental Surgery, Dental School, University of Maryland* 7 (September 1942): 21.]
17. Gilbert F. Gorsuch, a graduate of the Sparrows Point High School, graduated from the Baltimore College of Dental Surgery, Dental School, University of Maryland, in 1939. He practiced for a year and a half in Rockville and in Pocomoke City, Md. In 1941, he joined the naval reserves, and was promoted to lieutenant shortly before his death. [Robinson, "Dedication Address," 4-5.]

18. Herbert Friedberg interned at Beth Israel Hospital in Newark, and then attended a postgraduate course in oral surgery Northwestern University Dental School. After starting a practice in Atlantic City, N.J., he entered the Army Dental Corps in August 1942. He was first sent to Camp Sutton, N.C., and then transferred to duty with the 302nd Ordnance Battalion at Fort Ord, Ca.. His last assignment was with the 7th Medical Battalion, Armed Landing Force. On Attu, his field hospital was attacked by a force of 200 Japanese troops, who killed a medical officer, five corpsmen, and several patients. Reportedly, Lieut. Friedberg was asleep in his sleeping bag when he was shot and bayoneted. [Robinson, "Dedication Address," 5.]
19. Robinson, "Dedication Address," 4-5; Foley, *Proceedings of the 125th Anniversary Celebration*, pp. 243-44.
20. Robinson, "Dedication Address," 3.
21. "The Clarence J. Grieves Library Foundation: The Piperno Collection," *Journal of the Baltimore College of Dental Surgery* 6 (January 1942): 9-10.
22. Council on Dental Education, American Dental Association, "Survey of Dental Schools, 1942-43: Report on the Baltimore College of Dental Surgery, Dental School, University of Maryland," Dean's Office, Files.
23. Baltimore College of Dental Surgery, Dental School, University of Maryland, *Annual Catalogue Baltimore College of Dental Surgery, Dental School, University of Maryland, Session 1945–1946* (Baltimore: n.p., [1945]), 3-4.
24. Baltimore College of Dental Surgery, Dental School, University of Maryland, *Catalogue of the Baltimore College of Dental Surgery, Dental School, University of Maryland, Session 1949–1950* (Baltimore: n.p., [1949]), p, 15.
25. Baltimore College of Dental Surgery, Dental School, University of Maryland, *Catalogue of the Baltimore College of Dental Surgery, Dental School, University of Maryland, Session 1950–1951* (Baltimore: n.p., [1951]), p. 31 [insert]; "School Military Units," *Journal of the Baltimore College of Dental Surgery, Dental School, University of Maryland* 10 (May 1951): 54.
26. "The Endowment Fund of the National Alumni Association of the Baltimore College of Dental Surgery, Dental School, University of Maryland, Incorporated," Harry B. McCarthy Papers, National Museum of Dentistry Archives.
27. "600 Dentists and Students Watch Televised Operations," *The Sun*, November 14, 1950.
28. Baltimore College of Dental Surgery, Dental School, University of Maryland, *Catalogue of the Baltimore College of Dental Surgery, Dental School, University of Maryland, Session 1951–1952* (Baltimore: n.p., [1951]), pp.13, 35–36.
29. "Report on Major James Baido '46," *Journal of the Baltimore College of Dental Surgery, Dental School, University of Maryland* 11 (January 1952): 20.
30. Ralph W. Phillips, "Past, Present, and Future Composite Resin Systems," *Dental Clinics of North America* 25 (April 1981): 210–11.
31. Vincenzo Guerini was the author of *A History of Dentistry From the Most Ancient Times Until the End of the Eighteenth Century*, published under the auspices of the National Dental Association in 1909.
32. Letters, J. Ben Robinson to Vincenzo Guerini, March 21, 1950, July 18, December 1, 12, 1951, February 6, 1952; Vincenzo Guerini to J. Ben Robinson, March 28, May 5, July 26, October 30, December 4, 1950; December 18, 1951; January 8, February 21, March 28, 1952; Vincenzo Guerini, "Archaeological Dental Collection [list]," Baltimore College of Dental Surgery Papers, National Museum of Dentistry Archives.
33. Frederick S. McKay, "Fluorine and Mottled Enamel," in *Fluorine in Dental Public Health: A Symposium* (New York: New York Institute of Oral Pathology, 1944), pp. 10, 12.
34. The treatment at that time consisted of four applications of a topical solution of sodium fluoride to the dry and isolated teeth in each quadrant, no more than a week apart. [The author.]
35. H. Berton McCauley was an instructor in "clinical radiodontia" on from 1936 to1943. [Baltimore College of Dental Surgery, Dental School, University of Maryland, *Ninety-Sixth Annual Announcement and Catalogue Baltimore College of Dental Surgery, Dental School, University of Maryland, Session 1936–1937* (n,p., [1936]), p. 6.]
36. H. Berton McCauley, "Baltimore Fluoridates," *Maryland Medical Journal* 42 (August 1993): 745-46, 749.
37. Baltimore College of Dental Surgery, Dental School, University of Maryland, *Catalogue of the Baltimore College of Dental Surgery, Dental School, University of Maryland, Session 1953–1954* (Baltimore: n.p., [1953]), p. 6.

Myron S. Aisenberg

Chapter 17

The Aisenberg Years: 1953–63

"That the American Dental Association most respectfully recommend to our Dental Colleges the necessity of being more particular in requiring their matriculants a higher order of general literary and scientific education, and the strictest enforcement of their standard requirements for graduation."[1] **~Walter Webb Allport, 1860**

Myron S. Aisenberg: 1953–63

With the retirement of J. Ben Robinson, Myron Samson Aisenberg became the acting dean on July 1, 1953, and became dean in 1954. Actually, Dr. Aisenberg was not the first choice as dean. In the summer of 1954, Dr. H. C. "Curley" Byrd, the president of the University of Maryland, interviewed Dr. Harry B. McCarthy, the former director of clinics at the college, about the deanship. Dr. McCarthy had left the school two years previously to accept a position at Baylor University in Waco, Texas, and had been recommended for the deanship of that dental school. After discussing the situation with Dr. Byrd and the possible ramifications, McCarthy felt obligated to stay with Baylor and help build a new school and become accredited. Dr. Byrd reluctantly agreed with McCarthy's decision and selected Dr. Aisenberg as the new dean to replace Dr. Robinson.[2]

Dr. Aisenberg was born on October 30, 1899, in New Britain, Conn. He graduated with honors from the Dental Department, University of Maryland, in 1922. Dr. Timothy O. Heatwole, dean of the school, appointed him to the faculty as an assistant professor in science laboratories and clinical demonstrator. After the merger of the Baltimore College of Dental Surgery and the Dental Department, University of Maryland in 1923, he was made professor of embryology and histology, bacteriology and pathology at the combined school in 1924. In 1939, he was appointed assistant professor of bacteriology and pathology and in July 1940, he was promoted to professor of oral pathology. His title was changed in 1942 to professor of pathology. Since 1940, he served on the faculty council. He was president of the Maryland State Dental Association from 1943 to 1944 and the American Academy of Oral Pathology (founding fellow) in 1955. He was a diplomate of the American Board of Oral Pathology. Dr. Aisenberg was the recipient of the Fones Medal of the Connecticut State Dental Association and the Alpha Omega Distinguished Alumnus Award. He was also the Supreme Chancellor of Alpha Omega in 1955. His memberships included the Gorgas Odontological Society, Omicron Kappa Upsilon, Sigma Xi, American College of Dentists, the International Association for Dental Research, and honorary memberships in the Baltimore City and Maryland State Medical Pathology Societies. He was nationally known for his contributions to the dental literature, mainly in orthodontics, periodontics, oral surgery, and oral pathology, and was noted for his clinics and papers before national and local dental societies. Dr. Aisenberg died on April 12, 1986, after a brief illness at St. Joseph's Hospital in Baltimore.[3]

The Oral Surgery Clinic: 1950s

The oral surgery clinic had its own nurse, June G. Bingen, RN, and a secretary, Patricia R. Mall. At that time, the department had four operating rooms, located on the first floor opposite the Lombard Street entrance. Four senior students were assigned to the clinic each day, assisted by four junior students. The patients had no appointments; they just reported to the clinic each morning and after a quick examination of the offending tooth were sent to the X-ray department for radiographs. At that time, it was the only clinic in the school treating African-American patients. The instructors checked each patient before the student was allowed to proceed with anesthesia. At the time, anesthetic carpules were not used; the students had to make their own anesthetic solution from a procaine tablet mixed with Ringer's solution. The tablet was heated in a small porcelain crucible over a Bunsen burner. The instruments were sterilized by boiling, except for the syringe needles and suture needles, which were autoclaved. The clinic ran until the last patient was completed, which deviated from the other clinics (which closed at an appointed hour). For the 1957–59 sessions, now half-time (five mornings a week), John Hyson, Jr. [the author] was in charge of the oral surgery outpatient clinic at the old University Hospital Building on Lombard Street (which later became the site of the Student Union Building). Two senior dental students were assigned there each morning. In addition to local anesthesia in this clinic, trilene/nitrous oxide general anesthesia was used on children. The students thought it was a "big deal" to give intramuscular penicillin shots, as they had never done it before. For these five mornings, Hyson's payment was the sum of $2,000 for the entire year.[4]

University of Maryland Centennial: 1956

In 1956, the college participated in the centennial celebration of the founding of the Maryland Agricultural College at College Park, Md. Exhibits were set up in the Student Activities Building representing every school of the University and every department of the College Park Division. Dr. Aisenberg appointed a faculty committee to organize the school's exhibit, which included: Drs. Robert Biddington, Hugh Clement, Edward Dobbs, Calvin Gaver, and Mr. Gardner Foley, chairman. The presentation was in four booths. Booth 1 contained some of the rarest objects from the Dental Museum, including the Washington dentures made by John Greenwood in 1795 and Horace Hayden's 1810 dental license; Booth 2 illustrated the story of dental education from the founding of the Baltimore College of Dental Surgery in 1840 and included Robert Arthur's 1841 diploma; Booth 3: "Dental Health Problems" depicted with slides and moulage models the diseases that the dental student was trained to observe and treat; Booth 4: "Opportunities in Dentistry" illustrated the career opportunities in the dental profession. The dental presentation received special commendation from the centenary committee.[5]

In 1957, the tuition was increased to $400 for Maryland residents and $675 for non-residents. In addition, that year a student health service was established to supply medical and surgical care for its students. A student health clinic was located in the Dental School. Every student was required to undergo a complete physical examination. Any medical problems noted had to be corrected within the first school year. Each student had to have a statement from his ophthalmologist regarding the condition of his eyes. Hospital admission through the school physician was covered in University Hospital.[6]

Gardner P. H. Foley: Professor of Dental History

Now that Dr. Robinson had left the college, Gardner P. H. Foley assumed the professorship of dental history. Gardner Patrick Henry Foley was born in Gloucester, Mass., on March 18, 1902. He graduated from Clark University with a BA degree in 1923 and an MA in 1925. In 1925, he began his academic career at the University of Tennessee, and then in 1926 moved to the University of Mississippi. In 1928, he began a lifelong career of 41 years at the University of Maryland, during which time he reached approximately 3,000 dental students. His students made greater use of the library than those of any other department of the Dental School. In 1941, Foley was made an assistant professor of dental history; in 1949, he was promoted to associate professor; and in 1951, he was made a full professor. In 1953, at J. Ben Robinson's retirement, he assumed full responsibility for the history course. During his tenure, he was in charge of the Dental School's publications, being the associate editor of the *Journal of the Baltimore College of Dental Surgery* from 1938 to 1941 and editor from 1941 to 1964. Foley was also the faculty advisor for the student senate, and for the yearbook, *The Mirror*, for more than 30 years. He was responsible for the publication of the book on the School's 125th anniversary celebration. Foley was one of the founders of the *American Academy of the History of Dentistry* and wrote the first draft of its constitution. He was a regular contributor to the *Journal of the American Dental Association* with his "Foley's Footnotes" and authored a book on his footnotes. Professor Foley was elected as a fellow of the American College of Dentists, an honor rarely bestowed on a non-dentist. Professor Foley retired in 1969, but continued to lend his expertise on the school's history in an advisory capacity.[7] The formal course of history lectures was given in the sophomore year. In addition, the students were taught the use of libraries; compilation of bibliographies; oral presentation of papers; the collection, organization, and use of information; and uses of oral and written composition.[8] Professor Foley also made his students write a history paper with footnotes and a bibliography. His objective was to develop the students' skills to research and write a decent scientific paper.[9]

The High-Speed Era

In the early 1950s, the college acquired one of Dr. Robert B. Black's "airbrasive" machines marketed under the trade name "Airdent" by the S. S. White Company. The new drill was based on the principle of a finely focused stream of aluminum oxide abrasive particles to cut tooth structure. Its advantages were: increased cutting speed, no vibration, slight pressure, no heat generated, and no noise conducted by bone. Its disadvantages were: cost, space it occupied (large cabinet), required a rubber dam to control abrasive particles, incapability to remove soft carious dentin, necessity to revert to conventional rotary instruments in certain cases, and retraining the dentist.[10] The machine was located in the second floor demonstration room for the faculty to use to demonstrate the machine to the students. This failed technology would resurface some 40 years later.

Beginning in 1957, a number of changes were instituted in the Department of Operative Dentistry. These changes not only modified the didactic and clinical teaching, but improved the students' physical facilities. For the first time, the students were being taught to use a high-speed air-turbine hand piece[11] to cut cavity preparations and prepare crowns. The cavity preparations that formerly took the students hours to prepare with the old 5,000 rpm belt-driven handpieces was reduced to minutes.[12] The air-turbine handpiece was light and required no major changes in technique. With carbide burs and diamond stones, replacing the steel ones formerly used, enamel could be wiped away quickly with a series of gentle strokes. The air-turbine handpiece revolutionized dentistry. Dr. Ring best sums up its advantages: "It has made possible better restorations with less sacrifice of tooth structure. It has made the patient more comfortable not only by reducing vibration but also by cutting working time to a fraction of what it was before. And it has allowed dentists to do finer, more complicated work, of a delicacy and sophistication unimaginable just a few decades earlier."[13]

As a matter of interest, one of the Baltimore College of Dental Surgery's alumni, Dr. Basil Manly Wilkerson, Class of 1868, the inventor of the first hydraulic dental chair, also patented an air-turbine drill in 1877. His turbine drill was "automatically driven by water, steam, compressed air, or other motive power." It would be another 75 years before his invention became the standard.[14]

In addition to the high-speed equipment, the operative clinic was fitted with 14 jade-green Ritter H-5 units, which provided the student the use of the same type of equipment as the average dental office. Instruction also included the "didactic and clinical application" of elastic impression materials, the different types of amalgam and gold foil condensers, and the newer restorative materials.[15] On October 17 and 18, 1959, a postgraduate course in "High and Ultra High Speeds in Operative Dentistry" was presented by the operative department. There were 32 participants. The course was divided into didactic and clinical and was taught by Capt. George W. Ferguson, DC, USN; Capt. Arne G. Nielsen, DC, USN; Dr. Harold R. Stanley; Dr. Lloyd M. Armstrong; Dr. Julian J. Thomas; and the operative staff. The registrants were given the opportunity to evaluate nine different high-speed hand pieces on extracted teeth. Patients were also provided for clinical trials.[16]

The oral surgery department reported that from July 1, 1958, to June 30, 1959, there were 16,048 patients treated, 24,086 teeth extracted, and 39 fractured jaws treated in the school's oral surgery clinic, and the out- and inpatient departments of University Hospital.[17]

Dental Hygiene Department Rumors: 1959

In 1959, the first rumbling of the establishment of a school of dental hygiene surfaced, which Dr. Robinson had for so long opposed. On July 31, 1959, the National Alumni Association of the Baltimore College of Dental Surgery, Dental School, University of Maryland, notified

Dr. Elkins, the president of the university, that they had adopted a resolution requesting that a department of oral hygiene be organized. Dean Aisenberg and the faculty agreed that this training program should be established. The only problem was the lack of proper space for the program. As a new building was being planned, it was hoped that a hygiene program could be included. Meanwhile, Dr. Aisenberg was re-studying the current facilities to see if sufficient facilities could be provided for a hygiene program before construction of the new building.[18]

The Baltimore Union

In 1960, the Baltimore Union for professional school students was established on campus at 621 West Lombard Street. Accommodations for 195 male students was provided in the five-story, semi air-conditioned building, which had a cafeteria, fountain lounge, game room, bookstore, laundry room, barber shop, and meeting rooms. The rates were $150 per semester for double room, $60 per six weeks' summer session for a double room, and $45 per month for double room. The rate covered room furnishings, bed, chest of drawers, desk, chair, and lamp, book shelves, maid service, and change of linen.[19]

The Dental Library Transfer

In 1961, the Baltimore College of Dental Surgery's Grieves Library of more than 16,000 books and bound journals on dentistry and the collateral sciences, together with numerous pamphlets, reprints, unbound journals, and original prints were transferred to the campus Health Sciences Library, which included medicine, pharmacy, and nursing. The building was located at 111 South Greene Street, diagonally opposite the Dental School. The library contained more than 90,000 bound volumes and subscribed to more than 1,600 scientific periodicals. It was staffed by well-qualified professional librarians.[20]

For the 1962-63 session, the college added a graduate course in radiation biology to "familiarize the student with the techniques of handling radioactive isotopes as applied in biological research." The topics covered in the course were:

> The physics of radioactivity from the standpoint of the biological researcher, the selection of isotopes for specific investigations; the effects of radioactivity on cells, tissues, and systems; the effect of radioactivity on inheritance; the role of the environment on the effectiveness of radioactivity; and certain phases of laboratory health physics. The laboratory will be concerned with the use and location, as well as recording and interpreting data of isotopes as applied to biological research.[21]

Rumors of a New Building

In 1961, there was the first mention of a new building to replace the current one, which had served the college since 1930. It was reported that the University of Maryland had tentative plans to expand the Baltimore campus of the University. Specifically, the report stated that the planned expansion would increase the enrollment of the Baltimore school by 50 percent; the total cost of the project would be approximately $20,000,000; and that a new dental school building was included at a cost of $2,500,000. The American Council on Education had already surveyed dental education in the United States. One of the members of the commission was Charles P. McCormack, the chairman of the Board of Regents of the University of Maryland. Their official report contained the following observation:

> If the problem of financing dental education could be kept within the boundaries of the present enrollment, it would be relatively easy to solve, even though it would cost more money. However, the population of the United States is exploding and the demand for dental services grows constantly. Existing dental schools will have to be expanded and new schools must be constructed if there is to be sufficient manpower to care for the dental health of the people.[22]

The commission expressed the opinion that a building program of $35,000,000 would be necessary over the next 10 years to provide for the needs of dental education, just to keep up with the demands of the public. In 1961, a bill (S.1072) was introduced in the Senate to provide appropriations "to increase the opportunity for training of physicians, dentists, and professional public health personnel." In addition, the bill provided for dental school construction in the amount of $15,000,000 annually for 10 years, beginning July 1, 1961, and ending June 30, 1971. Construction was defined as: "The construction of new buildings, the expansion of existing buildings, and the remodeling, replacement, renovation, major repair or alteration of existing buildings." Grants to the Dental School could go up to 66⅔% of the total cost of construction.[23]

Retirement of Dean Aisenberg: 1963

In 1963, after serving as dean for 10 years, Dr. Aisenberg decided to retire from the deanship in September. Dean Aisenberg had presented papers before all of the national dental societies and a great many of the local and state societies.[24] His legacy was that he had the unenviable task of replacing the legendary J. Ben Robinson, yet stayed the course to keep the school among the upper echelon of dental education. In addition, his era ushered in the high-speed techniques of modern air-turbine dentistry for both operative and crown and bridge.

NOTES

1. J. S. Latimer, "Dental Education," in *Transactions of the American Dental Association* (Cincinnati: Wrightson & Co., 1863), p. 61.
2. Harry B. McCarthy, *Harry B. McCarthy, DDS, MA: an autobiography* (n.p., 1985), pp. 19–20.
3. Gardner P. H. Foley, ed. *Proceedings of the 125th Anniversary Celebration of the Baltimore College of Dental Surgery* (Baltimore: Horn-Shafer Co., 1966), p. 126; "Dr. Aisenberg '22 Appointed Acting Dean," *Journal of the Baltimore College of Dental Surgery, Dental School, University of Maryland* 13 (January 1954): 1; "In Memoriam [Dr. Myron Aisenberg]," *BCDS Forum* 7 (Fall 1986): 29.
4. The author.
5. "The School's Exhibit at the College Park Centenary," *Journal of the Baltimore College of Dental Surgery, Dental School, University of Maryland* 15 (May 1956): 68.
6. Baltimore College of Dental Surgery, Dental School, University of Maryland, *One Hundred and Seventeenth Catalogue with Announcements for the 1957–1958 Session Baltimore College of Dental Surgery, Dental School, University of Maryland* (Baltimore: n.p. [1957]), pp. 16, 18.
7. J. Ben Robinson, "A Testimonial to Gardner P. H. Foley," *Alma Mater* 11 (Spring 1970): 25–27; "Gardner P. H. Foley Honored," *Alma Mater* 13 (April 1972): 32.
8. Baltimore College of Dental Surgery, Dental School, University of Maryland, *One Hundred and Seventeenth Catalogue*, p. 23.
9. The author remembers writing a paper as a freshman student in 1946 for Foley's class on Dr. James Edmund Garretson, the "Father of Oral Surgery." In 1959, Professor Foley helped the author with his master's thesis, "The Use of Buccal Streptokinase in the Treatment of Infection and Edema." He had a great command of the English language and was a stickler for details such as comas, etc. He was a major influence on his students' writing skills. [The author.]
10. Robert B. Black, "Technic for Nonmechanical Preparation of Cavities and Prophylaxis," *Journal of the American Dental Association* 32 (August 1, 1945): 955, 956, 962.
11. Actually, the first successful, practical turbine handpiece was developed by Dr. Robert J. Nelsen, a research associate of the American Dental Association, and his staff at the National Bureau of Standards in Washington, D.C. Their handpiece was hydraulically powered, ran at a speed of 61,000 rpm, and was marketed as the "Turbo-jet." However, their effort was soon overshadowed by an air-turbine handpiece developed by Dr. John Borden of the Naval Dental School, which was marketed in 1957 as the "Airotor." The handpiece ran at a speed of 250,000 rpm. [Robert J. Nelsen, Carl E. Pelander, and John W. Kumpula, "Hydraulic turbine contra-angle handpiece,"

Journal of the American Dental Association 47 (September 1953): 324-29; Malvin E. Ring, "Behind the Dentist's Drill," *American Heritage of Invention & Technology*," 11 (Fall 1995): 31.]

12. Jose E. Medina, "Department of Operative Dentistry," *Alma Mater* 2 (February 1960): 39.
13. Ring, "Behind the Dentist's Drill," 31.
14. John M. Hyson, Jr., and Audrey B. Davis, "Basil Manly Wilkerson: Dental Inventor Extraordinaire," *Journal of the History of Dentistry* 47 (July 1999): 63.
15. Medina, "Department of Operative Dentistry," 39.
16. Jose E. Medina, "Postgraduate Course in Operative Dentistry," *Alma Mater* 2 (February 1960): 40.
17. Brice M. Dorsey, "Surgery Department," *Alma Mater* 2 (February 1960): 41–42.
18. "University of Maryland [Letter, A. O. Kuhn, Executive Vice President, to Joseph P. Cappuccio, Secretary, National Alumni Association, BCDS, n.d.]," *Alma Mater* 1 (March 1959): 9.
19. Baltimore College of Dental Surgery, Dental School, University of Maryland, *One Hundred and Twentieth Catalogue with Announcements for the 1960–1961 Session Baltimore College of Dental Surgery, Dental School, University of Maryland* (Baltimore, n.p., [1960]), pp. 20–21.
20. Baltimore College of Dental Surgery, Dental School, University of Maryland, *One Hundred and Twenty-First Catalogue with Announcements for the 1961–1962 Session Baltimore College of Dental Surgery, Dental School, University of Maryland* (Baltimore, n.p., [1961]), p. 11.
21. Baltimore College of Dental Surgery, Dental School, University of Maryland, *One Hundred and Twenty-Second Catalogue with Announcements for the 1962–1963 Session Baltimore College of Dental Surgery, Dental School, University of Maryland* (Baltimore, n.p., [1962]), p. 30.
22. [Kyrle W. Preis, ed.] "The Future—What!," *Alma Mater* 3 (June 1961): 2.
23. Ibid., 3
24. "Dr. Aisenberg Will Retire," *The Evening Sun* (Baltimore), May 23, 1963.

John J. Salley

Chapter 18

The Salley Years: 1963–74

"Knowledge is accumulating rapidly and technology is developing apace. Change is the most striking characteristic of this revolutionary era. In the present setting, any program, which fails to recognize the need to reevaluate and to revise, will soon be inadequate to serve its purpose. The modern university is under constant stress and strain. It must hold to lasting values, and must seek ways for adjustment and improvement. While the university as a whole must be committed to progress, the change can take place only within specific disciplines."[1] ~**Wilson H. Elkins**, President, University of Maryland, 1966

John J. Salley: 1963–74

In June 1962, Dr. Aisenberg[2] announced his intention to retire at the end of the next academic year. President Wilson H. Elkins appointed a search committee to find a successor. The committee was headed by Dr. R. Lee Hornbake, vice-president for the Department of Academic Affairs and included five faculty members, all of whom were department heads; namely, Drs. Biddix, Hahn, Preis, Vanden Bosche, and White.

By September 1962, the committee had begun to examine the credentials of 77 candidates for the position. Eventually the list was narrowed down to four candidates, who were interviewed by the committee and President Elkins at College Park. On March 21, 1963, President Elkins announced the appointment to the deanship of Dr. John J. Salley, professor and chairman of the Department of Oral Pathology, Medical College of Virginia, School of Dentistry. Dr. Aisenberg retired on September 30, 1963.[3]

Dr. Salley was born on October 29, 1926, in Richmond, Va. After attending public schools in Richmond, he entered the Virginia Military Institute in 1943. At the end of his sophomore year, he enlisted in the U.S. Army Air Force. After a year of service, he entered the Medical College of Virginia, School of Dentistry, and received his DDS degree in 1951. Contemplating a career in dental education, he received his PhD from the University of Rochester, School of Dentistry and Medicine, in 1954. During his postgraduate course of studies at Rochester, Dr. Salley was a United States Public Health Service (USPHS) postdoctoral fellow in pathology. From 1952 to 1954, he also served as an instructor in histology at the Eastman School of Dental Hygiene. He began his faculty affiliation with the Medical College of Virginia as an instructor in pathology, oral diagnosis, and therapeutics in 1954.

From 1955 to 1959, he was an assistant professor of pathology and dentistry; associate professor of pathology and dentistry (1959–62); chairman, Department of Oral Pathology (1960); and professor of oral pathology (1962). In 1956, Dr. Salley became the coordinator of cancer teaching and was a member of the tumor board at the Medical College of Virginia Hospitals.[4]

Dr. Salley was also a dental consultant, Office of the Chief Medical Examiner, Commonwealth of Virginia (1956); consultant on oral pathology, Richmond VA Hospital (1959); consultant to National Institute of Dental Research, USPHS, at Bethesda (1960); member of advisory editorial board, *Journal of Dental Research* (1960–62); chairman, American Cancer Society Institutional Grant Committee, Medical College of Virginia (1960); consultant, National Board of Dental Examiners (1961); and member of the Dental Study Section, National Institutes of Health (1962).[5]

In 1953, Dr. Salley received the Novice Award, International Association for Dental Research and in 1961, the Outstanding Civilian Service medal, Department of the Army. He held memberships in Sigma Zeta Science Society, 1950; Omicron Kappa Upsilon, 1951; Sigma Xi, 1954; American Dental Association; International Association for Dental Research; American Academy of Pathology; and the American Cancer Society. He contributed eight articles to the dental literature and collaborated on eight others before coming to Maryland. Dr. Salley had the distinction of being the second dean of a Maryland dental school who was not a graduate of a Maryland school. He assumed his duties on July 1, 1963.[6]

Almost immediately after assuming office, Dr. Salley's Committee on Curriculum and Building Planning adopted a series of objectives to revitalize the school. In September 1963, the committee announced the following three objectives:

1. To create the "highest quality of instruction in dental art and science."
2. To foster "an atmosphere of investigative spirit."
3. To present "an abiding attention to the service obligations incumbent on the dental profession."[7]

Integration of the Faculty: 1963

During Dr. Salley's first year, in November 1963, John E. Bonas, BS, MA, was hired as a research associate in the Department of Physiology. He was the first African American person to serve in a professional position at the school. As the only black professional at the school, he was well prepared from his experiences at the City University of New York, where he was frequently the only black student in class. Dr. Bonas recalled that any fears of discrimination were unfounded, as he was "treated like anybody else." Dr. John I. White, the professor of physiology, encouraged Bonas to pursue a doctorate and he then became the first black graduate student at the Dental School and later the first black faculty member as an instructor in physiology in 1968. After receiving his doctorate in 1972, he was promoted to assistant professor. Dr. Bonas credits Dean Salley with "bringing about the transition to a racially diverse faculty and student body," which ultimately led to the admission of the first black dental student, Elton Maddox in 1972.[8]

Meanwhile, Dr. Harvey Webb, Jr., a 1972 graduate of Howard University, became the first African American to serve as a part-time faculty member. Dean Salley appointed him an assistant professor, Department of Community Dentistry in July 1968.[9] In 1969, Dr. John Carr became the first recognized African-American dentist to serve as a full-time clinical faculty member of the school. Dr. Carr was a 1953 graduate of the Meharry Medical College, who had served for 28 years in the U.S. Army Dental Corps. He joined the Department of Restorative Dentistry as an assistant professor.[10]

The first African-American woman to join the faculty was Dr. Oswaldene E. Walker, a 1972 graduate of Howard University. She was appointed as an instructor in restorative dentistry in 1972.[11] The following year, 1973, another African-American woman, Gwendolyn F. Dunn, a 1970 graduate of Meharry Medical College, was appointed to the orthodontic department.[12]

The New Entrance Requirement

In 1965, applicants for admission to the college had to complete three years of academic study at an accredited college of arts and sciences, which included at least one year's credit in English, biology, physics, inorganic chemistry, and organic chemistry. The school's previous pre-dental requirement had been two years. The Board of Admissions gave preference to students with high scholastic records in secondary school and in college; who make satisfactory scores on the dental aptitude test; who have favorable recommendations from their instructors; and who "give every promise of becoming successful" dentists of high standing.[13]

125th Anniversary Celebration

In 1965, the college celebrated its 125th anniversary of its founding. More than 500 alumni and friends registered for the two-day meeting held on March 4 and 5, 1965. On March 4, Dr. Harold Hillenbrand delivered the first Hayden-Harris lecture on "The Past is Prologue."[14] Dr. Kyrle W. Preis served as general chairman of the celebration. The advisory committee consisted of Drs. George F. Anderson, C. Adam Bock, John H. Michael, Jessie Trager, and Dean John J. Salley. Actually, planning had begun as early as March 1963, when preliminary discussions were held. A budget of $5,000 was allotted for the celebration. In 1966, a book, *Proceedings of the 125th Anniversary Celebration of the Baltimore College of Dental Surgery*, edited by Gardner P. H. Foley, was published.[15]

The Smithsonian Loan

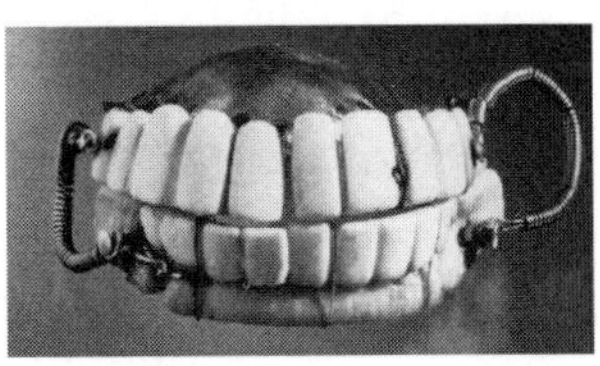

George Washington's dentures

In 1965, the University of Maryland reached an agreement with the Smithsonian Institution to loan artifacts from the collections of the Dental School Museum to the Smithsonian for an exhibit on dental history. On July 30, 1965, Dr. Emil G. Vanden Bosche,[16] chairman of the Museum Committee, submitted a report to the faculty council identifying the items desired by the Smithsonian, pending approval by the University's Board of Regents. The objects included George Washington's 1795 dentures, Dr. Robert Arthur's 1841 diploma and dental cabinet, Horace Hayden's 1810 Maryland dental license, Dr. Hollifield's 1830 dental cabinet, a Clarke 1905 octagonal dental cabinet, a profilograph of John Greenwood by Charles W. Peale, four pelicans, seven gold foil pluggers designed by Horace Hayden, and many examples of extraction keys, operative dental instruments, and dentures.[17] The Board of Regents approved the loan on November 19, 1965, as a "permanent loan basis and not as outright gifts."[18] On April 26, 1966, the objects were reported to have been sent to the Smithsonian on a 10-year minimum loan.[19]

The College's New Curriculum: 1966

In 1966, Dr. Salley announced his plans for a new "Dental Health Center." He believed that the dental profession had been "undergoing rapid changes during the past quarter of a century, both in its scientific knowledge and in its artistic principles." In addition, the ever-increasing public demand for services; the impact of federal, state, and local legislation; and rising "educational and economic status inherent in a progressive civilization," were factors affecting dental practice. These socioeconomic trends affected all health professionals. Furthermore, he predicted that dental practice would be different 20 years hence, and cited fluoridation and high-speed cutting devices, which had only recently come into prominence, as examples of the progress dental research had made. Dental education, he reasoned, also had to be reevaluated and designed to "meet the demands of society in future years" and Dr. Salley called for development of a "University Dental Health Center."[20]

In 1967, Dr. Brice M. Dorsey, professor of oral surgery, retired after 39 years of service. During World War II, while stationed in Australia, he had treated General Douglas MacArthur.[21] In 1968, Dr. Edward C. Dobbs, the long-time professor of pharmacology, retired after 43 years as a faculty member.[22] Also retiring the next year was Dr. Kyrle W. Preis, who headed the orthodontics department for more than 20 years,[23] and Gardner P. H. Foley, who retired after 41 years as a faculty member.[24]

The college's 1968 catalog stated the new methodology in dental education:

> The Baltimore College of Dental Surgery, Dental School, University of Maryland offers a course in dentistry devoted to instruction in the biomedical sciences, the dental sciences, and clinical practice. Instruction consists of didactic lectures, laboratory instruction, demonstrations, field visits, conferences, seminars and hospital ward rounds. Topics are assigned for collateral reading to educate the student in the value and use of dental literature.[25]

In 1968, an internship-residency program in pedodontics was initiated, which involved the school with the Children's Hospital of Baltimore and the Community Pediatric Center of the School of Medicine.[26] The tuition was now $650 for residents and $1,150 for non-residents.[27]

The Dental Auxiliary Program

In May 1968, representatives of the Baltimore College of Dental Surgery, Dental School, University of Maryland; Baltimore City Dental Society; Maryland State Dental Association; and the Community College of Baltimore met to finalize the curricula for courses in dental assisting and dental technology. In June 1968, Dr. Harry W. F. Dressel, Jr. (Class of 1945), was named as the head of the Department of Dental Auxiliaries, whose job would be to plan the facilities, select the faculty and equipment, and write the course syllabi. Mr. Ralph Steele, CDT, and Mrs. Barbara Eburg, CDA, were named as assistant professor of dental technology and dental assisting instructor, respectively. The greater part of the training programs was conducted at the Dental School. The dental assisting curriculum allowed a student to take a 35-week certificate program or a two-year course resulting in an associate of arts degree. In September 1969, evening courses were established to allow employed dental assistants to take the course.[28]

Community Dentistry: 1968

One of the new innovations in American dental schools in the late 1960s was the establishment of departments of community or "social dentistry." The purpose of these departments was teaching dental students health care delivery methods that would "enhance the quality and quantity of services in the community." At Maryland, the freshman students were given an "extramural experience," which bridges the "gap between theory and reality in the teaching of community health concepts." The community is used as "a living laboratory for observation and study." Maryland's program was both clinical and didactic and was chaired by Dr. Burton R. Pollack. There were two freshman, three sophomore and junior courses, and four senior-year courses.[29] The senior schedule included visits to a variety of community programs, such as those that provided "care for the handicapped, the chronically ill, and the aged." The seniors assisted in the dental care of patients at the Children's Hospital, Baltimore. Existing courses in "oral and written communications, ethics, jurisprudence, dental history, practice management, and public health" were integrated into the community dentistry program and new courses in "human behavior, biostatistics, and epidemiology" were added.[30] Later, in 1972, the department established a special clinic for special patients, including people with Down's syndrome, hydrocephalus, hemophilia, cleft palates, and other disabled individuals. White coats were not worn by the students because some of the patients had previous bad experiences with doctors in white jackets. Dr. Pollack described the program as the "first in the country to build special facilities for the education of undergraduate dental students in the treatment of these special patients." Dr. Arthur L. Hayden, assistant professor, was the director of the special clinic with Dr. Myron H. Sachs, a volunteer assistant professor who had been with the school for 17 years.[31]

Organizational Changes: 1968–69

In 1968, Dr. Salley revised the organization of the school by combining the operative, prosthetics (both fixed and removable), and endodontics departments into a restorative dentistry department under Dr. Wilbur O. Ramsey, the former professor of prosthetic dentistry. The newly organized department of about 30 full-time faculty members was designed around the "team-teaching concept, with small groups of students remaining under the supervision of a separate teaching team for each of the four semesters." The purpose of the change was to reduce "fragmentation of learning, simplify administration, and save time spent moving from clinic to clinic."[32]

The new assistant dean for curriculum affairs, Dr. Martin Lunin, was detailed to promote closer "integration and correlation of all learning experiences." The oral surgery program was enhanced by affiliations with the Baltimore City Hospitals, Crownsville State Hospital, and Provident Hospital. In addition, a new department of dentistry was established at the University of Maryland Hospital to provide dental services to hospital patients. The growth of continuing education, under Dr. Charles T. Pridgeon, was demonstrated by an increase from

1963–64 program that offered only four courses to a total of 29 separate courses for the college's next session.[33] Basically under Salley, the old "fragmented curriculum" was replaced with one that was "more integrated, one that builds and supplements the various programs rather than one that repeats, isolates, confuses and sometimes contradicts." The new philosophy "considers the student, helps the student, tries to reduce unnecessary physical movement resulting in waste of time, and above all permits students to participate in certain facets of decision making."[34]

In 1970, Gardner P. H. Foley, professor of dental history, expressed his views on inbreeding[35] of the dental faculty, as over a period of 125 years of inbreeding had been the case. The most obvious reason was that the alumni were willing to work for the unattractive salaries because of their loyalty to their alma mater; secondary was the proximately to their practices. Foley acknowledged that inbreeding had its faults and that graduates of other dental schools had something to contribute. However, the alumni faculty was likely to be "more generous with their time and far less likely to be concerned with offers from other schools." Foley encouraged recruiting a "strong phalanx of alumni members."[36] In 1970, postgraduate programs were instituted for the specialties of endodontics, orthodontics, periodontics, and prosthodontics.[37]

The Peruvian Connection

In 1970, the Dental School established a relationship with two Peruvian universities, Universidad National Mayor de San Marcos de Lima and Universidad Peruana Cayetano Heredia. Two BCDS faculty members were awarded Fulbright scholarships to lecture at San Marcos—Dr. McDonald K. Hamilton, head of the Department of Oral Surgery, and Dr. Irving I. Abramson, head of the Division of Endodontics in the Department of Restorative Dentistry. In September 1970, Dr. David Loza, another Fulbright Scholar of the Universidad Peruana, arrived in Baltimore to work with faculty members on a special course on occlusion. Dr. Salley, who had spent two weeks in May 1970 in Peru as a consultant to the Pan American Health Organization, had conferred with the administrators of the two universities on dental education and in 1971 established a formal affiliation with the Universidad Peruana Cayetano Heredia in Lima, Peru.[38]

Dental Hygiene Program Established

Patricia C. Stearns

At its May 1969 meeting, the Council on Dental Education granted accreditation classified as "accreditation eligible" to the dental hygiene education program proposed by the University of Maryland.[39] In July 1969, the Dental School Faculty Council approved a proposal to establish a baccalaureate dental curriculum in dental hygiene for transmission to the University Senate's Committee on Programs, Curricula and Courses.[40] In September 1970, a two-year baccalaureate degree program in dental hygiene was initiated under the direction of Patricia C. Stearns,[41] the first and only program of its kind in Maryland. The curriculum consisted of two years of preprofessional courses (chemistry, zoology, English, sociology, psychology, speech, mathematics, history, nutrition, and microbiology), a third year of basic dental and dental hygiene study with clinical application, and a fourth year of "advanced clinical practice and upper division electives in a recommended area of study, which constituted a minor related to a specialized area of dental hygiene practice."[42] At that time, the department's offices and clinics were on the ground floor, operating in separate facilities than the dental students. Modeling the interaction between hygiene and dental students after contemporary private practice would come later in the program. Hygiene students wore nurse's caps with white uniforms. The Class of 1970 had 10 students.[43] The first students were: Margaret Culbertson, Dorothy Duvall, Carol Grossman, Rebecca Howe, Kathleen Kochevar, Karen McGuffin, Janet Poehlman, Judith Schiller, Kathleen Smith, and Julia Wagner.[44] The same year, the Community College of Baltimore started a two-year dental hygiene program to complement the four-year program offered by the Dental School.[45] In June 1971, Barbara J. Vondrak, who held a master of science in dental hygiene degree from the University of Iowa, was added to the hygiene faculty as an assistant professor.[46] Finally, after a site visit in March 1972, the Council on Dental Education gave its official approval to the school's hygiene program on May 17, 1972.[47]

In 1971, the school lost another veteran teacher when Dr. Ernest B. Nuttall, a 1931 graduate and long-time professor of crown and bridge, retired after 40 years of service. After teaching at the school and maintaining a private practice, in 1942 Dr. Nuttall became the chair of crown and bridge. He was a past president of the Baltimore City Dental Society and the Maryland State Dental Association.[48]

The New Hayden-Harris Hall

In October 1965, Dr. Salley had reported on the current status of the proposed new dental building as rendered by the architect to the Capital Improvements Committee of the University. Final approval of the elevations was needed from the Board of Regents prior to completing "all detailed specifications." In November, Dr. Salley announced that Board of Regents had approved plans for the new building and an appropriation of an excess of \$5 million.[50] In January 1966, Dr. Salley announced that the federal contribution to the new building would be \$5,257,424 and the state of Maryland would contribute \$3,535,000 as part of the matching funds necessary. The bids were to go out around October 1, 1966, and construction to commence early in 1967.[51]

The new Hayden-Harris Hall plaque.

Finally, on Thursday, March 4, 1971, Hayden-Harris Hall, a six-story, 270,000 square-foot building, located in the block bounded by Baltimore, Arch, Fayette, and Pine Streets, was dedicated by Governor Marvin Mandell. The architects of this award-winning building were Cochran, Stephenson & Donkervoet of Baltimore. Federal participation in the project was \$5,257,424, with matching state funds of \$3,525,000.[52]

Dr. Louis L. Kaplan, chairman of the Board of Regents, in accepting the building for the University, offered these remarks:

> If ever patients are regarded as clinical material, this building will have been degraded and its use corrupted. We must never forget that the word patient comes from the Latin root which means 'to suffer.' Clinical material does not suffer. Human beings do. Human beings who will be coming here will bring with them . . . many emotional and physiological problems. In being sensitive to these human needs and feelings, those who learn and teach here will find their own humanity grow. Our personalities are honed and polished as we relate ourselves to others in human concern. There are people with hearts of stone and there are stones into which the pulsating warmth of the human heart can be infused. This is your great opportunity. Make the most of it.[53]

Dr. Salley, on behalf of the Dental School, offered these remarks:

> Because we are an integral part of a great University and its vast and versatile intellectual resources, today signifies the continuing opportunity to strengthen the reciprocal flow of knowledge between dentistry and other components of the academic community. Because we are part of a profession which fully commits itself to serving others, this day means renewal of the challenge and thus the opportunity to extend our service boundaries to include all who are in need. Because we live in an age which has one of its principal characteristics the constancy of change, today opens new vistas for probing and exploration beyond the present parameters of dental science and technology.[54]

Dr. Jessie L. Steinfeld, Surgeon General of the United States, then gave an address in which he stated that science was close to conquering the mystery of dental caries. In other events of the day, the Maryland Historical Society placed a marker on the grounds of the School designating it as the oldest dental school in the world and dentistry as the only educated profession to originate in the United States. The Maryland State Dental Association placed a marker plaque on the original site of the Baltimore College of Dental Surgery, then the Mercantile Bank and Trust Building at Hopkins Place.[55]

A three-day celebration followed the ceremonies. A tour of the new building was conducted from 10 a.m. to 12 p.m. From 1 p.m. to 5 p.m. scientific sessions were held after a welcome by Dr. Salley. The first lecturer was Dr. David B. Scott, Dean, Case-Western Reserve University and BCDS alumnus (Class of 1943); and the second, Lieut. Col. Simon Civjan, Chief, Division of Dental Materials, U.S. Army Institute of Dental Research. On March 5, a panel discussion was held from 9:30 a.m. to 12 p.m. on "The Interfaces of Dental Education." In the afternoon the dedication and Hayden-Harris Lecture were held. On the morning of March 6, after a breakfast, the historical marker of the dental school was placed on Hopkins Place at the site now occupied by the Mercantile-Trust Building.[56]

The new 266,000 square foot, five-story structure at 666 West Baltimore Street was planned and designed around the new curriculum at a final cost of $12,000,000 in state and federal funds. To include the new emphasis on public health programs, dental specialties and research, and the use of auxiliaries, the building was three times the size of the old building. The structure had five stories, plus an underground sixth floor and a foundation engineered to support an additional two floors for expansion, if needed. The building's "low rectangular configuration" was characterized by "a repetitive keypunch relief of brick and glass overlaid by a reticular lattice of contrasting concrete." In contrast to the earlier dental buildings, the new structure did not need the large windows and skylights to admit the natural light; modern lighting and equipment eliminated this need. Also missing was the large open clinic areas, which were replaced by individual treatment cubicles.[57]

The ground floor of the new, five-story building was fitted with a 48-chair preventative dental clinic, a student lounge, space for an independent learning center, a museum, student locker and toilet facilities, multidisciplinary laboratory spaces for the preclinical courses in the dental hygiene and dental assisting programs, an audiovisual section, including graphics, photography, photomicrography, a television facility, and a maintenance and repair shop. The first floor in its entirety was assigned to the undergraduate clinical teaching program; it contained a diagnosis clinic, suite for a physician and medical technician, radiology, oral surgery, and community dentistry clinics. The major portion of the first floor was taken up by two 128-cubicle general practice clinics. The second floor contained 16 multidisciplinary teaching laboratories, lecture halls, seminar rooms, and a central laboratory. The third floor contained faculty office space, a specialty clinic with 55 treatment rooms, and a faculty group practice area with 15 treatment rooms. The fourth floor was devoted to basic science faculty, administrative offices, and research facilities. The anatomy dissection laboratory and animal rooms completed the fifth floor.[58]

One of the features of the new building was the Division of Educational and Instructional Resources composed of a 2,000 square foot Independent Learning Center, closed-circuit color television system, and artistic and photographic support. The center housed 50 study carrels designed specifically for self-instruction, which enabled the students to study material in their courses in a variety of media at their own pace and timing. Educational and instructional resources freed the instructor for more student contact, whether it was independent conferences or small seminars, thus upgrading the quality of the teaching. A closed circuit television system distributed programs to approximately 100 monitors in various locations in the building. According to Dr. Ernest F. Moreland, who headed the department, the materials available in the center were not considered "supplementary to the student's education, but rather an integral part of the curriculum."[59]

The undergraduate courses now included: anatomy, basic dental science, biochemistry, clinical dentistry, community dentistry, conjoint sciences, dental auxiliary utilization, medicine, microbiology, oral pathology, orthodontics, pedodontics, periodontics, pharmacology, physiology, restorative dentistry, and surgery.[60]

The new building also allowed the school the capability to initiate more advanced dental education graduate programs. In the 1950s, the only clinical graduate degree the college offered was a master's degree in oral surgery[61] through the University of Maryland Graduate School. In 1968, pedodontics began and in September 1970 a full program of all disciplines was initiated. The school offered programs leading to eligibility for specialty boards in the following specialties: endodontics, oral surgery, orthodontics, pedodontics, periodontics, and prosthodontics. All the programs met the accreditation requirements of the Council on Dental Education of the American Dental Association. Successful completion of these programs resulted in the student receiving a certificate from the University of Maryland. Programs were also available for receiving the Master's Degree (MS) and the Doctor of Philosophy (PhD) from the Graduate School, University of Maryland.[62]

In 1971, the school adopted a complete pass-fail grading system for its students. Maryland was the first dental school to use it for all courses, both clinical and basic science. The purpose of the new system was to "permit students to study course material for its true value, rather than for a specific numerical grade."[63] In 1971, Dr. Salley combined the departments of anatomy and embryology into a single department chaired by Dr. Vincent D. Provenza. Also, dissection of the extremities was eliminated from the anatomy curriculum, to concentrate on the anatomy of the head and neck.[64] The same year, Dr. Salley established a formal affiliation with Universidad Peruana Cayetano Heredia, a dental school in Lima, Peru. The affiliation permitted the exchange of faculty and an eventual student's exchange program.[65]

In the early 1970s, another change in technology that would revolutionize operative dentistry was the introduction in 1969 of a composite resin restorative material by Johnson & Johnson, called "Adaptic." This material would eventually replace both the silicate cement and plastic materials as the restoration of choice for anterior teeth, where esthetics was most important. Later, future generations of composites would challenge even amalgam as a posterior filling material.[66]

Dean Salley vs. the Alumni: 1971

The dedication of the new school was not without incident. The Alumni Association was incensed over errors in the two historical markers commemorating the founding of the college, the first in the world, dedicated on March 6, 1971. One marker designed by the college was placed in the foyer of Hayden-Harris Hall and the other designed by the Maryland Historical Society was erected in front of the new building. The alumni found "serious historical errors" in both markers. When they called these errors to the dean's attention and asked him to rectify the errors, he did nothing. Finally in 1973, the president of the Alumni Association appointed a special committee to study the complaints of the alumni, the facts in the case, and orders to take the necessary steps to persuade the college authorities and the Historical Society to correct the errors. The committee of three was comprised of Dr. Gardner P. H. Foley, former professor of dental history; Dr. H. Berton McCauley, historian for the Maryland State Dental Association; and Dr. J. Ben Robinson, former professor of dental history and dean.[67]

In their report, the historians stated:

> Until recently, the Alumni Association and the College administration enjoyed a most amicable relationship. Unhappily, the present administration has manifested an unconcern for the presence of the Alumni Association and a willful disregard for the opinions of the alumni on questions relating to the history of the College. It has arrogated to itself an authority over important extramural matters which it has notionally exercised without regard for historical facts. It has arbitrarily acted: (1) to distort certain important facts of dental history and to record its errors upon a permanent marker which it placed upon exhibition in Hayden-Harris Hall; (2) to negate a solemn agreement made between the Trustees of the College and the Regents of the University that led to the consolidation of the College with the University; and (3) to violate specific provisions contained in the Act of the Maryland legislature in approving the consolidation of the College with the University. Officers and members of the Alumni Association have vigorously protested these imperious acts only to be met by a defiant attitude.[68]

Specifically, the alumni chief complaints over the two plaques concerned the text of the bronze plaque which was hung in the foyer of Hayden-Harris Hall. The inscription read: "The Baltimore College of Dental Surgery, the School of Dentistry of the University of Maryland, was founded on March 6, 1840. It is the first dental school in the world and thus occupies a unique place in the history of the dental profession. Its founders were Dr. Horace H. Hayden and Dr. Chapin A. Harris who were renowned dentists of the nineteenth century, and for whom this building is named." The committee found certain serious historical errors in the text, as well as "some careless omissions of facts," which would have improved its historical meaning, to wit:

1. The statement that the "Baltimore College of Dental Surgery, the School of Dentistry of the University of Maryland, was founded March 6, 1840," is simply not true. The University of Maryland was not in any way involved in the founding of the Baltimore College. The Dental Department of the University of Maryland was not founded until 1882 and it was not until the consolidation of the two schools in 1924 that both names were included in the official title of the school.
2. The contrived title, "The Baltimore College of Dental Surgery, School of Dentistry of the University of Maryland," was a distortion of the school's official title, "the Baltimore College of Dental Surgery, Dental School, University of Maryland," the use of which was authorized soon after the consolidation and which has since "become a tradition." The "deliberate, permanent display of a distorted version" of the College's official title could lead to much confusion.
3. The sentence, "It is the first dental school in the world," is ambiguous. It should be written in the past tense, not the present tense.
4. The statement that, "Its founders were Dr. Horace H. Hayden and Dr. Chapin A. Harris," conveyed the impression that the two men alone were the College's founders; whereas, there were actually four founders on the charter. This statement should have read, "principal founders." Also, it would have been better list them as "Horace H. Hayden, MD, DDS, and Chapin A. Harris, MD, DDS"; thus identifying both men as dentists.[69]

Similar problems were found in the Maryland Historical Society plaque, which referred to Chapin A. Harris as "Chapin H. Harris." Also, the location of the original BCDS building was not "Hopkins Plaza," but 13 South Sharp Street, Baltimore. The committee recommended that a copy of its report be sent to Dr. Salley and Dr. Albin C. Kuhn, Chancellor of the Baltimore campus.[70] On June 7, 1973, a copy of the alumni committee report was sent to Dean Salley and was acknowledged on June 22, 1973. By August 21, 1973, the committee had not received a reply from the dean. On September 7, 1973, the dean replied the submitted material was "still under study." Finally on May 17, 1974, Dean Salley replied that the Special Liaison Committee of the Faculty and Alumni, at its last meeting on March 28, 1974, agreed that the matter would "form an early agenda item for the permanent Faculty-Alumni Liaison Committee."[71]

Dean Salley Changes the School's Name

On May 5, 1971, Dr. H. Berton McCauley wrote to Dr. J. Ben Robinson, the former BCDS dean, concerning the apparent name change of the Dental School. No longer was it referred to in the catalog as the Baltimore College of Dental Surgery, Dental School, University of Maryland. The latest catalog called the school the "University of Maryland, School of Dentistry, Baltimore College of Dental Surgery." Dr. McCauley asked Dr. Robinson to clarify the official name of the school because Dr. Robinson was present during the merger of the BCDS with the University of Maryland.[72] Dr. Robinson replied that the official title of the school should be the "Baltimore College of Dental Surgery, Dental School, University of Maryland" as was first used in the *86th Annual Announcement* of the College, session of 1926–27.[73]

Dr. Salley, who had apparently been using the new name since 1967, said his reason for changing the name of the school to the "University of Maryland, School of Dentistry," followed by "Baltimore College of Dental Surgery" was that the new title was a "more inclusive, less cumbersome and contemporary" title. His intention was not to drop the Baltimore College as a portion of the official title, but to make the "University of Maryland" part more prominent by listing it first. The term "School of Dentistry" more accurately reflected the school's wider role in dental education than merely "Dental School," which connoted only a DDS program, which it was back in 1926 when the present title was adopted. Salley thought the new title would "reduce the confusion among dental educators, dental practitioners and laymen relative to the present status of dental education on Baltimore and Maryland."[74]

On November 20, 1971, Dr. Robinson wrote a letter clarifying the official name of the school to Kyrle W. Preis, the editor of the *Alma Mater*, the official BCDS alumni magazine, for publication in the April 1972 issue. Preis failed to publish the letter in an effort to avoid friction with Dean Salley. McCauley was left to his own devices as historian of the Maryland State Dental Association to confront Salley. Finally, in a conversation with Dean Salley on April 21, 1972, Dr. McCauley received "a commitment that the name BCDS would not be dropped." However, the dean still considered "Baltimore College of Dental Surgery, Dental School, University of Maryland" cumbersome.[75] Thus, the college's name remained the same as it had been since 1924, thanks mainly to Dr. McCauley's perseverance.

The Accelerated Professional Training Program: 1972

Another of the college's innovations was the establishment of an accelerated curriculum, called Accelerated Professional Training Program (APT), which was designed to satisfy the requirements for the DDS degree in three calendar years. The reduction in the time requirement was accomplished in the following manner:

1. Restructuring the traditional courses by "integration of subject matter to demonstrate correlations between basic science and clinical subjects."
2. Selection of course content "based upon clinical relevancy."
3. Adoption of "self-instructional methods reinforced by seminar discussions and close faculty support."[76]

The APT program was limited to 10 students per class and students were selected on their merits of their college record, better than average Dental Admissions Test scores, and a high level of motivation and maturity. The program's first class graduated in June 1975.[77] By contrast, through the STEP (Specially Tailored Educational Program), 10 students who were found to be "educationally, economically, and culturally less prepared" than the norm were allowed to progress through the school at their own rate, with special attention by the faculty. These students were given more than four years to complete their coursework, if necessary. The U.S. Public Health Service furnished a $1 million grant to the school's Division of Educational and Instructional Resources for these curriculum studies.[78]

The First African-American Graduate: 1972

In 1972, the University of Maryland at Baltimore issued its revised Affirmative Action Plan, which stated the campus administration's commitment "to provide equal opportunities for all, and to comply with federal regulations affecting equal employment opportunities."

Elton Maddox

Under this mandate, the campus set the "objective of assuring a major effort in each school to enroll and retain a representative number of qualified minority group and women students, and to identify, hire, retain, and promote a representative number of qualified minorities and women as faculty and staff." The goal was to achieve a staff and faculty that was "representative of the population of the State of Maryland."[79]

In 1972, Elton (Tony) Preston Maddox, Jr., became the first recognized African American to graduate from any of the Baltimore dental schools. Dr. Maddox was a graduate (BS) of Morgan State College in Baltimore.[80] The first African-American woman to graduate was Debra Antoinette Bass, another graduate of Morgan State University. She graduated in 1977.[81]

The State of the Museum

In July 1972, Dr. Robinson, the retired BCDS dean, sent a letter to Dr. Salley expressing his concerns for the dental museum's well-being. Robinson stated that he had left the museum in "good condition" when he retired in 1963; however, "I am deeply concerned about the present disordered condition of the College collection, particularly about the hazardous condition under which the bulk of the more valuable relics now lies in a state of neglect." Furthermore, Robinson cited the lack of "adequate floor, exhibit and storage space to be used in handling, organizing and displaying the collection." Robinson found the "multiuse room" within the Independent Learning Center on the ground floor of the dental building to which the Museum had been consigned "physically accessible, but not otherwise suitable." Currently, it contained a "mere token number of unmarked cabinets and a very few portraits" of early dentists. Its overall dimensions were "appreciably less" than the museum room in the old dental building on Greene Street. A second problem was the "neglected and perilous condition of a body of irreplaceable historical relics and rare museum pieces," which had been removed from the old museum and "unloaded promiscuously upon the floor of a store room where they still lie in complete disorder." Robinson said he was appalled at the situation and offered to serve in an advisory or "guidance" role if Dr. Salley wanted him to do so.[82]

On August 18, 1972, Dr. Salley replied and defended the exclusion in the plans for a museum in Hayden-Harris Hall on the basis of the fact that the federal government would not allow funds for a museum. The university was committed to at least 50 percent federal funding for Hayden-Harris Hall's construction and federal officials "flatly refused to support any space for museum purposes." However, there would be a "reading room" where museum objects could be displayed. Dr. Salley also mentioned the disarray of the collections.[83]

On September 15, 1972, Dr. Robinson replied that he was appalled by the federal government dictating Dr. Salley's right to make a decision in policy matters that he regarded "as a necessary part" of his plans for the "complete education" of dental students. He also commented that he was "unfamiliar with the poor state of organization" in which Salley found the museum when he arrived on campus.[84]

The TEAM Program

In 1972, a new program to train dental auxiliaries was inaugurated by the college, called "TEAM," an acronym for Training in Expanded Auxiliary Management. Historically, the program was initiated in 1961 by the U.S. Public Health Service. The purpose of the program was to provide "learning experiences for dental students in the proper management of a dental team which a dentist might utilize in his practice." The learning experience consisted of lectures, critiqued clinical practice, and seminars. Junior dental students received 27 lecture hours on management and senior students participated in the TEAM clinic. Students were exposed to working with expanded duty auxiliaries and learning "four-handed dentistry."[85]

The Faculty Practice Clinic

In 1973, a new Faculty Dental Service Plan was established in the school under the direction of Dr. George F. Buchness, assistant professor of restorative dentistry, to regulate faculty practice. Clinicians belonging to the group were allowed to spend a maximum of 10 hours per week (Monday through Friday, 8 a.m. to 5 p.m., and Saturday 8 a.m. to 2 p.m., of his own release time) working on their own patients. Because the faculty clinic was supposed to be self-sufficient, the fees charged were parallel to those received in private outside practice. A portion of the fees (12%) went into the School of Dentistry General Fund, which the dean could use for academic purposes; another (18%) went into fringe benefits, such as malpractice liability and life insurance; and an additional amount (20%) was allocated for dental and office supplies. Participants were responsible for their own laboratory bills.[86]

Accreditation of the School

In 1973, Dean Salley announced that the Council on Dental Accreditation of the American Dental Association gave "full approval" of all the school's dental educational programs. All the academic programs had been inspected by approximately 15 representatives of the council. Although the council's report "identified some areas which needed to be strengthened, the majority of the report was commendatory." Dean Salley commented: "The excellence identified on the council's evaluation is due in large measure to the fact that the University of Maryland has a dental faculty which is both dedicated and quite innovative in its approach to dental and dental hygiene education. The real credit must go to these fine people."[87]

The year 1973 saw the retirement of Dr. Irving I. Abramson, professor and head of the Department of Endodontics. Dr. Abramson was a 1932 alumnus of the school, who had been on the faculty since 1954.[88]

New Goals Study

During the 1973 academic year the faculty and students took on the time-consuming task of self-evaluation of the school's progress since the beginning of the Salley administration. The "plans, objectives, and goals" set in 1963 were probed to see how well they had been met, and what planning was necessary for the next decade. Two new staff members, Myra Land, administrative assistant to the dean, and Nell Savopoulos, research analyst, were hired for the project.[89]

In July 1973, a special committee of the Faculty Council for the "Development of New Goals and Objectives" was established to review the current program and to develop new objectives for the school's future guidelines. This type of planning was expected to foster "greater understanding among students, faculty, organized dentistry and the community at large." Eleven subcommittees were given "specific charges in a broad spectrum of investigation." Twenty-one students and 128 faculty members participated in more than 120 meetings. The salient findings, conclusions, and recommendations of all reports were transcribed into an "analytical anthology" concerning the Dental School. Its instructional programs, its faculty and students, and a blueprint of future directions, "patterned from anticipated trends in the delivery of dental health care and projected demand for dental manpower, particularly in the State of Maryland" were included. In the past 10 years, a new modern physical plant had been constructed; innovative programs in dental assistant utilization (DAU); training in expanded auxiliary management (TEAM); an accelerated professional training (APT); a specially tailored educational program (STEP) originated; curriculum units in basic dental science, conjoint science, biomedical science, and community dentistry conceived and implemented; a baccalaureate dental hygiene program initiated; an independent learning center established as a repository for audiovisual materials under a new Division of Educational and Instructional Resources; minority student recruitment originated; dental clerkships instituted to enrich the undergraduate dental program; and a faculty dental service plan, providing the facilities for intramural practice of the clinical faculty, initiated.[90]

Since 1963, postgraduate programs had been initiated in five specialties and course offerings in the continuing education program had been increased from 2 to 28 per year. In 1972, patient visits to the school's clinics reached approximately 93,000. Thus, in one decade, the school had moved forward and adapted to change. The "new goals" study gave evidence to the school's vitality as it searched for improvement and new dimensions in dental education.[91]

In the course of the evaluation, certain areas of weakness were identified in the dental undergraduate program; namely, a lack of emphasis on the teaching of preventative dentistry, failure to stimulate student interest in scientific literature, and failure to incorporate research into the undergraduate teaching program. Over the past decade, there had been a progressive cut in the number of hours allotted to the basic sciences as the emphasis shifted from "general training" to "specific instruction" in the basic sciences as they related to clinical dentistry. The student was provided with a "fundamental understanding of the functions of the human body," and the "close relationship between oral health and general health," as a basis for "sound and comprehensive patient treatment." The development of a closer relationship between the basic sciences and the clinical departments was seen as necessary to "effect [sic] a more viable curriculum." However, it was recommended that the feasibility of establishing a Department of Human Biology, encompassing all basic and conjoint sciences, be studied.[92]

In regard to the 1973 postgraduate programs, there were 600 applicants for the 18 positions available, and Maryland residents represented 50 percent of the total enrollment. The study found the oral surgery, orthodontic, and pedodontic programs satisfactory, but the periodontic program was hampered both by the lack of a permanent chair and a faculty composed of many part-time members. The endodontoc program also experienced insufficient faculty and was composed of mainly part-time faculty. There was no program in prosthodontics. The postgraduate clinic area lacked sufficient space and was poorly designed with old, outdated equipment. In general, the postgraduate programs suffered from insufficient faculty and funding.

The Changing Curriculum: 1973-74

Again, from 1973 to 1974, the college made more curriculum changes, copied after the revolutionary curriculum changes first introduced by Western Reserve University in the early 1950s. At that university, the "traditional lockstep, departmentally-oriented curriculum was replaced by a more flexible educational program stressing interdisciplinary approaches for both the biomedical sciences and clinical training." The movement spread rapidly because of the congressional mandates to "expand the level of biomedical research and the training of research scientists." By the 1960s, as the biomedical research effort became established, Congress and society turned their attention to "extending and expanding health care." A greater number of health care professionals were needed to satisfy the public demand for better health. The 1963 Health Professions Educational Assistance Act and the 1971 Comprehensive Health Manpower Training Act provided support for changes in the dental curriculum.[93] The College of Dentistry, University of Florida, was one of the first schools to adopt this new "modular approach to curriculum design."[94] Coincidently, Dr. Jose E. Medina, the dean of the Florida dental school, was a 1948 graduate of the Baltimore College and a former faculty member of that institution.[95]

Some of the school's new and innovative modification in the curriculum the past eight years were: Comprehensive or coordinated care for the clinical patient, which involves "examination, diagnosis, treatment planning, case presentation, appointment control, prevention, orientation, treatment performance, and patient recall." The curriculum emphasized these areas:

1. Community service as the State of Maryland's largest single provider of community dental care.
2. Computerized data retrieval of all information on both the patient and the student.
3. Special programs permitting the student to expand his basic knowledge of dental practice:
   a. Conjoint Science, a four-year interdepartmental program coordinating basic, applied, and clinical sciences.
   b. Biomedicine, a coordinated integration of oral and general pathology, internal medicine, physical and oral diagnosis, and dental radiology into one program.
   c. Independent Learning Center, a self-instructional center for independent activity for introduction of new modular learning units.
   d. Training in Expanded Auxiliary Management Program for advanced clinical students to obtain experience in the expanded function team clinic.
   e. Accelerated Professional Training for selected students to complete the dental degree in less than the conventional four-year program.
   f. Specially Tailored Educational Program for educationally, socially or culturally disadvantaged students was created to allow students additional time beyond the normal four years to complete their dental education.
   g. Special Patient Clinic for advanced student to experience working with the special or handicapped patient.
   h. Senior Clerkship Program to allow qualified seniors to devote up to 50 percent of their last year to a dental discipline of their choice.
   i. Dental Externship Program to devote eight weeks of field study in a Maryland practitioner's dental office.
   j. Community Dentistry Enrichment for all students to understand the dental care delivery system at the community level.[96]

Alumni Rumblings of Discontent

In 1973, the honeymoon was over between Dean Salley and the School's Alumni Association. On May 30, 1973, the president of the Alumni Association, Dr. Leon Seligman, wrote a letter to Dr. Louis L. Kaplan, chairman, Board of Regents, University of Maryland, expressing the association's concern with "certain alleged untoward conditions" at the School, which were "not in the best interests of either dental education or the dental profession." It was the opinion of the association that "many recent graduates of our dental school are not capable of producing efficient restorative clinical dentistry." Another complaint was the alumni's "inability to establish productive dialogue and rapport" with Dean Salley. The Alumni Association requested a hearing with the Board of Regents to "discuss these and other matters that are of vital concern to us."[97] Apparently, this letter was precipitated by an earlier attempt by the Alumni Association to engage in meaningful conversations with Dr. Salley without much success.[98]

Continuing Education: 1974

Before 1962, the school conducted an average of two continuing education courses a year. Up to 1963, there were no provisions in the budget for personnel or facilities to administer a continuing education program. In 1972, 25 percent of the courses operated at a loss as expenses exceeded tuition fees. In 1974, a $50,000 budget was provided for the administration and staffing of the program. During the academic year 1973–74, the school offered a total of 48 courses. The sum of $30,000 was allocated to provide an "ultra-modern auditorium" for the program's exclusive use.[99]

Senior Externship Program

A new concept in the undergraduate curriculum was initiated in 1974 with the establishment of a senior externship program under the direction of Dr. Jon K. Park, associate professor of oral diagnosis. The eight-week summer program was designed to "show senior dental students what private practice" was like before graduation. For the pilot program, 10 seniors were selected on the basis of their "academic standing and clinical competency" to work in the offices of 15 Maryland dentists (preceptors) who met certain criteria to be eligible. The requirements were: being a member in good standing in organized dentistry; conducting an active practice of a minimum of four days a week; maintaining two or more functioning operatories; and having been graduated from dental school at least three years before selection. The program had been approved by the faculty council and the Maryland State Legislature since a change in the Dental Practice Act was required before proceeding. Externs worked a minimum of 32 hours a week and received no clinical credit for their work; however, a record of specific services performed was maintained and became a part of the student's academic record. Experiences ranged from preventative treatment to complex restorative procedures.

Each student received a weekly salary from his preceptor.[100]

Dean Salley Resigns

Dean Salley announced his decision to leave the deanship in 1974, but before leaving, he sent a memorandum on August 30, 1974, to the Faculty Council urging it to petition the Board of Regents to approve as official the title, "University of Maryland School of Dentistry, Baltimore College of Dental Surgery," a title for the Dental School which he had been using "for the past seven years." On September 30, 1974, the Faculty Council recommended that the Liaison Committee discuss the petition with the Alumni Association.[101] Dr. Robinson called Salley's arguments for changing the name "irresponsible, specious arguments."[102]

Dr. Salley resigned his position as dean on April 26, 1974, effective September 30, 1974, to accept an appointment as associate vice-president for graduate studies and research at the Virginia Commonwealth University in Richmond. His new position entailed working with the 12 university schools to develop new graduate programs and improve the present programs, and to coordinate "all sponsored research programs" at the university.[103] In 1980, he was appointed dean of the newly created School of Graduate Studies at that institution.[104]

Despite his problems with the alumni, Dean Salley can be credited with building a new physical facility; integrating the faculty and student body; establishing a community dentistry program and a long overdue school of dental hygiene; establishing an accelerated program for dental students, an independent learning center, and televised instruction; upgrading the faculty from an inbred, closed, "old boy" network to a more diverse and talented group; and bringing the school's curriculum into the modern era of dental education. These achievements are his legacy.[105]

Dental Dean Search Committee: 1974

The University's Chancellor, Albin O. Kuhn, established a search committee to find a replacement for Dr. Salley. The committee chairman was Dr. Donald E. Shay, chairman, microbiology department. On September 1974, the committee began meeting every Friday and conducted interviews to screen candidates for the chancellor. The candidate selected had to be approved by the University of Maryland Board of Regents. The Dean Search Committee members were: Dr. John J. Berquist, professor and chair, periodontics; Dr. George F. Buchness, associate professor, restorative dentistry; Dr. Sidney O. Burnett, Jr., of the state Board of Dental Examiners; Dean John M. Dennis of the UMAB School of Medicine; Dr. Fred Gornick, chairman, chemistry department, UMBC; Dr. Robert W. Haroth, associate professor, restorative dentistry; Dr. John F. Hasler, professor and chairman, oral diagnosis and radiology; Dr. J. Martin Lunin, professor and chairman, oral pathology; Dr. Elton Preston Maddox, Jr., instructor, restorative dentistry; Dr. William R. Patteson, president, BCDS Alumni Association; Mrs. JoAnne I. Pepin, assistant professor and chairman, dental hygiene; Dr. Vincent D. Provenza, professor and chairman, anatomy; Lawrence Scheitler, dental student; and Dr. William T. Strahan, practicing dentist.[106]

NOTES

1. Wilson H. Elkins, "[Dental Health Center]," *Journal of the Baltimore College of Dental Surgery, Dental School, University of Maryland* 21 (December 1966): 48.
2. Dr. Aisenberg died at age 87 on April 12, 1986, in Baltimore, Md. ["In Memoriam (Dr. Myron Aisenberg)," *BCDS Forum* 7 (Fall 1986): 29.]
3. "Dr. Salley to Succeed Dr. Aisenberg as Dean," *Journal of the Baltimore College of Dental Surgery, Dental School, University of Maryland* 19 (May 1963): 13; Baltimore College of Dental Surgery, Dental School, University of Maryland, *Baltimore College of Dental Surgery, Dental School 1963–1964, The University of Maryland* (Baltimore: n.p., [1963]), p. v.
4. "Dr. Salley to Succeed Dr. Aisenberg," 13.

5. Ibid., 13–14.
6. Ibid., 14.
7. John J. Salley, "Progress Notes on Planning of the Baltimore College of Dental Surgery, Dental School, University of Maryland 1964," *Journal of the Maryland State Dental Association* 7 (April 1964): 13.
8. Henry N. Williams, "Dr. John Bonas: First black faculty, first black graduate student," unpublished document, Henry N. Williams file.
9. Letter, John J. Salley to Harvey Webb, Jr., July 23, 1968. Henry N. Williams' file.
10. Henry N. Williams, "Dr. John Carr: First full-time dentist hired as a faculty member," unpublished document, the files of Dr. Henry N. Williams.
11. Baltimore College of Dental Surgery, Dental School, University of Maryland, *1972–74 Bulletin University of Maryland School of Dentistry, Baltimore College of Dental Surgery* (n.p., [1972), p. 52.
12. Henry N. Williams, "Dr. Gwendolyn Dunn: One of first African American female instructors," unpublished document, the files of Dr. Henry N. Williams.
13. Baltimore College of Dental Surgery, Dental School, University of Maryland, *Baltimore College of Dental Surgery, Dental School 1965–66, The University of Maryland* (n.p., [1965]), pp. 3–4. *See* Appendix D for earlier admission requirements.
14. Kyrle W. Preis, "125th Anniversary Celebration," *Alma Mater* 7 (November 1965): 47.
15. Gardner P. H. Foley, ed., *Proceedings of the 125th Anniversary Celebration of the Baltimore College of Dental Surgery* (Baltimore: Horn-Shafer Co., 1966), pp. 3, 6, 7
16. Dr. Emil Gaston Vanden Bosche died on August 28, 1965. He had served on the faculty since 1924 teaching chemistry. ["Faculty Council Minutes, 1965–1966," December 1, 1965, Baltimore College of Dental Surgery Papers, National Museum of Dentistry Archives (*hereafter* cited as BCDSP, NMDA)]
17. "Faculty Council Minutes, 1965–1966," July 30, 1965, BCDSP, NMDA.
18. Ibid., November 23, 1965.
19. Ibid., April 26, 1966.
20. John J. Salley, "The Dental Health Center—A New Dimension in Dental Education at the University of Maryland," *Journal of the Baltimore College of Dental Surgery* 21 (December 1966): 49–50.
21. Joseph H. Seipp, Jr., "Dr. Brice Dorsey Retires," *Alma Mater* 9 (November 1967): 23.
22. "Dr. Dobbs, Pharmacology Head Retires After 43 Years Here," *Newsletter University of Maryland School of Dentistry* 1 (Spring 1968): 2.
23. "Dr. Preis to Retire as Head of Orthodontics: His Successor, Dr. John M. Grewe, to arrive July 1," *Newsletter University of Maryland School of Dentistry* 2 (Spring 1969): 1.
24. "Professor Gardner P. H. Foley Retires After 41 Years," *Newsletter University of Maryland School of Dentistry* 3 (Winter 1969): 3.
25. Baltimore College of Dental Surgery, Dental School, University of Maryland, *1968–1970 Catalog Baltimore College of Dental Surgery, Dental School, University of Maryland* (n.p., [1968]), p. 28.
26. Baltimore College of Dental Surgery, Dental School, University of Maryland, *1972–1974 Bulletin University of Maryland School of Dentistry, Baltimore College of Dental Surgery* (n.p., [1972]), p. 6.
27. Baltimore College of Dental Surgery, Dental School, University of Maryland, *1968–1970 Catalog*, p. 33.
28. "A Cooperative Effort in Dental Auxiliary Training," *Alma Mater* 11 (Spring 1970): 31–32.
29. Rosalynde K. Soble, Eli Shulman, and Burton R. Pollack, "Dental Education and the Community: A Field Experience," *Journal of the Baltimore College of Dental Surgery* 27 (July 1972): 36, 44; Baltimore College of Dental Surgery, Dental School, University of Maryland, *1968–1970 Catalog*, pp. 46-48.
30. Burton R. Pollack, "Students Learn of Social Problems in Community Dentistry," *Newsletter* 1 (Winter 1967): 4.
31. "Special Patient Clinic Trains Students to Treat Handicapped," *Newsletter University of Maryland School of Dentistry* 5 (Spring 1972): 3.
32. "Four Departments to Merge, Headed by Dr. W. O. Ramsey," *Newsletter University of Maryland School of Dentistry* 1 (Spring 1968): 1.
33. John J. Salley, "Greetings from the School of Dentistry," *Alma Mater* 10 (February 1969): 11; "Hospital Adds Dental Department," *Newsletter University of Maryland School of Dentistry* 1 (Spring 1968): 3.
34. Aaron Schaeffer, "Visitation to the University of Maryland Dental School," *Journal of the Maryland State Dental Association* 13 (August 1970): 113.
35. In 1963, 84 percent of the faculty was inbred (University of Maryland graduates), but by 1969, less than 50 percent of the staff were Maryland graduates. [Schaeffer, "Visitation to the University of Maryland Dental School," 114.]
36. Gardner P. H. Foley, "BCDS Notes." *Alma Mater* 11 (Spring 1970): 4.
37. Baltimore College of Dental Surgery, Dental School, University of Maryland, *1972–1974 Bulletin*, p. 6.
38. "Dental School Pursues Good Neighbor Policy," *Newsletter University of Maryland School of Dentistry* 4 (Fall 1970): 3; "Peru Affiliation Established," *Newsletter University of Maryland School of Dentistry* 4 (Spring 1971): 2.
39. Letter, Mario V. Santangelo, Assistant Secretary, Council on Dental Education, to John J. Salley, Dean, School of Dentistry, University of Maryland, June 24, 1971, Office of the Dean, Files (*hereafter* cited as BCDSOD).
40. Letter, John J. Salley, Dean, Dental School, University of Maryland, to Richard H. Jaquith, Chairman, Senate Committee on Programs, Curricula and Courses, University of Maryland, August 25, 1969, BCDSOD.
41. Patricia C. Stearns received a BS degree in dental hygiene from the University of Washington and an MS in dental hygiene administration from Columbia University. She served as an instructor in the Department of Dental Hygiene at Idaho State University and was the senior program director at the Dental Health Section of the Idaho Department of Health since 1953. In 1960, she served on the committee to organize a dental hygiene program at Idaho State University. ["Patricia Stearns to Head First Maryland Hygiene Program," *Newsletter University of Maryland School of Dentistry* 2 (Winter 1968): 2.]

42. Baltimore College of Dental Surgery, Dental School, University of Maryland, *1970–1972 Catalog University of Maryland School of Dentistry, Baltimore College of Dental Surgery* (n. p., [1970]), pp. 26, 57.
43. Rita Sutter, "Celebrating a Quarter Century of Dental Hygiene," *Forum* 16 (Fall 1995): 8–9.
44. "Report of Dental Hygiene Advancement Committee," Patricia C. Stearns, Chairman, June 15, 1971, BCDSOD.
45. "A Cooperative Effort in Dental Auxiliary Training," 32.
46. Letter, Patricia C. Stearns, Chairman, Department of Dental Hygiene, to Albin O. Kuhn, Chancellor of Baltimore Campus, University of Maryland, June 11, 1971, BCDSOD; "Curriculum Vitae," Barbara J. Vondrak, June 10, 1971, BCDSOD.
47. Letters, John J. Salley, Dean, Dental School, University of Maryland, to John M. Coady, Secretary, Council on Dental Education, January 18, 1972, Albin O. Kuhn, Chancellor, University of Maryland at Baltimore, to Mario V. Santangelo, Assistant Secretary, Council on Dental Education, May 24, 1972, BCDSOD.
48. Kyrle W. Preis, "Dr. Ernest B. Nuttall Retires," *Alma Mater* 12 (Spring 1971): 29.
49. "Faculty Council Minutes, 1965–1966," October 29, 1965, BCDSP, NMDA.
50. Ibid., November 23, 1965.
51. Ibid., January 21, 1966.
52. "U. of M. Dental School Project," *The Sun* (Baltimore), May 1, 1966, May 31, 1970.
53. "Science Close to Conquering Caries, Dedication Audience Told," *Newsletter University of Maryland School of Dentistry* 4 (Spring 1971): 1.
54. Baltimore College of Dental Surgery, Dental School, University of Maryland, *Dedication Hayden-Harris Hall* (n.p., 1971), p. 3.
55. Ibid.
56. "Dedication of Hayden-Harris Hall University of Maryland—School of Dentistry," *Alma Mater* 12 (Spring 1971): 20–21.
57. Marc D. Star, "Stones and Bricks: An Architectural Record of Maryland's Dental Colleges," senior thesis, Baltimore College of Dental Surgery, Dental School, University of Maryland, 1993, pp. 25, 28.
58. John J. Salley and James H. Stephenson, "Facilities for the University of Maryland Dental Health Center," *Journal of the Baltimore College of Dental Surgery* 23 (December 1968): 46–50, 53, 56, 58.
59. Baltimore College of Dental Surgery, Dental School, University of Maryland, *1972–1974 Bulletin*, p. 7; "Students Set Own Pace in Independent Learning Center," *Newsletter University of Maryland School of Dentistry* 5 (Winter 1071): 1.
60. Baltimore College of Dental Surgery, Dental School, University of Maryland, *1972–1974 Bulletin*, pp. 20–22, 24–29.
61. The first graduate to receive an MS degree in this program was Dr. John M. Hyson, Jr., a 1950 BCDS alumnus. [The author.]
62. Baltimore College of Dental Surgery, Dental School, University of Maryland, *1972–1974 Bulletin*, p. 31.
63. "Pass-Fail System Begins in September," *Newsletter University of Maryland School of Dentistry* 4 (Spring 1971): 3.
64. "Highlight: Department of Anatomy," *Dental Newsletter* 11 (Winter 1977): 2.
65. "Peru Affiliation Established," *Newsletter University of Maryland School of Dentistry* 4 (Spring 1971): 2.
66. Ralph W. Phillips, "Past, Present, and Future Composite Resin Systems," *Dental Clinics of North America* 25 (April 1981): 216–18.
67. Alumni Association, BCDS, "Report by a Special Study Committee," [1973], Gardner P. H. Foley Papers, National Museum of Dentistry Archives (*hereafter* cited as GPHFP, NMDA).
68. Ibid.
69. Ibid.
70. Ibid.
71. Ibid.
72. Letter, H. Berton McCauley, Historian, MSDA, to J. Ben Robinson, BCDS Dean, May 5, 1971, GPHFP, NMDA.
73. Letter, J. Ben Robinson to H. Berton McCauley, May 25, 1971, GPHFP, NMDA.
74. Memorandum, John J. Salley, BCDS Dean, to BCDS Faculty Council, August 30, 1974, GPHFP, NMDA.
75. Letter, J. Ben Robinson to Kyrle W. Preis, November 20, 1971, Letter, H. Berton McCauley to J. Ben Robinson, March 2, 1972, Notation, H. B. McCauley, April 21, 1972, H. Berton McCauley Papers.
76. Baltimore College of Dental Surgery, Dental School, University of Maryland, *1976-78 Bulletin Baltimore College of Dental Surgery, Dental School, University of Maryland at Baltimore* n.p., [1976], p. 30.
77. Ibid.
78. "Dental School to Try Innovative Curriculum for Selected Students," *Newsletter University of Maryland School of Dentistry* 6 (Winter 1972): 2.
79. "Affirmative Action Aims at Equal Opportunity for Minorities and Women," *Happenings* 2 (November 1972): 1.
80. Lawrence A. Kaplan, ed., *The 1972 Mirror* (n.p., 1972), p. 35.
81. T. Michael Payne, ed., *The Mirror 1977* (n.p., 1977), p. 46.
82. Letter, J. Ben Robinson to John J. Salley, July 24, 1972, GPHFP, NMDA.
83. Letter, John J. Salley, Dean, BCDS, to J. Ben Robinson, August 18, 1972, GPHFP, NMDA.
84. Letter, J. Ben Robinson to John J. Salley, September 15, 1972, GPHFP, NMDA.
85. Warren M. Morganstein and John J. Salley," The Team Program at the University of Maryland," *Journal of the Maryland State Dental Association* 16 (April 1973): 15, 16.
86. K. C. Sweeney, "Faculty Dental Clinic," *Maryland Probe* 2 (June 5, 1973): 1.
87. "Dean Salley Announces Accreditation of Dental School," *Dental Newsletter* 7 (Winter 1973): 3.
88. "Dr. Abramson to Retire," *Newsletter University of Maryland School of Dentistry* 6 (Spring 1973): 2.
89. "Dental School Evaluates Progress During Last Decade," *Newsletter University of Maryland School of Dentistry* 6 (Spring 1973): 1.

90. Baltimore College of Dental Surgery, Dental School, University of Maryland, "Initial Draft: Final Report Special Committee of the Faculty Council for the Development of New Goals and Objectives University of Maryland School of Dentistry July 1973," BCD-SOD.
91. Ibid.
92. Ibid.
93. John A. D. Cooper, "Curriculum Reforms in Medical Education," *Journal of Dental Education* 37 (January 1973): 13.
94. Arthur D. King, Don L. Allen, Richard S. Mackenzie, and Jose E. Medina, "A Modular Curriculum Design for Dentistry," *Journal of Dental Education* 36 (June 1972): 20.
95. In 1953, the author was an instructor in the Department of Operative Dentistry, BCDS, working with Dr. Medina who was an associate professor.
96. John F. Hasler and John J. Salley, "The Changing Faces of Dental Education: The Anatomy of the Clinical Dental Curriculum at the University of Maryland," *Bulletin University of Maryland School of Medicine* 59 (May 1974): 11–12.
97. Letter, Leon Seligman, President, BCDS Alumni Association, to Louis L. Kaplan, Chairman, Board of Regents, University of Maryland, May 30, 1973, GPHFP, NMDA.
98. Memorandum, unidentified, undated, GPHFP, NMDA.
99. Charles T. Pridgeon, "The Role and Involvement of the Dental School in Continuing Education," *Journal of the Maryland State Dental Association* 17 (August 1974): 100, 101.
100. "School of Dentistry Initiates Senior Externship Program," *Dental Newsletter* 8 (Winter 1974): 1.
101. Memorandum, J. Ben Robinson, "Dr. John J. Salley's Recommendation for Change in Official Title of the Dental School,"n.d., GPHFP, NMDA.
102. Letter, J. Ben Robinson to William R. Patteson, October 31, 1974, GPHFP, NMDA.
103. "Dean John J. Salley Resigns, Dr. Errol L. Reese Named Acting Dean," *Dental Newsletter* 8 (Winter 1974): 1; Larry Scheitler and Bernie French, "Dean Salley Resigns," *Maryland Probe* 3 (May 1974): 1.
104. "John Salley to Head New School of Graduate Studies," *Dental Newsletter* 13 (Spring 1980): 3.
105. Scheitler and French, "Dean Salley Resigns," 1.
106. "UMAB Chancellor Establishes Dental Dean Search Committee," *Dental Newsletter* 8 (Winter 1974): 1.

Errol L. Reese

Chapter 19

The Reese Years: 1974–90

"This school is responsible to the people of the State of Maryland; it exists for their benefit. It is the center for dentistry in this State. Its program is intended to strengthen the profession of dentistry in order to meet the needs of the population, not simply to perpetuate a profession based upon tradition. This school should become a central resource for the profession and extend the use of its creative and research capabilities to the community, allied institutions and professional organizations, in a cooperative campaign to eliminate oral disease."[1] **~Errol L. Reese, 1975**

Errol Reese Becomes Dean: 1974

Errol L. Reese, DDS, was appointed as the acting dean of the Dental School in 1974 and as dean on June 20, 1975. Dr. Reese was born on May 3, 1939, in Fairmont, W. Va. He was the son of a Baltimore College of Dental Surgery graduate, Dr. Edgar B. Reese, Class of 1931. Errol Reese received a BS degree from Fairmont State College in 1960 and a DDS degree from the West Virginia School of Dentistry in 1963. After graduation, he served in the U.S. Army and was stationed in Schweinfurt, Germany, for three years.

In 1966, Reese was awarded an NIH postdoctoral training grant in physiological prosthodontics and received his MS degree and specialty certificate from the University of Detroit and Wayne State Medical School. In 1968, he began his career at the Baltimore College of Dental Surgery as an associate professor. He was appointed associate dean in 1973. He was a fellow of the American College of Dentists and International College of Dentists, and held high offices in the Council of Dental School Deans and the American Association of Dental Schools (now American Dental Education Association), including serving as its president. Reese served as a consultant to many international, national, and local institutions and was a board member of several national foundations. He also served as a consultant to the Human Performance Institute in Atami, Japan, and was a member of a World Health Organization Expert Panel to study performance simulation in dentistry. Reese received the Martin Luther King Humanitarian Award and the J. Ben Robinson Memorial Award from the American College of Dentists.[2]

Dr. Reese's first year began during a period of severe reduction in federal fiscal support, including a 24 percent decrease in capitation funds. In addition, "spiraling inflation without a concurrent increase in the level of state funding resulted in the erosion of base support from state appropriations." The school had to tighten its belt and reexamine its options for survival.[3] At the same time, the rate of overall dental school enrollment was reduced in the 1975–76 academic year, whereas enrollments of women and minority students continued to climb. In the previous two years, enrollment of women in dental schools more than doubled, comprising nine percent of all predoctoral dental students. Minority students comprised 11 percent of the incoming freshman dental class.[4]

First Women Full Professors: 1975

Immediately after his appointment, Dean Reese addressed the faculty on the future direction of the school and the revisions in the academic structure he deemed necessary to "streamline administrative support to the faculty with the desire of increasing and improving all educational programs, research, and service aspects of the School."[5] In one of his first moves, in July 1975, Dr. Reese appointed the first two women full professors in the history of the school. Dr. Frieda Rudo, Department of Pharmacology, and Dr. Sue-ning Barry, Department of Anatomy, were promoted to the rank of full professors.[6]

Dr. Rudo came to the University in 1955 as a technical consultant in the cardio-pulmonary laboratory and in 1960 was appointed an instructor in experimental surgery at the School of Medicine. For eight years, she remained at the medical school, teaching and researching with Dr. John D. Krantz and served as a research fellow in the pharmacology of anesthetics and as assistant professor of pharmacology. In 1968, she accepted an assistant professorship in pharmacology at the Dental School and within two years was promoted to associate professor. Dr. Rudo was a 1944 graduate of Goucher College and held master's degrees in pharmacology and biochemistry and PhD degrees in both pharmacology and physiology from the University of Maryland School of Medicine. She authored chapters on pharmacology and anesthetics for three textbooks; published articles in many of the country's top professional journals; and developed films and videotapes for educational purposes. Her research activities resulted in the development of two inhalation anesthetics (Ethrane and Forane), and over a five-year period her research support totaled $135,000.[7]

Dr. Barry, a graduate of Barat College in Illinois and the PhD program in zoology at the University of Maryland, College Park, joined the Dental School's Department of Histology and Embryology in 1961. While working as a research fellow on a National Institutes of Health grant, she was appointed as an assistant professor in 1962 and was later promoted to associate professor in 1968. Dr. Barry became a professor of anatomy, teaching the microscopic and developmental aspects. Her special interest was the field of cell physiology, under contract with the National Institute of Dental Research.[8]

Another noteworthy event in 1975 was the retirement of Dr. William E. Hahn, the director of admissions and former professor of anatomy. An alumnus of the School, Dr. Hahn had served on the faculty for 44 years, beginning in the early 1930s as an anatomy instructor to professor of anatomy in the 1940s. In 1956, he became the first full-time chairman of the Department of Anatomy. In 1965, he was appointed as the director of admissions. In June of 1971, he resigned his anatomy chairmanship to devote his full attention to admissions.

Dr. Hahn was replaced by Dr. Charles B. Leonard, Jr., associate professor of biochemistry, as admissions director on July 1, 1975.[9]

The Accelerated Program Graduation

One of the school's innovative programs was initiated in 1971, called the Accelerated Professional Training Program (APT), which was designed to satisfy the requirements for the DDS degree in three calendar years, graduated its first class in 1975. The lessons learned from the program benefited the traditional curriculum, by providing a rotation of other dental faculty members through the program. This "school within a school" not only satisfied the federal requirement for increased enrollment, but "served as a unique method of educational research, wherein lies its future promise." The three-year program continued until 1983.[10]

New Administrative Appointments

Dean Reese announced a number of "modifications to the administrative structure" of the School in June 1975 in response to the recommendations of the accreditation report of the Council on Dental Education. Changes were made to strengthen the school's programs and service capabilities. The revisions in the administrative organization were as follows:

1. Dr. Warren M. Morganstein was appointed as associate dean.
2. Dr. John F. Hasler, formerly chairman of the division of oral diagnosis and radiology and assistant dean for clinical affairs, was appointed as associate dean for clinical affairs. He was responsible for the "coordination and supervision of existing intra and extramural clinical programs, and for the development and implementation of new clinical programs."
3. Dr. Ernest F. Moreland, formerly director of the Division of Educational and Instructional Resources, was appointed as associate dean for academic affairs. He was responsible for the "effective implementation of all academic programs and for curriculum development." His job was to "work with faculty and students to develop methods of improving and refining the educational programs of the Dental School."
4. Dr. Wilbur O. Ramsey, professor of removable prosthodontics, was appointed as director of "advanced specialty education and special clinical programs." As director of "advanced specialty education," it was his task to "serve as administrator and coordinator of the didactic and clinical aspects of postdoctoral training in the disciplines of orthodontics, pediatric dentistry, oral surgery, endodontics, periodontics and prosthodontics." He was also responsible for the general administrative supervision of the dental externship program and the special clinic for the disabled.
5. Dr. Donald E. Shay, chairman of the Department of Microbiology, was appointed as assistant dean for biological sciences. He was responsible for ensuring the "relevance of course content in the biological sciences to that in the clinical sciences" and encouraging the "increased participation of the biological science departments in all educational programs and to see realized the integration of research into the undergraduate dental and postdoctoral programs."
6. Dr. Charles T. Pridgeon, professor of periodontics, was appointed as associate dean for continuing education and alumni affairs, and Dr. Robert W. Haroth, associate professor of fixed restorative dentistry, was appointed as Dr. Pridgeon's assistant director. Their roles were

to expand the continuing education programs and to increase the "effort to serve the alumni and the practicing dentist."

7. The Department of Restorative Dentistry was subdivided by elevating to departmental status the former divisions of fixed restorative dentistry, removable prosthodontics, and endodontics. Dr. Alvan M. Holston was named the acting chairman of the new Department of Fixed Restorative Dentistry. Dr. Frank C. Jerbi remained the chairman of the new Department of Removable Prosthodontics, and Dr. Stanley S. Andrews continued as acting chairman of the new Department of Endodontics.

8. Dr. C. Daniel Overholser was named the acting chairman of the Division of Oral Diagnosis and Radiology.

9. Dr. James F. Craig was appointed the director of the Division of Educational and Instructional Resources.

10. The Department of Pedodontics became the Department of Pediatric Dentistry.

11. The Department of Community Dentistry became the Department of Oral Health Care Delivery under Dr. Thomas L. Snyder, the acting director.

12. Dr. Rodger F. Sisca was appointed as the director of conjoint sciences and interdisciplinary studies. Although conjoint sciences was not a new course, it was the first time a director had been appointed for its coordination.[11]

Satellite Centers Established

A 1975 grant of $2,000 from the Maryland Regional Medical Program (MRMP) made it possible for the school to "usher in a new dimension in Continuing Education for the practicing dentists and dental auxiliaries" in the Baltimore area. The grant helped subsidize the establishment of "satellite learning centers" at selected community colleges throughout the state for the use of the members of the Maryland State Dental Association (MSDA). Professional, self-instruction material was now available to local dentists and dental auxiliaries through the medium of the learning centers at the participating colleges. Each satellite center provided access to continuing education material, including videotapes, 8 mm film, slide presentations, books, records, and audiotapes. In this manner, a practitioner could participate at his own convenience in self-instructional continuing education. The Dental School's campus Independent Learning Center was also available to the dental community. The community colleges that eventually subscribed to the program were: Allegany, Frederick, Harford, and Prince George community colleges and Hagerstown Junior and Salisbury State colleges.[12]

The project was called "A New Adventure in Continuing Education" and marked the "introduction to the dental community and the utilization of the independent learning system for purposes of continuing education." The MRMP and the MSDA provided funds to make the school's center open one night a week for dentists and their auxiliaries. Later, the center was available to the dental community on a daily basis. The "teaching/learning process via independent learning resources, as opposed to the traditional classroom lecture" experienced tremendous acceptance and growth in all phases of education and the Dental School was in the forefront of this educational trend.[13]

Self-Study

In June 1975, university system President Wilson H. Elkins requested that each division and department of the university undergo a period of self-analysis to recommend ways and means to improve the university. In the 1975–76 academic year, Dr. Reese and the executive committee established a task force to generate the required data. The study focused on the goals and priorities of the Dental School. The steps identified to correct the deficiencies in the areas of faculty positions and funding, were as follows:

1. Each department should review and evaluate its use of resources in relation to both department and school priorities and submit a report.
2. Reallocate 15 percent of operating funds to support the clinical program.
3. Request additional state support for the clinical program.
4. Redistribute state-supported positions based on actual teaching load and seek additional positions.
5. Seek additional support staff.
6. Reallocate departmental resources to provide for future goals.
7. Seek additional alumni funding to provide for development of new goals.
8. Study methods of passing on additional costs to students and patients.[14]

Independent Learning Center

The 1970s saw an increased use of the Independent Learning Center. Although not the first of its kind, the center was "the most comprehensive, in terms of its scope and the degree to which students are expected to make use of it." Consisting of 3,200 square feet containing 100 study carrels, where students worked with all different kinds of self-instructional media, each carrel became a place where the student was literally "in a class of one." The center was open 15–18 hours a day, and on weekends and holidays, and the students could work on their own time schedule and "rate of intensity" according to their personal needs. Meanwhile, the faculty developed the program material, monitored the student responses, and revised and updated material. Teachers could take a "broader and very much more personal role in each student's education."[15]

In July 1976, Dr. James F. Craig was named chairman of the Department of Educational and Instructional Resources, which included the Independent Learning Center, with its 1,600 titles and more than 8,000 total programs used as "an integral part of the dental curriculum." Now the school was recognized nationally and internationally for its self-instructional programs and was receiving requests from all over the world for them. In the "new goals study" of 1973, it was predicted that by 1983, 85–90 percent of the school's curriculum would be self-instructional.[16]

Dr. Craig was also involved in the development of continuing education programs via the Communications Technology Satellite (CTS), a joint NASA and Canadian government satellite. The School was able to transmit and receive from the Lister Hill Center located at the National Library of Medicine at Bethesda. The process had been set up by a grant awarded by the Department of Health, Education and Welfare, Public Health Service, Health Resources Administration, Bureau of Health Resources. The school was one of four universities in the country selected for this program. The others were the universities of Colorado in Denver, Washington in Seattle, and Kentucky in Lexington. The purpose of the 13-month grant was to "experiment with and evaluate the use of satellites for continuing education in dentistry." The Maryland school's part of the experiment was titled "People Problems in Office Management." Dental practitioners within the immediate vicinity of the transmission area were given the opportunity to take the course, which if successful, would lead to the use of satellite technology for continuing education throughout the world.[17] Twenty dentists from Southern Maryland and Washington, D.C., were selected for the initial control group to evaluate the effectiveness of this new medium in continuing education.[18]

Other Changes: 1976–78

In July 1976, Dr. Reese revised the organization of the Faculty Assembly to include non-faculty alumni representation on several key committees of the Faculty Council—the dental admissions and dental hygiene admissions subcommittees, the subcommittee on continuing education, the faculty-alumni liaison committee, and a newly created Committee of Nine.[19]

For the 1977–78 session, the school decided to begin to phase out federal capitation support. Upon completion of this "phase-out," the school would "regain its independence to control and direct the curriculum and its various educational programs, as well as to determine enrollment." This decision was made with the belief that both the state of Maryland and the alumni and friends of the Dental School would provide "sufficient support so that the loss of the federal capitation support" would not be detrimental to the institution. The state of Maryland responded by providing "additional faculty and classified personnel support and operating funds." Alumni contributions increased substantially in 1977 and 1978.[20]

In the fall of 1977, the university's Dental Hygiene Department offered its students, through its Bachelor of Science curriculum, specialized training in public health, consisting of 18 credit hours. Twelve of these core hours were offered at the Dental School and six hours at the University of Maryland Baltimore County or other nearby academic institutions. Courses were included in statistics, community development, health administration, psychology, and sociology.[21] In July the same year, the school announced the appointment of Cheryl T. Metzger as assistant professor and chairperson of the Hygiene Department.[22]

In 1977, the school established a Center for Treatment of Dento-Facial Abnormalities, whose purpose was to "study, diagnose, and treat acquired and congenital dento-facial abnormalities disturbing the biological and social well-being of affected patients." This treatment required a multidisciplinary approach with oral surgeons, orthodontists, dental hygienists, periodontists, a psychologist, and restorative dentists. Medical specialty coverage of "anesthesia, psychiatry, otolaryngology, neurosurgery, plastic surgery and internal medicine" was also available at the center on a consulting basis. The center was directed by Dr. Donald M. Tilghman, associate professor of oral surgery, and Dr. Ronald J. Scornavacca, assistant clinical professor of orthodontics.[23]

The general practice residency in dentistry program at the University of Maryland Hospital received a three-year grant of $363,000 in 1978 awarded by the Bureau of Health Manpower, Department of Health, Education and Welfare. The mission of the program was to "provide residents with advanced knowledge of dentistry so that upon completion they may go into general practice with less dependence upon other dental specialists." In addition to gaining experience in treating patients in a hospital setting, the residents gained "knowledge and skills in treating medically compromised patients."[24]

Dean Reese announced the appointment of two new chairmen in 1978; Dr. James T. Rule, Department of Pediatric Dentistry, and Dr. William M. Davidson, Department of Orthodontics.[25]

In 1978, the annual tuition for dental students was $1,750 for Maryland residents and $3,550 for non-residents; hygiene students paid $620 for residents and $2,050 for out-of-state. In addition, instruments and supplies cost the dental student $2,249 for freshmen, $1,827 for sophomores, $490 for juniors, and $100 for seniors. As in the past, the oral surgery instruments were provided by the school. The purchase of textbooks was not required, although it was encouraged. Textbooks ran about $300 for freshmen and sophomores, $200 for juniors, and $50 for seniors.[26] The Class of 1978 was special because it included 16 women, six more than any previous class in the history of the school.[27]

The late 1970s also saw the implementation of the Specially Tailored Educational Program (STEP), allowing students to spend up to three years to complete the first two years of dental school. The program was developed for students, who, "because of academic difficulty, illness or other circumstances, need special assistance and/or additional time to fulfill the academic requirements." The first- or second-year advancement committees could offer the student the option of STEP or assign any student whose progress was unsatisfactory to STEP. Those students assigned to STEP were placed under the supervision of the Special Academic Programs Committee, whose function was to carefully monitor the students' progress. Faculty counselors in the basic sciences and preclinical sciences were also made available.[28] At the same time, the Accelerated Professional Training Program (APT) was still available to complete the curriculum in three years.[29]

Meanwhile in October 1977, Dr. Joseph P. Cappuccio, long-time clinical professor of oral surgery, was elected president-elect of the American Dental Association (ADA) at its 118th annual session held at Miami Beach, Fla. Dr. Cappuccio had previously served as a delegate to the ADA's House of Delegates (for 18 years before 1971), chairman of the Maryland delegation, and currently was trustee of the 4th district. He assumed the presidency in 1978.[30]

In 1979, a new master of science program in oral biology was approved by the State Board for Higher Education for the Dental School. The program was developed by Dr. Donald E. Shay and the administrative staff of the Advanced Specialty Education Program to allow candidates seeking certificates of advanced education in "recognized specialties" to extend their programs into areas of "education, biological and clinical sciences and research." The accepted students had to hold a DDS degree.[31]

Death of Katherine Toomey

The year 1979 was an especially sad one for the college, as it signified the death of a legend—Katherine (Kate) Toomey, who, as the dean's secretary (1917–61), provided major administrative support for three deans, Drs. Heatwole, Robinson, and Aisenberg. Kate was beloved by the students, alumni, and faculty. In 1958, Mount Saint Mary's College, Emmitsburg, Md., awarded her an honorary Doctor of Laws degree. In conferring the degree, the college said: "With easy grace and modest reserve you have been content to work your magic behind the scenes, finding your satisfaction in the bright careers which are the fruit of your devotion. The scores of men and women who have passed from the University of Maryland Dental School bear the lasting imprint of your genuine kindness."[32] The *Alma Mater* in the January 1980 issue perhaps best summarized her stature at the college:

Katherine (Kate) Toomey

> If there was ever person dedicated to the interests of dentistry—educationally, organizationally, and socially—it is Katherine Toomey. Her entire adult life was devoted to our profession. It was a full-time job and she more than met its demands with intelligence, energy and enthusiasm. Serving three Deans—Timothy Heatwole, J. Ben Robinson, and Myron Aisenberg—was for her a joyous experience of which she was quite proud. Little wonder that with time, and confidence in her judgment fully justified, she occupied a unique position of administrative influence and fully earned the respect of dental leaders.
>
> Perhaps she shall be remembered best by the hosts of former students each having benefited in countless little ways from kindness which only they knew.[33]

Decreased Enrollment of Undergraduates: 1980

During the late 1960s and early 1970s, the federal government was interested in increasing dental manpower in primary care and in providing dentistry for underserved areas. It provided financial support to dental schools if they increased their enrollment to a designated level. In 1980, the school was no longer obligated to the federal government "to increase enrollment and maintain that enrollment for a 10-year period, in return for federal funds to construct Hayden-Harris Hall." In addition, the school had agreed to the increased enrollment to take advantage of federal capitation funds, which paid for many of the educational programs that enhanced the School's curriculum. Now, it could make adjustments in enrollment that it deemed appropriate. Dean Reese requested the Maryland State Dental Association to ascertain the manpower needs of the state, and set up an ad hoc committee to carry out this study. The Faculty Council also appointed a committee to study enrollment. These studies were ongoing while the school phased out capitation and fulfilled the last two years of the building contract. Finally, in July 1980, the Executive Committee approved a recommendation to "effect a reduction in enrollment in the undergraduate DDS program beginning with the class entering in 1981." This plan was called, "The Enrollment Plan for the '80's," and was approved by Chancellor T. Albert Farmer on November 17, 1980. This reduction was proposed to last until 1983 at which time the Executive Committee could review the impact of this reduction. As enrollment in the undergraduate program was reduced, an increase was planned for the postdoctoral programs. The enrollment quota for undergraduate freshmen students was set at 96 and the accelerated professional training program (APT) was phased out. In addition, it was decided to expand the advanced dental education program by developing a Master of Science curriculum in oral biology and dental hygiene, and an advanced general dentistry program.[34]

Patient-Centered Care

As dental schools throughout the United States were facing growing problems related to funding and operating their predoctoral clinical training programs, Dean Reese, in 1980, assigned the school's Associate Dean for Clinical Affairs, Dr. John F. Hasler, the responsibility of reviewing its clinical programs and recommending appropriate changes to meet these emerging challenges. Working with the school's Clinical and Basic Sciences Councils, it was determined that a new emphasis was needed, focusing on creating and maintaining an environment that was conducive to patient- and student-centered clinical care, emulating (where possible) private dental practice. All members of the school's Executive Committee were asked to embrace this patient-centered approach, placing the patients' needs first, and concurrently focusing on a student-centered mentoring approach. These early shifts in clinical emphasis led to the subsequent development, in the early 1990s of the school's widely admired General Practice Program, using dentist managers and patient care coordinators. Maryland was one of the first, if not the first dental school, to initiate such a program, and over the years many other U.S. dental schools adopted similar patient-centered programs.[35]

Beginning with the Class of 1980, the extramural training program became a required part of the curriculum for students. The program consisted of six weeks, of which two weeks were spread over the first three years and four weeks during the senior year. Seniors were allowed to practice in private dental offices, hospitals, U.S. Coast Guard dental clinics, medical facilities for senior citizens, etc., under the supervision of licensed dentists serving as preceptors. The program was directed by Dr. George H. Williams, assistant professor.[36] Oddly enough, this method of teaching had been used as the very first method of teaching dentistry to students before the advent of the Baltimore College of Dental Surgery; however, now the major difference was that the apprentices were all nearly fully trained graduate dentists.

The Maryland Bridge

In 1980, two faculty members of the Department of Fixed Restorative Dentistry, Drs. Gus J. Livaditis and Van P. Thompson, collaborated on the development of a resin-bonded bridge called the "Maryland Bridge." The etched metal resin-bonded retainers had many advantages over conventional bridgework. Tooth enamel reduction was kept to a minimum and dentinal involvement was eliminated. The restorations were designed to be supragingival and the restorations were bonded to the lingual surfaces; thus, maintaining the esthetics of the natural enamel. In addition, the restorations were relatively low cost when compared with other bridgework. Another advantage of the resin-bonded bridge was its reversibility leaving the teeth virtually unaltered. In February 1981, Livaditis and Thompson presented their findings before the American Prosthodontic Society and the American Academy of Crown and Bridge Prosthodontics.[37]

Drug Abuse Program

In 1980, the school became the first dental school in the United States to be awarded a training grant to support a program to study the problems of alcoholism and drug abuse among dental patients. Dr. Mark S. Arthur, assistant professor, was selected to be the first career teacher in the program under the direction of Dr. Paul D. Thut of the Department of Pharmacology. A comprehensive curriculum in drug and alcohol abuse was to be included in the course for all dental and dental hygiene students for them to understand the role they played in the treatment and/or referral of substance abusing patients. This information was also to be made available to all practicing dentists and dental hygienists in the community.[38]

The Loss of the Washington Denture: 1981

The Dental School Museum was located in the Independent Learning Center on the ground floor of Hayden-Harris Hall. On exhibition were antique instruments, chairs, cabinets, dentures, replicas of ancient prostheses, and portraits of the leaders in the development of the profession. The museum was open Monday through Friday from 8:30 a.m. to 4:30 p.m., with extended hours evenings and Saturdays during the regular academic year.[39] However, the museum suffered its greatest loss in its 140-year history in 1981, when the 1795 Washington dentures were reported stolen from the Smithsonian Institution in Washington, D.C. The dentures had been loaned to the Smithsonian in 1965 for an exhibition on the history of dentistry at the Museum of History and Technology, which had opened in October 1967. On June 19, 1981, the dentures were reported stolen, while they were in a locked storage room accessible only to Smithsonian employees. It was believed that they were stolen for their gold content, as the price of gold was high at the time. On May 3, 1982, the Washington mandibular ivory denture mysteriously reappeared at the Smithsonian storage room, anonymously returned. However, the maxillary swedged-gold denture was not to be found. The Federal Bureau of Investigation made no announcement until it was leaked to the press in August 1982. The denture was never recovered.[40]

Several questions can be raised concerning this occurrence. The dentures had been safely stored in the college's museum since at least the 1860s without incident. Reportedly, the dentures could only be removed from the university campus with the consent of the University Board of Regents. Then too, the Smithsonian carried no liability insurance on borrowed items. And lastly, why were the dentures not returned to the college at the end of the exhibition? In any event, the museum lost its most precious item, a probable $3 million icon.

The Accreditation Site Visit: 1981

Every seven years, dental schools in the United States were visited by the Commission on Dental Accreditation of the American Dental Association. The Commission provided general guidelines for collecting information and conducting the self-study survey. Administrative planning began in August 1979 and was completed by August 1980. In January 1981, the college was visited by the Commission. Before the visit, the faculty had prepared an extensive self-study document. The DDS program alone contained some 4,000 pages and the advanced specialty education and dental hygiene programs comprised another 4,000 pages.[41] The accreditation visit was very successful; in fact, the committee was very impressed: "The visiting committee was most impressed with the academic and professional backgrounds and qualifications of both basic science clinical science faculty. The faculty's general, professional and advanced education preparation and experience in education and research are generally excellent." The committee also commented on the clinical program: "Among the strengths observed in the clinical science programs of the dental school are the quality of the faculty and its dedication at all levels of instruction to create an environment for their students that is conducive to the attainment of the best possible educational experience in all aspects of the clinical sciences at varying levels of student proficiency."[42]

However, the committee did recommend the following changes be implemented:

1. Strengthen the dental hygiene and advanced oral and maxillofacial surgery programs. They were given "conditional approval" for a one-year period so that the modifications recommended by the commission could be carried out.
2. Develop the conjoint science program to integrate the basic sciences into clinical dentistry.
3. Increase minority recruitment activities, as well as financial assistance to students.
4. Begin a program of renovation and replacement of clinical space and equipment for the 10-year-old Hayden-Harris Hall.
5. Increase security in and around the Dental School.
6. Reevaluate faculty distribution to ensure a better student-faculty ratio.
7. Recruit a formally trained dental radiologist.
8. Strengthen the student preclinical experience in "prevention, dietary analysis, counseling, behavioral modification, patient motivation."
9. Increase research opportunities and productivity in both basic science and clinical areas.[43]

In 1981, the college faculty presented a successful series of lectures for the U.S. Armed Forces in Germany.[44]

The year 1981 was also noteworthy for the retirement of Dr. Donald E. Shay, the chairman of the department of microbiology and the assistant dean for biological sciences. Since 1945, Dr. Shay had been associated with the dental and pharmacy as an associate professor of microbiology. In 1948, he was appointed as professor and chairman of the Department of Microbiology at the Dental School, a position he held for 33 years until his retirement. In 1975, he was appointed as assistant dean for biological sciences by Dean Reese. Dr. Shay was "widely recognized for his research in the areas of oral microbiology, antibiotics, antiseptics and disinfectants.[45]

Student-Faculty Group Practice

In 1982, the school initiated a "Dental Practice Systems" (DPS) to provide a realistic practice experience for dental students. Evolving from the earlier "dental auxiliary utilization" and "expanded auxiliary management" programs, the new program was designed to "provide a realistic private practice environment" for the student. The program, under the direction of Dr. Gary A. Colangelo, allowed the students to work with dental auxiliaries, give them experience in financial and personnel management, and practice dentistry in a group practice environment. All third- and fourth-year students rotated through the practice and performed procedures "appropriate for their skill level." Each fourth-year student was assigned to act as manager of the practice for one day and work with the business manager and auxiliary supervisor in "assuring the smooth operation of the clinic" for that day. The student manager was responsible for such tasks as managing patient flow, handling emergencies, patient scheduling, bookkeeping, recall system, and supply management. In addition, five fourth-year students were selected as "DPS Clerks," whose duties included practicing in the clinic one full day a week, treatment planning, and treating their own patients, as well as performing managerial duties. Clerks were allowed to refer patients to specialists. A dental hygiene clerkship was also instituted for one hygiene student to practice one day a week for the entire year.[46]

DPS used 24 operatories in a clinic on the ground floor of Hayden-Harris Hall. Changes made for the program included a redesigned reception area, addition of a second radiographic unit, and the development of a nearby basic dental laboratory. Five full-time and six part-time faculty members, including general dentists, prosthodontists, endodontists, a periodontist; a part-time hygienist; nine certified dental assistants; three expanded function dental auxiliaries; a part-time laboratory technician; and four administrative personnel were assigned to the clinic. In addition, four volunteer dentists from the community assisted the staff. Revenues generated from the clinic were used to pay the salaries of the professional and support staff, as well as purchase both dental and office supplies.[47]

Dominican Dental Mission Project: 1982

The Dominican Dental Mission Project was founded in 1982 by Assistant Professor of Oral Health Care Delivery Dr. Francis G. Serio, under the auspices of the Catholic Medical Mission Board, as an "individual effort to provide dental care to some of the world's poor." What began as a solo trip by Dr. Serio to the Catholic mission of Centro Padre Arturo located in the town of San Jose de Ocoa in the south central mountains of the Dominican Republic expanded into a trip the following July by Dr. Serio with three dental students and a hygienist. The group spent three weeks working in and around Ocoa and setting up shop in the surrounding villages. They had a small portable dental unit and compressor with a generator to supply power in villages with no electricity. By 1985, the trip had expanded to include 14 volunteers and became an annual event. By 1991—the tenth anniversary—the project included 26 dentists and dental students and Dr. Serio was recognized by President George Herbert Walker Bush as a recipient of the President's Volunteer Action Award, one of only 19 Americans so honored nationwide. By 1999, in its 18 years of operation, more than 270 students and graduates of the University of Maryland, the University of Mississippi, the Medical University of South Carolina, and other dentists had volunteered their time to provide the needed dental services. More than 36,500 people had received treatment consisting of exodontia, restorative, prosthetic, endodontic, preventive, and periodontal services. The estimated value of these services was in excess of five million U.S. dollars. The Dominican awareness of oral health consciousness was raised by the program. Seven Dominican dental students, who were initially inspired to become dentists by the program, were provided with instruments, books, supplies, and financial support for their education.[48]

The Advanced General Dentistry Program: 1982

An Advanced General Dentistry Program (AGD) was initiated in 1982 under the direction of Dr. Alvan M. Holston, Jr., assistant professor, Department of Fixed Restorative Dentistry, with five students. The new one-year program was the first Dental School-based program to be initiated in the United States. The new postdoctoral program was established to provide recent graduates with an opportunity to "increase their knowledge in all disciplines and develop speed, confidence, and advanced techniques under faculty supervision." The program was developed around the concept of comprehensive patient care based on a private practice model. The students received clinical experiences in endodontics, fixed and removable prosthetics, oral and maxillofacial surgery, oral diagnosis and medicine, orthodontics, pediatric dentistry, periodontics, restorative dentistry, and practice management. In addition to the clinical disciplines, the students attended seminars in all the clinical specialties, practice management, applied biological sciences, literature review, treatment planning, and a journal club. The students were provided with detailed information concerning the operational costs and the income produced to gain insight into the "appreciation for the business and financial management of a practice."[49]

In 1983, the predoctoral Senior Clerkship Program was expanded to include approximately 90 students. Also that year, three other new programs were finally initiated: A Center for the Study of Human Performance in Dentistry, a Facial Pain Center, and a Master of Science Degree Program in Dental Hygiene.[50]

Contributions of Non-Dental Faculty: 1980s

One of the highlights of the 1980s was the contributions of three non-dental members of the Department of Educational and Instructional Resources, namely: Ernest F. Moreland, EdD, professor; James F. Craig, EdD, associate professor; and Elaine Romberg, PhD, assistant professor. They were instrumental in presenting innovative programs on educational research at the AADS sessions. Such topics as: "The Influence of Dentist and Nondentist Parents on Dental Students: Reinforcement, Interaction, and Perceptions"; "Lesson Plans: An Effective Method for Improving Instruction and the Curriculum"; "Relationship of Recruitment Strategies Used By Baccalaureate Dental Hygiene Programs to Applicant Pool Size"; "The Development and Evaluation of a Performance Simulation Training System for Dental Education"; "Teaching Preclinical Operative Dentistry Using Performance Logic"; and "Student Evaluation of Teaching: Relative Ratings of Five Areas," were among the various presentations.[51]

In addition, during this period Dr. Craig initiated the development into the curriculum of a "Generic Dental Disc," for interactive videodisc technology, representing the major disciplines in dentistry. The faculty members' "constant need for professionally produced graphic slides for their lectures and presentations," was now satisfied by the new technology. As many as 54,000 slides could be put on just one side of a videodisc and access to any one of them gained in less than a second.[52]

Center for Human Performance

The Center for the Study of Human Performance in Dentistry was dedicated on September 21, 1983; it was the first of its kind in North America. The center was a "unique educational, research, and treatment complex for the study of advanced concepts of dental care delivery, with primary focus on the principles of human performance." The program was developed through the collaborative efforts of the college and the Center for Human Performance in Dentistry in the United States, the Human Performance Institute, and the J. Morita Corporation in Japan. The center had three distinct, but integrated phases: the Performance Simulation Unit, the Clinical Research Unit, and the Optimum Management Unit. Collectively, they formed a "controlled state-of-the-art environment for undergraduate and postgraduate education, clinical research, and the optimal delivery of patient care." The first concept studied by the center was "performance logic," a "scientific paradigm developed by Dr. Daryl R. Beach at the Human Performance Institute in Atami, Japan."[53] Finally in 1989, the new clinical simulation unit was ready for student use in an expanded facility near the center for the Study of Human Performance in Dentistry. The simulators replicated a human head and jaws, complete with realistic teeth. Both the dental and dental hygiene students received training on the simulator. The new unit was dedicated to Dr. Daryl Beach, who was involved with the study of "human performance" for many decades.[54]

According to Dr. Michael Belenky, director of the unit, "Performance logic is a scientific paradigm based on the human inclination to perform procedures from a balanced reference posture most natural for the task." After 1983, the school "formally committed" to teaching performance logic and provided continuing education courses in its application for dental practitioners. Participants attended from all parts of the United States and many foreign countries to learn how "proper posture can prevent back pain and disability and help them achieve greater efficiency in their professional lives."[55]

Quest for Care Fund

The Quest for Care Fund, a charitable program of comprehensive dental care to "provide a resource of perpetual financial support for medically, physically, and mentally compromised patients," was initiated in 1984 by four dental students at the Baltimore College of Dental Surgery. Those founders were Drs. Michael Gaglio, Rudy Klima, Al Grzch, and Jody Waddell. These students recognized that there were "very few sources for funding oral health care services for individuals with physical, medical and/or mental health challenges."[56]

Increase in Women and Minority Students

In 1984, first-year enrollment among women at the school reached 43 percent, bringing the total number of female students in attendance to 120. This number exceeded the total number of women graduates between 1951 and 1975, when there were only 27 women graduates; the total number from 1976 to 1983 was 130. Twelve women graduated in the 1950s, only six in the 1960s, and no women graduates in five of the ten years. In the 1970s, the number of women graduates ranged from 0 to 22 annually. The school's 1984 figures compared most favorably with the national figure of 25 percent first-year woman enrollment.[57]

In 1985, after Howard University College of Dentistry and Meharry Medical College, the Baltimore College ranked number one in the number of African-American students enrolled for non-minority dental schools, beginning with only three percent in 1970. That year, on January 14, Bertrand Bonnick, a third-year dental student, honored the birthday of Dr. Martin Luther King, Jr., by presenting a special exhibit honoring both Dr. King and Dr. Robert Tanner Freeman, the first black dental graduate (Harvard 1869). Dr. Elton Maddox, Class of 1972, the school's first recognized African-American graduate, provided the keynote speech.[58]

In 1985, the college was selected by the American Association of Dental Schools and the American Dental Association House of Delegates to participate in a program called "SELECT." This program was a pilot project to encourage practicing dentists and alumni in the community in attracting "quality applicants" to the dental profession. Two other schools were involved in the project in addition to Maryland: the University of Minnesota and the Medical College of Georgia.[59]

In February of the same year, Dr. Reese established a Grant's Management Office under the direction of Dr. Thomas M. Hassell, associate professor of anatomy and periodontics, to assist the faculty in preparation of their research grant proposals. Government support at the school had climbed from $65,000 in 1973 to more than $2 million in 1985. Total research funding from both federal and private sources for ongoing projects exceeded $5 million annually. At the time, approximately 15 research projects at the school were funded by private (corporate) sources.[60]

Strategic Planning: 1986

The college was 1 of 21 institutions chosen in 1986 to receive a five-year strategic planning grant funded by the Pew National Dental Education Program. Started in 1985, the project sought to assist dental schools in "making strategic shifts to accommodate themselves to the dramatic changes occurring in health care, and particularly dental health care." A grant of up to $100,000 for two years was to be given to the schools to help them "incorporate strategic planning mechanisms into their management structures." Another phase was to provide seven selected schools, including the Dental School, up to one million dollars to implement the innovations. The $8.7 million program was supported by the Pew Memorial Trust of Philadelphia and was managed by the Dental Foundation at the University of North Carolina School of Dentistry at Chapel Hill, N.C.[6] The initial step for the 24-month process was taken by groups from the Dental School faculty, the university staff, practicing dental and medical professionals, local community representatives, and national experts in strategic planning, who conducted four independent surveys. Next, a series of meetings were held by full- and part-time faculty, associate staff members, and students, followed by meetings of an External Environment Analysis Group, which examined "present and future societal, political, technological and financial impacts on dentistry and dental education." After these meetings, a Competitive Environment Analysis Group identified and accessed the school's competition, in student, faculty, and patient recruitment, research funding and financial support. Lastly, a Strength and Weakness Analysis Group surveyed the school's strongest and weakest points. From all these reports, a strategic plan was drafted and adopted to wit:

1. Graduate an independent, self-directed individual who is capable of life-long learning and solving critical problems through scientific knowledge.
2. Integrate clinical programs into patient-centered practice settings.
3. Expand the use of simulation into pre-clinical and clinical settings.
4. Establish for an international reputation for research and collaborative research both interdepartmentally and with the other campus schools.
5. Develop a continuing education program for dental graduates.
6. Expand and promote faculty development in education and research.[62]

Phase II of the Pew grant finally came through in 1988 to implement the strategic plan for the next three years. The school was awarded a total of $748,000 to develop and implement its strategic plan by the Pew Foundation. Several courses were revised and re-sequenced to provided a "more evenly balanced course load and a more logical progression." This Pew grant also facilitated a dental informatics initiative at the Dental School.[63] The same year, the School received a $1.4 million dollar grant from the National Institutes of Health to fund a study of the factor of inheritance in periodontal disease.[64]

First Generic Dental Disc Developed

In 1986, the school created its first division of Dental Informatics as a reflection of the influx of computers into dentistry. BCDS was the only school in the country with 18 interactive videodisc systems using videodisc and computer technology to deliver interactive instruction to students.[65]

Hayden-Harris Hall Renovation

In 1987, the school initiated a total renovation of the student clinics. The project was expected to take three years to complete at an estimated cost of $11.6 million, of which approximately $7,100,000 was projected for construction costs. Dr. John F. Hasler, associate dean for clinical affairs, was the project manager. The renovation called for complete redesign and renovation of the entire first floor predoctoral clinics. An emphasis was placed on "establishing an environmental ambience conducive to patient satisfaction and modern practice dynamics." Each of the eight treatment modules of 32 units was to be reconfigured to produce eight group practice clinics of 24 units, each with a private business office, waiting, consultation, radiography, and isolation treatment rooms, laboratory, and dispensing area. A central sterilization center supported all clinics. A networked automated information system provided patient and student tracking and business support. In addition, the first floor saw a refurbishing of the admissions and patient areas. The third floor specialty clinics were redesigned to provide an integrated advanced dental education facility. A contract for these renovations was awarded in 1989. The renovation costs were to be supported by the state and the dental equipment costs by university appropriations.[66]

The school finally launched its $14 million building renovation project on June 1, 1989. The 20-year lifespan of dental equipment, plus the 1981 accreditation site visit prompted the need for change in clinic improvement. Hasler, the coordinator of the three-phased renovations, said: "Because of our work in performance logic and the Optimal Management Unit and because of changes in the delivery of dentistry since the building opened, we felt our job involved much more than just equipment replacement. The objective of the renovation was to provide a dental school environment which would simulate the way dentistry will be practiced into the 21st century."[67]

The smaller class size called for a reduction in the number of operatories in the new clinic and allowed space for practice management, central sterilization, materials management, and business services. Instruments for particular procedures would be pre-packaged and sterilized. Phase I of the renovation, half of the lobby and east half of the first floor clinics, was scheduled for completion on December 23, 1989; Phase II, west half of the first floor clinics, for August 1, 1990; and phase III, third floor graduate clinic, February 1, 1991.[68]

The National Museum of Dentistry

1989 also saw the birth of the National Museum of Dentistry at the Baltimore College of Dental Surgery. The museum was under the direction of Dr. Ben Z. Swanson, Jr., one of only two dentists in the country with a master's degree in dental history. Dr. Swanson, a retired Air Force dentist, was a graduate of the University of Texas at Houston, and the Welcome Institute for the History of Medicine in London. The museum was originally planned to be an addition to the fifth floor of Hayden-Harris Hall, cantilevering out eight feet beyond the face of the building. It was to feature a domed circular rotunda from which visitors could view the campus and the Baltimore City skyline. Wings on either side of the foyer were to contain long vaulted galleries for exhibition space. Plans called for a wood-paneled library, a bookstore, research, conservation, and audiovisual rooms. The main gallery was to feature an exhibit on the history of dentistry. The college agreed to loan indefinitely its extensive collections of historic artifacts and records to the museum, and pledged $150,000 annually to the operation and staffing. The American Academy of the History of Dentistry pledged to raise $100,000 for the museum.[69]

The BCDS Sesquicentennial: 1990

The year 1990 was the 150th anniversary of the founding of the Baltimore College of Dental Surgery. Appropriately, plans were made for its celebration. Whereas other schools were struggling for survival and some even had to close their doors, the Dental School thrived and even launched the aforementioned $14 million clinic renovation. The Commission on Dental Accreditation was scheduled to visit the campus in the fall of 1990, and the completion of the strategic planning Phase II of the Pew grant was also expected the same year.[70] The sesquicentennial celebration was officially launched in January 1990 at a reception and dinner honoring the 150th anniversary of the presentation to the 1840 Maryland Legislature of the act incorporating the Baltimore College of Dental Surgery. For the occasion, the National Museum of Dentistry mounted an exhibition, "Dentistry and the U.S. Military," curated by Dr. John M. Hyson, Jr., Class of 1950. A reception was held in the museum for the military representatives, alumni, and university officials.[71]

The college received another honor in 1990 when Dean Reese was appointed president of the University of Maryland, Baltimore. The Board of Regents and Dr. Donald N. Langenberg, Chancellor of the University of Maryland System, announced his appointment, effective December 11, 1990. Dr. Warren M. Morganstein was appointed as acting dean of the Dental School.[72]

The Morganstein Year: 1990–91

Dr. Warren M. Morganstein was a 1969 graduate of the Baltimore College of Dental Surgery. He received a certificate from the General Practice Residency Program at the U.S. Public Health Service Hospital in San Francisco (USPHS) and his MPH degree from the Johns Hopkins University in 1975. After serving at the USPHS outpatient clinic in Greenwich Village, N.Y., he joined the dental faculty in 1971 as the director of the dental auxiliary utilization (DAU) and training in expanded auxiliary management (TEAM) programs. Three years later, he was appointed chairman of the oral health care delivery department. In 1980, he was as appointed associate dean. In 1986, he returned from sabbatical leave in Israel, where he was the director of the advanced general dentistry residency program at the Jerusalem Luba Slome Dental Center. He also served as a visiting professor at the Hebrew University-Hadassah School of Dental Medicine and the School of Dental Medicine, Tel Aviv University. He was a fellow of both the American and International College of Dentists and served as a consultant to the U.S. Public Health Service, the World Health Organization, and the American Dental Association. He was a past president of the Baltimore City Dental Society and a member of the House of Delegates of the Maryland State Dental Association.[73]

During Dr. Morganstein's tenure as acting dean, the college became the recipient of the country's first periodontal regeneration and implant research center located in a university setting. The center was established to "research bone regeneration and the replacement of teeth via implants" through faculty and postgraduate work. The mission was to study the regeneration of tissues around the teeth and develop better techniques for regeneration of the bone before teeth are lost. The center started with $500,000, with a goal of raising $2 million.[74]

NOTES

1. Baltimore College of Dental Surgery, Dental School, University of Maryland, "Annual Report 1975–76 Academic Year," p. 2, Office of the Dean, Files (*hereafter* cited as BCDSOD).
2. Joyce L. Tarrant, "Reese Takes the Helm: Errol Reese Named President of UMAB Campus," *Baltimore College of Dental Surgery Forum* 11 (Spring 1991): 7; University of Maryland at Baltimore, "Presidential Profile [Errol L. Reese]," Office of Institutional Development, n.d.
3. "Annual Report: 1975–76 Academic Year," p. 3, BCDSOD.
4. "Rate of Dental School Enrollment Slowing," *Maryland Probe* 5 (May 1976): 5.
5. Ibid., p. 2.
6. "Two Women Faculty Members Promoted to Full Professor," *Dental Newsletter* 9 (Winter 1975): 5.
7. Ibid.
8. Ibid.
9. "Dr. Hahn Retires, Dr. Leonard Named Admissions Director," *Dental Newsletter* 8 (Spring 1975): 2.
10. James C. Gingell, James R. Swancar, and Gregory G. Zeller, "The Accelerated Professional Training Program—An Alternative Method of Dental Education," *Journal of the Baltimore College of Dental Surgery* 34 (February 1981): 10, 12.
11. "New Administrative Appointments Announced at Faculty Retreat," *Dental Newsletter* 9 (Winter 1975): 2, 3, 6; "Alumni Affairs Incorporated into Duties of Associate Dean, Assistant Director of Continuing Education," *Dental Newsletter* 9 (Winter 1975): 4; "Annual Report: 1975–76 Academic Year," pp. 2–3, BCDSOD.
12. Letter, Charles T. Pridgeon to Edward Davens, Coordinator, Maryland Regional Medical Program, January 20, 1975, James F. Craig Papers (*hereafter* cited as JFCP); "Satellite Centers to Localize Independent Learning," *Dental Newsletter* 8 (Spring 1975): 1.
13. Letter, Pridgeon to Davens, January 20, 1975, JFCP.
14. Errol L. Reese and Nell Savopoulos, "An Introspective Evaluation of Expenditures of Resources at the Baltimore College of Dental Surgery, Dental School, University of Maryland," *Alma Mater* 18 (May 1977): 5–7.
15. Baltimore College of Dental Surgery, Dental School, University of Maryland, *A Class of One*, 1976[?].
16. "Dr. James F. Craig Department of Educational and Instructional Resources," *Dental Newsletter* 10 (Winter 1976): 2.

17. "Dental School Participates in Satellite Project, Experiments in Continuing Education," *Dental Newsletter* 10 (Winter 1976): 5.
18. "Continuing Education Program Transmitted Via CTS Satellite," *Dental Newsletter* 11 (Winter 1977): 4.
19. Errol L. Reese, "Dean's Report," *Alma Mater* 18 (May 1977): 3.
20. Baltimore College of Dental Surgery, Dental School, University of Maryland, "Annual Report 1977–78," p. 2. BCDSOD.
21. Jacquelyn L. Singer, "The Dental Hygiene Public Health Concentration," *The Journal of the Baltimore College of Dental Surgery* 33 (June 1980): 5.
22. "Department of Dental Hygiene Names Chairperson," *Dental Newsletter* 11 (Winter 1977): 3.
23. "Comprehensive Orthognathic Surgery Center Becomes a Reality at the Dental School," *Dental Newsletter* 10 (Spring 1977): 2, 7.
24. "General Practice Residency Grant," *Dental Newsletter* 12 (Winter 1978): 2.
25. "Two New Department Chairmen Named," *Dental Newsletter* 12 (Winter 1978): 4.
26. Baltimore College of Dental Surgery, Dental School, University of Maryland, *Dental School Bulletin 1978–80 Baltimore College of Dental Surgery, University of Maryland at Baltimore* (n.p., [1978]), pp. 9, 21.
27. Frederick Smith, "Sixteen Women in the Freshmen Class," *Alma Mater* 16 (April 1975): 17.
28. Baltimore College of Dental Surgery, Dental School, University of Maryland, *Dental School Bulletin 1980–1982, Baltimore College of Dental Surgery, University of Maryland at Baltimore* (n.p., [1980]), p. 21.
29. Ibid., p. 38.
30. "Dr. Cappuccio Wins ADA Election," *Dental Newsletter* 11 (Winter 1977): 2; "Dr. Joseph P. Cappuccio Announces Candidacy for President-Elect of ADA," *Dental Newsletter* 10 (Spring 1977): 1.
31. "New Master of Science Program to Begin," *Dental Newsletter* 13 (Winter 1979): 2, 4.
32. Mount St. Mary's College (program), *Sesquicentennial Convocation Mount Saint Mary's College, Emmitsburg, Maryland, April 12, 1958,* Emmetsburg, Md.
33. "Katherine (Kate) Toomey LLD." *Alma Mater* 21 (January 1980): 51. Katherine Toomey was born on April 20, 1891 in Baltimore, Md. She received her early education at Western High School in Baltimore, and later attended Eastern College of Commerce, and night classes at Johns Hopkins University, and Loyola College of Baltimore. She was a charter member and president of the Quota Club of Baltimore; one of founders and treasurer of the Women of Psi Omega, Alpha Chapter; member and secretary-treasurer of the Faculty Assembly of the BCDS; honorary member of the Alumni Association of the BCDS, and the University of Maryland Alumni Club of Baltimore. She attended 42 commencement exercises and saw more than 3,000 dentists graduate before her retirement in 1962. Kate Toomey died on July 4, 1979. [Letter, Barbara Toomey Hauschka to author, December 12, 2003.]
34. Errol L. Reese, "Open Forum," *BCDS Forum* 1 (Fall 1980): 2–3; Idem, "Dental School Enrollment—A Look at the Past and Plans for the Future," *Baltimore College of Dental Surgery Forum* 9 (Fall 1988): 2.
35. John F. Hasler, "Patient-Centered Care: 1980," unpublished document, 2004.
36. "The Extramural Training Program," *Dental Newsletter* 12 (Spring 1979): 1.
37. Gus J. Livaditis, and Van P. Thompson," The Maryland Bridge Technique," *BCDS Forum* 2 (Winter 1982): 6.
38. "Alcoholism, Drug Abuse and the Dentist," *Dental Newsletter* 13 (Spring 1980): 4.
39. Baltimore College of Dental Surgery, Dental School, University of Maryland, *1976–78 Bulletin*, p. 7.
40. [Alfred W. Chandler], "George Washington's Dentures," *Journal of the American Dental Association* 76 (May 1968): 961; Ron Davis, "Loss of historic 'teeth' saddens official at UM: FBI probes loss of dentures," *Baltimore Sun*, June 21, 1981; "Vanishing Teeth," *New York Times*, April 17, 1983; Irvin Molotsky, "A Crime Half Solved: Part of Washington's Teeth Reappear," *New York Times*, August 30, 1982.
41. Dorothy S. Linthicum and Ernest F. Moreland, "Accreditation Process: Its Effectiveness at the University of Maryland Dental School," *Journal of the Baltimore College of Dental Surgery* 35 (June 1981): 19; Errol L. Reese, "Dean's Report: 'The Accreditation Site Visit'," *Alma Mater* 22 (January 1981): 3–4.
42. Errol L. Reese, "Open Forum," *BCDS Forum* 2 (Fall 1981): 2.
43. Ibid., 3.
44. Errol L. Reese, "Dean's Report: 'Facing the 80s—Can We Continue Our Progress?' "*Alma Mater* 23 (February 1982): 3–4.
45. Baltimore College of Dental Surgery, Dental School, University of Maryland, *Retirement Dinner and Tribute to Donald E. Shay, PhD*, June 26, 1981.
46. Gary A. Colangelo and Leonard A. Cohen, "Dental Practice Systems: A Student-Faculty Group Practice," *BCDS Forum* 4 (Fall 1983): 6.
47. Ibid., 6–7.
48. Francis G. Serio, "The Dominican Dental Mission Project: Serving the dental needs of the poor of the Dominican Republic, Summary 1982–1999," unpublished document. Currently, Dr. Serio is professor and chairman, Department of Periodontics, University of Mississippi, School of Dentistry [Ibid.].
49. "Advanced General Dentistry Program," *BCDS Forum* 3 (Fall 1982): 24; Douglas M. Barnes, John F. Hasler, and Alvan M. Holston, "Advanced General Dentistry Program," *Journal of Dental Education* 35 (May 1988): 271–72.
50. Errol L. Reese, "Dean's Report—1984," *Alma Mater* 25 (March 1984): 3.
51. "Abstracts of Educational Research and New Programs Presentations," *Journal of Dental Education* 46 (January 1982): 28, 42; 46 (January 1984): 44, 49; 49 (January 1985): 51; 51 (January 1987): 39.
52. James F. Craig, and Jeffrey I. Plotkin, "Integrating the Use of Interactive Videodisc Technology into the Curriculum: A Case Study in Dental Education," *Journal of Medical Education Technologies* 2 (Winter 1992): 18, 20; James F. Craig, "Potential for Computer and Optical Videodisc Technology in Dental Education," *Dental Clinics of North America* 30 (October 1986): 714, 719.
53. Michael M. Belenky, "First Again," *BCDS Forum* 4 (Fall 1983): 2.
54. "New clinical simulation unit dedicated," *Baltimore College of Dental Surgery Forum* 9 (Spring 1989): 3.
55. Ruth Walsh, "Dental School Expands Performance Logic Center," *The Voice* 6 (December 20, 1988): 1–2.

56. Quest for Care Committee, "Twentieth Anniversary Gala Celebrating Twenty Years of Caring 1984–2004," 2004; Letter, Quest for Care Committee to "Dear Sir/Madam," September 2003, Werner Seibel Papers. By 2004, the Quest for Care Fund had provided more than $200,000 in financial assistance for more than 300 patients [Ibid.].
57. "More Women Finding Dentistry an Attractive Career," *BCDS Forum* 5 (Fall 1984): 10. On the lighter side, a fourth year BCDS student, Mary Elizabeth Haroth, who entered the contest as Miss Towson, was crowned "Miss Maryland" in 1984. Her father, Dr. Robert W. Haroth, was a BCDS faculty member, serving as associate dean of continuing education. ["First Again: BCDS Student Crowned Miss Maryland," *BCDS Forum* 5 (Fall 1984): 9.]
58. Errol L. Reese, "Exhibit Honors Black Leaders," *BCDS Forum* 5 (Spring 1985): 2; Baltimore College of Dental Surgery, Dental School, University of Maryland, "Two Decades of Progress," [1985?], p. 17.
59. Errol L. Reese, "Dean's Report," *Alma Mater* 26 (April 1985): 3.
60. "Grants Management Office Assists Faculty with Funded Research," *BCDS Forum* 6 (Fall 1985): 24.
61. "BCDS Chosen for Pew Foundation Grant," *BCDS Forum* 6 (Spring 1986): 15.
62. Eleanor M. Henry, "Strategic Plan Taking Shape," *Baltimore College of Dental Surgery Forum* 7 (Spring 1987): 7.
63. Eleanor M. Henry, "A Blueprint for the Future: Building on our Strengths," *Baltimore College of Dental Surgery Forum* 8 (Spring 1988): 7, 9.
64. "Dental School Receives $1.4 Million Grant for Periodontics Study," *Baltimore College of Dental Surgery Forum* 9 (Fall 1988): 4.
65. James F. Craig and Ernest F. Moreland, "The Technology Assisted Learning Environment," in Louis M. Abbey and John L. Zimmerman, eds., *Dental Informatics: Integrating Technology into the Dental Environment* (New York: Springer-Verlag, 1992), pp. 194–96.
66. John F. Hasler, "Hayden-Harris Hall: Into the Twenty-First Century," *Baltimore College of Dental Surgery Forum* 8 (Fall 1987): 3.
67. "The Construction Production," *Baltimore College of Dental Surgery Forum* 10 (Fall 1989): 14–15.
68. Ibid.
69. Mary Love, "The National Museum of Dentistry: Preserving Our Past for the Nation," *Baltimore College of Dental Surgery Forum* 9 (Spring 1989): 12, 14–15; "Dr. Swanson Appointed Curator of Museum," *Baltimore College of Dental Surgery Forum* 8 (Spring 1988): 20.
70. Errol L. Reese, "A Time for Celebration," *Baltimore College of Dental Surgery Forum* 10 (Fall 1989): 2.
71. "Year-Long Sesquicentennial is Underway," *Baltimore College of Dental Surgery Forum* 10 (Spring 1990): 2–3.
72. Bernard Gordon, "President Errol L. Reese," *Journal of the Maryland Sate Dental Association* 34 (Spring 1991): 7. After serving as University president until December 31, 1993, Dr. Reese was appointed as a tenured professor in the Department of Restorative Dentistry, Dental School. In 1997, he was appointed a professor emeritus in the School. [Letters, Richard R. Ranney to Errol L. Reese, November 4, 1994; David J. Ramsay to Richard R. Ranney, April 2, 1997, BCDS, Dental School, University of Maryland, Office of the Dean, files.]
73. "Dr. Morganstein Named Acting Dean," *Baltimore College of Dental Surgery Forum* 11 (Spring 1991): 7.
74. "Another first: BCDS to House New Periodontal Research Center," *Baltimore College of Dental Surgery Forum* 11 (Spring 1991): 15.

Richard R. Ranney

Chapter 20

The Ranney Years: 1991–2003

"Dental education is challenged by each of these new opportunities as it prepares practitioners for the early to middle decades of the first century in the next millennium, and each is stimulating for an intellectually curious dental faculty."[1] **~Richard R. Ranney, 1992**

Dr. Ranney Assumes the Deanship: 1991

Dr. Richard R. Ranney was appointed as dean of the Baltimore College of Dental Surgery, Dental School, University of Maryland, effective October 1, 1991. Before his appointment at BCDS, Dr. Ranney was a professor of periodontics and former dean of the University of Alabama School of Dentistry. He had been a productive researcher, credited with more than 130 journal articles, abstracts, and book chapters on the clinical, bacteriological, and immunological aspects of periodontal diseases. University president and former dental dean, Dr. Errol L. Reese, in making the announcement said: "I am very pleased to have Dr. Ranney join our university to lead our dental school toward international eminence. He is a dental researcher of the highest caliber and a fine administrator, and we look forward to the new dimension his leadership will bring to the dental school."[2] Dr. Reese realized that the school was "very strong in the clinical area, very strong in service, but very weak in research." He wanted to strengthen its programs in research to be "competitive and to survive." Dr. Ranney's background in research made him an ideal choice for the position.[3]

Richard R. Ranney, DDS, MS

Dr. Ranney was born in Atlanta, Ga., on July 11, 1939. He received his DDS degree from the University of Iowa College of Dentistry and served an internship at a U.S. Public Health Service (USPHS) hospital in San Francisco. Subsequently, he became the chief dental officer of a clinical USPHS outpatient facility in Cincinnati. At this point, he realized that to pursue his academic and clinical interests in periodontics, his undergraduate education was insufficient for the purposes he had in mind. Therefore, he left the USPHS and enrolled in the periodontics program at the Eastman Dental Center in Rochester, N.Y. He received an MS from the University of Rochester School of Medicine and Dentistry and a certificate in periodontics at the Eastman Dental Center. Dr. Ranney began his teaching career in 1969 as an assistant professor in the department of periodontics at the University of Oregon. From 1972 to 1986, he was an associate professor and then professor of periodontics at the Virginia Commonwealth University School of Dentistry, where he developed a periodontal graduate program. He served in a number of positions at VCU, including assistant dean for research, 1984–86; assistant dean for research and graduate affairs, 1977–84; director, clinical research center for periodontal diseases, 1978–86; chairman, periodontics, 1974–77; and director, graduate periodontics, 1972–76. In 1986 he was appointed dean and professor of periodontics at the University of Alabama School of Dentistry, University of Alabama at Birmingham. After serving as dean from 1986 to 1989, he gave up the deanship to return to faculty duties. Dr. Ranney served as past president both the American and International Associations for Dental Research, and was involved in various capacities with the American Association of Dental Schools, American Dental Association, American Academy of Periodontology, and the National Institutes of Health, including the National Institute of Dental Research.[4]

Dr. Ranney received the Balint Orban Prize from the American Academy of Periodontology, the IADR Basic Research in Periodontology Award, and an Eastman Dental Center Alumni Award for special distinction in dental research. He received fellowships from the American and International Colleges of Dentistry and the American Association for the Advancement of Science.[5]

The Budget Cuts: 1992–93

Dr. Ranney's arrival coincided with a state budget crisis that directly affected the Dental School's fiscal support. At the outset of his deanship, he was forced to make "painful cuts in school programs and staffing as well as handle State instituted furloughs." Dr. Ranney believed the school had to improve its ability to generate its own support and reduce its dependency on the state. He also believed that the school needed a "more balanced educational curriculum" and needed to enlarge its presence in the community to attract "new and innovative research opportunities." A new philosophy was required to "better complement its clinical curriculum with quality interdisciplinary research activities and meaningful community initiatives." More research was needed to include the whole orofacial region and "target functions that can affect individuals' systemic well-being and quality of life."[6] With changes initiated in 1992, revenues from student clinic activities were increased by 29 percent, and income from grant and contract awards increased by 19 percent over the preceding year. Dr. Ranney said at the time that adding other changes in "funding of selected activities and an increase in tuition,[7] our working FY93 budget as compared to FY92 already has moved nearly $1 million from state appropriated funds to other sources."[8]

In conjunction with the budget cuts, Dr. Ranney decided to combine three offices that formerly dealt with continuing education, fund raising, and alumni affairs into one Office of Professional Alumni Resources (OPAR). Another change was the establishment of the Office of Admissions and Student Affairs by the combination of two formerly separate offices. Dr. Margaret B. Wilson was selected to head the new office. Curriculum and academic performance were moved to the "purview" of the senior associate dean. Third, the dean established new graduate programs (PhD and MS) focusing on biology and diseases of the oral and craniofacial region. The dean requested that the university's Graduate School establish a new degree in oral and craniofacial biological science. To support the new programs, Dr. Ranney consolidated the current departments of anatomy, biochemistry, microbiology, pharmacology, and physiology into a department of oral and craniofacial biological sciences.[9] He also combined the departments of general dentistry and prosthetic dentistry into a department of restorative dentistry. This move was made for cost savings and the fact that the two department chairs were vacant. Then too, operative dentistry as measured by "significantly lower performance" by students on national board exams was lower than any other section on the boards. Placing operative dentistry together with prosthetics was thought to "upgrade operative through collegial interactions." The major activities relating to general dentistry would be relocated to the Department of Oral Health Care Delivery.[10]

The Osaka Agreement

On November 11, 1993, the dean of Faculty of Dentistry, Osaka University, Dr. Masayoshi Sakuda, and Dean Ranney, desiring to promote cooperation and collaboration in education and academic research concluded a five-year agreement for academic exchange between the two faculties. The agreement encouraged: (1) Development of "collaborative research, joint symposia, lectures and exchange of scholars to promote these programs." (2) Development of "mechanisms for exchange of information and academic materials" that were of mutual interest. (3) Exchange of "scholars and researchers in field of specific interest to both institutions."[11]

Navajo Indian Denture Externship

In November 1994, Dean Ranney wrote to Dr. Samia A. Elias, an associate professor in the Department of Restorative Dentistry, regarding his concerns about the Navajo Indian Complete Denture Externship Program. In particular, he questioned the liability and logistic difficulties. Dr. Ranney wanted an advance contract from the U.S. Public Health Service describing the work to be performed and providing for the financial arrangements. These stipulations would ensure that the rules and regulations of the University of Maryland; the University of Maryland, Baltimore campus; the Dental School; and the laws of the state of Maryland, were in compliance. The project had to be approved by the Predoctorial Education Committee and by Dr. Gary A. Colangelo, Director of Community Programs, to be recognized as an academic program of the Dental School.[12]

With the necessary contracts in order, the externship continued another summer with the Tuba City and Chinle Indian Health Center Clinics, Arizona, as part of the elective curriculum, with 19 rising senior students participating in two summer sessions. In a three-week period, 92 patients received their dentures.[13]

Maryland School Children Study

Between 1994 and 1995, Dr. Mark L. Wagner, a professor of pediatric dentistry, conducted a survey of the oral health status of Maryland school children for the Office of Child Health, Department of Health Mental Hygiene. The survey was conducted during the 1994–95 school year and continued through the fall term of 1995. Fifty-one public elementary, middle, and high schools were visited throughout the state and 3,500 children were examined. The five grades selected for the study were kindergarten, third, ninth, and twelfth grade. Some disturbing results were obtained from the study. The average Maryland school child had nearly four cavities, and the percentage of children with decay was 60 percent. More than 70 percent of high school seniors had cavities in their permanent teeth. Children living in non-fluoridated water areas had 50 percent more teeth with caries than their peers living in fluoridated areas. Children eligible for Medicaid and the free lunch program had over 30 percent more cavities than the average child in the state. Only 20 percent of the school children had sealants placed on one or more teeth. The survey revealed that approximately 75 percent of decay was in 25 percent of the children, and 15 percent of the children had 50 percent of the decay. In conclusion, Maryland children had more untreated cavities than the national average; Maryland showed 55 percent untreated decay compared to 21 percent nationwide.[14] As a consequence of the Wagner report, a committee of pediatric and general dentists recommended that the Office of Oral Health provide increased funding for eligible children, under the guidance of the "Maryland Partnership for Oral Health," a broad-based advisory group.[15]

Dr. Dubner Joins the Faculty

In his efforts to strengthen the school's research and education programs, Dr. Ranney recruited Dr. Ronald Dubner to chair the newly consolidated basic science department, Oral and Craniofacial Biological Sciences, effective June 1, 1995. The purpose of the consolidation was to "foster the integration of the basic and clinical sciences and strengthen research training" in the school. As part of the consolidation, "graduate degree programs in Oral and Craniofacial Biological Sciences (OCBS), including the PhD, the MS, and the DDS-PhD" were approved by the university. These new graduate degree offerings were "viewed as a programmatic expansion designed to provide highly motivated and qualified dental clinicians with rigorous research training in those areas of modern biological inquiry that are relevant to their clinical interests." The need for traditional PhD students was recognized as vital to "facilitate creation of new knowledge relevant to the overall improvement of oral health." Both basic science and clinical educators are necessary to "help alleviate the critical shortage" of dental school faculty.[16]

Ronald Dubner, DDS, PhD, was the former chief of the Neurobiology and Anesthesiology Branch of the National Institute of Dental and Craniofacial Research (NIDCR). He "combines the perspective and goals of a clinician with the methods of a scientist into a comprehensive vision of dentistry's future. He brings with him the promise for outstanding leadership in basic sciences related to oral and craniofacial health."[17] At NIDCR, Dr. Dubner directed a multidisciplinary program of more than 30 "basic and clinical scientists who conducted research on pain mechanisms and where he directed the only pain clinic in the world devoted exclusively to research on pain." He had authored more than 225 journal and book articles, co-authored one book, and co-edited six books in the field. He was the chief editor of the journal, *Pain*, the official journal of the International Association for the Study of Pain (IASP), and a past president of the American Pain Society and the Neuroscience Group of the International Association for Dental Research.[18]

Shortly after his arrival on campus, Dr. Dubner began to develop the "three primary areas of research and training focus for the newly created graduate degree programs," e.g., cell and molecular biology, infectious disease and immunology, and neuroscience. In addition, the combined DDS/PhD program (originally a program in the physiology department in the 1980s) was restructured to "facilitate coordination between basic and clinical science components of the program." The department also offered an MS program designed for dentists who wished to pursue the degree without being enrolled in a clinical specialty program. In addition, to the PhD, the MS, and the combined DDS/PhD, the department offered post-doctoral training in oral biology and neuroscience.[19]

Dr. Dubner continued the tradition at the school, which differed from most other U.S. dental schools by having its own faculty teach the basic sciences; most schools had the medical faculty do it. Continuing reductions in state support resulted in an increased emphasis on external funding. By 1997, Dubner's two-year-old department had become the "most externally funded department and one of the largest departments in the school."[20] In September 2003 the oral and craniofacial biology department's name was officially changed to the Department of Biomedical Sciences, a name more appropriately "describing the programmatic and research interests of the faculty." Dubner's department's funding, $800,000 in 1995 when he was appointed, would eventually increase to $10,600,000 in 2004. The school achieved the rank of sixth among dental educational institutions in extramural funding from the NIH during Dr. Ranney's deanship.[21]

Hayden-Harris Hall Problems

Dr. Ranney also dealt with "a crisis with respect to capital needs" from the beginning of his deanship. The more than 20-year-old Hayden-Harris Hall was demonstrating its age and inherent structural deficiencies. Although relatively recently renovated (1987–92), teaching clinics were superficially adequate; they were "suffering along with the rest of the building from a crumbling infrastructure." Alarms, sprinklers, air handling, fume hoods, asbestos, plumbing, and vacuum systems were all problems. These problems were to have been addressed in phases III and IV of a capital improvement plan approved by the state in the mid-1980s, but the plan was eliminated from the state's capital budget plan for FY 1996 and beyond. Unfortunately, funding had been delayed at state or University of Maryland levels until they were literally "off the horizon."[22]

These deficiencies not only made it difficult to "conduct teaching, research and service programs" adequately, but they included a "number of health and safety hazards." During the past few years the school had to "shut down operations repetitively on an emergency basis because of mechanical or fire safety failures." On many occasions, the faculty, staff, and patients had to wait outside on the street after evacuating the building, awaiting the return of "reasonably safe conditions."[23] This problem was Dr. Ranney's dilemma; where to get the funds?

ICD Exchange Program

In July 1995, the college and the USA Section of the International College of Dentists (ICD) participated in the International Exchange Program. The program was funded by a grant from the USA Section and enabled BCDS to link up with dental schools in Cork, Ireland, and Dundee, Scotland. Two students from BCDS were selected to represent the school at the dental school of the University of College Cork (UCC), and the dental college at the University of Dundee (UD). In return, two students from the European schools were sent to the BCDS. The students were able to observe the methods of education, clinical work, research activities, and health care systems as well as the culture of the respective countries.[24]

Death of Dr. Ruskin

Dr. Frieda G. Rudo Ruskin, the first woman to have attained the rank of full professor at the School (1975), died on January 16, 1996, of a brain tumor. Dr. Ruskin was the professor emeritus of pharmacology. She had received her AB from Goucher College in 1944 and a PhD in 1963 and worked with Dr. John C. Krantz in the Department of Pharmacology of the university's medical school before joining the dental faculty. When Dr. Ruskin retired in 1985, her research had been supported by more than $2.5 million in grants, and had expanded to include research in parenteral analgesics and muscle relaxants. She was known internationally for her work on anesthetic drugs, particularly the inhalation agents, Ethrane and Forane. Dr Ruskin was a mentor and role model to female dental students in an era when women were just beginning to enter the profession.[25]

Announcements and Changes

In 1996 Dr. Ranney announced that the applicant numbers for the fall 1996 class were again increased over the preceding year, probably reaching 2,000 for the 96 enrolled. The advanced education program in oral and maxillofacial surgery received full accreditation in 1996; and the new PhD program in oral and craniofacial biological sciences was approved by the Graduate School. Dr. Ranney announced that Ms. Kathleen Reasinger would be the director of the reorganized Office of Development and Alumni Relations. Dr. Ranney noted that the BCDS Alumni Association was an external organization, with its governance separate from the Dental School, "existing for the support of the school." Dr. Ranney expected the new office to "provide a complementary internal structure to facilitate cooperative efforts with the Alumni Association and enhance relationships with all alumni."[26]

Dr. Ranney also announced in 1996 that the Department of Oral and Craniofacial Biological Sciences (OCBS) had raised $1.6 million from external research grants and contract support for FY96, double the figure for FY95. The student clinical revenues for FY96 totaled more than $4.6 million, or 91 percent greater than FY91 when Dr. Ranney became dean. With the reductions in state appropriations and enhanced other revenues, the majority of revenues for supporting the school were now no longer received from the state, but from the school's entrepreneurial activities.[27]

The Class of 1996 job placement rate was overwhelmingly in favor of private practice (36%) and general practice residency (33%). The other career choices were: advanced education in general dentistry (11%); specialty programs (11%); military (7%); public health (1%); and unknown (2%).[28]

Medical University of Lodz

In November 1996, Dean Ranney and nine other faculty visited the Institute of Dentistry, Medical University of Lodz, Poland, for the purpose of initiating a collaborative relationship with the Dental School. Travel costs were provided by the institute, primarily from commercial sources in Poland and other European countries. Dr. Ranney signed an agreement for collegial relationship, which provided for "future collaboration of mutual benefit to both institutions," on November 15, 1996. The collaborative ventures included reciprocal faculty visitations, joint ventures in research, and faculty and student exchanges.[29]

Drs. Gartner and Hiatt's Textbooks: 1997

In 1997, Drs. Leslie P. Gartner and James L. Hiatt, Associate Professors, Oral and Craniofacial Biological Sciences, published their second book, *Color Textbook of Histology.* In 1994, they had published their first book, *Color Atlas of Histology.* These two books were selected in a survey of medical students as being among the top medical textbooks available (*Anatomical Reviews*). In addition to the English version, the first book has been translated into Chinese (Mandarin), French, Greek, Indonesian, Italian, Portuguese, and Spanish, and enjoys a world-wide market that these translations suggest. It is currently in its third edition, including a CD-ROM version. The second book has been translated into Italian, Greek, Portuguese, and Spanish. Another text with co-author Judy Strum, *Cell Biology and Histology* is also available in Indonesian, Greek, and Japanese. In addition, Dr. Gartner's other books include, *Essentials of Oral Histology and Embryology, Textbook of Head and Neck Anatomy, A Review of Histology, Oral Histology, Histology Slide Set I,* and *Histology Slide Set II.* Nearly all of Gartner's books have had multiple editions and have been standard textbooks in dental and medical schools around the world. Dr. Gartner, who has served on the faculty since 1970, was selected by the students as their outstanding teacher on three separate occasions, the latest being in 1999.[30]

Board of Visitors

In 1997, Dr. Ranney formed a board of visitors for the school, consisting of professional and community leaders. The new group was to provide "critically important advice, advocacy, and support to help the School enhance its resources and pursue its mission." It would work in conjunction with similar boards at the other five professional schools on the campus of the University of Maryland and the board of visitors which assisted the UMB president, David J. Ramsay. The second quarter of FY97 was 66 percent ahead of the previous year for grants and contracts. In fact, the Dental School was the UMB campus leader in the rate in increase of research funding for the first half of FY97.[31]

In 1997, Dr. Ranney announced that the school's 1997 DDS graduates ranked first among all schools in overall results of the licensing examination administered by the Northeast Regional Board of Dental Examiners. Progress was also being made in the research programs. The $5.3 million in sponsored program funding for FY97 was nearly a 50 percent increase over the preceding year and the best year that records showed ever.[32] The same year, the college signed an agreement with the Institute of Dentistry, Medical University of Lodz, Poland, to collaborate in "joint research and teaching for the advancement of dental education in both nations." In November, Dr. Ranney met with Dr. Henryk Stepien, rector of the Medical University of Lodz, and Dr. Stanislaw Suliborski, director of the Institute of Dentistry, in Lodz to sign the formal agreement.[33]

Accreditation

The school successfully completed its accreditation visit in September 1997 by the Commission on Dental Education, which ensured that the "graduates' licensure eligibility, certification of completion of advanced general dental education programs, and recognition of specialty status" were valid. The process also provided "peer review and feedback" for all of the school's programs as measured against national standards. The commission commented on the healthy condition of the school. The visiting committee also noted that the "Dental School was an integral part of the University of Maryland, Baltimore. There was strong support for the school from the university administration, and the school had excellent representation and interaction with the university."[34] Furthermore, the school had done an "outstanding job in recruiting and enrolling an extremely diverse student body, which enriched the dental school community."[35]

Brotman Facial Pain Clinic and Clinical Studies Unit

The Brotman Facial Pain Clinic was created in 1997, along with the establishment of a regional pain center in a cooperative effort by the Dental School, University of Maryland Medical System, the Baltimore Veterans Affairs Medical Center, and Johns Hopkins Medical Center, aided by a gift from alumni Drs. Don-N and Solomon Brotman. Dr. Ronald Dubner, chairman, oral and craniofacial biological sciences, was chosen as director of the group, as they conducted "basic biological, cellular, and clinical research." The Facial Pain Center was co-located in the former Center for the Study of Human Performance in Dentistry together with a new Clinical Studies Unit renovated with assistance from UMB President David J. Ramsay. Dr. Edward G. Grace headed the Facial Pain Clinic (responsible for the diagnosis and treatment of acute and chronic pain, especially temporomandibular joint pain) and the Clinical Studies Unit was co-directed by Drs. John C. Gunsolley and Leonard J. Litkowski.[36]

The Gunther Gift

In 1997 the school received a record-breaking gift for the Dean's Fund for Excellence Endowment from Dr. Edgar Gunther, a retired U.S. Air Force Dental Corps officer. Colonel Gunther, a 1931 BCDS graduate, and his wife, Dorothy, gave a total contribution of $900,000 to the school, the largest gift from an alumnus in the history of the school (at that time). Unfortunately, Dr. Gunther passed away on November 25, 1996, while arrangements were being negotiated for the gift. "The first thing Dr. Gunther did after his arrival [at the school] was to institute a rotation system whereby the boys on the 'amalgam line' were given a chance to do some surgery and prosthetic work for a change. The clinic's morale picked up immediately and needless to say, he became a very popular commanding officer."[37]

Operation Smile

In January 1997 the school's faculty and students participated in "Operation Smile" in Vietnam. This program was an externship experience for senior students under faculty supervision. Dr. Gary A. Colangelo, assistant professor in the oral health care delivery department, was director of this external program.[38]

Renewal of Osaka Agreement

In 1997, as a result of the Osaka agreement, Dr. Koichi Iwata from Osaka University (later, chair of the Department of Physiology at Nihon University, Tokyo) spent the month of March working with Dr. Dubner in his laboratory.[39] The following November 11, 1998, the dean of the Faculty of Dentistry, Osaka University, Dr. Toshifumi Morimoto, and Dean Ranney signed a renewal agreement for academic exchange between the two faculties for another five-year period.[40]

Dr. Morimoto returned in July 1998 to work another five weeks with Dubner, and returned for a third visit in 1999 as a visiting associate professor. He collaborated with Drs. Dubner and Ke Ren from July 10 to August 18, 1999, on the following research projects: the effects of inflammatory agents injected into the perioral region, the TMJ area on neuronal activity, and the behavior and neurochemistry of the trigeminal medullary dorsal horn.[41]

The School's Role with the Maryland Health Advisory Committee

In December 1997 Senator Gloria Lawlah (Prince Georges County) commissioned a workgroup of individuals from the "University of Maryland President's Office, University of Maryland Dental School, Maryland State Dental Association, Maryland Academy of Pediatric Dentistry, Maryland Association of Local and County Dental Public Health Officers and other oral health advocates to develop a five-year plan to address the oral health access problem for Medicaid-eligible children and pregnant women in Maryland." Legislation was developed that became Senate Bill 590.[42]

An Oral Health Advisory Committee (OHAC) was developed in 1998 as the result of Senate Bill 590. Legislation passed by the Maryland General Assembly stated that the "Department of Health and Mental Hygiene (DHMH) shall collaborate with representatives of the dental community, dental managed care organizations, and managed care organizations in the State in the design and implementation of the assessment process (HealthChoice dental program) and statewide survey . . ." The OHAC was comprised of the DHMH secretary, Dr. Ranney, and other representatives from DHMH public health and health care financing (i.e., Maryland Medical Assistance Program) programs, managed care organizations, dental managed care organizations, professional dental organizations, local health departments, community advocates, and individual practitioners.[43]

One of the significant programs developed as a result of the OHAC was the establishment by the University of a Pediatric Dental Fellowship Program which placed trained pediatric fellows into Maryland "public health facilities to treat Maryland's underserved, young and special care needs children." A 2000 survey of Maryland Head Start children conducted by the Dental School found that over half of these children had dental caries, of which 96 percent was untreated decay. In addition, the Office of Oral Health decided to annually award the Dental School a grant to organize an Eastern Shore Oral Health Outreach Project to increase access to oral health services. Finally, the university worked through the OHAC to develop a landmark loan assistance repayment program for dentists if they provided care for a certain percentage of Medicaid patients in their practices.[44]

The New Alumni Association

Recognition of the alumni association that was originally affiliated with the Baltimore College of Dental Surgery was withdrawn by the University System of Maryland's Board of Regents (USM) in the fall of 1997, consequent to a request from UMB President David J. Ramsay, for failures to comply with the USM required agreement (1995) between the university and the association. Without an official agreement in place, the university's rules required Dr. Ranney to disallow use of university space by the association, which he did on September 9, 1997. In April of 1998, as directed by President Ramsay in a letter to the dean, a new alumni association "recognized and authorized by the Board of Regents" was formed by those attending a called meeting of alumni. The result was confusion engendered by perceptions of a school with two alumni associations.[45] The old alumni association's "constant refusal to make changes which could have attracted a larger and more representative base of support among alumni and enabled more effective working relationship with the School," was the primary reason for the split.[46] The only alumni reunion organized for 1999 "in cooperation with the Dental School" was to be held on June 4–5, 1999, in Baltimore.[47] Finally, the issues between the two factions were resolved and on May 31, 2003, the internal alumni organization was dissolved at the "first Annual Meeting of the 1849 Alumni Association" after restoration of its recognition by the university on October 11, 2002.[48]

The High School Programs

In 1997 Dr. Norbert R. Myslinski, associate professor in the Department of Oral and Craniofacial Biological Sciences, conceived the idea of a neuroscience competition, called a "Brain Bee," for high school students. The first competition was held in Baltimore in 1998 and led to an international competition in 1999, where hundreds of students, parents, teachers, judges, and presenters took part in a two-day event at the University of Maryland and the National Institutes of Health to crown a champion. The first champion came from Ontario (1999), then Arizona (2000), New Jersey (2001), Ontario (2003), and New York (2003). The Brain Bee attracted national media attention, including National Public Radio and Maryland Public Television.[49] As early as 1988, Dr. Myslinski had developed a program for high school students called the "High School Biomedical Research Program." Students spent eight weeks during the summer working on a neuroscience project in a neuroscience laboratory under a mentor. Eighty-two Maryland high schools and 84 mentors have participated in the program.[50]

Management of HIV Patients

In April 1998 Dr. James T. Rule, a professor of pediatric dentistry, lectured to the junior students on the "ethical issues in the management of HIV patients." Afterward, some of the students described "inconsistencies between the CDC recommendations for management of HIV patients" compared with the standards of management at the Dental School. The automatic "space-man look," double gowning and gloving, gave them concern for their safety in treating HIV patients. Dr. Rule thought that the school should adopt a "uniform school-wide policy" that was more in keeping with the CDC recommendations and was "procedure-based, or pathology-based rather than diagnosis-based." As a consequence of this student concern, the Infection Control Committee addressed the issue of "appropriate precautions, including barrier procedures," for management of these patients with a view toward the development of a "universal policy" for the school's clinics.[51]

Professor of Dental Hygiene

In 1999 Dr. Ranney proposed that Linda E. DeVore, associate professor and chair (1993) of dental hygiene, be promoted to the rank of professor. She was a nationally recognized professional in dental hygiene, who had served on the faculty since 1976 and was president of the American Association of Dental Schools, the only hygienist to ever hold that elected position. In 1961, she completed a certificate program in dental hygiene at Ohio State University and later earned a BS in dental hygiene at the University of Maryland in 1976. She also was awarded an MA degree in 1982 in instructional systems development and an advanced certificate in health and public policy from UMBC.[52] University President David J. Ramsay approved the promotion effective November 15, 1999.[53]

The New Building

The year 2000 brought some exciting news for the Baltimore College of Dental Surgery, Dental School, University of Maryland, when Maryland's Governor Parris N. Glendening announced in December 1999 that he was committing $94 million in state funding for the construction of a new facility for the school. On July 1, 2000, the Maryland General Assembly confirmed the governor's budget for the new dental building and appropriated the first installment of $22 million. On September 20, the Board of Public Works approved the construction and issued contracts to Bohlin Cywinski Jackson (BCJ) of Philadelphia as the prime architectural/engineering firm and Barton Malow Company of Baltimore as construction manager. Supporting design was assigned to Bard, Rao & Athans of Boston, Anshen & Allen of Baltimore, and RFD Lab Planning of San Diego. Groundbreaking was scheduled for 2002, with a completion date targeted for late 2005.[54] Dr. John F. Hasler, associate dean of clinical affairs, was named as the school's project manager.[55]

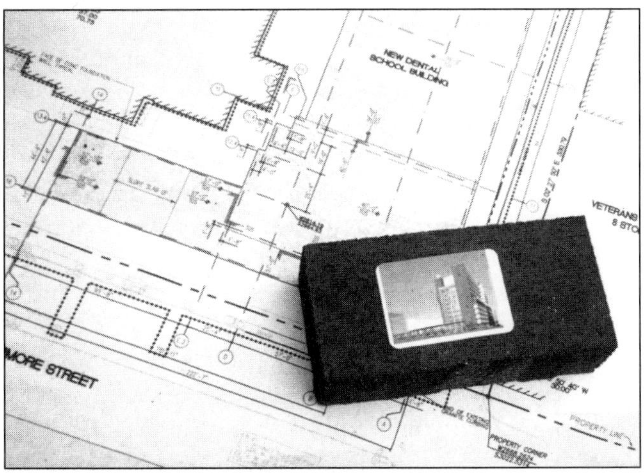

Plans for a new future

To upgrade the continuing education (CE) program, the school formed a partnership in 2001 with the Chesapeake Health Education Program (CHEP) at the Veterans Administration Hospital in Perryville, Md. The partnership combined the BCDS tradition with the network of Maryland's "premier provider of continuing education." BCDS faculty and visiting faculty would provide the educational courses.[56]

Collaboration with Foreign Dental Schools

In May 2002 the Affiliation and Collaboration with Foreign Dental Schools Committee, chaired by Dr. Michael M. Belenky, reported on agreements with Poland, Thailand, Korea, Mexico, and Russia. The standing collegial relationships with foreign dental schools carried the image of the world's oldest dental college to many areas of the globe. The countries collaborating with the school included:

1. **Poland.** In March 2001, Drs. Ronald B. Gunderson, Neville J. McDonald, and Bhavna Shroff visited the Institute of Dentistry, Medical University of Lodz, Poland, accompanied by 10 volunteer senior dental students. They presented lectures in prosthodontics, endodontics, and orthodontics to the faculty and students of the Institute, and the Maryland students became acquainted with the various aspects of Polish dental education and oral health. In September 2001, Drs. Douglas M. Barnes, Michael M. Belenky, Bradley L. Phillips, Michael A. Siegel, and Bhavna Shroff were scheduled to present papers at the Central European Dental Exhibition and provide hands-on continuing dental education courses at the Lodz Institute of Dentistry, Poland; however, the tragic events of September 11, 2001, prevented Drs. Barnes and Phillips and several members of the North American team from attending. Drs. Belenky, Siegel, and Shroff extended the scope and breadth of their presentations to accommodate the missing material. In November 2001, Drs. Belenky and Tomasz Dzieniakowski presented a paper on human-centered ergonomics and musculoskeletal disorders to a section of the Polish Academy of Sciences in Lodz.[57]
2. **Thailand.** In January 2001, Dr. Warren M. Morganstein, Senior Associate Dean, visited the School of Dentistry, Thammasat University, Bangkok, Thailand, to advise the school's dean and faculty on implementation of a new curriculum, based in the SATV (skill acquisition, test, and evaluation), using the principles of performance logic and human-centered ergonomics. Dr. Morganstein's previous background and experience in this system at Maryland provided the Thai school with valuable assistance in their implementation of the new curriculum.[58]
3. **Korea.** In 2001, two faculty members of the School of Dentistry, Kyung Hee University, Seoul, Korea, began a two-year collaboration in the Department of Oral and Craniofacial Biologic Sciences. In October 2001, Drs. Belenky and William M. Davidson, professor of orthodontics, were scheduled to present papers at the First World Edgewise Orthodontic Conference (WEOC) at the Kyung Hee University in Seoul; however, they were unable to attend because of the impact of the global terrorist threat.[59]
4. **Mexico.** During the year 2001, because of economics, no collaborative activities were conducted with the faculty of Odontology, International University, Thalpan, Mexico City, Mexico.[60]
5. **Russia.** Dr. Belenky received communication from the Institute of Postgraduate Education, Moscow State University of Medicine and Dentistry, Moscow, Russia, of their interest in establishing a collegial relationship with the BCDS.[61]

Minority Enrollment

Since the 1970s, the school's enrollment of "under-represented minorities" had compared favorably with peer institutions. As recently as 1998, in spite of a national shortage of qualified black applicants, the school's freshman enrollment of 10 black students ranked first among the majority institutions, and third among all U.S. dental schools (behind Howard University and Meharry Medical College). At the same time, enrollment of Hispanic/Latino students also showed an increase.[62]

Oral and Craniofacial Biological Sciences

The Department of Oral and Craniofacial Biological Sciences (OCBS) was awarded a $2.5 million training grant from the National Institutes of Dental and Craniofacial Research in 2001. The goal of the department was to "provide rich research opportunities to a diverse population of college, graduate, dental, medical, postgraduate and combined DDS/PhD and MD/PhD students, and to junior and mid-career faculty seeking new research initiatives." More than 50 faculty mentors from the University of Maryland, Johns Hopkins University, and the National Institutes of Health were associated with the grant program. Hard tissue and neoplastic disease, infectious and autoimmune diseases, oral and craniofacial chronic sensory disorders, and oral and craniofacial motor disorders were the themes for clinical and basic science research. Primary emphasis was placed on "cross-disciplinary approaches, stressing the integration of basic, translational and clinical research" in the selected student programs. Stipends for the students were available.[63]

Mission Statement

The 2002–2004 catalog re-stated the school's mission and vision statement:

> The Baltimore College of Dental Surgery, Dental School, University of Maryland (BCDS), will build on its tradition as the world's first dental school to become a full partner with the University of Maryland, Baltimore and the University of Maryland Medical System (UMMS) in achieving eminence in education, science, and practice related to health, with special emphasis on health of the oral-facial region. Embraced by and subscribing to the University and UMMS visions, BCDS will be a leader for dentistry in:
>
> - Developing innovative educational offerings in dentistry and related disciplines
> - Devising and adopting technological advances in dental education and practice
> - Producing new basic and applied knowledge
> - Preparing practitioner-scholars for leadership in the future
> - Integrating service activities with the needs of the community
> - Initiating programs that cross school, university, state, and national boundaries
> - Preparing practitioners and educators capable of functioning competently at the fullest breadth and depth of their professional areas of expertise
> - Influencing oral health care policies
>
> In living this vision, BCDS will achieve greater prominence through activities that bring recognition. Students will find excellent opportunities; faculty, unexcelled intellectual stimulation; and patients, high quality and caring treatment. BCDS will continually contribute to the resolution of health-related problems that plague mankind and, through special concentration in the oral-facial region, improve the quality of life.[64]

For the 2002–2003 academic year, 379 students were enrolled in the predoctoral dental education program. The total enrollment of 546 students included 59 hygiene, 41 graduate, and 67 advanced dental education students.[65]

Dr. Dubner's Grant

In 2002 Dr. Ronald Dubner, professor and chair of the Department of Oral and Craniofacial Biological Sciences, and colleagues received a $6.8 million grant from the U.S. Department of Health and Human Services to "study how the body's response to pain is shaped by previous experiences with pain." It was the largest grant ever received by the college. Over a five-year period, Dubner's researchers would study rat models to "study how the development of the nociceptive (the part of the nervous system that transmits pain signals) is affected by the pain experienced by newborns (neonates), especially those born prematurely and requiring extensive, painful procedures." Dr. Dubner said that one of the big questions is "whether neonatal pain experience has an impact on pain experience in adult life. . . . Pain induces changes in the nociceptive system, which in neonates is not fully developed. Neonatal tissue injury and pain might lead to changes in how pain is 'modulated' by the nervous system. What the effect of that modulation is on pain experience in adults is at the heart of our research." Hopefully, Dubner's research will have an impact on giving adult chronic pain sufferers relief.[66]

Dr. Ranney Resigns as Dean

On January 31, 2002, Dr. David J. Ramsay, President, University of Maryland Baltimore, announced that Dr. Ranney was resigning his post as dean of the Baltimore College of Dental Surgery, effective at the end of the calendar year, to pursue other professional opportunities. Dr. Ramsay commented that during the 10 years of his deanship:

> Dr. Ranney influenced, championed, and oversaw important initiatives for the School. From community outreach programs to groundbreaking research, under his direction, the School has maintained its tradition of excellence. . . . Dean Ranney leaves with the assurance that the long-awaited new dental school building will become a reality, set to open in 2005. He can be proud of this lasting achievement for the School, which will use the new facility to push the limits of dental science and technology. His insightful leadership was key to the School's consistently high rankings among other dental institutions nationwide.[67]

The dental dean search committee began screening applicants for Dr. Ranney's replacement in May 2002.[68]

Groundbreaking for the New Building

The groundbreaking ceremony for the new building was held on May 23, 2002. Dr. David Ramsay, President of the Baltimore campus of the University of Maryland welcomed the crowd of over 400 and was joined on the podium by Parris N. Glendening, governor of Maryland; Martin O'Malley, mayor of Baltimore; the late Howard Rawlings, state delegate and chair of the House Appropriations Committee; and Dr. Richard Ranney. Governor Glendening stated, "Today marks the first physical step on the single largest commitment to an academic building in Maryland's history." Dr. Ranney called the new building a "landmark" for oral health care professionals and said the new building was important for Marylanders. He stated: "Put simply, our 546 students, 28,000 patients, faculty, and staff, and our more than 6,000 alumni deserve it and need it."[69]

Among the many milestones during the Ranney era, perhaps these four major achievements will be his legacy:

The late Howard 'Pete' Rawlings, Parris N. Glendening, David J. Ramsay, Martin O'Malley, and Richard R. Ranney.

1. The merger of the school's five basic sciences departments into one department, the department of oral and craniofacial biological sciences under Dr. Dubner.
2. The gaining of "graduate medical education support for postdoctoral and postgraduate training programs through an arrangement with York Hospital."
3. The tripling of externally funded research support by "bringing world-class faculty to the school who established strong research programs." When Dean Ranney came to the school, it was in the "middle of the pack or lower in terms of National Institutes of Health funding." By FY 1999, it had become number six. The added emphasis on research moved the school to the "top tier of dental schools in the country."
4. The securing of the $94 million commitment from the state for the new dental school building.[70]

Dean Ranney made a significant impact on the Dental School, and the stage was set to usher in another era of excellence.

NOTES

1. Richard R. Ranney, "Open Forum: Reflections on Opportunity," Baltimore *College of Dental Surgery Forum* 12 (Spring 1992): 2.
2. "New Dental Dean Named at U.M.A.B.," *Journal of the Maryland State Dental Association* 34 (Winter 1991): 33.
3. Deborah K. Rager, "A Decade of Dedication: Richard R. Ranney, DDS, MS, Dean of the Baltimore College of Dental Surgery, Dental School, University of Maryland." *Forum* 20 (Winter 2002): 16.
4. Ibid.; Harold S. Goodman, "A Conversation with Dean Richard R. Ranney," *Journal of the Maryland State Dental Association* 35 (Summer 1992): 32–33.
5. Goodman, "A Conversation with Dean Richard R. Ranney," 33.
6. Ibid., 33–34.
7. The dental school tuition for the 1990–92 session was $6,778 per year for in-state students and $15,550 for out-of-state; for 1992–94 the in-state tuition was $8,274 and out-of-state $18, 979. For dental hygiene students in 1990–92 the tuition per year was $1,788 for in-state and out-of-state $5,736; for 1992–94 the tuition was $2,104 for in-state and $7,004 for out-of-state. [Baltimore College of

Dental Surgery, Dental School, University of Maryland, *Dental School Catalog 1990–1992* (n.p., [1990]), p. 34; Idem, *Dental School 1992–94 Catalog* (n.p., [1992]), pp. 39–40.]

8. Richard R. Ranney, "Quality with Declining Resources," *Forum* 13 (Fall 1992): 2.
9. Richard R. Ranney, "Open Forum: Fall 1993—Three New Approaches," *Forum* 14 (Fall 1993): 2–3.
10. Letter, Richard R. Ranney to Errol L. Reese, February 13, 1992, BCDS Papers, National Museum of Dentistry Archives.
11. "Agreement for Scholarly Exchange and Collaboration Between Osaka University, Faculty of Dentistry, Baltimore College of Dental Surgery, Dental School, University of Maryland at Baltimore," November 11, 1993, unpublished internal document.
12. Letter, Richard R. Ranney, BCDS Dean, to Samia A. Elias, November 18, 1994, Baltimore College of Dental Surgery, Dental School, University of Maryland, Office of the Dean, Files (hereafter cited as BCDSOD).
13. Letters, Richard R. Ranney to Samia A. Elias, August 31, 1995, Samia A. Elias to Richard R. Ranney, August 21, 1995, BCDSOD.
14. Mark L. Wagner, "Executive Summary: Oral; Health Status of Maryland School Children," 1995, BCDSOD.
15. James T. Rule, "Five Year Children's Oral Health Plan," December 1, 1997, BCDSOD.
16. Baltimore College of Dental Surgery, Dental School, University of Maryland, Department of Biomedical Sciences. "Background and History," unpublished internal document, 2 lvs., n.d.
17. Richard R. Ranney, "News from the Dean . . .," *Forum* 15 (Spring 1995): 2.
18. "OCBS—a Step Ahead," *Forum* 18 (Fall 1997): 12, 13.
19. Baltimore College of Dental Surgery, Dental School, University of Maryland, Department of Biomedical Sciences, "Background and History."
20. "OCBS—a Step Ahead," 12, 13.
21. Baltimore College of Dental Surgery, Dental School, University of Maryland, Department of Biomedical Sciences, "Background and History."
22. Richard R. Ranney, "News from the Dean . . .," *Forum* 16 (Fall 1995): 3.
23. Memorandum, Richard R. Ranney, Dean, to Elza Harrison, Executive Director, MSDA, December 15, 1995, BCDSOD.
24. "ICD Exchange Program in Second Year," *Forum* 16 (Spring 1996): 3.
25. "Frieda G. Rudo Ruskin, PhD: November 13, 1923-January 16, 1996," *Forum* 16 ((Spring 1996): 7.
26. Richard R. Ranney, "News from the Dean . . .". *Forum* 16 (Spring 1996): 2.
27. Richard R. Ranney, "Open Forum: It's working!" *Forum* 17 (Fall 1996): i.
28. "Job Placement Rates—Class of 1996)," 1996, BCDSOD.
29. Memorandum, Richard R. Ranney, Dean, to David J. Ramsay, President, UMAB, November 20, 1996, BCDSOD.
30. Letter, Richard R. Ranney, BCDS dean, to Stephen Leeper Award Committee, September 25, 2000, BCDSOD.
31. Richard R. Ranney, "Open Forum," *Forum* 17 (Spring 1997): i.
32. Richard R. Ranney, "Open Forum," *Forum* 18 (Fall 1997): i.
33. Michael M. Belenky, "Global Partners in Education," *Forum* 17 (Spring 1997): 11.
34. Richard R. Ranney, "Open Forum," *Forum* 18 (Spring 1998): i.
35. Commission on Dental Accreditation, "Formal Report of the Commission on Dental Accreditation to the Administration of University of Maryland, Baltimore on the Evaluation of the Dental, Allied and Advanced Dental Education Programs Baltimore, Maryland," January 30, 1998, BCDSOD.
36. Edward G. Grace, "Facial Pain Clinic Opening," *Forum* 17 (Spring 1997): 15.
37. "Gunthers enhance Dean's Fund for Excellence Endowment," *Forum* 17 (Spring 1997): 29; Letter, Richard R. Ranney to Dr. and Mrs. Harold Brest, October 10, 2002, BCDSOD.
38. Memorandum, Richard R. Ranney, Dean, to Michael M. Belenky, February 17, 1997, BCDSOD.
39. Ronald Dubner, "Osaka University collaboration," unpublished internal document, 2004.
40. "Memorandum Concerning Agreement on Academic Exchange Between Osaka University, Faculty of Dentistry, Baltimore College of Dental Surgery, Dental School, University of Maryland," November 11, 1998, unpublished internal document.
41. Ronald Dubner, "Osaka University collaboration," statement to author.
42. Baltimore College of Dental Surgery, Dental School, University of Maryland, "The Maryland Oral Health Advisory Committee: An Assessment of its Utility and Value to the Citizens of Maryland," unpublished internal document.
43. Baltimore College of Dental Surgery, Dental School, University of Maryland, "Executive Summary: The Maryland Oral Health Advisory Committee," unpublished internal document.
44. Baltimore College of Dental Surgery, Dental School, University of Maryland, "The Maryland Oral Health Advisory Committee."
45. Richard R. Ranney, "Open Forum," *Forum* 18 (Spring 1999): i.
46. H. B[erton] McCauley, "The Beginning and End of the Internal Alumni Association of the Baltimore College of Dental Surgery," June 3, 2003, H. Berton McCauley Papers. (*hereafter* cited as HBMP).
47. Ranney, "Open Forum [1999],"i.
48. McCauley, "The Beginning and End of the Internal Alumni Association," HBMP.
49. Norbert R. Myslinski, "The Revolution in 'Brain literacy'," *Cerebrum* 3 (March 2001): 60–73.
50. David J. Ramsay, "Presidents Column," *Voice* 15 (June 1998): 1.
51. Memoranda, James T. Rule to Richard R. Ranney, April 1, 1998, Richard R. Ranney to Louis G. DePaola, June 9, 1998, BCDSOD.
52. Letter, Richard R. Ranney, BCDS dean, to Mark W. Wagner, Chair, Committee on Appointments, Promotion and Tenure, September 29, 1999, BCDSOD.
53. Letter, Richard R. Ranney to Linda E. DeVore, November 18, 1999, BCDSOD.
54. Richard R. Ranney, "Open Forum," *Forum* 19 (Fall 2000): i.

55. Memo, Richard R. Ranney, BCDS dean, to Steering Committee for New Building, March 29, 2000, BCDSOD.
56. "BCDS Launches New CE Program," *Forum* 19 (Summer 2001): 3.
57. Belenky, Michael M., "Affiliation and Collaboration with Foreign Dental Schools Committee Report to the Executive Board," May 20, 2002, unpublished internal document.
58. Ibid.
59. Ibid.
60. Ibid.
61. Ibid.
62. Letter, Richard R. Ranney to Judy Stavisky, Senior Program Officer, Robert Wood Johnson Foundation, December 10, 2001, BCDSOD.
63. "Training Program Integrate basic and clinical training," *What's on at OCBS?* 2 (Summer 2001): 1.
64. Baltimore College of Dental Surgery, Dental School, University of Maryland, *Baltimore College of Dental Surgery, Dental School, University of Maryland Baltimore 2002–2004 Catalog* (n.p., [2002]), p. 5.
65. Ibid., p. 7.
66. "School Receives Largest Grant to Study Pain: $6.8 Million Awarded," *Forum* 20 (Winter 2002): 3.
67. David J. Ramsay, "Best Wishes to Our Dean," *Forum* 20 (Summer 2002): 3.
68. "Dean's Search," *Forum* 20 (Summer 2002): 3.
69. "The World's First to Become the World's Newest," *Forum* 20 (Summer 2002): 6–7.
70. Rager, "A Decade of Dedication," 16.

Christian S. Stohler

Chapter 21

A New Beginning: 2003

The future of dental education at the Baltimore College of Dental Surgery will rely on the continued support of alumni, the creativity of faculty, the innovation of our research programs, and the excellence of all students who leave these walls as the best oral health professionals they can be. The partnership between the school, its faculty, alumni, staff, and students is key to meeting the future needs of dental education in Maryland.[1] ~**Christian S. Stohler, 2003**

Christian S. Stohler Becomes Dean: 2003

The year 2003 saw the change of leadership at the Baltimore College of Dental Surgery, Dental School, University of Maryland, from Richard R. Ranney to Christian S. Stohler, DMD, DrMedDent. Dr. Stohler, who was appointed on January 1, 2003, received his DMD degree from the University of Bern, Switzerland, in 1972 and his DrMedDent degree from the same institution in 1975. In addition, he holds a certificate in oral surgery (1976) and a certificate in prosthodontics (1979). His previous teaching experience was at the University of Michigan, where he served as an associate professor from 1984 to 1990, professor (1990–2003), director of research (1994–97) and chair (1995–2003) of the Department of Biologic and Material Sciences, professor and chair, Department of Removable Prosthetics, University of Geneva (1986).

By way of honors, he received the William R. Mann and the Roy & Natalie Roberts endowed professorships award; was president of two national research groups, the International Academy of Dental Research (IADR) and the American Academy of Dental Research (AADR); associate editor of the *Journal of Orofacial Pain*; member of the National Institute of Dental and Craniofacial Research Board of Scientific Counselors; author of more than 75 journal articles or book chapters since 1975. On November 6, 2002, he was appointed as professor with tenure in the Department of Restorative Dentistry at the Baltimore College of Dental Surgery, Dental School, University of Maryland. Dr. Stohler's primary field of interest was focused on pain, specifically pain associated with the temporomandibular joint.[2]

Dean Stohler's Curriculum Changes

Dean Stohler did not hesitate to make necessary changes in the curriculum. One of the first he made was to combine community dentistry, pediatrics, and hygiene into one department under the chair of pediatrics. Next, he merged endodontics and periodontics under the chair of periodontics. His next move—for fiscal reasons—was to eliminate the Development Department and transfer its functions to the central campus operations in the Office of External Affairs.[3]

NIH Pain Grant

In 2003, the National Institutes of Health (NIH), National Institute of Arthritis and Musculoskeletal and Skin Diseases, awarded the school a five-year, $5.36 million grant to research how men and women respond to pain differently. The grant established a NIH Specialized Center of Research on Women's Health in the school's Department of Oral and Craniofacial Biological Sciences, called the Research Center for Neuroendocrine Influences on Pain. This center was only one of eleven established by NIH in the country, and the only one devoted to pain. The researchers were to study how the different sexes respond to pain and the how "sex hormones influence the intensity of pain."[4]

The majority of the clinical research on chronic pain in temporomandibular joint disease and disorders was based on the research of Ronald Dubner, DDS, PhD, professor and chair of the Department of Biomedical Sciences and director of the Research Center on Persistent Pain.[5] Much more research on pain is still needed, as Dr. Stohler emphasized that "the best pain medications that we have today only reduce about 50 percent of pain in 50 percent of the people." Furthermore, he stated that, "In the future, if a physician offers a single treatment that provides relief even for 60 percent of patients, people will look for another physician." The answer probably lies in tailoring the pain medication to the "genetic makeup of a particular person for his molecular individuality."[6]

The New Building

In 2000 engineering surveys had concluded that Hayden-Harris Hall, with "most of its major mechanical and electrical systems failing," was in need of $60 million in repairs to its infrastructure. It was increasingly apparent that the school's present facility challenged the faculty's teaching efforts, the clinical care of patients, community service initiatives, and research programs. The school expected the new building to:

1. Attract the "brightest students and most talented faculty."
2. Provide the students with the best dental education.
3. Provide clinicians with the facilities to practice the "highest standards of oral health care."
4. Facilitate "cutting-edge research."
5. Provide a comfortable, open, bright, accessible environment.
6. Enable the school to "maintain its competitive edge."[7]

The new 12-story building designed by award-winning architects Bohlin, Cywinski, and Jackson and constructed by Barton-Malow, was scheduled for occupancy in the summer of

2005. It was to feature an atrium encompassing the building's façade, fronting Baltimore Street, and a transverse atrium in the building's center rising from the fifth floor to the roofline. Both atria would allow natural light to penetrate the building and create a comfortable environment for both patients and staff.[8]

A $21-million capital campaign was needed for the building's successful completion, which would allow the BCDS to remain "a recognized leader in the field of oral health care."[9]

Oral and Craniofacial Biological Sciences

In 2003, the Department of Oral and Craniofacial Biological Sciences (OCBS), through a cooperative effort with local colleges and universities, expanded the "Short-Term Research Training Program" to include undergraduate students trained during the summer. These college students, as well as incoming freshman and sophomore dental students in NIH-supported programs, were provided with research training opportunities designed according to their educational levels. All of the trainees, regardless of background, were treated as full-time participants in his/her mentor's research program. The goal of the program was to discover students qualified for an academic research career in dentistry and medicine.[10]

Global Maryland

The Baltimore College of Dental Surgery is determined to remain a leader in dental education among its peers by "undertaking new programs to fulfill the expectations of a 'World Class' institution, and broaden the preparation of its graduates for their responsibilities as oral health professionals in a rapidly changing world." The Global Maryland program of "extramural ventures for faculty and students" is designed to achieve this objective. The goals of "Global Maryland" are:

1. To prepare both the faculty and students for the "challenges, opportunities, and responsibilities" in the global community.
2. To provide the faculty and students with opportunities for contributing to the oral health needs of underserved patients of other nations.
3. To provide the faculty opportunities for collaborative exchange with the dental schools with which the BCDS has established formal collegial relationships for research and teaching in areas of common interest.
4. To provide students with exchange programs for study in a foreign country.
5. To enlist the support and cooperation of governmental and non-governmental agencies involved in service to the global community.
6. To "encourage and engage the participation, support, and participation" of the BCDS alumni, the Maryland State Dental Association (MSDA), and other agencies of organized dentistry in the "aforementioned extramural ventures."
7. To develop sources of extramural financial support for Global Maryland.
8. To establish a director and an Office of International Relations to conduct the operations of Global Maryland.[11]

Funding Project for the New Building

On April 28, 2004, James T. Hill, Vice President for Administration and Finance at UMB, sent a memorandum to President David J. Ramsay concerning the shortage of funding for the Dental School's new building. The school had been required to raise \$21.6 million toward the project; however, a \$2 million NIH grant reduced the funding requirement to \$19.6 million. By the April date, no significant funds had been raised to meet the deadline of December 2004. Therefore, the campus needed to provide a "bridge loan" in the amount of \$19.6 million to the Dental School "until such time as they can raise the required funds." In addition, Dean Stohler was desirous of making several "scope changes to the building that would address some programmatic issues and deal with certain realities that did not exist when the project started." However, the cost of the project could not be increased. Any change that increased the cost had to be met with a change that decreased the cost. Furthermore, any idea of using Hayden-Harris Hall once the new building was completed had to be dismissed as impractical. The primary reason for constructing the new building was to replace the "outdated and awful HHH;" its continued use after the new building was completed would destroy the credibility of the 20-year argument for its replacement.[12]

Oral Cancer and Reconstructive Surgery

During the early 2000s, the Dental School became an active partner with the Medical School in treating oral cancer patients. The Department of Oral-Maxillofacial Surgery under its chair, Robert A. Ord, MD, DDS, combined its talents with the School of Medicine's Division of Otolaryngology-Head and Neck Surgery to treat patients ravaged by the disease. Dr. Ord performs the "ablative (tissue removal) part of the surgery" before other procedures, such as mircovascular surgery, are carried out.[13]

The Dean's Faculty

In 2004 Dr. Stohler continued to fight the mounting state budget deficits and fiscal problems by creating a "Dean's Faculty" of dedicated alumni and non-alumni volunteer dentists who would "contribute significantly to the mission of the Dental School by playing an active and important part in the School's programs of education, research, service and development." Projections estimated "an 8–10 % annual deficit in funding for faculty positions in the foreseeable future." Dr. Stohler's goal was to provide more resources for his students at the time the state was providing less. The Dean's Faculty would provide a "resource stream of additional faculty" while enhancing the "current and future full-time faculty's opportunity to expand their scholarly and professional activities." This partnership with the dental community would, in the short-term (1–5 years), allow the Dental School to acquire "an important new resource in terms of enriched faculty expertise through increased quantity, practical experience and diversity of faculty." In the long-term, the school, the university, and the dental community would "reap the mutual benefits of the development of a strong long-term personal and professional relationship," which would be a model for other campus schools and other dental schools throughout the country. The Dean's Faculty would include the following core activities: admissions, teaching, externship, student mentoring, research, ethics and professionalism, delivery of oral health care, practice management, and development.[14]

The Dean's Faculty members would include current and retired practitioners (dentists and hygienists), retired faculty, and other interested individuals who could contribute to the school's agenda. They would serve as "role models" for the students; fill the gap between the "number of faculty required to achieve" the school's mission; and allow full-time faculty to "engage in significant scholarly and professional achievements not attainable with current resources." As many of the mutual benefits of the program to the participating members, the school would offer continuing education credits; invitations to faculty events, study club presentations, and social activities; use of campus computers and e-mail accounts; and campus parking accommodations. The Dean's Faculty program was directed and developed by Dr. Warren M. Morganstein, senior associate dean, with Debbie Horstman as program coordinator.[15]

As of October 2004, 40 new volunteer faculty members had joined the Dean's Faculty Program since it began in April 2004. In addition, 57 Dean's Faculty members served as preceptors in extramural sites; in all, the program had recruited 120 volunteers for school activities.[16]

State-of-the-School Address

On June 23, 2004, Dean Stohler gave his state-of-the-school address in historic Davidge Hall, where Horace Hayden first lectured to medical students in 1819. The mission statement of the school now read:

> The Baltimore College of Dental Surgery, Dental School, University of Maryland, Baltimore, seeks to graduate exceptional oral health care professionals, contribute to the scientific basis of treatments for diseases of the orofacial complex, and deliver comprehensive dental care. These accomplishments will promote, maintain, and improve the overall health of the people within Maryland and have a national and international impact.[17]

These are the stated goals toward fulfilling the mission:

1. The school's graduates will be sought-after as "clinicians, educators, and researchers."
2. Major discoveries arising from the school's research will lead to "new therapies and cures for diseases."
3. The school will devise and implement "new strategies to increase access to health care and enhance health promotion and disease prevention.
4. The school's academic oral health center will "become a trusted source of care for the most complex problems."
5. The school's alumni will hold it in high regard and recognize its "commitment to their personal professional development."
6. The school will build "local, state, and national alliances with lay and professional partners interested in enhancing oral health care."
7. The school will have "ample financial support" from its "alumni, research, and educational partners and grateful patients."
8. Overall, the school will have a "top national ranking in education, research, and service."[18]

Dr. Stohler mentioned that the decreased state support for the Dental School, instead of being a liability, had the possibility of being potentially positive, as he remarked: "This is a challenge that sets the University free by getting away from the idea that you have to wait for Annapolis to tell you how much you can do. You think much more freely and in the long term."[19]

As for the future, the school promised to become a full partner with the other campus entities with the resulting multidisciplinary ventures contributing to its "prominence in scientific discovery, scholarly activity, and service to the community." Global outreach efforts would be increased, and an "atmosphere of collegiality and intellectual stimulation" would be stressed to nurture students, faculty, and staff. The organizational structure will help foster "creativity and responsiveness" to a wide range of opportunities for students, faculty, and staff to achieve these goals. The school promised the world's first dental school "will take its place as the premier dental school of the 21st century."[20]

Meanwhile, according to the National Institutes of Health (NIH), the school ranked second among all dental schools, based on "NIH monetary awards in FY03" and had received 31 grants totaling $11.4 million in funding for the year. This included 25 research grants, 2 training grants, 3 fellowships, and 1 award in the "other" category. In a nine-year period, the school had risen from the 26th position, with a grant total of $2.3 million in Fiscal Year 1996 to the seventh position in the rankings by Fiscal Year 2001. The school enhanced its research ranking by its emphasis on programs in diseases of the orofacial complex, "neuroscience and pain, oral-pharyngeal cancer, microbial pathogenesis, and health policy."[21]

Preparations for Accreditation Site Visit

In February 2004, the Dental School was visited by a team of accreditation consultants in preparation for the September 2004 visit by the American Dental Association's Council on Dental Education (CODA) team to evaluate the dental programs, predoctoral, dental hygiene, and specialty curricula. The specific aspects of each program were to be reviewed, including stated mission, curricula, and "resources in relation to specific approved standards." Ad-hoc committees of faculty and students had already evaluated the school's compliance with each standard and proposed "suggestions to better meet them." A steering committee ensured the faculty, students, staff, and "other interested parties" had input into the self-study. The CODA team would forward the results of the site visit in January 2005 to the ADA and the School was notified of its status in March 2005.[22]

The results of the visit were good overall. According to the report, all minimal standards were met, but there was a recommendation to ". . . improve appointment, promotion, and tenure communication."[23] The school also received several commendations in the areas of mentoring DDS/PhD students, infection control and compliance, basic science, and for the new building. The Advanced Dental Education programs received no recommendations and 19 commendations. The Division of Dental Hygiene received no recommendations and two commendations.[24]

Death of Dr. Provenza

The year 2004 saw the death of Dr. D. Vincent Provenza, the long-time teacher of anatomy, embryology, and histology, who had retired in 1987. Dr. Provenza had received his PhD from the University of Maryland in 1955, and served on the board of the *American Journal of Anatomy* and the Maryland Anatomy Board for more than 20 years. His specialty was the study of "cells, membranes and tissues and how they interact." Dr. Provenza was fluent in French, German, and Italian and lectured at conferences in Europe and Israel. He died on August 12, 2004. [25]

Emphasis on Oral Cancer

Under the direction of Robert Ord, DDS, MD, MS, chair of the Department of Oral and Maxillofacial Surgery, the school placed a renewed emphasis on the detection and treatment of oral cancer in 2004. Ord and his colleagues saw "approximately one-fifth of the 570 new cases," involving cancers of the mouth, throat, and pharynx, in Maryland in 2003. Oral cancer, he has noted, is the "sixth most common form of cancer in men and the 14th most common in women." Traditionally there has been a 10–1 ratio of male to female oral cancer diagnoses, but unfortunately that gap has closed to a 3–2 ratio. Because of increased smoking and drinking, "women have caught up rapidly." Ord says that biologically women react differently to these substances than men, and that, "Women seem to be more susceptible to tobacco and alcohol, and perhaps metabolize the carcinogens differently." However unexplainably, in Ord's study of 500 oral cancer cases, nonsmokers and nondrinkers made up 20 percent of the cases. Early detection by screening is critical to long-term survival of these patients and the School is doing its part in the treatment, construction of prosthetic appliances, and research on the "molecular events that underlie tumor development and progression."[26]

The UMB Bridge Loan

In January 2005, UMB President Dr. David J. Ramsay announced a $16 million "bridge loan" to the Dental School to finance the completion of the new dental building. The loan was to cover the remaining balance on the $141 million project, which was originally "funded with $120 [million] in state money." The money was to come from the university's cash fund balance, which was used "to pay salaries and other operating expenses." Dr Stohler had had the unenviable task of raising $21.5 million for the project. Stohler's dilemma was blamed on the controversy between the previous dean and the old alumni association.[27] However, the next month, Dr. Ramsay announced that the $16 million would be raised through "donations and equipment discounts rather than with a loan." Ramsay said that the school's status as the number two dental school in the country should assure that the necessary funds would be raised.[28]

Changes in the Faculty and Administration

On January 1, 2005, the dean announced the formation of a Clinical Operations Board, created to provide enhanced service to patients and student education. The original members included Drs. Harry Goodman (chair), George Williams, David George, Louis DePaola, and Roger Eldridge. (Dr. Linda Otis was added in 2006.) In creating a hospital-like environment, Dean Stohler noted that, "The new structure will help identify and address areas that will allow us to deliver optimal patient care, provide an exceptional framework for students, and facilitate an ideal work environment for clinic staff."[29]

In March 2005, Dr. Stohler announced that Drs. John C. Gunsolley and Morton Wood had stepped down from the posts as chairs of their respective departments of endodontics and periodontics and restorative dentistry. Drs. Mark A. Reynolds and Ashraf Fouad assumed the chair positions; Dr. Fouad to chair a department of the combined disciplines of endodontics, prosthodontics, and operative dentistry; Dr. Reynolds to chair the Department of Periodontics. Dr. Stuart Josell was to serve as the interim chair of orthodontics.[30]

In the Office of Admissions, Dr. Andrea Morgan ('90) joined the admissions operations as the dental recruitment coordinator. A member of the faculty since 2002, Morgan continued to teach in the Department of Endodontics, Prosthodontics, and Operative Dentistry along with her duties in admissions. The admissions director, Dr. Patricia E. Meehan ('93), assumed her role as head of admissions in 2004.

Fundraising Increases

Beginning in latter half of 2005, fundraising picked up momentum, and the Dental School began to make serious inroads toward financing the school's $21 million obligation to the state. Bequests from two alumni in particular—Drs. Harry W. F. Dressel ('45) and Maurice G. Lussier ('55)—totaled $1.5 million.

In addition, a group of largely African-American alumni led by Drs. Derek E. Brown and Kweli Carson launched a fundraising effort to name a $100,000 conference room in the new building to honor Wilhelma Garner-Brown, MEd. Garner-Brown, who spent more than 25 years helping to recruit and retain students, played a key role in the lives of many alumni. "As an African-American, I felt a personal responsibility to recruit to this Dental School qualified young black people who wanted to be dentists," said Garner-Brown.[31] By February of 2006, the group had raised more than $155,000.

Corporate agreements were notable in 2006 as well. On April 3, 2006, the Dental School signed an institutional agreement with implant manufacturer Nobel Biocare for $2 million. The three-year partnership was designed to help launch new initiatives in the curriculum, patient care, research, and development. Key areas supported by the grant included treatment planning, esthetic dentistry, complex prosthetic rehabilitation, and three-dimensional imaging technologies.[32] Also, discounts from Planmeca, the supplier of the dental operaties and related technologies in the new building, total more than $2 million toward the school's fundraising goals.

Notable Accomplishments

Aside from fundraising successes, the Dental School made strides in several other key areas. The Department of Oral Maxillofacial Surgery Residency Program completed a successful accreditation site visit in December 2005. Every five years, the program undergoes accreditation, and the 2005 visit garnered several commendations for the department. Also in 2005, the Division of Dental Hygiene received a program award from the Maryland Association for Higher Education. By the fall of 2006, the hygiene program had successfully launched a distance learning program for students on Maryland's Eastern Shore to "meet the needs of the dental community, students, and the public," stated Jacquelyn Fried, RDH, MS, director of the Division of Dental Hygiene.[33]

Researchers in the Department of Biomedical Sciences (BMS) reaped much positive attention for the Dental School. As part of a $19 million NIH pain study, researchers in BMS will participate with four other institutions in a long-term investigation of temporomandibular joint disorders (TMJD). The Dental School's component of the seven-year study is led by

Principal Investigator Dr. Joel D. Greenspan and Dr. Ronald Dubner, chair of the BMS department.[34] In addition, three BMS faculty members—Drs. Michael S. Gold, Joel D. Greenspan, and Richard J. Traub—led a three-day, international conference on pain, titled The Painful Truth: A Conference on Gender and Pain Research. Held in September 2006, the event attracted leading pain experts from around the world to discuss gender-based pain research.[35]

Other BMS faculty members were published in leading scholarly journals during 2006. The *New England Journal of Medicine* and *The Lancet* featured articles by Dr. Cyril O. Enwonwu on noma, the orofacial gangrene disease that contributes to the deaths of thousands of children in Africa and other parts of the world. Enwonwu, who stated that noma is largely a "disease of extreme poverty,"[36] was also interviewed by the BBC radio in June 2006. Dr. Patrik Bavoil, a noted Chlamydia researcher, was published in *Scientific American* and the *Proceedings of the National Academy of Sciences.*

Other individual accomplishments were also noteworthy during 2005 and 2006. Department of Oral Maxillofacial Surgery faculty members Drs. John F. Caccamese, Jr., and Domenick P. Coletti each received $100,000 Faculty Educator Development Awards in 2005 from the American Association of Oral Maxillofacial Surgeons. The awards are given to four outstanding young faculty members in the United States to encourage retention in academia.[37]

BCDS 1986 alumna Leslie E. Grant was formally installed as president of the National Dental Association on December 2, 2005. Grant's one-year tenure emphasized health equity for the underserved.

In March of 2006, Anna Muench, a second-year dental student, became a Howard Hughes Medical Institute Fellow. The award, mainly given to medical students, carried a $25,000 grant and gave Muench the opportunity to spend a year researching up-regulated biofilm genes.

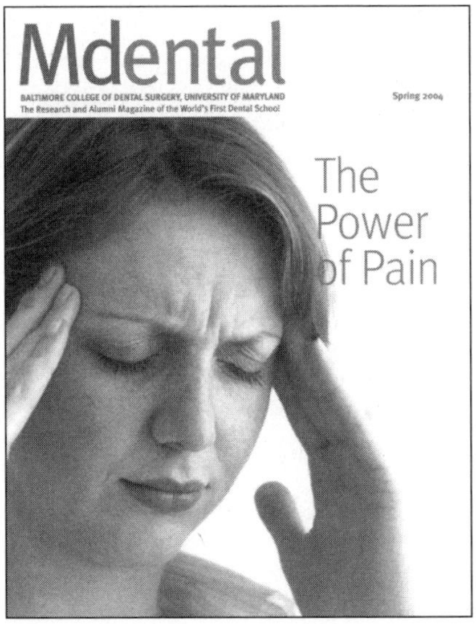

Mdental, the Dental School's new publication

The state of Maryland recognized Dr. Valli Meeks in August 2006 with a Certificate of Appreciation signed by Maryland Senator Barbara A. Mikulski. The certificate acknowledged the ". . . outstanding oral health care . . . provided to people living in Maryland with HIV/AIDS . . ."[38]

Mdental, the Dental School's new publication proved to hold its own among other publications before its second anniversary. In 2005, the magazine received the Silver Scroll Award from the International College of Dentists in the category of most improved publications (for its transformation from the *Forum* to *Mdental*). Three awards were earned in 2006: 1) the Best in Maryland award from the Public Relations Society of America (Maryland Chapter)—magazine division; 2) APEX Award of Excellence; and 3) Magnum Opus Award (Silver).

The Transformation

In September 2006, the long-awaited move to the new Dental School building became a reality. Students, faculty, staff, patients, and alumni were the beneficiaries of this transition to a new site and a new culture of technology-based teaching and care.

The all-digital facility at 650 West Baltimore Street included two atria, wireless network connections, ceiling-mounted cameras, hearing assisted technology, and remote communication to various classrooms, UMB sites, or other U.S. or international locations. The sophisticated digital technology was largely supported by UMB's Center for Information Technology Services, headed by UMB Vice President and Chief Information Officer Peter J. Murray, PhD.

The new school became an international blueprint for the future of dental education. State-of-the-art operatories and simulation rooms would facilitate enhanced levels of patient care and learning. Schools worldwide used the standards introduced at the new BCDS as a model, or gold standard, for their institutions.

A formal dedication ceremony was held on October 24, 2006. The years of hard work and patience were finally translated into a place that could provide the best level of patient care for thousands of Marylanders and an environment that stimulated more interactive learning and sophisticated research. The school now held the promise of living up to the words of UMB President David J. Ramsay:

"We are the oldest dental school in the world. Why not be the best?"[39]

The center atrium of the new building brings in natural light.

NOTES

1. Christian S. Stohler, "Dean's Message," *Forum* 21 (Spring 2003): 1.
2. Kelley Ray, "A Talk with the New Dean," *Forum* 21 (Spring 2003): 10; Letter, Richard R. Ranney to David J. Ramsay, November 8, 2002, Baltimore College of Dental Surgery, Dental School, University of Maryland, Office of the Dean, Files (*hereafter* cited as BCDSOD).
3. Presentation, Christian S. Stohler to MSDA Board of Trustees, February 11, 2004.
4. Mike Lurie, "NIH Funds Pain Study: Researchers examine how men and women respond to pain differently," *Forum* 21 (Spring 2003): 2
5. Regina Lavette Davis, "Facing Pain—Head On," *Mdental* (Spring 2004): 6, 8.
6. Regina L. Davis, "Understanding Pain: Gender, Genetics, and Treatment," *University of Maryland Baltimore* (2005): 2, 6.
7. Baltimore College of Dental Surgery, Dental School, University of Maryland, *Building for the Future: Raising the Bar* (Baltimore: n.p., 2003), p. 2.
8 Ibid., p. 4.
9. Ibid., p. 7.
10. "Summer Student Research Training Update," *What's on at OCBS?* 3 (Winter 2003): 1.

11. Baltimore College of Dental Surgery, Dental School, University of Maryland, "Global Maryland: Challenges, Opportunities, and Responsibilities in the 21st Century, A Global Perspective for Dental Education," unpublished internal document.
12. Memorandum, James T. Hill to David J. Ramsay, April 28, 2004, BCDSOD.
13. Regina Lavette Davis, "Jaws of Life," *University of Maryland Baltimore* (2004): 16, 18.
14. "Dean Stohler's Strategy Against an Uncertain Future," *MSDA Newsletter* 39 (June 2004): 1, 9.
15. Ibid., p. 9
16. "Dean's Faculty Progress Report," *Mdental* (Winter 2004–2005): 7.
17. Christian S. Stohler, "State of the School," June 23, 2004.
18. Ibid.
19. Regina Lavette Davis, "Stohler Outlines Challenges," *VOICE* (Summer 2004): 3.
20. Stohler, "State of the School."
21. "Dental School Rises to No. 2," *VOICE* (Summer 2004): 6. [In 2005, the school was ranked number three by the NIH.]
22. "Dental School Prepares for Accreditation Site Visit." *Mdental* (Spring 2004): 2.
23. "Accreditation Update." *Mdental* (Winter 2004–2005): 2
24. Ibid.
25. "Dr. D. Vincent Provenza, 85, UM Dental professor," *The Sun* (Baltimore), August 14, 2004.
26. Regina L. Davis, "Oral Cancer: Pathways to Diagnosis and Treatment," *Mdental,* Winter 2004–2005, pp. 9–11.
27. Ivan Penn, "UMB lends dental school $16 million to bridge funding gap," *The Sun* (Baltimore), January 23, 2005.
28. Ivan Penn, "Dental school to raise funds for new facility, UMB head says," *The Sun* (Baltimore), February 11, 2005.
29. "Dental School Reorganizes." *Mdental,* Spring 2005, p. 2.
30. Announcement, March 28, 2005, Office of the Dean, Files.
31. Regina Lavette Davis. "In Loco Parentis." *Mdental,* Spring, 2005, p. 24.
32. "Dental School & Nobel Biocare Sign $2 Million Agreement." *Mdental,* Spring, 2006, p 3.
33. "Bridging a Dental Hygiene Gap." Ibid, p. 2.
34. "Dental School Part of Major NIH Pain Study." Ibid, p. 7.
35. *The Painful Truth: A Conference on Gender and Pain Research,* Brochure, August 2006
36. "The Prestigious *New England Journal of Medicine* Features Dental School Researcher." *Mdental,* Spring 2006, p. 12.
37. "OMS Faculty Members Earn National Distinction," *Mdental,* Spring 2005, p. 11.
38. Letter, Maryland Department of Health and Mental Hygiene, August 1, 2006.
39. "The Relevance of Technology," *Mdental,* Summer 2006, p. 3.

Appendix A

Graduates of the Baltimore Schools Who Have Served as Dean of a Dental School

Aisenberg, Myron S. University of Maryland, 1922—Baltimore College of Dental Surgery, Dental School, University of Maryland

Arnold, J. P. University of Maryland, 1900—Texas Dental College

Arthur, Robert. Baltimore College of Dental Surgery, 1841—Philadelphia College of Dental Surgery; Pennsylvania College of Dental Surgery

Austen, Philip. Baltimore College of Dental Surgery, 1849—Baltimore College of Dental Surgery

Biddington, W. Robert. Baltimore College of Dentistry, Dental School, University of Maryland, 1948—School of Dentistry, West Virginia University

Cheaney, Price. Baltimore College of Dental Surgery, 1884—Northwestern College of Dental Surgery

Cowardin, Louis M. Baltimore College of Dental Surgery, 1874—School of Dentistry of the College of Physicians and Surgeons (VA)

Crenshaw, William. Baltimore College of Dental Surgery, 1884—Atlanta Dental College, Dental Department of Southern Medical College

DeFord, William H. Baltimore College of Dental Surgery, 1882—Drake University College of Dentistry

Dufour, John Francis Ruter. Baltimore College of Dental Surgery, 1867—Howard University, College of Dentistry

Foster, William G. Baltimore College of Dental Surgery,1881—Baltimore College of Dental Surgery

Fox, Lewis. Baltimore College of Dental Surgery, 1927—University of Connecticut, School of Dental Medicine

Frew, Athol L. University of Maryland, 1905—-Baylor University, School of Dentistry

Gorgas, Ferdinand J. S. Baltimore College of Dental Surgery, 1855—Baltimore College of Dental Surgery; Dental Department, University of Maryland

Haddock, Fernando, Jr. Baltimore College of Dental Surgery, Dental School, University of Maryland, 1958— University of Puerto Rico School of Dentistry

Heatwole, Timothy O. University of Maryland, 1895—Dental Department, University of Maryland; Baltimore College of Dental Surgery, Dental School, University of Maryland

Houghton, Frank J. Baltimore College of Dental Surgery, 1917—Loyola University, School of Dentistry (New Orleans)

Hovland, Eric J. Baltimore College of Dental Surgery, Dental School, University of Maryland [YEAR]—School of Dentistry, Louisiana State University Health Science Center

Jones, Henry C. Baltimore College of Dental Surgery, 1871—Dental Department, Medical College of Virginia

Lewis, Hall. Baltimore College of Dental Surgery, 1879—Columbian University, Dental Department (DC)

McCarthy, Harry B. University of Maryland, 1923—Baylor University, College of Dentistry

Medina, Jose E. Baltimore College of Dental Surgery, Dental School, University of Maryland, 1948— University of Florida, College of Dentistry

Montell, William A. Baltimore College of Dental Surgery, 1884—Baltimore Medical College, Dental Department

Morgan, William H. Baltimore College of Dental Surgery, 1848—Department of Dentistry, Vanderbilt University

Orrison, J. Edgar. Baltimore College of Dental Surgery, 1886—Baltimore Medical College, Dental Department

Perez, Bienvenido Jr. Baltimore College of Dental Surgery, Dental School, University of Maryland, 1958— University of Puerto Rico School of Dentistry

Pollack, Burton R. Baltimore College of Dental Surgery, Dental School, University of Maryland, 1946— School of Dental Medicine at Stony Brook

Randolph, Kenneth V. Baltimore College of Dental Surgery, Dental School, University of Maryland, 1939—School of Dentistry, West Virginia University; Baylor University, College of Dentistry

Robinson, J. Ben. University of Maryland, 1914—Baltimore College of Dental Surgery, Dental School, University of Maryland; School of Dentistry, West Virginia University

Sarrazin, Jules J. Baltimore College of Dental Surgery, 1887—New Orleans College of Dentistry; Loyola University, School of Dentistry

Scott, David B. Baltimore College of Dental Surgery, Dental School, University of Maryland, 1943—Case Western Reserve University School of Dentistry

Simpson, Richard L. University of Maryland, 1896—University College of Medicine, Dental Department; School of Dentistry, Medical College of Virginia

Smith, J. William. Baltimore College of Dental Surgery, 1888—Baltimore Medical College, Dental Department

Stuart, James T. Baltimore College of Dental Surgery, 1892—Milwaukee Medical College, Dental Department (Marquette University, Dental School)

Van Hassel, Henry J. Baltimore College of Dental Surgery, Dental School, University of Maryland, 1963—School of Dentistry, Oregon Health Sciences University

Walker, William E. Baltimore College of Dental Surgery, 1889—New Orleans College of Dentistry (Tulane University, School of Dentistry)

Walton, J. Roland Baltimore College of Dentistry, 1888—George Washington University, Department of Dentistry; National University, Dental Department

Weiser, Reuben B. Baltimore College of Dental Surgery, 1868—Denver College of Dentistry

Winder, Richard B. Baltimore College of Dental Surgery, 1869—Maryland Dental College; Baltimore College of Dental Surgery

Source: "Graduates of the B.C.D.S. Who Have Served or Are Serving as Deans of Dental Schools," *Journal of the Baltimore College of Dental Surgery, Dental School, University of Maryland* 15 (May 1956): 69; "Dean Fox Assumes Duties," *Alma Mater* 6 (November 1964): 35; Gardner P. H. Foley, "The Legacy of a School," *Alma Mater* 10 (February 1969): 3–4; "Dr. Randolph Succeeds Dr. McCarthy as Dean of Baylor University College of Dentistry," *Alma Mater* 10 (February 1969): 55; Deborah K. Rager, "The 'Alumni Deans'," *Forum* 20 (Summer 2002): 19–24.

Appendix B

Graduates of the Baltimore Schools Who Have Served as President of the American Dental Association

Morgan, William H. BCDS, Class of 1848, President ADA, 1870.

Rehwinkel, Frederick H. BCDS, Class of 1855, President ADA, 1877.

Shepard, Luther D. BCDS, Class of 1861, President ADA, 1879.

Walker, William W. BCDS, Class of 1884, President ADA, 1891.

Burkhart, Harvey J. BCDS, Class of 1890, President NDA, 1898.

Smith, B. Holly. BCDS, Class of 1881, President NDA, 1899.

Turner, Vines E. BCDS, Class of 1858, President NDA, 1908.

Robinson, J. Ben. University of Maryland, Class of 1914, President ADA, 1942.

Lynch, Daniel F. BCDS, Dental School, University of Maryland, Class of 1925, President ADA, 1954.

Cappuccio, Joseph P. BCDS, Dental School, University of Maryland, Class of 1946, President ADA, 1978.

Source: Gardner P. H. Foley, "Heritage," *Alma Mater* 19 (January 1978): 40.

Appendix C

Deans of the Baltimore Dental Schools

	Baltimore College of Dental Surgery
Chapin A. Harris	1840–1841
Thomas E. Bond	1841–1842
Washington R. Handy	1842–1853
Philip H. Austen	1853–1865
Ferdinand J. S. Gorgas	1865–1882
Richard B. Winder	1882–1894
M. Whilldin Foster	1894–1914
William G. Foster	1914–1923
Maryland Dental College *1873–1878 (Merged with BCDS)*	
Richard B. Winder	1873–1878
University of Maryland *(Founded 1882)*	
Ferdinand J. S. Gorgas	1882–1911
Timothy O. Heatwole	1911–1923
Baltimore Medical College *1895–1913 (Merged with University of Maryland)*	
J. William Smith	1895–1901
William A. Montell	1901–1903
J. Edgar Orrison	1903–1904
J. William Smith	1904–1913
Baltimore College of Dental Surgery Dental School University of Maryland *(BCDS joined the University of Maryland, 1923)*	
Timothy O. Heatwole	1923–1924

J. Ben Robinson	1924–1953
Myron S. Aisenberg	1953–1963
John J. Salley	1963–1974
Errol L. Reese (Acting)	1974–1975
Errol L. Reese	1975–1990
Warren M. Morgenstein (Acting)	1990–1991
Richard R. Ranney	1991–2003
Christian S. Stohler	2003–

Source: Gardner P. H. Foley, ed., *Proceedings of the 125th Anniversary Celebration of the Baltimore College of Dental Surgery* (Baltimore: Horn–Shafer Co., 1966), p. 124.

Appendix D

Admission Requirements and Length of Dental Curriculum

Admission Requirements

1840–1882	None (assumed applicants could read and write)
1884–1900	Rudimentary English
1900–1902	One year of high school or equivalent
1902–1907	Two years of high school
1907–1925	Four years of high school
1926–1935	One year of college
1935–1965	Two years of college
1965–	Three years of college

Length of Dental Curriculum

Period	**No. of Years**	**Months/Year**
1840–1882	2	4
1882–1891	2	5
1892–1896	3	5½
1896–1899	3	6
1899–1903	3	7
1903–1904	4	7
1904–1909	3	7½
1909–1917	3	8
1917–	4	8

Source: Letter, H. Berton McCauley to John M. Hyson, Jr., May 1, 2003.

Appendix E

Presidents of the National Alumni Association

Society of Alumni of BCDS

Harvey Colburn	1849–50
J. H. A. Fehr	1850–51

Alumni Association of BCDS

Samuel J. Cocheville	1876–78

Alumni Association of BCDS Merged with Alumni Association of Maryland Dental College

Samuel J. Cocheville	1878–79
C. S. Hulburt	1879–80
S. J. Cocheville	1880–81
Ferdinand S. J. Gorgas	1881–82
Walter S. Harban	1882–83
James B. Hodgkin	1883–84
W. W. Waller	1889–90
Charles A. Meeker	1895–96
George E. Adams	1896–97
Harvey J. Burkhart	1905–06
James H. Ferguson, Jr.	1921–22

Alumni Association of Dental Department, University of Maryland

Robert A. Hungerford	1885–86
R. Delamer Dodson	1886–87
A. Hungerford	1887–88
R. D. Dodson	1888–89
E. D. Beavis	1889–90
Clarence J. Grieves	1904–05

National Alumni Association Since Merger of BCDS with Dental School, University of Maryland

Frank P. Duffy	1923–30
B. Lucien Brun	1930–33
Wiley W. Smith	1933–34
B. Sargent Wells	1934–35
George M. Anderson	1935–36
Author I. Bell	1936–39
Harry E. Kelsey	1939–40
Brice M. Dorsey	1940–41
Leonard I. Davis	1941–42
James H. Samuel	1942–44
F. Noel Smith	1944–45
Elmer F. Corey	1945–46
C. Adam Bock	1946–47
Paul A. Deems	1947–48
Arthur L. Davenport	1948–49
Conrad L. Inman	1949–50
Harry B. McCarthy	1950–51
Thomas J. Bland, Jr.	1951–52
Harry Levin	1952–53
Eugene L. Pessagno, Jr.	1953–54
Albert C. Cook	1954–55
Lawrence W. Bimestefer	1955–56
Frank Hurst	1956–57
Daniel E. Shehan	1957–58
Edwin G. Gail	1958–59
Harry Dressel	1959–60
Daniel Lynch	1960–61
Joseph Cappuccio	1961–62
Lewis Toomey	1962–63
L. Lynn Emmart	1963–64
Calvin Gaver	1964–65
Irving Abramson	1965–66
Ashur Chavoor	1966–67
J. Philip Norris	1967–68
Eugene Leatherman	1968–69
Meyer Eggnatz	1969–70
Ernest Nuttall	1970–71
Joseph Seipp	1971–72
Leon Seligman	1972–73
Francis Veltre	1973–74
William Patteson	1974–75
Kyrle Preis	1975–76

Conrad Inman, Jr.	1976–77
Michael Ventura	1977–78
Charles Page, Jr.	1978–79
George H. Williams III	1979–80
Robert Bates	1980–81
Joe N. Price	1981–82
William T. Strahan	1982–83
Raymond W. Palmer	1983–84
Robert E. Murphy	1984–85
Gerald V. Eskow	1985–86
John F. Patterson	1986–87
Don–N Brotman	1987–88
Howard E. Schunick	1988–89
Edwin L. Morris	1989–90
James R. Sullivan	1990–91
M. Eugene Hinds	1991–92
D. Michael Brown	1992–93
Frank A. Dolle	1993–94
Stanley E. Block	1994–95
Frank J. Romeo	1995–96
Ronald M. Reichart	1996–97
Sheldon Silverman	1997–98
John D. Denney	1998–99
Sylvan Feldman	1998–2000
Robert J. Wilson, Sr.	1999–2000
Robin R. Gaber	2000–2001
Melvin F. Kushner	2000–2002
Bruce E. Yuille	2001–2002
Stephen J. Friedman	2002–2003
Harry W. F. Dressel, Jr.	2003–2004
Melvin F. Kushner	2004–2005
J. Roedel Jaeger, Jr.	2005–2006

Source: "Presidents of National Alumni Association Since Time of Merger of the BCDS with Dental School, Univ. of Maryland," BCDS Papers, NMDA; "Past Presidents of the Alumni Association," *Alma Mater* 23 (February 1982): 48; "Past Presidents of the Alumni Association," Office of the Dean, Files.

Appendix F

Endowed Lectures

The Grayson W. Gaver Memorial Lecture, an endowed lectureship, was established in memory of the late Dr. Grayson W. Gaver, an "outstanding leader in the field of prosthetics and a distinguished member of the faculty for many years," through the generosity of both his family and the school alumni. The Gaver Lecture is presented biennially as part of the Student-Faculty Day activities.

The Stephen E. and Jeffrey A. Kleiman Lectures in Dentistry and Medicine were established by Dr. Bernard S. Kleiman as a tribute to the two health professions chosen by his sons. This endowed annual lecture alternates between the University's Dental and Medical schools. The Kleiman Lecture alternates with the Gaver Lecture as part of Student Faculty Day activities.

The William B. and Elizabeth S. Powell Lecture was established in 1965 by a generous contribution from two alumni, Drs. William B. and Elizabeth S. Powell. The first lecture was presented in April 1966. These lectures are intended to broaden the "total academic program."

The Jane Boswell Toomey and Lewis Cole Toomey, DDS Memorial Lecture was endowed in 1983 by a major gift from the Toomey family with contributions by friends and associates of Dr. and Mrs. Toomey. The biennial lecture was initiated during the 1984–85 academic year. The Toomey Lecture enables the school to invite distinguished clinicians and researchers to speak on timely topics useful to both students and faculty.

The John E. Fogarty Memorial Lecture, sponsored by the Rhode Island Section of the Alumni Association, is presented on a rotating basis once every three years as part of the Commencement/Alumni Week activities.

The Hayden-Harris Memorial Lecture, sponsored by the Alumni Association, is presented on a rotating basis once every three years as part of the Commencement/Alumni Week activities.

The J. Ben Robinson Memorial Lecture, sponsored by the Maryland Section of the American College of Dentists, is presented on a rotating basis once every three years as part of the Commencement/Alumni Week activities.

Source: Baltimore College of Dental Surgery, Dental School, University of Maryland, *Advanced Dental Education Programs* (n.p., 1984), pp. 3–4.

Appendix 9

Faculty Emeriti of the Baltimore College of Dental Surgery, Dental School, University of Maryland

Irving I. Abramson, DDS, *Professor Emeritus*
* Myron S. Aisenberg, DDS, *Dean Emeritus*
Sophia Balis, DDS, *Professor Emeritus*
John M. Berquist, DDS, *Professor Emeritus*
* Joseph C. Biddix, DDS, *Professor Emeritus*
Gerald M. Bowers, DDS, *Professor Emeritus*
Raymond M. Burgison, PhD, *Professor Emeritus*
John J. Berquist, DDS, *Professor Emeritus*
Jerome D. Buxbaum, DDS, *Professor Emeritus*
Joseph P. Cappuccio, DDS, *Professor Emeritus*
Harold L. Crossley, DDS, PhD, *Professor Emeritus*
* Edward C. Dobbs, DDS, BS, *Professor Emeritus*
* Frank A. Dolle, PhD, DDS, *Professor Emeritus*
* Brice M. Dorsey, DDS, *Professor Emeritus*
Thomas C. Dumsha, DDS, MS, *Professor Emeritus*
* Gardner P. H. Foley, AM, AB, *Professor Emeritus*
* William B. Finney, DDS, *Professor Emeritus of Prosthetic Dentistry*
* M. Whilldin Foster, MD, DDS, *Professor Emeritus of Therapeutics and Pathology*
* William E. Hahn, DDS, NS, AB, *Professor Emeritus*
Charles E. Hawley, DDS, PhD, *Professor Emeritus*
John J. Salley, DDS, PhD, *Dean Emeritus*
Frank A. Dolle, DDS, PhD, *Professor Emeritus*
William A. Falkler, Jr., PhD, *Professor Emeritus*
Gerald W. Gaston, DDS, PhD, *Professor Emeritus*
Marvin M. Graham, DDS, *Clinical Professor Emeritus*
Charles E. Hawley, DDS, PhD, *Professor Emeritus*
James L. Hiatt, PhD, *Professor Emeritus*
* Burt B. Ide, DDS, *Professor Emeritus*
Frank C. Jerbi, DDS, *Professor Emeritus*

* E. Frank Kelley, PharD, DSc, *Professor Emeritus of Chemistry*
John P. Lambooy, PhD, *Professor Emeritus*
Charles B. Leonard, Jr., PhD, *Professor Emeritus*
Robert J. Leupold, DMD, *Professor Emeritus*
Martin Lunin, DDS, *Professor Emeritus*
* George McLean, MD, *Associate Professor Emeritus*
William C. Moffitt, DDS, *Professor Emeritus*
Robert K. Nauman, PhD, *Professor Emeritus*
Ernest B. Nuttall, DDS, *Professor Emeritus*
* J. Edgar Orrison, DDS, *Professor Emeritus of Chemistry*
* Kyrle W. Preis, DDS, *Professor Emeritus*
Charles T. Pridgeon, DDS, *Professor Emeritus*
* D. Vincent Provenza, PhD, *Professor Emeritus*
Wilbur O. Ramsey, DDS, *Professor Emeritus*
Richard R. Ranney, DDS, MS, *Dean Emeritus*
Errol L. Reese, DDS, *Professor Emeritus*
Ida M. Robinson, AB, BSLS, *Librarian Emeritus*
* J. Ben Robinson, DDS, DSc, *Dean Emeritus*
Frieda G. Rudo, PhD, *Professor Emeritus*
James T. Rule, DMD, *Professor Emeritus*
John J. Salley, DDS, PhD, *Dean Emeritus*
Donald E. Shay, PhD, *Professor Emeritus*
Paul D. Thut, PhD, *Peofessor Emeritus*
Mark L. Wagner, DDS, *Professor Emeritus*
* L. Edward Warner, DDS, *Professor Emeritus*
John I. White, PhD, *Professor Emeritus*
Henry N. Williams, PhD, *Professor Emeritus*
Riley S. Williamson, Jr., DDS, *Professor Emeritus*

**Deceased*

Source: Baltimore College of Dental Surgery, *75th Annual Catalogue of the Baltimore College of Dental Surgery* (n.p., [1914]), p. 2; Idem, *Eighty-Second Annual Catalogue of the Baltimore College of Dental Surgery* (n.p., [1922]), p. 2; Baltimore College of Dental Surgery, Dental School, University of Maryland, *Eighty-Seventh Annual Announcement and Catalogue University of Maryland School of Dentistry and the Baltimore College of Dental Surgery* (n.p., [1927]), p. 3; Idem, *Annual Catalogue of the Baltimore College of Dental Surgery, Dental School, University of Maryland, Session 1947–1948* (n.p., [1947]), p. 5; Idem, *1976–78 Bulletin Baltimore College of Dental Surgery, Dental School, University of Maryland at Baltimore* (n.p., [1976]), p. 56; Idem, *Dental School Bulletin 1980–1982 Baltimore College of Dental Surgery, University of Maryland at Baltimore* (n.p., [1980]), p. 66; Idem, *Dental School Bulletin 1982–1984 Baltimore College of Dental Surgery, University of Maryland at Baltimore* (n.p., [1982]), p. 47; Idem, *Dental School Bulletin 1984–1986 Baltimore College of Dental Surgery, University of Maryland at Baltimore* (n.p., [1984]), p. 59; Idem, *Dental School 1992-94 Catalog* (n.p., [1992]), p. 45; Idem, *Baltimore College of Dental Surgery, Dental School, University of Maryland Baltimore 2002–2004 Catalog* (n.p., [2002]), p. 99; "Faculty Emeritus Professors," *What's on at BMS?* 4 (Summer 2004): 1.

Appendix H

BCDS and Alumni Publications

The first publication of the Alumni Association of the Baltimore College of Dental Surgery was *The Bulletin*, edited by Oren H. Gaver, DDS. The first issue appeared in August 1926, followed by two in 1927, one in April, and another in December, edited by Myron S. Aisenberg, DDS. There were also two issues in 1928, one in May and one in December. This final issue listed all the alumni on record, with the intent of gathering eventually a more complete list. All 659 graduates of the Baltimore College of Dental Surgery, 394 of the University of Maryland, and 169 of the Baltimore Medical College were named. Actually, the Dental Department, University of Maryland, had published an earlier publication, *The University Orist*, beginning in 1904.

In March 1937, the *Journal of the Baltimore College of Dental Surgery, Dental School, University of Maryland* was launched, edited by Brice M. Dorsey, DDS. It was published by the faculty and contained in addition to alumni activities, article, and case reports of significant interest authored by faculty members, guest lecturers, researchers, and writers connected and unconnected with the school. There were two issues annually, July and December, subsequently edited by Gardner P. H. Foley, MA, and finally by D. Vincent Provenza, PhD. The last issue as published in July 1985.

In March 1959, the Alumni Association of the Baltimore College of Dental Surgery, Dental School, University of Maryland, decided to publish its own journal, *The Alma Mater*, edited by Kyrle W. Preis, DDS. The issues of February 1962 through November 1967 were edited by Joseph H. Seipp, Jr., DDS. Anthony Bravos, DDS, edited the issues to the spring of 1971, and afterward Dr. Preis resumed editorial responsibility. Frank J. Romeo, DDS, became the editor, starting with the March 1984 issue and continued in that capacity until the final issue in March 1990.

In 1967, the Office of University Relations published the *Newsletter, University of Maryland School of Dentistry*, the first issue dated winter 1967. Later in the 1980s, the publication became the *Dental Newsletter. Another publication, edited by William Bennett,* The Maryland Probe, was initiated by the school's dental students in 1974.

In the fall of 1980, there appeared a publication, *BCDS Form*, ostensibly in response to suggestions and requests of many alumni and friends for up-to-date practical information of use in everyday practice, plus news about classmates, colleagues, and faculty members. The executive editor was Errol L. Reese, dean of the school and the editor, Nell M. Savopoulos. There were two annual issues, produced by the school's Office of Development and Alumni Relations, variously edited. Later issues were simply titled *Forum*, boldly imprinted over the name of the school, finally acquiring a subtitle, "The Alumni Magazine of the World's First Dental School." The last issue of spring 2003 appeared early in the administration of Dean Christian S. Stohler, edited by Kelley Ray, MA.

In 2004 Dean Stohler originated a new publication, *Mdental*, and subtitled "The Research and Alumni Magazine of the World's First Dental School." Produced by the University's Office of External Affairs, the first issue appeared in the spring of 2004 and the editorial responsibility was assumed by Regina Lavette Davis, MA.

Source: H. Berton McCauley, "A Summary History of the World's First Dental Alumni," H. Berton McCauley Papers.

Bibliography

Books

Adjutant General of New York State. *New York in the Spanish-American War 1898: Part of the Report of the Adjutant General of the State for 1900.* Vol.1. Albany, NY: James B. Lyon, 1900.

Ambler, Henry L., comp., ed. *Facts, Fads and Fancies about Teeth.* Cleveland: Helman-Taylor Co., 1900.

American Academy of Dental Science. *History of Dental and Oral Science in America.* Philadelphia: Samuel S. White, 1876.

American Association of Dental Schools. *A Course of Study in Dentistry.* Chicago: Curriculum Survey Committee, 1935.

American Dental Convention. *Transactions of the American Dental Convention.* New York: Sears and Cole, 1875.

Anderson, George M., ed. *Proceedings Dental Centenary Celebration 1849–1940.* Baltimore: Waverly Press, Inc., 1940.

__________. *The Work of Adalbert Johann Volck 1828–1912: who chose for his name the anagram V. Blada 1861–1865* (Baltimore: George M. Anderson, 1970.

Asbell, Milton B. *Dentistry: A Historical Perspective.* Bryn Mawr, PA: Dorance & Co., Inc., 1988.

Baltimore College of Dental Surgery. *The 1934 Mirror.* Baltimore: n. p., 1934.

Base Hospital 18 Association. *History of Base Hospital No. 18 American Expeditionary Forces (Johns Hopkins Unit).* Baltimore: Thomsen-Ellis Co., 1919.

Beirne, Francis F. *Baltimore: a picture history 1858–1968.* Baltimore: Bodine & Associates, Inc., 1968.

Blanton, Wyndham B. *Medicine in Virginia in the Nineteenth Century.* Richmond: Garrett & Massey, Inc., 1933.

Bourguignon-Frasseto, Claude. *Betsy Bonaparte: The Belle of Baltimore.* Translated by Elborg Forster. Baltimore: Maryland Historical Society, 2003.

Bowman, John. *Pictorial History of the American Presidency.* New York: Gallery Books, 1986.

Bremner, M.D.K. *The Story of Dentistry.* 3rd ed., rev. Brooklyn, NY: Dental Items of Interest Publishing Co., 1954.

[Brophy, Truman W.]. "Section IX: Education, Literature, and History [Chairman's Address]." In *Transactions of the Fourth International Dental Congress* [1904]. Vol. 3. Philadelphia: S.S. White Dental Mfg. Co., 1905. [pp. 213–22.]

Brown, George W. *Baltimore and the Nineteenth of April, 1861: A Study of the War.* Baltimore: Johns Hopkins University, 1887. Reprint. Baltimore: Maclay & Associates, 1982.

Browne, Gary Larson. *Baltimore in the Nation, 1789–1861.* Chapel Hill, NC: University of North Carolina Press, 1980.

Callcott, George H. *A History of the University of Maryland.* Baltimore: Maryland Historical Society, 1966.

Camalier, C. Willard, Sr. *100 Years of Dental Progress in the Nation's Capital.* Washington, DC: C. Willard Camalier, 1966.

Campbell, J. Menzies. *Dentistry Then and Now.* Glasgow: Bell & Bain, Ltd., 1981.

Chapelle, Howard I. *The History of the American Sailing Navy: The Ships and their Development.* New York: Bonanza Books, 1949.

Chesnut, Mary B. *A Diary from Dixie.* Edited by Ben A. Williams. Boston: Houghton Mifflin Co., 1949.

Cordell, Eugene F. *The Medical Annals of Maryland 1799–1899.* Baltimore: Williams & Wilkins Co., 1903.

__________. *University of Maryland 1807–1907: Its History, Influence, Equipment and Characteristics with Biographical Sketches and Portraits of Its Founders, Benefactors, Regents, Faculty and Alumni.* 2 Vols. New York: Lewis Publishing Co., 1907.

Craig, James F., and Ernest F. Moreland. "The Technology Assisted Learning Environment." In *Dental Informatics: Integrating Technology into the Dental Environment.* New York: Springer-Verlag, 1992. [pp. 179–200.]

De Ford, William H. *Lectures on General Anaesthetics in Dentistry.* 2d ed. Pittsburgh, PA: Lee S. Smith & Son, 1912.

Department of the Army. *U.S. Army Register.* Vol. 1. Washington, DC: U.S. Government Printing Office, 1966.

Department of the Navy, Bureau of Medicine and Surgery. *The Dental Corps of the United States Navy: A Chronology 1912–1962.* Washington: Bureau of Medicine and Surgery, 1962.

Dietrich, Fred W., comp. *A History of Dentistry in Arkansas: A Story of Progress.* Camden, AK: Hurley Co., Inc., 1957.

Dow, Thomas D., comp., and Madison Jones. *History of the Tennessee State Dental Association.* Nashville: Tennessee Dental Association, 1958.

Faust, Patricia L., ed. *Historical Times Illustrated Encyclopedia of the Civil War.* 1st ed. New York: Harper & Row, 1986.

Fleming, J. Martin. *The History of the North Carolina Dental Society: With Biographies of its Founders.* Raleigh, NC: North Carolina Dental Society, 1939.

Foley, Gardner, P.H., ed. *Proceeding of the 125th Anniversary Celebration of the Baltimore College of Dental Surgery.* Baltimore: Horn-Shafer Co., 1966.

__________. *Hall of Fame of Great American Dentists.* Baltimore: Maryland State Dental Association, 1976.

Georgia Dental Association. *History of Dentistry in Georgia.* Macon, GA: Southern Press, Inc., 1962.

Gies, William J. *Dental Education in the United States and Canada.* New York: Carnegie Foundation for the Advancement of Teaching, 1926.

Gluckman, Arcadi. *United States Muskets, Rifles and Carbines.* Harrisburg, PA: Stackpole Co., 1959.

Griffith, Thomas W. *Annals of Baltimore.* Baltimore: William Wooddy, 1824.

Haines, Helen S., and Robert Thoburn. *75 Years of Dentistry.* Gainesville: University of Florida Press, 1960.

Handy, W[ashington] R. *Valedictory Address, Delivered Before the Baltimore College of Dental Surgery, at its Second Annual Commencement, February 18, 1842.* Baltimore: Woods and Crane, 1842.

__________. *A Textbook of Anatomy, and Guide in Dissection, for the Use of Students of Medicine and Dental Surgery.* Philadelphia: Lindsay & Blackiston, 1854.

Hapgood, Richard L. *History of Harvard Dental School.* Boston: Harvard University Dental School, 1930.

Harris, Chapin A. *The Principles and Practice of Dental Surgery.* 2nd ed. Philadelphia: Lindsay & Blakiston, 1845.

Hartzler, Daniel D. *Medical Doctors of Maryland in the C.S.A.* 1st ed. Funkstown, MD: Tri-State Printing, Inc., 1979.

Hayward, Mary Ellen, and Frank R. Shivers, Jr., eds. *The Architecture of Baltimore: An Illustrated History* Baltimore, MD: The Johns Hopkins University Press, 2004.

Hodgkin, J[ames] B., and R[ichard] B. Winder. *A Series of Questions Pertaining to the Course of Lectures on Dental Mechanism and Metallurgy by Prof. J. B. Hodgkin and on Dental Surgery by Prof. R. B. Winder.* Baltimore: Snowden & Cowman, 1881.

Hoffmann-Axthelm, Walter. *History of Dentistry.* Chicago: Quintessence Publishing Co., Inc., 1981.

Hollander, Morton H., ed. *The Mirror of November*, 1943. N.P., 1943.

Horner, Harlan H. *Dental Education Today.* Chicago: University of Chicago Press, 1947.

Houlihan, John J. "Ice Hockey." In *The 1932 Mirror.* Baltimore: n.p., 1932.

Hungerford, Edward . *The Story of the Baltimore & Ohio Railroad 1827–1927.* 2 Vols. New York: G.P. Putnam's Sons, 1928.

Hyson, John M. Jr. *The United States Military Academy Dental Service: A History 1825–1920.* West Point, NY: United States Military Academy, United States Army, 1989.

Jeffcott, George F. *A History of the United States Army Dental Service in World War II.* Washington, DC: U.S. Government Printing Office, 1955.

Jersey State Dental Society. *Transactions of the New Jersey State Dental Society.* Philadelphia: J. B. Lippincott Co., 1888.

Johnson, Paul. *A History of the American People.* New York: Harper Perennial, 1999.

Johnson, Herbert T., comp. *Vermont in the Spanish-American War.* Montpelier, VT: The General Assembly, 1929.

Kaplan, Lawrence A., ed. *The 1972 Mirror.* n.p., 1972.

Kauffman, Michael W. *American Brutus: John Wilkes Booth and the Lincoln Conspiracies.* New York: Random House, 2004.

Keating, Bern. *The Flamboyant Mr. Colt and His Deadly Six-Shooter.* Garden City, NY: Doubleday & Co., Inc., 1978.

Kelly, Howard A., and Walter L. Burrage. *American Medical Biographies.* Baltimore: Norman Remington Co., 1920

King, Thompson. *Consolidated of Baltimore 1816–1950: A History of Consolidated Gas Electric Light and Power Company of Baltimore.* Baltimore: Consolidated Gas Electric Light and Power Company, 1950.

Koch, Charles R.E., ed. *History of Dental Surgery.* 3 Vols. Fort Wayne, IN: National Art Publishing Co., 1910.

Koch, Tom. *The Wreck of the William Brown: A True Tale of Overcrowded Lifeboats and Murder at Sea.* Camden, ME: International Marine/McGraw-Hill, 2004.

Latimer, J. S. "Dental Education." In *Transactions of the American Dental Association.* Cincinnati: Wrightson & Co., 1863.

Levine, Walter I. *Fifty Year History of Alpha Omega Fraternity 1907–1957.* Philadelphia: Bingham Co., 1957.

McKay, Frederick S. "Fluorine and Mottled Enamel." In *Fluorine in Dental Public Health: A Symposium.* New York: New York Institute of Oral Pathology, 1944.

Macaulay, Neill W. *History of the South Carolina Dental Association: Centennial Edition 1869–1969.* Columbia, SC: R. L. Bryan Co., 1969.

Maryland War Records Commission. *Maryland in the World War 1917–1919: Military and Naval Service Records.* 2 Vols. Baltimore: Twentieth Century Press, 1933.

Massey, Mary E. *Ersatz in the Confederacy: Shortages and Substitutes in the Southern Homefront.* Columbia, SC: University of South Carolina Press, 1952.

Meekins, Geo[rge] A. *Fifth Regiment, Infantry, Md. Nat. Guard, U.S. Volunteer: A History of the Regiment from its First Organization to the Present Time, Illustrated.* Baltimore: A. Hoen & Co., 1899.

Missouri State Dental Association. *The History of Dentistry in Missouri.* Foulton, MO: Ovid Bell Press, Inc., 1938.

Monica, Woodrow S. *Outline of Dental History.* Hackensack, NJ: Fairleigh Dickinson University, School of Dentistry, 1967.

New York State. *New York in the Spanish-American War 1898: Part of the Report of the Adjutant General of the State for 1900.* Vol. 1. Albany, NY: James B. Lyon, State Printer, 1900.

Olson, Sherry H. *Baltimore: The Building of an American City.* Rev. ed. Baltimore: Johns Hopkins University Press, 1997.

O'Rourke, John T., and Leroy M.S. Miner. *Dental Education in the United States.* Philadelphia: W.B. Saunders Co., 1941.

Parry, Melanie, ed. *Chambers Biographical Dictionary.* Reprint. Edinburgh, UK: Chambers Harrap Publishers Ltd., 1998.

Payne, T. Michael, ed. *The Mirror 1977.* n.p., 1977.

Polk, R.L. *Polk's Dental Register and Directory of the United States and Canada.* 5th ed. Detroit: R.L. Polk Co., 1902.

Polk, R.L. *Polk's Dental Register and Directory of the United States and Dominion of Canada.* 14th ed. Chicago: R.L. Polk Co., 1928.

Powell, Hermie W., comp., ed. *100 Years of Dentistry in Virginia.* n.p., n.d.

Quinan, John R. *Medical Annals of Baltimore from 1608 to 1880, Including Events, Men and Literature.* Baltimore: Isaac Friedenwald, 1884.

Robinson, J. Ben. "The Beginnings of Institutional Dental Education in America." In *Proceedings of the Fourteenth Annual Meeting of the American Association of Dental Schools.* American Association of Dental Schools, 1937. [pp. 23–40].

__________. *The Foundations of Professional Dentistry.* Baltimore: Waverly Press, Inc., 1940.

Rukert, Norman G. *Federal Hill: A Baltimore National Historic District.* Baltimore: Bodine & Associates, Inc., 1980.

Scharf, J. Thomas. *History of Baltimore City and County from the Earliest Period to the Present Day: Including Biographical Sketches of Their Representative Men.* Philadelphia: Louis Everts, 1881.

Shaw, David W. *The Sea Shall Embrace Them: The Tragic Story of the Steamship Artic.* New York: Free Press, 2002.

Sheads, Scott. *Fort McHenry.* Baltimore: Nautical & Aviation Publishing Co. of America, Inc., 1995.

Sheads, Scott S., and Daniel C. Toomey. *Baltimore During the Civil War.* Linthicum, MD: Toomey Press, 1997.

Silverman, Kenneth. *Edgar A. Poe: Mournful and Never-Ending Remembrance.* New York: Harper Perennial, 1992.

Simon, William. "History of the Baltimore College of Dental Surgery." In *Transactions of the Fourth International Dental Congress* [1904]. Vol. 3. Philadelphia: S.S. White Dental Mfg. Co., 1905 [pp. 290–323].

Stanton, Elizabeth C., Susan B. Anthony, and Matilda J. Gage, eds. *History of Woman Suffrage.* Vol. 3. New York: Charles Mann, 1886. Quoted in "Women in Dentistry," Odontographic Journal 7 (April 1886): 39–45.

State of Maryland. *Laws Made and Passed by the General Assembly of the State of Maryland.* Annapolis, MD: William M'Neir, 1840.

Stickley, Robert P., and Jack D. Amowitz. *The Lynchburg Dental Society presents One Hundred and Forty-Three Years of Dentistry 1820–1963.* Lynchburg, VA: J. P. Bell Co., Inc., 1964.

Stout, Walter C. *The First Hundred Years: A History of Dentistry in Texas.* Dallas: Eagan Co., 1969.

Swartz, Theodore A., Walter E. Karfgin, Clarence G. Luther, et al, eds. *The 42nd General Hospital in World War II.* Brisbane, Australia: Truth and Sportsman Ltd., [1945].

Taylor, J. A. *History of Dentistry: A Practical Treatise for the Use of Dental Students and Practitioners.* Philadelphia: Lea & Febiger, 1922.

Thompson, A.H. "Scientific Instruction in Our Colleges." In *Transactions of the American Dental Association.* Chicago: H.D. Justi—The Dental Review Co., 1890.

Thorpe, Burton Lee. "A Biographical Review of the Careers of Hayden and Harris." In *Transactions of the Fourth International Dental Congress* [1904]. Vol. 3. Philadelphia: S.S. White Dental Mfg. Co., 1905 [pp. 413–24].

Tignor, Edwin P. "The Educational Value of Oral Hygiene in the Army." In *Transactions of the Panama Pacific Dental Congress.* Vol. 1. n.p., 1915 [pp. 265–68].

Thrall, Ralph B., ed. "Hockey Team." In *The 1933 Mirror* Baltimore: n.p., 1933.

University of Maryland. *Bones Molars and Briefs.* Baltimore: Senior Department of Medicine, Dentistry, and Law, 1901.

U.S. War Department. *General Orders and Bulletins.* Washington, DC: U.S. Government Printing Office, 1919.

Van Sickle, Ron R., ed., comp. *General Index to Official Army Register of the Volunteer Force of the United States, 1861–1865.* Gaithersburg, MD: Ron R. Van Sickle, 1987.

Warner, Ezara J. *General's in Blue: Lives of the Union Commanders.* Baton Rouge, LA: Louisiana State University Press, 1964.

Weed, Frank W., ed. *The Medical Department of the United States Army in the World War: Administration American Expeditionary Forces.* Vol. 2. Washington, DC: U.S. Government Printing Office, 1927.

Whitehorne, Joseph A. *The Battle for Baltimore 1814.* Baltimore: Nautical & Aviation Publishing Company of America, Inc., 1997.

Wiley, Bell J. *The Life of Johnny Reb.* Baton Rouge, LA: Louisiana State University Press, 1988.

Williams, Harold A. *Baltimore Afire.* Baltimore: Schneidereith & Sons, 1954.

Wilson, W[illia]m H. , ed., comp. *Medical and Dental Register of the City of Baltimore with Medical Directory of Maryland.* n.p., 1884.

Winder, Richard B. "Causes of the Deterioration of the Teeth." In *Transactions of the American Dental Convention* (New York: Sears and Cole, 1874. [pp. 311–23.]

__________. "Treating Burnishers." (*Southern Dental Journal). Quoted in* Catching's Compendium of Practical Dentistry for 1893. Atlanta, GA: Franklin Printing & Publishing Co., 1894. [p. 279].

Catalogs

Baltimore College of Dental Surgery. *Annual Announcement of the Board of Visitors of the Baltimore College of Dental Surgery.* Baltimore: Woods and Crane, Printers, 1840.

__________. *Fifth Annual Announcement of the Baltimore College of Dental Surgery.* Baltimore: Woods & Crane, Printers, 1844.

__________. *Sixth Annual Announcement of the Baltimore College of Dental Surgery.* Baltimore: John W. Woods, Printer, 1845.

__________. *Eighth Annual Announcement of the Baltimore College of Dental Surgery.* Baltimore: John W. Woods, Printer, 1847.

__________. *Ninth Annual Announcement of the Baltimore College of Dental Surgery.* Baltimore: John W. Woods, Printer, 1848.

__________. *Tenth Annual Announcement of the Baltimore College of Dental Surgery.* Baltimore: John W. Woods, Printer, 1849.

__________. *Eleventh Annual Announcement of the Baltimore College of Dental Surgery.* Baltimore: John D. Toy, 1850.

__________. *Thirteenth Annual Announcement of the Baltimore College of Dental Surgery.* Baltimore: John W. Woods, Printer, 1852.

__________. *Fourteenth Annual Announcement and Catalogue of the Baltimore College of Dental Surgery.* Baltimore: John W. Woods, Printer, 1853.

__________. *Fifteenth Annual Announcement and Catalogue of the Baltimore College of Dental Surgery.* Baltimore: John W. Woods, Printer, 1854.

__________. *Sixteenth Annual Announcement and Catalogue of the Baltimore College of Dental Surgery.* Baltimore: John W. Woods, Printer, 1855.

__________. *Seventeenth Annual Announcement and Catalogue of the Baltimore College of Dental Surgery.* Baltimore: John W. Woods, Printer, 1856.

__________. *Nineteenth Annual Announcement of the Baltimore College of Dental Surgery.* Baltimore: John W. Woods, Printer, 1858.

__________. *Twenty-First Annual Circular and Catalogue of the Baltimore College of Dental Surgery.* Baltimore: James Lucas & Son, 1860.

__________. *Twenty-Seventh Annual Circular & Catalogue of the Baltimore College of Dental Surgery.* Baltimore: John W. Woods, Printer, 1866.

__________. *Twenty-Eighth Annual Circular of the Baltimore College of Dental Surgery.* Baltimore: John W. Woods, Printer, 1867.

__________. *Twenty-Ninth Annual Circular of the Baltimore College of Dental Surgery.* Baltimore: John W. Woods, Printer, 1868.

__________. *Thirtieth Annual Circular of the Baltimore College of Dental Surgery.* Baltimore: Office American Journal of Dental Science, 1869.
__________. *Thirty-First Annual Circular of the Baltimore College of Dental Surgery.* Baltimore: Office American Journal of Dental Science, 1870.
__________. *Thirty-Third Annual Circular of the Baltimore College of Dental Surgery.* Baltimore: Snowden & Cowman, 1872.
__________. *Thirty-Fourth Annual Circular of the Baltimore College of Dental Surgery.* Baltimore: Snowden & Cowman, 1873.
__________. *Thirty-Seventh Annual Catalogue of the Baltimore College of Dental Surgery.* Baltimore: n.p., [1876].
__________. *Thirty-Eighth Annual Catalogue of the Baltimore College of Dental Surgery.* Baltimore: n.p., [1877].
__________. *Thirty-Ninth Annual Catalogue of the Baltimore College of Dental Surgery.* Baltimore: n.p., [1878].
__________. *Fortieth Annual Catalogue of the Baltimore College of Dental Surgery.* Baltimore: n.p., [1879].
__________. *Forty-Second Annual Catalogue of the Baltimore College of Dental Surgery.* Baltimore: n.p., [1881].
__________. *Forty-Six Annual Catalogue of the Baltimore College of Dental Surgery.* Baltimore: n.p., [1885].
__________. *Forty-Seventh Annual Catalogue of the Baltimore College of Dental Surgery.* Baltimore: n.p., [1886].
__________. *By-Laws of the Alumni Association of the Baltimore College f Dental Surgery.* Baltimore: Griffin, Curley & Co., 1888.
__________. *Fifty-second Annual Catalogue of the Baltimore College of Dental Surgery.* Baltimore: Snowden & Cowman, 1891.
__________. *Fifty-third Annual Catalogue of the Baltimore College of Dental Surgery.* Baltimore: Snowden & Cowman, 1892.
__________. *Fifty-sixth Annual Catalogue of the Baltimore College of Dental Surgery.* Baltimore: Snowden & Cowman Mfg. Co., 1895.
__________. *Fifty-Eighty Annual Catalogue of the Baltimore College of Dental Surgery.* Baltimore: Snowden & Cowman Mfg. Co., 1897.
__________. *Sixtieth Annual Catalogue of the Baltimore College of Dental Surgery.* Baltimore: n.p., [1898].
__________. *Sixty-First Annual Catalogue of the Baltimore College of Dental Surgery.* Baltimore: n.p., [1900].
__________. *Sixty-Second Annual Catalogue of the Baltimore College of Dental Surgery.* Baltimore: n.p., [1901].
__________. *63rd Annual Catalogue of the Baltimore College of Dental Surgery.* Baltimore: n.p., [1902].
__________. *66th Annual Catalogue of the Baltimore College of Dental Surgery.* Baltimore: n.p., [1905].
__________. *68th Annual Catalogue of the Baltimore College of Dental Surgery.* Baltimore: n.p., [1907].
__________. *71st Annual Catalogue of the Baltimore College of Dental Surgery.* Baltimore: n.p., [1910].
__________. *72nd Annual Catalogue of the Baltimore College of Dental Surgery.* Baltimore: n.p., [1911].
__________. *75th Annual Catalogue of the Baltimore College of Dental Surgery.* Baltimore: n.p., [1914].
__________. *78th Annual Catalogue of the Baltimore College of Dental Surgery.* Baltimore: n.p., [1917].
__________. *79th Annual Catalogue of the Baltimore College of Dental Surgery.* Baltimore: n.p., [1918].
__________. *Eighty-First Annual Catalogue of the Baltimore College of Dental Surgery.* Baltimore: n.p., [1921].
__________. *Eighty-Second Annual Catalogue of the Baltimore College of Dental Surgery.* Baltimore: n.p., [1922].
Baltimore College of Dental Surgery, Dental School, University of Maryland. *Eighty-Fifth Annual Announcement and Catalogue University of Maryland School of Dentistry and the Baltimore College of Dental Surgery.* n.p., [1925].
__________. *Eighty-Sixth Annual Announcement and Catalogue University of Maryland School of Dentistry and the Baltimore College of Dental Surgery.* n.p., [1926].
__________. *Eighty-Seventh Annual Announcement and Catalogue University of Maryland School of Dentistry and the Baltimore College of Dental Surgery.* n.p., [1927].
__________. *Eighty-Ninth Annual Announcement and Catalogue University of Maryland School of Dentistry and the Baltimore College of Dental Surgery.* n.p., [1929].
__________. *Ninety-First Annual Announcement and Catalogue University of Maryland School of Dentistry and the Baltimore College of Dental Surgery, Session of 1931–1932.* n.p., [1931].
__________. *Ninety-Second Annual Announcement and Catalogue University of Maryland School of Dentistry and the Baltimore College of Dental Surgery, Session of 1932–1933.* n.p., [1932].
__________. *Ninety-Fourth Annual Announcement and Catalogue University of Maryland School of Dentistry and the Baltimore College of Dental Surgery, Session of 1934–1935.* n.p., [1934].
__________. *Ninety-Fifth Annual Announcement and Catalogue University of Maryland School of Dentistry and the Baltimore College of Dental Surgery, Session of 1935–1936.* n.p., [1935].
__________. *Ninety-Sixth Annual Announcement and Catalogue Baltimore College of Dental Surgery, Dental School, University of Maryland, Session 1936–1937.* n.p., [1936].

__________. *Ninety-Ninth Annual Announcement and Catalogue Baltimore College of Dental Surgery, Dental School, University of Maryland, Session 1938–1939.* n.p., [1938].

__________. *Centennial Number. Annual Announcement and Catalogue Baltimore College of Dental Surgery, Dental School, University of Maryland, Session 1939–1940.* Baltimore: n.p., [1939].

__________. *Annual Announcement and Catalogue Baltimore College of Dental Surgery, Dental School, University of Maryland, Session 1941–1942.* Baltimore: n.p., [1941].

__________. *Announcement of Accelerated Course of Instruction Offered by the Baltimore College of Dental Surgery, Dental School, University of Maryland.* Baltimore: n.p., [1942].

__________. *Annual Catalogue Baltimore College of Dental Surgery, Dental School, University of Maryland, Session 1943–1944.* Baltimore: n.p., [1943].

__________. *Annual Catalogue Baltimore College of Dental Surgery, Dental School, University of Maryland, Session 1944–1945.* Baltimore: n.p., [1944]

__________. *Annual Catalogue Baltimore College of Dental Surgery, Dental School, University of Maryland, Session 1945–1946.* Baltimore: n.p., [1945].

__________. *Annual Catalogue of the Baltimore College of Dental Surgery, Dental School, University of Maryland, Session 1947–1948.* Baltimore: n.p., [1947].

__________. *Catalogue of the Baltimore College of Dental Surgery, Dental School, University of Maryland, Session 1949–1950.* Baltimore: n.p., [1949].

__________. *Catalogue of the Baltimore College of Dental Surgery, Dental School, University of Maryland, Session 1950–1951.* Baltimore: n.p., [1950].

__________. *Catalogue of the Baltimore College of Dental Surgery, Dental School, University of Maryland, Session 1951–1952.* Baltimore: n.p., [1951].

__________. *Catalogue of the Baltimore College of Dental Surgery, Dental School, University of Maryland, Session 1953–1954.* Baltimore: n.p., [1953].

__________. *One Hundred and Seventeenth Catalogue with Announcements for the 1957–1958 Session Baltimore College of Dental Surgery, Dental School, University of Maryland.* Baltimore: n.p., [1957].

__________. *One Hundred and Twentieth Catalogue with Announcements for the 1960–1961 Session Baltimore College of Dental Surgery, Dental School, University of Maryland.* Baltimore: n.p., [1960].

__________. *One Hundred and Twenty-First Catalogue with Announcements for the 1961–1962 Session Baltimore College of Dental Surgery, Dental School, University of Maryland.* Baltimore: n.p., [1961].

__________. *One Hundred and Twenty-Second Catalogue with Announcements for the 1962–1963 Session Baltimore College of Dental Surgery, Dental School, University of Maryland.* Baltimore: n.p., [1962].

__________. *Baltimore College of Dental Surgery, Dental School 1963–1964, The University of Maryland.* Baltimore: n.p., [1963].

__________. *Baltimore College of Dental Surgery, Dental School 1965–66, The University of Maryland.* n.p., [1965.

__________. *1968–1970 Catalog Baltimore College of Dental Surgery, Dental School, University of Maryland.* n.p., [1968].

__________. *1970–1972 Catalog University of Maryland School of Dentistry, Baltimore College of Dental Surgery.* n.p., [1970].

__________. *1972–74 Bulletin University of Maryland School of Dentistry, Baltimore College of Dental Surgery.* n.p., [1972].

__________. *1976–78 Bulletin Baltimore College of Dental Surgery, Dental School, University of Maryland at Baltimore.* n.p., [1976].

__________. *Dental School Bulletin 1978–1980 Baltimore College of Dental Surgery, University of Maryland at Baltimore.* n.p., [1978].

__________. *Dental School Bulletin 1980–1982 Baltimore College of Dental Surgery, , University of Maryland at Baltimore.* n.p., [1980].

__________. *Dental School Bulletin 1982–1984 Baltimore College of Dental Surgery, , University of Maryland at Baltimore.* n.p., [1982].

__________. *Dental School Bulletin 1984–1986 Baltimore College of Dental Surgery, , University of Maryland at Baltimore.* n.p., [1984].

__________. *Advanced Dental Education Programs.* n.p., 1984.

__________. *Dental School Catalog 1990–1992.* n.p., [1990].

__________. *Dental School 1992–94 Catalog.* n.p., [1992].

__________. *Baltimore College of Dental Surgery, Dental School, University of Maryland 2002–2004 Baltimore Catalog.* n.p., [2002].

Dental Department of the Baltimore Medical College. *Annual Announcement. Dental Department of the Baltimore Medical College. Session 1896–97.* Baltimore: n.p., [1896].

__________. *Annual Announcement. Dental Department of the Baltimore Medical College. Session 1897–98.* Baltimore: n.p., [1897].
__________. *Dental Department of the Baltimore Medical College. Session 1900–1901.* Baltimore: n.p., [1900].
__________. *Dental Department of the Baltimore Medical College. Session 1901–1902.* Baltimore: n.p., [1901].
__________. *Dental Department of the Baltimore Medical College. Session 1902–1903.* Baltimore: n.p., [1902].
__________. *Dental Department of the Baltimore Medical College. Session 1903–1904.* Baltimore: n.p., [1903].
__________. *Dental Department of the Baltimore Medical College. Session 1905–1906.* Baltimore: n.p., [1905].
__________. *Annual Catalogue and Announcement. Dental Department of the Baltimore Medical College. Thirteenth Annual Session 1907–1908.* Baltimore: n.p., [1907].
__________. *Annual Catalogue and Announcement. Dental Department of the Baltimore Medical College. Seventeenth Annual Session 1911–1912.* Baltimore: n.p., [1911].
__________. *Annual Catalogue and Announcement. Dental Department of the Baltimore Medical College. Eighteenth Annual Session 1912–1913.* Baltimore: n.p., [1912].
Dental Department of the University of Maryland. *Announcement of the Dental Department of the University of Maryland for the Session 1882–3.* Baltimore: William K. Boyle & Son, 1882.
__________. *Annual Circular of the Dental Department of the University of Maryland for the Session 1883–4.* Baltimore: Isaac Friedenwald, 1883.
__________. *Annual Circular and Catalogue of the Dental Department of the University of Maryland for the Session 1886–7.* Baltimore: Guggenheimer , Weil & Co., 1886.
__________. *Eighth Annual Circular and Catalogue of the Dental Department of the University of Maryland for the Session 1889–90.* Baltimore: Munder Bros., 1889.
__________. *Ninth Annual Circular and Catalogue of the Dental Department of the University of Maryland for the Session 1890–91.* Baltimore: Munder Bros., 1889.
__________. *Twenty-Second Annual Announcement and Catalogue of the Dental Department of the University of Maryland. Session 1903–1904.* Baltimore: n.p., [1903].
__________. *Twenty-Sixth Annual Announcement and Catalogue of the Dental Department of the University of Maryland. Session 1907–1908.* Baltimore: n.p., [1907].
__________. *Twenty-Eighth Annual Announcement and Catalogue of the Dental Department of the University of Maryland. Session 1909–1910.* Baltimore: n.p., [1909].
__________. *Twenty-Ninth Annual Announcement and Catalogue of the Dental Department of the University of Maryland Session 1910–1911.* Baltimore: n.p., [1910].
__________. *Thirtieth Annual Announcement and Catalogue of the Dental Department of the University of Maryland, Session 1911–1912.* Baltimore: n.p., [1911].
__________. *Thirty-First Annual Announcement and Catalogue of the Dental Department of the University of Maryland, Session 1912–1913.* Baltimore: n.p., [1912].
__________. *Thirty-Third Annual Announcement and Catalogue of the Dental Department of the University of Maryland, Session 1914–1915.* Baltimore: n.p., [1914].
__________. *Thirty-Fourth Annual Announcement and Catalogue of the Dental Department of the University of Maryland, Session 1915–1916.* Baltimore: n.p., [1915].
__________. *Thirty-Sixth Annual Announcement and Catalogue of the Dental Department of the University of Maryland Session 1917–1918.* Baltimore: n.p., [1917].
__________. *Thirty-Ninth Annual Announcement and Catalogue School of Dentistry, University of Maryland, Session of 1920–1921.* Baltimore: n.p., [1920].
Maryland Dental College. *Annual Circular and Catalogue of the Maryland Dental College.* Baltimore: Snowden & Cowman, 1874, 1875, 1876, 1877, 1878.
Maryland State Dental Association, and American Dental Association. *1840–1940 Dental Centenary Celebration.* Baltimore: 20th Century Printing Co., 1940.
New York Dental Centennial. *Catalogue Exhibition of Historical and Scientific Dentistry.* N.P, 1934.
School of Medicine, University of Maryland. *Ninety-Fourth Annual Announcement of the School of Medicine, Session 1900–1901.* Baltimore: Kohn & Pollock, 1900.
University of Maryland. *Catalogue 1922–1923.* College Park, MD: n.p., [1922].
White, S.S. *Illustrated Catalogue Dental Engines and Equipments.* Philadelphia: S.S. White Dental Mfg. Co., 1892.

Articles

"Abstracts of Educational Research and New Programs Presentations." *Journal of Dental Education* 46 (January 1982): 28, 42; 46 (January 1984): 44, 49; 49 (January 1985): 51; 51 (January 1987): 39.

"Advanced General Dentistry Program." *BCDS Forum* 3 (Fall 1982): 24.

"Affirmative Action Aims at Equal Opportunity for Minorities and Women." *Happenings* 2 (November 1972): 1, 6.

"Alcoholism, Drug Abuse and the Dentist." *Dental Newsletter* 13 (Spring 1980): 4.

Allen, C[harles] C. "A Society of Dental Surgeons in New York." *New York Dental Recorder* 2 (October 1, 1847): 2–3.

"Alpha Omega." *Maryland Probe* 3 (October 19, 1973): 4.

"Alumni Affairs Incorporated into Duties of Associate Dean, Assistant Director of Continuing Education," *Dental Newsletter* 9 (Winter 1975): 4.

"Alumni Breakfast in Washington." *Journal of the Baltimore College of Dental Surgery, Dental School, University of Maryland* 15 (May 1956): 55–56.

"Alumni Meeting." *Dental Cosmos* 18 (May 1876): 262.

"American Dental Association. Twenty-Seventh Annual Meeting [Proceedings]." *Independent Practitioner* 8 (September 1887): 480–87.

"American Dental Convention— Twenty-First Annual Session [Proceedings]. *Dental Cosmos* 17 (November 1875): 593–604.

"American Dental Convention—Twenty-Second Annual Session [Proceedings]." *Dental Cosmos* 18 (November 1876): 601–8; 19 (January 1877): 26–35

"The American Journal of Dental Science." *Maryland Medical and Surgical Journal* 1 (October 1839): 110–11.

Anderson, Bert G. "Philip H. Austen: A Voice in the Wilderness." *Journal of Dental Education* 3 (October 1938): 11–19.

"Annual Banquet Baltimore College of Dental Surgery Alumni Association, February 26th." *American Dentist* 8 (February 15, 1919): 10.

"Annual Commencement of the Baltimore College of Dental Surgery, Session, 1849–50." *American Journal of Dental Science* 10 (April 1850): 211–16.

Annual Commencement of the Baltimore College of Dental Surgery." *American Journal of Dental Science*, n.s., 1 (April 1851): 403–4; n.s., 2 (April 1852): 500–501; n.s., 3 (April 1853): 505–7; n.s., 4 (July 1854): 675–76.

"Annual Commencement of the Baltimore College of Dental Surgery." *Dental News Letter* 5 (April 1852): 332–33; 9 (April 1856): 196.

"Annual Meeting of the Dental Society of the State of Maryland and District of Columbia." *Dental Cosmos* 17 (December 1875): 652–53.

"Another first: BCDS to house new periodontal research center." *Baltimore College of Dental Surgery Forum* 11 (Spring 1991): 15.

"April 1850 [American Society of Dental Surgeons]." *Dental News Letter* 3 (April 1850): 69.

Armstrong, R.W. "Proceedings of the First Annual Meeting of the Society of the Alumni of the Baltimore College of Dental Surgery: furnished for the American Journal and Library of Dental Science." *American Journal of Dental Science* 9 (January 1849): 261–62.

Arthur, Robert. " Dental Education." *Dental Cosmos* 17 (May 1875): 229–36.

__________. "Practical Dentistry." *American Journal of Dental Science*, n.s. 10 (April 1860): 176–81.

Atkinson, W[illia]m B., comp. "Society Proceedings. American Medical Association." *Journal of the American Medical Association* 8 (June 25, 1887): 707–22.

Baker, E. "Letter from Dr. Baker." *American Journal of Dental Science* 6 (June 1846): 302–10.

Ballard, Charles W. "Dental Education." *American Journal of Dental Science*. n.s., 2 (October 1851): 59–71.

Baltimore College of Dental Surgery." *American Journal of Dental Science* 2 (March 1842): 261; 5 (March 1845): 249–50; 7 (March 1847): 282–84; n.s., 2 (July 1852): 672; n.s., 5 (April 1855): 340–41; 3rd ser., 1 (May 1867): 40–41; 27 (April 1894): 570.

"Baltimore College of Dental Surgery." *Dental Times and Advertiser* 1 (August 1851): 35; 1 (June 1852): 200.

"Baltimore College of Dental Surgery." *Dental News Letter* 9 (July 1856): 275; 10 (April 1857): 223; 11 (April 1858): 190–91; 12 (April 1859): 204.

"Baltimore College of Dental Surgery." *Dental Cosmos*, n.s., 1 (April 1860): 480; n.s., 6 (May 1865): 560; n.s., 7 (April 1866): 483; n.s., 10 (April 1868): 207–8; n.s., 11 (April 1869): 194–95; n.s., 12 (April 1870): 204; n.s., 13 (April 1871): 196; 14 (April 1872): 198; 15 (May 1873): 247; 16 (April 1874): 190; 17 (April 1875): 206; 18 (April 1876): 202; 19 (April 1877): 207; 20 (April 1878): 232–33; 21 (April 1879): 219–20; 22 (April 1880): 202; 23 (April 1881): 212; 24 (April 1882): 213; 25 (April 1883): 208; 26 (April 1884): 240–41; 27 (April 1885): 247; 28 (April 1886): 247; 29 (April 1887): 270; 30 (April 1888): 284; 31 (April 1889): 306; 32 (April 1890): 319; 33 (May 1891): 406;

34 (May 1892): 396–97; 35 (April 1893): 319; 37 (June 1895): 534; 38 (April 1896): 429; 40 (May 1898): 391; 41 (May 1899): 499; 42 (June 1900): 599; 43 (June 1901): 676; 44 (June 1902): 633; 45 (June 1903): 520; 46 (June 1904): 527–28; 47 (June 1905): 744; 48 (June 1906): 706; 49 (June 1907): 659; 50 (July 1908): 765; 51 (June 1909): 774; 52 (June 1910): 708–9; 53 (June 1911): 744; 54 (July 1912): 840; 56 (July 1914): 895; 57 (August 1915): 956; 58 (July 1916): 843; 59 (September 1917): 946; 60 (July 1918): 643; 61 (August 1919): 804; 62 (August 1920): 1030; 63 (July 1921): 756; 64 (August 1922): 909; 75 (July 1933)¨724.

"Baltimore College of Dental Surgery." *Dental Register* 51 (July 1897): 350.

"Baltimore College of Dental Surgery—Spring Lectures." *American Journal of Dental Science* 3 (December 1842): 151–52.

"Baltimore Medical College, Dental Department." *Dental Cosmos* 40 (July 1898): 587; 41 (May 1899): 498; 42 (June 1900): 596; 43 (June 1901): 681; 44 (June 1902): 632; 45 (July 1903): 603; 46 (June 1904): 524; 47 (July 1905): 906–7; 48 (July 1906): 802; 49 (July 1907): 779; 50 (July 1908): 769; 51 (July 1909): 908; 52 (July 1910): 817; 53 (August 1911): 973; 54 (August 1912): 959.

Barnes, Douglas M., John F. Hasler, and Alvan M. Holston. "Advanced General Dentistry Program." *Journal of Dental Education* 52 (May 1988): 271–75.

Baxley, H. Willis. "The First Dental College." *Items of Interest* 11 (January 1888): 1–3.

"BCDS alumnus helped make history in World War I." *Forum* 15 (Spring 1995): 26.

"BCDS Chosen for Pew Foundation Grant." *BCDS Forum* 6 (Spring 1986): 15.

"BCDS Launches New CE Program." *Forum* 19 (Summer 2001): 3.

Belenky, Michael M. "First Again." *BCDS Forum* 4 (Fall 1983): 2–3.

__________. "Global Partners in Education." *Forum* 17 (Spring 1997): 11.

Bethel, L[ouis] P. "Congress Gives Dentistry the Same Recognition as Medicine." *Dental Summary* 37 (November 1917): 855–57.

Black, Robert B. "Technic for Nonmechanical Preparation of Cavities and Prophylaxis." *Journal of the American Dental Association* 32 (August 1, 1945): 955–65.

Blount, A. A. "The Merits of Soft and Cohesive Gold, as Filling Materials." (*Ohio State Journal of Dental Science*), quoted in *Dental Advertiser* 13 (January 1882): 1–4.

Bond, Thomas E. "Valedictory Address," *American Journal of Dental Science* 1 (August/September 1841): 241–57.

Bond, Tho[ma]s E., Jr. "Obituary of Prof. Horace H. Hayden, being a Valedictory Address to the Graduating Class of the Baltimore College of Dental Surgery," *American Journal of Dental Science* 4 (June 1844): 221–30.

"Brief Necrology [Dr. E. Treat Payne]." *Dental Cosmos* 52 (June 1910): 706.

"Brief Necrology [Dr. John Akin Millard]." *Dental Cosmos* 56 (November 1914): 1287.

"Brigadier General Robert H. Mills. *Army Dental Bulletin* 13 (April 1942): 142.

Brown, J. P. H. "Objects and Aims." *Southern Dental Examiner* 1 (May 1860): 1–2.

__________. "To Our Readers." *Southern Dental Examiner* 2 (January 1862): 107.

Brown, Lawrence Parmly. "New Light on Dental History." *Dental Cosmos* 62 (August 1920): 936–58.

__________. "The Horace H. Hayden—John Harris Controversy: Hayden's Priority as a Dental Educator." *Dental Cosmos* 75 (August 1933): 794–99.

__________. "The Antiquities of Dental Prosthesis, Part III, Section II, Eighteenth Century." *Dental Cosmos* 76 (November 1934): 1155–65.

Brown, Solyman. "Remarks on Professional Morality." *American Journal of Dental Science* 1 (August 1839): 1–9.

__________. comp. "National Dentists' Society." *American Journal of Dental Science* 1, no. 7 (1840): 157–70.

__________. "Information Concerning the American Society of Dental Surgeons." *American Journal of Dental Science* 1 (January-February 1841): 190–96.

Burton, W. Leigh. "Dental Surgery as Applied in the Armies of the late Confederate States." *American Journal of Dental Science*, 3rd ser., 1 (August 1867): 180–89.

__________. "Dental Notes on the late Civil War." *American Journal of Dental Science*, 3rd ser., 1 (January 1868): 440–48.

Carr, Malcolm Wallace. "Thomas W. Evans: His Life and Influence on the Development of Dentistry as a Learned Profession." *Journal of the American College of Dentists* 46 (April 1979): 87–100.

Cattell, D. M. "Amalgam: Its History and Metallurgic Phenomena." *Dental Cosmos* 64 (August 1922): 855–62.

[Chandler, Alfred W.]. "George Washington's Dentures." *Journal of the American Dental Association* 76 (May 1968): 961.

"The Chapin A. Harris Memorial." *Dental Digest* 28 (May 1922): 299.

"The Chapin A. Harris Memorial Fund." *Dental Digest* 18 (January 1912): 20.

Cigrand, B.J. "Abraham Lincoln and Dentists." *American Dental Journal* 10 (February 15, 1913): 343–46.

"The Clarence J. Grieves Library Foundation: The Piperno Collection." *Journal of the Baltimore College of Dental Surgery* 6 (January 1942): 9–10.

Colangelo, Gary A., and Leonard A. Cohen. "Dental Practice Systems: A Student-Faculty Group Practice." *BCDS Forum* 4 (Fall 1983): 6–7.
"College of Dental Surgery." (*Boston Med. & Surg. Journal*), quoted in *American Journal of Dental Science* 5 (December 1844): 158.
"Comprehensive Orthognathic Surgery Center Become a Reality at the Dental School." *Dental Newsletter* 10 (Spring 1977): 2, 7.
"Constitution and By-Laws of the Society of the Alumni of the Baltimore College of Dental Surgery." *American Journal of Dental Science* 9 (January 1849): 248–50.
"The Construction Production." *Baltimore College of Dental Surgery Forum* 10 (Fall 1989): 14–15.
"Continuing Education Program Transmitted Via CTS Satellite." *Dental Newsletter* 11 (Winter 1977): 4.
Copper, John A. D. "Curriculum Reforms in Medical Education." *Journal of Dental Education* 37 (January 1973): 13–16.
"A Cooperative Effort in Dental Auxiliary Training." *Alma Mater* 11 (Spring 1970): 31–32.
Craig, James F. "Potential for Computer and Optical Videodisc Technology in Dental Education." *Dental Clinics of North America* 30 (October 1986): 713–20.
__________. "The First Dental College: A Faculty Without a Building." *Baltimore College of Dental Surgery Forum* 7 (Spring 1987): 2, 9.
__________. "Integrating the Use of Interactive Videodisc Technology into the Curriculum: A Case Study in Dental Education." *Journal of Medical Education Technologies* 2 (Winter 1992): 18–25.
"Curiosities of Dentistry." *Dental News Letter.* 4 (October 1850): 20–22.
"Cyrus Orlando Cone." *Dental Radiology and Photography* 36, no. 2 (1963): i, 44.
Davis, Regina Lavette. "Jaws of Life." *University of Maryland Baltimore* (2004): 16–19.
__________. "Facing Pain—Head On." *Mdental* (Spring 2004): 6–11.
__________. "Stohler Outlines Challenges." *Voice* (Summer 2004): 3.
__________. "Understanding Pain: Gender, Genetics, and Treatment." *University of Maryland Baltimore* (2005): 2–6.
__________. "Oral Cancer: Pathways to Diagnosis and Treatment." *Mdental* (Winter 2004–2005): 9–12.
Davy, T[omas] H. "Alumni Meeting." *Dental Cosmos* 18 (May 1876): 262.
"Dean Fox Assumes Duties." *Alma Mater* 6 (November 1964): 35.
"Dean Salley Announces Accreditation of Dental School." *Dental Newsletter* 7 (Winter 1973): 3.
"Dean John J Salley Resigns, Dr. Errol L. Reese Named Acting Dean." *Dental Newsletter* 8 (Winter 1974): 1–2.
"Dean Stohler's Strategy Against an Uncertain Future." *MSDA Newsletter* 39 (June 2004): 1, 9.
"Dean's Faculty Progress Report." *Mdental* (Winter 2004–2005): 7.
"Dean's Search." *Forum* 20 (Summer 2002): 3.
"Death Claims Dr. Lankford." *New Mexico Dental Journal* 13 (February 1963): 12
"Deaths [Fred C. House]." *Journal of the American Dental Association* 14 (July 1927): 1327.
"Dedication of Hayden-Harris Hall University of Maryland—School of Dentistry." *Alma Mater* 12 (Spring 1971): 20–21
"The Defamatory Article in the Dental Times." *American Journal of Dental Science*, 3rd ser., 2 (August 1868): 208–10.
De Moulin, Daniel. "A Historical-Phenomenological Study of Bodily Pain in Western Man." *Bulletin of the History of Medicine* 48 (Winter 1974): 540–70.
"Dental Alumni Association of Maryland Dental College." *Dental Cosmos* 17 (May 1875): 267; 18 (April 1876): 202.
"Dental Commencement." *Dental Cosmos*, n.s., 2 (April 1861): 498.
"Dental Department of the University of Maryland." *Dental Cosmos* 25 (April 1883): 213.
"The Dental Exhibit at the Centennial." *Dental Advertiser* 7 (October 1876): 165–68.
"Dental School Enrollment, 1940–41." *Journal of Dental Education* 5 (October 1940): 6.
"Dental School Evaluates Progress During Last Decade." *Newsletter University of Maryland School of Dentistry* 6 (Spring 1973): 1.
"Dental School Participates in Satellite Project, Experiments in Continuing Education." *Dental Newsletter* 10 (Winter 1976): 5.
"Dental School Prepares for Accreditation Site Visit." *Mdental* (Spring 2004): 2.
"Dental School Pursued Good Neighbor Policy." *Newsletter University of Maryland School of Dentistry* 4 (Fall 1970): 3.
"Dental School Receives $1.4 Million Grant for Periodontics Study." *Baltimore College of Dental Surgery Forum* 9 (Fall 1988): 4.
"Dental School Rises to No. 2." *Voice* (Summer 2004): 6.
"Dental School to Try Innovative Curriculum for Selected Students." *Newsletter University of Maryland School of Dentistry* 6 (Winter 1972): 2.
"Dental Society of the State of New York. Sixteenth Annual Meeting [Proceedings]." *Odontographic Journal* 5 (July 1884): 49–92.

"Dental Society of the State of New York. Seventeenth Annual Meeting [Proceedings]." *Odontographic Journal* 6 (July 1885): 65–128.

DePaola, Louis G. "Dental Honorary Society." *Maryland Probe* 4 (March 1975): 4.

"Department of Dental Hygiene Names Chairperson." *Dental Newsletter* 11 (Winter 1977): 3.

"Dinner in Honor of Dr. Timothy I. Heatwole." *The Bulletin the National Alumni Association of the Baltimore College of Dental Surgery* 2 (April 1927): 7.

"Do You Know." *The Vanguard* 2 (February 17, 1928): 2.

Dorsey, Brice M. "Surgery Department." *Alma Mater* 2 (February 1960): 41–42.

"Dr. Abramson to Retire." *Newsletter University of Maryland School of Dentistry* 6 (Spring 1973): 2.

"Dr. Aisenberg 22' Appointed Acting Dean." *Journal of the Baltimore College of Dental Surgery, Dental School, University of Maryland* 13 (January 1954): 1.

"Dr. Biddington Named Dean." *Alma Mater* 10 (February 1969): 54.

"Dr. C.C. Allen's Letter in Reply to our Remarks in Vol. 6, No. 2, upon the 'Resolutions of the American Society of Dental Surgeons, in Relation to the Use of Amalgams for Filling Teeth." *American Journal of Dental Science* 6 (June 1846): 267–82.

"Dr. Cappuccio Wins ADA Election." *Dental Newsletter* 11 (Winter 1977): 2.

"Dr. Dobbs, Pharmacology Head Retires After 43 Years Here." *Newsletter University of Maryland School of Dentistry* 1 (Spring 1968): 2.

"Dr. Hahn Retires, Dr. Leonard Named Admissions Dean." *Dental Newsletter* 8 (Spring 1975): 2.

"Dr. Edward Maynard." *Dental Cosmos* 33 (June 1891): 493.

"Dr. J. Ben Robinson Retires as Dean on May 1." *Journal of the Baltimore College of Dental Surgery, Dental School, University of Maryland* 12 (May 1953): 35–38.

"Dr. James F. Craig Department of Educational and Instructional Resources." *Dental Newsletter* 10 (Winter 1976): 2.

"Dr. Joseph P. Cappuccio Announces Candidacy for President-Elect of ADA." *Dental Newsletter* 10 (Spring 1977): 1.

"Dr. Medina Appointed Dean at Florida Dental School." *Alma Mater* 11 (Spring 1970): 29.

"Dr. Morganstein named acting dean." *Baltimore College of Dental Surgery Forum* 11 (Spring1991): 7.

"Dr. Preis to Retire as Head of Orthodontics: His Successor, Dr. John M. Grewe, to Arrive July 1." *Newsletter University of Maryland School of Dentistry* 2 (Spring 1969): 1.

"Dr. Randolph Succeeds Dr. McCarthy as Dean of Baylor University College of Dentistry." *Alma Mater* 10 (February 1969): 55.

"Dr. Salley to Succeed Dr. Aisenberg as Dean." *Journal of the Baltimore College of Dental Surgery, Dental School, University of Maryland* 19 (May 1963): 13–14

"Dr. Swanson Appointed Curator of Museum." *Baltimore College of Dental Surgery Forum 8* (Spring 1988): 20.

"Dr. T. O. Walton." *Dental Cosmos* 43 (April 1901): 442.

Dunbracco, W.W. "Baltimore College of Dental Surgery Alumni." *Dental Cosmos* 32 (May 1890): 398–99.

__________. "Alumni Association of Baltimore College of Dental Surgery." *Items of Interest* 28 (March 1906): 239.

"Editorial Department." *American Journal of Dental Science*, n.s., 10 (October 1860): 588–91.

Elkins, Wilson H. "[Dental Health Center]." *Journal of the Baltimore College of Dental Surgery, Dental School, University of Maryland* 21 (December 1966):48.

Erlick, David P. "The Peales and Gas Lights in Baltimore" *Maryland Historical Magazine* 80 (Spring 1985): 9–18.

Eskin, Albert C. "Dr. Henry Willis Baxley." *Journal of the Baltimore College of Dental Surgery, Dental School, University of Maryland* 5 (March 1941): 5–6.

"The Extramural Training Program." *Dental Newsletter* 12 (Spring 1979): 1.

"Faculty Emeritus Professors." *What's on at BMS?* 4 (Summer 2004): 1–2.

Farinholt, L[eroy] W. "Alumni Association, Dental Department, University of Maryland." *Items of Interest* 28 (May 1906): 392.

"Farewell to Miss Toomey." *Journal of the Baltimore College of Dental Surgery, Dental School, University of Maryland* 20 (May 1961): 3–4.

"Farm Boy to Dentist, via Engineering and Medicine [Amos Westcott, BS, CE, MD, DDS]." *Dental Radiology and Photography* 29, no. 3. 1956: i, 50.

Federation of American Women Dentists. "Women in Dentistry—1855–1880." *Journal of the American Dental Association* 15 (September 1928): 1735–56.

"First Alumni Meeting." *Alma Mater* 1 (March 1959): 6.

"First Again: BCDS Student Crowned Miss Maryland." *BCDS Forum* 5 (Fall 1984): 9.

Foley, Gardner P.H. "Dental Exhibits at the Pratt Library." *Journal of the Baltimore College of Dental Surgery, Dental School, University of Maryland* 9 (September 1945):3.

__________. "The Dental Sections of the University Hospital Units." *Journal of the Baltimore College of Dental Surgery, Dental School, University of Maryland* 9 (November 1946): 66–67.
__________. "Adalbert Volck dentist and artist." (*Journal American College Dentists*), quoted in *Dental Radiography and Photography* 35, no. 4 (1962): 74, 87–89.
__________, "The Legacy of a School." *Alma Mater* 10 (February 1969): 3–4.
__________. "B.C.D.S. Notes." *Alma Mater* 11 (Spring 1970): 4–5; 12 (Spring 1971): 5–6.
__________. "Heritage." *Alma Mater* 19 (January 1978): 40.
__________. "The Granting of Honorary DDS Degrees by the Baltimore College of Dental Surgery." *Bulletin of the History of Dentistry* 33 (April 1985): 13–17.
__________. "The World's First Dental College: Why? When? And Where?" *Journal of the Maryland State Dental Association* 33 (Spring 1990): 8–9.
Foster, J.H. "Address, delivered before the Society of the Alumni of the Baltimore College of Dental Surgery, at their First Annual Meeting." *American Journal of Dental Science* 9 (April 1849): 265–300.
"Four Departments to Merge, Headed by Dr. W.O. Ramsey," *Newsletter University of Maryland School of Dentistry* 1 (Spring 1968): 1.
"Frieda G. Rudo Ruskin, PhD: November 13, 1923-January 16, 1996." *Forum* 16 (Spring 1996): 7.
Gardette, E[mile] B. "On the Importance of Establishing a Lectureship on Dental Surgery in Medical Colleges." (*American Journal of Medical Sciences*). Quoted in *American Journal of Dental Science*, n.s., 1 (April 1851): 305–97.
"Gardner P. H. Foley Honored." *Alma Mater* 13 (April 1972): 32.
"General Medical Council." *British Journal of Dental Science* 36 (June 15, 1893): 562–74.
"General Practice Residency Grant." *Dental Newsletter* 12 (Winter 1978): 2.
Gies, William J. "Dental Education: Including a Study of the Alleged Influence of Derogatory Medical Opinion on Its Institutional Initiation in 1840." *Journal of the American Dental Association* 27 (January 1940): 99–109.
Gingel, James C., James R. Swancar, and Gregory G. Zeller. "The Accelerated Professional Training Program—An Alternative Method of Dental Education." *Journal of the Baltimore College of Dental Surgery* 34 (February 1981): 10–12.
Goodman, Harold S. "A Conversation with Dean Richard R. Ranney." *Journal of the Maryland State Dental Association* 35 (Summer 1992): 32–34
"A Good Time in Baltimore." *Missouri Dental Journal* 11 (March 1879): 177.
Gordon, Bernard. "President Errol L. Reese." *Journal of the Maryland State Dental Association* 34 (Spring 1991): 7.
Gorgas, F[erdinand] J. S. "Dental Education." *Independent Practitioner* 5 (August 1884): 414–21.
__________. "University of Maryland." *Dental Advertiser* 16 (October 1885): 120.
__________. "The Museum of the Dental Department of the University of Maryland." *University Orist* 1 (September 1904): 3–4.
Grace, Edward G. "Facial Pain Clinic Opening." *Forum* 17 (Spring 1997): 15.
"Graduates of the BCDS Who Have Served or Are Serving as Deans of Dental Schools." *Journal of the Baltimore College of Dental Surgery, Dental School, University of Maryland* 15 (May 1956): 69.
"Grants Management Office Assists Faculty with Funded Research." *BCDS Forum* 6 (Fall 1985): 24.
"Gunthers enhance Dean's Fund for Excellence Endowment." *Forum* 17 (Spring 1997): 29.
H., F. L. "Obituary. Dr. Henry J.B. McKellops," *Dental Cosmos* 43 (June 1901): 702–6.
H., F. N. "North Carolina State Dental Association, Raleigh, N.C." *Archives of Dentistry*, n.s., 5 (August 1888): 390–94.
Hahn, William E. "Department of Anatomy." *Alma Mater* 2 (February 1960): 37–38.
Handy, Geo[rge] E. "Doctor Clarence Jones Grieves." *The Bulletin the National Alumni Association of the Baltimore College of Dental Surgery* 2 (December 1927): 13–17.
Harris, Chapin A. "Observations on the qualifications necessary to a Practitioner of Dental Surgery—and on the manner in which they should be obtained." *American Journal of Dental Science* 1, no. 3 (1839): 49–57.
__________. "Ulceration of the gums and exfoliation of the Alveolar processes of children—resulting from general debility or defective nutrition." *Maryland Medical and Surgical Journal* 1 (October 1840): 424–29.
__________."Introductory Lecture." *American Journal of Dental Science* 1 (January 1841): 198–216.
__________. "Baltimore College of Dental Surgery." *American Journal and Library of Dental Science* 2 (December 1841): 207–08.
__________. "Answers to Questions of a Correspondent." *American Journal and Library of Dental Science* 2 (March 1842): 264.
__________. "Dissertation on the Diseases of the Maxillary Sinus." *American Journal of Dental Science* 3 (September 1842): 20–64.
__________. "Artificial Teeth Worn by Washington." *American Journal of Dental Science* 3 (September 1842): 76–77.
__________. "Dr. Hayden's 'Comments'." *American Journal of Dental Science* 3 (June 1843): 286–90.

__________. "Baltimore College of Dental Surgery." *American Journal of Dental Science* 4 (June 1844): 298–300.

__________. "Baltimore College of Dental Surgery." *American Journal of Dental Science* 5 (March 1845): 249–50.

__________. "Museum of the Baltimore College of Dental Surgery." *American Journal of Dental Science* 6 (December 1845): 181–82.

__________. "Baltimore College of Dental Surgery." *American Journal of Dental Science* 7 (September 1846): 112.

__________. "Contributions to the Museum of the Baltimore College of Dental Surgery." *American Journal of Dental Science* 8 (October 1847): 110–11.

__________. "The Diploma of the Baltimore College of Dental Surgery." *American Journal of Dental Science* 10 (January 1850): 139.

__________. "An Imposter." *American Journal of Dental Science* 10 (January 1850): 140–41

__________. "Dr. Gardette on the Propriety of Abolishing Dental Colleges, and substituting for them a Lectureship on Dentistry in each of the Medical Schools." *American Journal of Dental Science*, n.s., 1 (April 1851): 395–401.

__________. "Osseous Union of Teeth." *American Journal of Dental Science*, n.s., 3 (January 1853): 333.

__________. "Ancient Dental Instruments." *American Journal of Dental Science*, n.s., 3 (January 1853): 333–34.

__________. "Baltimore College of Dental Surgery." *American Journal of Dental Science*, n.s., 8 (October 1858): 584–85.

__________. "Importance of Army and Navy Dentists." *American Journal of Dental Science*, n.s., 9 (July 1859): 444–45.

Hasler, John F., and John J. Salley. "The Changing Faces of Dental Education: The Anatomy of the Clinical Dental Curriculum at the University of Maryland." *Bulletin University of Maryland School of Medicine* 59 (May 1974): 10–12.

Hasler, John F. "Hayden-Harris Hall: Into the Twenty-First Century." *Baltimore College of Dental Surgery Forum* 8 (Fall 1987): 3.

Hayden, Horace H. "The following comments were elicited by the perusal of an Essay, read in part, by Dr. C.A. Harris, of Baltimore, before the American Society of Dental Surgeons, at their annual meeting, held in Boston, July 20th 1842." *American Journal of Dental Science* 3 (December 1842): 203–26.

" 'He Lent Charm and Dignity to His Calling' [William W. H. Thackston, MD, DDS]." *Dental Radiography and Photography* 26, no. 1 (1953): ii, 19.

Henry, Eleanor M. "Strategic Plan Taking Shape." *Baltimore College of Dental Surgery Forum* 7 (Spring 1987): 7

__________. "A Blueprint for the Future: Building on Our Strengths." *Baltimore College of Dental Surgery Forum* 8 (Spring 1988): 7–10.

"Highlight: Department of Anatomy." *Dental Newsletter* 11 (Winter 1977): 2.

"Historical Review of the Progress of Dental Surgery in the United States, with Reflections upon the Causes that have Accelerated it, and the means Necessary for its further Advancement." *American Journal of Dental Science.* n,s., 2 (October 1851): 92–101.

Hodgkin, J[ames] B., and R[ichard] B. Winder. *A Series of Questions Pertaining to the Course of Lectures on Dental Mechanism and Metallurgy by Prof. J. B. Hodgkin and on Dental Surgery by Prof. R. B. Winder.* Baltimore: Snowden & Cowmam, 1881.

Hodgkin, James B., et al. "Dental Education." *Independent Practitioner* 5 (July 1884): 358–68.

"Honor Roll of Alumni in Active Service." *Journal of the Baltimore College of Dental Surgery, Dental School, University of Maryland* 8 (December 1943): 4–18; 8 (November 1944): 52–56; 9 (September 1945): 4–8; 9 (November 1946): 69–70.

Hopkinson, B. Merrill. "Dental Education." *Independent Practitioner* 5 (June 1884): 291–97.

"Hospital Adds Dental Department." *Newsletter University of Maryland School of Dentistry* 1 (Spring 1968): 3.

Hyson, John M., Jr. "Women Dentists: The Origins." *CDA Journal* 30 (June 2002): 444–53.

__________. "Dental Service Base Hospital No. 18: Johns Hopkins Hospital 1917–19." *Journal of the History of Dentistry* 51 (November 2003): 115–17.

Hyson, John M. Jr., and Ben Z. Swanson, Jr. "Portrait of a Confederate Secret Service Agent: Henry A. Parr, DDS." *Journal of the History of Dentistry* 44 (July 1996): 53–60.

Hyson, John M., Jr., and Gardner P. H. Foley. "Thomas Brian Gunning and His Splint for Jaw Fractures." *MSDA Journal* 40 (Winter 1997): 35–38.

__________. "James Baxter Bean: The first military maxillofacial hospital." *MSDA Journal* 40 (Spring 1997): 77–81.

__________. "Richard Bayly Winder: Andersonville Quartermaster and Dental College Dean." *MSDA Journal* 40 (Fall 1997): 163–68.

Hyson, John M., Jr., and Audrey B. Davis. "Basil Manly Wilkerson: Dental Inventor Extraodinaire." *Journal of the History Dentistry* 47 (July 1999): 61–64.

Hyson, John M., Jr., and Scott D. Swank. "Dr. Newell Sill Jenkins Progenitor of Cosmetic Dentistry." *CDA Journal* 31 (August 2005): 626–29.

"ICD Exchange Program in Second Year." *Forum* 16 (Spring 1996): 3–4.

"In Memoriam [Dr. Myron Aisenberg]." *BCDS Forum* 7 (Fall 1986): 29.
"In Memoriam. Dr. R.B. Winder Dead." *Southern Dental Journal and Luminary* 13 (September 1, 1894): 392.
"In Memoriam. Dr. Vines Edmunds Turner." *Items of Interest* 36 (July 1914): 552.
"In Memory of Dr. Timothy O. Heatwole (1865–1949)." *Alma Mater* 2 (February 1960): 43.
"An International Dental Family (Eleazar Parmly, MD, DDS)." *Dental Radiography and Photography* 32, no. 3 (1959): i, 59–60.
"John Salley to Head New School of Graduate Studies." *Dental Newsletter* 13 (Spring 1980): 3.
"Journalistic." *Missouri Dental Journal* 5 (June 1873): 230–33.
"Katherine (Kate) Toomey L.L.D." *Alma Mater* 21 (January 1980): 51.
Kelsey, Charles C. "Dental Fraternities at Michigan." *School of Dentistry Alumni Bulletin* (1977–78): 66.
Kempton, [H.M.]. "Ohio State Dental Society [Proceedings]." *Archives of Dentistry*, n.s., 7 (January 1890): 29–32.
King, Arthur D., Don L. Allen, Richard S. Mackenzie, and Jose E. Medina. "A Modular Curriculum Design for Dentistry." *Journal of Dental Education* 36 (June 1972): 20–23.
[King, Otto U]. "Demobilization of the Student Army Training Corps Between December 1 and 21, 1918." *Journal of the National Dental Association* 5 (December 1918): 1287–88.
[Kirk, Edward C.]. "The Chapin A. Harris Memorial." *Dental Cosmos* 55 (March 1913):330–33.
__________. "Committee on Dentistry, General Medical Board of Council of National Defense." *Journal of the National Dental Association* 4 (June 1917): 640–44.
Lankford, Arthur. "The Principles Involved in Interchangeable Interdental Splints with Attachment for Extra-facial tension in Maxillo-facial Surgery." *Dental Cosmos* 61 (September 1919): 839–45.
Lee, Fred C. "The Amateur Ice Hockey Association of Baltimore." *Sports Centre News* (1933): 6–10, 14.
Lewis, Carl P., Jr. "The Baltimore College of Dental Surgery and the Birth of Professional Dentistry, 1840." *Maryland Historical Magazine* 59 (September 1964): 268–85.
"Lieut. Tignor Represents the Army Dental Corps." *University Orist [University of Maryland]* 1 (September 1904): 7.
Linthicum, Dorothy S., and Ernest F. Moreland. "Accreditation Process: Its Effectiveness at the University of Maryland Dental School." *Journal of the Baltimore College of Dental Surgery* 35 (June 1981): 19–23.
Livaditis, Gus J., and Van P. Thompson. "The Maryland Bridge Technique." *BCDS Forum* 2 (Winter 1982): 6–8.
Love, Mary. "The National Museum of Dentistry: Preserving Our Past for the Nation." *Baltimore College of Dental Surgery Forum* 9 (Spring 1989): 12–15.
Lurie, Mike. "NIH Funds Pain Study: Researchers examine how men and women respond to pain differently." *Forum* 21 (Spring 2003): 2.
McCarthy, Harry B. "Former Director of Clinics Remembers Peers." *Journal of the Maryland State Dental Association* 26 (August 1983): 64–66.
McCauley, H. Berton. "Professional Dentistry and the University of Maryland at Baltimore." *Bulletin of the History of Dentistry* 30 (October 1982): 73–91.
__________. "The Century-Old Dental Department of the University of Maryland at Baltimore." *Journal of the Maryland State Dental Association* 25 (December 1982): 96–102.
__________. "The Maryland State Dental Association: In the Beginning." *Journal of the Maryland State Dental Association* 26 (August 1983): 74–78.
__________. "Dental Education Institutionalized: The 'What' of the Baltimore College of Dental Surgery." *Journal of the Maryland State Dental Association* 33 (Spring 1990): 10–13.
__________. "Baltimore fluoridates." *Maryland Medical Journal* 42 (August 1993): 745–49.
McDonald, Norval H. "The Clarence J. Grieves Library Foundation of the Maryland State Dental Association." *The Bulletin the National Alumni Association of the Baltimore College of Dental Surgery* 1 (August 1, 1926): 8–9.
[Mackall, Leonard]. "Obituary [Anson B. Hayden]." *American Journal of Dental Science* 3 (September 1842): 80.
Marshall, John S. "Technical vs. Theoretic Training." *Dental Brief* 5 (September 1900): 506–9.
"Maryland Dental College." *Dental Cosmos* 16 (April 1874): 193–94; 17 (April 1875): 210; 18 (April 1876): 205; 19 (April 1877): 211; 20 (April 1878): 236.
Medina, Jose E. "Department of Operative Dentistry." *Alma Mater* 2 (February 1960): 39–40.
__________. "Postgraduate Course in Operative Dentistry." *Alma Mater* 2 (February 1960): 40.
"[Meeting Alumni of Baltimore College of Dental Surgery]". *Dental Facts for Dentists* 8 (August 1920): 26.
"Meeting of the Alumni of the Maryland Dental College." *Dental Cosmos* 20 (February 1878): 120..
Mills, Edward C. "John Harris, MD, DDS." *Bulletin of the Ohio State Dental Society* 1 (November 1927): 106–111.
Mills, Robert H. "Factors in the Development and Progress of the Army Dental Corps." *Journal of the American Dental Association* 31 (April 1, 1944): 531–36.

"Miss Toomey Honored by Mount St. Mary's College." *Journal of the Baltimore College of Dental Surgery, Dental School, University of Maryland* 17 (May 1958): 53.

"More Women Finding Dentistry an Attractive Career." *BCDS Forum* 5 (Fall 1984): 10.

Morganstein, Warren M., and John J. Salley. "The Team Program at the University of Maryland." *Journal of the Maryland State Dental Association* 16 (April 1973): 15–21.

Myslinski, Norbert R. "The Revolution in 'Brain Literacy'." *Cerebrum* 3 (March 2001): 60–73.

"National Alumni Association of the Baltimore College of Dental Surgery." *Dental Cosmos* 64 (December 1922): 1336–45; 65 (January 1923): 86–95.

"National Association of Dental Faculties [Proceedings]." *Dental Cosmos* 26 (August 1884): 560–64; 31 (September 1889): 727–29.

"National Dental Association of the United States of America—Second Annual Session [Proceedings]." *Dental Cosmos* 23 (September 1881): 476–84.

Nelsen, Robert J., Carl E. Pelander, and John W. Kumpula. "Hydraulic turbine contra-angle handpiece." *Journal of the American Dental Association* 47 (September 1953): 324–29.

Nevin, Mendel. "The History and Development of Local Anesthesia." *Dental Items of Interest* 65 (July 1943): 674–77.

"New Administrative Appointments Announced at Faculty Retreat," *Dental Newsletter* 9 (Winter 1975): 2, 3–4.

"New clinical simulation unit dedicated." *Baltimore College of Dental Surgery Forum* 9 (Spring 1989): 3.

"New Dental College." *Dental Advertiser* 4 (July 1873): 119.

"New Dental Dean Named at UMAB." *Journal of the Maryland State Dental Association* 34 (Winter 1991): 33.

"New Master of Science Program to Begin." *Dental Newsletter* 13 (Winter 1979): 2.

"New Orleans Dental College." *Dental Cosmos*, n.s., 9 (October 1867): 151–52.

"New York Odontological Society [Proceedings]." *Dental Cosmos* 17 (July 1875): 358–72.

"Not the occupation that honors this man—he honors his occupation [Norman William Kingsley, MDS, DDS]" *Dental Radiography and Photography* 26, no. 3, (1953): i, 64.

"Obituary. Arthur Langford (sic), DDS." *Journal of the Maryland State Dental Association* 28 (April 1985): 32.

"Obituary [Dr. Alexander Gordon Lyle]." *Journal of the Baltimore College of Dental Surgery, Dental School, University of Maryland* 15 (January 1956): 13.

"Obituary [Dr. B. Lucien Brun]." *Journal of the Baltimore College of Surgery, Dental School, University of Maryland* 13 (May 1954): 44–45.

"Obituary. Dr. Basil Manly Wilkerson." *Dental Cosmos* 52 (October 1910): 1176.

"Obituary [Dr. Chapin A. Harris]." *Cincinnati Dental Lamp* 2, no. 1 (1860): 17–19.

"Obituary. Dr. Edward Maynard." *International Dental Journal* 12 (June 1891): 414–16.

"Obituary. Dr. E. L. Hunter." *Dental Cosmos* 51 (October 1909): 1238.

"Obituary. Dr. E. Parmly Brown." *Dental Cosmos* 58 (April 1916): 464–66.

"Obituary. Dr. Edward C. McSherry." *Dental Cosmos* 42 (October 1900): 1092.

"Obituary. Dr. F. H. Rehwinkel, MD, DDS." *Dental Cosmos* 31 (July 1889): 562–63.

"Obituary. Dr. Ferdinand J. S. Gorgas." *Dental Cosmos* 56 (June 1914): 771–72.

"Obituary. Dr. H. A. Parr." *Dental Cosmos* 74 (September 1932): 926.

"Obituary. Dr. Homer Judd." *Dental Cosmos* 32 (July 1890): 574.

"Obituary. Dr. Howard Emory Topping." *Journal of the Baltimore College of Dental Surgery, Dental School, University of Maryland* 14 (May 1955): 57.

"Obituary. Dr. Hugh W. Arthur." *Dental Cosmos* 70 (January 1928): 118–19.

"Obituary. Dr. J. S. Boak." (*Martinsburg Evening World*), quoted in Dental Brief 12 (January 1907): 54–55.

"Obituary. Dr. J. W. Hunter." *Dental Cosmos* 45 (January 1903): 70.

"Obituary. Dr. John W. Holt." *Dental Cosmos* 36 (November 1894): 952.

"Obituary. Dr. John W. Meng." *Dental Cosmos* 59 (June 1917): 667.

"Obituary. Dr. R. B. Winder." *Dental Cosmos* 36 (September 1894: 758–59.

"Obituary. Dr. Richard C. Mackall." *Dental Cosmos* 44 (May 1902): 523–24.

"Obituary. Dr. S. C. Wilkerson." *Dental Cosmos* 39 (December 1897): 1053–54.

"Obituary. Dr. Samuel Johnstone Cockerille." *Dental Cosmos* 46 (December 1904): 1093.

"Obituary. Dr. Vines Edmunds Turner." *Dental Cosmos* 56 (June 1914): 770–71.

"Obituary. Dr. Willis Perry Burt." *Dental Cosmos* 48 (August 1906): 891–92

"Obituary. Dr. William Crenshaw." *Dental Cosmos* 63 (April 1921): 437–38.

"Obituary. Dr. Wm. S. Carruthers." *Dental Cosmos* 56 (May 56 (May 1914): 645.

"Obituary. Jacob Zollinger Hoffer, DDS." *Dental Cosmos* 43 (July 1901): 835.

"Obituary. [Prof. R. B. Winder]." *American Journal of Dental Science* 28 (August 1894): 186–87.

"Obituary. Prof. Richard Bayly Winder." *Dental Review* 8 (August 15, 1894): 607.
"OCBS—a Step Ahead." *Forum* 18 (Fall 1997): 12–17.
"Officers: The National Alumni Association of the Baltimore College of Dental Surgery," *Bulletin* 3 (May 1928): i, ii.
"Originator of the Rubber Dam [Sanford Christie Barnum, DDS]." *Dental Radiography and Photography* 43, no. 4 (1970): ii, 82.
[Ottolengui, Rodrigues]. "The Present Status of Dental Service in the United States Army, and the Effect of War Conditions upon Education." *Dental Items of Interest* 40 (October 1918): 823–27.
P., R. I. "Obituary. Dr. Amzi W. Alexander." *Dental Cosmos* 52 (April 1910): 503.
"Pass-Fail System Begins in September." *Newsletter University of Maryland School of Dentistry* 4 (Spring 1971): 3.
"Past Presidents of the Alumni Association." *Alma Mater* 23 (February 1982): 48.
"Patricia Stearns to Head First Maryland Hygiene Program." *Newsletter University of Maryland School of Dentistry* 2 (Winter 1968): 2..
Peace, Ann Louise. "James Howell Harris—DDS, MD, 1834–1910." *Alma Mater* 14 (April 1973): 3–4.
"Pennsylvania College of Dental Surgery." *Dental Cosmos* 20 (April 1878): 233.
"Peru Affiliation Established." *Newsletter University of Maryland School of Dentistry* 4 (Spring 1971): 2.
Phillips, Ralph W. "Past, Present, and Future Composite Resin Systems." *Dental Clinics of North America* 25 (April 1981): 209–18.
"Poet Laureate of Dentistry [Solyman Brown, AM, DD, MD, DDS]." *Dental Radiography and Photography* 27, no. 4 (1954): i, 72.
Pollack, Burton R. "Students Learn of Social Problems in Community Dentistry." *Newsletter* 1 (Winter 1967): 4.
[Preis, Kyrle W.] "The Future—What!" *Alma Mater* 3 (June 1961): 2–3.
__________. "125th Anniversary Celebration." *Alma Mater* 7 (November 1965): 47.
__________. "Dr. Ernest B. Nuttall Retires." *Alma Mater* 12 (Spring 1971): 29–30.
Pridgeon, Charles T. "The Role and Involvement of the Dental School in Continuing Education." *Journal of the Maryland State Dental Association* 17 (August 1974): 99–103.
"Proceedings of the Society of the Alumni of the Baltimore College of Dental Surgery." *Dental News Letter* 3 (April 1850): 66–68.
"Professor Gardner P.H. Foley Retires After 41 Years." *Newsletter University of Maryland School of Dentistry* 3 (Winter 1969): 3.
Pryor, W. J. "The Closed Bite Relation of the Jaws of George Washington, with Comments on his Tooth Troubles and General Health." *Journal of the American Dental Association* 20 (April 1933): 567–79.
Rager, Deborah K. "A Decade of Dedication: Richard R. Ranney, DDS, MS, Dean of the Baltimore College of Dental Surgery, Dental School, University of Maryland." *Forum* 20 (Winter 2002): 15–17.
__________. "The 'Alumni Deans'." *Forum* 20 (Summer 2002): 19–24.
Ramsay, David J. "President's Column." *Voice* 15 (June 1998):1.
__________. "Best Wishes to Our Dean." *Forum* 20 (Summer 2002): 3.
Ranney, Richard R. "Open Forum: Reflections on Opportunity." *Baltimore College of Dental Surgery Forum* 12 (Spring 1992): 2–3.
__________. "Quality with Declining Resources." *Forum* 13 (Fall 1992): 2
__________. "Open Forum: Fall 1993—Three New Approaches." *Forum* 14 (Fall 1993): 2–3.
__________. "From the desk . . .". *Forum* 15 (Fall 1994): 2.
__________. "News from the Dean . . .". *Forum* 15 (Spring 1995): 2; 16 (Fall 1995): 3;
16 (Spring 1996): 2.
__________. "Open Forum: It's working!" *Forum* 17 (Fall 1996): i; 17 (Spring 1997): i;
18 (Fall 1997): i; 18 (Spring 1998): i; 18 ((Spring 1999): i; 19 (Fall 2000): i.
Raper, Howard R. "The Teaching of Dental Radiography." *Dental Brief* 18 (September 1913): 602–17.
"Rate of Dental School Enrollment Slowing." *Maryland Probe* 5 (May 1976): 5.
Ray, Kelley. "A Talk with the New Dean." *Forum* 21 (Spring 2003): 10–11.
Reese, Errol L. "Dean's Report." *Alma Mater* 18 (May 1977): 3–4.
Reese, Errol L., and Nell Savopoulos. "An Introspective Evaluation of Expenditures of Resources at the Baltimore College of Dental Surgery, Dental School, University of Maryland." *Alma Mater* 18 (May 1977): 5–7.
Reese, Errol L. "Open Forum." *BCDS Forum* 1 (Fall 1980): 2–3.
__________. "Dean's Report: 'The Accreditation Site Visit'." *Alma Mater* 22 (January 1981): 3–4.
__________. "Open Forum." *BCDS Forum* 2 (Fall 1981): 2–3.
__________. "Dean's Report: 'Facing the 80s—Can We Continue Our Progress'?" *Alma Mater* 23 (February 1982): 3–4.
__________. "Dean's Report—1984." *Alma Mater* 25 (March 1984): 3; 26 (April 1985): 3–4.
__________. "Exhibit Honors Black Leaders." *BCDS Forum* 5 (Spring 1985): 2–3.

__________. "Dental School Enrollment—A Look at the Past and Plans for the Future." *Baltimore College of Dental Surgery Forum* 9 (Fall 1988): 2–3.

__________. "A Time for Celebration." *Baltimore College of Dental Surgery Forum* 10 (Fall 1989): 2.

Rehert, Isaac. "Forget that Myth about Washington's Set of Wooden Teeth." *Alma Mater* 17 (May 1975): 6–8.

"Report of the Commencement of the Baltimore College." *Dental News Letter* 2 (April 1849): 59–60.

"Report on Major Baido '46." *Journal of the Baltimore College of Dental Surgery, Dental School, University of Maryland* 11 (January 1952): 20.

Ring, Malvin E. "Behind the Dentist's Drill." *American Heritage of Invention & Technology* 11 (Fall 1995): 24–29, 31.

Robertson, William. "A Practical Treatise on the Human Teeth, showing the causes of their Destruction , and the means of their Preservation." *American Journal and Library of Dental Science* 2 (September 1841): 150–51.

Robinson, J. Ben. "Dr. Horace H. Hayden and His Influence on Dental Education." *Dental Cosmos* 74 (August 1932): 783–87.

__________. "Testing Certain Evidence Relating to Horace H. Hayden's Influence on Dental Education." *Dental Cosmos* 75 (September 1933): 853–64.

__________. "Dr. Benjamin Fendall (1753–1818): A Pioneer American Dentist." *Journal of the Baltimore College of Dental Surgery, Dental School, University of Maryland.* 2 (March 1938): 1–4.

__________. "Dedication Address by Dean Robinson." *Journal of the Baltimore College of Dental Surgery, Dental School, University of Maryland* 8 (December 1943): 4–5.

__________. "Some Highlights in the History of the Maryland State Dental Association." *Journal of the Maryland State Dental Association* 1 (April 1958): 5–16.

__________. "Let's Keep the Records Straight." *Alma Mater* 1 (May 1959): 28–33.

__________. "General Robert H. Mills Honored." *Alma Mater* 2 (October 1960): 31–32.

__________. "A Testimonial to Gardner P. H. Foley." *Alma Mater* 11 (Spring 1970): 25–27.

__________. "The Baltimore College of Dental Surgery and the Baltimore College of Dental Surgery, Dental School, University of Maryland." *Journal of the Maryland State Dental Association* 18 (August 1975): 98–101.

__________. "Early Dentists in Baltimore who Probably Practiced their Profession at Fell's Point." *MSDA Journal* 19 (December 1976):166–67.

Rodgers, Charles W. "Lieutenant-Commander Richard Grady, U.S.N. Dental Surgeon." *Dental Cosmos* 66 (August 1924): 912–13.

Salley, John J. "Progress Notes on Planning of the Baltimore College of Dental Surgery, Dental School, University of Maryland 1964." *Journal of the Maryland State Dental*
Association 7 (April 1964): 13–15.

__________. "The Dental Health Center—A New Dimension in Dental Education at the University of Maryland." *Journal of the Baltimore College of Dental Surgery* 21 (December 1966): 49–102.

__________. "Greetings from the School of Dentistry." *Alma Mater* 10 (February 1969): 11.

Salley, John J., and James H. Stephenson. "Facilities for the University of Maryland Dental Health Center." *Journal of the Baltimore College of Dental Surgery* 23 (December 1968): 45–59.

"Satellite Centers to Localize Independent Learning." *Dental Newsletter* 8 (Spring 1975): 1, 4.

Schaeffer, Aaron. "Visitation to the University of Maryland Dental School." *Journal of the Maryland State Dental Association* 13 (August 1970): 113–16.

Scheitler, Larry, and Bernie French. "Dean Salley Resigns." *Maryland Probe* 3 (May 1974): 1, 6.

"School of Dentistry Initiates Senior Externship Program." *Dental Newsletter* 8 (Winter 1974): 1.

"School Military Units." *Journal of the Baltimore College of Dental Surgery, Dental School, University of Maryland* 10 (May 1951): 54.

"School Receives Largest Grant to Study Pain: $6.8 Million Awarded." *Forum* 20 (Winter 2002): 3.

"The School's Exhibit at the College Park Centenary." *Journal of the Baltimore College of Dental Surgery, Dental School, University of Maryland* 15 (May 1956): 68.

Schwartz, L. Laszlo. "War Problems of Dentistry: The South in the Civil War." *Journal of the American Dental Association* 32 (January 1, 1945): 37–42.

"Science Close to Conquering Caries, Dedication Audience Told." *Newsletter University of Maryland School of Dentistry* 4 (Spring 1971): 1.

"Searching East and West for knowledge and adventure, he found both . . . [Homer Judd, MD, DDS]." *Dental Radiography and Photography* 25, no. 3 (1952): ii, 60.

Seipp, Joseph H., Jr. "A Brief History of the First Dental Alumni Association in the World (Organizations Associated with the Baltimore College of Dental Surgery)." *Alma Mater* 8 (November 1966): 4–9.

__________. "Dr. Brice Dorsey Retires." *Alma Mater* 9 (November 1967): 23.

"Simon P. Hullihen, MD, DDS." *Dental Radiography and Photography,* 22, no. 4 (1949): i, 80.
Singer, Jacquelyn L. "The Dental Hygiene Public Health Concentration." *Journal of the Baltimore College of Dental Surgery* 33 (June 1980): 5–6.
Smith, B. Holly. "The Chapin A. Harris Memorial Association." *Dental Review* 3 (August 15, 1889): 531–32.
Smith, Frederick. "Sixteen Women in the Freshmen Class." *Alma Mater* 16 (April 1975): 17.
Soble, Rosalynde K., Eli Shulman, and Burton R. Pollack. "Dental Education and the Community: A Field Experience." *Journal of the Baltimore College of Dental Surgery* 27 (July 1972): 36–44.
"Southern Dental Association. Annual Meeting (Conjointly with the North Carolina State Dental Association) [Proceedings]." *American Journal of Dental Science,* 3d ser., 15 (October 1881): 269–75.
"Southern Dental Association—Fifteenth Annual Session [Proceedings]. *Dental Cosmos* 26 (September 1883): 475–85.
"Southern Dental Association—Sixteenth Annual Session [Proceedings]. *Dental Cosmos* 26 (July 1884): 423–34.
"Special Patient Clinic Trains Students to Treat Handicapped." *Newsletter University of Maryland School of Dentistry* 5 (Spring 1972): 3.
Stohler, Christian S. "Dean's Message." *Forum* 21 (Spring 2003): 1.
"Students Set Own Pace in Independent Learning Center." *Newsletter University of Maryland School of Dentistry* 5 (Winter 1971): 1.
"Summer Student Research Training Update." *What's on at OCBS?* 3 (Winter 2003): 1–2.
Sutter, Rita. "Celebrating a Quarter Century of Dental Hygiene." *Forum* 16 (Fall 1995): 8–9.
Sweeney, K.C. "Faculty Dental Clinic." *Maryland Probe* 2 (June 5, 1073): 1.
Sweet, A. Porter, "Amalgam and the 'New Departure'." *Dental Radiography and Photography* 32, no. 4 (1959): 66–70.
Taft, J[onathan]. "American Journal of Dental Science." *Dental Register of the West* 15 (November 1861): 666.
__________. "Association of the Colleges of Dentistry [Proceedings]."*Dental Register* 21 (January 1867): 29–33.
__________. "The Association of the Colleges of Dentistry [Proceedings]." *Dental Register* 21 (April 1867): 179–84.
__________. "Proceedings of the Association of the Colleges of Dentistry." *Dental Register* 22 (May 1868): 197–202.
__________. "Dental Education—Office Pupilage." *Dental Register* 44 (February 1890): 57–60.
Tarrant, Joyce L. "Reese Takes the Helm: Errol Reese Named President of UMAB Campus." *Baltimore College of Dental Surgery Forum* 11 (Spring 1991): 6–7.
Taylor, James. "Obituary [Dr. Chapin A. Harris]." *Cincinnati Dental Lamp* 2, no. 1 (1860): 17–19.
__________. "Life and Character of Chapin A. Harris, MD, DDS: An Address." *Dental Register of the West* 15 (February 1861): 79–90.
"Thomas William Evans, MD, DDS, PhD." *Dental Radiography and Photography* 21, no. 3 (1948): i.
Thorpe, Burton Lee. "In Memoriam: Dr. James Albert Price." *Western Dental Journal* 30 (October 1916): 3–5.
"Training Program Integrate basic and clinical research training." *What's on at OCBS?* 2 (Summer 2001): 1–2.
T[ruman], J. "Obituary. Prof. Richard Bayly Winder, MD, DDS." *International Dental Journal* 15 (September 1894): 604–5.
"Twenty-Fifth Annual Union Convention of the Sixth, Seventh, and Eighth District Dental Societies of the State of New York." *Dental Cosmos* 35 (December 1893): 1315–41.
"Two New Department Chairmen Named." D*ental Newsletter* 12 (Winter 1978): 4.
"Two Women Faculty Members Promoted to Full Professor." *Dental Newsletter* 9 (Winter 1975): 5.
"UMAB Chancellor Establishes Dental Dean Search Committee." *Dental Newsletter* 8 (Winter 1974): 2.
"Union Meeting of the Maryland State Dental Association and the District of Columbia Dental Society." *Dental Cosmos* 44 (November 1902): 1163–81.
"University of Maryland." *Alma Mater* 1 (March 1959): 9.
"University of Maryland—Department of Dental Surgery." *Dental Cosmos* 26 (April 1884): 245–46; 35 (April 1893): 319; 36 (June 1894): 477; 38 (April 1896): 434; 39 (June 1897): 501; 40 (May 1898): 396–97; 41 (May 1899): 497–98; 46 (June 1904): 525; 47 (June 1905): 743; 48 (June 1906): 706–7; 49 (August 1907): 890.
"University of Maryland—Dental Department." *Dental Cosmos* 27 (April 1885): 252; 28 (April 1886): 250; 29 (April 1887): 273–74; 30 (April 1888): 291; 31 (April 1889): 312–13; 32 (April 1890): 321; 33 (April 1891): 312; 34 (May 1892): 397–98; 37 (May 1895): 455; 42 (June 1900): 594; 43 (June 1901): 679–80; 44 (June 1902): 628; 45 (June 1903): 514; 50 (July 1908): 775; 51 (July 1909): 909; 52 (July 1910): 820; 53 (August 1911): 970; 56 (August 1914): 1012; 58 (July 1916): 847; 59 (October 1917): 1053; 60 (September 1918): 848; 61 (August 1919): 797; 62 (September 1920): 1153; 63 (July 1921): 756; 64 (July 1922): 802; 65 (August 1923): 896.
"Wadsworth C. Trojakowski." *Journal of the Baltimore College of Dental Surgery, Dental School, University of Maryland* 7 (September 1942): 21.
Waite, Frederick C. "The Background of Modern American Dentistry." *Journal of Dental Education* 1 (February 1937): 91–108.

Walker, [Mrs.] J. M. "An Interesting Supreme Court Decision." *Dental Brief* 4 (October 1899): 573.
Walsh, Ruth. "Dental School Expands Performance Logic Center." *The Voice* 6 (December 20, 1988): 1–2.
"Watchmaker—Actor—Dentist [Elisha Townsend, MD, DDS]. *Dental Radiography and Photography* 30, no. 3 (1957): I, 60.
Weinberger, Bernhard Wolf. "The Educational Evolution of the Dental Surgeon: Development and Progress toward the Formation of the First Dental College." *Dental Cosmos* 71 (May 1929): 516–26; (June 1929): 565–75.
Werterfield, T. L. "In Memoriam. John C. Story, MD, DDS." *Items of Interest* 19 (June 1897): 467–68.
Westcott, A[mos], comp. "Tenth Annual Meeting of the American Society of Dental Surgeons, held in the City of Baltimore, the 25, 26, 27 days of March, 1850." *American Journal of Dental Science* 10 (April 1850): 208–11.
W[hite], J[ohn] D. "Dental Colleges." *Dental News Letter* 10 (April 1857): 220–21.
__________. "Dental Colleges." *Dental Cosmos*, n.s., 2 (May 1861): 560–61.
Wilson, Courtney B. "The B&O Railroad Museum." *The Courier* 2 (Spring/Summer 2003): 11, 13.
Winder, Richard B. "Dental Education." *American Journal of Dental Science*, 3d ser., 2 (April 1869): 575–81.
__________. "A National Dental Association." *Dental Cosmos* 21 (September 1879): 500–06.
__________. "Dental Education." *Southern Dental Journal* 3 (June 1884): 188–97.
__________. "Anchylosed Maxillaries—A Remarkable Case." Odontographic *Journal* 6 (July 1885): 130.
__________. "German Dental Education." *Items of Interest* 10 (January 1888): 35.
__________. "The Teeth As An Index of Civilization." *American Journal of Dental Science* 27 (December 1893): 337–39.
Woolverton, Deborah K. "The Medical and Chirurgical Faculty of the State of Maryland and the Evolution of Professional Dentistry in Maryland: An Exhibition Celebrating the Maryland State Dental Association's Centennial Meeting, Convention Center, Baltimore, Maryland, September 22–25, 1983," *Journal of the Maryland State Dental Association* 26 (December 1983): 120–21.
"Women Dentists in Germany." (Cincinnati Gazette). Quoted in *Johnston's Dental Miscellany* 1 (June 1874): 239.
"The World's First to Become the World's Newest." *Forum* 20 (Summer 2002): 6–10.
"Year-Long Sesquicentennial is Underway." *Baltimore College of Dental Surgery Forum>P> 10 (Spring 1990): 2–3.*

Advertisements
"Baltimore College of Dental Surgery." In *American Journal of Dental Science* 1 (July 1840): 7.
"Baltimore College of Dental Surgery, Fifteenth Session, 1854–5." In *Dental News Letter* 8 (January 1855): n.p.n.

Dissertations & Unpublished Documents
Baltimore College of Dental Surgery, Dental School, University of Maryland. "Agreement for Scholarly Exchange and Collaboration Between Osaka University, Faculty of Dentistry, Baltimore College of Dental Surgery, Dental School, University of Maryland." November 11, 1993.
__________. "Department of Biomedical Sciences: Background and History." 2 lvs.
__________. Department of Health Promotion and Policy, "Executive Summary: The Maryland Oral Health Advisory Committee."
__________. Department of Health Promotion and Policy, "The Maryland Oral Health Advisory Committee: An Assessment of its Utility and Value to the Citizens of Maryland."
__________. "Global Maryland: Challenges, Opportunities, and Responsibilities in the 21st Century, a Global Perspective for Dental Education."
__________. "Memorandum Concerning Agreement on Academic Exchange Between Osaka University, Faculty of Dentistry, Baltimore College of Dental Surgery, Dental School, University of Maryland." November 11, 1998.
__________. Office of the Dean, Files (BCDSOD).
__________. "Two Decades of Progress." [1985?].
Belenky, Michael M. "Affiliation and Collaboration with Foreign Dental Schools Committee Report to the Executive Board." May 20, 2002.
Commission on Dental Accreditation. "Formal Report of the Commission on Dental Accreditation to the Administration of the University of Maryland, Baltimore on the Evaluation of the Dental, Allied and Advanced Dental Education Programs, Baltimore, Maryland." January 30, 1998.
Dubner, Ronald. "Osaka University collaboration." 2004.
Eckels, Claire W. "Baltimore's Earliest Architects 1785–1820." PhD Dissertation. Johns Hopkins University, 1950.
Hasler, John F. "Patient-Centered Care: 1980." 2004.
McCarthy, Harry B. "A History of Dental Education in Maryland." Master's Thesis. Graduate School, University of Maryland, 1948.
__________. "Harry B. McCarthy, DDS, MA: An Autobiography." n.p., 1985.

Milner, John Associates. "Architecture as History: The Formative Years of the Baltimore College of Dental Surgery as Recorded in the Housing History." Final Report. John Milner Associates, West Chester, PA, 1980.
Serio, Francis G. "The Dominican Dental Mission Project: Serving the dental needs of the poor of the Dominican Republic. Summary, 1982–1999."
Star, Marc D. "Stones and Bricks: An Architectural Record of Maryland's Dental Colleges." Senior Thesis. Baltimore College of Dental Surgery, Dental School, University of Maryland, 1993.
Williams, Henry N. "Dr. Gwendolyn Dunn: One of First African American female instructors."
__________."Dr. John Bonas: First black faculty, first black graduate student."
__________. "Dr. John Carr: First full-time dentist hired as a faculty member."
__________. Letter, John J. Salley to Harvey Webb, Jr. July 23, 1968.

National Museum of Dentistry Archives (NMDA)
American Society of Dental Surgeons. "Minutes, 1840–56."
Baltimore College of Dental Surgery Papers (BCDSP):
Alumni Association of the Baltimore College of Dental Surgery. *Alumni Banquet.* March 19, 1896.
__________. *Second Annual Banquet Baltimore College of Dental Surgery at the "Severn," Baltimore Thursday Evening March 18, 1897.*
__________. *Program of the Alumni Meeting and Class Reunion Baltimore College of Dental Surgery may 10th and 11th 1906.*
__________. *Re-Union May 30th, 31st and June 1st, One –Nine—Two—Two.*
__________. *Reunion Dinner National Alumni Association of the Baltimore College of Dental Surgery, Penn Athletic Club, Philadelphia, Pennsylvania, Tuesday Evening, August Twenty-Fourth Nineteen Hundred Twenty-Six.*
Certificate of Incorporation, Maryland Dental Association of Baltimore City, Superior Court of Baltimore City, November 3, 1883.
Baltimore College of Dental Surgery Alumni Card File.
Correspondence, various documents.
"Faculty Council Minutes, 1965–1966."
Hayden, Horace H. "A Reply to Dr. C.A. Harris, on 'Hayden's Comments'." n.p. (n.d.): 1–21.
"[History of the Dental Department, Baltimore Medical College]." 5 pp. typed manuscript, N.d.
Maryland Dental College. Commencement Invitation, 1877.
__________. Commencement Program, 1879.
__________. Maryland Dental College Faculty. "To the Dental Profession," [1879].
Record of the Proceedings of the Faculty of the Baltimore College of Dental Surgery.
Reese, Errol L. Letter [J. Ben Robinson's curriculum vitae] to Albin O. Kuhn, Chancellor, University of Maryland at Baltimore, November 13, 1975.
Record of the Proceedings of the Faculty of the Baltimore College of Dental Surgery.
Foley, Gardner P.H., Papers (GPHFP):
Cadden, J.J. "Richard Bayly Winder." Unpublished student paper, 1945.
"Faculty Minutes of B.C.D.S." February 21, 25, 1879.
Foley, Gardner P. H. "Alumni Records (Foley File), Baltimore College of Dental Surgery."
__________. "Civil War File."
Heatwole, Timothy O. "Timothy O. Heatwole Memoirs." 1940.
Klingelhofer, Charles L. "Reminiscences of the Baltimore College of Dental Surgery in the Years 1891–1894." N.d.
Rapoport, Leonard. "Dentistry in the Eighteenth Century." Unpublished student paper.
Schaeffer, Aaron. "Dentistry in Maryland: 1800–1840." Unpublished student paper.
Williamson, Riley S. "Washington R. Handy, MD" Unpublished student paper.

Craig, James F. Papers (JFCP)
Correspondence, various.

McCauley, H. Berton Papers (HBMP)
Correspondence, various.
"The Beginning and End of the Internal Alumni Association of the Baltimore College of Dental Surgery." June 3, 2003.
"A Summary History of the World's First Dental Alumni." N.d.

National Archives and Records Administration (NARA)

Record Group 15 (Bureau of Pensions and Veterans Administration):

Pension record, John L. McGee.

Pension record, Robert W. Morgan

Record Group 94 (Adjutant General's Office):

Microcopy 384. Compiled Service Records of Volunteer Union Soldiers Who Served in Organizations from the State of Maryland.

Microcopy 405. Compiled Service Records of Volunteer Union Soldiers Who Served in Organizations from the State of Missouri.

Microcopy 508. Compiled Service Records of Volunteer Union Soldiers Who Served in Organizations from the State of West Virginia.

Microcopy 535. Compiled Service Records of Volunteer Union Soldiers Who Served in Organizations from the State of Connecticut.

Micro copy 602. Index to Compiled Service Records of Volunteer Soldiers who Served during the War of 1812. (roll 95).

Compiled Military Service Record. Horace H. Hayden, 39 Regiment (Fowler's) Maryland Militia (War of 1812).

Compiled Military Service Records (Civil War)

Compiled Military Service Records (Spanish War).

Entry 25. Document File, 1890–1917.

Entry 26. Record Cards, 1890–1917.

Entry 91. Enlistment Papers, 1798-Oct. 31, 1912.

Entry 561. Personal Papers, Medical Officers and Physicians, ("Medical Officer's File"), Prior to 1912.

Record Group 109 (War Department Collection of Confederate Records):

Microcopy 253. Consolidated Index to Compiled Service Records of Confederate Soldiers

Microcopy 258. Compiled Service Records of Confederate Soldiers Who Served in Organizations Raised Directly by the Confederate Government.

Micro copy 266. Compiled Service Records of Confederate Soldiers Who Served in Organizations from the State of Georgia.

Micro copy 267. Compiled Service Records of Confederate Soldiers Who Served in Organizations from the State of South Carolina.

Micro copy 268. Compiled Service Records of Confederate Soldiers Who Served in Organizations from the State of Tennessee.

Micro copy 269. Compiled Service Records of Confederate Soldiers Who Served in Organizations from the State of Mississippi.

Micro copy 270. Compiled Service Records of Confederate Soldiers Who Served in Organizations from the State of North Carolina.

Micro copy 311. Compiled Service Records of Confederate Soldiers Who Served in Organizations from the State of Alabama.

Micro copy 320. Compiled Service Records of Confederate Soldiers Who Served in Organizations from the State of Louisiana.

Micro copy 321. Compiled Service Records of Confederate Soldiers Who Served in Organizations from the State of Maryland.

Micro copy 322. Compiled Service Records of Confederate Soldiers Who Served in Organizations from the State of Missouri.

Micro copy 323. Compiled Service Records of Confederate Soldiers Who Served in Organizations from the State of Texas.

Micro copy 324. Compiled Service Records of Confederate Soldiers Who Served in Organizations from the State of Virginia.

Micro copy 324. Compiled Service Records of Confederate Soldiers Who Served in Organizations from the State of Virginia.

Micro copy 331. Compiled Service Records of Confederate General and Staff Officers and Non-Regimental Enlisted Men.

Micro copy 405. Compiled Service Records of Confederate Soldiers Who Served in Organizations from the State of Missouri.

Record Group 112 (Surgeon General's Office):
Entry 12. Letters Received, 1818–89.
Entry 25. Record Cards for General Correspondence, 1894–1917.
Entry 26. General Correspondence, 1894–1917.
Entry 101. Case Files of Persons Examined for Appointment as Dental Surgeons, 1900–1917.
Entry 134. Personal Data Cards of Candidates Seeking Appointment to the Dental Reserve Corps, 1917–1918.

Record Group 120 (American Expeditionary Forces, World War I):
Entry 2130. Records of Base Hospitals, 1917–19.
Entry 2398. General Correspondence of the Section Surgeon, Base Section No. 2, 1917–19.

Seibel, Werner Papers (WSP)
Correspondence, various.

University of Maryland Health Sciences and Human Services Library (HSL)
Baltimore College of Dental Surgery. "Faculty Minutes Jan. 15, 1875 to and incl. April 26, 1916."
Heatwole, T[imothy] O. "An Abbreviated Biography of Ferdinand J.S. Gorgas, MA, DDS, MD." Special Collections.
"Records of Papers—Letters, etc. in connection with Conduct of Dr. F.J.S. Gorgas in regard to Mail matters—Treachery and Falsehood affecting the interests of the Baltimore College of Dental Surgery—after the resignation of his position as Dean on April 27th 1882,"
University of Maryland, Dental Department. "U. of M. Faculty Minutes, April 28, 1882 to March 15, 1911."
__________. "Minutes of Faculty Meetings, May 11, 1911, to June 22, 1922, incl."

Winder, Bayly Philip Papers (BPWP)
"The Dental Profession Alarmed: A Bill Imposing Fine or Imprisonment for Refusal to Answer Census Queries." New York Sun, May 12, 1892.
Maryland State Dental Society Committee. "To the Senators and Representatives of Maryland, and other states in Congress Assembled, May 9–10, 1892."

Newspapers
American & Commercial Daily Advertiser
Baltimore American
Baltimore Advertiser
Baltimore Evening Post
Baltimore Evening Sun
Baltimore Daily Intelligencer
Baltimore Daily Repository
Baltimore Republican or Anti-Democrat
Baltimore Sun
Boston Daily Advertiser
Evening Star (Washington, DC)
Federal Gazette and Baltimore Daily Advertiser
Federal Intelligencer and Baltimore Daily Gazette
Maryland Gazette
Maryland Journal and Baltimore Advertiser
New York Gazette and Weekly Mercury
New York Times
News and Daily Advance (Lynchburg, VA)
Washington Star

Pamphlets & Programs
Baltimore College of Dental Surgery, Dental School, University of Maryland. *Dedication Hayden-Harris Hall.* n.p., 1971.
__________. *A Class of One.* 1976.
__________. *Retirement Dinner and Tribute to Donald E. Shay, PhD.* June 26, 1981.
__________. *Building for the Future: Raising the Bar.* Baltimore: n.p., 2003.
Foley, Gardner P.H., ed. *Hall of Fame of Great Maryland Dentists.* Maryland State Dental Association, 1976.
"History in brief of Base Hospital No. 18." In *Base Hospital Eighteen Thanksgiving Dinner,* November 28, 1918. n.p., 1918.

Mount St. Mary's College. *Sesquicentennial Convocation, Mount Saint Mary's College, Emmitsburg, Maryland, April 12, 1958.* Emmitsburg, MD: Mount St. Mary's College, 1958.
Quest for Care Committee. "Twentieth Anniversary Gala Celebrating Twenty Years of Caring 1984–2004."
[Christian S. Stohler]. "State of the School." June 23, 2004.
University of Maryland at Baltimore. "Presidential Profile [Errol L. Reese]." Office for Institutional Development. n.d.
U.S. Army. *Dedication Ceremony Tignor Army Dental Clinic, in Honor of Colonel Edwin Payne Tignor, Fort Eustis, Virginia, May 22, 1964.* n.p., 1964.
__________. *Dedication LaFlamme Army Dental Clinic, Fort Bragg, North Carolina, December 16, 1969.* n.p., 1969.
West Virginia University. *J. Ben Robinson Recognition.* Morgantown, WV: West Virginia University, 1976.

Personal Correspondence & Interviews

Ames, E. Almer, Jr. Letter to author, July 28, 1980.
Burke, Robert. Photo released to editor. September 2006.
Hauschka, Barbara Toomey. Letter to author, December 2, 2003.
Hillard, Jerome. Photos released to editor. September 2006.
McCauley, H. Berton. Letters to author, October 10, 1998, May 1, 2003.
Moriyami, Norinaga. Letters to author, July 6, August 16, December 6, 12, 2004.
Tignor, Lorraine. Interview by author, Wicomico Church, VA, August 5, 1986.